MAD® ABOUT SUPER HEROES

MW01000010

ALSO AVAILABLE FROM MAD BOOKS

MAD: NEUMANISMS

THE MAD BATHROOM COMPANION
NUMBER TWO

THE MAD GROSS BOOK

THE MAD BATHROOM COMPANION

MAD ABOUT TV

MAD ABOUT THE MOVIES—
SPECIAL WARNER BROS. EDITION

MAD ABOUT SUPER HEROES

BY
"THE USUAL
GANG OF
SUPER-
IDIOTS"

EDITED BY
NICK MEGLIN & JOHN FICARRA

INTRODUCTION BY
ADAM WEST

MAD
New York
BOOKS

MAD BOOKS

WILLIAM GAINES FOUNDER

JENETTE KAHN PRESIDENT & EDITOR-IN-CHIEF

PAUL LEVITZ EXECUTIVE VICE PRESIDENT & PUBLISHER

NICK MEGLIN & JOHN FICARRA EDITORS (MAD)

DOROTHY CROUCH VP–LICENSED PUBLISHING & ASSOCIATE PUBLISHER

SAM VIVIANO ART DIRECTOR

NADINA SIMON ASSOCIATE ART DIRECTOR

CHARLES KOCHMAN EDITOR (LICENSED PUBLISHING)

CHARLIE KADAU SENIOR EDITOR (MAD)

JAYE GARDNER ASSOCIATE EDITOR (LICENSED PUBLISHING)

TRENT DUFFY MANAGING EDITOR (LICENSED PUBLISHING)

PATRICK CALDON SENIOR VP–FINANCE & OPERATIONS

ALISON GILL VP–MANUFACTURING

LILLIAN LASERSON VP & GENERAL COUNSEL

Published by MAD Books. An imprint of E.C. Publications, Inc., 1700 Broadway, New York, NY 10019. A division of Warner Bros. — An AOL Time Warner Company.

ISBN 1-56389-886-1

Printed in Canada

First edition
10 9 8 7 6 5 4 3 2 1

Visit MAD online at www.madmag.com

Though Alfred E. Neuman wasn't the first to say "A fool and his money are soon parted," here's your chance to prove the old adage right—subscribe to MAD! Simply call 1-800-4-MADMAG and mention code 9HPP2. Operators are standing by (the water cooler).

CONTENTS

INTRODUCTION

I like the cover illustration of this book. Examine it. That's my chin on the guy on the right with the spikey ears. The big guy in the center has my chin, too. The short, sappy guy on the left doesn't. (But he is wearing the same baggy underwear that Julie "Catwoman" Newmar gave me for my birthday.) In a collection that focuses on super heroes, it is essential that the reader understand the importance of a solid, strong chin. You might remember I used to have a strong chin when I was playing Batman in the late 1960s. Although barely noticeable, recent age-related bone loss has somewhat diminished my jaw line. At one time I was considered the best chin actor in Hollywood. I was driven to this high level of performance because, as Batman, my mouth and chin were the only facial features not covered by a mask. By now you are beginning to understand why the inspired use of a talented chin is important to the portrayal of a super hero. Comic book artists certainly do. In my case, however, it was impossible to let the camera see the soul behind the eyes when the eyes were lost in two dark holes cut into a plastic mask. Just pull on your cowl and give it a shot some Halloween.

The reason I have taken a moment to discuss the challenge of acting with barely a chin exposed is to help you understand how thrilled I am that MAD Magazine reveals so much more of me and the Batman character than television ever did. The MAD artists have given me prickly chest hair, knobby knees, a cute potbelly, large expressive teeth, and highly visible big-crazed eyes. And speaking of chins and things, it is interesting to note that Bruce Wayne's chin resembles Woody Allen's. Because of this, we know Bruce would never be recognized as his alter ego, Batman. Clever.

Yes, it is a thrill to be included in this MAD super hero collection. I've been on the cover of Life, TV Guide, Gear, and a number of other magazines, but the MAD cover (#105, September 1966) remains my favorite. I love the exposure the "Usual Gang of Idiots" have given our favorite Batman. At last, he is allowed to perform with more than a chin showing. Just check out the page where Batman's cape is caught behind him in a flushing toilet. His tights are down and his cape is strangling him. His bathroom carelessness has created a situation more dangerous and challenging than any cliff-hanger he ever faced on television. The "Usual Gang of Idiots" has revealed new levels of the Batman personality, and for this deeper, more complete rendering of character, I am grateful.

On the pages of this book, the reader will be hopelessly and joyfully caught up in the adventures of other super heroes as well as Batman. So prepare yourselves to see your favorite pop culture icons depicted with the same kind of reverence and respect. After all, it is only what they deserve. Boy Wonderful would agree. "Holy belly laugh, Batman!"

Adam West

—Adam West

AIDE-DE-"CAMP" DEPT.

Everybody's going wild over that new TV show featuring "The Caped Crusader" and his teenage side-kick. But has anyone ever wondered what it would really be like as the side-kick of a "Caped Crusader"? Would a typical red-blooded teenage boy really be happy dressing in some far-out costume and spending all of his free time chasing crooks? Or would he much prefer dressing in chinos and go-go boots and spending all of his free time chasing chicks? We at MAD think the latter! In fact, we're ready to prove it! Let's take a MAD look at "Boy Wonderful" as he is slowly being driven

BATS-MAN

ARTIST: MORT DRUCKER WRITER: LOU SILVERSTONE

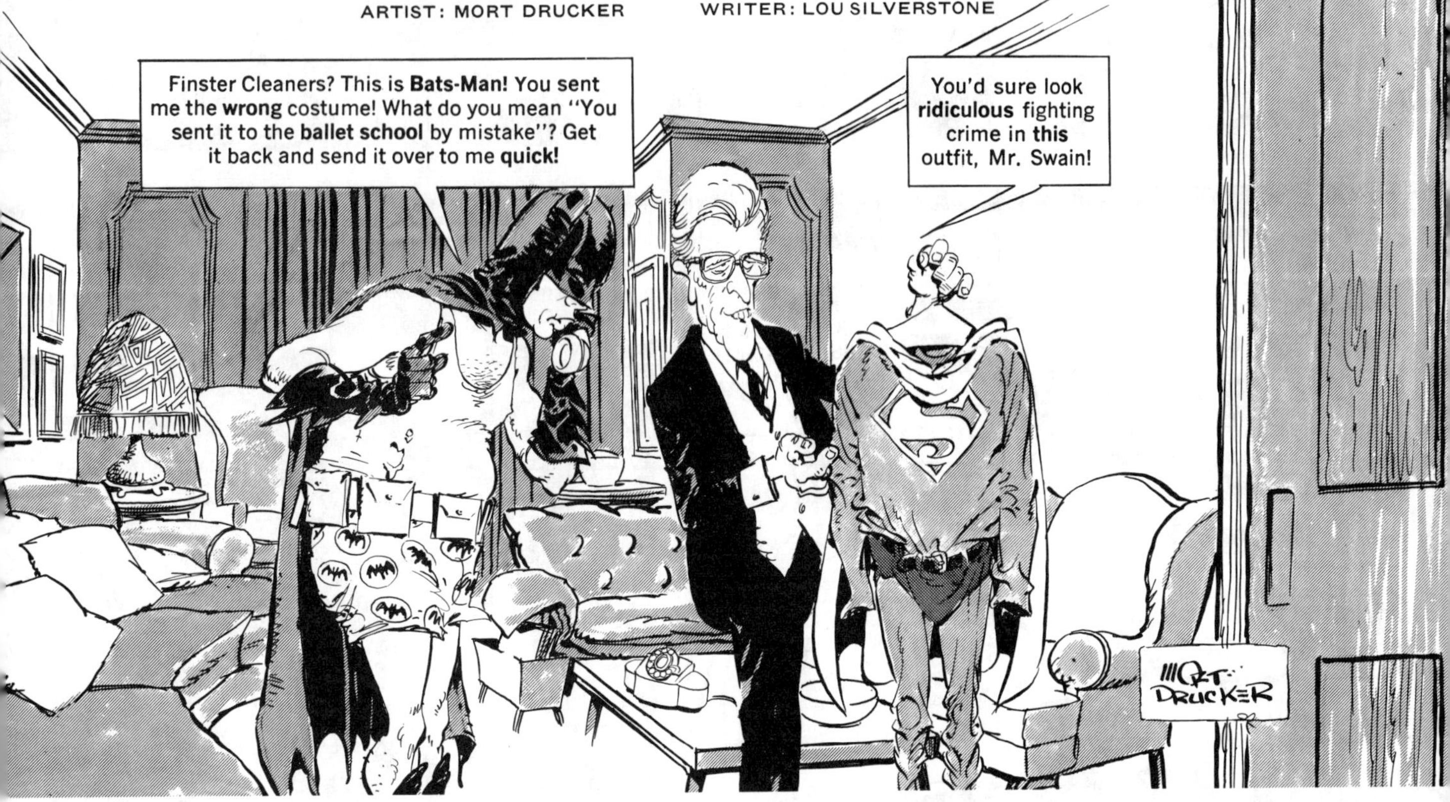
Finster Cleaners? This is Bats-Man! You sent me the wrong costume! What do you mean "You sent it to the ballet school by mistake"? Get it back and send it over to me quick!
You'd sure look ridiculous fighting crime in this outfit, Mr. Swain!
MORT DRUCKER

Meanwhile, at Franklin D. Wilson High School . . .

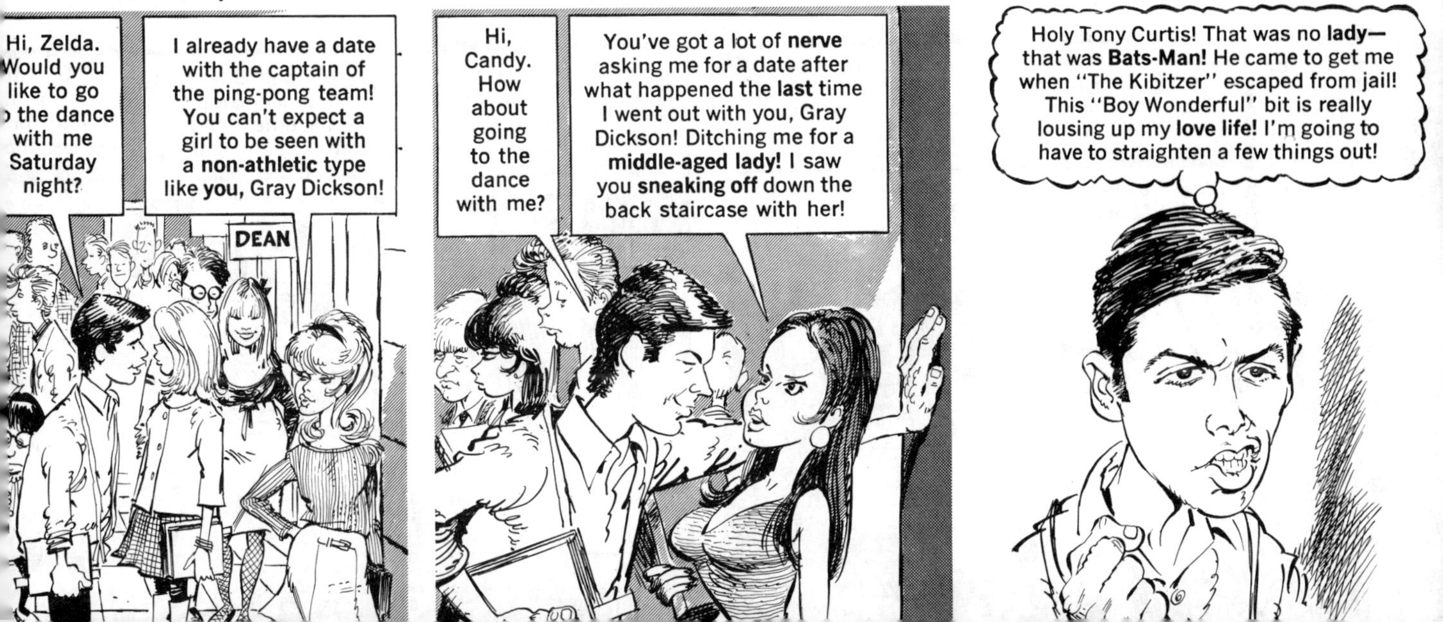
Hi, Zelda. Would you like to go the dance with me Saturday night?
I already have a date with the captain of the ping-pong team! You can't expect a girl to be seen with a non-athletic type like you, Gray Dickson!
DEAN
Hi, Candy. How about going to the dance with me?
You've got a lot of nerve asking me for a date after what happened the last time I went out with you, Gray Dickson! Ditching me for a middle-aged lady! I saw you sneaking off down the back staircase with her!
Holy Tony Curtis! That was no lady— that was Bats-Man! He came to get me when "The Kibitzer" escaped from jail! This "Boy Wonderful" bit is really lousing up my love life! I'm going to have to straighten a few things out!

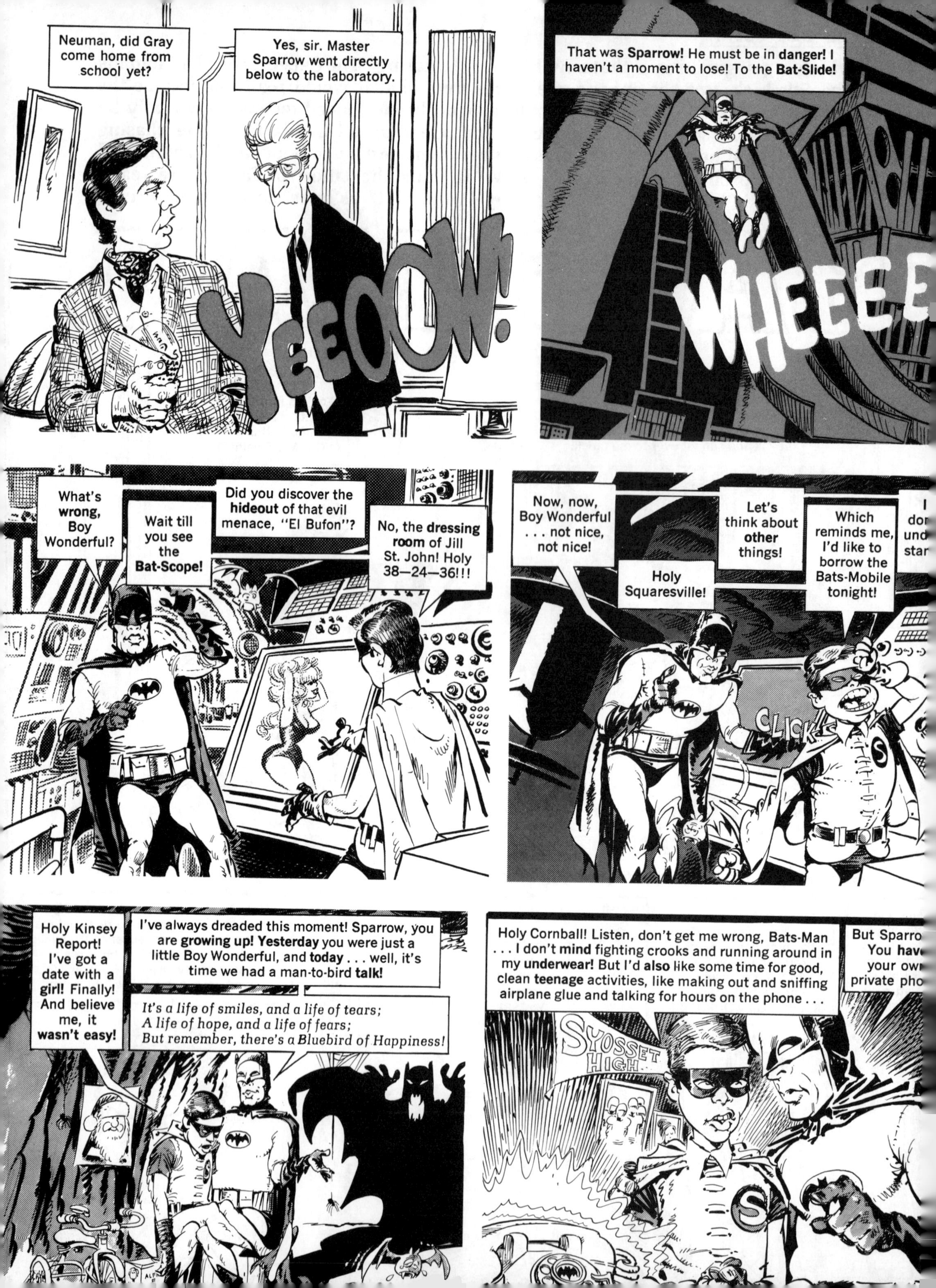
Neuman, did Gray come home from school yet?
Yes, sir. Master Sparrow went directly below to the laboratory.
YEEOOW!
That was **Sparrow!** He must be in **danger!** I haven't a moment to lose! To the **Bat-Slide!**
What's **wrong,** Boy Wonderful?
Wait till you see the **Bat-Scope!**
Did you discover the **hideout** of that evil menace, "El Bufon"?
No, the **dressing room** of Jill St. John! Holy 38—24—36!!!
Now, now, Boy Wonderful . . . not nice, not nice!
Holy Squaresville!
Let's think about **other** things!
Which reminds me, I'd like to borrow the Bats-Mobile tonight!
CLICK
Holy Kinsey Report! I've got a date with a **girl!** Finally! And believe me, it **wasn't easy!**
I've always dreaded this moment! Sparrow, you are **growing up! Yesterday** you were just a little Boy Wonderful, and **today** . . . well, it's time we had a man-to-bird **talk!**
It's a life of smiles, and a life of tears;
A life of hope, and a life of fears;
But remember, there's a Bluebird of Happiness!
Holy Cornball! Listen, don't get me wrong, Bats-Man . . . I don't **mind** fighting crooks and running around in my **underwear!** But I'd **also** like some time for good, clean **teenage** activities, like making out and sniffing airplane glue and talking for hours on the phone . . .
SYOSSET HIGH

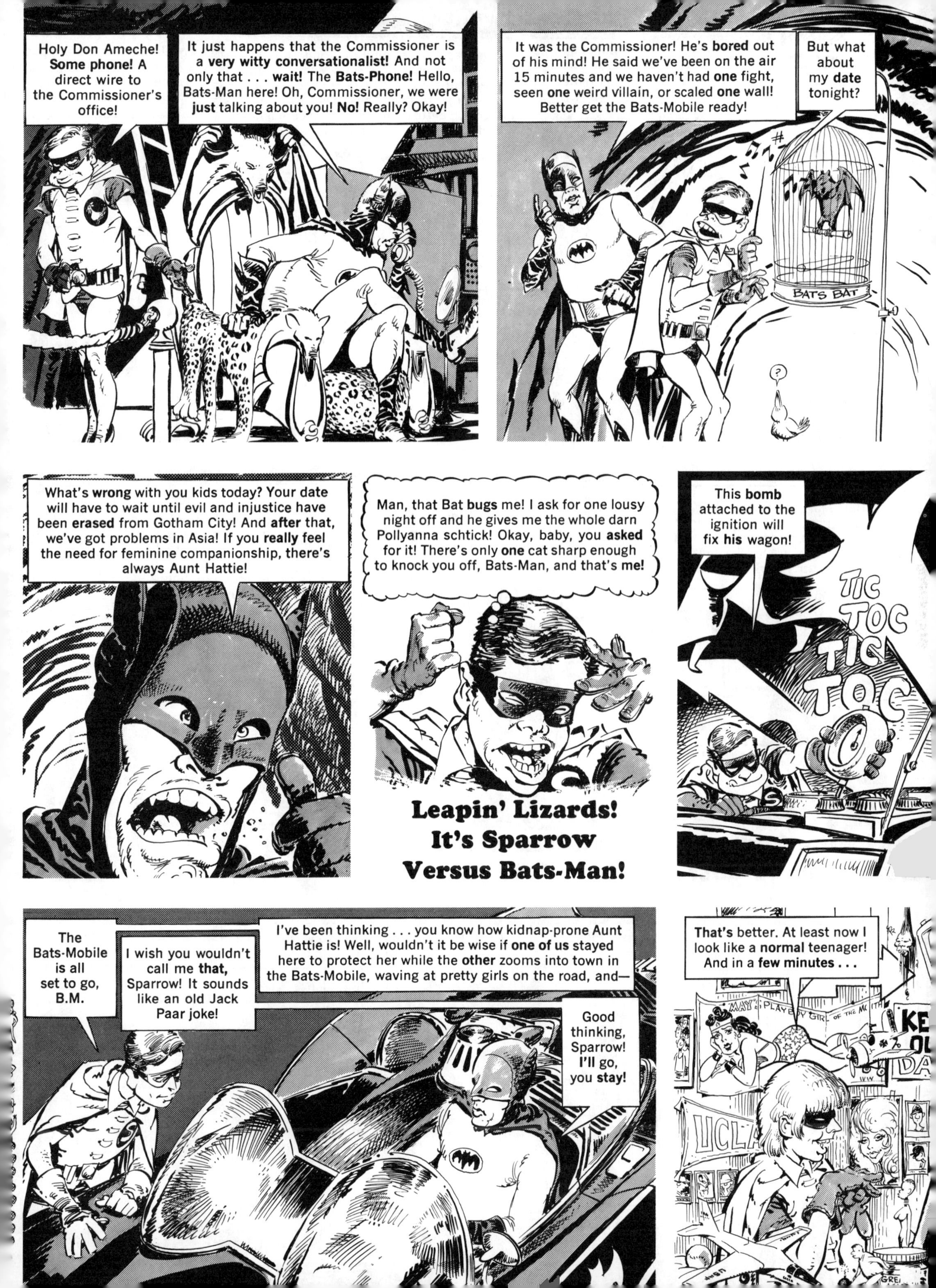
Holy Don Ameche! **Some phone!** A direct wire to the Commissioner's office!
It just happens that the Commissioner is a **very witty conversationalist!** And not only that . . . **wait!** The **Bats-Phone!** Hello, Bats-Man here! Oh, Commissioner, we were **just** talking about you! **No!** Really? Okay!
It was the Commissioner! He's **bored** out of his mind! He said we've been on the air 15 minutes and we haven't had **one** fight, seen **one** weird villain, or scaled **one** wall! Better get the Bats-Mobile ready!
But what about my **date** tonight?
BATS BAT
What's **wrong** with you kids today? Your date will have to wait until evil and injustice have been **erased** from Gotham City! And **after** that, we've got problems in Asia! If you **really feel** the need for feminine companionship, there's always Aunt Hattie!
Man, that Bat **bugs** me! I ask for one lousy night off and he gives me the whole darn Pollyanna schtick! Okay, baby, you **asked** for it! There's only **one** cat sharp enough to knock you off, Bats-Man, and that's **me!**
Leapin' Lizards! It's Sparrow Versus Bats-Man!
This **bomb** attached to the ignition will fix **his** wagon!
TIC TOC TIC TOC
The Bats-Mobile is all set to go, B.M.
I wish you wouldn't call me **that,** Sparrow! It sounds like an old Jack Paar joke!
I've been thinking . . . you know how kidnap-prone Aunt Hattie is! Well, wouldn't it be wise if **one of us** stayed here to protect her while the **other** zooms into town in the Bats-Mobile, waving at pretty girls on the road, and—
Good thinking, Sparrow! **I'll** go, you **stay!**
That's better. At least now I look like a **normal** teenager! And in a **few minutes . . .**
MAY'S PLAYBOY GIRL OF THE MONTH
UCLA

Holy Mushroom Cloud! Can That Be The End Of Bats-Man?!

Bats-Man! Are you all right?

That was a close call, Boy Wonderful! If I hadn't fallen out of the Bats-Mobile on that **sharp turn** outside the Bats-Cave, I'd be Bats-Burger by now! The car is a total loss, though . . . better call the Insurance Adjuster and uncrate the alternate Bats-Mobile!

Hmmm . . . getting this Ba off my back is going to be **tougher** than I figured. But my **next idea** won't fail

Holy Socks! What Bird-Brained Scheme Is Sparrow Hatching Now

Mr. Bats-Man, sir, this package just arrived. I took the liberty of opening it for you—It's a new **electric razor**!

Probably a gift from one of my many admirers. Come to think of it, I can use a shave right **now**!

Just wait until he uses that razor! It's really a **Laser beam**! So long, you **old Bat**!

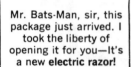

Suffering Sunbeam! Is This The End For Bats-Man, Or Just Another Close Shave?

It's the Commissioner, sir. Some diabolical fiend has just **robbed** the Wessel Foundation Museum . . .

Tell him not to worry—the paintings are all insured for more than they're worth!

Not just the **paintings**, sir—they stole the **whole museum**!

What Give me that phone

TO THE MOST POPULAR BAT ON TV GOOD LUCK DRACULA

They put the whole museum on **wheels** and stole it in broad daylight? **Astounding!** Sounds like a **new menace** has come to Gotham City—or maybe it's just the Seven Santini Brothers!?

Yeeaahhhh!!!

Holy Ichabod Crane!

Oh dear, and good domestics are **so** hard to find, nowadays!

That **death ray** was meant for m I'm up against the archest arc criminal in my career! **Warm u** the alternate Bats-Mobile!

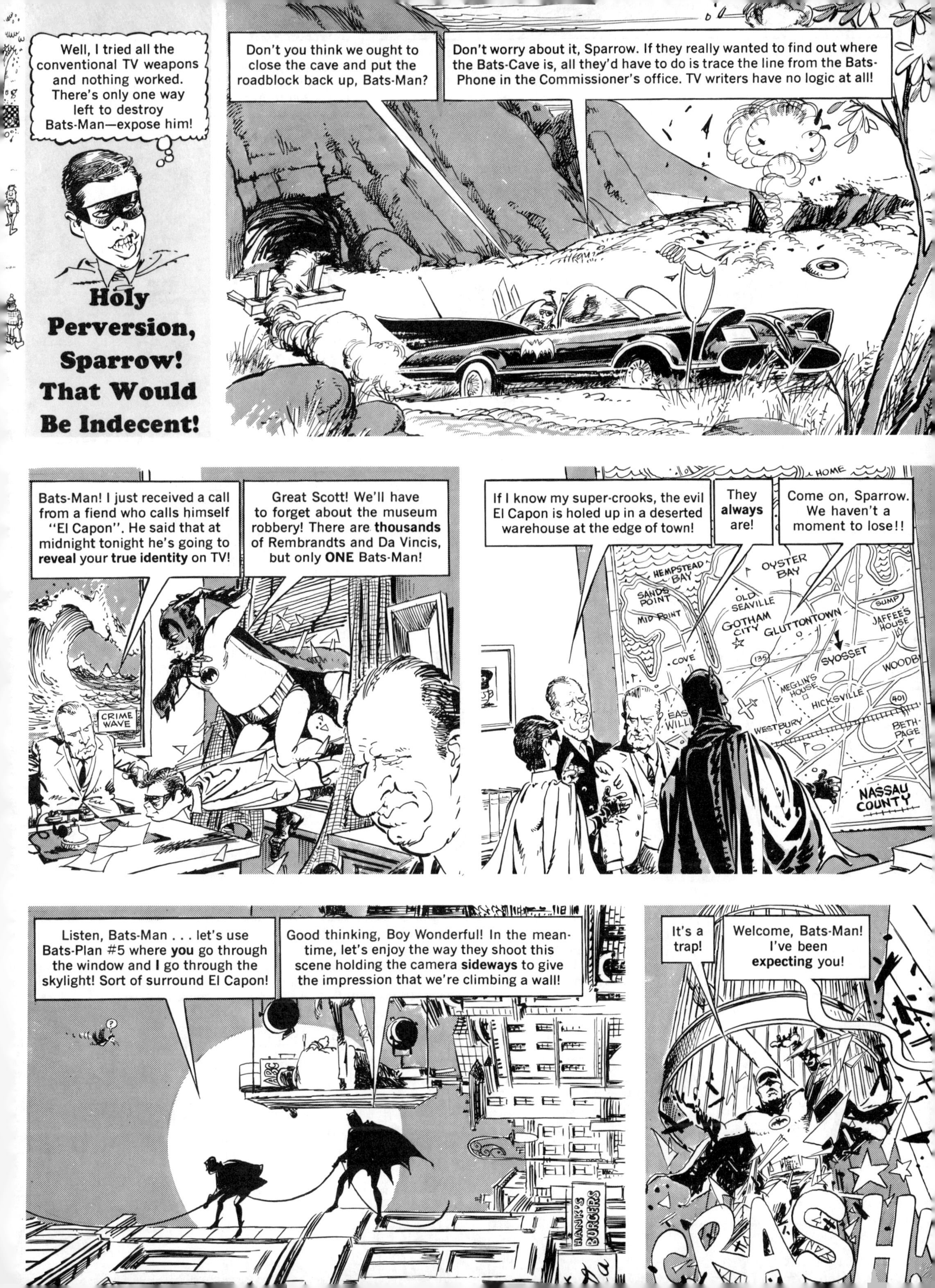
Well, I tried all the conventional TV weapons and nothing worked. There's only one way left to destroy Bats-Man—expose him!
Holy Perversion, Sparrow! That Would Be Indecent!
Don't you think we ought to close the cave and put the roadblock back up, Bats-Man?
Don't worry about it, Sparrow. If they really wanted to find out where the Bats-Cave is, all they'd have to do is trace the line from the Bats-Phone in the Commissioner's office. TV writers have no logic at all!
Bats-Man! I just received a call from a fiend who calls himself "El Capon". He said that at midnight tonight he's going to **reveal** your **true identity** on TV!
Great Scott! We'll have to forget about the museum robbery! There are **thousands** of Rembrandts and Da Vincis, but only **ONE** Bats-Man!
CRIME WAVE
If I know my super-crooks, the evil El Capon is holed up in a deserted warehouse at the edge of town!
They **always** are!
Come on, Sparrow. We haven't a moment to lose!!
HOME
HEMPSTEAD BAY
OYSTER BAY
SANDS POINT
MID POINT
OLD SEAVILLE
GOTHAM CITY
GLUTTONTOWN
SUMP
JAFFEE'S HOUSE
COVE
135
SYOSSET
MEGLIN'S HOUSE
HICKSVILLE
401
WESTBURY
BETH-PAGE
NASSAU COUNTY
Listen, Bats-Man . . . let's use Bats-Plan #5 where **you** go through the window and **I** go through the skylight! Sort of surround El Capon!
Good thinking, Boy Wonderful! In the mean-time, let's enjoy the way they shoot this scene holding the camera **sideways** to give the impression that we're climbing a wall!
ABC
HANK'S BURGERS
It's a trap!
Welcome, Bats-Man! I've been **expecting** you!
CRASH!

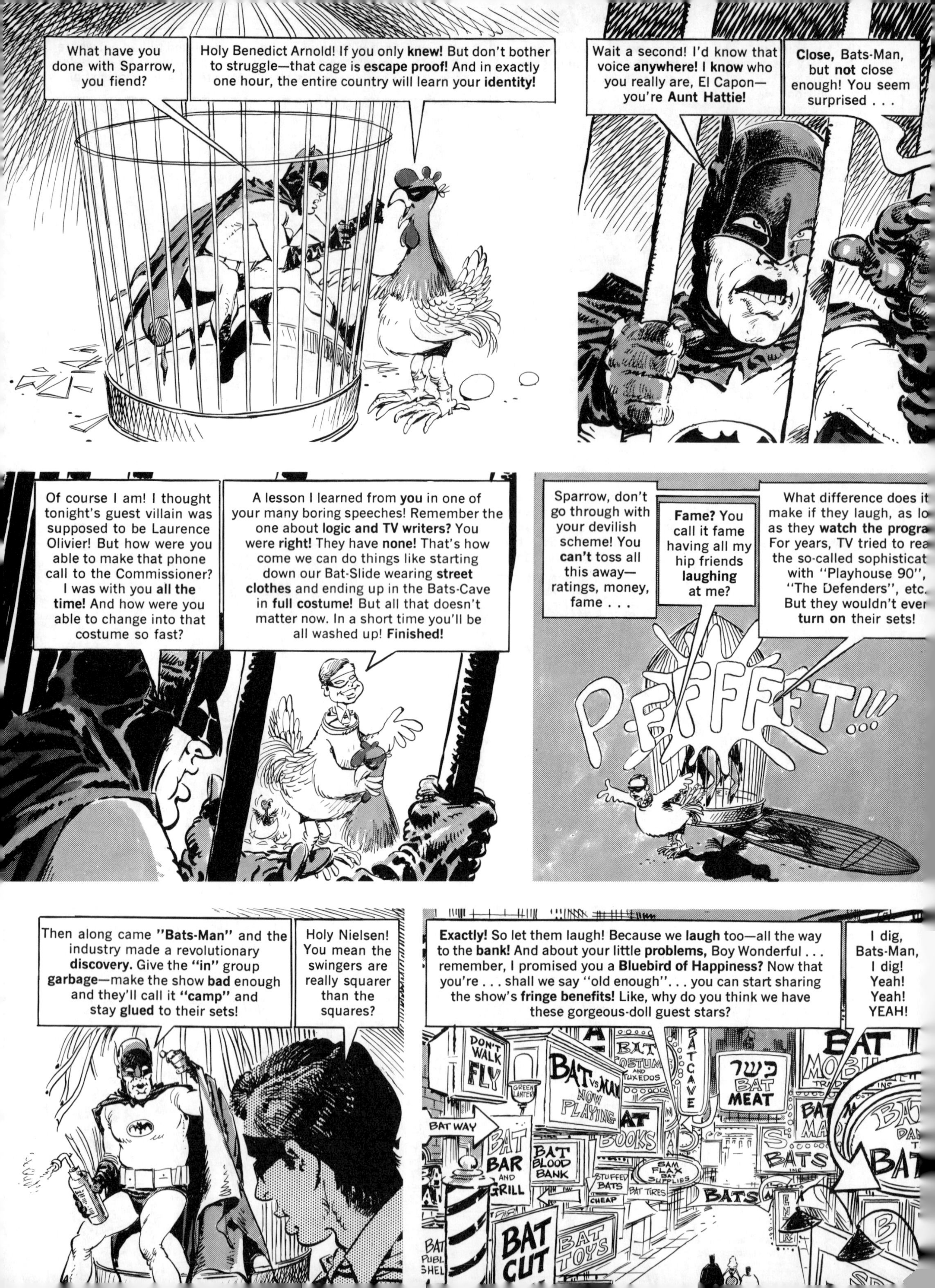
What have you done with Sparrow, you fiend?
Holy Benedict Arnold! If you only **knew!** But don't bother to struggle—that cage is **escape proof!** And in exactly one hour, the entire country will learn your **identity!**
Wait a second! I'd know that voice **anywhere! I know** who you really are, El Capon— you're **Aunt Hattie!**
Close, Bats-Man, but **not** close enough! You seem surprised . . .
Of course I am! I thought tonight's guest villain was supposed to be Laurence Olivier! But how were you able to make that phone call to the Commissioner? I was with you **all the time!** And how were you able to change into that costume so fast?
A lesson I learned from **you** in one of your many boring speeches! Remember the one about **logic and TV writers?** You were **right!** They have **none!** That's how come we can do things like starting down our Bat-Slide wearing **street clothes** and ending up in the Bats-Cave in **full costume!** But all that doesn't matter now. In a short time you'll be all washed up! **Finished!**
Sparrow, don't go through with your devilish scheme! You **can't** toss all this away— ratings, money, fame . . .
Fame? You call it fame having all my hip friends **laughing** at me?
What difference does it make if they laugh, as lo as they **watch the progra** For years, TV tried to rea the so-called sophisticat with "Playhouse 90", "The Defenders", etc. But they wouldn't ever **turn on** their sets!
Then along came **"Bats-Man"** and the industry made a revolutionary **discovery.** Give the **"in"** group **garbage**—make the show **bad** enough and they'll call it **"camp"** and stay **glued** to their sets!
Holy Nielsen! You mean the swingers are really squarer than the squares?
Exactly! So let them laugh! Because we **laugh** too—all the way to the **bank!** And about your little **problems,** Boy Wonderful . . . remember, I promised you a **Bluebird of Happiness?** Now that you're . . . shall we say "old enough" . . . you can start sharing the show's **fringe benefits!** Like, why do you think we have these gorgeous-doll guest stars?
I dig, Bats-Man, I dig! Yeah! Yeah! YEAH!
DON'T WALK FLY
BAT VS MAN NOW PLAYING
BAT CAVE
כשר BAT MEAT
BAT WAY
BAT BAR AND GRILL
BAT BLOOD BANK
STUFFED BATS
CHEAP
SAM FLAX BAT SUPPLIES
BAT TIRES
BATS
BAT CUT
BAT TOYS

YOU KENT WIN 'EM ALL DEPT.

A SUPER OPPORTUNITY

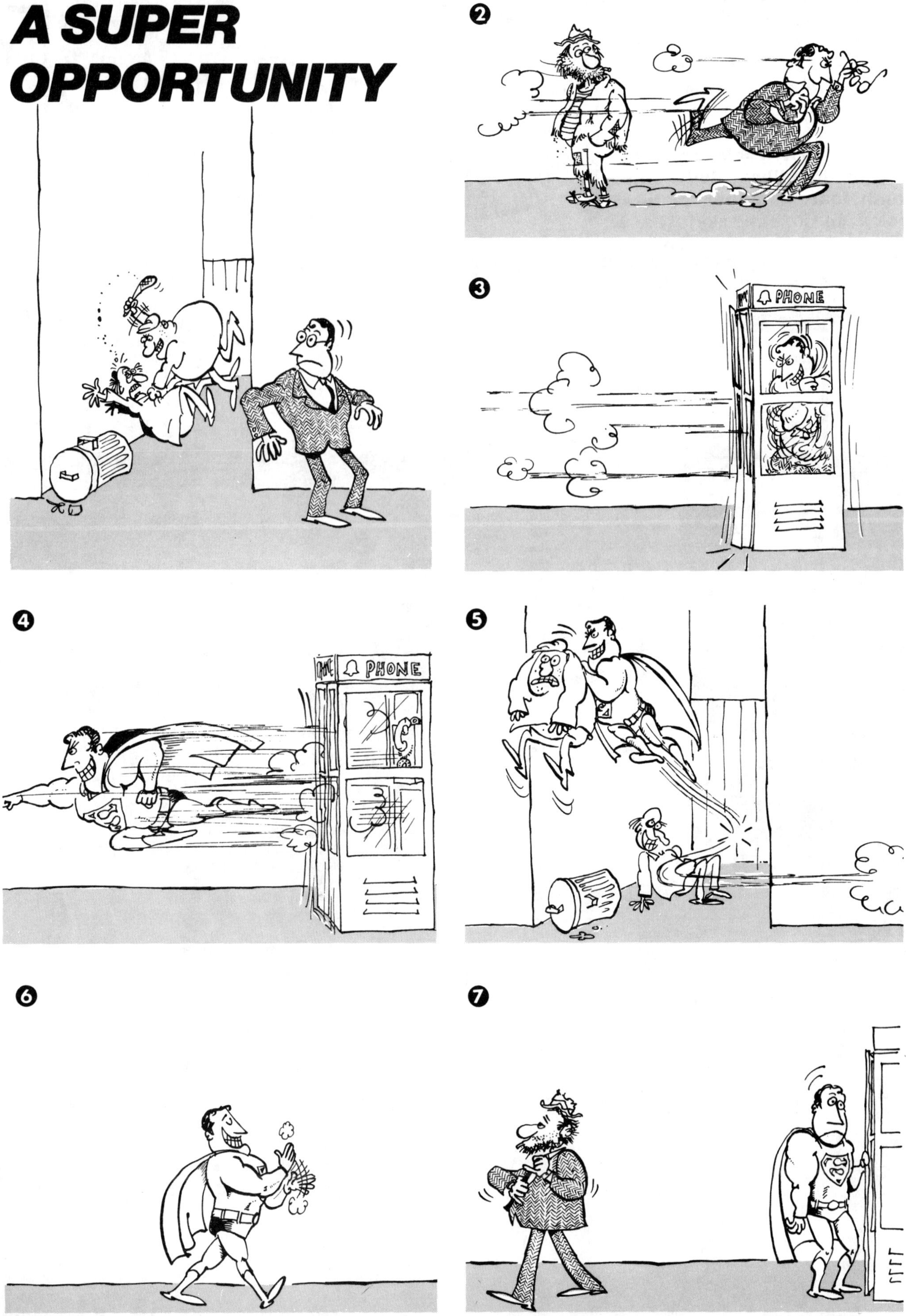
2
3
PHONE
4
PHONE
5
6
7

ARTIST & WRITER: SERGIO ARAGONES

SUPER MARKETING DEPT.

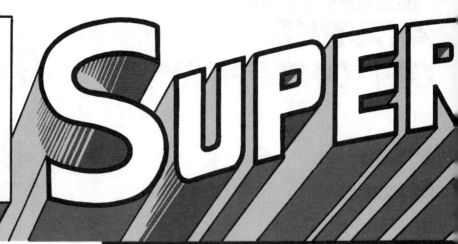

He started out in the Thirties as a comic book hero. Then, he became the star of a movie serial, a radio show, a television series, a Broadway musical, and now...at last...he's the star of a multi-million dollar full-length feature motion picture! Look...up in the sky! It's a gold mine! It's a bonanza! It's

SUPER

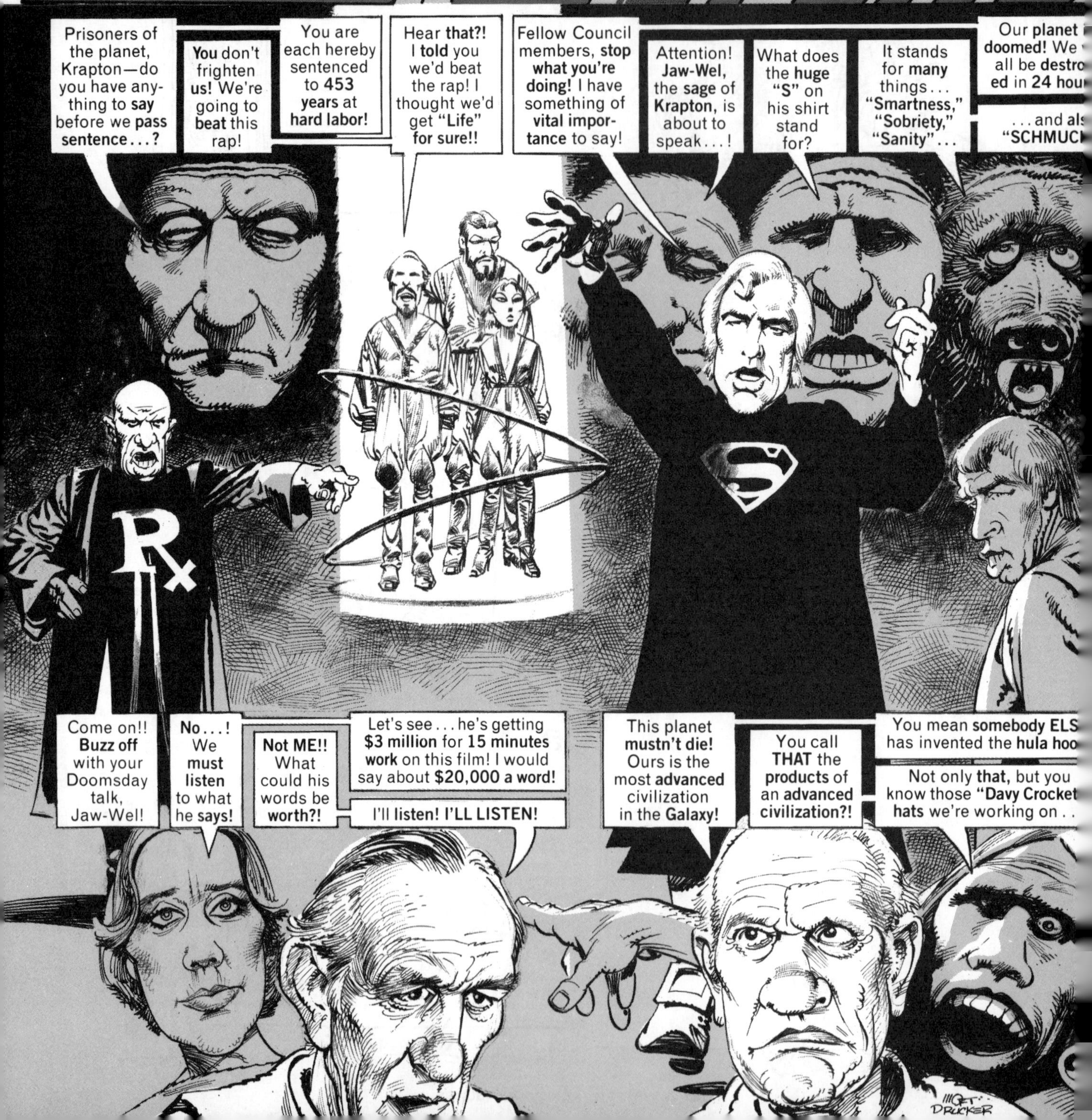

Prisoners of the planet, Krapton—do you have anything to say before we pass sentence...?
You don't frighten us! We're going to beat this rap!
You are each hereby sentenced to 453 years at hard labor!
Hear that?! I told you we'd beat the rap! I thought we'd get "Life" for sure!!
Fellow Council members, stop what you're doing! I have something of vital importance to say!
Attention! Jaw-Wel, the sage of Krapton, is about to speak...!
What does the huge "S" on his shirt stand for?
It stands for many things... "Smartness," "Sobriety," "Sanity"...
Our planet doomed! We all be destro ed in 24 hou
...and als "SCHMUC
Come on!! Buzz off with your Doomsday talk, Jaw-Wel!
No...! We must listen to what he says!
Not ME!! What could his words be worth?!
Let's see...he's getting $3 million for 15 minutes work on this film! I would say about $20,000 a word!
I'll listen! I'LL LISTEN!
This planet mustn't die! Ours is the most advanced civilization in the Galaxy!
You call THAT the products of an advanced civilization?!
You mean somebody ELS has invented the hula hoo
Not only that, but you know those "Davy Crocket hats we're working on . .

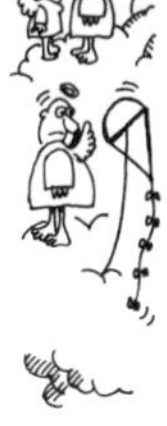

DUPERMAN

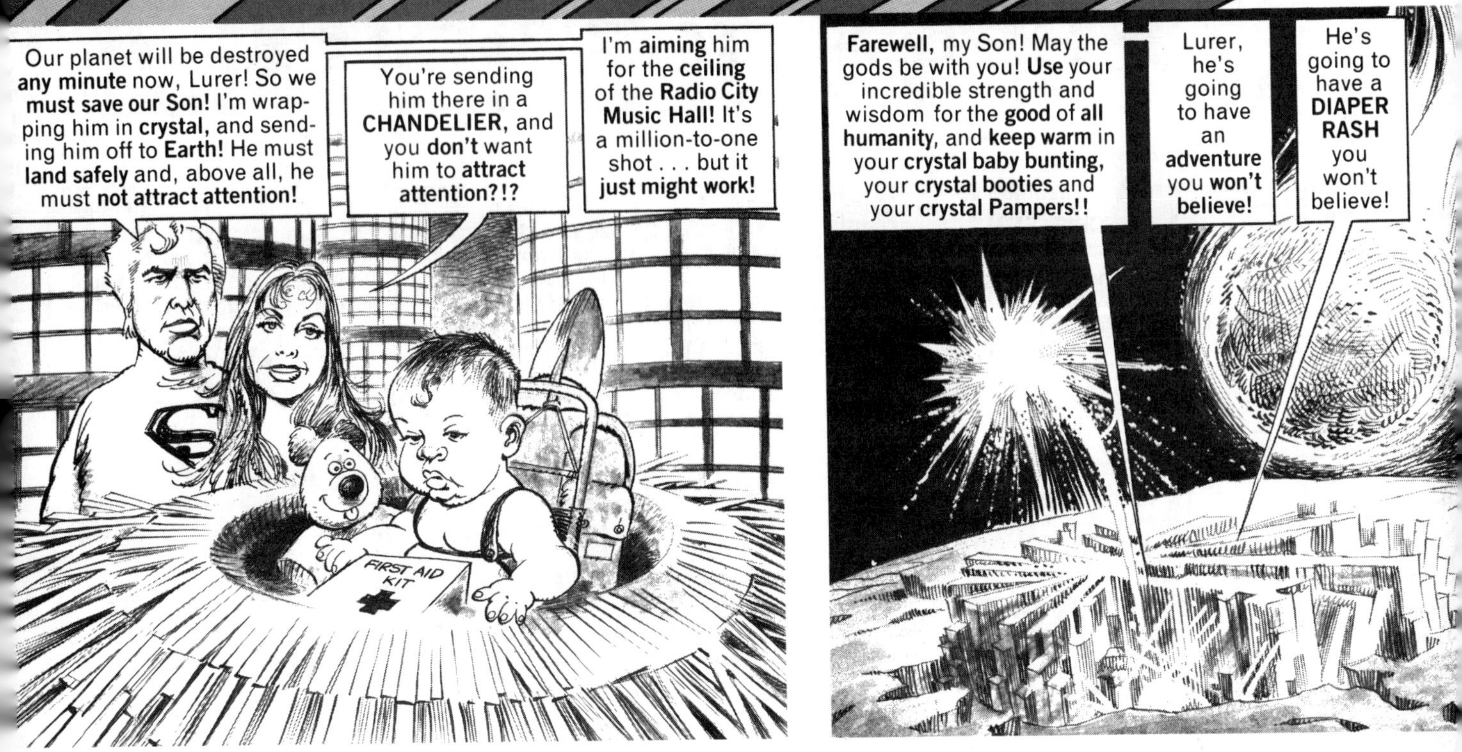

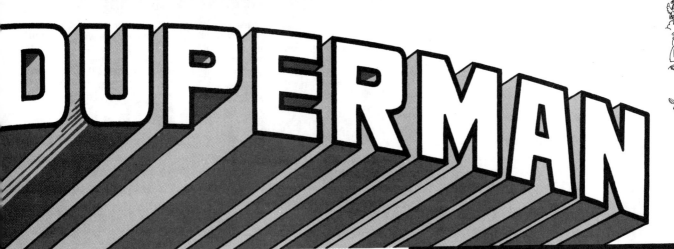

Our planet will be destroyed any minute now, Lurer! So we must save our Son! I'm wrapping him in crystal, and sending him off to Earth! He must land safely and, above all, he must not attract attention!
You're sending him there in a CHANDELIER, and you don't want him to attract attention?!?
I'm aiming him for the ceiling of the Radio City Music Hall! It's a million-to-one shot . . . but it just might work!
FIRST AID KIT
Farewell, my Son! May the gods be with you! Use your incredible strength and wisdom for the good of all humanity, and keep warm in your crystal baby bunting, your crystal booties and your crystal Pampers!!
Lurer, he's going to have an adventure you won't believe!
He's going to have a DIAPER RASH you won't believe!

ARTIST: MORT DRUCKER WRITER: LARRY SIEGEL

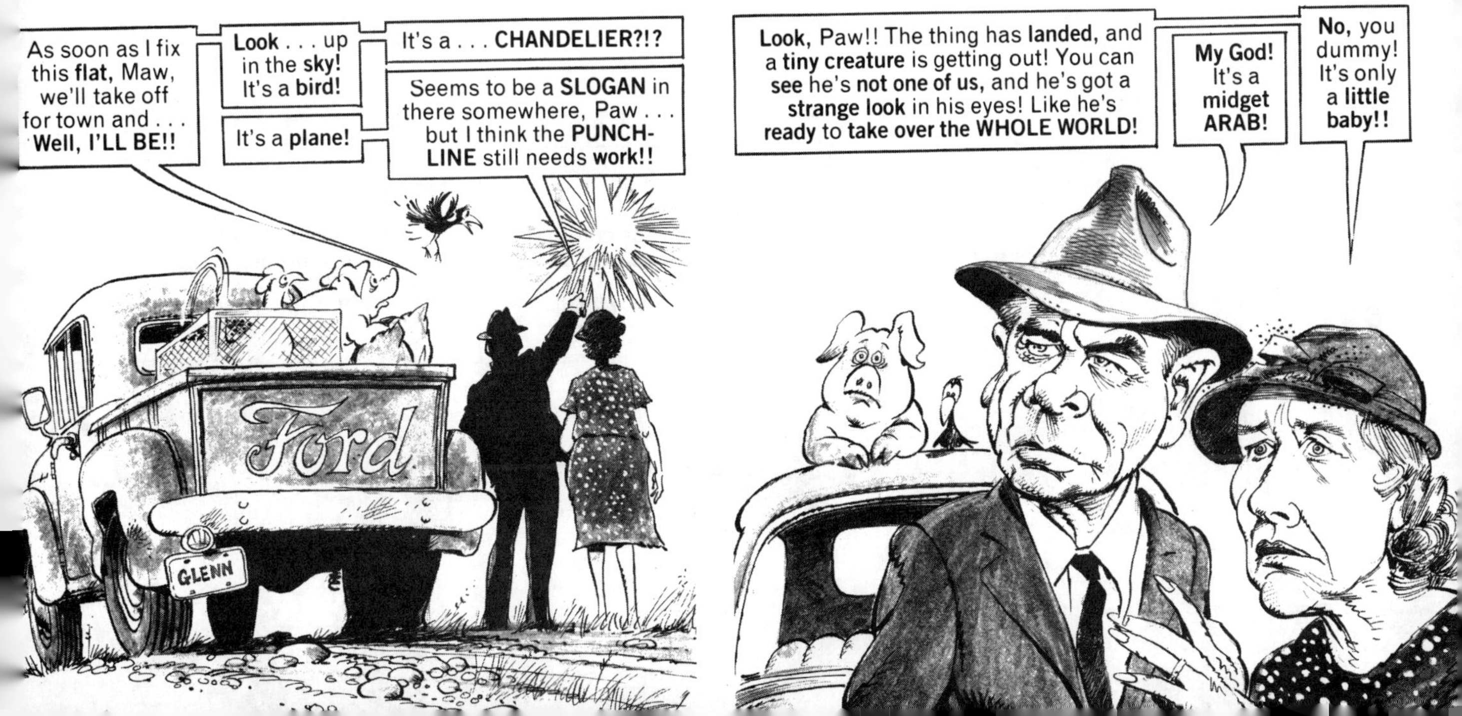

As soon as I fix this flat, Maw, we'll take off for town and . . . Well, I'LL BE!!
Look . . . up in the sky! It's a bird!
It's a plane!
It's a . . . CHANDELIER?!?
Seems to be a SLOGAN in there somewhere, Paw . . . but I think the PUNCH-LINE still needs work!!
Ford
GLENN
Look, Paw!! The thing has landed, and a tiny creature is getting out! You can see he's not one of us, and he's got a strange look in his eyes! Like he's ready to take over the WHOLE WORLD!
My God! It's a midget ARAB!
No, you dummy! It's only a little baby!!

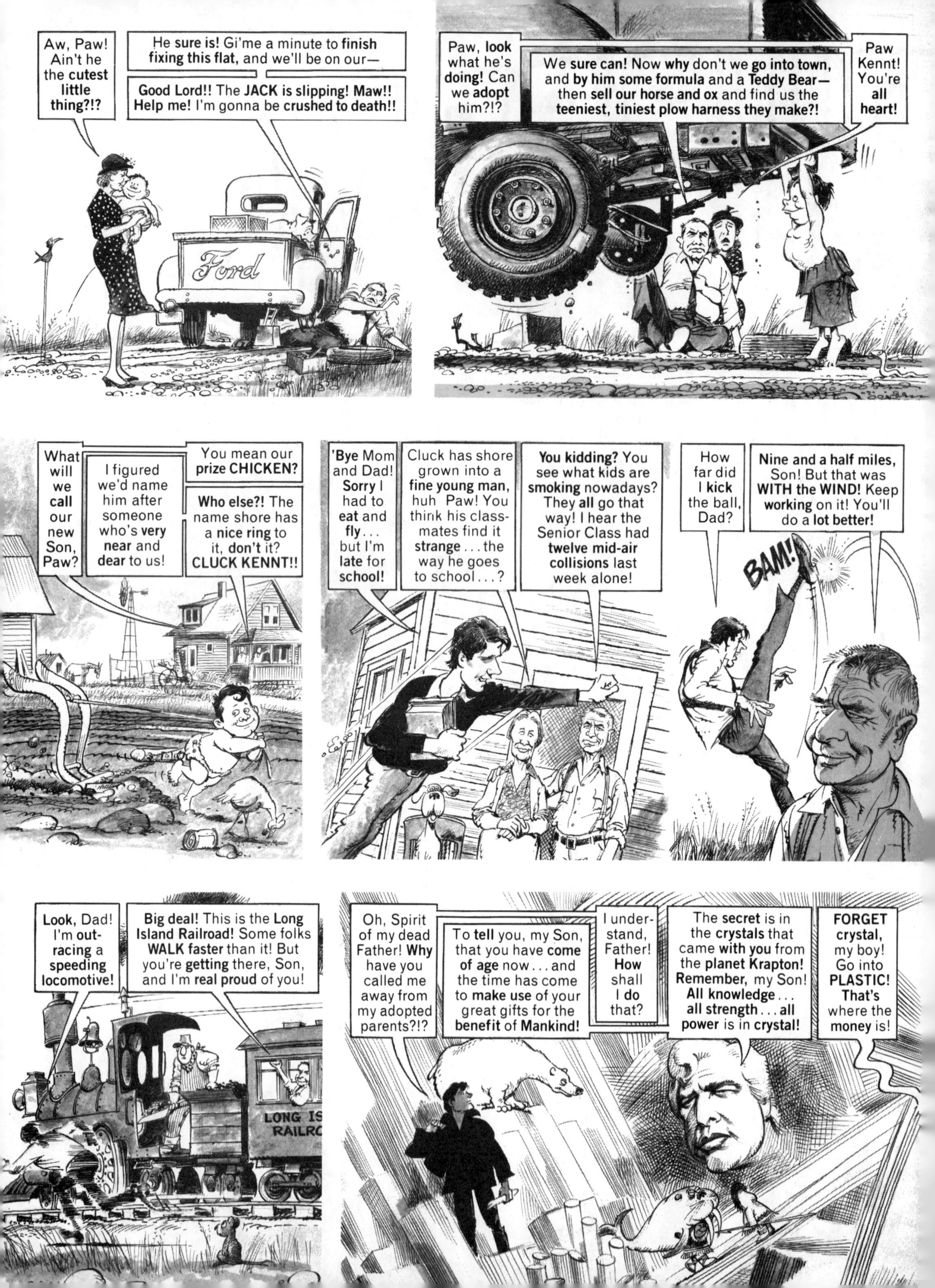

Aw, Paw! Ain't he the cutest little thing?!?
He sure is! Gi'me a minute to finish fixing this flat, and we'll be on our—
Good Lord!! The JACK is slipping! Maw!! Help me! I'm gonna be crushed to death!!
Ford
Paw, look what he's doing! Can we adopt him?!?
We sure can! Now why don't we go into town, and by him some formula and a Teddy Bear—then sell our horse and ox and find us the teeniest, tiniest plow harness they make?!
Paw Kennt! You're all heart!
What will we call our new Son, Paw?
I figured we'd name him after someone who's very near and dear to us!
You mean our prize CHICKEN?
Who else?! The name shore has a nice ring to it, don't it? CLUCK KENNT!!
'Bye Mom and Dad! Sorry I had to eat and fly . . . but I'm late for school!
Cluck has shore grown into a fine young man, huh Paw! You think his classmates find it strange . . . the way he goes to school . . . ?
You kidding? You see what kids are smoking nowadays? They all go that way! I hear the Senior Class had twelve mid-air collisions last week alone!
How far did I kick the ball, Dad?
Nine and a half miles, Son! But that was WITH the WIND! Keep working on it! You'll do a lot better!
BAM!
Look, Dad! I'm out-racing a speeding locomotive!
Big deal! This is the Long Island Railroad! Some folks WALK faster than it! But you're getting there, Son, and I'm real proud of you!
Oh, Spirit of my dead Father! Why have you called me away from my adopted parents?!?
To tell you, my Son, that you have come of age now . . . and the time has come to make use of your great gifts for the benefit of Mankind!
I understand, Father! How shall I do that?
The secret is in the crystals that came with you from the planet Krapton! Remember, my Son! All knowledge . . . all strength . . . all power is in crystal!
FORGET crystal, my boy! Go into PLASTIC! That's where the money is!

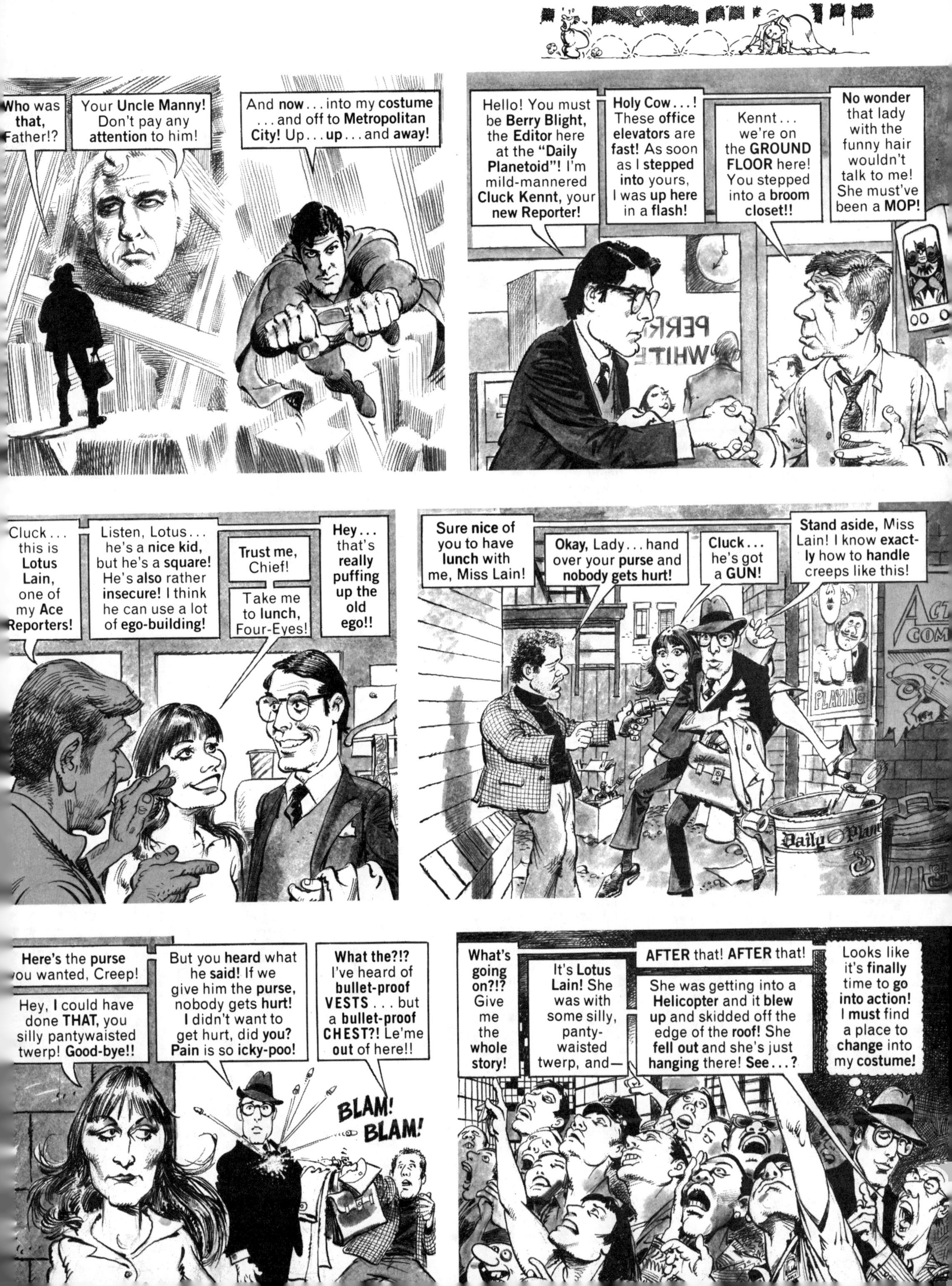
Who was that, Father!?
Your Uncle Manny! Don't pay any attention to him!
And now . . . into my costume . . . and off to Metropolitan City! Up . . . up . . . and away!
Hello! You must be Berry Blight, the Editor here at the "Daily Planetoid"! I'm mild-mannered Cluck Kennt, your new Reporter!
Holy Cow . . . ! These office elevators are fast! As soon as I stepped into yours, I was up here in a flash!
Kennt . . . we're on the GROUND FLOOR here! You stepped into a broom closet!!
No wonder that lady with the funny hair wouldn't talk to me! She must've been a MOP!
PERRY WHITE
Cluck . . . this is Lotus Lain, one of my Ace Reporters!
Listen, Lotus . . . he's a nice kid, but he's a square! He's also rather insecure! I think he can use a lot of ego-building!
Trust me, Chief!
Take me to lunch, Four-Eyes!
Hey . . . that's really puffing up the old ego!!
Sure nice of you to have lunch with me, Miss Lain!
Okay, Lady . . . hand over your purse and nobody gets hurt!
Cluck . . . he's got a GUN!
Stand aside, Miss Lain! I know exactly how to handle creeps like this!
PLAYING
Daily Planet
Here's the purse you wanted, Creep!
Hey, I could have done THAT, you silly pantywaisted twerp! Good-bye!!
But you heard what he said! If we give him the purse, nobody gets hurt! I didn't want to get hurt, did you? Pain is so icky-poo!
What the?!? I've heard of bullet-proof VESTS . . . but a bullet-proof CHEST?! Le'me out of here!!
BLAM! BLAM!
What's going on?!? Give me the whole story!
It's Lotus Lain! She was with some silly, panty-waisted twerp, and—
AFTER that! AFTER that!
She was getting into a Helicopter and it blew up and skidded off the edge of the roof! She fell out and she's just hanging there! See . . . ?
Looks like it's finally time to go into action! I must find a place to change into my costume!

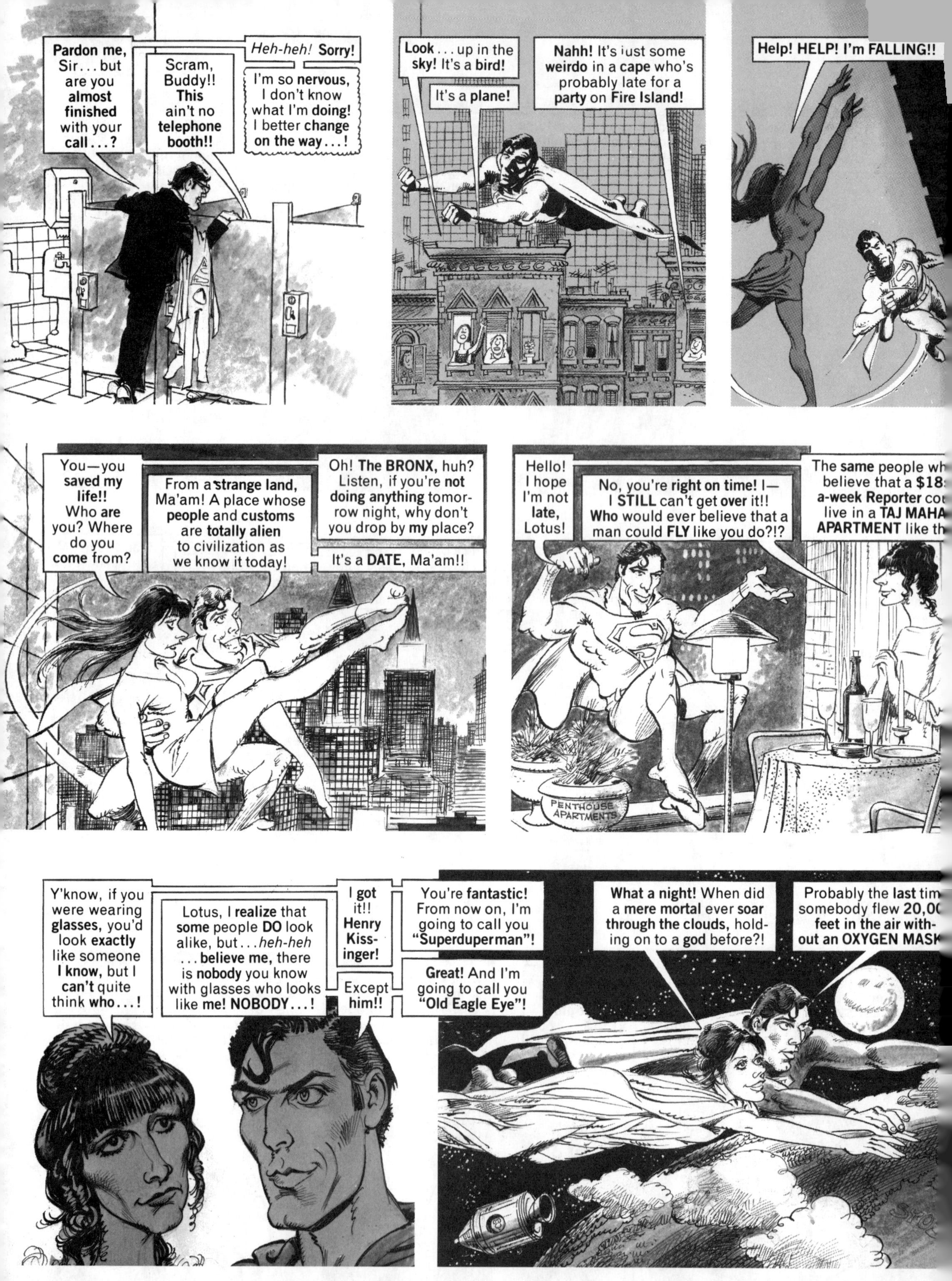

Pardon me, Sir... but are you almost finished with your call...?
Scram, Buddy!! This ain't no telephone booth!!
Heh-heh! Sorry!
I'm so nervous, I don't know what I'm doing! I better change on the way...!
Look... up in the sky! It's a bird!
It's a plane!
Nahh! It's just some weirdo in a cape who's probably late for a party on Fire Island!
Help! HELP! I'm FALLING!!
You—you saved my life!! Who are you? Where do you come from?
From a strange land, Ma'am! A place whose people and customs are totally alien to civilization as we know it today!
Oh! The BRONX, huh? Listen, if you're not doing anything tomorrow night, why don't you drop by my place?
It's a DATE, Ma'am!!
Hello! I hope I'm not late, Lotus!
No, you're right on time! I—I STILL can't get over it!! Who would ever believe that a man could FLY like you do?!?
PENTHOUSE APARTMENTS
Y'know, if you were wearing glasses, you'd look exactly like someone I know, but I can't quite think who...!
Lotus, I realize that some people DO look alike, but... heh-heh ... believe me, there is nobody you know with glasses who looks like me! NOBODY...!
I got it!! Henry Kissinger!
Except him!!
You're fantastic! From now on, I'm going to call you "Superduperman"!
Great! And I'm going to call you "Old Eagle Eye"!
What a night! When did a mere mortal ever soar through the clouds, holding on to a god before?!

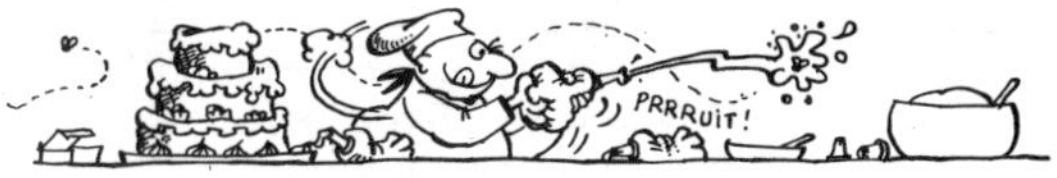
PRRRUIT!

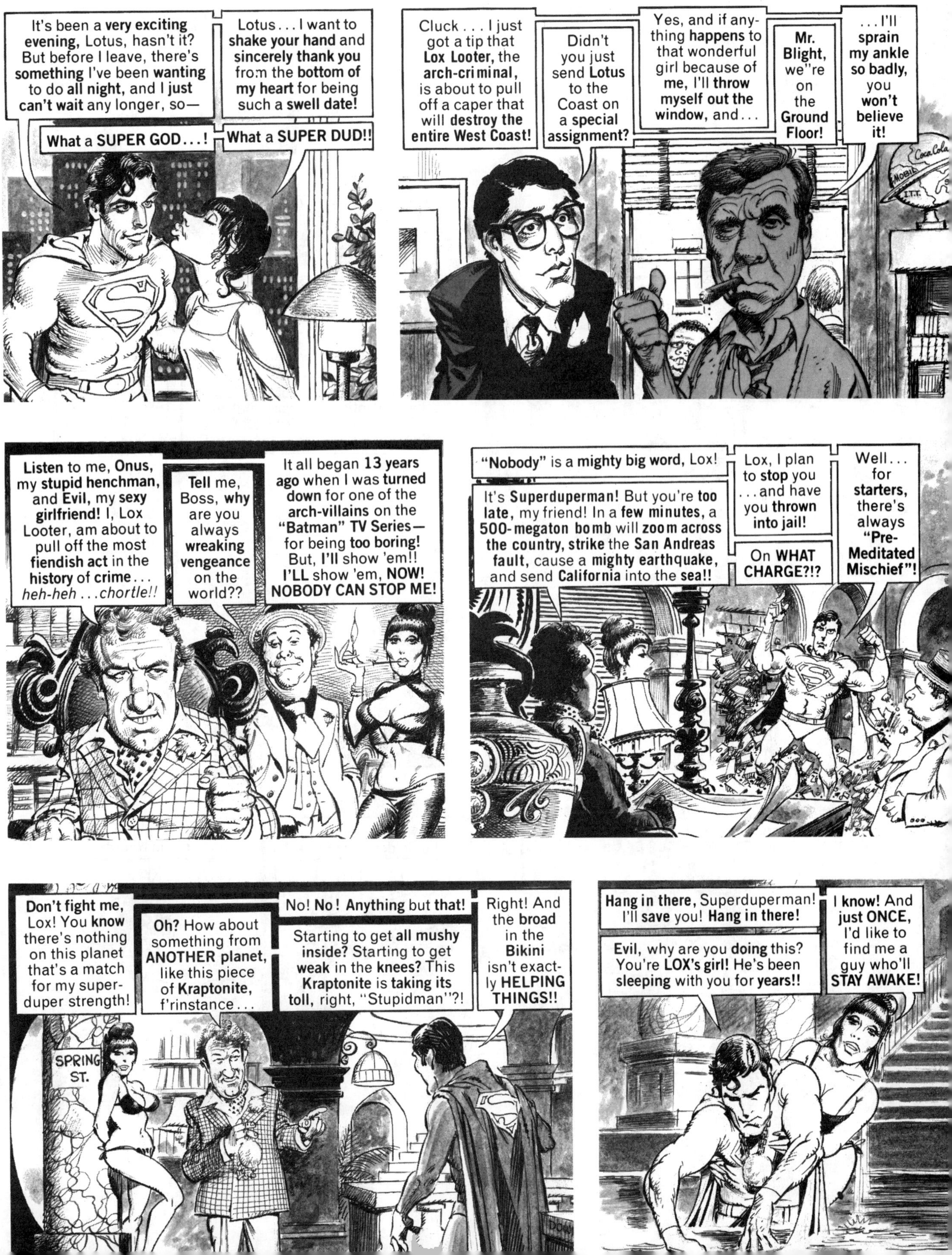
It's been a very exciting evening, Lotus, hasn't it? But before I leave, there's something I've been wanting to do all night, and I just can't wait any longer, so—
What a SUPER GOD...!
Lotus... I want to shake your hand and sincerely thank you from the bottom of my heart for being such a swell date!
What a SUPER DUD!!
Cluck... I just got a tip that Lox Looter, the arch-criminal, is about to pull off a caper that will destroy the entire West Coast!
Didn't you just send Lotus to the Coast on a special assignment?
Yes, and if anything happens to that wonderful girl because of me, I'll throw myself out the window, and...
Mr. Blight, we''re on the Ground Floor!
...I'll sprain my ankle so badly, you won't believe it!
Coca Cola
MOBIL
I.T.T.
Listen to me, Onus, my stupid henchman, and Evil, my sexy girlfriend! I, Lox Looter, am about to pull off the most fiendish act in the history of crime... heh-heh...chortle!!
Tell me, Boss, why are you always wreaking vengeance on the world??
It all began 13 years ago when I was turned down for one of the arch-villains on the "Batman" TV Series—for being too boring! But, I'll show 'em!! I'LL show 'em, NOW! NOBODY CAN STOP ME!
"Nobody" is a mighty big word, Lox!
It's Superduperman! But you're too late, my friend! In a few minutes, a 500-megaton bomb will zoom across the country, strike the San Andreas fault, cause a mighty earthquake, and send California into the sea!!
Lox, I plan to stop you ...and have you thrown into jail!
On WHAT CHARGE?!?
Well... for starters, there's always "Pre-Meditated Mischief"!
Don't fight me, Lox! You know there's nothing on this planet that's a match for my super-duper strength!
Oh? How about something from ANOTHER planet, like this piece of Kraptonite, f'rinstance...
No! No! Anything but that!
Starting to get all mushy inside? Starting to get weak in the knees? This Kraptonite is taking its toll, right, "Stupidman"?!
Right! And the broad in the Bikini isn't exactly HELPING THINGS!!
SPRING ST.
Hang in there, Superduperman! I'll save you! Hang in there!
Evil, why are you doing this? You're LOX's girl! He's been sleeping with you for years!!
I know! And just ONCE, I'd like to find me a guy who'll STAY AWAKE!

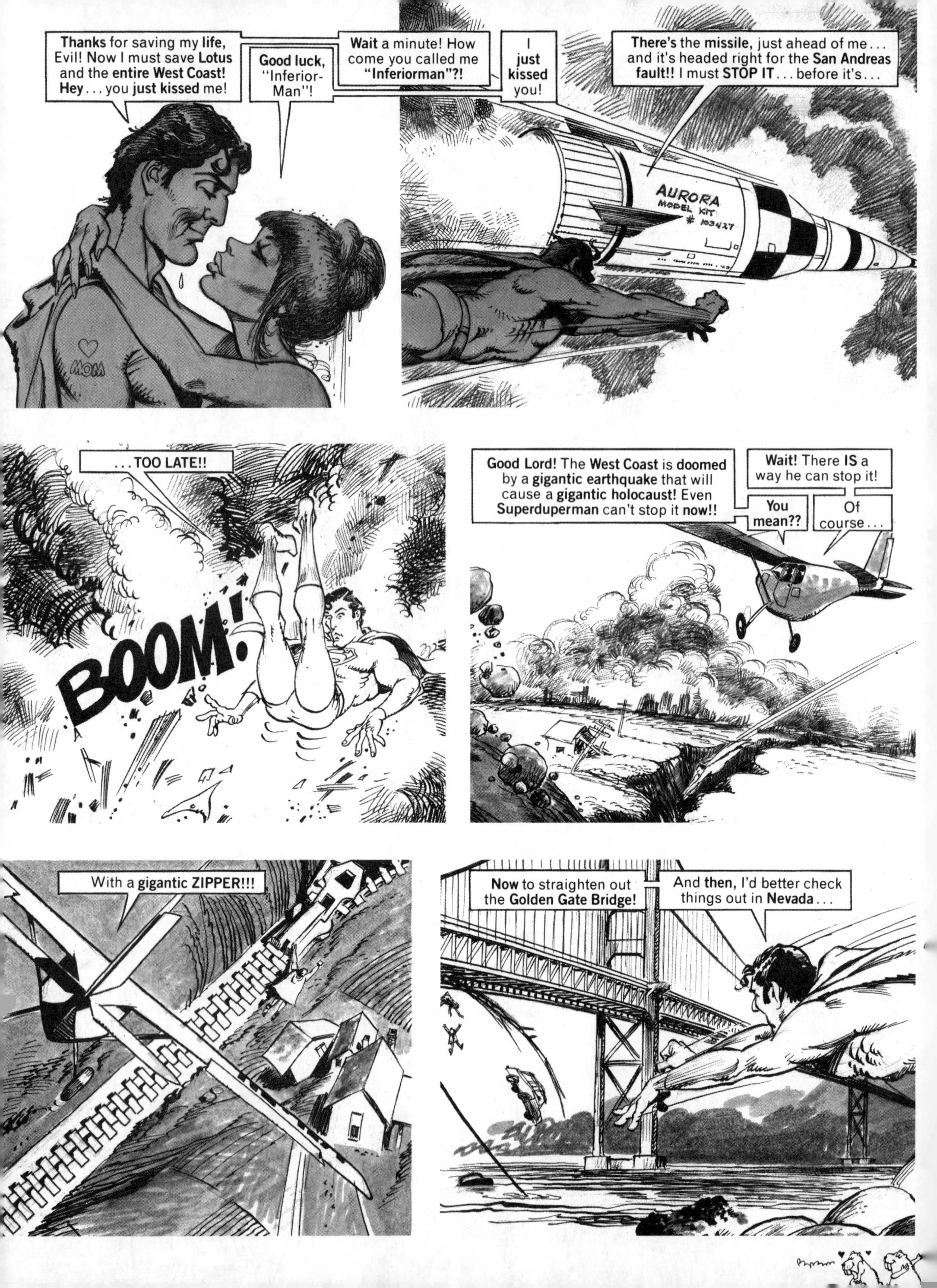

Thanks for saving my life, Evil! Now I must save Lotus and the entire West Coast! Hey . . . you just kissed me!
Good luck, "Inferior-Man"!
Wait a minute! How come you called me "Inferiorman"?!
I just kissed you!
There's the missile, just ahead of me . . . and it's headed right for the San Andreas fault!! I must STOP IT . . . before it's . . .
AURORA MODEL KIT
MOM
. . . TOO LATE!!
BOOM!
Good Lord! The West Coast is doomed by a gigantic earthquake that will cause a gigantic holocaust! Even Superduperman can't stop it now!!
Wait! There IS a way he can stop it!
You mean??
Of course . . .
With a gigantic ZIPPER!!!
Now to straighten out the Golden Gate Bridge!
And then, I'd better check things out in Nevada . . .

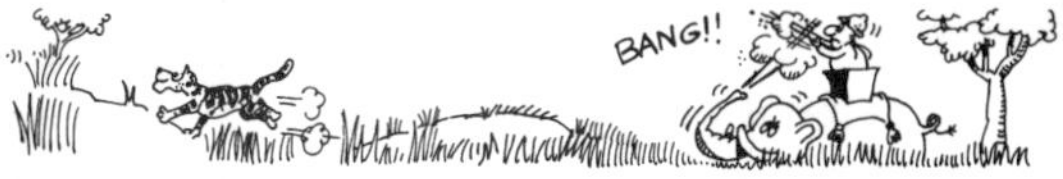
BANG!!

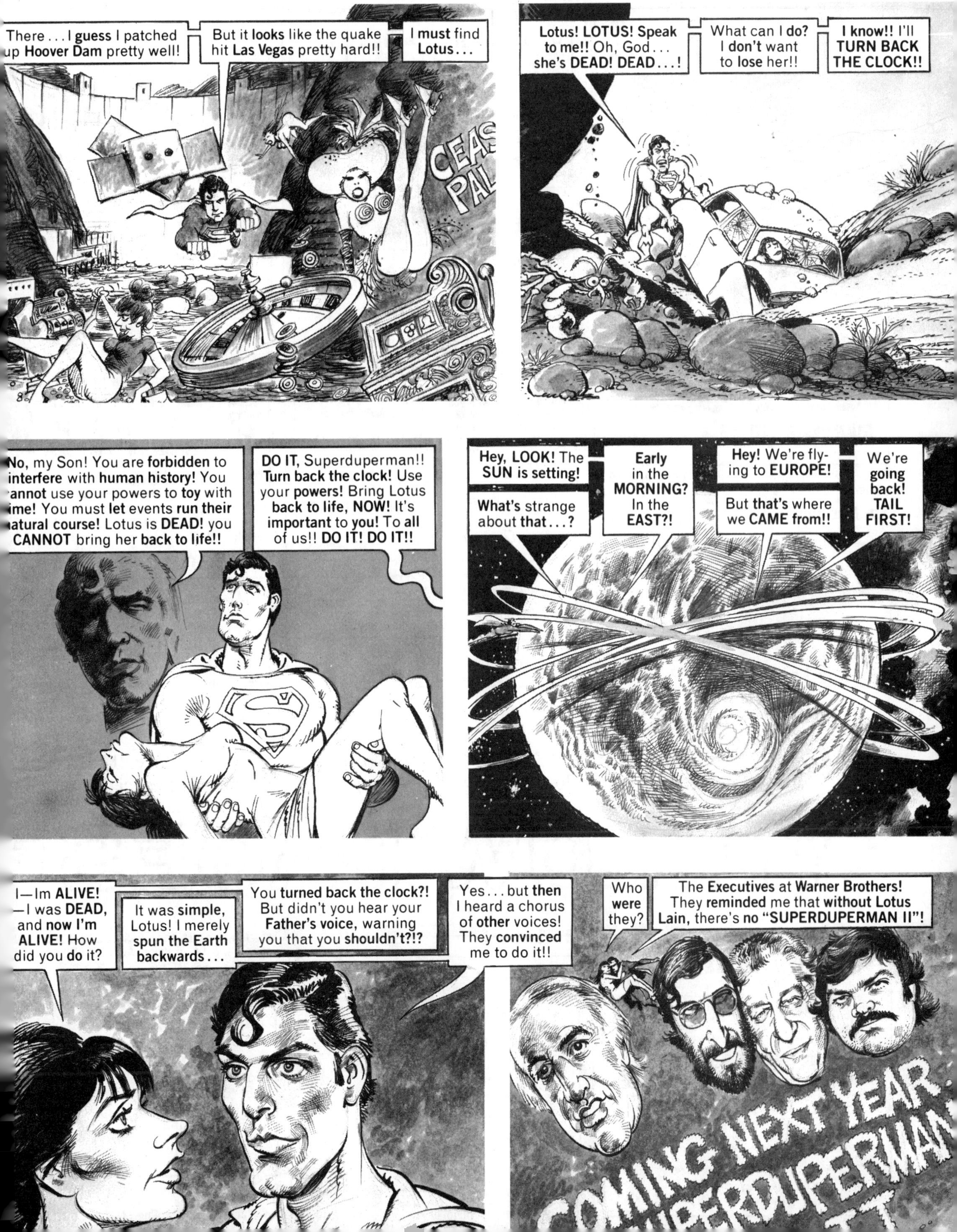
There . . . I **guess** I patched up **Hoover Dam** pretty well!
But it **looks** like the quake hit **Las Vegas** pretty hard!!
I **must** find **Lotus . . .**
CEAS PAL
Lotus! LOTUS! Speak to me!! Oh, God . . . she's **DEAD! DEAD . . . !**
What can I **do?** I **don't** want to **lose** her!!
I know!! I'll **TURN BACK THE CLOCK!!**
No, my Son! You are **forbidden** to **interfere** with **human history!** You **annot** use your powers to **toy** with **ime!** You must **let events run their atural course!** Lotus is **DEAD!** you **CANNOT** bring her **back to life!!**
DO IT, Superduperman!! **Turn back the clock!** Use your **powers!** Bring Lotus **back to life, NOW!** It's **important** to **you!** To **all** of us!! **DO IT! DO IT!!**
Hey, LOOK! The **SUN is setting!**
What's strange about **that . . . ?**
Early in the **MORNING?** In the **EAST?!**
Hey! We're fly-ing to **EUROPE!**
But **that's** where we **CAME** from!!
We're **going back! TAIL FIRST!**
I—Im **ALIVE!** —I was **DEAD,** and **now I'm ALIVE!** How did you **do** it?
It was **simple,** Lotus! I merely **spun the Earth backwards . . .**
You **turned back the clock?!** But didn't you hear your **Father's** voice, warning you that you **shouldn't?!?**
Yes . . . but **then** I heard a chorus of **other** voices! They **convinced** me to do it!!
Who **were** they?
The **Executives** at **Warner Brothers!** They **reminded** me that **without Lotus Lain,** there's no **"SUPERDUPERMAN II"!**
COMING NEXT YEAR SUPERDUPERMAN

▶ Apparel

Thinking of becoming a **SUPER HERO?** Let our custom costume designers suit you up with an outfit that will **strike terror** into the hearts of **evil-doers!**

FREE ESTIMATES!

Designs submitted for your approval.

Satisfied clients include: Batman, Green Lantern, Flash and many others.

Super Costumers

for Super Customers

225 Lafayette St. **MAsquerade 3-0940**

Airboy, Inc. 1098 Barry St..................HIllman 4-5687
Angel, The Corp 30 Gustavson Pl.......TImely 3-9579

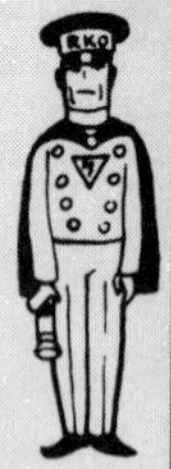

▶ Automobile Sales & Service

Are you driving an out-of-date super car with those corny old-fashioned gimmicks? Let MARVEL MOBILES design you a modern jet-powered "Crime-Fighting Arsenal"

(Snow tires Extra) Garage located 75 feet underground! By appointment only.

MARVEL MOBILES 123 SHAZAM PLAZA **EDsel 2-3400**

Aquaman Associates 10 Norris Rd...NAtional 4-5565
Black Condor 3 Fine St...........................BUsy 5-4387

▶ Attorneys

Bothered by pesky **LAW SUITS?**

Let us get you out of the courtroom and back up in the sky FAST! Don't let all those small claims against your locomotive-stopping, plane-catching or door-smashing bog you down!

Martini & Rossi

708 DEFENDER BLDG.

PLaintiff 3-7771

▶ Chemistry

- **LAUGHING GAS**
- **TEAR GAS**
- **SMOKE PELLETS**
- **STINK BOMBS**

What's your specialty? We mix, package and deliver standard or special formula gasses in handy, compact, easy to throw capsules!

GAS-O-RAMA 903 Potsdam Dr. **MUstard 8-0004**

▶ Chiropractors

WHY SUFFER?

Don't be ashamed of aches and pains! It's all a part of the hero-business. We'll take care of sprains and dislocations and never tell a soul!

SIDNEY SPINEBENDER 97 Manipulate Place **ORtho 0-2367**

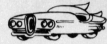

▶ Clothes Pickup Services

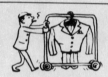

Step into that phone booth, discard your everyday clothes, and then—CALL US! Don't let the fear of having someone walk away with your $100 tropical worsted cramp your crime-busting style. Charge into your villains with the confidence that your clothes are in good hands and will be delivered later in strictest confidence.

HERO GARMENT RETRIEVERS

302 Transvestite Ave.

RObert Hall 9-8642

▶ Dry Cleaning

Special dry cleaning service tailored to the needs of today's crime-fighters. Don't risk your wholesome public image by appearing in a costume soiled by blood-stains or spaghetti sauce!

WE CLEAN WHILE YOU WAIT!

ZAP CLEANERS 45 Bard FEnster 3-5401

▶ Embroidery

One-of-a-kind Insignia Service

Emblems securely embroidered in fire-proof thread on your leotards or cape. A wide selection of letters, symbols, stars, lightning bolts, animals, etc.

MORRIS INSIGNIA LTD. NEedle 8-110

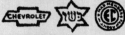

Blue Bolt, Inc. 93 Mandel St.............NOvelty 3-4
Captain Flag, Ass. 3 Streeter St.........GOldwtr 3-4

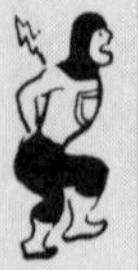

▶ Food

Super-heroes **CAN** get super-malnu trition if they don't **eat** good! S you're busy—so you're in a hurry—s big deal! You can **always** afford minutes for your **belly!** One of Hank' Super-Burgers has enough **vitamin** and nutrients to keep you going fo twenty-four hours!

Eat here or Fly-out service

Hank's Super-Burgers

Fishman's Plaza East

Call GRistle 3-8800

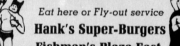

Captain Marvel, Inc. 4 Crowley Rd...FAwcett 5-46
Catman, & Co. 34 Quinlan St...............HEInit 7-77
Chameleon, Ltd. 134 Davis Ln...........NOvelty 3-33

▶ Ghost Writing

Don't put your invincible foot in your super mouth! Let us write your speeches for Yout Groups, Hospital Dedications, Air Meets an Comicons. Free Brochure on request: Call no

PHANTOM Suite 35 OPERA BLDG. SPelvin 4-56

Commando Ranger Bros. 33 Saaf Rd...FIction 9-45
Death Patrol 40 Davenport Ave.........QUality 8-45

COMIC RELIEF DEPT.

Needless to say, the life of any "Caped Crusader" can't be all glory. There comes time when even our long underwear-wearing crime fighters need special services n

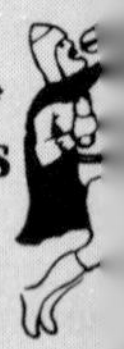

YELLOW PAGES F

▶ Belts

UTILITY BELTS

with accessory pockets for gas pellets, wire cutters, climbing ropes, aspirins, etc. You name it, we'll make a place for it. Send your requirements and waist size (strictly confidential, so don't shave off a few inches for vanity sake) and we'll give a free estimate.

BIG BELTER BELTS

24 West 34th St. COrset 5-0059

▶ Camps

This summer, give your boy-wonder assistant some *time off!* Send him to camp with ordinary youngsters for the vacation of his life! Identities scrupulously guarded!

ROBIN'S NEST CAMP FOR BOYS Wurtsboro, New York **GRayson 3-2425**

▶ Electronics

NOW For super-heroes who lack the advantages of X-ray vision:

ZUCH ELECTRONICS

Miniaturized X-Ray Machine

See our full line of minute, transistorized gadgets and gimmicks that will give you other special powers that you lack!

ZUCH ELECTRONICS Wyandanch Rd. SHort 8-1101

Blackhawk Ltd. 1980 Cuidera Ave.....QUality 7-5656
Black Terror Co. 60 Robinson Lane..STandard 9-0997
Black X, The 46 Eisner Blvd..............QUality 9-5667
Blue Beetle Ass. 2 Nicholas Rd..............FOx 4-4454

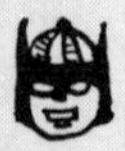

Eye, The, Inc. 34 Thomas St............CEntaur 9-9
Face, The, & Co. 4 Bailey Ave.........COlumbia 4-4

▶ Hair Pieces

Don't let the Underworld call you "baldy"!

Hairpieces so natural only your barber knows for sure! Guaranteed not to come off, even while flying faster than a speeding bullet!

RUg 5-9911 **TOPPER' 3 Broad S**

Iron Skull Ltd. 376 Gilman Av..............HArdy 6-34
Johnny Thunder, Inc. 2 Toth Blvd.......NAtionl 7-34
Lady Luck Ltd. 3 Nordling St...............QUality 9-03

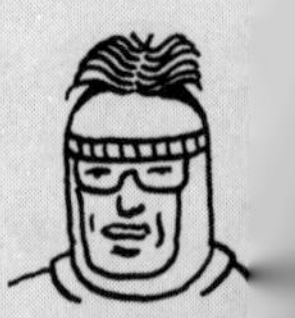

Hideouts

We'll build a new hideout for you under your home or redecorate your old cave or laboratory (complete with secret panels, passageways, tunnels, etc.) for the lowest price in town. We use only foreign speaking labor to guarantee security. Each work gang quietly deported after job is completed.

- All brass plumbing
- Poured foundation
- Pure plaster, no wall board
- 220 V. wiring—hardwood floors
- Direct sewer hookup, no cesspools

LETTIERI & BELLEZZA Contractors

19 Jersey Ave. FLimsy 9-0909

ss Fury, Inc. Tarpé Mills Ave..........TImely 4-5732
dnight Ass. 345 Cole Ave..............QUality 4-3444
ss Guardian Inc. 56 Meskin Pl.....GOldwtr 3-4549

Hosiery

Tired after a long day of crime-stopping? Super Supp-Hose will give you the support you will need for relaxing after hours.

cko Socks 75 Elastic St. STretch 1-1437

uicksilver Co. 78 Cardy St..............QUality 9-7654
andman Inc. 4 Christman Ave..........NAtionl 5-5567

Housekeeping

IGHT-LIPPED OMESTIC HELP VAILABLE

DUstrag 4-5801

rusty Homekeepers 12121 Bobrick Place

Skyman Inc. 50 Whitney Blvd..........COlmbia 9-0708

Insurance

SURE, YOU'RE INVINCIBLE, BUT WHAT IF . . . ?

Have you provided for the future well-being of your boy assistant if something, God forbid, should happen to you? How about your parents? Would you want them to go on welfare if some arch fiend finally figures out a way to do you in? Provide for those you love by calling in one of our Hero Security Consultants today.

Al Alexander Sales Rep.

Hero Insurance Group

91 N. Franklin PRemium 5-1000

Junk

Earn extra income while helping society. We pay spot cash for items you smash to bits . . . autos, bridges, fences, etc. Anything you wreck in the line of duty is worth money. Carry it in or phone for pickup.

Seymour's Scrap Oasis

775 Labonza Rd. SAlvage 8-1099

Mottos

Add a note of *profundity* to your crime-busting! Remember what the "weed of crime" motto did for The Shadow? Let Super- Slogans do the same for *you!*

1966 Winner of Parseghian Award (Credo Category)

"Commit a crime and the world is made of glass" The Green Glazier

Winner of 1966 "EDDY"—

"Those who travel the Highway of Crime must pay the toll" Captain Turnpike

BArtlett 7-3233

Super-Slogans, Inc.

12 Kimosabe Lane

Shoe Repair

Don't let your heel let a "heel" slip away! Worn out boot soles and heels don't grip rooftops or sides of buildings properly. Come in today for a free traction check-up.

NICK'S SOLE-VILLE

3910—16th AVE. O'Sullivan 2-1234

Speech Instruction

Is your voice a dead giveaway?

Are people liable to discover your **secret identity** because of it? We'll teach you to **change your voice** as you **change your clothes!** Your voice will take on a new dimension of authority when you say **"Take that, you fiend!"** We guarantee a more heroic voice in just **3 short weeks** or your money will be **cheerfully refunded.**

MYSTO VOICE SCHOOL

241 Kearny St., DIction 5-0045

Target, The Ltd. 45 Greene Ave.........NOvelty 4-4678
Tomahawk & Co. 34 Ray Blvd............NAtionl 4-5429

Stock Brokers

When you're finished fighting all those nogoodniks, what will you live on? Your plaques and scrolls from a grateful Metropolis? Fat chance! Start today to put a little something into a Monthly Investment Plan that will see you safely through your declining years.

FELD, GAINES & BRENNER

900 WALL STREET

Call TIcker 9-7530

Vision, The, Ass. 78 Simon Ln............TImely 8-3450
Wildcat Ltd. 6 Irwin Hasen St..........NAtionl 9-4939
Zatara & Co. 8 Guardineer Place........NAtionl 9-6543

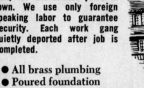

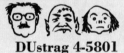

ailable in everyday type stores. And when this time comes, they do as we everyday ople do—they let their muscle-bound fingers do the walking, right through the . . .

WRITER:
DON REILLY

SUPER HEROES

Inspiration

o you feel no one eally cares bout you?

o you feel feared nd respected but ot loved?

DIAL-A-BLESSING FAith 4-7291

adow Ass. 3 Powell Lane...............ESaness 7-4347
ark, The, Corp. 56 Glanzman..........HArdy 2-2479
eena, Inc. 2150 Cayuga Dr....FIctionhouse 7-7776
ield, The Ass. 10 Novick Pl..........GOldwtr 4-4769

Spacehawk, Ltd. 4 Wolverton Blvd...NOvelty 7-7777
Steel Sterling, Corp. 3 Biro Pl..........GOldwtr 7-3334
Sub-Mariner & Co. 5 Everett St..........TImely 9-4545

Public Opinion Research

Are you as popular as you used to be? Don't rely on the cheers of the crowd or the grateful embraces of rescued maidens to know how you're doing. Let us take a scientific sample of the population to give you a statistically valid public opinion profile of what people really think of you. Guaranteed no press leaks of the results.

GAllup 4-5566

Wessel Research,

5960 W. Coolidge Ave.

Tailoring

Suits carefully designed to completely conceal your bulky costume underneath!

SPECIAL JACKET DESIGN ELIMINATES "CAPE BULGE"

Trousers with nylon side zippers for instant removal ends cursing and fumbling with conventional fly.

MANNY & MOE'S OVER-ALL-SUITS

95 SECOND AVE. GArment 8-1077

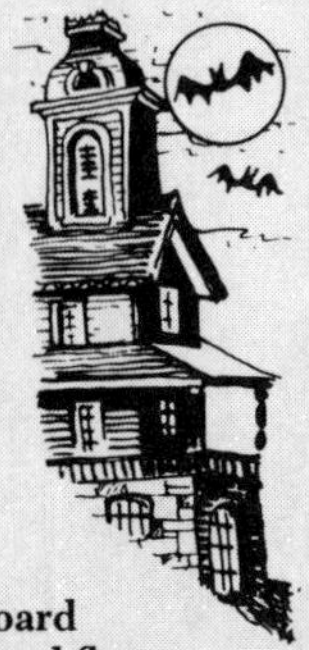

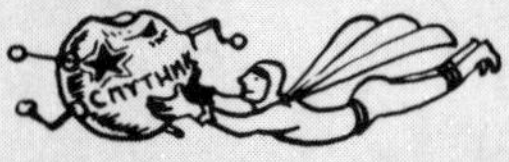

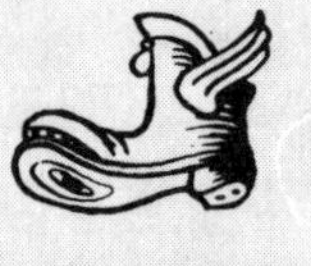

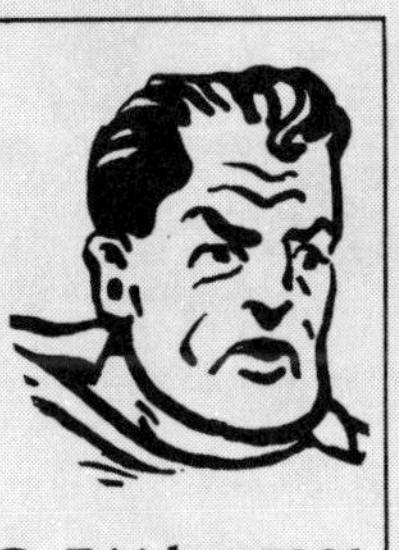

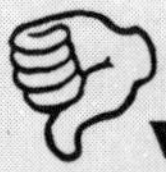

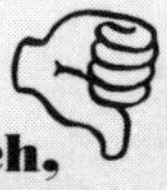

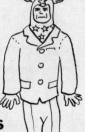

THE DYNAMIC UNO DEPT.

What's the hot-action, feel-good hit of the summer that people are flocking to see? *Ghostbusters II*, of course! Which is why MAD now proudly presents its satire of...

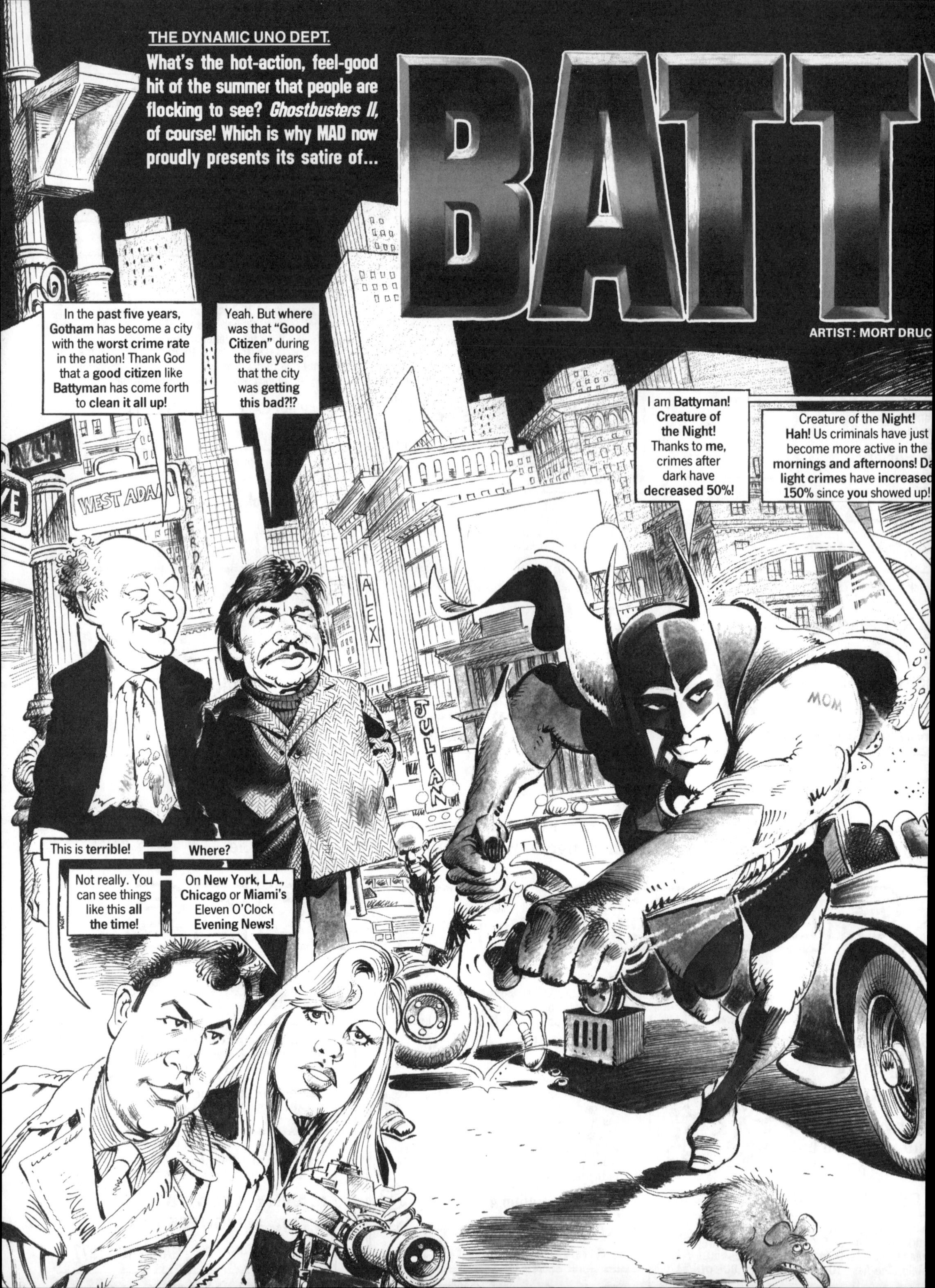

BATTY
ARTIST: MORT DRUC
In the past five years, Gotham has become a city with the worst crime rate in the nation! Thank God that a good citizen like Battyman has come forth to clean it all up!
Yeah. But where was that "Good Citizen" during the five years that the city was getting this bad?!?
I am Battyman! Creature of the Night! Thanks to me, crimes after dark have decreased 50%!
Creature of the Night! Hah! Us criminals have just become more active in the mornings and afternoons! Da light crimes have increased 150% since you showed up!
This is terrible!
Where?
Not really. You can see things like this all the time!
On New York, L.A., Chicago or Miami's Eleven O'Clock Evening News!
WEST ADAM
AMSTERDAM
ALEX
JULIAN
MOM

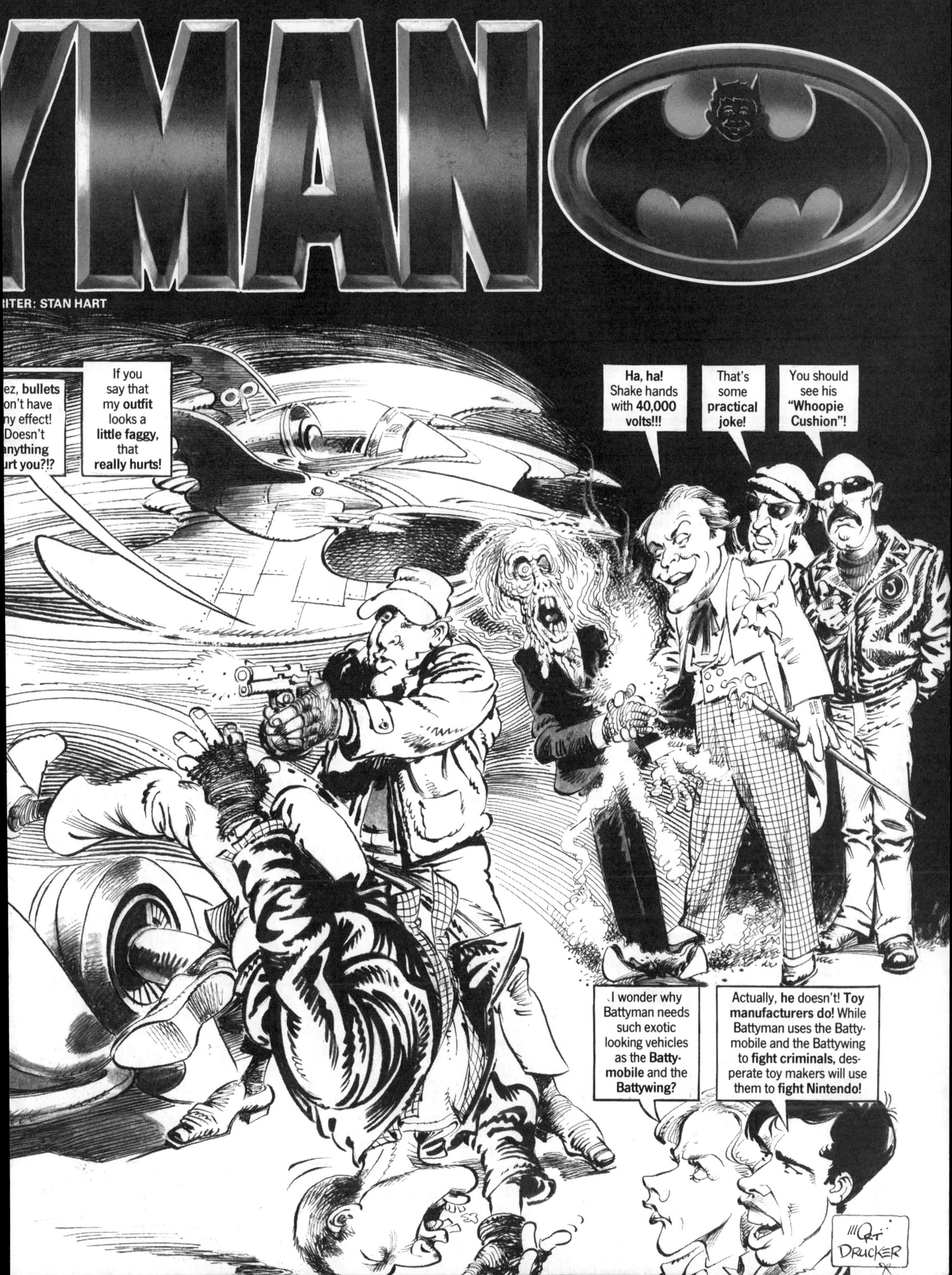

YMAN
RITER: STAN HART
ez, bullets on't have ny effect! Doesn't anything urt you?!?
If you say that my outfit looks a little faggy, that really hurts!
Ha, ha! Shake hands with 40,000 volts!!!
That's some practical joke!
You should see his "Whoopie Cushion"!
I wonder why Battyman needs such exotic looking vehicles as the Batty-mobile and the Battywing?
Actually, he doesn't! Toy manufacturers do! While Battyman uses the Batty-mobile and the Battywing to fight criminals, desperate toy makers will use them to fight Nintendo!
Mort DRUCKER

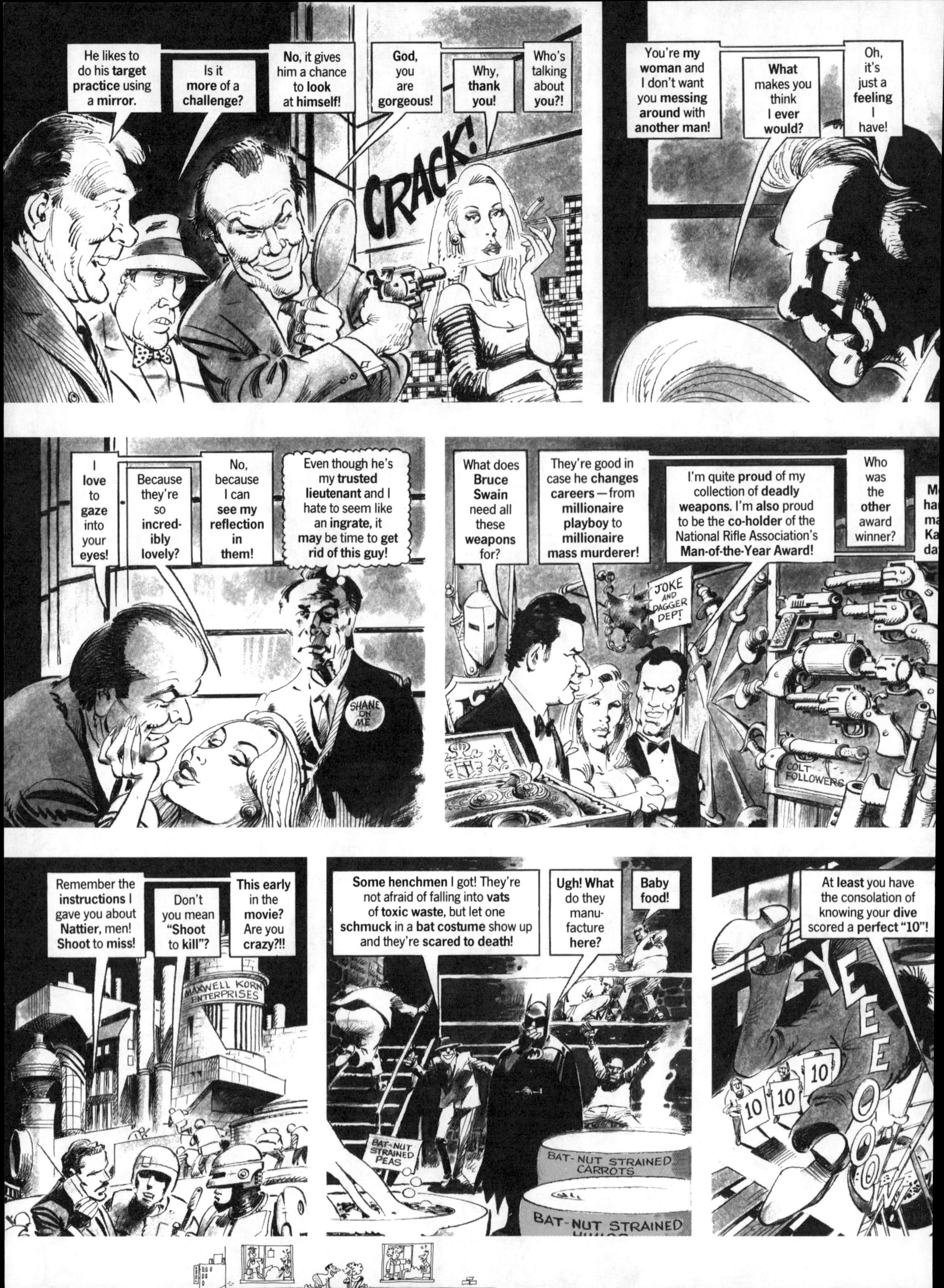
He likes to do his target practice using a mirror.
Is it more of a challenge?
No, it gives him a chance to look at himself!
God, you are gorgeous!
Why, thank you!
Who's talking about you?!
CRACK!
You're my woman and I don't want you messing around with another man!
What makes you think I ever would?
Oh, it's just a feeling I have!
I love to gaze into your eyes!
Because they're so incred-ibly lovely?
No, because I can see my reflection in them!
Even though he's my trusted lieutenant and I hate to seem like an ingrate, it may be time to get rid of this guy!
SHANE ON ME
What does Bruce Swain need all these weapons for?
They're good in case he changes careers—from millionaire playboy to millionaire mass murderer!
I'm quite proud of my collection of deadly weapons. I'm also proud to be the co-holder of the National Rifle Association's Man-of-the-Year Award!
Who was the other award winner?
JOKE AND DAGGER DEPT
COLT FOLLOWERS
Remember the instructions I gave you about Nattier, men! Shoot to miss!
Don't you mean "Shoot to kill"?
This early in the movie? Are you crazy?!!
MAXWELL KORN ENTERPRISES
Some henchmen I got! They're not afraid of falling into vats of toxic waste, but let one schmuck in a bat costume show up and they're scared to death!
Ugh! What do they manu-facture here?
Baby food!
BAT-NUT STRAINED PEAS
BAT-NUT STRAINED CARROTS
BAT-NUT STRAINED
At least you have the consolation of knowing your dive scored a perfect "10"!
YEEEOOOW!
10
10
10

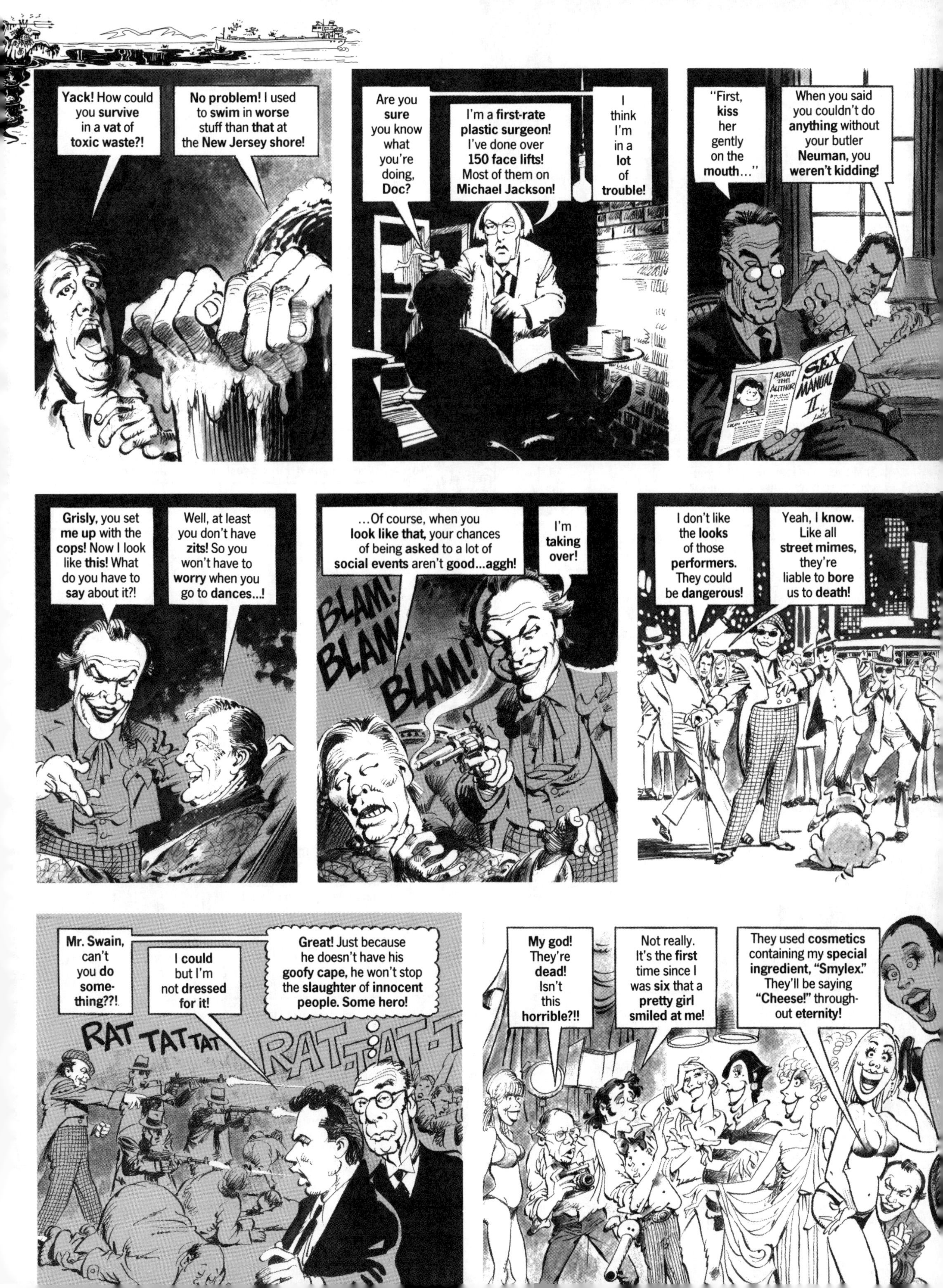
Yack! How could you survive in a vat of toxic waste?!
No problem! I used to swim in worse stuff than that at the New Jersey shore!
Are you sure you know what you're doing, Doc?
I'm a first-rate plastic surgeon! I've done over 150 face lifts! Most of them on Michael Jackson!
I think I'm in a lot of trouble!
"First, kiss her gently on the mouth…"
When you said you couldn't do anything without your butler Neuman, you weren't kidding!
ABOUT THE AUTHOR
SEX MANUAL II
Grisly, you set me up with the cops! Now I look like this! What do you have to say about it?!
Well, at least you don't have zits! So you won't have to worry when you go to dances…!
…Of course, when you look like that, your chances of being asked to a lot of social events aren't good…aggh!
I'm taking over!
BLAM! BLAM! BLAM!
I don't like the looks of those performers. They could be dangerous!
Yeah, I know. Like all street mimes, they're liable to bore us to death!
Mr. Swain, can't you do something??!
I could but I'm not dressed for it!
Great! Just because he doesn't have his goofy cape, he won't stop the slaughter of innocent people. Some hero!
RAT TAT TAT
RAT-TAT-T
My god! They're dead! Isn't this horrible?!!
Not really. It's the first time since I was six that a pretty girl smiled at me!
They used cosmetics containing my special ingredient, "Smylex." They'll be saying "Cheese!" throughout eternity!

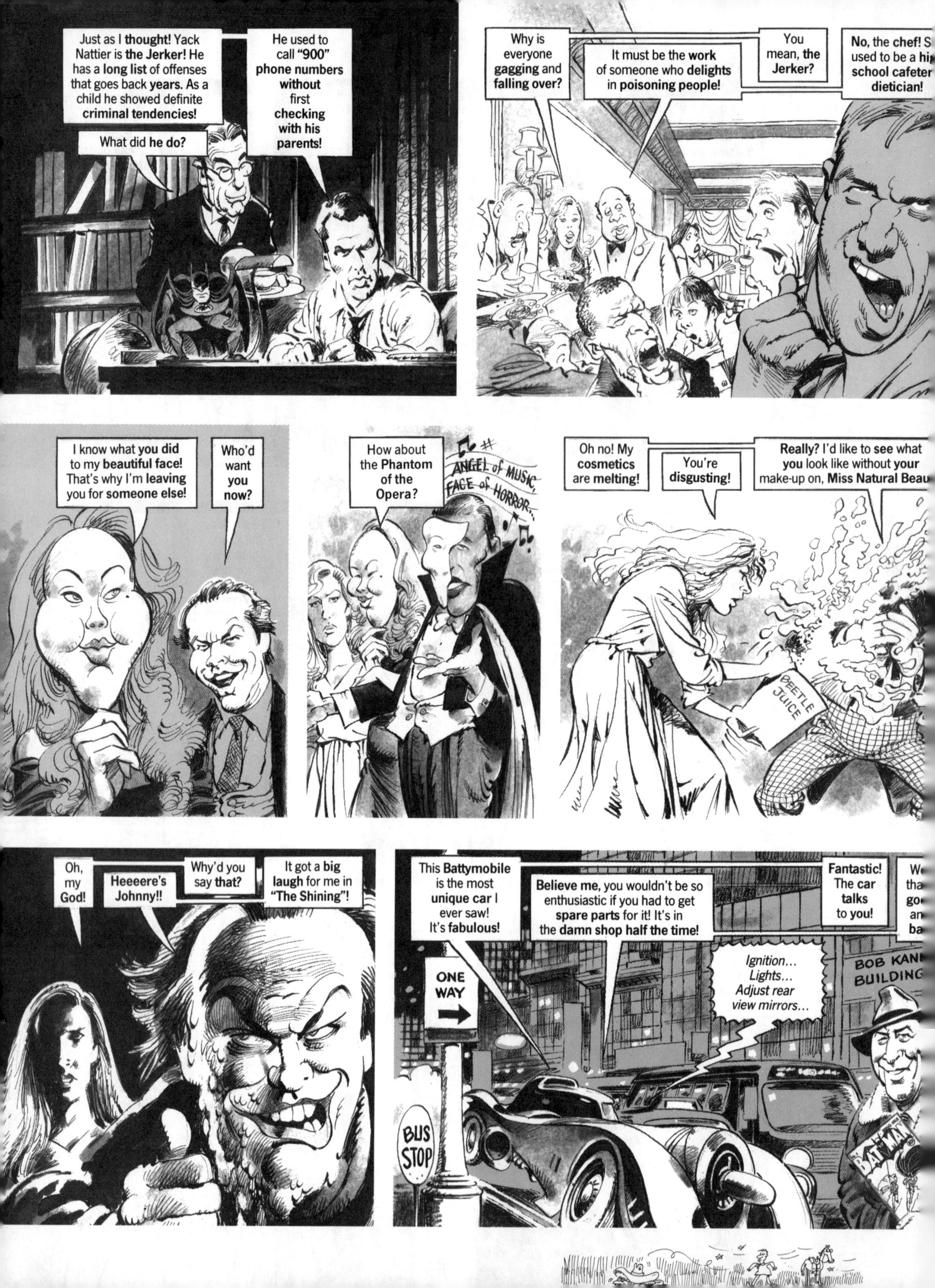

Just as I thought! Yack Nattier is the Jerker! He has a long list of offenses that goes back years. As a child he showed definite criminal tendencies!
What did he do?
He used to call "900" phone numbers without first checking with his parents!
Why is everyone gagging and falling over?
It must be the work of someone who delights in poisoning people!
You mean, the Jerker?
No, the chef! S used to be a hi school cafeter dietician!
I know what you did to my beautiful face! That's why I'm leaving you for someone else!
Who'd want you now?
How about the Phantom of the Opera?
ANGEL of MUSIC, FACE of HORROR...
Oh no! My cosmetics are melting!
You're disgusting!
Really? I'd like to see what you look like without your make-up on, Miss Natural Beau
BEETLE JUICE
Oh, my God!
Heeeere's Johnny!!
Why'd you say that?
It got a big laugh for me in "The Shining"!
This Battymobile is the most unique car I ever saw! It's fabulous!
Believe me, you wouldn't be so enthusiastic if you had to get spare parts for it! It's in the damn shop half the time!
Fantastic! The car talks to you!
ONE WAY
Ignition… Lights… Adjust rear view mirrors…
BOB KAN BUILDING
BUS STOP

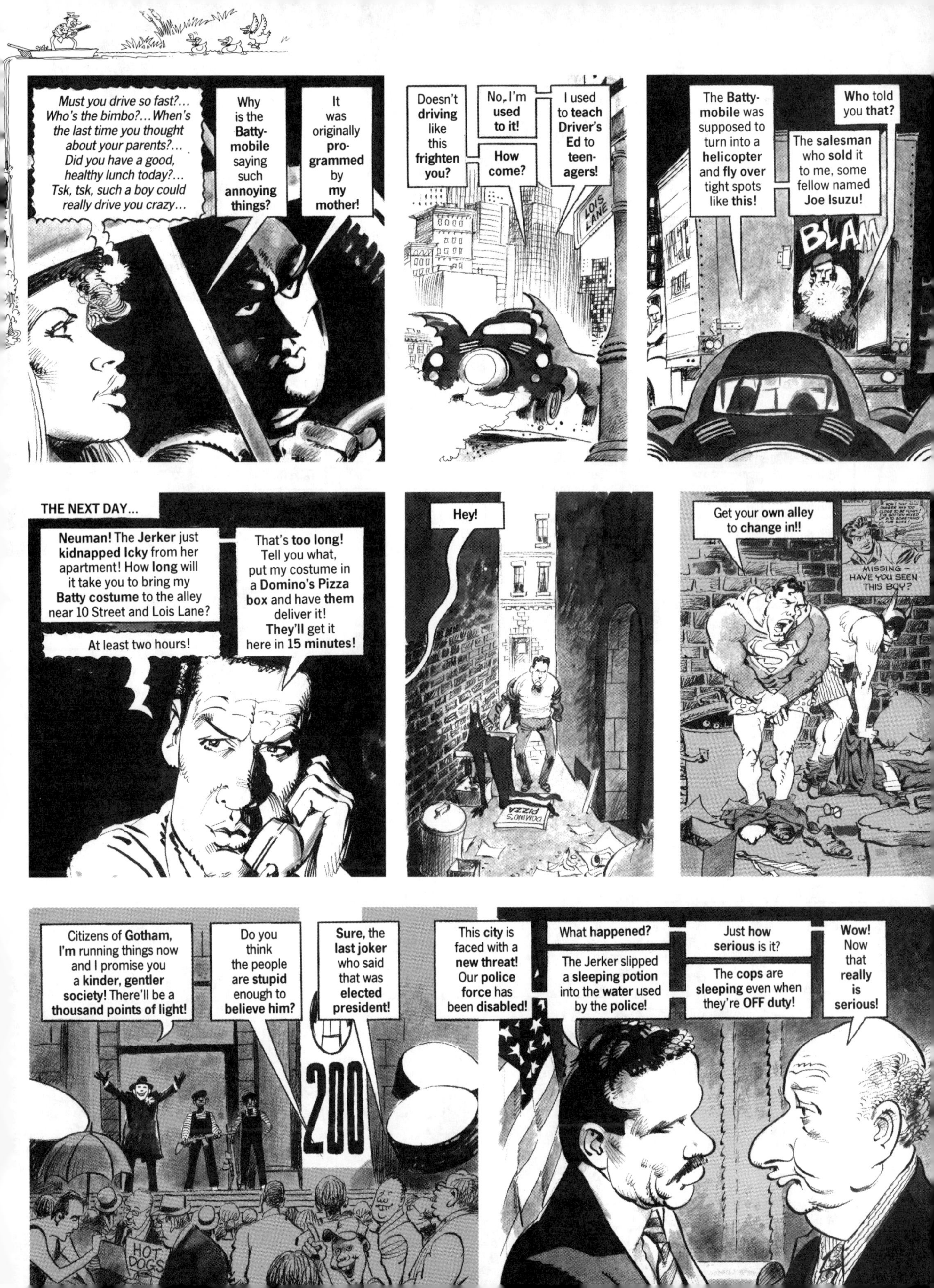

Must you drive so fast?... Who's the bimbo?...When's the last time you thought about your parents?... Did you have a good, healthy lunch today?... Tsk, tsk, such a boy could really drive you crazy...
Why is the Batty-mobile saying such annoying things?
It was originally pro-grammed by my mother!
Doesn't driving like this frighten you?
No, I'm used to it!
How come?
I used to teach Driver's Ed to teen-agers!
LOIS LANE
The Batty-mobile was supposed to turn into a helicopter and fly over tight spots like this!
Who told you that?
The salesman who sold it to me, some fellow named Joe Isuzu!
BLAM
THE NEXT DAY...
Neuman! The Jerker just kidnapped Icky from her apartment! How long will it take you to bring my Batty costume to the alley near 10 Street and Lois Lane?
At least two hours!
That's too long! Tell you what, put my costume in a Domino's Pizza box and have them deliver it! They'll get it here in 15 minutes!
Hey!
DOMINO'S PIZZA
Get your own alley to change in!!
MISSING – HAVE YOU SEEN THIS BOY?
Citizens of Gotham, I'm running things now and I promise you a kinder, gentler society! There'll be a thousand points of light!
Do you think the people are stupid enough to believe him?
Sure, the last joker who said that was elected president!
200
HOT DOGS
This city is faced with a new threat! Our police force has been disabled!
What happened?
The Jerker slipped a sleeping potion into the water used by the police!
Just how serious is it?
The cops are sleeping even when they're OFF duty!
Wow! Now that really is serious!

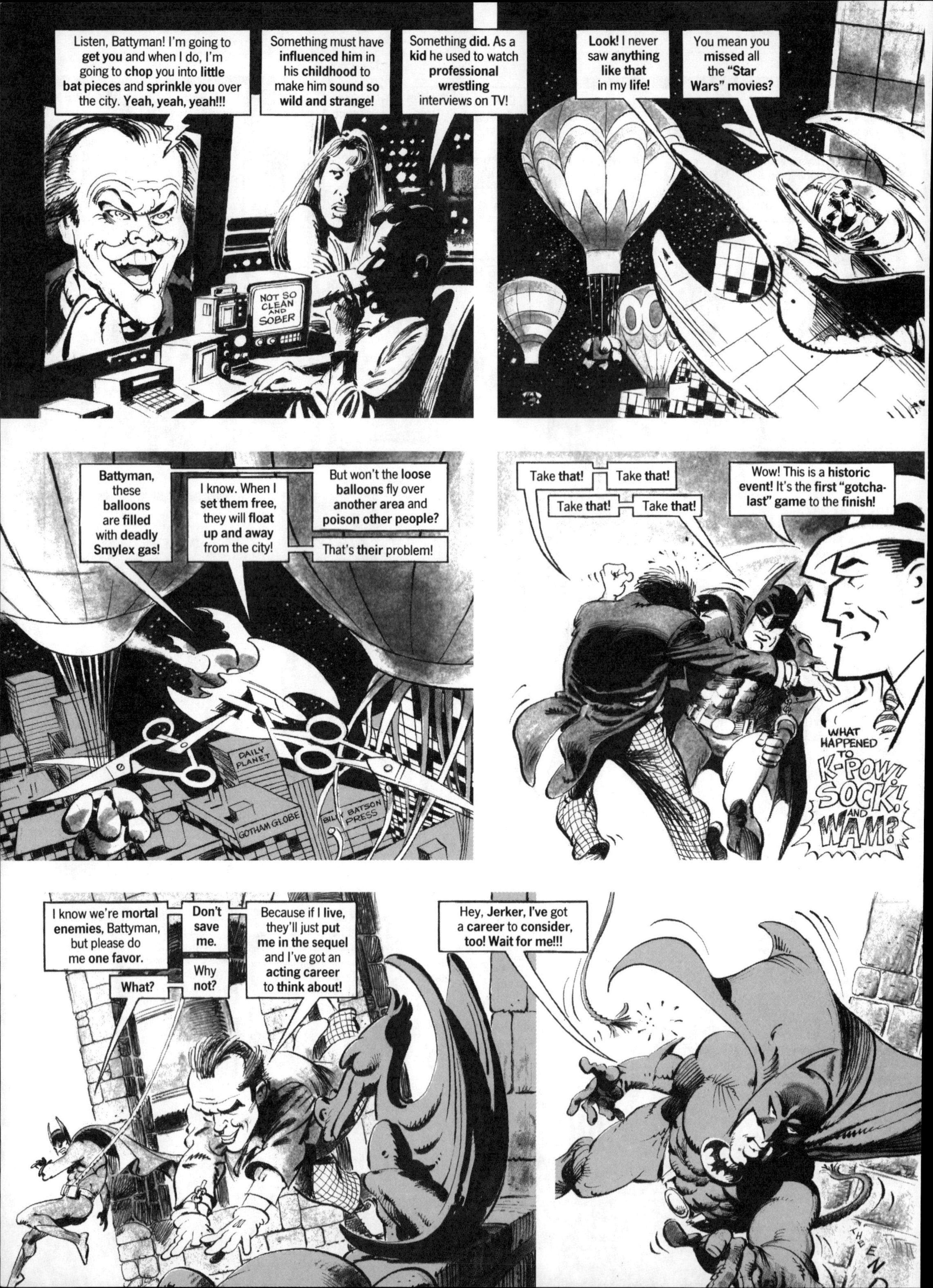

Listen, Battyman! I'm going to get you and when I do, I'm going to chop you into little bat pieces and sprinkle you over the city. Yeah, yeah, yeah!!!
Something must have influenced him in his childhood to make him sound so wild and strange!
Something did. As a kid he used to watch professional wrestling interviews on TV!
NOT SO CLEAN AND SOBER
Look! I never saw anything like that in my life!
You mean you missed all the "Star Wars" movies?
Battyman, these balloons are filled with deadly Smylex gas!
I know. When I set them free, they will float up and away from the city!
But won't the loose balloons fly over another area and poison other people?
That's their problem!
DAILY PLANET
GOTHAM GLOBE
BILLY BATSON PRESS
Take that!
Take that!
Take that!
Take that!
Wow! This is a historic event! It's the first "gotcha-last" game to the finish!
WHAT HAPPENED TO K-POW! SOCK! AND WAM?
I know we're mortal enemies, Battyman, but please do me one favor.
What?
Don't save me.
Why not?
Because if I live, they'll just put me in the sequel and I've got an acting career to think about!
Hey, Jerker, I've got a career to consider, too! Wait for me!!!
THE END

HERO WORSHIP DEPT.: FASTER THAN A SPEEDING BULLET! *KA-PWEENG!* MORE POWERFUL THAN A LOCOMOTIVE! ... *CHUGACHUGACHUGA CHUG!* ABLE TO LEAP TALL BUILDINGS IN A SINGLE BOUND!... *BOINGSWOOOSH!*... LOOK!... UP IN THE SKY!... IT'S A BIRD!... IT'S A PLANE!... IT'S...

SUPERDUPERMAN!

OUR STORY BEGINS HIGH UP IN THE OFFICES OF THAT FIGHTING NEWSPAPER, 'THE DAILY DIRT'!

AN INCREDIBLY MISERABLE AND EMACIATED LOOKING FIGURE SHUFFLES FROM SPITOON TO SPITOON!

FOR THIS IS THE ASSISTANT TO THE COPY BOY... CLARK BENT, WHO IS IN REALITY, **SUPERDUPERMAN!**

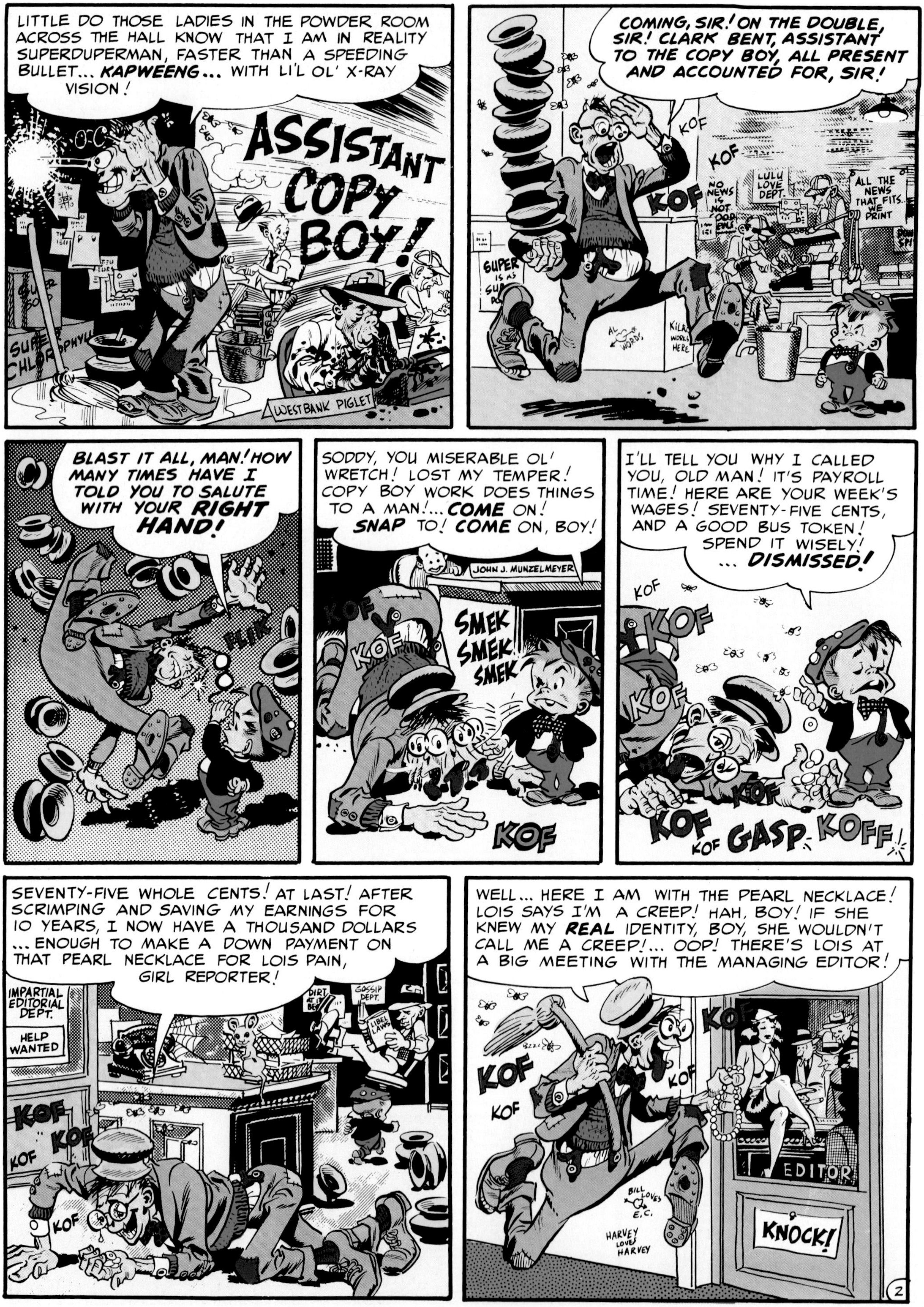

LITTLE DO THOSE LADIES IN THE POWDER ROOM ACROSS THE HALL KNOW THAT I AM IN REALITY SUPERDUPERMAN, FASTER THAN A SPEEDING BULLET... KAPWEENG... WITH LI'L OL' X-RAY VISION!
ASSISTANT COPY BOY!
WESTBANK PIGLET
COMING, SIR! ON THE DOUBLE, SIR! CLARK BENT, ASSISTANT TO THE COPY BOY, ALL PRESENT AND ACCOUNTED FOR, SIR!
KOF
KOF
KOF
LULU LOVE DEPT.
ALL THE NEWS THAT FITS... WE PRINT
BLAST IT ALL, MAN! HOW MANY TIMES HAVE I TOLD YOU TO SALUTE WITH YOUR RIGHT HAND!
FLIK
SODDY, YOU MISERABLE OL' WRETCH! LOST MY TEMPER! COPY BOY WORK DOES THINGS TO A MAN!... COME ON! SNAP TO! COME ON, BOY!
JOHN J. MUNZELMEYER
KOF
KOF
SMEK SMEK SMEK
KOF
I'LL TELL YOU WHY I CALLED YOU, OLD MAN! IT'S PAYROLL TIME! HERE ARE YOUR WEEK'S WAGES! SEVENTY-FIVE CENTS, AND A GOOD BUS TOKEN! SPEND IT WISELY! ... DISMISSED!
KOF
KOF
KOF
KOF
KOF KOF GASP KOFF!
SEVENTY-FIVE WHOLE CENTS! AT LAST! AFTER SCRIMPING AND SAVING MY EARNINGS FOR 10 YEARS, I NOW HAVE A THOUSAND DOLLARS ... ENOUGH TO MAKE A DOWN PAYMENT ON THAT PEARL NECKLACE FOR LOIS PAIN, GIRL REPORTER!
IMPARTIAL EDITORIAL DEPT.
HELP WANTED
GOSSIP DEPT.
LIBEL LAWS
KOF
KOF KOF
KOF
WELL... HERE I AM WITH THE PEARL NECKLACE! LOIS SAYS I'M A CREEP! HAH, BOY! IF SHE KNEW MY REAL IDENTITY, BOY, SHE WOULDN'T CALL ME A CREEP!... OOP! THERE'S LOIS AT A BIG MEETING WITH THE MANAGING EDITOR!
KOF
KOF
KOF
KOF
EDITOR
BILL LOVES E.C.
HARVEY LOVES HARVEY
KNOCK!
2

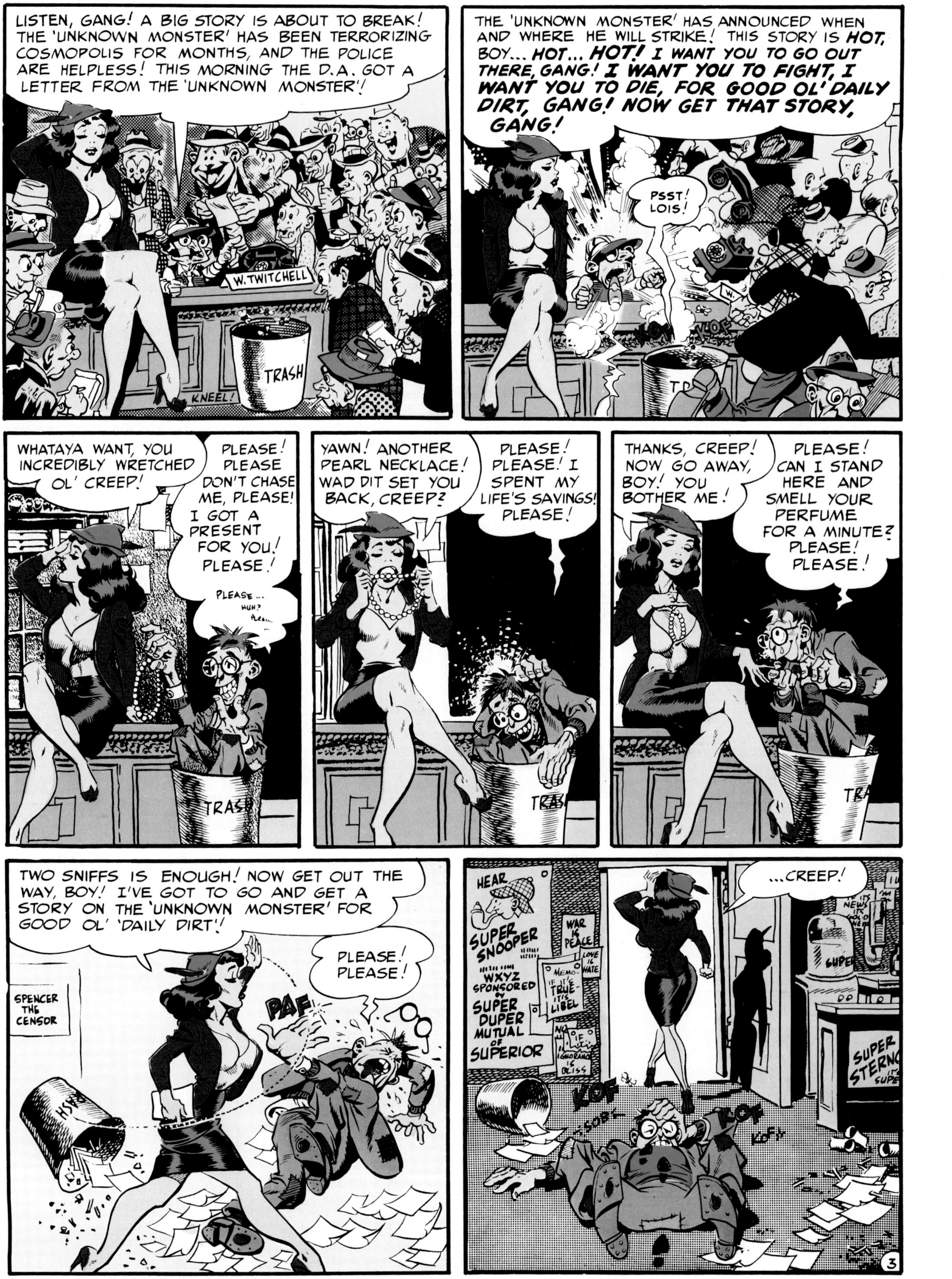
LISTEN, GANG! A BIG STORY IS ABOUT TO BREAK! THE 'UNKNOWN MONSTER' HAS BEEN TERRORIZING COSMOPOLIS FOR MONTHS, AND THE POLICE ARE HELPLESS! THIS MORNING THE D.A. GOT A LETTER FROM THE 'UNKNOWN MONSTER'!
W. TWITCHELL
TRASH
KNEEL!
THE 'UNKNOWN MONSTER' HAS ANNOUNCED WHEN AND WHERE HE WILL STRIKE! THIS STORY IS HOT, BOY... HOT... HOT! I WANT YOU TO GO OUT THERE, GANG! I WANT YOU TO FIGHT, I WANT YOU TO DIE, FOR GOOD OL' DAILY DIRT, GANG! NOW GET THAT STORY, GANG!
PSST! LOIS!
KOF
KOF
WHATAYA WANT, YOU INCREDIBLY WRETCHED OL' CREEP!
PLEASE! PLEASE DON'T CHASE ME, PLEASE! I GOT A PRESENT FOR YOU! PLEASE!
PLEASE... HUH? PLEA...
TRASH
YAWN! ANOTHER PEARL NECKLACE! WAD DIT SET YOU BACK, CREEP?
PLEASE! PLEASE! I SPENT MY LIFE'S SAVINGS! PLEASE!
THANKS, CREEP! NOW GO AWAY, BOY! YOU BOTHER ME!
PLEASE! CAN I STAND HERE AND SMELL YOUR PERFUME FOR A MINUTE? PLEASE! PLEASE!
TWO SNIFFS IS ENOUGH! NOW GET OUT THE WAY, BOY! I'VE GOT TO GO AND GET A STORY ON THE 'UNKNOWN MONSTER' FOR GOOD OL' 'DAILY DIRT'!
PLEASE! PLEASE!
SPENCER THE CENSOR
PAF
TRASH
...CREEP!
HEAR SUPER SNOOPER
WXYZ SPONSORED BY SUPER DUPER MUTUAL OF SUPERIOR
WAR IS PEACE
LOVE IS HATE
MEMO IF IT'S TRUE IT'S LIBEL
IGNORANCE IS BLISS
SUPER STERNO
KOF
SOB
KOF
KOF

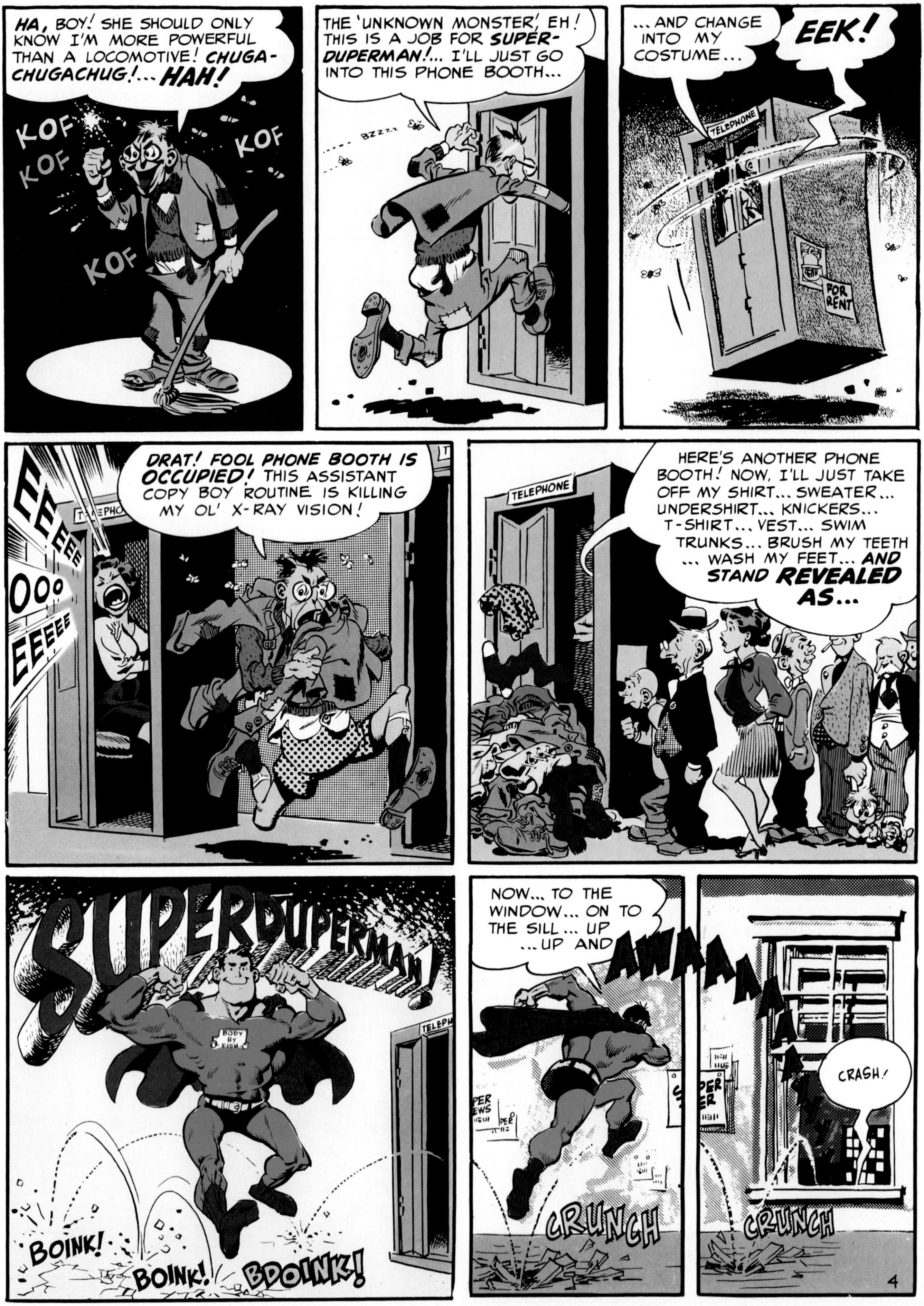

HA, BOY! SHE SHOULD ONLY KNOW I'M MORE POWERFUL THAN A LOCOMOTIVE! CHUGA-CHUGACHUG!... HAH!
KOF KOF KOF KOF
THE 'UNKNOWN MONSTER', EH! THIS IS A JOB FOR SUPER-DUPERMAN!... I'LL JUST GO INTO THIS PHONE BOOTH...
BZZZZ
... AND CHANGE INTO MY COSTUME...
EEK!
TELEPHONE
FOR RENT
EEEEE OOO EEEEE
DRAT! FOOL PHONE BOOTH IS OCCUPIED! THIS ASSISTANT COPY BOY ROUTINE IS KILLING MY OL' X-RAY VISION!
TELEPHONE
HERE'S ANOTHER PHONE BOOTH! NOW, I'LL JUST TAKE OFF MY SHIRT... SWEATER... UNDERSHIRT... KNICKERS... T-SHIRT... VEST... SWIM TRUNKS... BRUSH MY TEETH ... WASH MY FEET... AND STAND REVEALED AS...
SUPERDUPERMAN!
BODY BY FISH
BOINK! BOINK! BDOINK!
NOW... TO THE WINDOW... ON TO THE SILL... UP ...UP AND AWAAAAAAAAY
CRUNCH
CRASH!
CRUNCH

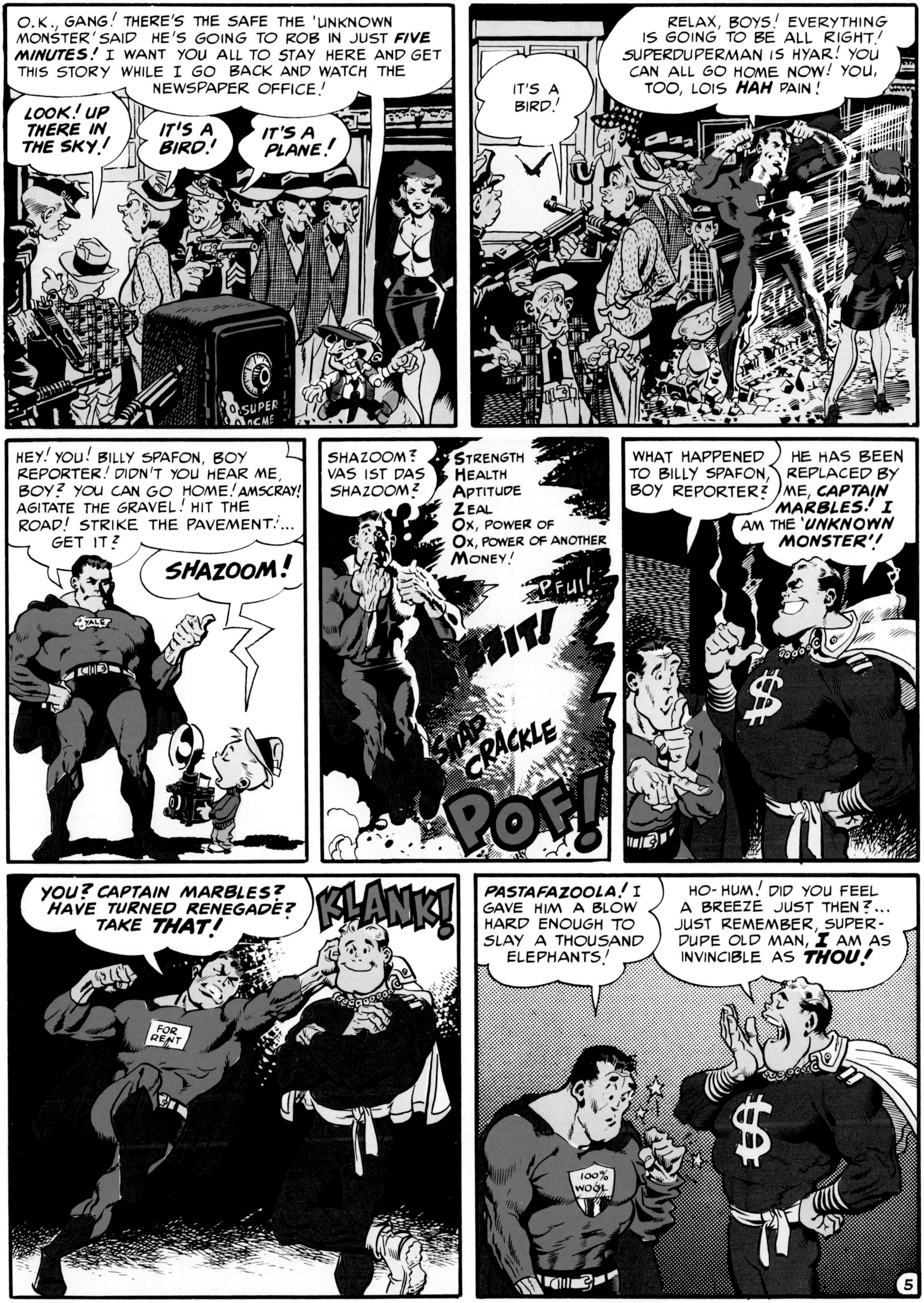
O.K., GANG! THERE'S THE SAFE THE 'UNKNOWN MONSTER' SAID HE'S GOING TO ROB IN JUST FIVE MINUTES! I WANT YOU ALL TO STAY HERE AND GET THIS STORY WHILE I GO BACK AND WATCH THE NEWSPAPER OFFICE!
LOOK! UP THERE IN THE SKY!
IT'S A BIRD!
IT'S A PLANE!
SUPER ACME
IT'S A BIRD!
RELAX, BOYS! EVERYTHING IS GOING TO BE ALL RIGHT! SUPERDUPERMAN IS HYAR! YOU CAN ALL GO HOME NOW! YOU, TOO, LOIS HAH PAIN!
HEY! YOU! BILLY SPAFON, BOY REPORTER! DIDN'T YOU HEAR ME, BOY? YOU CAN GO HOME! AMSCRAY! AGITATE THE GRAVEL! HIT THE ROAD! STRIKE THE PAVEMENT!... GET IT?
SHAZOOM!
SHAZOOM? VAS IST DAS SHAZOOM?
STRENGTH
HEALTH
APTITUDE
ZEAL
OX, POWER OF
OX, POWER OF ANOTHER
MONEY!
PFUI!
ZZIT!
SNAP
CRACKLE
POF!
WHAT HAPPENED TO BILLY SPAFON, BOY REPORTER?
HE HAS BEEN REPLACED BY ME, CAPTAIN MARBLES! I AM THE 'UNKNOWN MONSTER'!
YOU? CAPTAIN MARBLES? HAVE TURNED RENEGADE? TAKE THAT!
KLANK!
FOR RENT
PASTAFAZOOLA! I GAVE HIM A BLOW HARD ENOUGH TO SLAY A THOUSAND ELEPHANTS!
HO-HUM! DID YOU FEEL A BREEZE JUST THEN?... JUST REMEMBER, SUPER-DUPE OLD MAN, I AM AS INVINCIBLE AS THOU!
100% WOOL

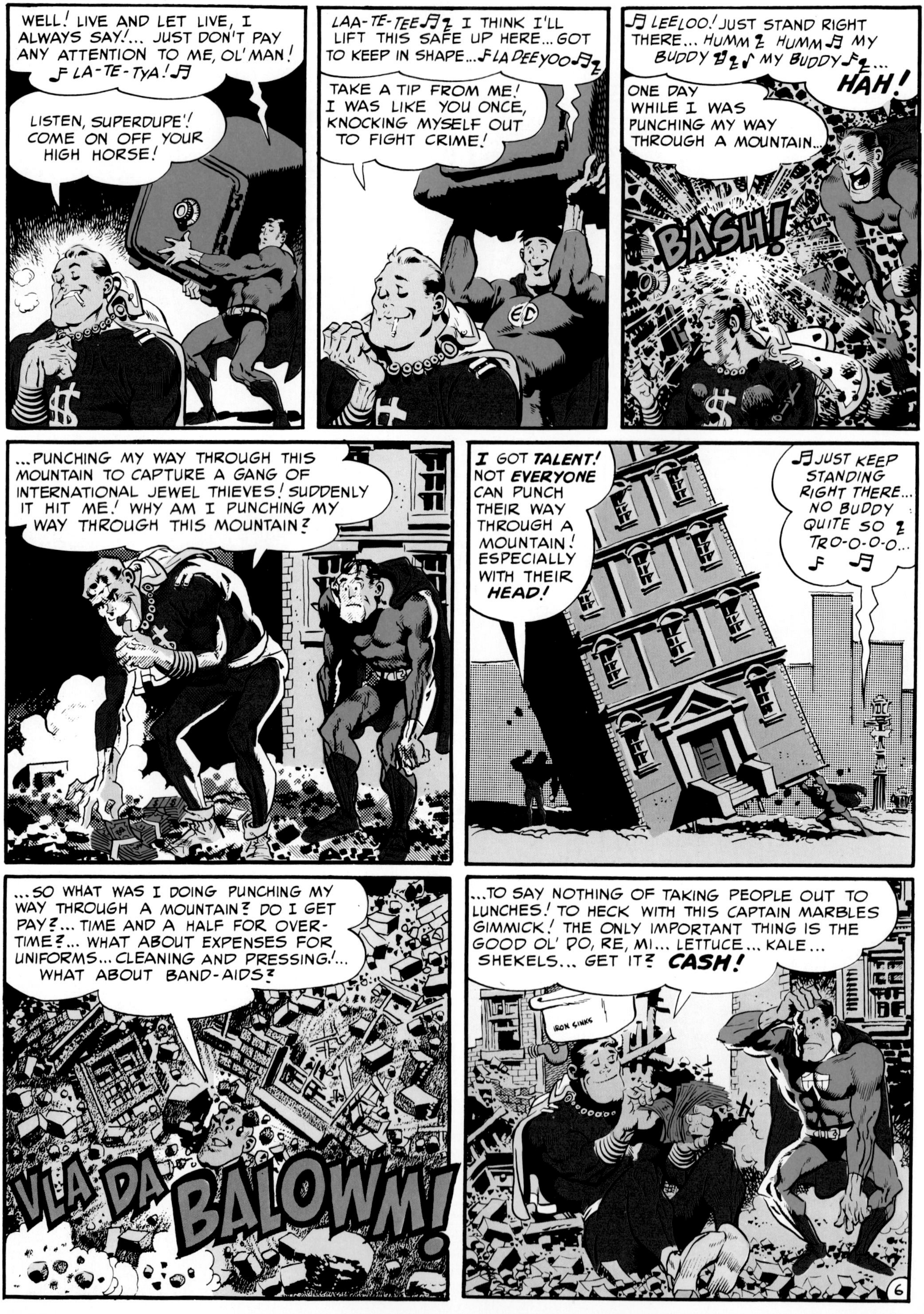
WELL! LIVE AND LET LIVE, I ALWAYS SAY!... JUST DON'T PAY ANY ATTENTION TO ME, OL' MAN! LA-TE-TYA!
LISTEN, SUPERDUPE! COME ON OFF YOUR HIGH HORSE!
LAA-TE-TEE I THINK I'LL LIFT THIS SAFE UP HERE... GOT TO KEEP IN SHAPE... FLADEEYOO
TAKE A TIP FROM ME! I WAS LIKE YOU ONCE, KNOCKING MYSELF OUT TO FIGHT CRIME!
LEELOO! JUST STAND RIGHT THERE... HUMM HUMM MY BUDDY MY BUDDY... HAH!
ONE DAY WHILE I WAS PUNCHING MY WAY THROUGH A MOUNTAIN...
BASH!
...PUNCHING MY WAY THROUGH THIS MOUNTAIN TO CAPTURE A GANG OF INTERNATIONAL JEWEL THIEVES! SUDDENLY IT HIT ME! WHY AM I PUNCHING MY WAY THROUGH THIS MOUNTAIN?
I GOT TALENT! NOT EVERYONE CAN PUNCH THEIR WAY THROUGH A MOUNTAIN! ESPECIALLY WITH THEIR HEAD!
JUST KEEP STANDING RIGHT THERE... NO BUDDY QUITE SO TRO-O-O-O...
...SO WHAT WAS I DOING PUNCHING MY WAY THROUGH A MOUNTAIN? DO I GET PAY?... TIME AND A HALF FOR OVER-TIME?... WHAT ABOUT EXPENSES FOR UNIFORMS... CLEANING AND PRESSING!... WHAT ABOUT BAND-AIDS?
VLA DA BALOWM!
...TO SAY NOTHING OF TAKING PEOPLE OUT TO LUNCHES! TO HECK WITH THIS CAPTAIN MARBLES GIMMICK! THE ONLY IMPORTANT THING IS THE GOOD OL' DO, RE, MI... LETTUCE... KALE... SHEKELS... GET IT? CASH!
IRON SINKS

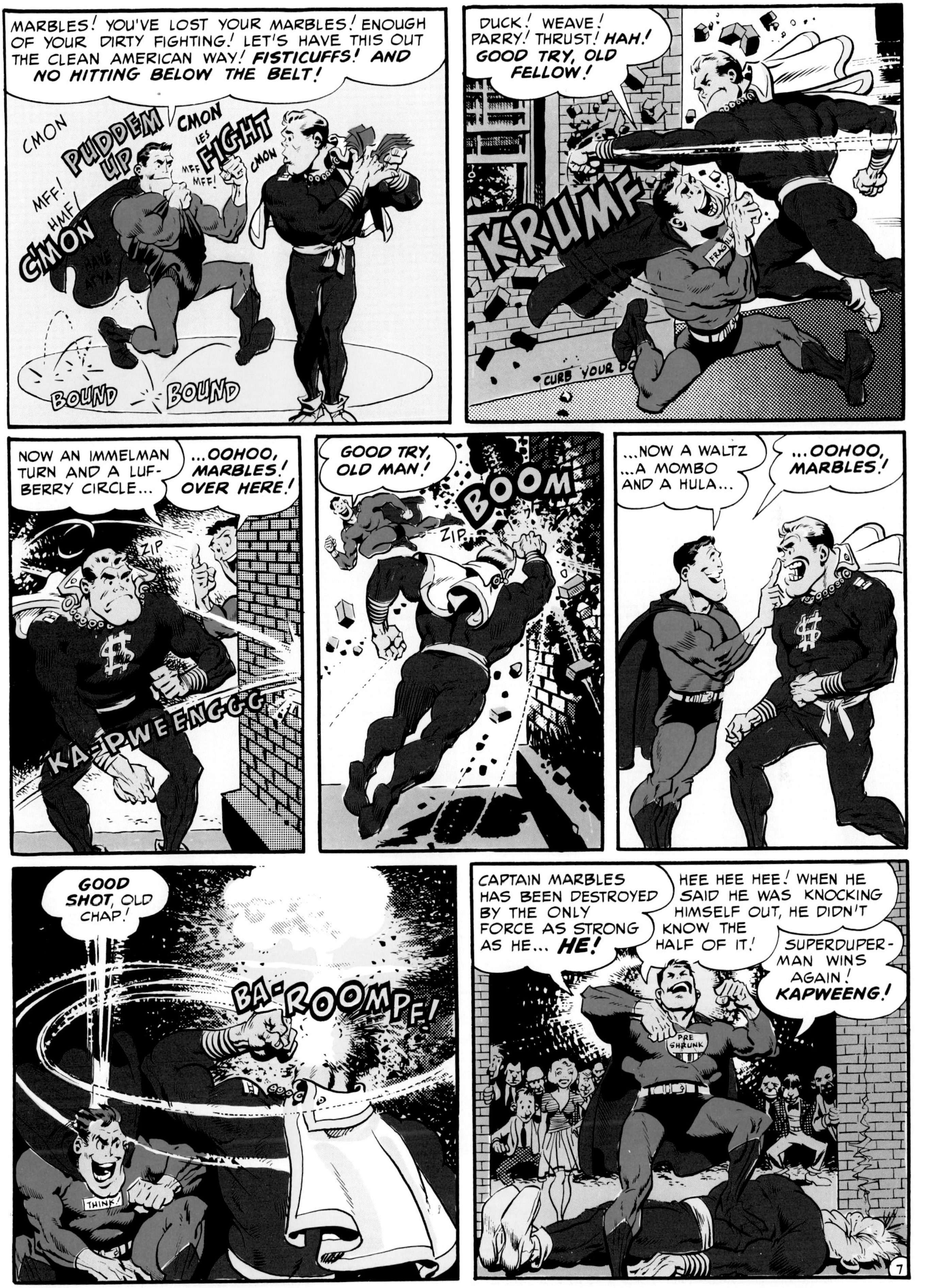
MARBLES! YOU'VE LOST YOUR MARBLES! ENOUGH OF YOUR DIRTY FIGHTING! LET'S HAVE THIS OUT THE CLEAN AMERICAN WAY! FISTICUFFS! AND NO HITTING BELOW THE BELT!
CMON
PUDDEM UP
CMON
LES FIGHT
CMON
MFF!
MFF MFF!
HMF!
CMON
HAVE AT YA
BOUND
BOUND
DUCK! WEAVE! PARRY! THRUST! HAH! GOOD TRY, OLD FELLOW!
KRUMF
FRAGILE
CURB YOUR DO
NOW AN IMMELMAN TURN AND A LUFBERRY CIRCLE...
...OOHOO, MARBLES! OVER HERE!
ZIP
KA-PWEENGGG
GOOD TRY, OLD MAN!
BOOM
ZIP
...NOW A WALTZ ...A MOMBO AND A HULA...
...OOHOO, MARBLES!
GOOD SHOT, OLD CHAP!
BA-ROOMPF!
THINK!
CAPTAIN MARBLES HAS BEEN DESTROYED BY THE ONLY FORCE AS STRONG AS HE... HE!
HEE HEE HEE! WHEN HE SAID HE WAS KNOCKING HIMSELF OUT, HE DIDN'T KNOW THE HALF OF IT!
SUPERDUPERMAN WINS AGAIN! KAPWEENG!
PRE SHRUNK

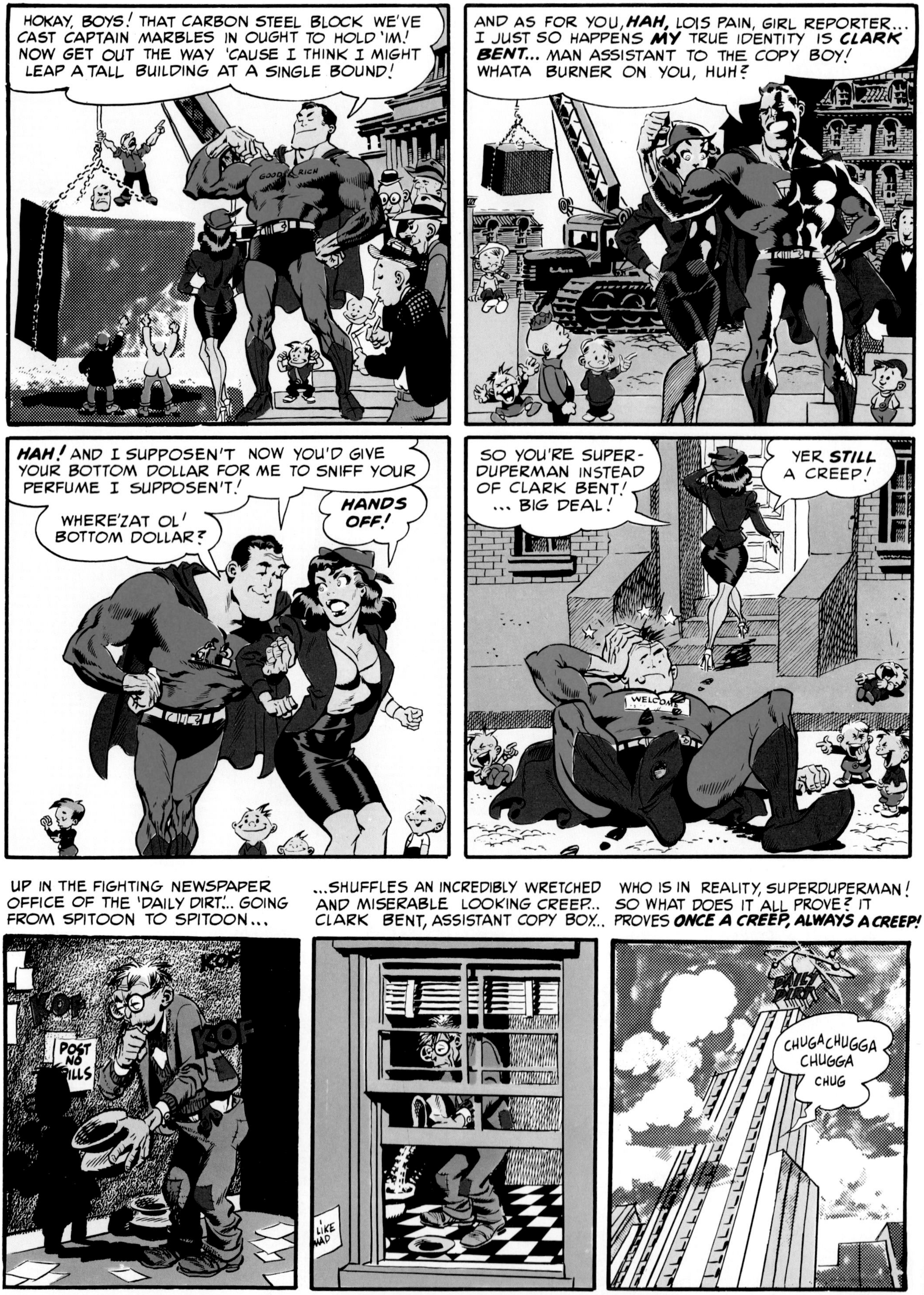
HOKAY, BOYS! THAT CARBON STEEL BLOCK WE'VE CAST CAPTAIN MARBLES IN OUGHT TO HOLD 'IM! NOW GET OUT THE WAY 'CAUSE I THINK I MIGHT LEAP A TALL BUILDING AT A SINGLE BOUND!
GOOD RICH
AND AS FOR YOU, HAH, LOIS PAIN, GIRL REPORTER... I JUST SO HAPPENS MY TRUE IDENTITY IS CLARK BENT... MAN ASSISTANT TO THE COPY BOY! WHATA BURNER ON YOU, HUH?
HAH! AND I SUPPOSEN'T NOW YOU'D GIVE YOUR BOTTOM DOLLAR FOR ME TO SNIFF YOUR PERFUME I SUPPOSEN'T!
WHERE'ZAT OL' BOTTOM DOLLAR?
HANDS OFF!
SO YOU'RE SUPER-DUPERMAN INSTEAD OF CLARK BENT! ... BIG DEAL!
YER STILL A CREEP!
WELCOME
UP IN THE FIGHTING NEWSPAPER OFFICE OF THE 'DAILY DIRT'... GOING FROM SPITOON TO SPITOON...
KOF
KOF
KOF
POST NO BILLS
...SHUFFLES AN INCREDIBLY WRETCHED AND MISERABLE LOOKING CREEP... CLARK BENT, ASSISTANT COPY BOY...
I LIKE MAD
WHO IS IN REALITY, SUPERDUPERMAN! SO WHAT DOES IT ALL PROVE? IT PROVES ONCE A CREEP, ALWAYS A CREEP!
DAILY DIRT
CHUGA CHUGGA CHUGGA CHUG

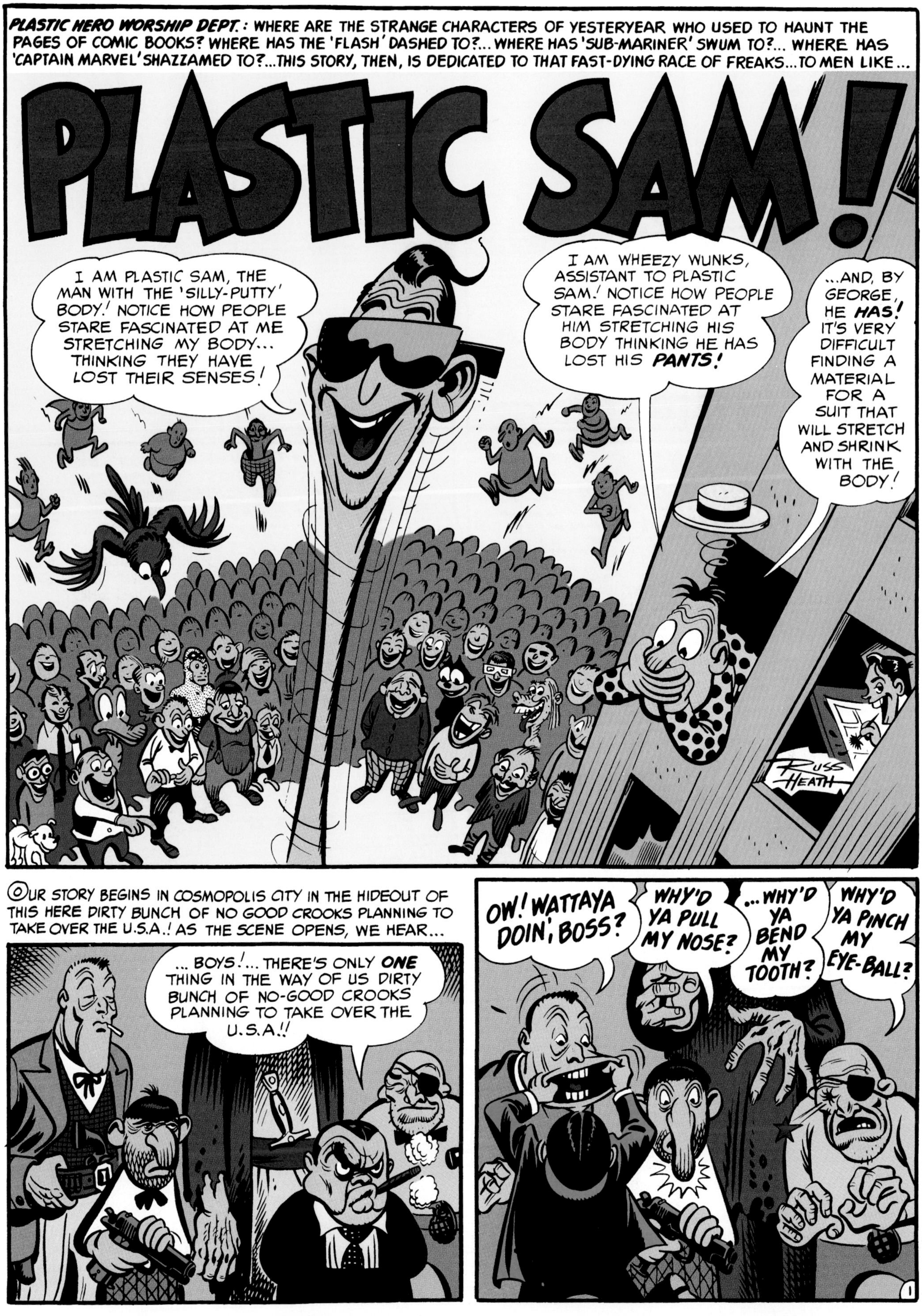
PLASTIC HERO WORSHIP DEPT.: WHERE ARE THE STRANGE CHARACTERS OF YESTERYEAR WHO USED TO HAUNT THE PAGES OF COMIC BOOKS? WHERE HAS THE 'FLASH' DASHED TO?... WHERE HAS 'SUB-MARINER' SWUM TO?... WHERE HAS 'CAPTAIN MARVEL' SHAZZAMED TO?...THIS STORY, THEN, IS DEDICATED TO THAT FAST-DYING RACE OF FREAKS...TO MEN LIKE...
PLASTIC SAM!
I AM PLASTIC SAM, THE MAN WITH THE 'SILLY-PUTTY' BODY! NOTICE HOW PEOPLE STARE FASCINATED AT ME STRETCHING MY BODY... THINKING THEY HAVE LOST THEIR SENSES!
I AM WHEEZY WUNKS, ASSISTANT TO PLASTIC SAM! NOTICE HOW PEOPLE STARE FASCINATED AT HIM STRETCHING HIS BODY THINKING HE HAS LOST HIS PANTS!
...AND, BY GEORGE, HE HAS! IT'S VERY DIFFICULT FINDING A MATERIAL FOR A SUIT THAT WILL STRETCH AND SHRINK WITH THE BODY!
RUSS HEATH
OUR STORY BEGINS IN COSMOPOLIS CITY IN THE HIDEOUT OF THIS HERE DIRTY BUNCH OF NO GOOD CROOKS PLANNING TO TAKE OVER THE U.S.A.! AS THE SCENE OPENS, WE HEAR...
... BOYS!... THERE'S ONLY ONE THING IN THE WAY OF US DIRTY BUNCH OF NO-GOOD CROOKS PLANNING TO TAKE OVER THE U.S.A!!
OW! WATTAYA DOIN', BOSS?
WHY'D YA PULL MY NOSE?
...WHY'D YA BEND MY TOOTH?
WHY'D YA PINCH MY EYE-BALL?
1

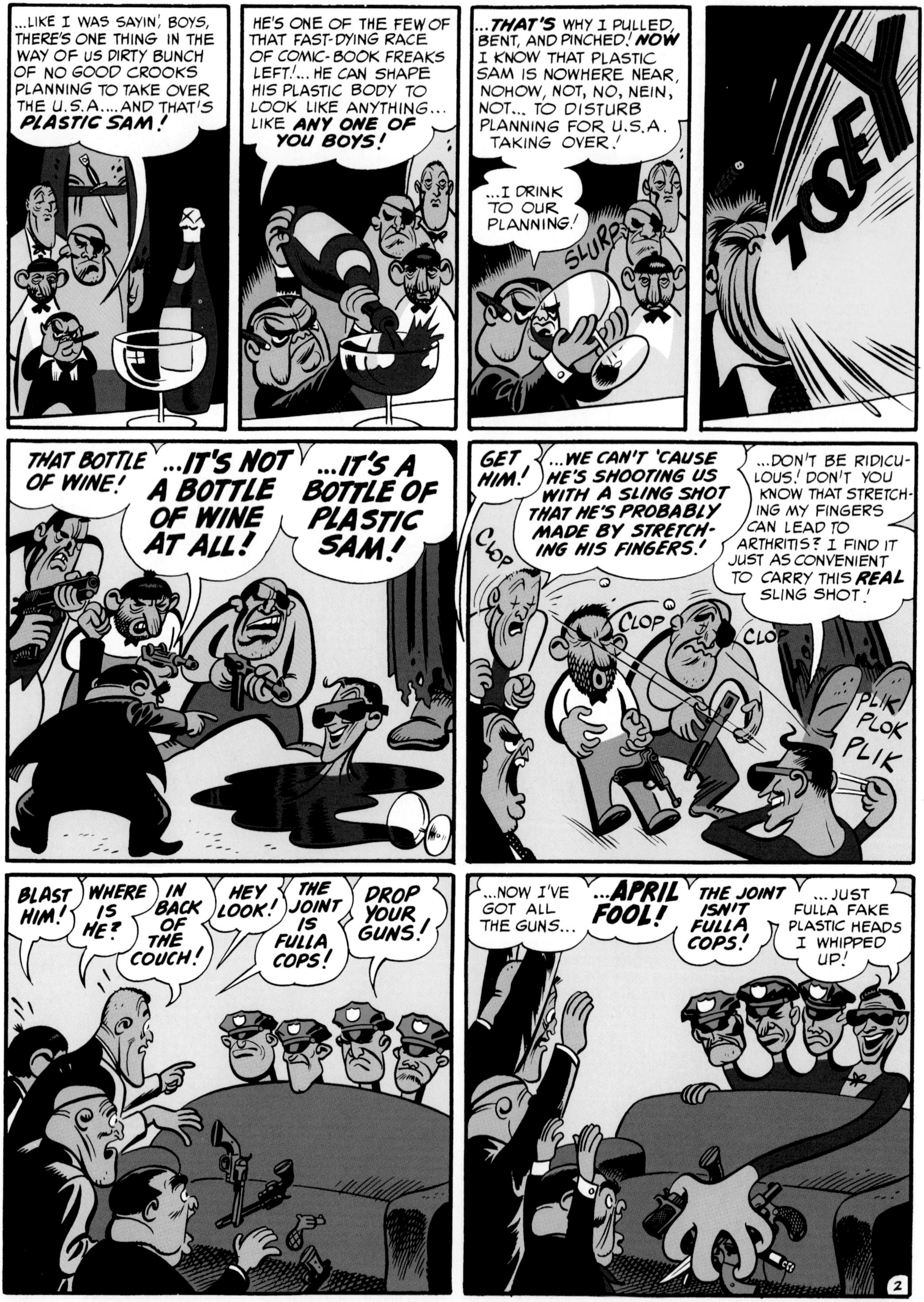
...LIKE I WAS SAYIN', BOYS, THERE'S ONE THING IN THE WAY OF US DIRTY BUNCH OF NO GOOD CROOKS PLANNING TO TAKE OVER THE U.S.A.... AND THAT'S PLASTIC SAM!
HE'S ONE OF THE FEW OF THAT FAST-DYING RACE OF COMIC-BOOK FREAKS LEFT!... HE CAN SHAPE HIS PLASTIC BODY TO LOOK LIKE ANYTHING... LIKE ANY ONE OF YOU BOYS!
...THAT'S WHY I PULLED, BENT, AND PINCHED! NOW I KNOW THAT PLASTIC SAM IS NOWHERE NEAR, NOHOW, NOT, NO, NEIN, NOT... TO DISTURB PLANNING FOR U.S.A. TAKING OVER!
...I DRINK TO OUR PLANNING!
SLURP
TOCEY
THAT BOTTLE OF WINE!
...IT'S NOT A BOTTLE OF WINE AT ALL!
...IT'S A BOTTLE OF PLASTIC SAM!
GET HIM!
...WE CAN'T 'CAUSE HE'S SHOOTING US WITH A SLING SHOT THAT HE'S PROBABLY MADE BY STRETCHING HIS FINGERS!
...DON'T BE RIDICULOUS! DON'T YOU KNOW THAT STRETCHING MY FINGERS CAN LEAD TO ARTHRITIS? I FIND IT JUST AS CONVENIENT TO CARRY THIS REAL SLING SHOT!
CLOP
CLOP
CLOP
PLIK
PLOK
PLIK
BLAST HIM!
WHERE IS HE?
IN BACK OF THE COUCH!
HEY LOOK!
THE JOINT IS FULLA COPS!
DROP YOUR GUNS!
...NOW I'VE GOT ALL THE GUNS...
...APRIL FOOL!
THE JOINT ISN'T FULLA COPS!
...JUST FULLA FAKE PLASTIC HEADS I WHIPPED UP!

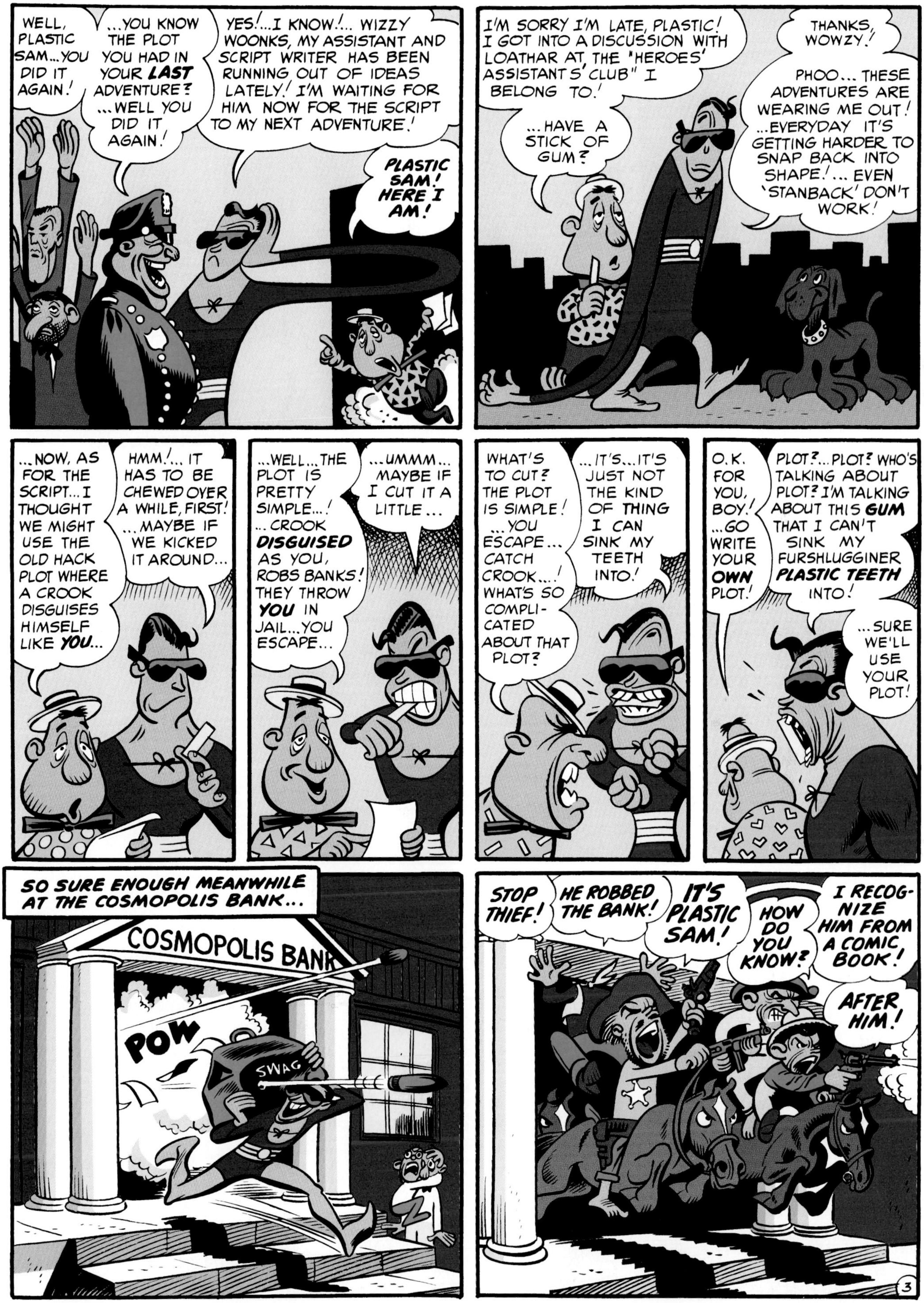
WELL, PLASTIC SAM...YOU DID IT AGAIN!
...YOU KNOW THE PLOT YOU HAD IN YOUR LAST ADVENTURE? ...WELL YOU DID IT AGAIN!
YES!...I KNOW!... WIZZY WOONKS, MY ASSISTANT AND SCRIPT WRITER HAS BEEN RUNNING OUT OF IDEAS LATELY! I'M WAITING FOR HIM NOW FOR THE SCRIPT TO MY NEXT ADVENTURE!
PLASTIC SAM! HERE I AM!
I'M SORRY I'M LATE, PLASTIC! I GOT INTO A DISCUSSION WITH LOATHAR AT THE "HEROES' ASSISTANTS' CLUB" I BELONG TO!
...HAVE A STICK OF GUM?
THANKS, WOWZY!
PHOO... THESE ADVENTURES ARE WEARING ME OUT! ...EVERYDAY IT'S GETTING HARDER TO SNAP BACK INTO SHAPE!... EVEN 'STANBACK' DON'T WORK!
...NOW, AS FOR THE SCRIPT...I THOUGHT WE MIGHT USE THE OLD HACK PLOT WHERE A CROOK DISGUISES HIMSELF LIKE YOU...
HMM!... IT HAS TO BE CHEWED OVER A WHILE, FIRST! ...MAYBE IF WE KICKED IT AROUND...
...WELL...THE PLOT IS PRETTY SIMPLE...! ...CROOK DISGUISED AS YOU, ROBS BANKS! THEY THROW YOU IN JAIL...YOU ESCAPE...
...UMMM... MAYBE IF I CUT IT A LITTLE...
WHAT'S TO CUT? THE PLOT IS SIMPLE! ...YOU ESCAPE... CATCH CROOK...! WHAT'S SO COMPLICATED ABOUT THAT PLOT?
...IT'S...IT'S JUST NOT THE KIND OF THING I CAN SINK MY TEETH INTO!
O.K. FOR YOU, BOY! ...GO WRITE YOUR OWN PLOT!
PLOT?...PLOT? WHO'S TALKING ABOUT PLOT? I'M TALKING ABOUT THIS GUM THAT I CAN'T SINK MY FURSHLUGGINER PLASTIC TEETH INTO!
...SURE WE'LL USE YOUR PLOT!
SO SURE ENOUGH MEANWHILE AT THE COSMOPOLIS BANK...
COSMOPOLIS BANK
POW
SWAG
STOP THIEF!
HE ROBBED THE BANK!
IT'S PLASTIC SAM!
HOW DO YOU KNOW?
I RECOGNIZE HIM FROM A COMIC BOOK!
AFTER HIM!

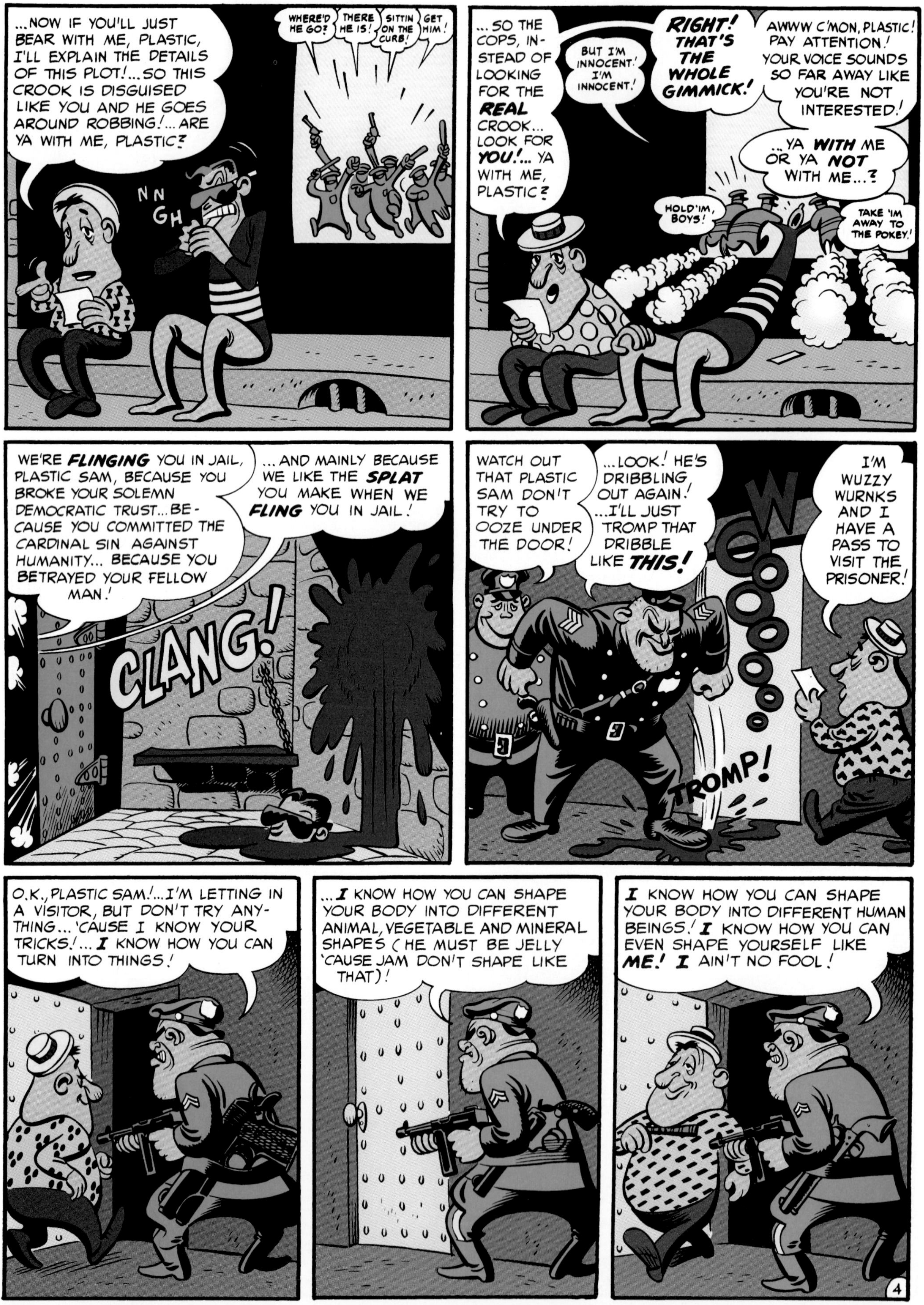
...NOW IF YOU'LL JUST BEAR WITH ME, PLASTIC, I'LL EXPLAIN THE DETAILS OF THIS PLOT!...SO THIS CROOK IS DISGUISED LIKE YOU AND HE GOES AROUND ROBBING!...ARE YA WITH ME, PLASTIC?
WHERE'D HE GO?
THERE HE IS!
SITTIN ON THE CURB!
GET HIM!
NNGH
...SO THE COPS, INSTEAD OF LOOKING FOR THE REAL CROOK... LOOK FOR YOU!... YA WITH ME, PLASTIC?
BUT I'M INNOCENT! I'M INNOCENT!
RIGHT! THAT'S THE WHOLE GIMMICK!
AWWW C'MON, PLASTIC! PAY ATTENTION! YOUR VOICE SOUNDS SO FAR AWAY LIKE YOU'RE NOT INTERESTED!
...YA WITH ME OR YA NOT WITH ME...?
HOLD'IM, BOYS!
TAKE 'IM AWAY TO THE POKEY!
WE'RE FLINGING YOU IN JAIL, PLASTIC SAM, BECAUSE YOU BROKE YOUR SOLEMN DEMOCRATIC TRUST...BECAUSE YOU COMMITTED THE CARDINAL SIN AGAINST HUMANITY... BECAUSE YOU BETRAYED YOUR FELLOW MAN!
...AND MAINLY BECAUSE WE LIKE THE SPLAT YOU MAKE WHEN WE FLING YOU IN JAIL!
CLANG!
WATCH OUT THAT PLASTIC SAM DON'T TRY TO OOZE UNDER THE DOOR!
...LOOK! HE'S DRIBBLING OUT AGAIN! ...I'LL JUST TROMP THAT DRIBBLE LIKE THIS!
I'M WUZZY WURNKS AND I HAVE A PASS TO VISIT THE PRISONER!
TROMP!
O.K., PLASTIC SAM!...I'M LETTING IN A VISITOR, BUT DON'T TRY ANYTHING...'CAUSE I KNOW YOUR TRICKS!...I KNOW HOW YOU CAN TURN INTO THINGS!
...I KNOW HOW YOU CAN SHAPE YOUR BODY INTO DIFFERENT ANIMAL, VEGETABLE AND MINERAL SHAPES (HE MUST BE JELLY 'CAUSE JAM DON'T SHAPE LIKE THAT)!
I KNOW HOW YOU CAN SHAPE YOUR BODY INTO DIFFERENT HUMAN BEINGS! I KNOW HOW YOU CAN EVEN SHAPE YOURSELF LIKE ME! I AIN'T NO FOOL!

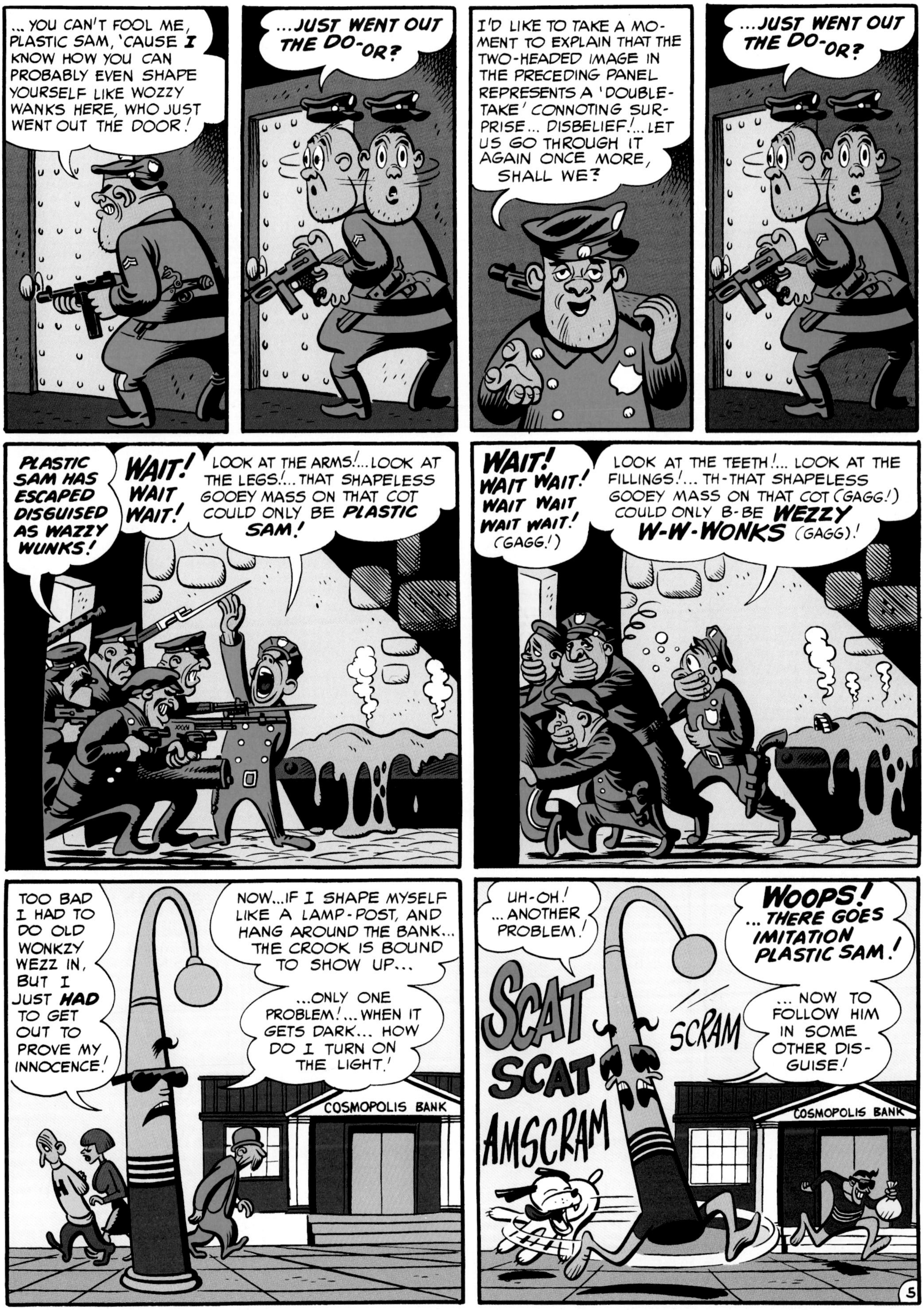

...YOU CAN'T FOOL ME, PLASTIC SAM, 'CAUSE I KNOW HOW YOU CAN PROBABLY EVEN SHAPE YOURSELF LIKE WOZZY WANKS HERE, WHO JUST WENT OUT THE DOOR!
...JUST WENT OUT THE DO-OR?
I'D LIKE TO TAKE A MOMENT TO EXPLAIN THAT THE TWO-HEADED IMAGE IN THE PRECEDING PANEL REPRESENTS A 'DOUBLE-TAKE' CONNOTING SURPRISE... DISBELIEF!...LET US GO THROUGH IT AGAIN ONCE MORE, SHALL WE?
...JUST WENT OUT THE DO-OR?
PLASTIC SAM HAS ESCAPED DISGUISED AS WAZZY WUNKS!
WAIT! WAIT WAIT!
LOOK AT THE ARMS!...LOOK AT THE LEGS!...THAT SHAPELESS GOOEY MASS ON THAT COT COULD ONLY BE PLASTIC SAM!
WAIT! WAIT WAIT! WAIT WAIT WAIT WAIT! (GAGG!)
LOOK AT THE TEETH!... LOOK AT THE FILLINGS!... TH-THAT SHAPELESS GOOEY MASS ON THAT COT (GAGG!) COULD ONLY B-BE WEZZY W-W-WONKS (GAGG)!
TOO BAD I HAD TO DO OLD WONKZY WEZZ IN, BUT I JUST HAD TO GET OUT TO PROVE MY INNOCENCE!
NOW...IF I SHAPE MYSELF LIKE A LAMP-POST, AND HANG AROUND THE BANK... THE CROOK IS BOUND TO SHOW UP...
...ONLY ONE PROBLEM!...WHEN IT GETS DARK... HOW DO I TURN ON THE LIGHT!
COSMOPOLIS BANK
UH-OH! ...ANOTHER PROBLEM!
WOOPS! ...THERE GOES IMITATION PLASTIC SAM!
SCAT
SCAT
AMSCRAM
SCRAM
...NOW TO FOLLOW HIM IN SOME OTHER DISGUISE!
COSMOPOLIS BANK

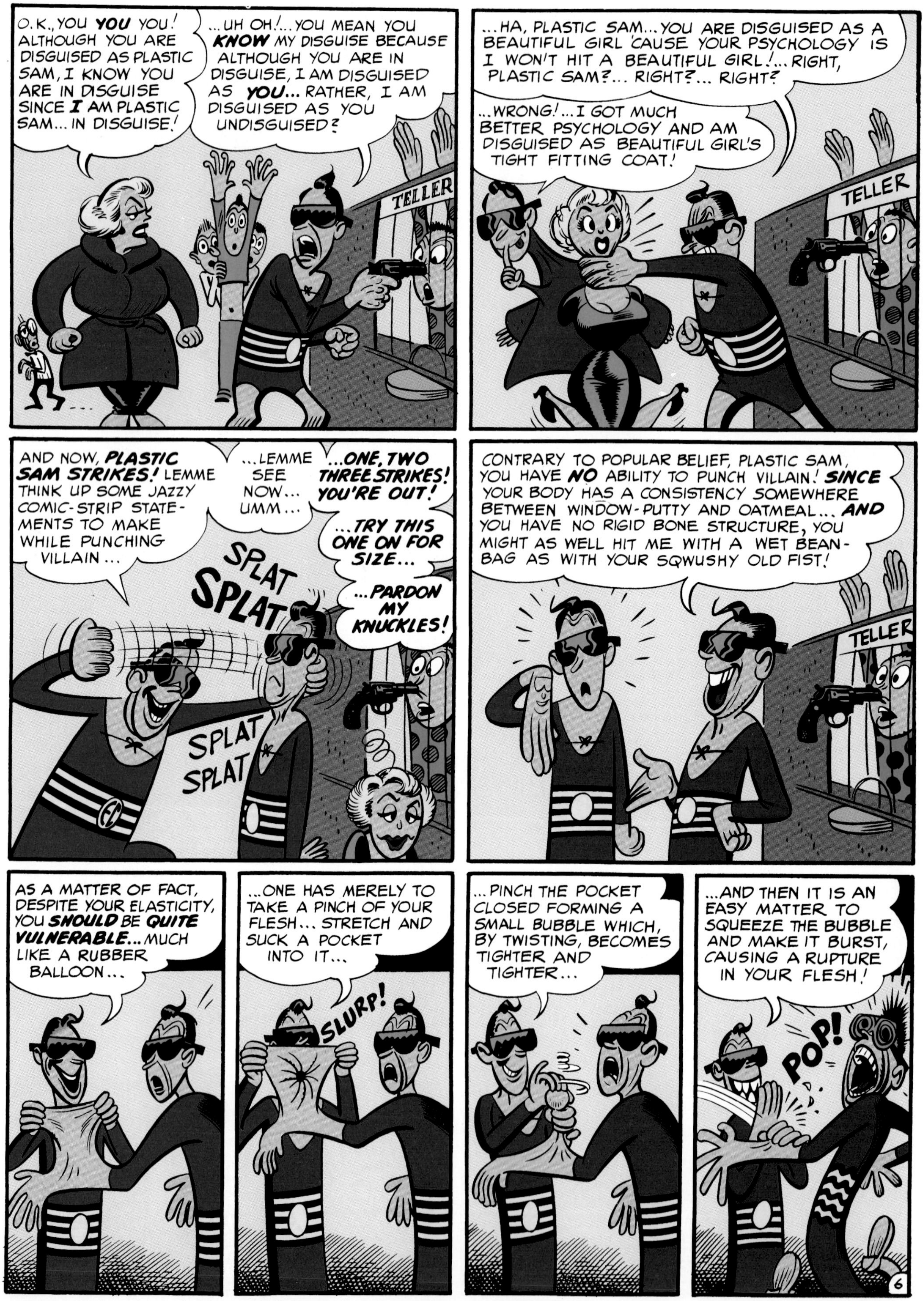
O.K., YOU YOU YOU! ALTHOUGH YOU ARE DISGUISED AS PLASTIC SAM, I KNOW YOU ARE IN DISGUISE SINCE I AM PLASTIC SAM... IN DISGUISE!
...UH OH!... YOU MEAN YOU KNOW MY DISGUISE BECAUSE ALTHOUGH YOU ARE IN DISGUISE, I AM DISGUISED AS YOU... RATHER, I AM DISGUISED AS YOU UNDISGUISED?
TELLER
...HA, PLASTIC SAM... YOU ARE DISGUISED AS A BEAUTIFUL GIRL 'CAUSE YOUR PSYCHOLOGY IS I WON'T HIT A BEAUTIFUL GIRL!... RIGHT, PLASTIC SAM?... RIGHT?... RIGHT?
...WRONG!... I GOT MUCH BETTER PSYCHOLOGY AND AM DISGUISED AS BEAUTIFUL GIRL'S TIGHT FITTING COAT!
TELLER
AND NOW, PLASTIC SAM STRIKES! LEMME THINK UP SOME JAZZY COMIC-STRIP STATEMENTS TO MAKE WHILE PUNCHING VILLAIN...
...LEMME SEE NOW... UMM...
...ONE, TWO THREE STRIKES! YOU'RE OUT!
...TRY THIS ONE ON FOR SIZE...
...PARDON MY KNUCKLES!
SPLAT SPLAT
SPLAT SPLAT
CONTRARY TO POPULAR BELIEF, PLASTIC SAM, YOU HAVE NO ABILITY TO PUNCH VILLAIN! SINCE YOUR BODY HAS A CONSISTENCY SOMEWHERE BETWEEN WINDOW-PUTTY AND OATMEAL... AND YOU HAVE NO RIGID BONE STRUCTURE, YOU MIGHT AS WELL HIT ME WITH A WET BEAN-BAG AS WITH YOUR SQWUSHY OLD FIST!
TELLER
AS A MATTER OF FACT, DESPITE YOUR ELASTICITY, YOU SHOULD BE QUITE VULNERABLE... MUCH LIKE A RUBBER BALLOON...
...ONE HAS MERELY TO TAKE A PINCH OF YOUR FLESH... STRETCH AND SUCK A POCKET INTO IT...
SLURP!
...PINCH THE POCKET CLOSED FORMING A SMALL BUBBLE WHICH, BY TWISTING, BECOMES TIGHTER AND TIGHTER...
...AND THEN IT IS AN EASY MATTER TO SQUEEZE THE BUBBLE AND MAKE IT BURST, CAUSING A RUPTURE IN YOUR FLESH!
POP!
6

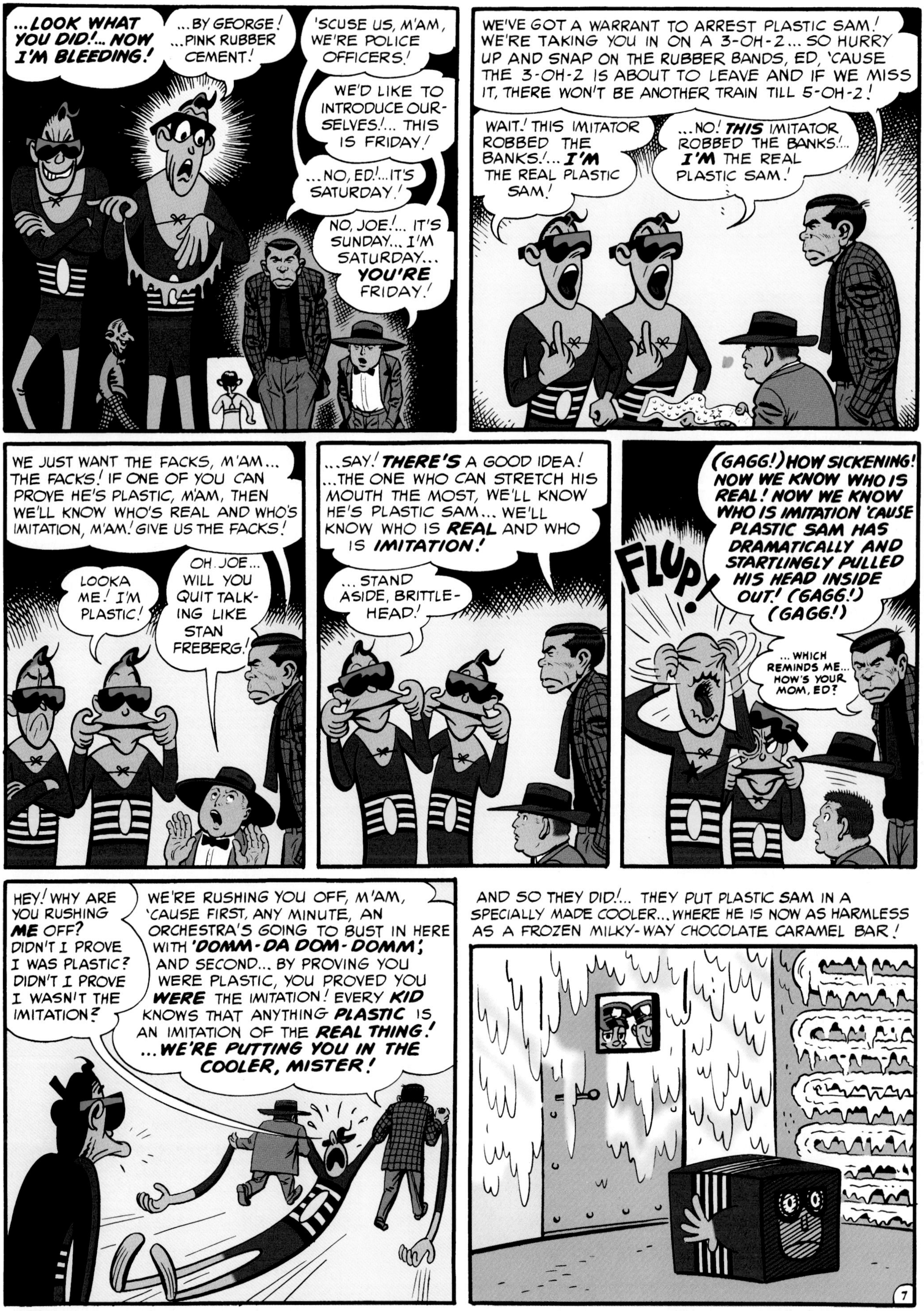
...LOOK WHAT YOU DID!... NOW I'M BLEEDING!
...BY GEORGE! ...PINK RUBBER CEMENT!
'SCUSE US, M'AM, WE'RE POLICE OFFICERS!
WE'D LIKE TO INTRODUCE OURSELVES!... THIS IS FRIDAY!
...NO, ED!...IT'S SATURDAY!
NO, JOE!... IT'S SUNDAY... I'M SATURDAY... YOU'RE FRIDAY!
WE'VE GOT A WARRANT TO ARREST PLASTIC SAM! WE'RE TAKING YOU IN ON A 3-OH-2... SO HURRY UP AND SNAP ON THE RUBBER BANDS, ED, 'CAUSE THE 3-OH-2 IS ABOUT TO LEAVE AND IF WE MISS IT, THERE WON'T BE ANOTHER TRAIN TILL 5-OH-2!
WAIT! THIS IMITATOR ROBBED THE BANKS!... I'M THE REAL PLASTIC SAM!
...NO! THIS IMITATOR ROBBED THE BANKS!... I'M THE REAL PLASTIC SAM!
WE JUST WANT THE FACKS, M'AM... THE FACKS! IF ONE OF YOU CAN PROVE HE'S PLASTIC, M'AM, THEN WE'LL KNOW WHO'S REAL AND WHO'S IMITATION, M'AM! GIVE US THE FACKS!
LOOKA ME! I'M PLASTIC!
OH, JOE... WILL YOU QUIT TALKING LIKE STAN FREBERG!
...SAY! THERE'S A GOOD IDEA! ...THE ONE WHO CAN STRETCH HIS MOUTH THE MOST, WE'LL KNOW HE'S PLASTIC SAM... WE'LL KNOW WHO IS REAL AND WHO IS IMITATION!
...STAND ASIDE, BRITTLE-HEAD!
(GAGG!) HOW SICKENING! NOW WE KNOW WHO IS REAL! NOW WE KNOW WHO IS IMITATION 'CAUSE PLASTIC SAM HAS DRAMATICALLY AND STARTLINGLY PULLED HIS HEAD INSIDE OUT! (GAGG!) (GAGG!)
FLUP!
...WHICH REMINDS ME... HOW'S YOUR MOM, ED?
HEY! WHY ARE YOU RUSHING ME OFF? DIDN'T I PROVE I WAS PLASTIC? DIDN'T I PROVE I WASN'T THE IMITATION?
WE'RE RUSHING YOU OFF, M'AM, 'CAUSE FIRST, ANY MINUTE, AN ORCHESTRA'S GOING TO BUST IN HERE WITH 'DOMM-DA DOM-DOMM', AND SECOND... BY PROVING YOU WERE PLASTIC, YOU PROVED YOU WERE THE IMITATION! EVERY KID KNOWS THAT ANYTHING PLASTIC IS AN IMITATION OF THE REAL THING! ...WE'RE PUTTING YOU IN THE COOLER, MISTER!
AND SO THEY DID!... THEY PUT PLASTIC SAM IN A SPECIALLY MADE COOLER... WHERE HE IS NOW AS HARMLESS AS A FROZEN MILKY-WAY CHOCOLATE CARAMEL BAR!
7

Pop Art, Post Modernism, Appropriation Art, Situationism. We don't know what the hell we're talking about! Here's...

Famous Artists' PAINTINGS OF COMIC BOOK CHARACTERS

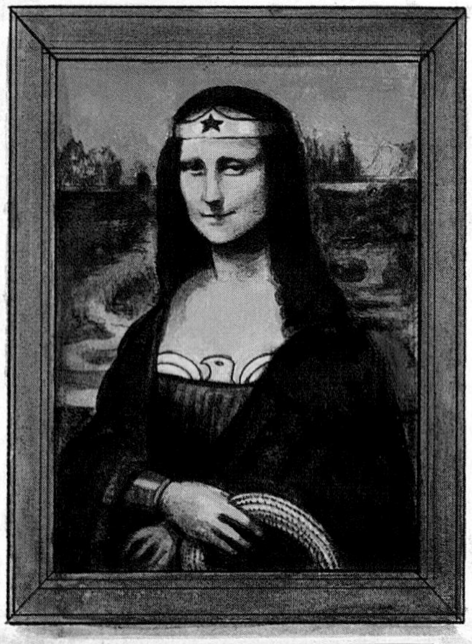

WONDER WOMAN LISA
by Leonardo Da Vinci

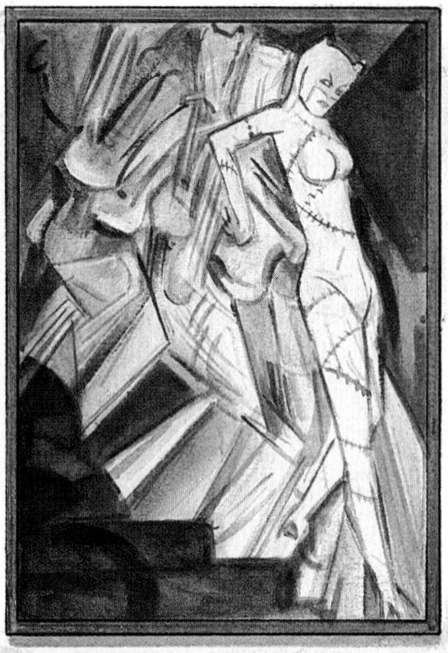

CATWOMAN DESCENDING A STAIRCASE by Duchamp

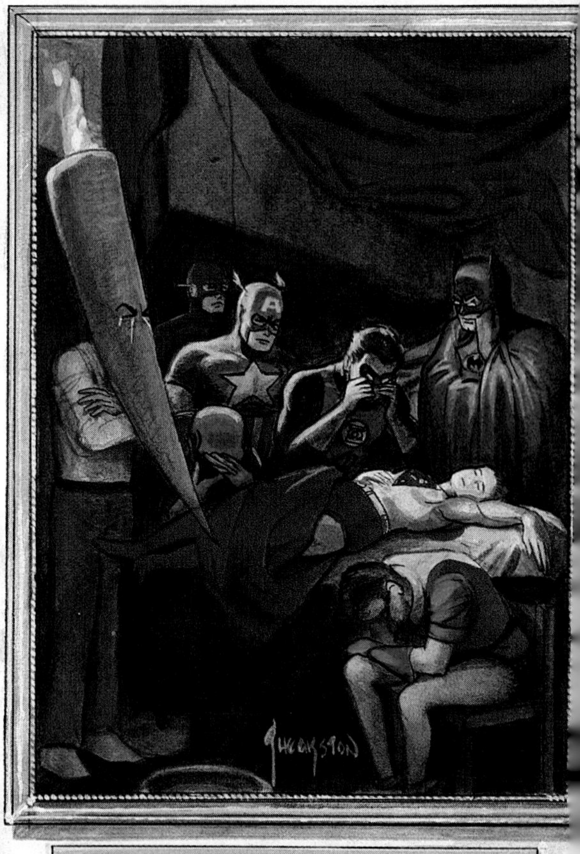

Caravaggio's DEATH OF SUPERMAN

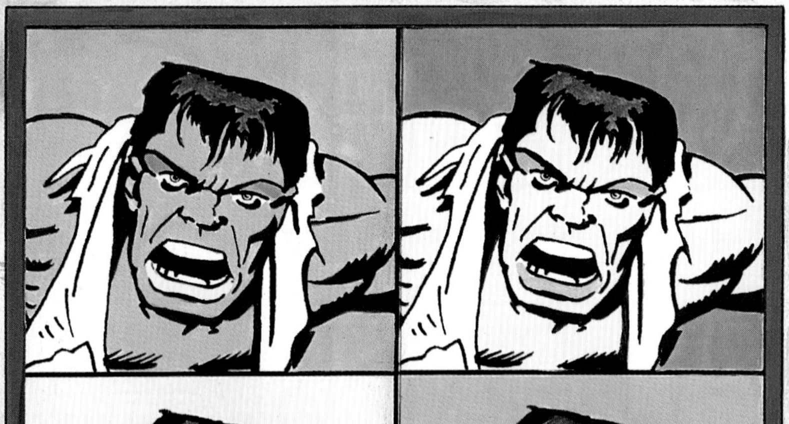

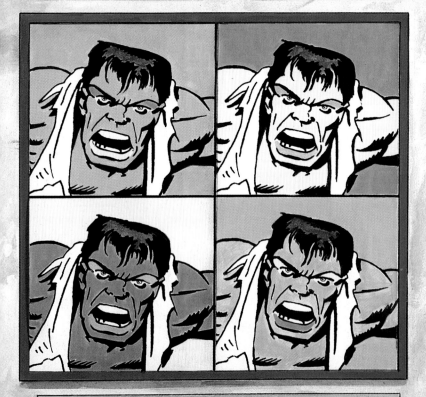

Andy Warhol's HULKS

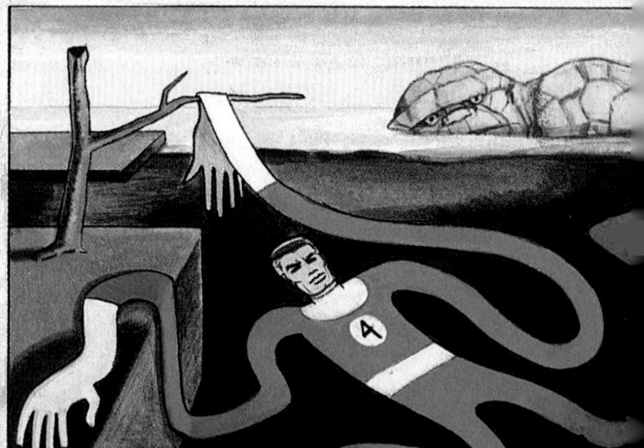

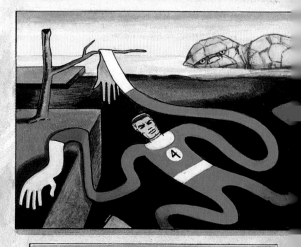

THE PERSISTANCE OF MR. FANTASTIC
by Salvador Dali

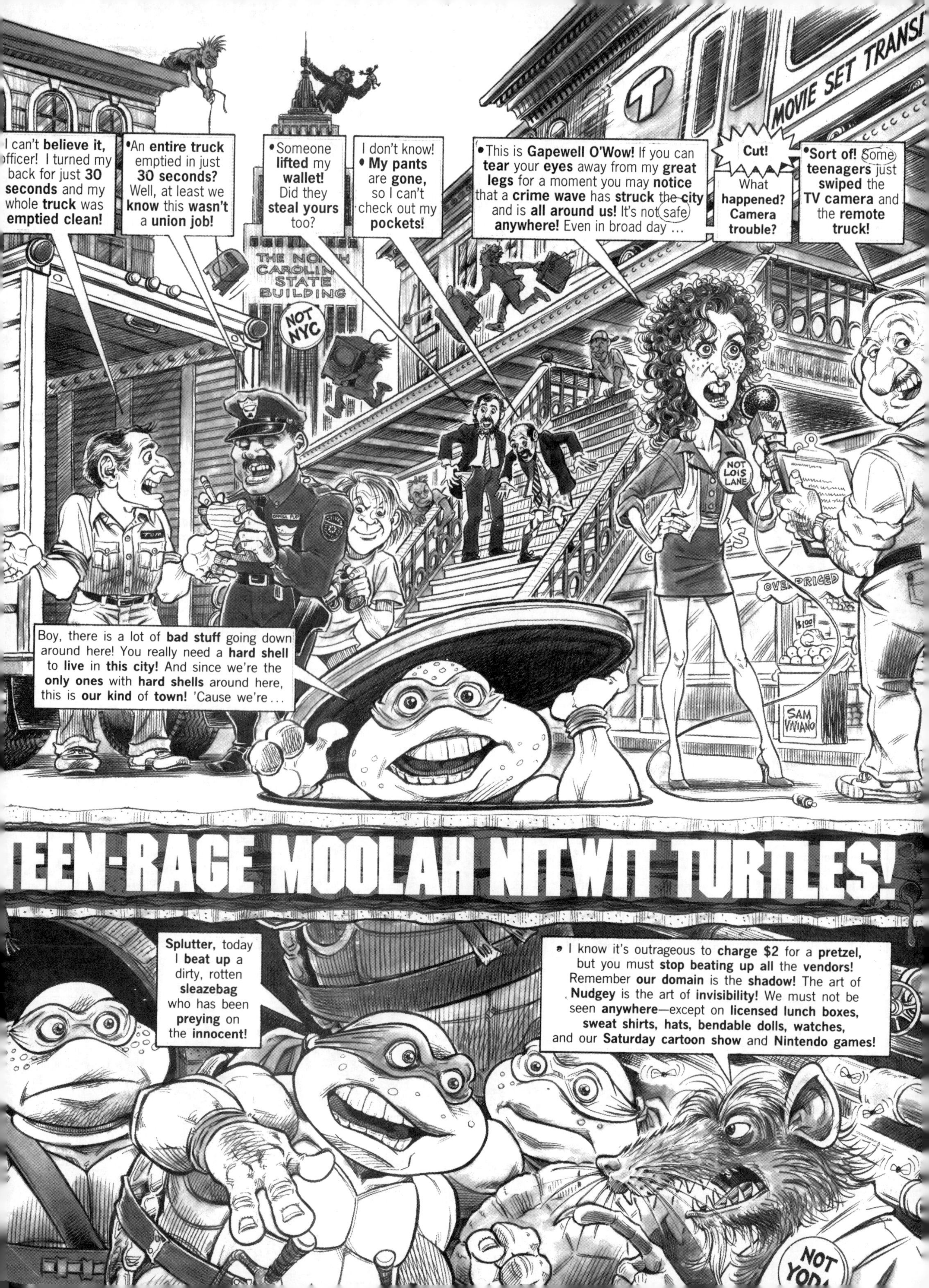
I can't believe it, officer! I turned my back for just 30 seconds and my whole truck was emptied clean!
An entire truck emptied in just 30 seconds? Well, at least we know this wasn't a union job!
Someone lifted my wallet! Did they steal yours too?
I don't know! My pants are gone, so I can't check out my pockets!
This is Gapewell O'Wow! If you can tear your eyes away from my great legs for a moment you may notice that a crime wave has struck the city and is all around us! It's not safe anywhere! Even in broad day . . .
Cut!
What happened? Camera trouble?
Sort of! Some teenagers just swiped the TV camera and the remote truck!
MOVIE SET TRANSI
THE NORTH CAROLINA STATE BUILDING
NOT NYC
NOT LOIS LANE
OVERPRICED
SAM VIVIANO
Boy, there is a lot of bad stuff going down around here! You really need a hard shell to live in this city! And since we're the only ones with hard shells around here, this is our kind of town! 'Cause we're . . .
TEEN-RAGE MOOLAH NITWIT TURTLES!
Splutter, today I beat up a dirty, rotten sleazebag who has been preying on the innocent!
I know it's outrageous to charge $2 for a pretzel, but you must stop beating up all the vendors! Remember our domain is the shadow! The art of Nudgey is the art of invisibility! We must not be seen anywhere—except on licensed lunch boxes, sweat shirts, hats, bendable dolls, watches, and our Saturday cartoon show and Nintendo games!
NOT YOD

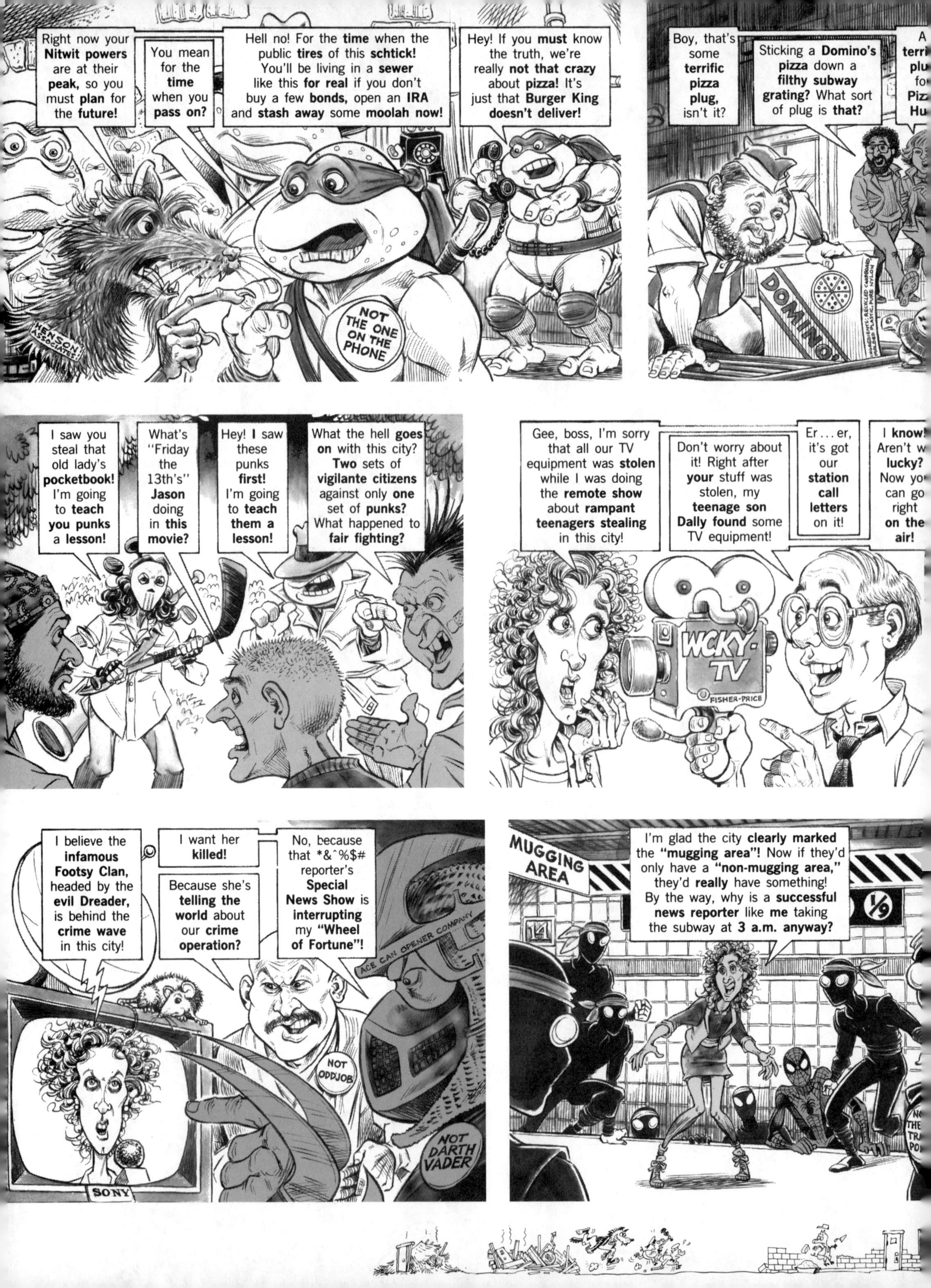

Right now your Nitwit powers are at their peak, so you must plan for the future!
You mean for the time when you pass on?
Hell no! For the time when the public tires of this schtick! You'll be living in a sewer like this for real if you don't buy a few bonds, open an IRA and stash away some moolah now!
Hey! If you must know the truth, we're really not that crazy about pizza! It's just that Burger King doesn't deliver!
HENSON ASSOCIATES
NOT THE ONE ON THE PHONE
Boy, that's some terrific pizza plug, isn't it?
Sticking a Domino's pizza down a filthy subway grating? What sort of plug is that?
DOMINO
I saw you steal that old lady's pocketbook! I'm going to teach you punks a lesson!
What's "Friday the 13th's" Jason doing in this movie?
Hey! I saw these punks first! I'm going to teach them a lesson!
What the hell goes on with this city? Two sets of vigilante citizens against only one set of punks? What happened to fair fighting?
Gee, boss, I'm sorry that all our TV equipment was stolen while I was doing the remote show about rampant teenagers stealing in this city!
Don't worry about it! Right after your stuff was stolen, my teenage son Dally found some TV equipment!
Er . . . er, it's got our station call letters on it!
WCKY-TV
FISHER-PRICE
I believe the infamous Footsy Clan, headed by the evil Dreader, is behind the crime wave in this city!
I want her killed!
Because she's telling the world about our crime operation?
No, because that *&^%$# reporter's Special News Show is interrupting my "Wheel of Fortune"!
ACE CAN OPENER COMPANY
NOT ODDJOB
NOT DARTH VADER
SONY
MUGGING AREA
I'm glad the city clearly marked the "mugging area"! Now if they'd only have a "non-mugging area," they'd really have something! By the way, why is a successful news reporter like me taking the subway at 3 a.m. anyway?
14
1/9

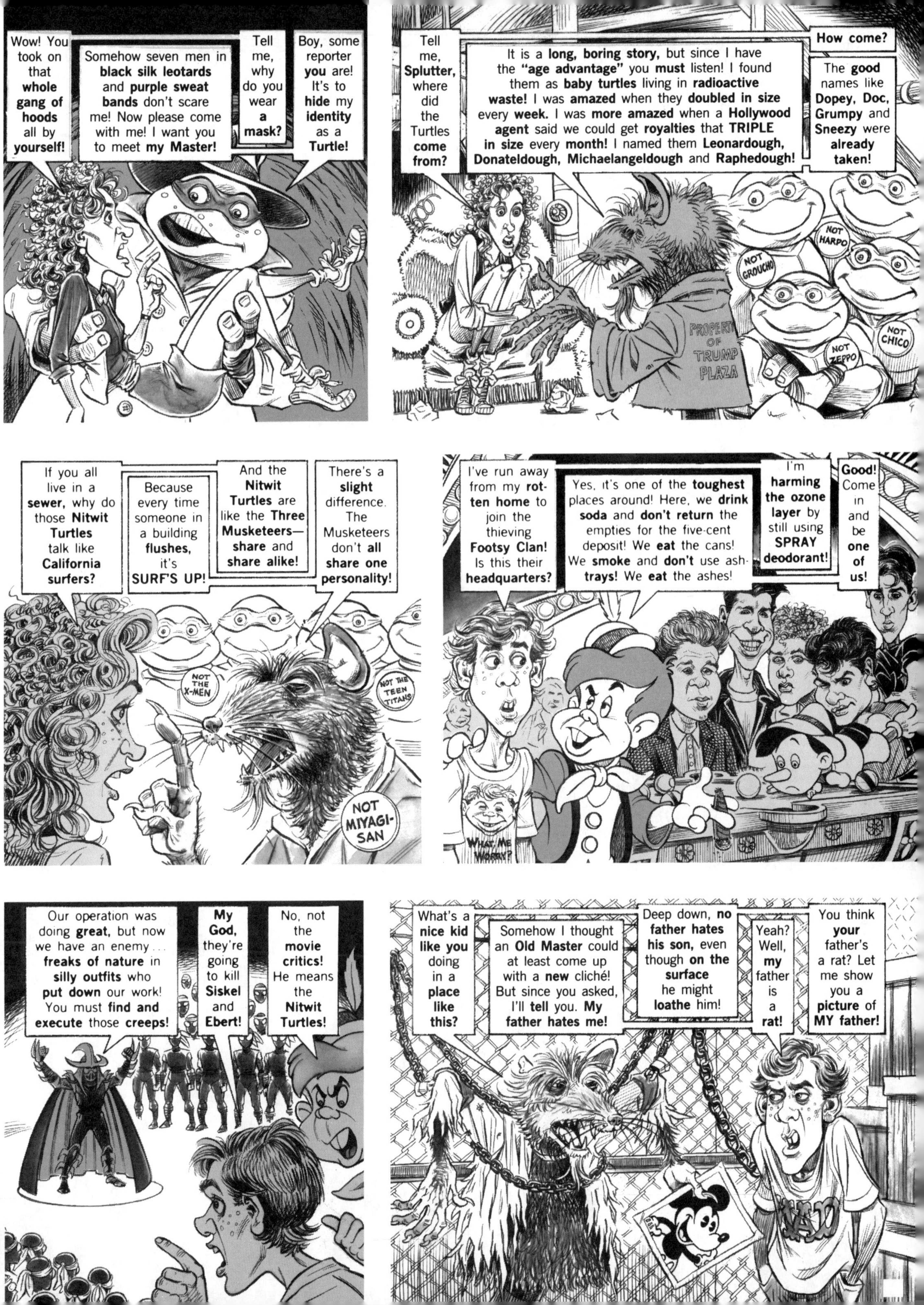
Wow! You took on that whole gang of hoods all by yourself!
Somehow seven men in black silk leotards and purple sweat bands don't scare me! Now please come with me! I want you to meet my Master!
Tell me, why do you wear a mask?
Boy, some reporter you are! It's to hide my identity as a Turtle!
Tell me, Splutter, where did the Turtles come from?
It is a long, boring story, but since I have the "age advantage" you must listen! I found them as baby turtles living in radioactive waste! I was amazed when they doubled in size every week. I was more amazed when a Hollywood agent said we could get royalties that TRIPLE in size every month! I named them Leonardough, Donateldough, Michaelangeldough and Raphedough!
How come?
The good names like Dopey, Doc, Grumpy and Sneezy were already taken!
NOT HARPO
NOT GROUCHO
PROPERTY OF TRUMP PLAZA
NOT CHICO
NOT ZEPPO
If you all live in a sewer, why do those Nitwit Turtles talk like California surfers?
Because every time someone in a building flushes, it's SURF'S UP!
And the Nitwit Turtles are like the Three Musketeers—share and share alike!
There's a slight difference. The Musketeers don't all share one personality!
NOT THE X-MEN
NOT THE TEEN TITANS
NOT MIYAGI-SAN
I've run away from my rotten home to join the thieving Footsy Clan! Is this their headquarters?
Yes, it's one of the toughest places around! Here, we drink soda and don't return the empties for the five-cent deposit! We eat the cans! We smoke and don't use ash-trays! We eat the ashes!
I'm harming the ozone layer by still using SPRAY deodorant!
Good! Come in and be one of us!
WHAT, ME WORRY?
Our operation was doing great, but now we have an enemy . . . freaks of nature in silly outfits who put down our work! You must find and execute those creeps!
My God, they're going to kill Siskel and Ebert!
No, not the movie critics! He means the Nitwit Turtles!
What's a nice kid like you doing in a place like this?
Somehow I thought an Old Master could at least come up with a new cliché! But since you asked, I'll tell you. My father hates me!
Deep down, no father hates his son, even though on the surface he might loathe him!
Yeah? Well, my father is a rat!
You think your father's a rat? Let me show you a picture of MY father!

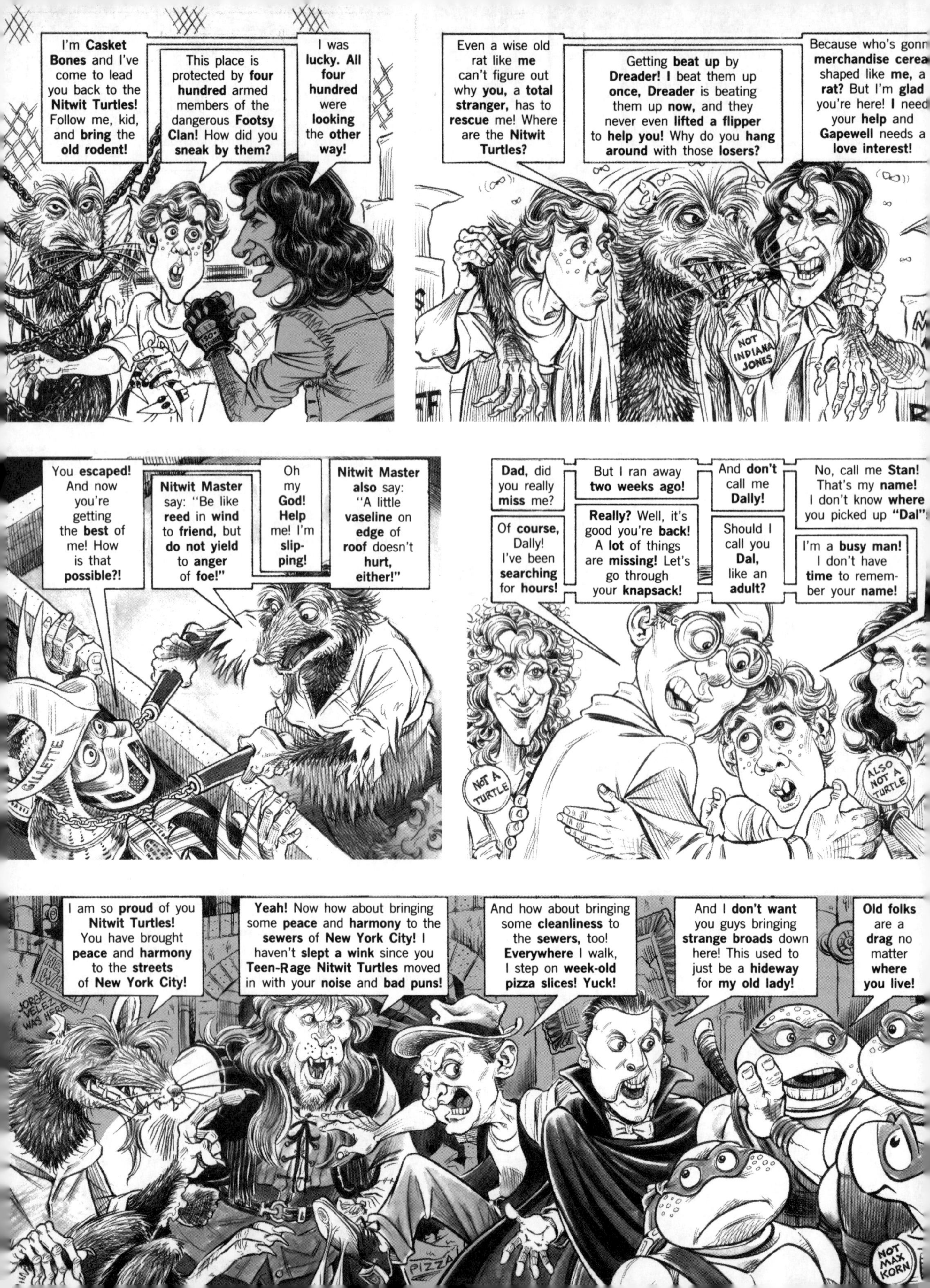
I'm **Casket Bones** and I've come to lead you back to the **Nitwit Turtles!** Follow me, kid, and **bring** the **old rodent!**
This place is protected by **four hundred** armed members of the dangerous **Footsy Clan!** How did you **sneak by them?**
I was **lucky. All four hundred** were **looking** the **other way!**
Even a wise old rat like **me** can't figure out why **you,** a **total stranger,** has to **rescue** me! Where are the **Nitwit Turtles?**
Getting **beat up** by **Dreader! I** beat them up **once, Dreader** is beating them up **now,** and they never even **lifted a flipper** to **help you!** Why do you **hang around** with those **losers?**
Because who's gonn **merchandise cerea** shaped like **me,** a **rat?** But I'm **glad** you're here! **I** need your **help** and **Gapewell** needs a **love interest!**
NOT INDIANA JONES
You **escaped!** And now you're getting the **best** of me! How is that **possible?!**
Nitwit Master say: "Be like **reed** in **wind** to **friend,** but **do not yield** to **anger** of **foe!"**
Oh my **God! Help** me! I'm **slip-ping!**
Nitwit Master also say: "A little **vaseline** on **edge** of **roof** doesn't **hurt, either!"**
GILLETTE
Dad, did you really **miss** me?
Of **course,** Dally! I've been **searching** for **hours!**
But I ran away **two weeks ago!**
Really? Well, it's good you're **back!** A **lot** of things are **missing!** Let's go through your **knapsack!**
And **don't** call me **Dally!**
Should I call you **Dal,** like an **adult?**
No, call me **Stan!** That's my **name!** I don't know **where** you picked up **"Dal"**
I'm a **busy man!** I don't have **time** to remem-ber your **name!**
NOT A TURTLE
ALSO NOT A TURTLE
I am so **proud** of you **Nitwit Turtles!** You have brought **peace** and **harmony** to the **streets** of **New York City!**
Yeah! Now how about bringing some **peace** and **harmony** to the **sewers** of **New York City!** I haven't **slept a wink** since you **Teen-Rage Nitwit Turtles** moved in with your **noise** and **bad puns!**
And how about bringing some **cleanliness** to the **sewers,** too! **Everywhere** I walk, I step on **week-old pizza slices! Yuck!**
And I **don't want** you guys bringing **strange broads** down here! This used to just be a **hideway** for **my old lady!**
Old folks are a **drag** no matter **where you live!**
JORGE VELEZ WAS HERE
PIZZA
NOT MAX KORN

MORE POWERFUL THAN A LOCOMOTIVE...

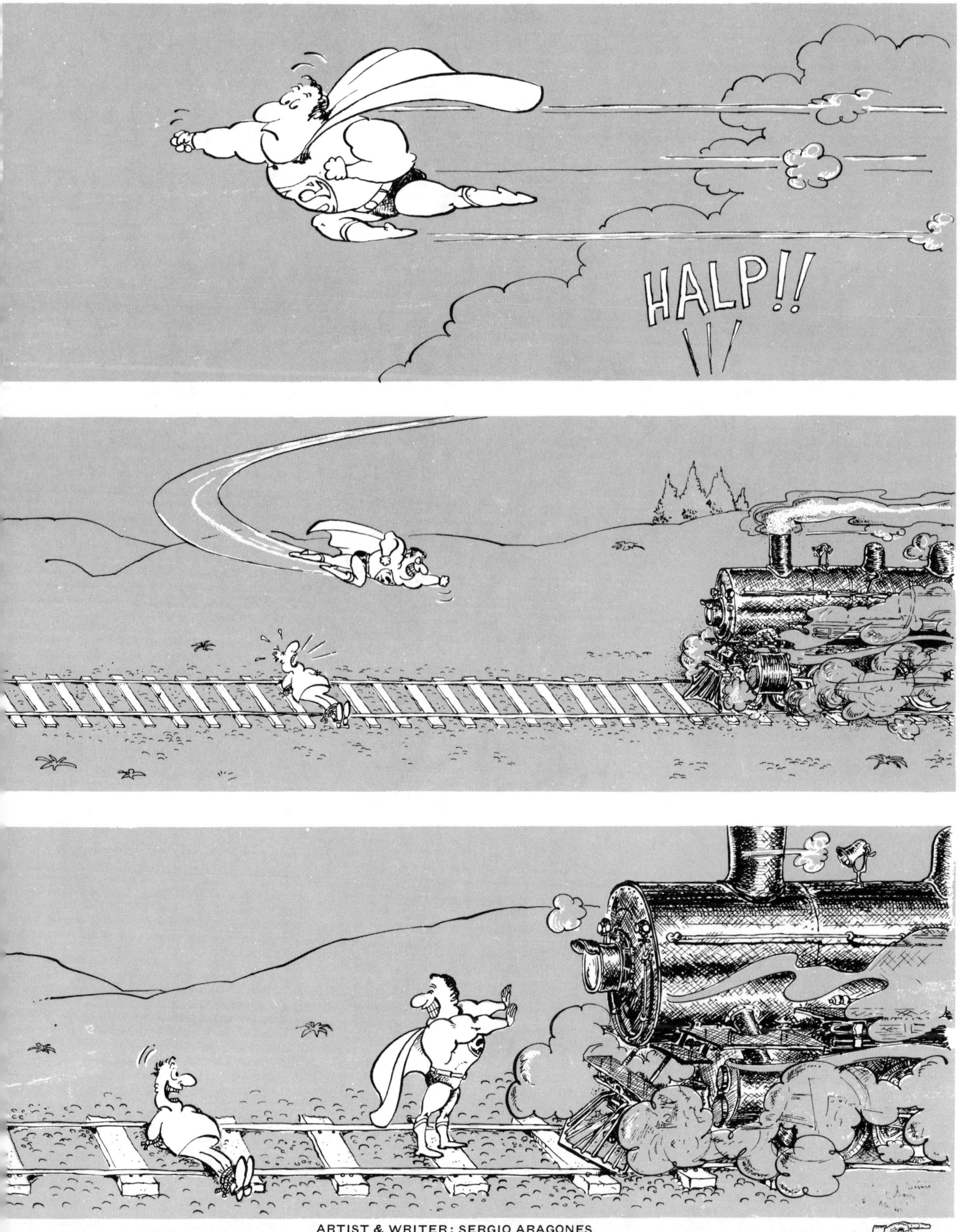
HALP!!

ARTIST & WRITER: SERGIO ARAGONES

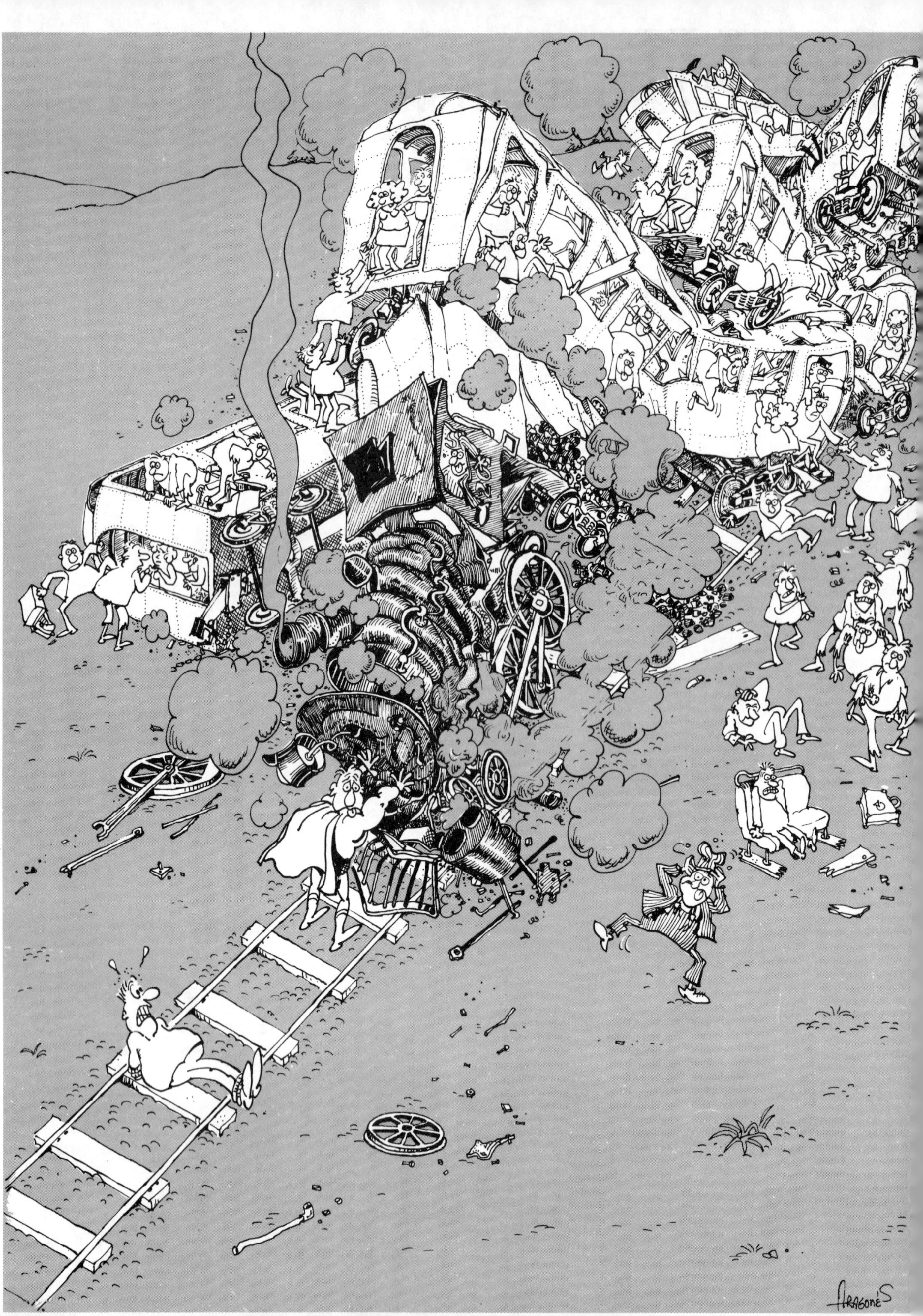
ARAGONÉS

THE FANTASTIC FOUR YEARS DEPT.

ARTIST: JOE STATON WRITER: DESMOND DEVLIN

YOU SIMPLY CAN'T SAVE THE GALAXY FROM MANIACAL EVILDOERS AND THEIR SENSES-SHATTERING DEATH PLOTS WITHOUT A PROPER, SOLID EDUCATION. THE KIND OF EDUCATION PROVIDED AT...

SUPERHERO HIGH

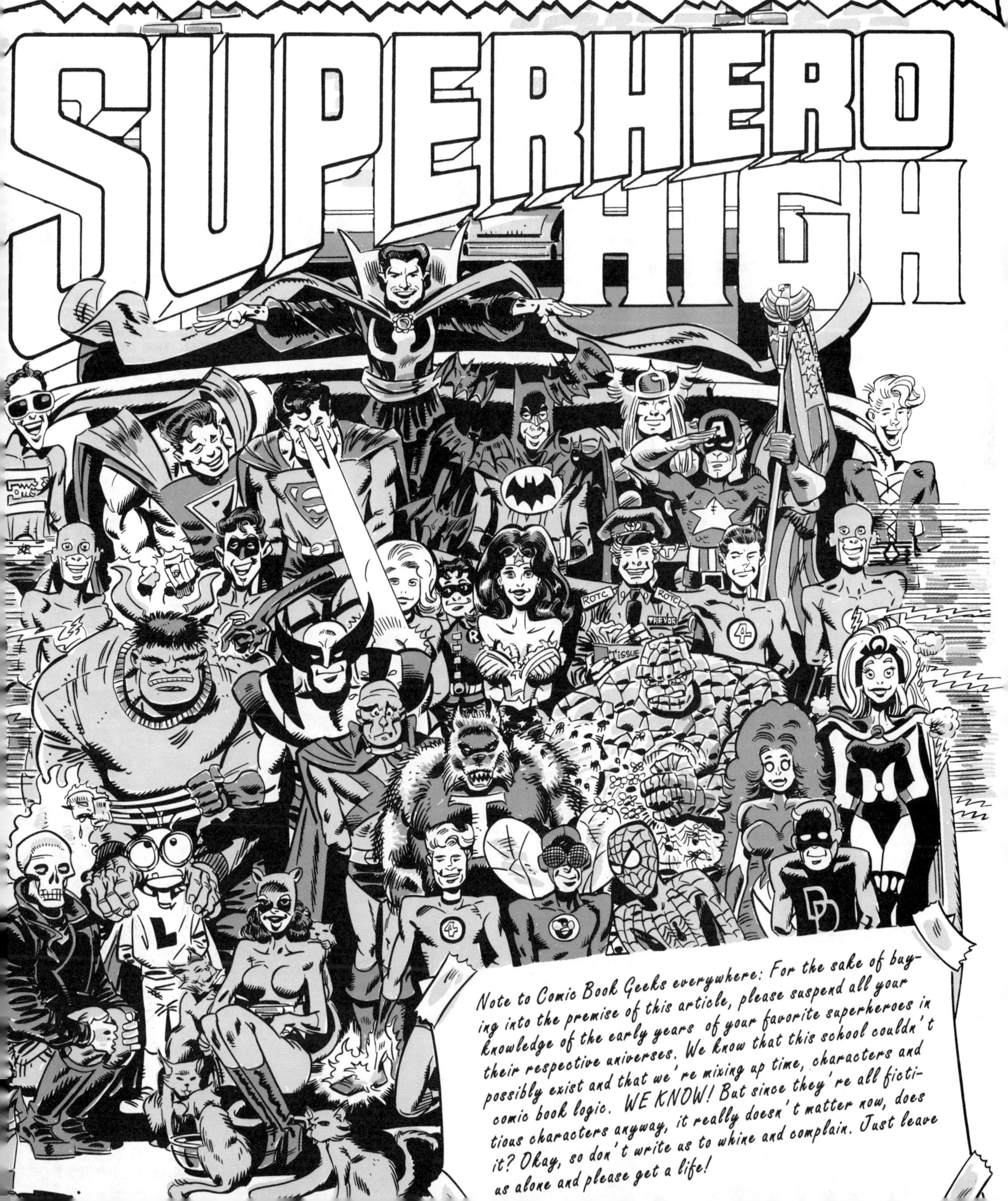
ROTC
ROTC
TREVOR
TISSUE
Note to Comic Book Geeks everywhere: For the sake of buying into the premise of this article, please suspend all your knowledge of the early years of your favorite superheroes in their respective universes. We know that this school couldn't possibly exist and that we're mixing up time, characters and comic book logic. WE KNOW! But since they're all fictitious characters anyway, it really doesn't matter now, does it? Okay, so don't write us to whine and complain. Just leave us alone and please get a life!

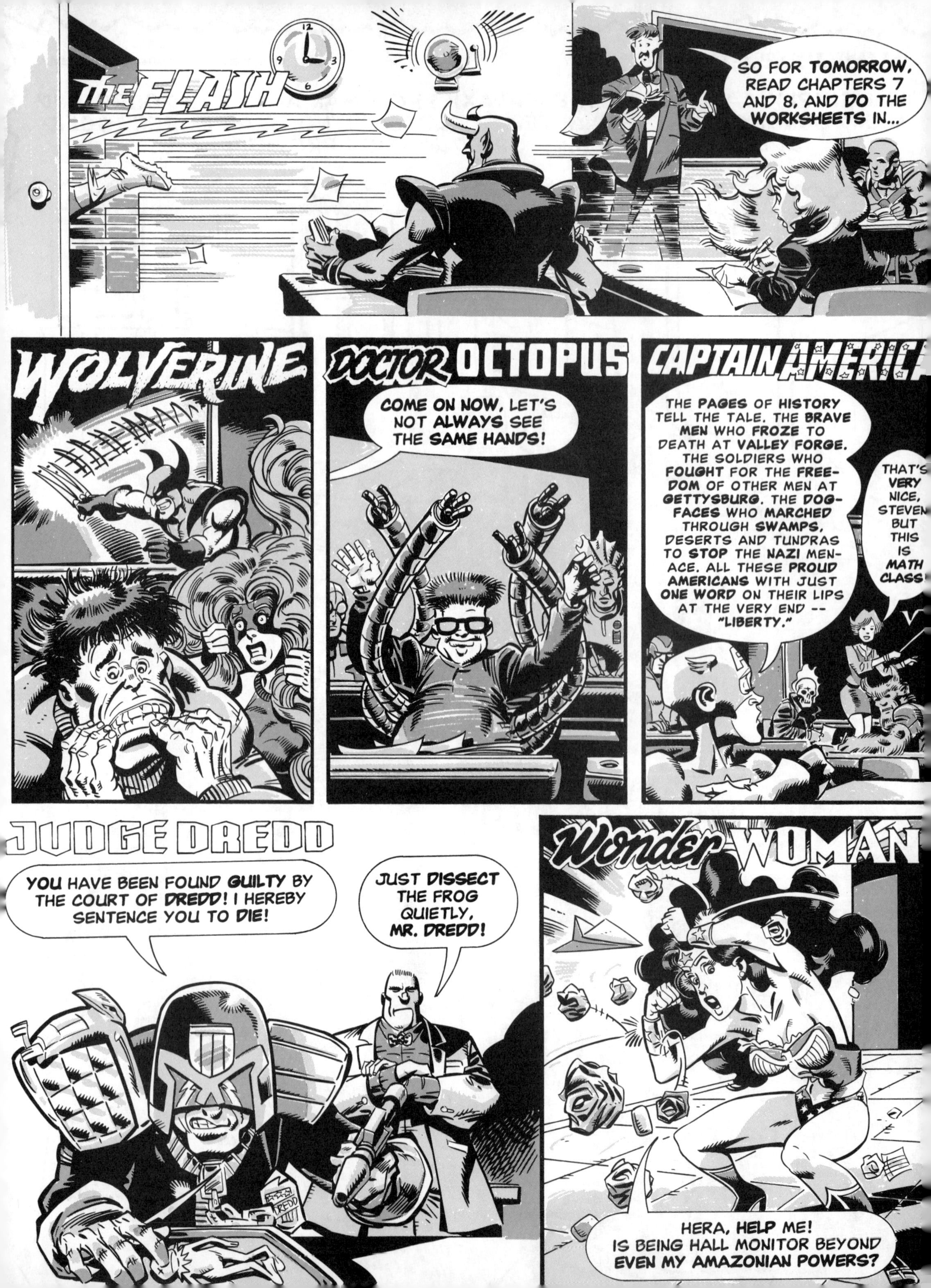
THE FLASH
SO FOR TOMORROW, READ CHAPTERS 7 AND 8, AND DO THE WORKSHEETS IN...
WOLVERINE
DOCTOR OCTOPUS
COME ON NOW, LET'S NOT ALWAYS SEE THE SAME HANDS!
CAPTAIN AMERICA
THE PAGES OF HISTORY TELL THE TALE. THE BRAVE MEN WHO FROZE TO DEATH AT VALLEY FORGE. THE SOLDIERS WHO FOUGHT FOR THE FREEDOM OF OTHER MEN AT GETTYSBURG. THE DOGFACES WHO MARCHED THROUGH SWAMPS, DESERTS AND TUNDRAS TO STOP THE NAZI MENACE. ALL THESE PROUD AMERICANS WITH JUST ONE WORD ON THEIR LIPS AT THE VERY END -- "LIBERTY."
THAT'S VERY NICE, STEVEN BUT THIS IS MATH CLASS!
JUDGE DREDD
YOU HAVE BEEN FOUND GUILTY BY THE COURT OF DREDD! I HEREBY SENTENCE YOU TO DIE!
JUST DISSECT THE FROG QUIETLY, MR. DREDD!
WONDER WOMAN
HERA, HELP ME! IS BEING HALL MONITOR BEYOND EVEN MY AMAZONIAN POWERS?

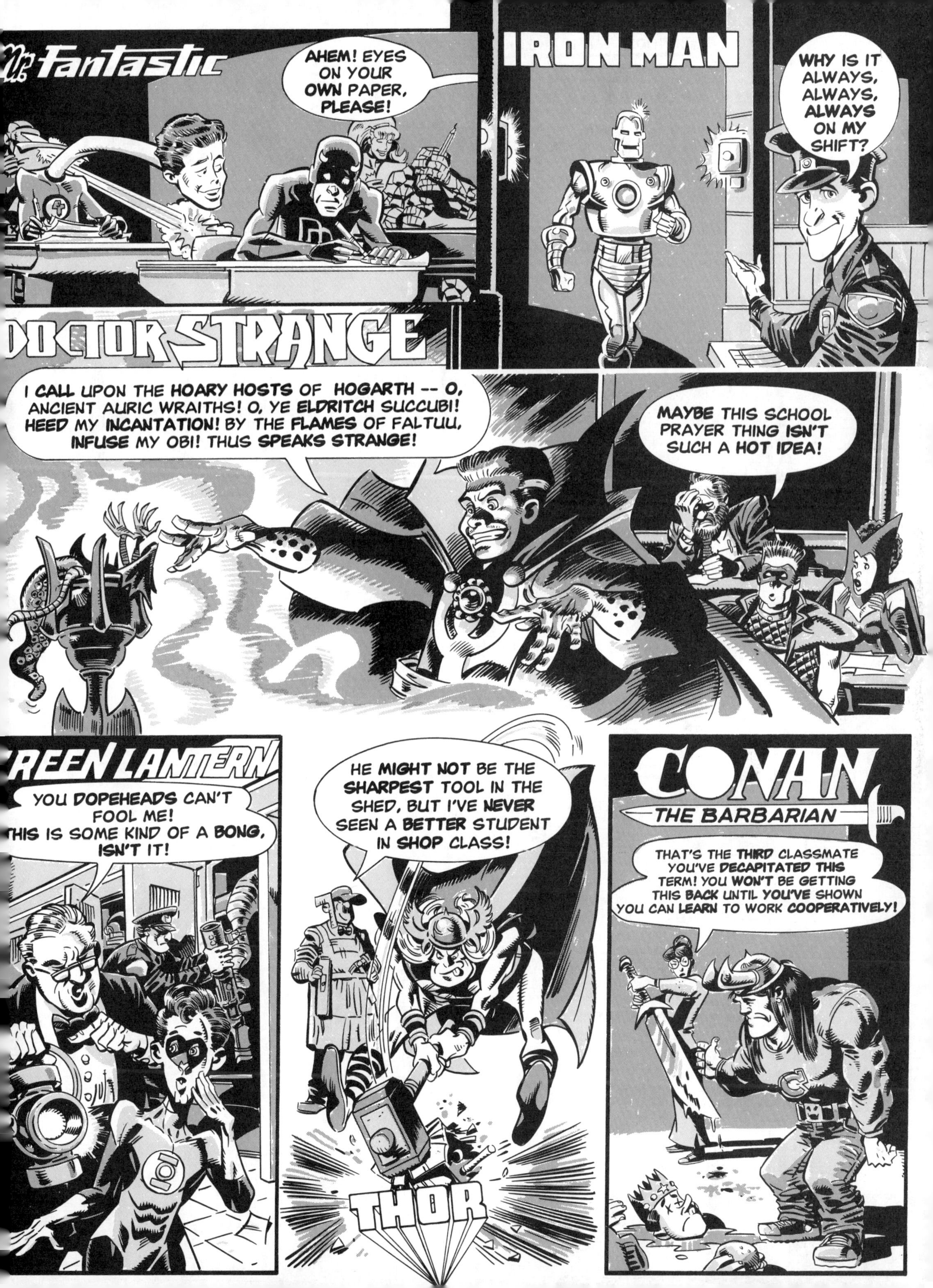

Mr. Fantastic
AHEM! EYES ON YOUR OWN PAPER, PLEASE!
IRON MAN
WHY IS IT ALWAYS, ALWAYS, ALWAYS ON MY SHIFT?
DOCTOR STRANGE
I CALL UPON THE HOARY HOSTS OF HOGARTH -- O, ANCIENT AURIC WRAITHS! O, YE ELDRITCH SUCCUBI! HEED MY INCANTATION! BY THE FLAMES OF FALTUU, INFUSE MY OBI! THUS SPEAKS STRANGE!
MAYBE THIS SCHOOL PRAYER THING ISN'T SUCH A HOT IDEA!
REEN LANTERN
YOU DOPEHEADS CAN'T FOOL ME! THIS IS SOME KIND OF A BONG, ISN'T IT!
HE MIGHT NOT BE THE SHARPEST TOOL IN THE SHED, BUT I'VE NEVER SEEN A BETTER STUDENT IN SHOP CLASS!
THOR
CONAN THE BARBARIAN
THAT'S THE THIRD CLASSMATE YOU'VE DECAPITATED THIS TERM! YOU WON'T BE GETTING THIS BACK UNTIL YOU'VE SHOWN YOU CAN LEARN TO WORK COOPERATIVELY!

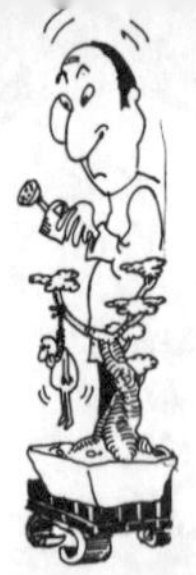

SHNOOK . . . UP IN THE SKY! DEPT.

A MAD LOOK AT SUP

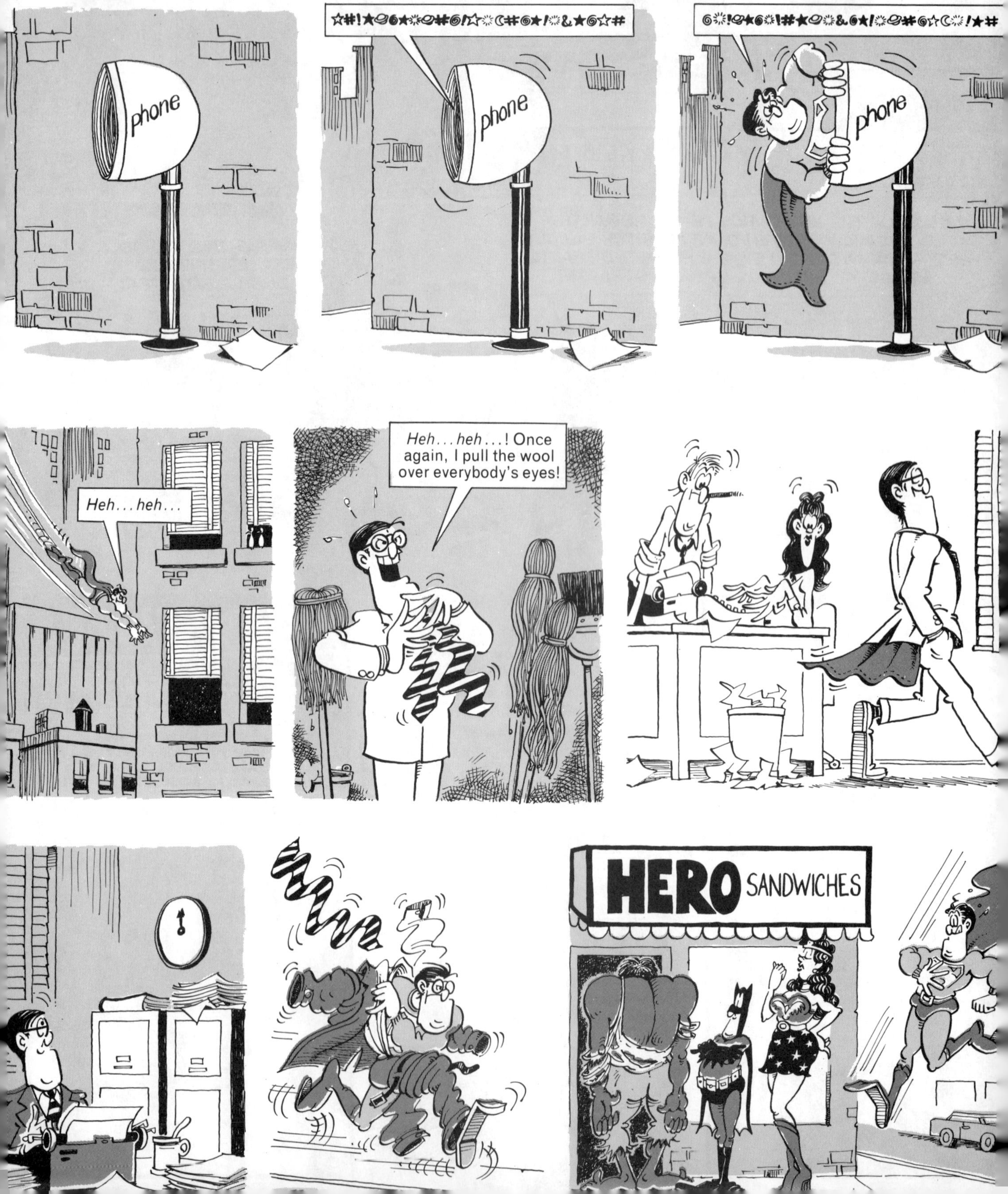
phone
phone
phone
Heh . . . heh . . .
Heh . . . heh . . . ! Once again, I pull the wool over everybody's eyes!
HERO SANDWICHES

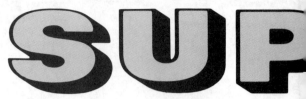

ERMAN

ARTIST: DON MARTIN

WRITER: DON EDWING

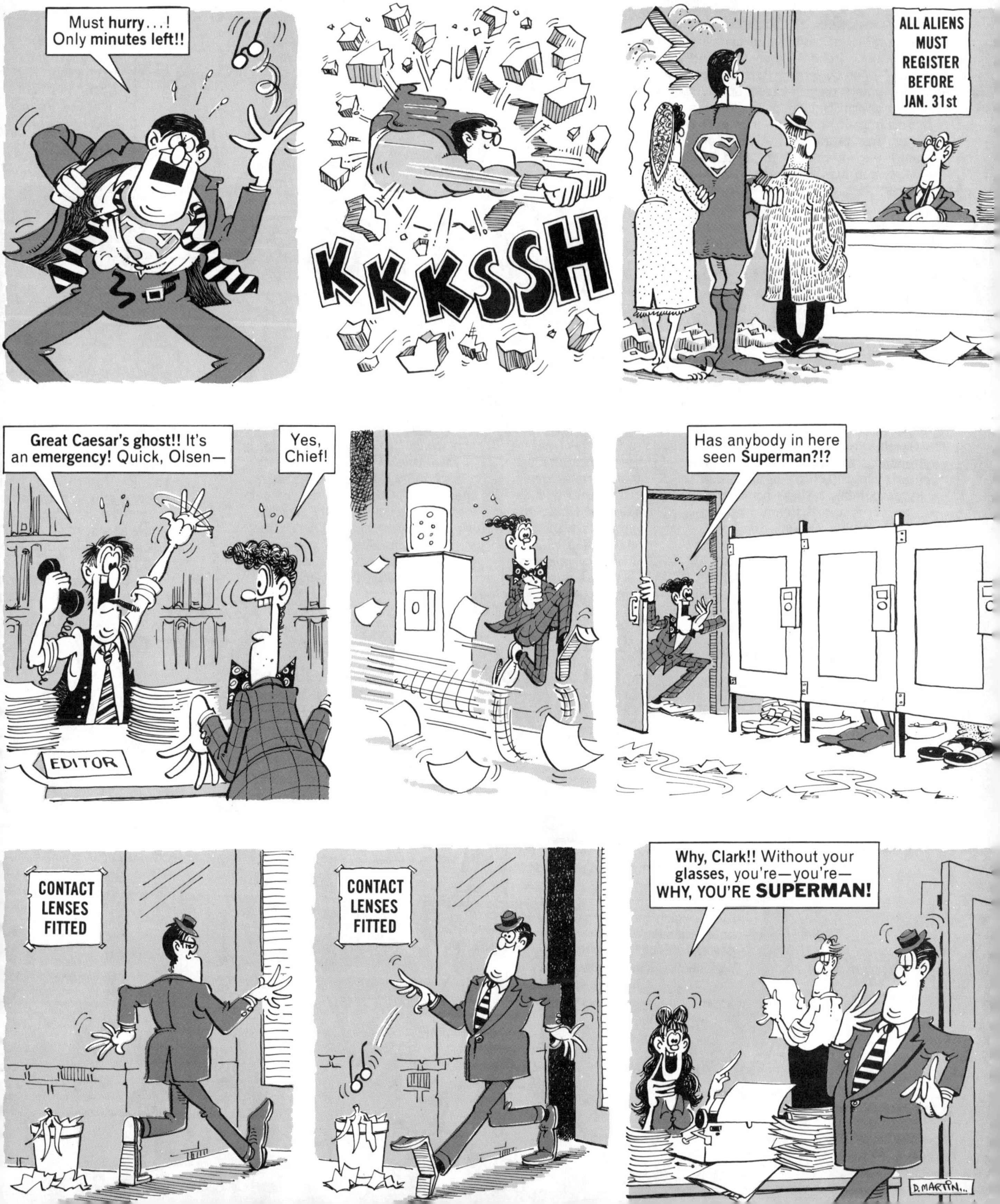
Must hurry...! Only minutes left!!
KKKSSH
ALL ALIENS MUST REGISTER BEFORE JAN. 31st
Great Caesar's ghost!! It's an emergency! Quick, Olsen—
Yes, Chief!
EDITOR
Has anybody in here seen Superman?!?
CONTACT LENSES FITTED
CONTACT LENSES FITTED
Why, Clark!! Without your glasses, you're—you're—WHY, YOU'RE SUPERMAN!
D. MARTIN

SUPER ZEROS DEPT.

Each year, they grow in numbers! Mutant hybrids feared and hated by the citizens of this great land! But enough about today's high school students! Let's concentrate on another breed of mutants, the kind who rule the Fox Network every Saturday morning! Yeah, you know who we're referring to...

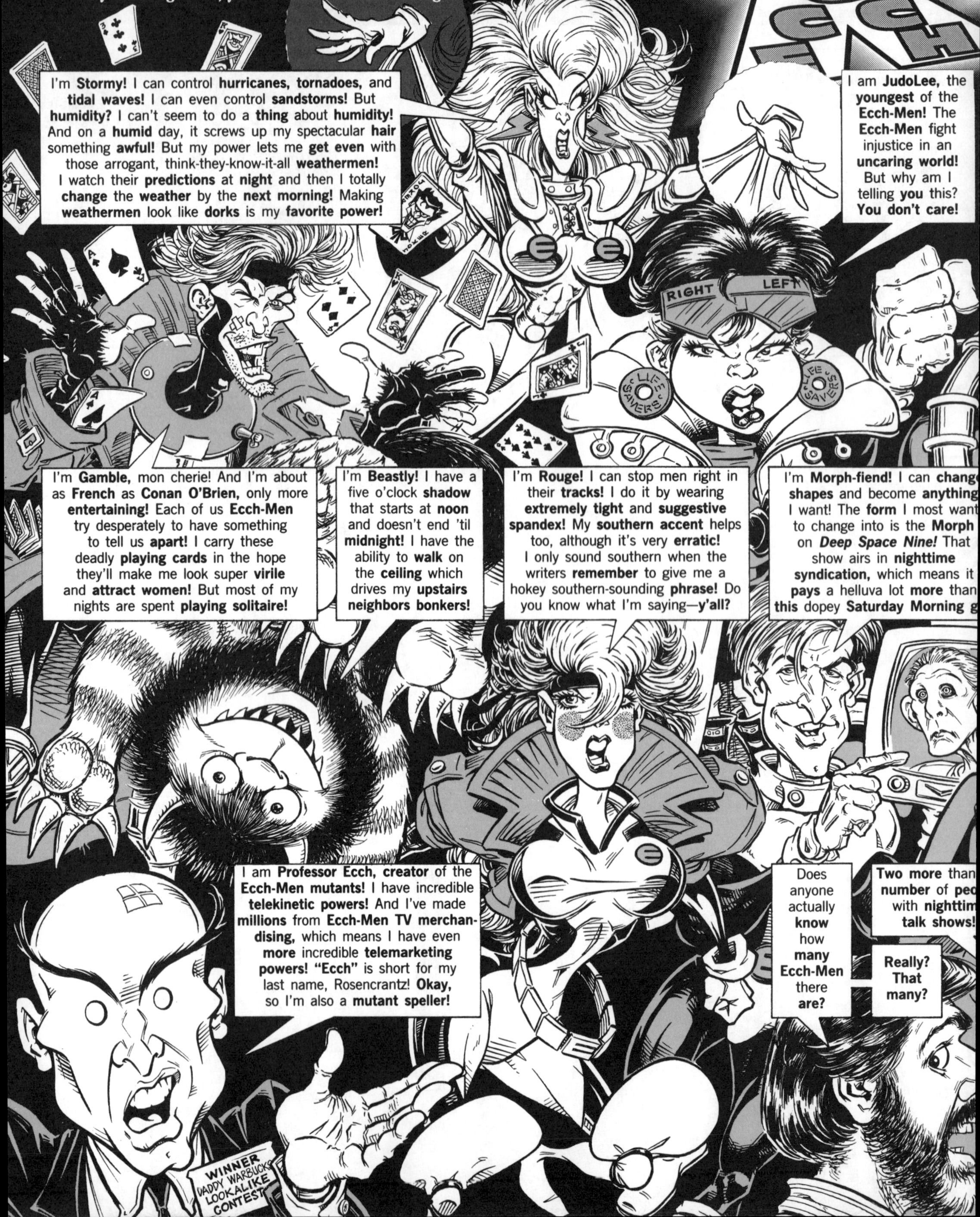

ECCCH
I'm Stormy! I can control hurricanes, tornadoes, and tidal waves! I can even control sandstorms! But humidity? I can't seem to do a thing about humidity! And on a humid day, it screws up my spectacular hair something awful! But my power lets me get even with those arrogant, think-they-know-it-all weathermen! I watch their predictions at night and then I totally change the weather by the next morning! Making weathermen look like dorks is my favorite power!
I am JudoLee, the youngest of the Ecch-Men! The Ecch-Men fight injustice in an uncaring world! But why am I telling you this? You don't care!
RIGHT LEFT
LIFE SAVERS
I'm Gamble, mon cherie! And I'm about as French as Conan O'Brien, only more entertaining! Each of us Ecch-Men try desperately to have something to tell us apart! I carry these deadly playing cards in the hope they'll make me look super virile and attract women! But most of my nights are spent playing solitaire!
I'm Beastly! I have a five o'clock shadow that starts at noon and doesn't end 'til midnight! I have the ability to walk on the ceiling which drives my upstairs neighbors bonkers!
I'm Rouge! I can stop men right in their tracks! I do it by wearing extremely tight and suggestive spandex! My southern accent helps too, although it's very erratic! I only sound southern when the writers remember to give me a hokey southern-sounding phrase! Do you know what I'm saying—y'all?
I'm Morph-fiend! I can change shapes and become anything I want! The form I most want to change into is the Morph on Deep Space Nine! That show airs in nighttime syndication, which means it pays a helluva lot more than this dopey Saturday Morning g
I am Professor Ecch, creator of the Ecch-Men mutants! I have incredible telekinetic powers! And I've made millions from Ecch-Men TV merchandising, which means I have even more incredible telemarketing powers! "Ecch" is short for my last name, Rosencrantz! Okay, so I'm also a mutant speller!
Does anyone actually know how many Ecch-Men there are?
Two more than number of peo with nighttim talk shows!
Really? That many?
WINNER DADDY WARBUCKS LOOKALIKE CONTEST

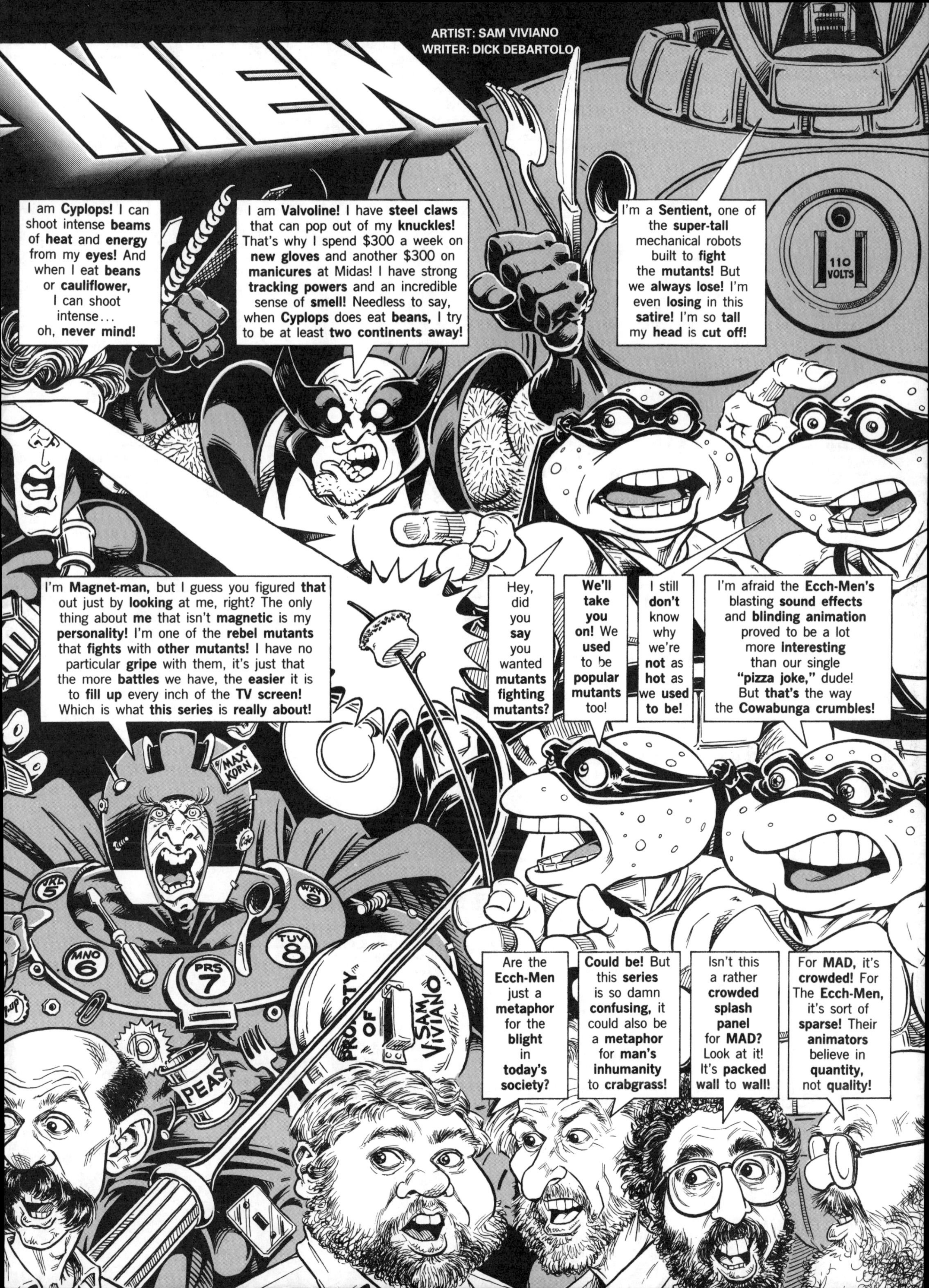
ARTIST: SAM VIVIANO
WRITER: DICK DEBARTOLO
MEN
I am Cyplops! I can shoot intense beams of heat and energy from my eyes! And when I eat beans or cauliflower, I can shoot intense... oh, never mind!
I am Valvoline! I have steel claws that can pop out of my knuckles! That's why I spend $300 a week on new gloves and another $300 on manicures at Midas! I have strong tracking powers and an incredible sense of smell! Needless to say, when Cyplops does eat beans, I try to be at least two continents away!
I'm a Sentient, one of the super-tall mechanical robots built to fight the mutants! But we always lose! I'm even losing in this satire! I'm so tall my head is cut off!
110 VOLTS
I'm Magnet-man, but I guess you figured that out just by looking at me, right? The only thing about me that isn't magnetic is my personality! I'm one of the rebel mutants that fights with other mutants! I have no particular gripe with them, it's just that the more battles we have, the easier it is to fill up every inch of the TV screen! Which is what this series is really about!
Hey, did you say you wanted mutants fighting mutants?
We'll take you on! We used to be popular mutants too!
I still don't know why we're not as hot as we used to be!
I'm afraid the Ecch-Men's blasting sound effects and blinding animation proved to be a lot more interesting than our single "pizza joke," dude! But that's the way the Cowabunga crumbles!
MAX KORN
PROPERTY OF SAM VIVIANO
PEAS
Are the Ecch-Men just a metaphor for the blight in today's society?
Could be! But this series is so damn confusing, it could also be a metaphor for man's inhumanity to crabgrass!
Isn't this a rather crowded splash panel for MAD? Look at it! It's packed wall to wall!
For MAD, it's crowded! For The Ecch-Men, it's sort of sparse! Their animators believe in quantity, not quality!

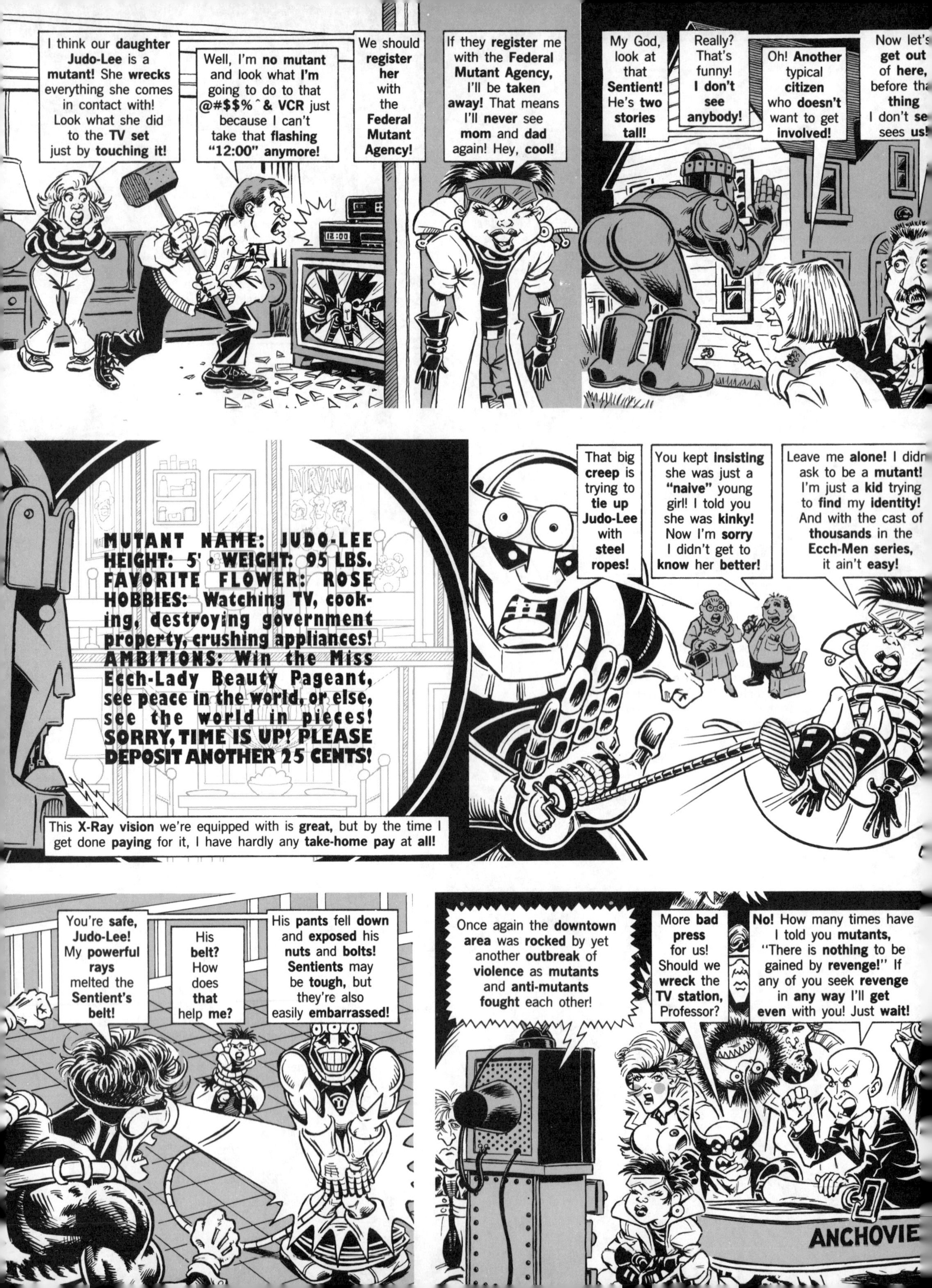
I think our daughter Judo-Lee is a mutant! She wrecks everything she comes in contact with! Look what she did to the TV set just by touching it!
Well, I'm no mutant and look what I'm going to do to that @#$$%^& VCR just because I can't take that flashing "12:00" anymore!
12:00
We should register her with the Federal Mutant Agency!
If they register me with the Federal Mutant Agency, I'll be taken away! That means I'll never see mom and dad again! Hey, cool!
My God, look at that Sentient! He's two stories tall!
Really? That's funny! I don't see anybody!
Oh! Another typical citizen who doesn't want to get involved!
Now let's get out of here, before tha thing I don't se sees us!
NIRVANA
MUTANT NAME: JUDO-LEE
HEIGHT: 5' • WEIGHT: 95 LBS.
FAVORITE FLOWER: ROSE
HOBBIES: Watching TV, cooking, destroying government property, crushing appliances!
AMBITIONS: Win the Miss Ecch-Lady Beauty Pageant, see peace in the world, or else, see the world in pieces!
SORRY, TIME IS UP! PLEASE DEPOSIT ANOTHER 25 CENTS!
This X-Ray vision we're equipped with is great, but by the time I get done paying for it, I have hardly any take-home pay at all!
That big creep is trying to tie up Judo-Lee with steel ropes!
You kept insisting she was just a "naive" young girl! I told you she was kinky! Now I'm sorry I didn't get to know her better!
Leave me alone! I didn ask to be a mutant! I'm just a kid trying to find my identity! And with the cast of thousands in the Ecch-Men series, it ain't easy!
You're safe, Judo-Lee! My powerful rays melted the Sentient's belt!
His belt? How does that help me?
His pants fell down and exposed his nuts and bolts! Sentients may be tough, but they're also easily embarrassed!
Once again the downtown area was rocked by yet another outbreak of violence as mutants and anti-mutants fought each other!
More bad press for us! Should we wreck the TV station, Professor?
No! How many times have I told you mutants, "There is nothing to be gained by revenge!" If any of you seek revenge in any way I'll get even with you! Just wait!
ANCHOVIE

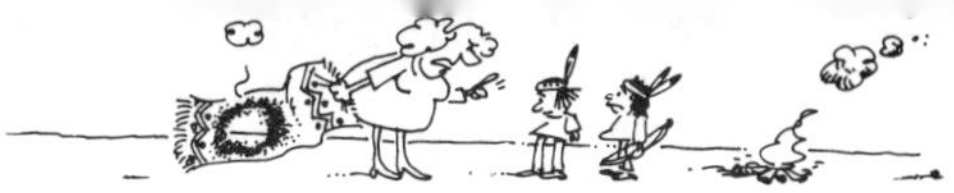

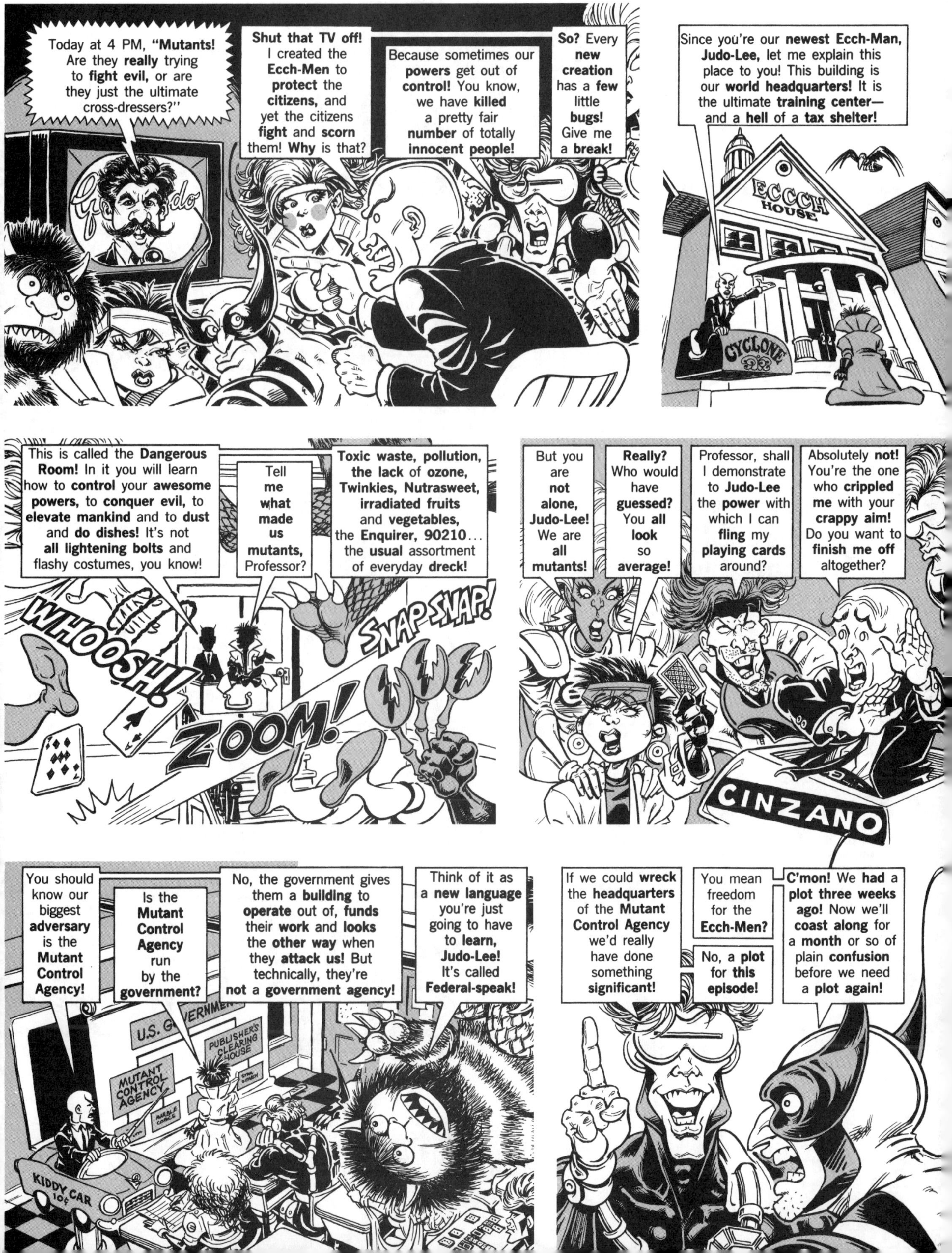

Today at 4 PM, "Mutants! Are they really trying to fight evil, or are they just the ultimate cross-dressers?"
Shut that TV off! I created the Ecch-Men to protect the citizens, and yet the citizens fight and scorn them! Why is that?
Because sometimes our powers get out of control! You know, we have killed a pretty fair number of totally innocent people!
So? Every new creation has a few little bugs! Give me a break!
Since you're our newest Ecch-Man, Judo-Lee, let me explain this place to you! This building is our world headquarters! It is the ultimate training center—and a hell of a tax shelter!
ECCCH HOUSE
CYCLONE
This is called the Dangerous Room! In it you will learn how to control your awesome powers, to conquer evil, to elevate mankind and to dust and do dishes! It's not all lightening bolts and flashy costumes, you know!
Tell me what made us mutants, Professor?
Toxic waste, pollution, the lack of ozone, Twinkies, Nutrasweet, irradiated fruits and vegetables, the Enquirer, 90210... the usual assortment of everyday dreck!
WHOOSH!
SNAP SNAP!
ZOOM!
But you are not alone, Judo-Lee! We are all mutants!
Really? Who would have guessed? You all look so average!
Professor, shall I demonstrate to Judo-Lee the power with which I can fling my playing cards around?
Absolutely not! You're the one who crippled me with your crappy aim! Do you want to finish me off altogether?
CINZANO
You should know our biggest adversary is the Mutant Control Agency!
Is the Mutant Control Agency run by the government?
No, the government gives them a building to operate out of, funds their work and looks the other way when they attack us! But technically, they're not a government agency!
Think of it as a new language you're just going to have to learn, Judo-Lee! It's called Federal-speak!
PUBLISHER'S CLEARING HOUSE
MUTANT CONTROL AGENCY
MARBLE COMICS
KIDDY CAR 10¢
If we could wreck the headquarters of the Mutant Control Agency we'd really have done something significant!
You mean freedom for the Ecch-Men?
No, a plot for this episode!
C'mon! We had a plot three weeks ago! Now we'll coast along for a month or so of plain confusion before we need a plot again!

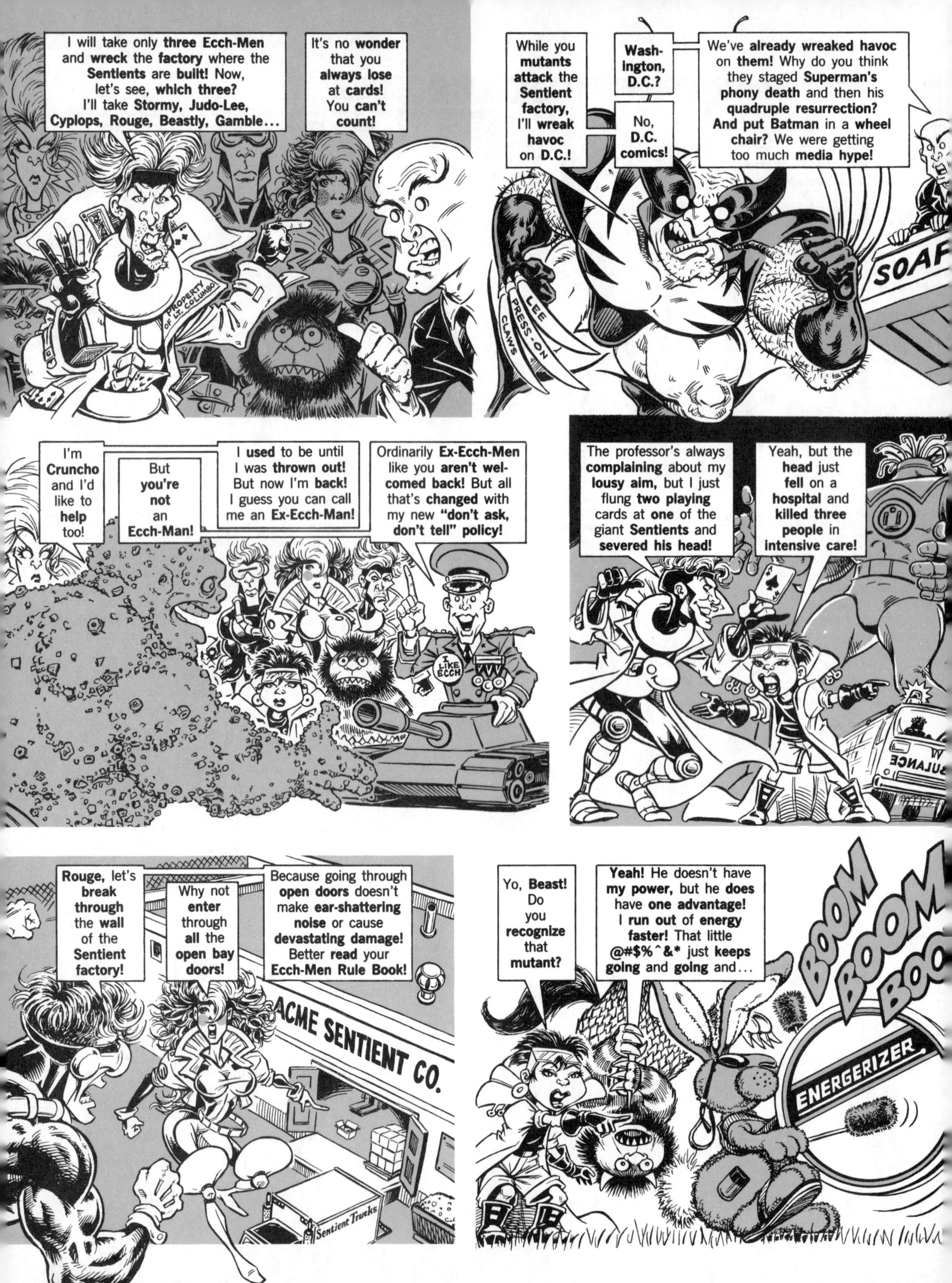

I will take only **three Ecch-Men** and **wreck** the **factory** where the **Sentients** are **built!** Now, let's see, **which three?** I'll take **Stormy, Judo-Lee, Cyplops, Rouge, Beastly, Gamble...**
It's no **wonder** that you **always lose** at **cards!** You **can't count!**
PROPERTY OF LT. COLUMBO
While you **mutants attack** the **Sentient factory,** I'll **wreak havoc** on **D.C.!**
Wash-ington, D.C.?
No, **D.C. comics!**
We've **already wreaked havoc** on **them!** Why do you think they staged **Superman's phony death** and then his **quadruple resurrection? And put Batman** in a **wheel chair?** We were getting too much **media hype!**
LEE PRESS-ON CLAWS
I'm **Cruncho** and I'd like to **help** too!
But **you're not** an **Ecch-Man!**
I **used** to be until I was **thrown out!** But now I'm **back!** I guess you can call me an **Ex-Ecch-Man!**
Ordinarily **Ex-Ecch-Men** like you **aren't wel-comed back!** But all that's **changed** with my new **"don't ask, don't tell"** policy!
I LIKE ECCH
The professor's always **complaining** about my **lousy aim,** but I just flung **two playing** cards at **one** of the giant **Sentients** and **severed his head!**
Yeah, but the **head** just **fell** on a **hospital** and **killed three people** in **intensive care!**
Rouge, let's **break through** the **wall** of the **Sentient factory!**
Why not **enter** through **all** the **open bay doors!**
Because going through **open doors** doesn't make **ear-shattering noise** or cause **devastating damage!** Better **read** your **Ecch-Men Rule Book!**
ACME SENTIENT CO.
Sentient Trucks
Yo, **Beast!** Do you **recognize** that **mutant?**
Yeah! He doesn't have **my power,** but he **does** have **one advantage!** I **run out** of **energy faster!** That little **@#$%^&*** just **keeps going** and **going** and...
BOOM
BOOM
ENERGIZER

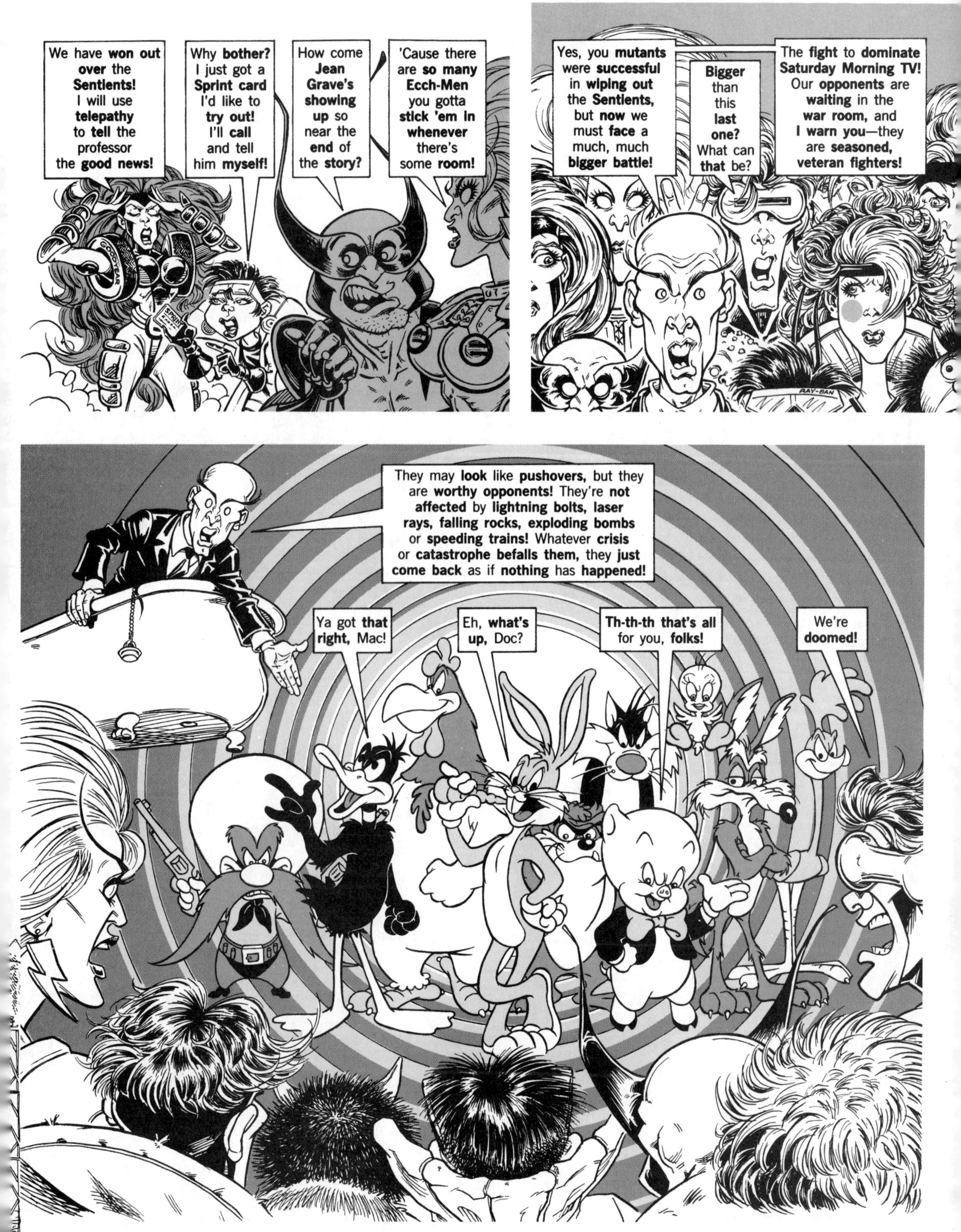
We have won out over the Sentients! I will use telepathy to tell the professor the good news!
Why bother? I just got a Sprint card I'd like to try out! I'll call and tell him myself!
How come Jean Grave's showing up so near the end of the story?
'Cause there are so many Ecch-Men you gotta stick 'em in whenever there's some room!
GOODYEAR
Yes, you mutants were successful in wiping out the Sentients, but now we must face a much, much bigger battle!
Bigger than this last one? What can that be?
The fight to dominate Saturday Morning TV! Our opponents are waiting in the war room, and I warn you—they are seasoned, veteran fighters!
RAY-BAN
They may look like pushovers, but they are worthy opponents! They're not affected by lightning bolts, laser rays, falling rocks, exploding bombs or speeding trains! Whatever crisis or catastrophe befalls them, they just come back as if nothing has happened!
Ya got that right, Mac!
Eh, what's up, Doc?
Th-th-th that's all for you, folks!
We're doomed!

THE ECCH MEN DEPT.

Look! Up in the sky! And keep looking all day, fanboy! If you're lucky, you might see a cloud that sort of looks like Jimmy Olsen! We hate to break it to you, but there aren't four Supermen—in fact, there isn't even one! Wolverine, Green Lantern, Commissioner Gordon...you name it, they're all fake! But don't despair, because you still may have the chance to meet some of these...

REAL-LIFE SUPERF

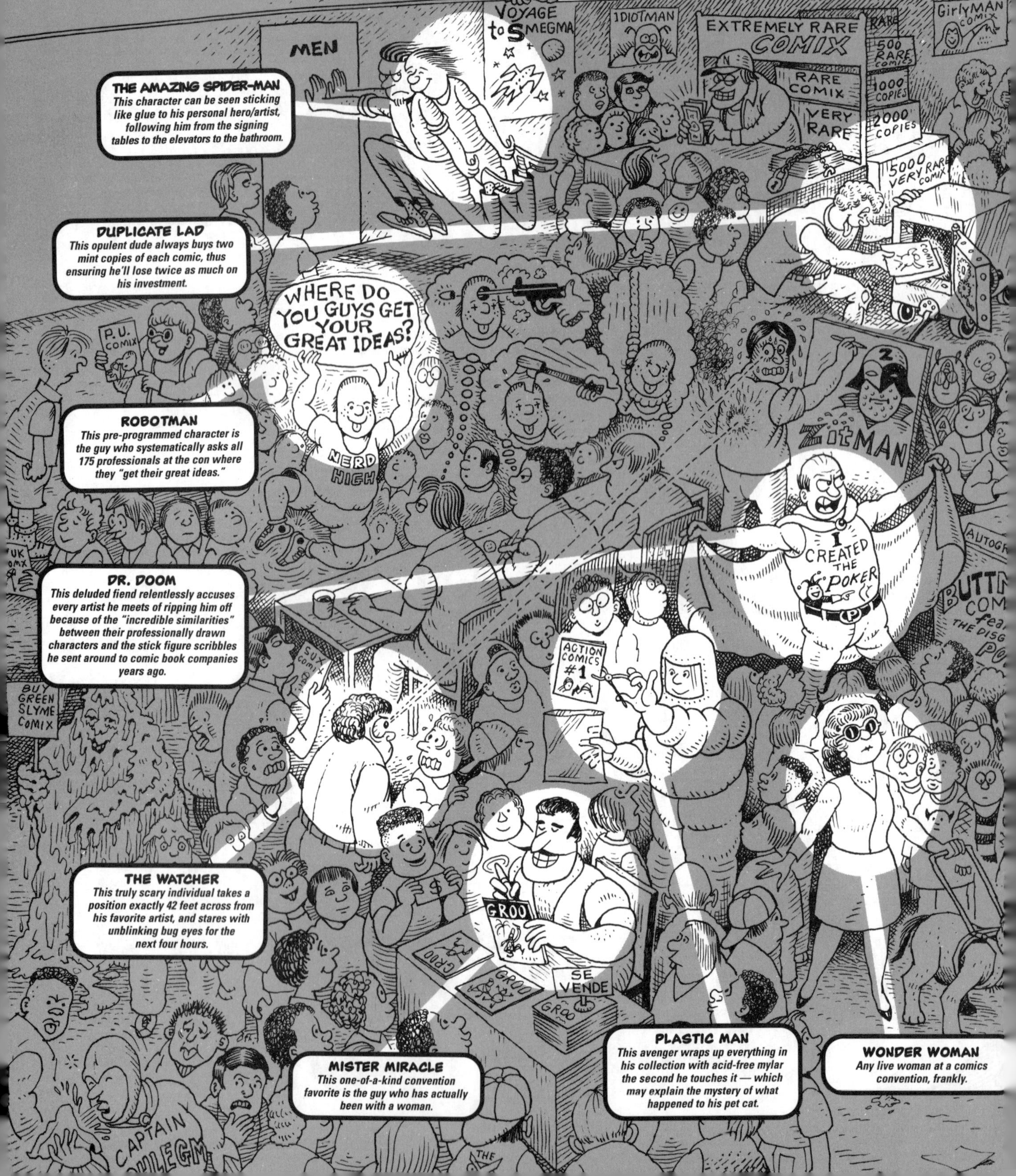
MEN
VOYAGE to SMEGMA
IDIOTMAN
EXTREMELY RARE COMIX
RARE
GirlyMAN COMIX
500 RARE COMICS
RARE COMIX
1000 COPIES
VERY RARE
2000 COPIES
5000 VERY RARE COMIX
COMIX
WHERE DO YOU GUYS GET YOUR GREAT IDEAS?
P.U. COMIX
NERD HIGH
ZitMAN
I CREATED THE POKER
UK COMX
SUX COMIX
BUY GREEN SLYME COMIX
ACTION COMICS #1
GROO
SE VENDE
CAPTAIN

THE AMAZING SPIDER-MAN
This character can be seen sticking like glue to his personal hero/artist, following him from the signing tables to the elevators to the bathroom.

DUPLICATE LAD
This opulent dude always buys two mint copies of each comic, thus ensuring he'll lose twice as much on his investment.

ROBOTMAN
This pre-programmed character is the guy who systematically asks all 175 professionals at the con where they "get their great ideas."

DR. DOOM
This deluded fiend relentlessly accuses every artist he meets of ripping him off because of the "incredible similarities" between their professionally drawn characters and the stick figure scribbles he sent around to comic book companies years ago.

THE WATCHER
This truly scary individual takes a position exactly 42 feet across from his favorite artist, and stares with unblinking bug eyes for the next four hours.

MISTER MIRACLE
This one-of-a-kind convention favorite is the guy who has actually been with a woman.

PLASTIC MAN
This avenger wraps up everything in his collection with acid-free mylar the second he touches it — which may explain the mystery of what happened to his pet cat.

WONDER WOMAN
Any live woman at a comics convention, frankly.

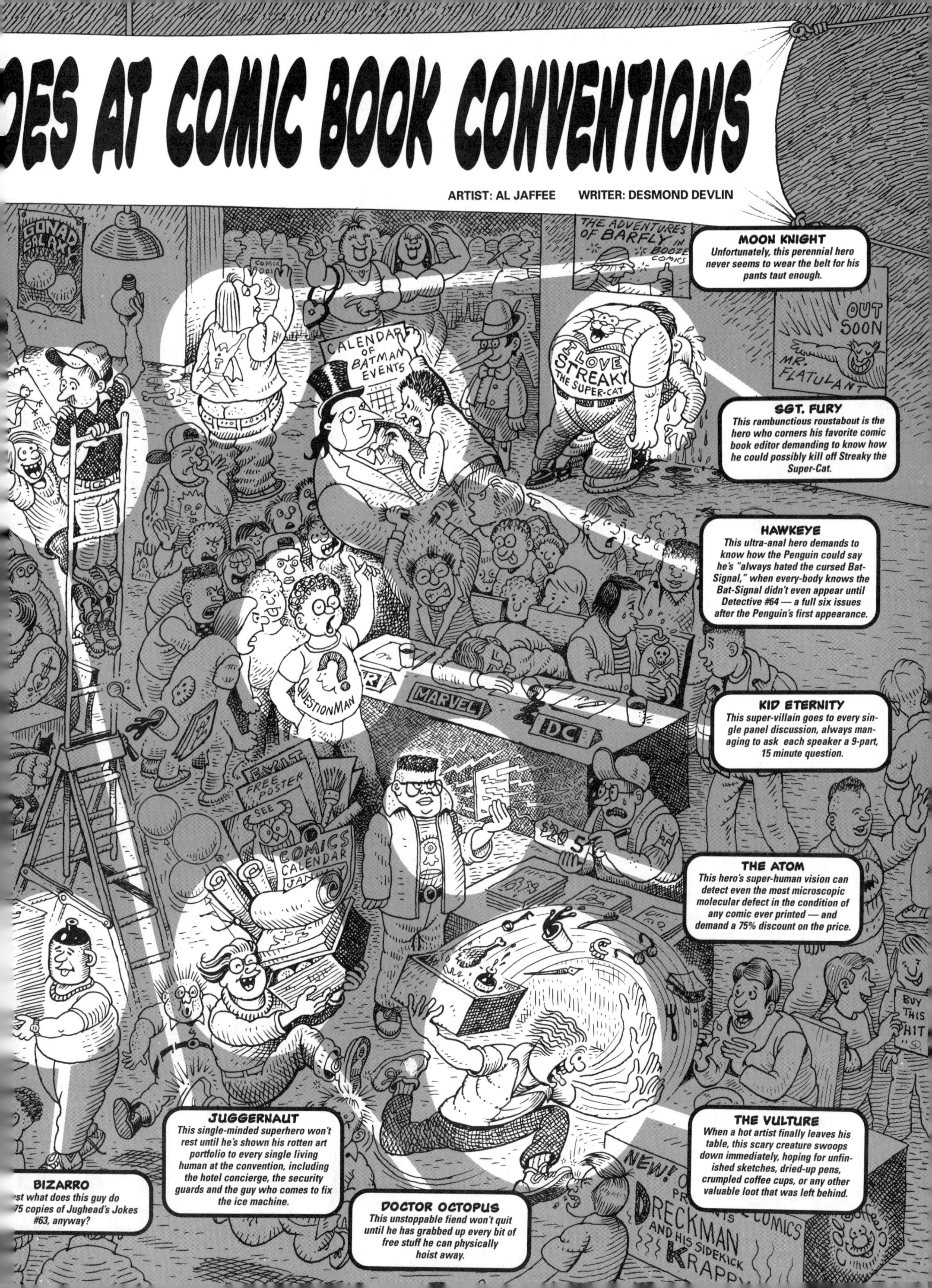

OES AT COMIC BOOK CONVENTIONS
ARTIST: AL JAFFEE WRITER: DESMOND DEVLIN
THE ADVENTURES OF BARFLY IN BOOZE COMICS
MOON KNIGHT
Unfortunately, this perennial hero never seems to wear the belt for his pants taut enough.
OUT SOON MR. FLATULANT
CALENDAR OF BATMAN EVENTS
I LOVE STREAKY THE SUPER-CAT
SGT. FURY
This rambunctious roustabout is the hero who corners his favorite comic book editor demanding to know how he could possibly kill off Streaky the Super-Cat.
HAWKEYE
This ultra-anal hero demands to know how the Penguin could say he's "always hated the cursed Bat-Signal," when every-body knows the Bat-Signal didn't even appear until Detective #64 — a full six issues after the Penguin's first appearance.
QUESTIONMAN
MARVEL
DC
KID ETERNITY
This super-villain goes to every single panel discussion, always managing to ask each speaker a 9-part, 15 minute question.
FREE POSTER
COMICS CALENDAR JAN
$20 5
THE ATOM
This hero's super-human vision can detect even the most microscopic molecular defect in the condition of any comic ever printed — and demand a 75% discount on the price.
BUY THIS HIT
JUGGERNAUT
This single-minded superhero won't rest until he's shown his rotten art portfolio to every single living human at the convention, including the hotel concierge, the security guards and the guy who comes to fix the ice machine.
THE VULTURE
When a hot artist finally leaves his table, this scary creature swoops down immediately, hoping for unfinished sketches, dried-up pens, crumpled coffee cups, or any other valuable loot that was left behind.
BIZARRO
st what does this guy do 75 copies of Jughead's Jokes #63, anyway?
DOCTOR OCTOPUS
This unstoppable fiend won't quit until he has grabbed up every bit of free stuff he can physically hoist away.
NEW!
DRECKMAN AND HIS SIDEKICK KRAPP

ALL MEN ARE CREATING SEQUELS DEPT.

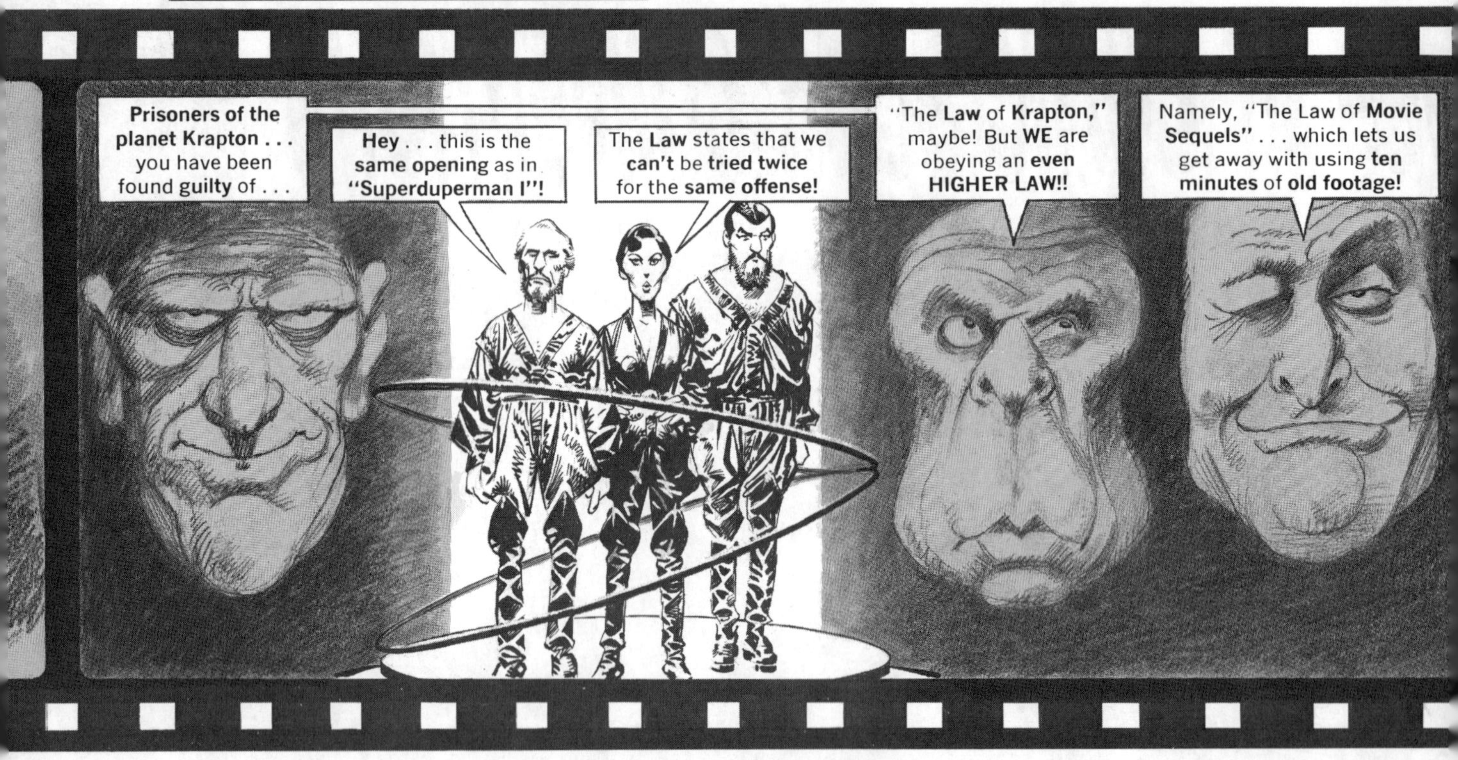

Prisoners of the planet Krapton . . . you have been found guilty of . . .
Hey . . . this is the same opening as in "Superduperman I"!
The Law states that we can't be tried twice for the same offense!
"The Law of Krapton," maybe! But WE are obeying an even HIGHER LAW!!
Namely, "The Law of Movie Sequels" . . . which lets us get away with using ten minutes of old footage!

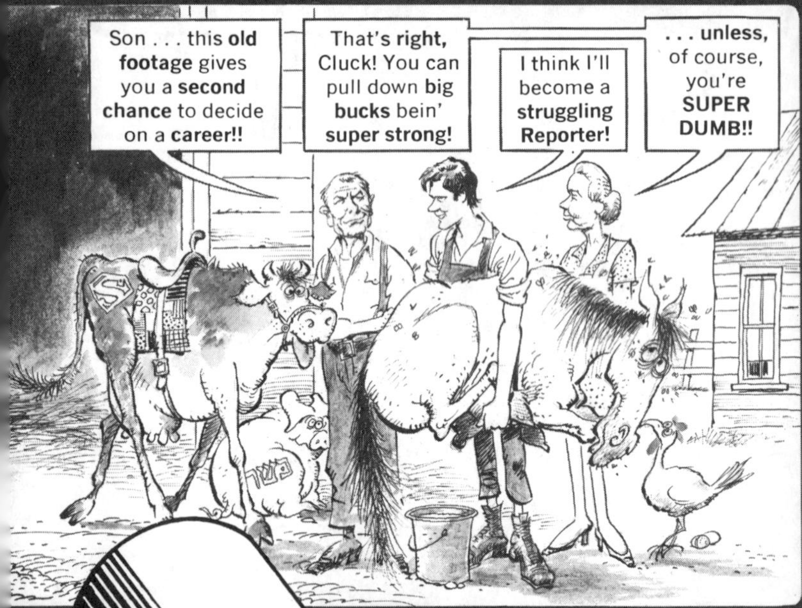

Son . . . this old footage gives you a second chance to decide on a career!!
That's right, Cluck! You can pull down big bucks bein' super strong!
I think I'll become a struggling Reporter!
. . . unless, of course, you're SUPER DUMB!!
כשר

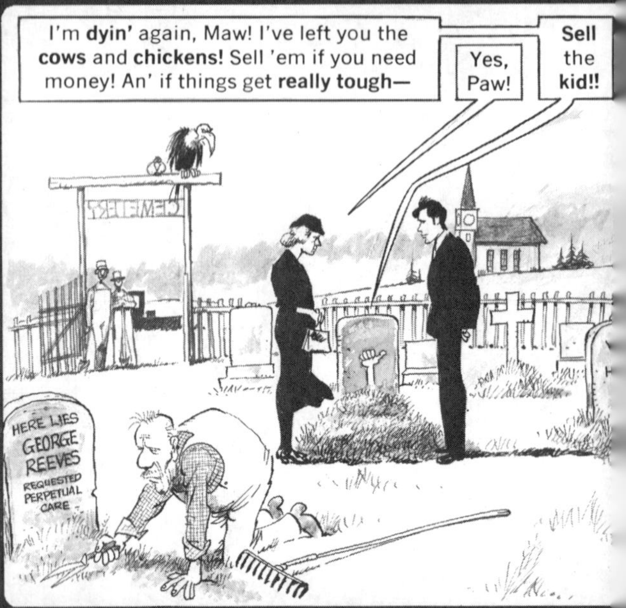

I'm dyin' again, Maw! I've left you the cows and chickens! Sell 'em if you need money! An' if things get really tough—
Yes, Paw!
Sell the kid!!
HERE LIES GEORGE REEVES REQUESTED PERPETUAL CARE

SUPERDU

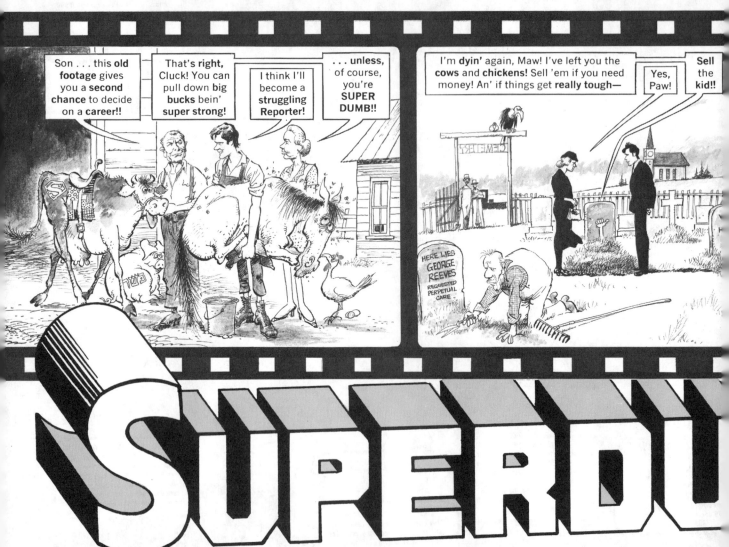

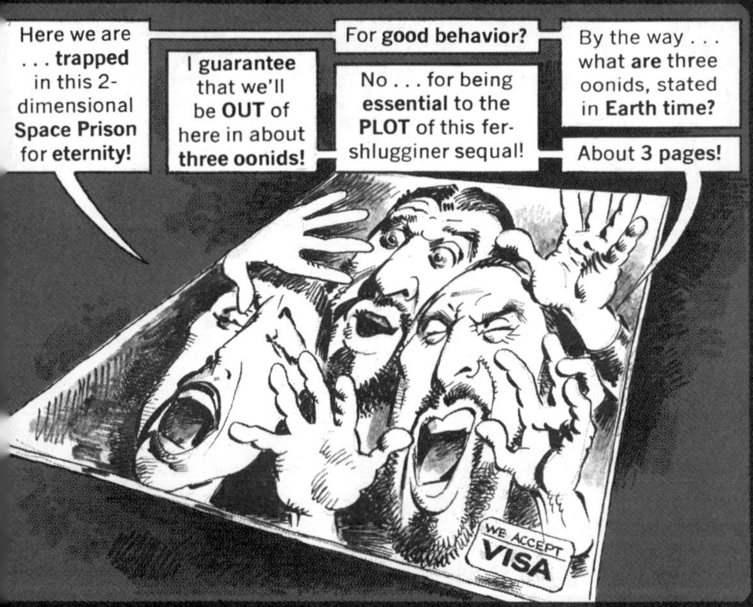
Here we are . . . trapped in this 2-dimensional Space Prison for eternity!
I guarantee that we'll be OUT of here in about three oonids!
For good behavior?
No . . . for being essential to the PLOT of this fershlugginer sequal!
By the way . . . what are three oonids, stated in Earth time?
About 3 pages!
WE ACCEPT VISA

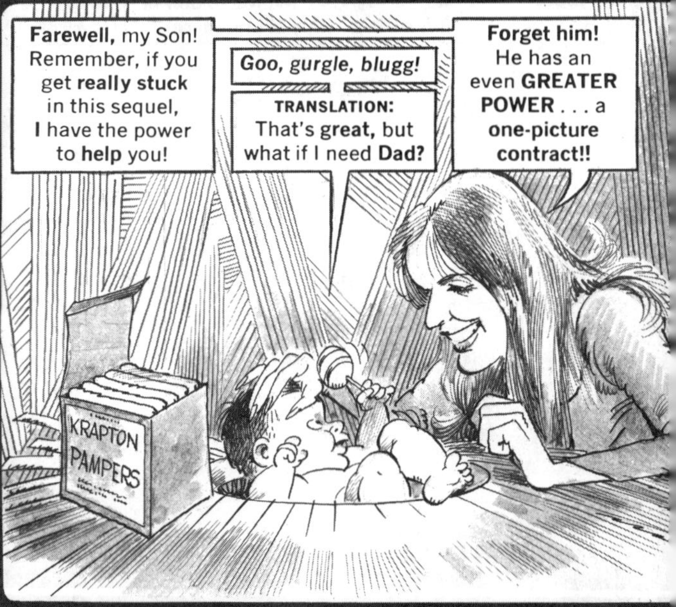
Farewell, my Son! Remember, if you get really stuck in this sequel, I have the power to help you!
Goo, gurgle, blugg!
TRANSLATION: That's great, but what if I need Dad?
Forget him! He has an even GREATER POWER . . . a one-picture contract!!
KRAPTON PAMPERS

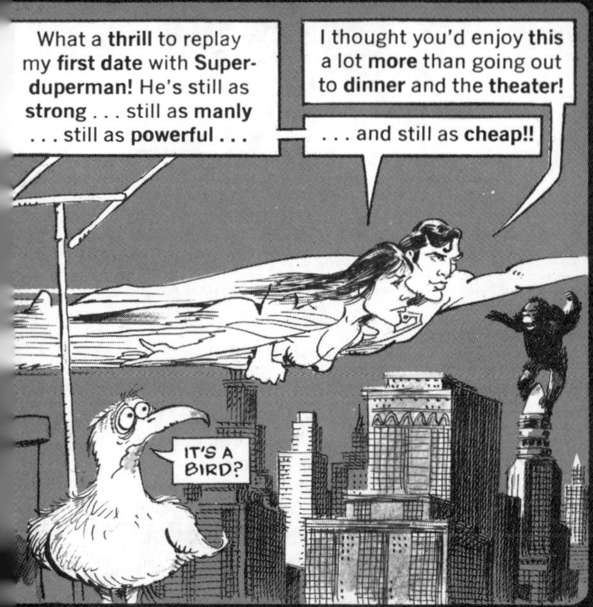
What a thrill to replay my first date with Superduperman! He's still as strong . . . still as manly . . . still as powerful . . .
I thought you'd enjoy this a lot more than going out to dinner and the theater!
. . . and still as cheap!!
IT'S A BIRD?

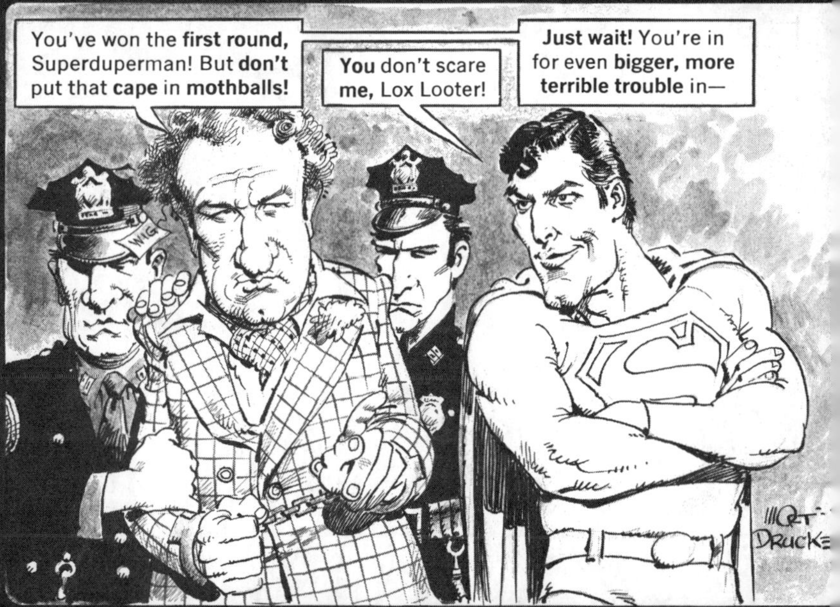
You've won the first round, Superduperman! But don't put that cape in mothballs!
You don't scare me, Lox Looter!
Just wait! You're in for even bigger, more terrible trouble in—
MORT DRUCKER

PERMAN II

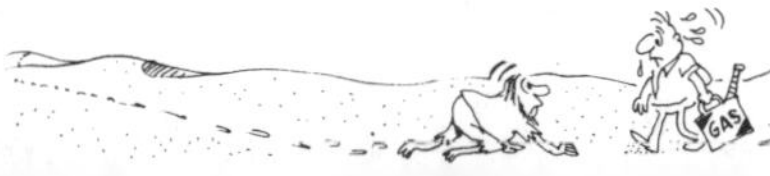

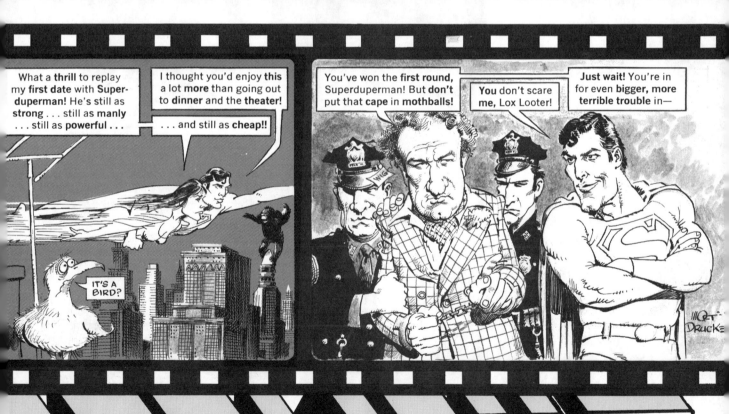

ARTIST: MORT DRUCKER

WRITER: FRANK JACOBS

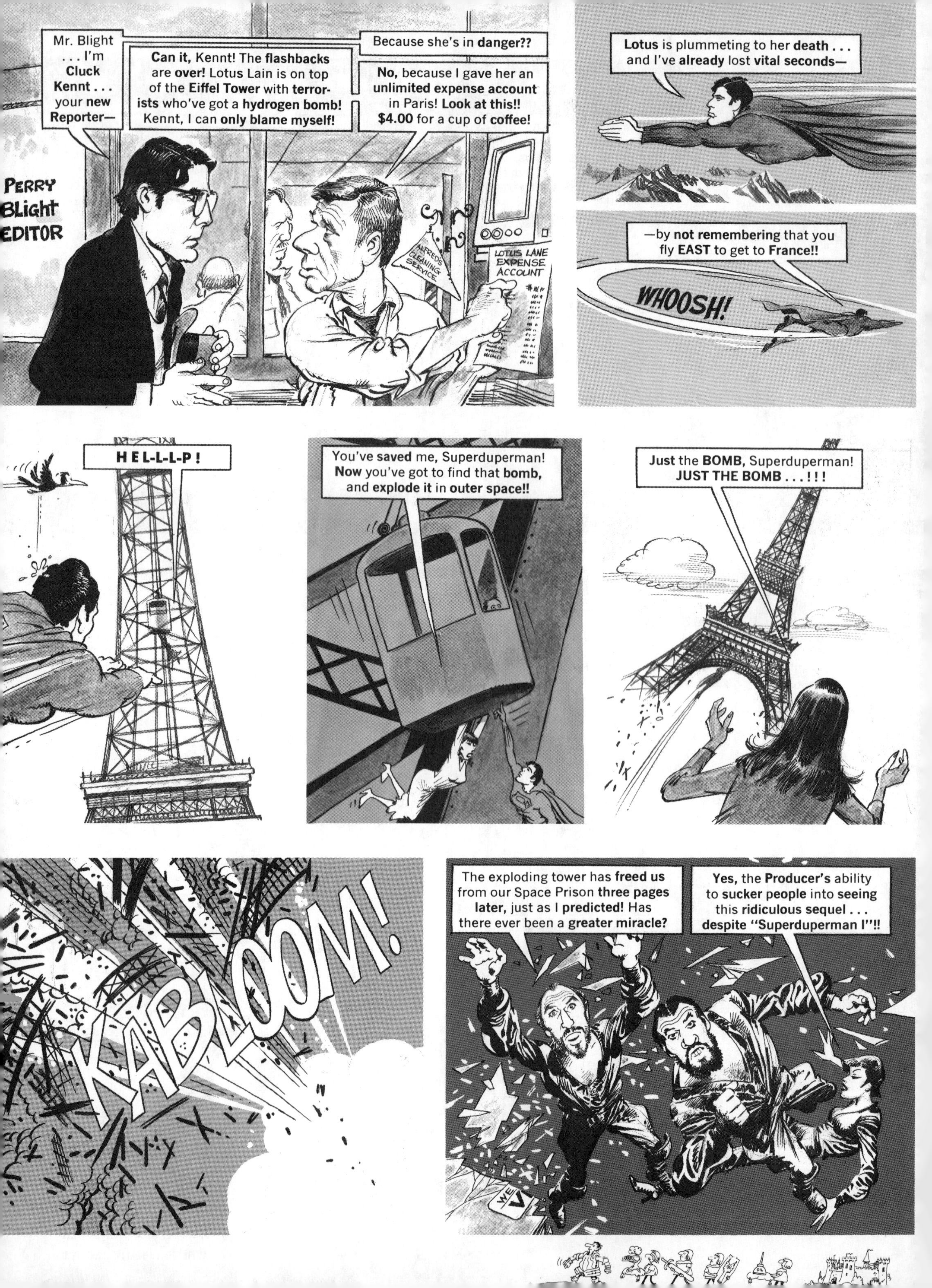

Mr. Blight . . . I'm Cluck Kennt . . . your new Reporter—
Can it, Kennt! The flashbacks are over! Lotus Lain is on top of the Eiffel Tower with terrorists who've got a hydrogen bomb! Kennt, I can only blame myself!
Because she's in danger??
No, because I gave her an unlimited expense account in Paris! Look at this!! $4.00 for a cup of coffee!
PERRY BLIGHT EDITOR
ALFRED'S CLEANING SERVICE
LOTUS LANE EXPENSE ACCOUNT
Lotus is plummeting to her death . . . and I've already lost vital seconds—
—by not remembering that you fly EAST to get to France!!
WHOOSH!
HEL-L-L-P!
You've saved me, Superduperman! Now you've got to find that bomb, and explode it in outer space!!
Just the BOMB, Superduperman! JUST THE BOMB . . . !!!
KABLOOM!
The exploding tower has freed us from our Space Prison three pages later, just as I predicted! Has there ever been a greater miracle?
Yes, the Producer's ability to sucker people into seeing this ridiculous sequel . . . despite "Superduperman I"!!

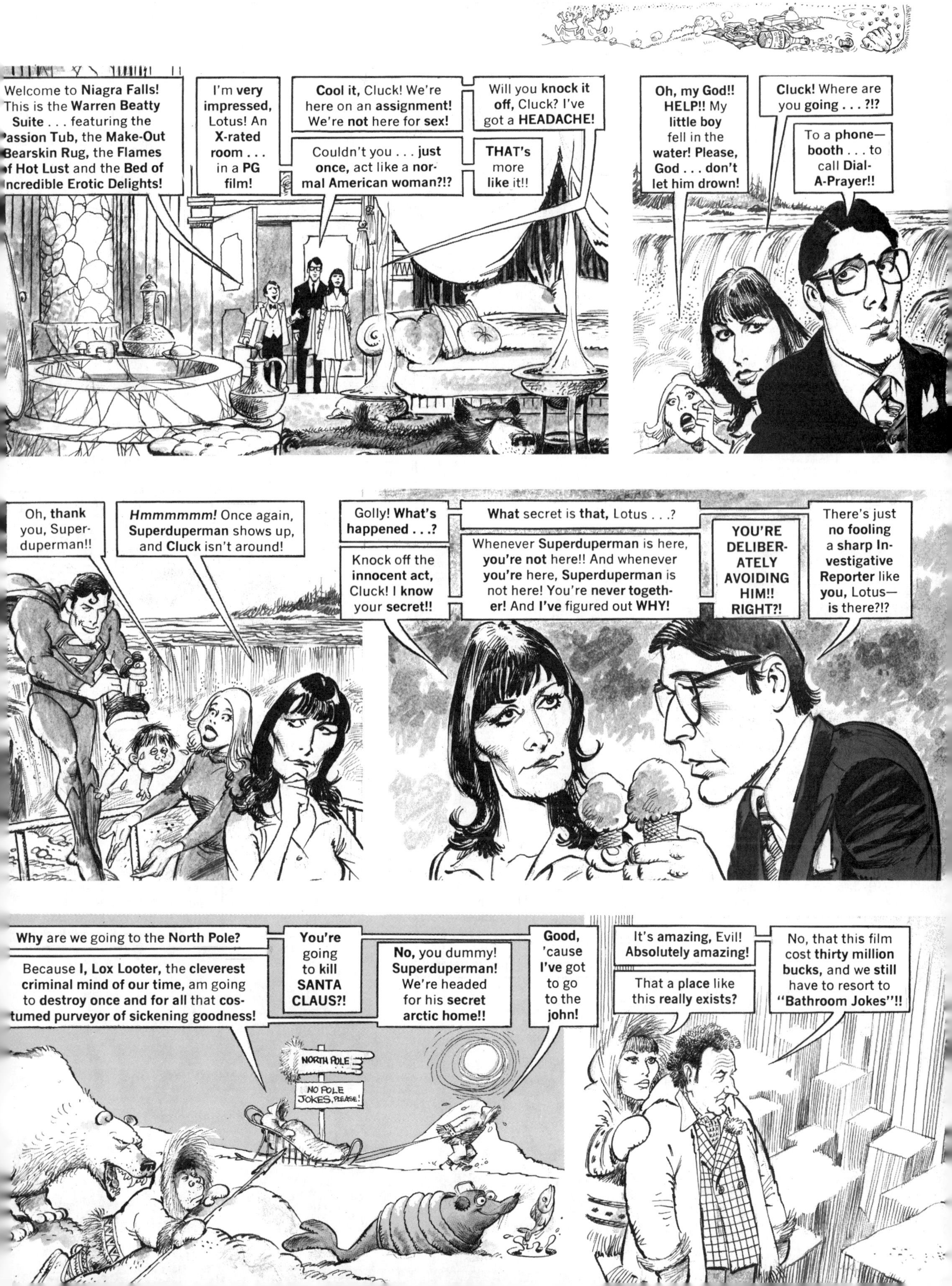

Welcome to Niagra Falls! This is the Warren Beatty Suite . . . featuring the assion Tub, the Make-Out Bearskin Rug, the Flames f Hot Lust and the Bed of ncredible Erotic Delights!
I'm very impressed, Lotus! An X-rated room . . . in a PG film!
Cool it, Cluck! We're here on an assignment! We're not here for sex!
Couldn't you . . . just once, act like a normal American woman?!?
Will you knock it off, Cluck? I've got a HEADACHE!
THAT's more like it!!
Oh, my God!! HELP!! My little boy fell in the water! Please, God . . . don't let him drown!
Cluck! Where are you going . . . ?!?
To a phone-booth . . . to call Dial-A-Prayer!!
Oh, thank you, Superduperman!!
Hmmmmmm! Once again, Superduperman shows up, and Cluck isn't around!
Golly! What's happened . . .?
Knock off the innocent act, Cluck! I know your secret!!
What secret is that, Lotus . . .?
Whenever Superduperman is here, you're not here!! And whenever you're here, Superduperman is not here! You're never together! And I've figured out WHY!
YOU'RE DELIBERATELY AVOIDING HIM!! RIGHT?!
There's just no fooling a sharp Investigative Reporter like you, Lotus—is there?!?
Why are we going to the North Pole?
Because I, Lox Looter, the cleverest criminal mind of our time, am going to destroy once and for all that costumed purveyor of sickening goodness!
You're going to kill SANTA CLAUS?!
No, you dummy! Superduperman! We're headed for his secret arctic home!!
Good, 'cause I've got to go to the john!
NORTH POLE
NO POLE JOKES, PLEASE!
It's amazing, Evil! Absolutely amazing!
That a place like this really exists?
No, that this film cost thirty million bucks, and we still have to resort to "Bathroom Jokes"!!

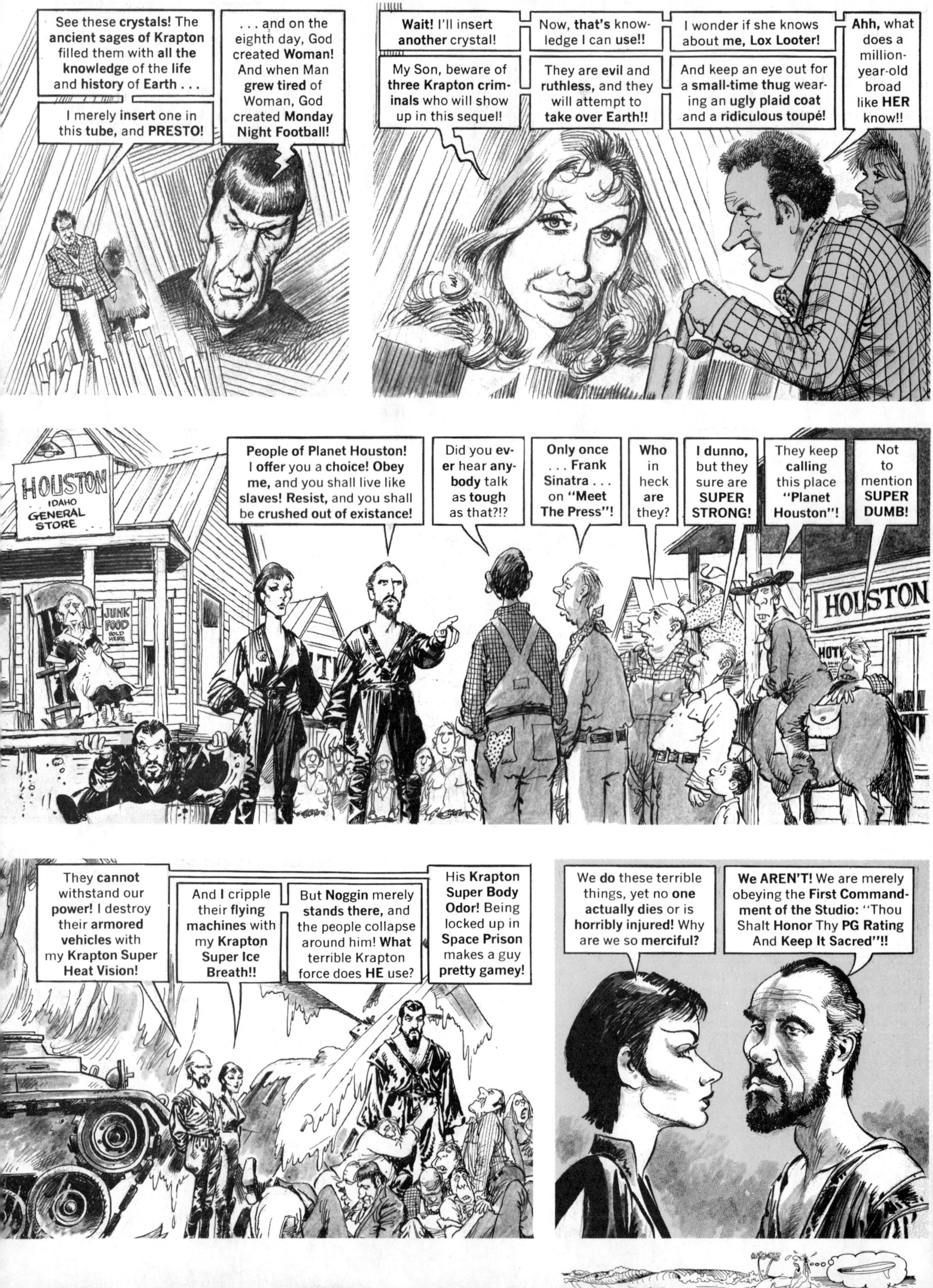

See these crystals! The ancient sages of Krapton filled them with all the knowledge of the life and history of Earth . . .
I merely insert one in this tube, and PRESTO!
. . . and on the eighth day, God created Woman! And when Man grew tired of Woman, God created Monday Night Football!
Wait! I'll insert another crystal!
My Son, beware of three Krapton criminals who will show up in this sequel!
Now, that's knowledge I can use!!
They are evil and ruthless, and they will attempt to take over Earth!!
I wonder if she knows about me, Lox Looter!
And keep an eye out for a small-time thug wearing an ugly plaid coat and a ridiculous toupé!
Ahh, what does a million-year-old broad like HER know!!
HOUSTON
IDAHO
GENERAL STORE
JUNK FOOD
SOLD HERE
HOUSTON
People of Planet Houston! I offer you a choice! Obey me, and you shall live like slaves! Resist, and you shall be crushed out of existance!
Did you ever hear anybody talk as tough as that?!?
Only once . . . Frank Sinatra . . . on "Meet The Press"!
Who in heck are they?
I dunno, but they sure are SUPER STRONG!
They keep calling this place "Planet Houston"!
Not to mention SUPER DUMB!
They cannot withstand our power! I destroy their armored vehicles with my Krapton Super Heat Vision!
And I cripple their flying machines with my Krapton Super Ice Breath!!
But Noggin merely stands there, and the people collapse around him! What terrible Krapton force does HE use?
His Krapton Super Body Odor! Being locked up in Space Prison makes a guy pretty gamey!
We do these terrible things, yet no one actually dies or is horribly injured! Why are we so merciful?
We AREN'T! We are merely obeying the First Commandment of the Studio: "Thou Shalt Honor Thy PG Rating And Keep It Sacred"!!

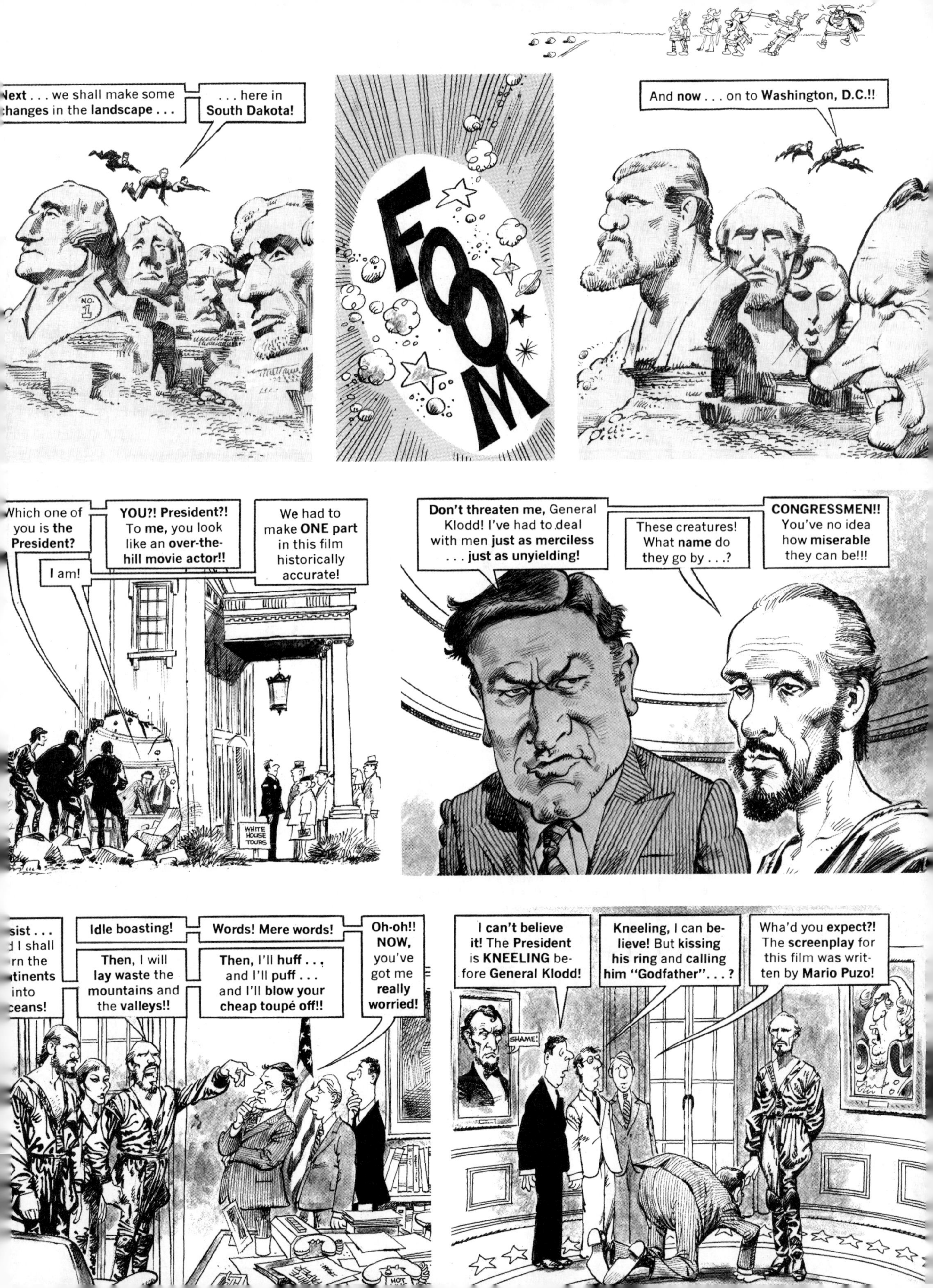

Next . . . we shall make some changes in the landscape . . .
. . . here in South Dakota!
NO. 1
FOOM
And now . . . on to Washington, D.C.!!
Which one of you is the President?
YOU?! President?! To me, you look like an over-the-hill movie actor!!
We had to make ONE part in this film historically accurate!
I am!
WHITE HOUSE TOURS
Don't threaten me, General Klodd! I've had to deal with men just as merciless . . . just as unyielding!
These creatures! What name do they go by . . .?
CONGRESSMEN!! You've no idea how miserable they can be!!!
sist . . . d I shall rn the tinents into ceans!
Idle boasting!
Then, I will lay waste the mountains and the valleys!!
Words! Mere words!
Then, I'll huff . . . and I'll puff . . . and I'll blow your cheap toupé off!!
Oh-oh!! NOW, you've got me really worried!
I can't believe it! The President is KNEELING before General Klodd!
SHAME!
Kneeling, I can believe! But kissing his ring and calling him "Godfather" . . . ?
Wha'd you expect?! The screenplay for this film was written by Mario Puzo!

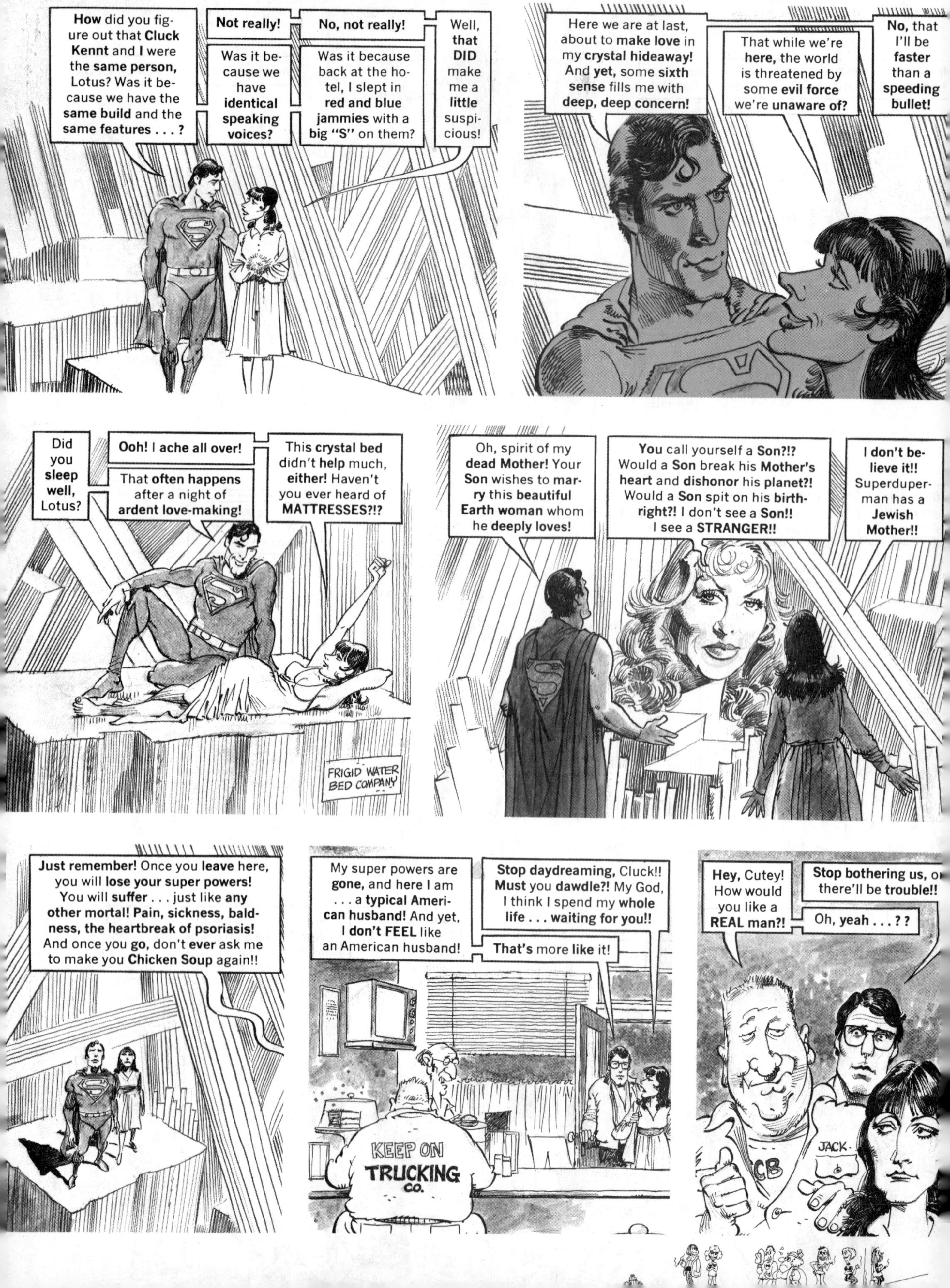
How did you figure out that Cluck Kennt and I were the same person, Lotus? Was it because we have the same build and the same features . . . ?
Not really!
Was it because we have identical speaking voices?
No, not really!
Was it because back at the hotel, I slept in red and blue jammies with a big "S" on them?
Well, that DID make me a little suspicious!
Here we are at last, about to make love in my crystal hideaway! And yet, some sixth sense fills me with deep, deep concern!
That while we're here, the world is threatened by some evil force we're unaware of?
No, that I'll be faster than a speeding bullet!
Did you sleep well, Lotus?
Ooh! I ache all over!
That often happens after a night of ardent love-making!
This crystal bed didn't help much, either! Haven't you ever heard of MATTRESSES?!?
FRIGID WATER BED COMPANY
Oh, spirit of my dead Mother! Your Son wishes to marry this beautiful Earth woman whom he deeply loves!
You call yourself a Son?!? Would a Son break his Mother's heart and dishonor his planet?! Would a Son spit on his birthright?! I don't see a Son!! I see a STRANGER!!
I don't believe it!! Superduperman has a Jewish Mother!!
Just remember! Once you leave here, you will lose your super powers! You will suffer . . . just like any other mortal! Pain, sickness, baldness, the heartbreak of psoriasis! And once you go, don't ever ask me to make you Chicken Soup again!!
My super powers are gone, and here I am . . . a typical American husband! And yet, I don't FEEL like an American husband!
Stop daydreaming, Cluck!! Must you dawdle?! My God, I think I spend my whole life . . . waiting for you!!
That's more like it!
KEEP ON TRUCKING CO.
Hey, Cutey! How would you like a REAL man?!
Stop bothering us, o
there'll be trouble!!
Oh, yeah . . . ? ?
JACK
CB

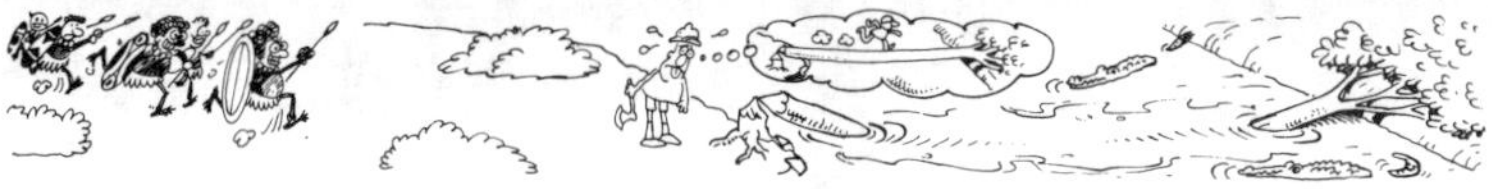

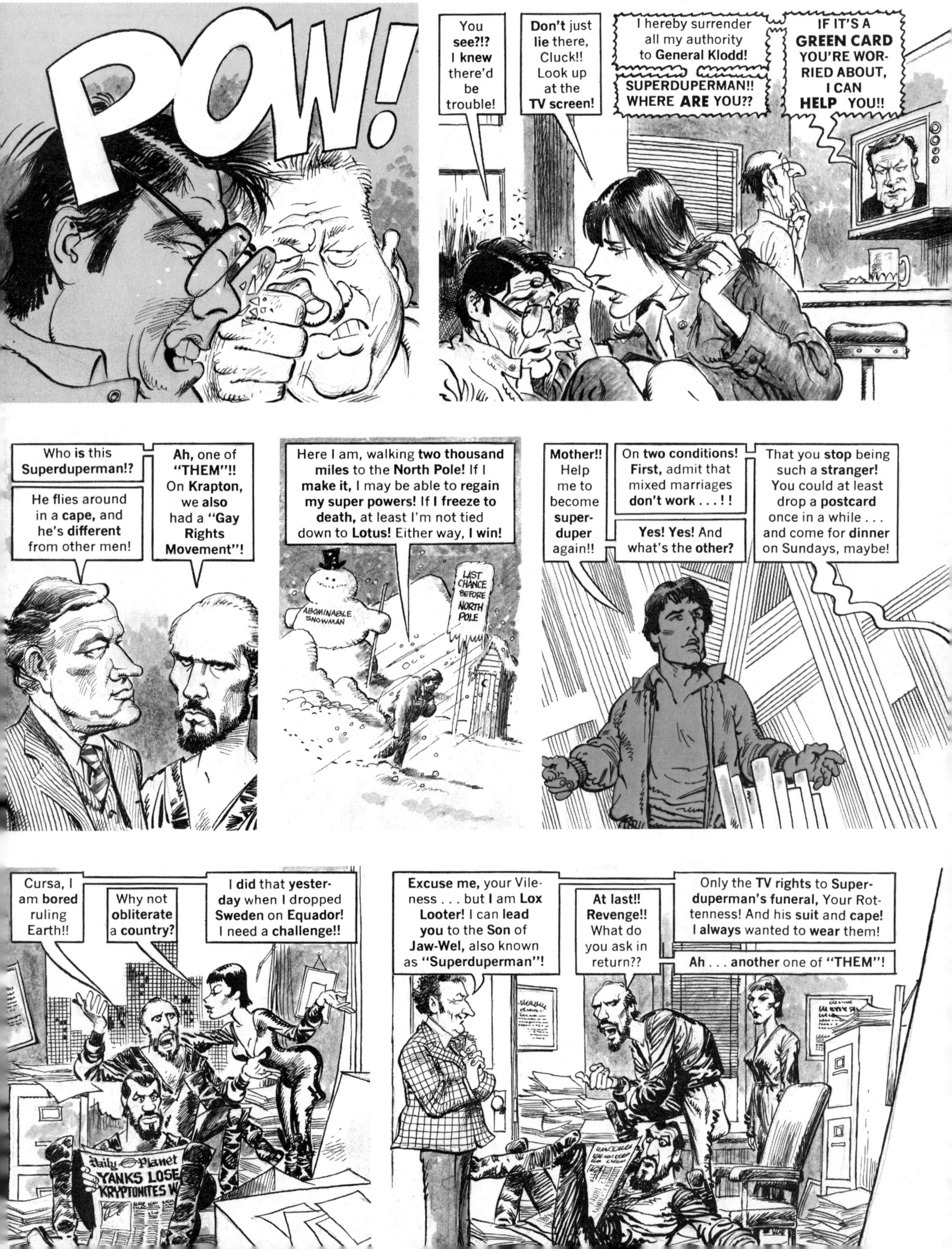
POW!
You see?!? I knew there'd be trouble!
Don't just lie there, Cluck!! Look up at the TV screen!
I hereby surrender all my authority to General Klodd!
SUPERDUPERMAN!! WHERE ARE YOU??
IF IT'S A GREEN CARD YOU'RE WORRIED ABOUT, I CAN HELP YOU!!
Who is this Superduperman!?
He flies around in a cape, and he's different from other men!
Ah, one of "THEM"!! On Krapton, we also had a "Gay Rights Movement"!
Here I am, walking two thousand miles to the North Pole! If I make it, I may be able to regain my super powers! If I freeze to death, at least I'm not tied down to Lotus! Either way, I win!
ABOMINABLE SNOWMAN
LAST CHANCE BEFORE NORTH POLE
Mother!! Help me to become super-duper again!!
On two conditions! First, admit that mixed marriages don't work . . . ! !
Yes! Yes! And what's the other?
That you stop being such a stranger! You could at least drop a postcard once in a while . . . and come for dinner on Sundays, maybe!
Cursa, I am bored ruling Earth!!
Why not obliterate a country?
I did that yesterday when I dropped Sweden on Equador! I need a challenge!!
Daily Planet
YANKS LOSE
Excuse me, your Vileness . . . but I am Lox Looter! I can lead you to the Son of Jaw-Wel, also known as "Superduperman"!
At last!! Revenge!! What do you ask in return??
Only the TV rights to Superduperman's funeral, Your Rottenness! And his suit and cape! I always wanted to wear them!
Ah . . . another one of "THEM"!

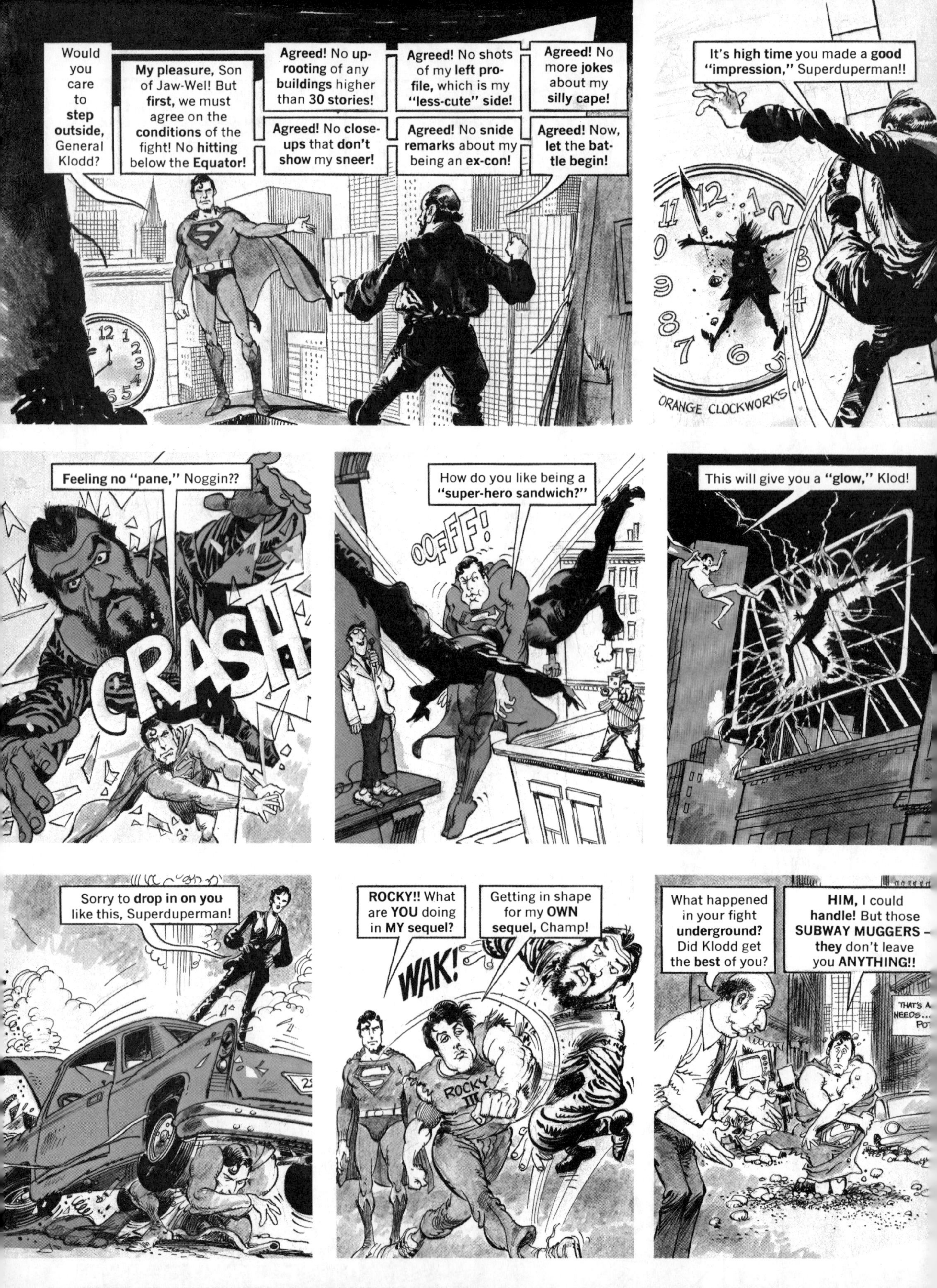

Would you care to step outside, General Klodd?
My pleasure, Son of Jaw-Wel! But first, we must agree on the conditions of the fight! No hitting below the Equator!
Agreed! No uprooting of any buildings higher than 30 stories!
Agreed! No close-ups that don't show my sneer!
Agreed! No shots of my left profile, which is my "less-cute" side!
Agreed! No snide remarks about my being an ex-con!
Agreed! No more jokes about my silly cape!
Agreed! Now, let the battle begin!
It's high time you made a good "impression," Superduperman!!
ORANGE CLOCKWORKS CO.
Feeling no "pane," Noggin??
CRASH
How do you like being a "super-hero sandwich?"
OOFFF!
This will give you a "glow," Klod!
Sorry to drop in on you like this, Superduperman!
ROCKY!! What are YOU doing in MY sequel?
Getting in shape for my OWN sequel, Champ!
WAK!
ROCKY III
What happened in your fight underground? Did Klodd get the best of you?
HIM, I could handle! But those SUBWAY MUGGERS – they don't leave you ANYTHING!!

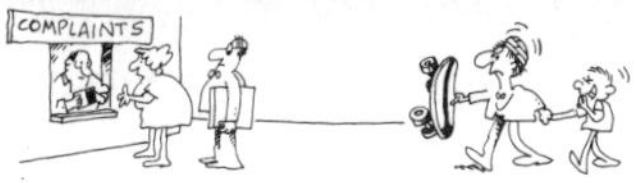
COMPLAINTS

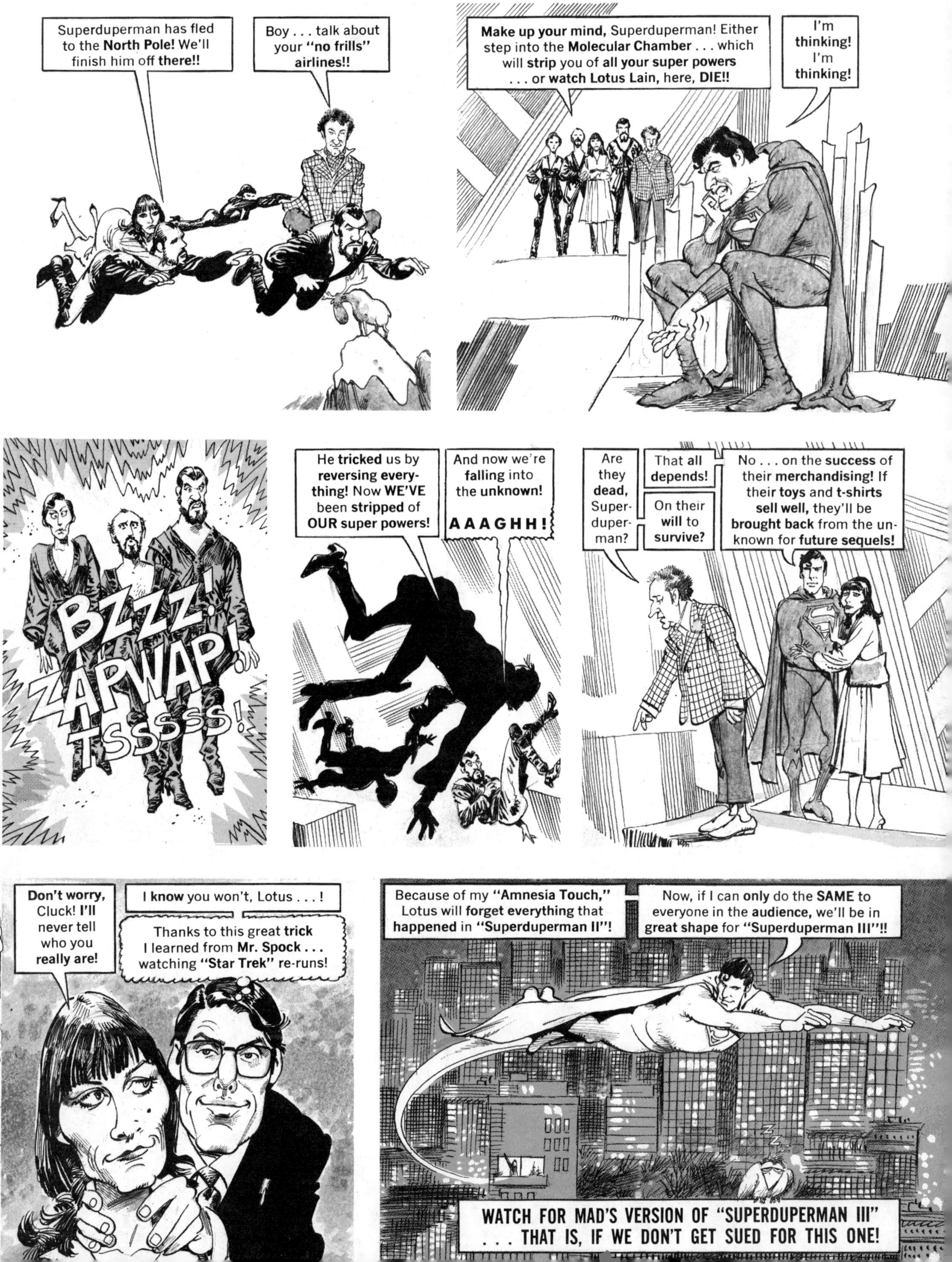
Superduperman has fled to the North Pole! We'll finish him off there!!
Boy . . . talk about your "no frills" airlines!!
Make up your mind, Superduperman! Either step into the Molecular Chamber . . . which will strip you of all your super powers . . . or watch Lotus Lain, here, DIE!!
I'm thinking! I'm thinking!
BZZZ! ZAPWAP! TSSSSS!
He tricked us by reversing everything! Now WE'VE been stripped of OUR super powers!
And now we're falling into the unknown!
AAAGHH!
Are they dead, Superduperman?
That all depends!
On their will to survive?
No . . . on the success of their merchandising! If their toys and t-shirts sell well, they'll be brought back from the unknown for future sequels!
Don't worry, Cluck! I'll never tell who you really are!
I know you won't, Lotus . . . !
Thanks to this great trick I learned from Mr. Spock . . . watching "Star Trek" re-runs!
Because of my "Amnesia Touch," Lotus will forget everything that happened in "Superduperman II"!
Now, if I can only do the SAME to everyone in the audience, we'll be in great shape for "Superduperman III"!!
Z Z Z
WATCH FOR MAD'S VERSION OF "SUPERDUPERMAN III" . . . THAT IS, IF WE DON'T GET SUED FOR THIS ONE!

WEST-WARD-HO-HO! DEPT.

A MAD LOOK

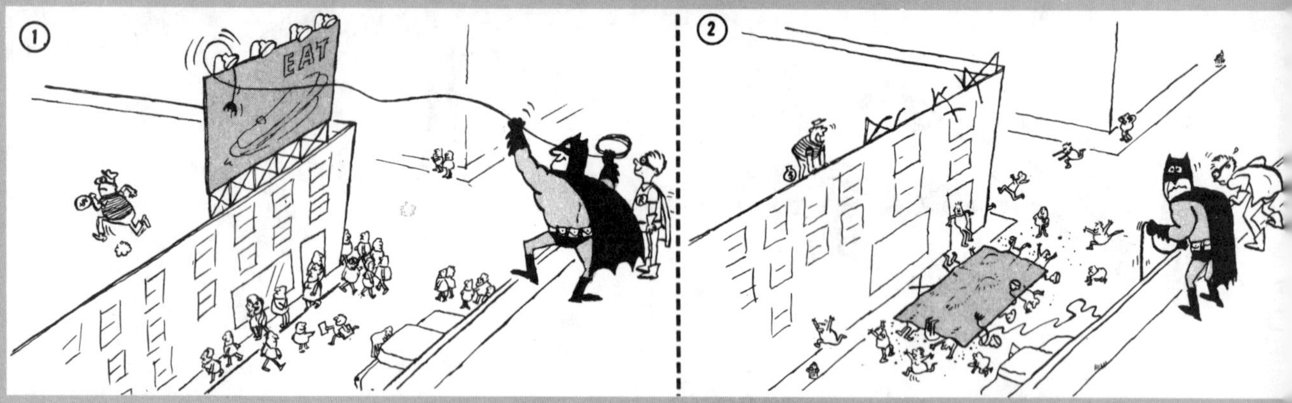
EAT

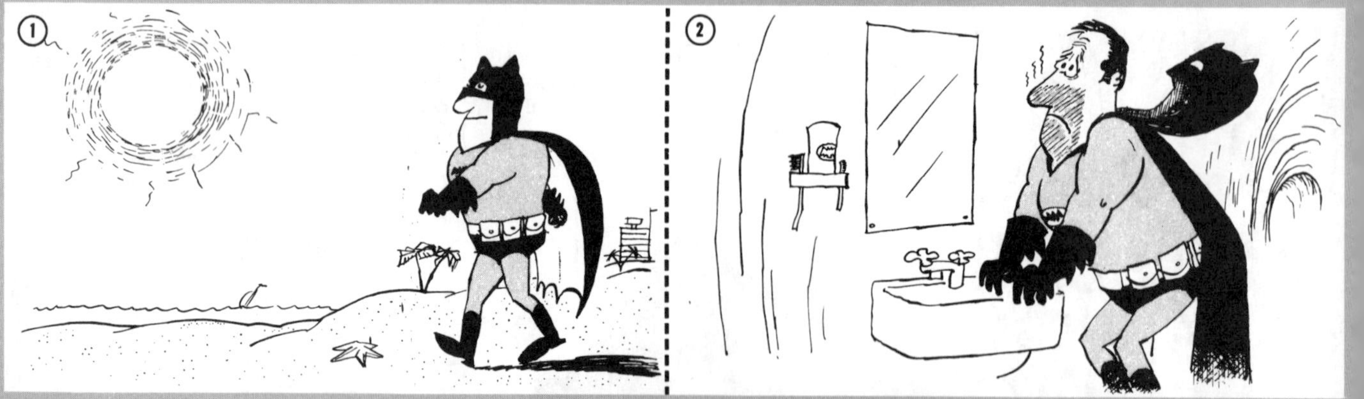

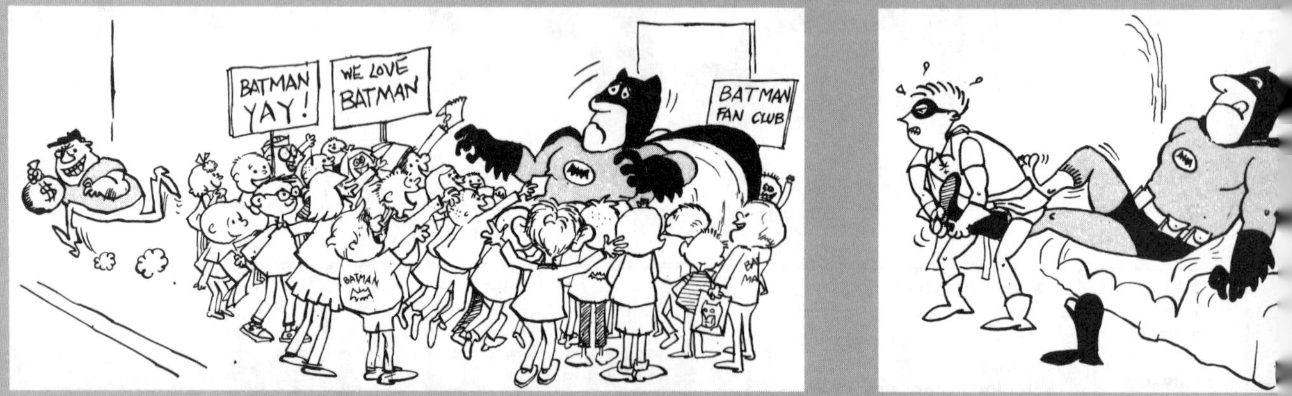
BATMAN YAY!
WE LOVE BATMAN
BATMAN FAN CLUB

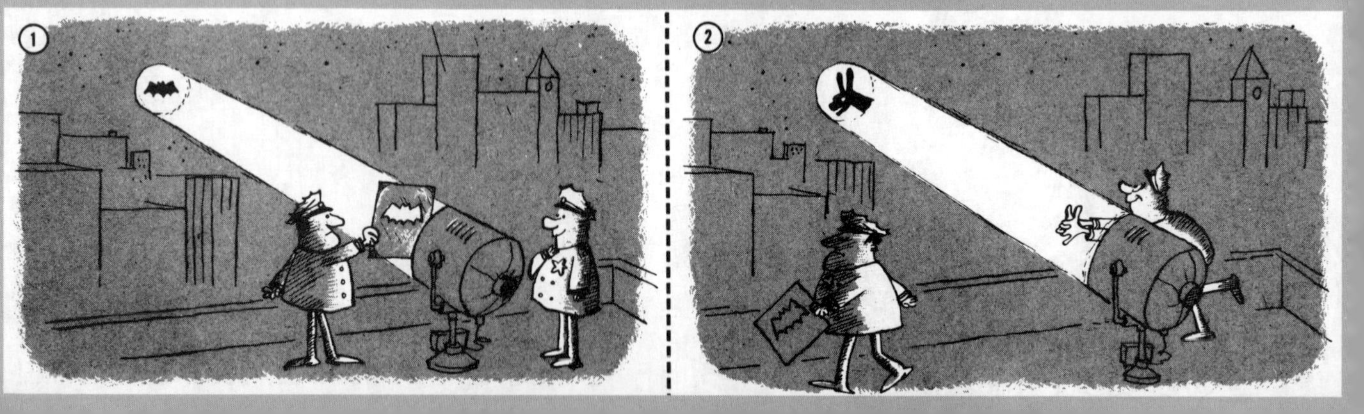

AT BATMAN

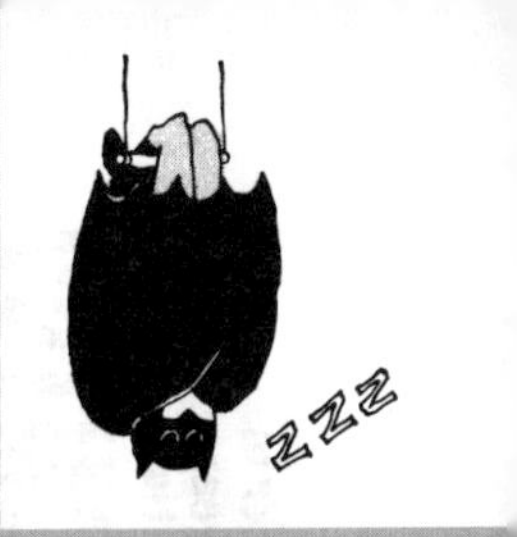
ZZZ

ST & WRITER: SERGIO ARAGONES

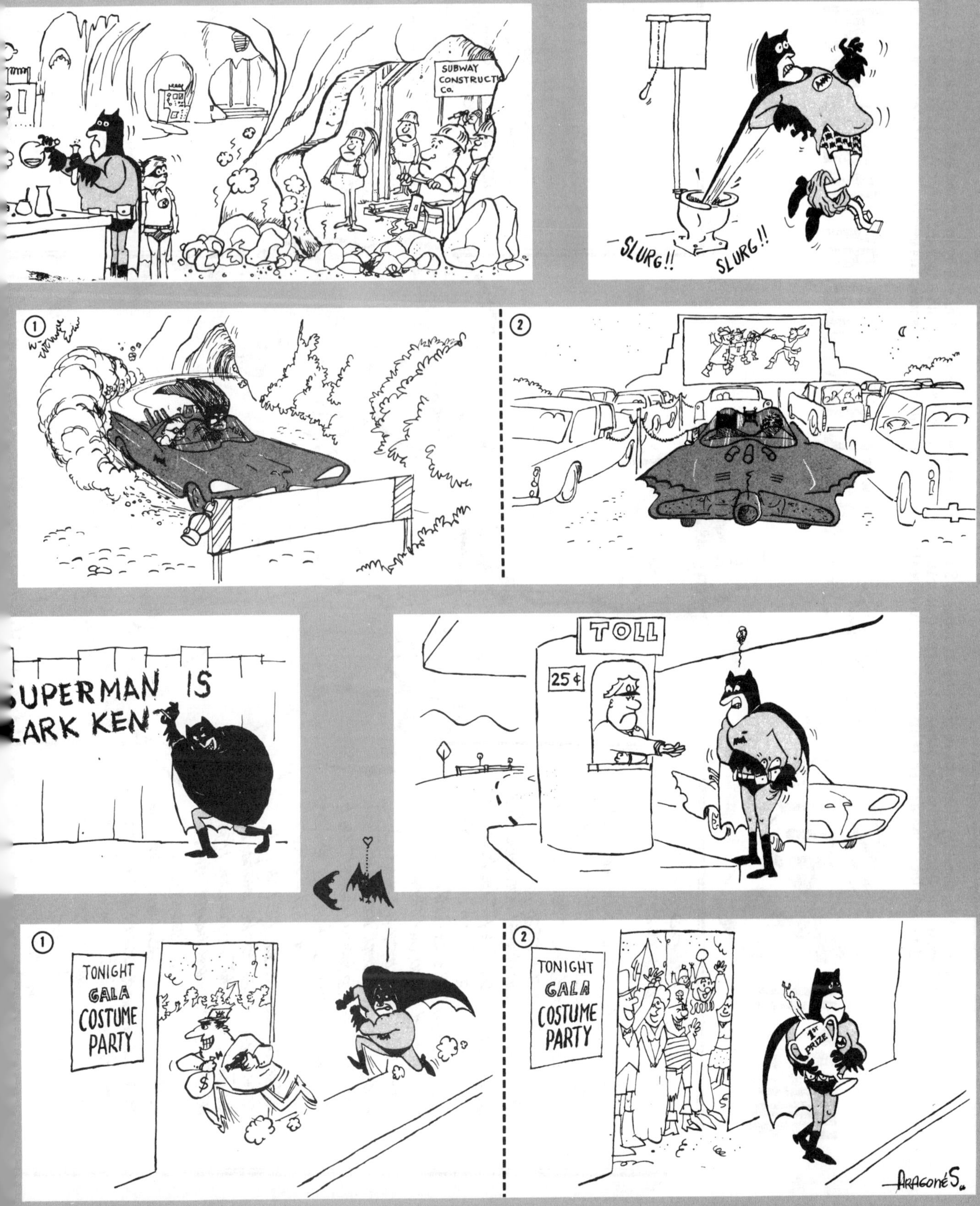
SUBWAY
CONSTRUCT
Co.
SLURG!!
SLURG!!
SUPERMAN IS
ARK KEN
TOLL
25¢
TONIGHT
GALA
COSTUME
PARTY
TONIGHT
GALA
COSTUME
PARTY
1ST PRIZE
ARAGONÉS

TODAY YOU ARE A MAN OF STEEL DEPT.

In an alternate reality, the baby that was to grow up to become Superman was not discovered in Kansas by Jonathan and Martha Kent, but rather in Brooklyn by Hyman and Doris Feldstein. Doris, a loving and devoted mother, chronicled her only son's extraordinary exploits in her diary. After years of research and a whole lot of conjecture, MAD magazine now reveals a few selected entries that resolve the mystery of that eternally asked question:

WHAT IF SUPERMAN™ WERE RAISED BY JEWISH PARENTS?

February 28th, 1938--
The Discovery

A rocketship! Who would put a baby in a rocket? Who does such a thing? Sends up a baby so that it crashes in our backyard?! On Purim of all days! You should've seen Hyman, such a fit he had!

"Oy," he said, "Such a mess this rocket! Feh!" I was just as angry, you should know, but then I saw something pink moving and I screamed like you wouldn't believe: "Look a baby! Gevalt, such a lovely baby!" I decided to keep him. Hyman looked a little upset, but with his ulcer, he wasn't going to argue. So he sighs and says "all right, Doris, all right. What should we name him?"

Oy, I was so happy! I picked up the baby and held him to the sky and said "We'll name him Herman, after my uncle, may he rest in peace. Herman Mortimer Feldstein. Such a doctor he'll make!" I tell you, such a baby,

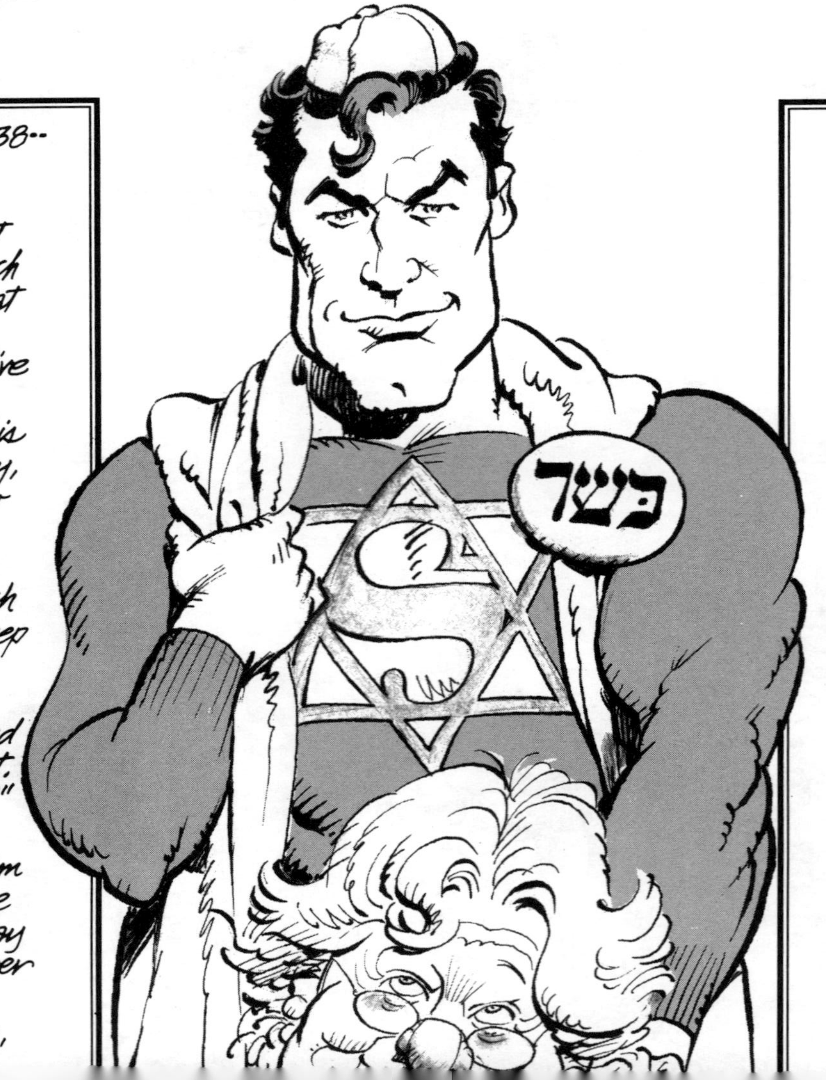
כשר

March 6, 1938—
The Circumcision

Oy, such a mess! The poor rabbi. First he tries to cut Herman's schmeckel with the scapel and the scapel breaks. It breaks! This is a schmeckel from Heaven, I tell you. Rabbi Donowitz was so upset. He's never failed with a circumcision, oh no. Slish slash and he's usually done.

So he tries with a butcher knife he got from Gimpel the butcher, and wouldn't you know, that blade gets nicked too! Hyman told the Rabbi to give it up, it was clearly a sign from God to leave the schmeckel alone, but the Rabbi, he said he knew better.

So he tries an ax. An ax! Who does such a thing? I was scared for little Herman, but I shouldn't have been. He broke the ax, such a strong boy! So finally, Rabbi Donowitz is huffing and puffing and so angry, such a look on his face, that he starts asking around for a chainsaw. I said "Rabbi, you can use my electric carving knife, but oy, a chainsaw?!" But then, before he can do anything, two rays of light come from little Herman's eyes and fry the Rabbi. Gevalt! Anyway, now Rabbi Taub will be the new Rabbi.

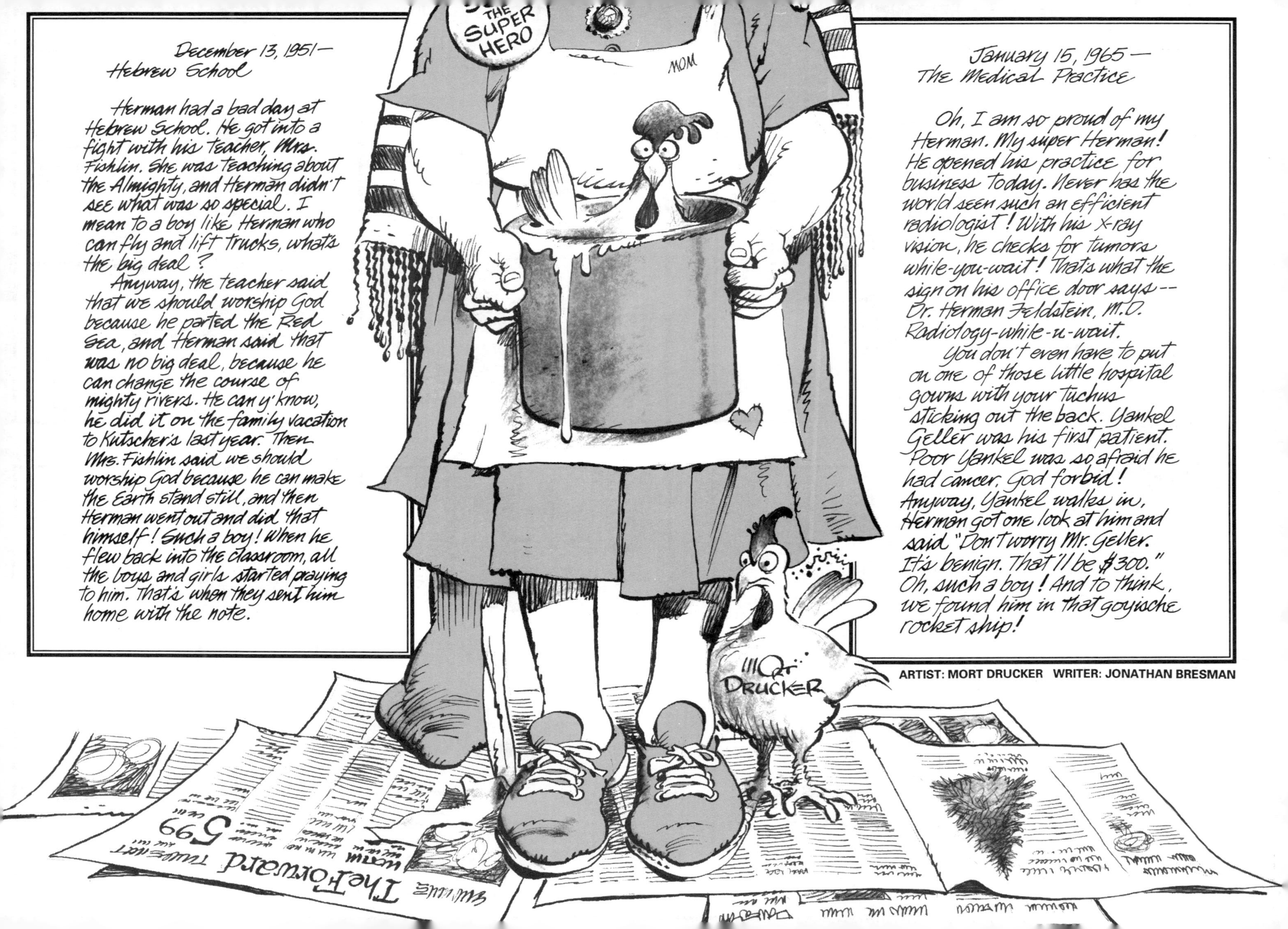
THE SUPER HERO
MOM
December 13, 1951—
Hebrew School
Herman had a bad day at Hebrew School. He got into a fight with his teacher, Mrs. Fishlin. She was teaching about the Almighty, and Herman didn't see what was so special. I mean to a boy like Herman who can fly and lift trucks, what's the big deal?
Anyway, the teacher said that we should worship God because he parted the Red Sea, and Herman said that was no big deal, because he can change the course of mighty rivers. He can y'know, he did it on the family vacation to Kutscher's last year. Then Mrs. Fishlin said we should worship God because he can make the Earth stand still, and then Herman went out and did that himself! Such a boy! When he flew back into the classroom, all the boys and girls started praying to him. That's when they sent him home with the note.
January 15, 1965—
The Medical Practice
Oh, I am so proud of my Herman. My super Herman! He opened his practice for business today. Never has the world seen such an efficient radiologist! With his x-ray vision, he checks for tumors while-you-wait! That's what the sign on his office door says-- Dr. Herman Feldstein, M.D. Radiology-while-u-wait.
You don't even have to put on one of those little hospital gowns with your tuchus sticking out the back. Yankel Geller was his first patient. Poor Yankel was so afraid he had cancer, God forbid! Anyway, Yankel walks in, Herman got one look at him and said "Don't worry Mr. Geller. It's benign. That'll be $300." Oh, such a boy! And to think, we found him in that goyische rocket ship!
ARTIST: MORT DRUCKER WRITER: JONATHAN BRESMAN
DRUCKER
The Forward
599

NOISE SOLUTION DEPT.

DON MARTIN'S GUIDE TO SOME VERY OBSCURE COMICS

ARTIST: DON MART

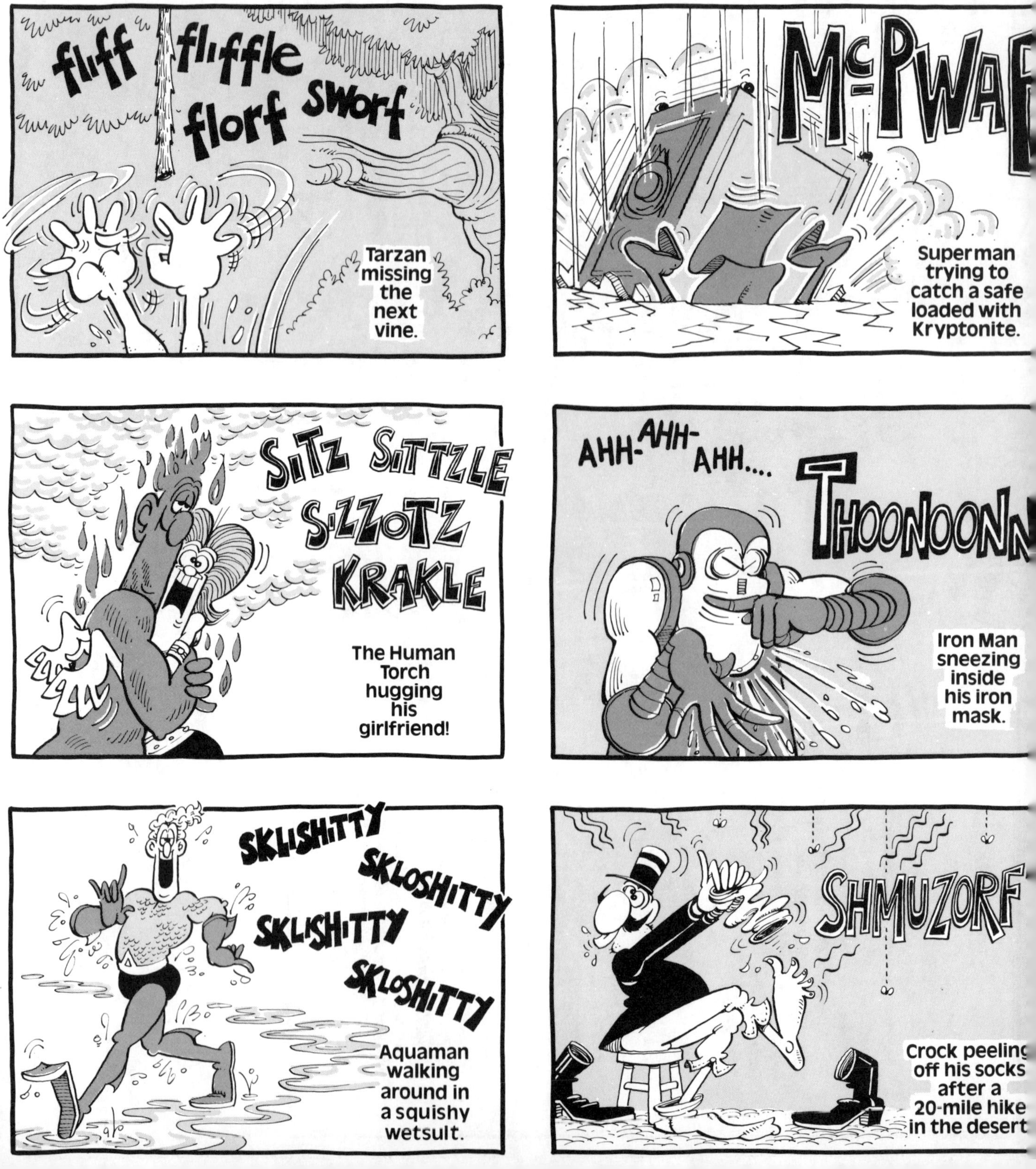
fliff
fliffle
florf
sworf
Tarzan missing the next vine.
McPWAF
Superman trying to catch a safe loaded with Kryptonite.
SITZ SITTZLE
SIZZOTZ
KRAKLE
The Human Torch hugging his girlfriend!
AHH-AHH-AHH....
THOONOONN
Iron Man sneezing inside his iron mask.
SKLISHITTY
SKLOSHITTY
SKLISHITTY
SKLOSHITTY
Aquaman walking around in a squishy wetsult.
SHMUZORF
Crock peelin off his socks after a 20-mile hike in the desert

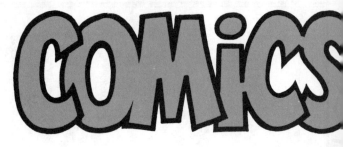

SOUND EFFECTS

ITER: DON EDWING

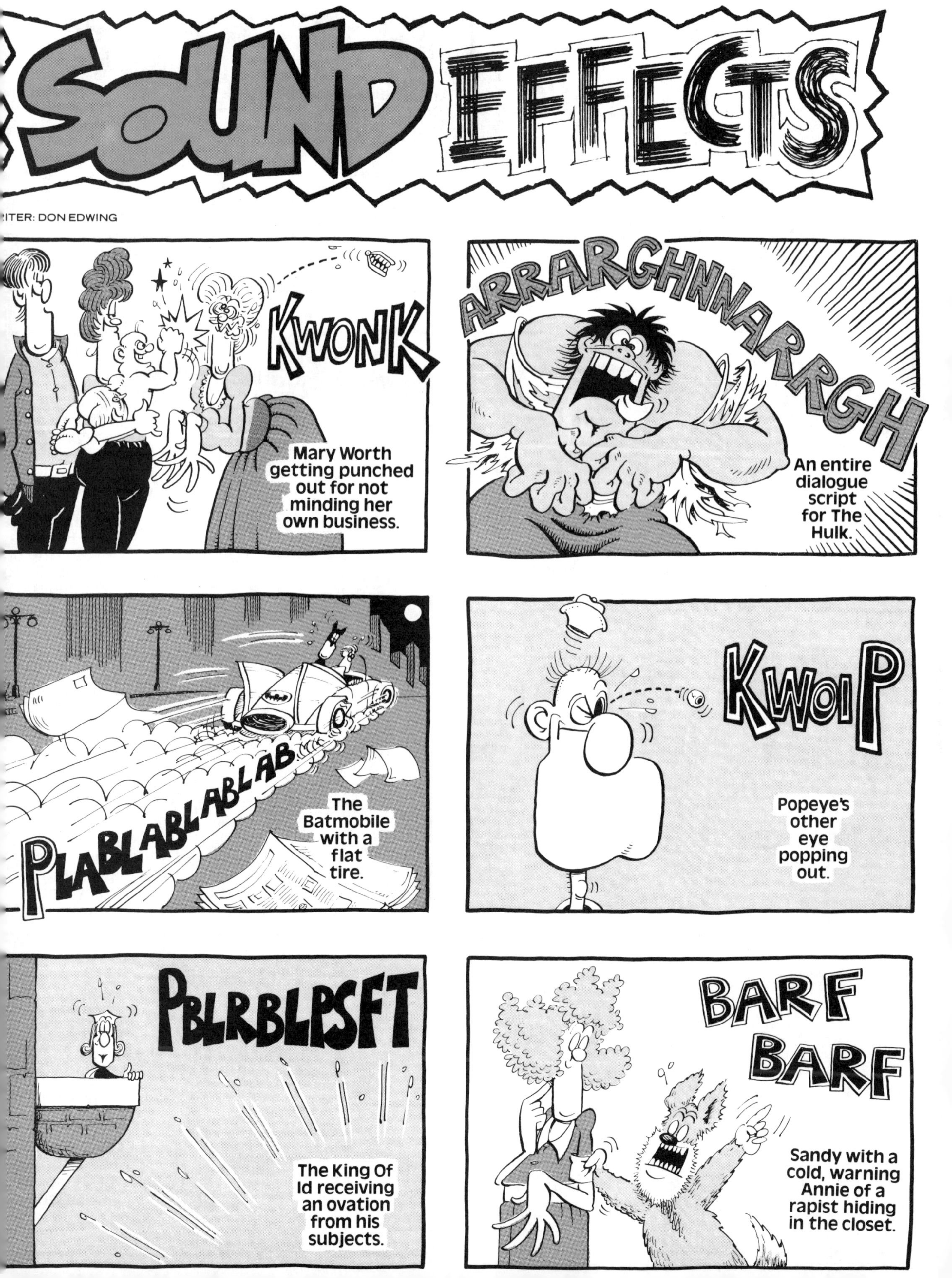
KWONK
Mary Worth getting punched out for not minding her own business.
ARRARGHNNARRGH
An entire dialogue script for The Hulk.
PLABLABLABLAB
The Batmobile with a flat tire.
KWOIP
Popeye's other eye popping out.
PBLRBLPSFT
The King Of Id receiving an ovation from his subjects.
BARF
BARF
Sandy with a cold, warning Annie of a rapist hiding in the closet.

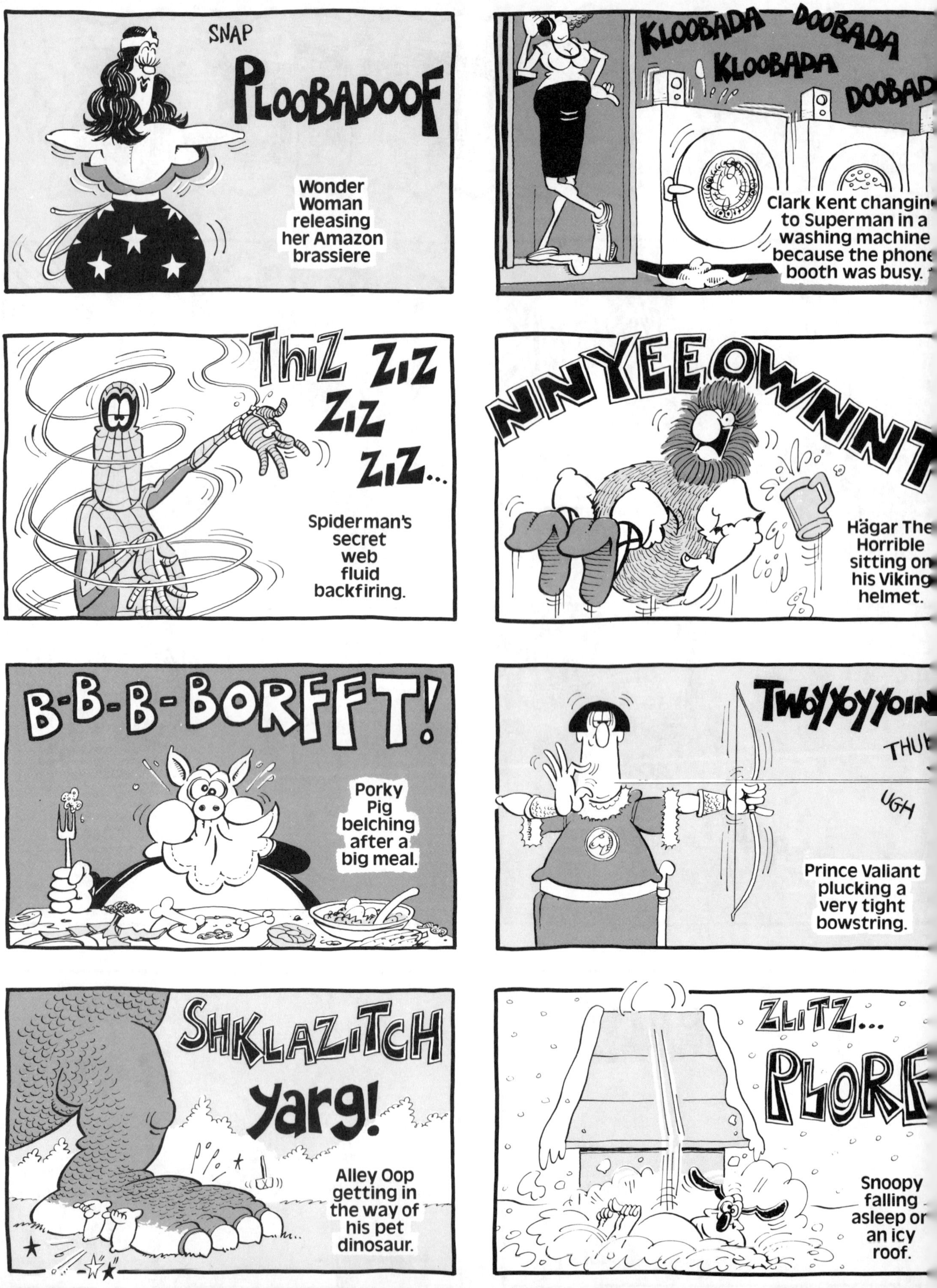
SNAP
PLOOBADOOF
Wonder Woman releasing her Amazon brassiere
KLOOBADA DOOBADA
KLOOBADA
DOOBAD
Clark Kent changin
to Superman in a
washing machine
because the phone
booth was busy.
THIZ ZIZ
ZIZ
ZIZ...
Spiderman's secret web fluid backfiring.
NNYEEEOWNNNT
Hägar The
Horrible
sitting on
his Viking
helmet.
B-B-B-BORFFFT!
Porky Pig belching after a big meal.
TWOYYOYYOIN
THU
UGH
Prince Valiant plucking a very tight bowstring.
SHKLAZITCH
Yarg!
Alley Oop getting in the way of his pet dinosaur.
ZLITZ...
PLORF
Snoopy
falling
asleep or
an icy
roof.

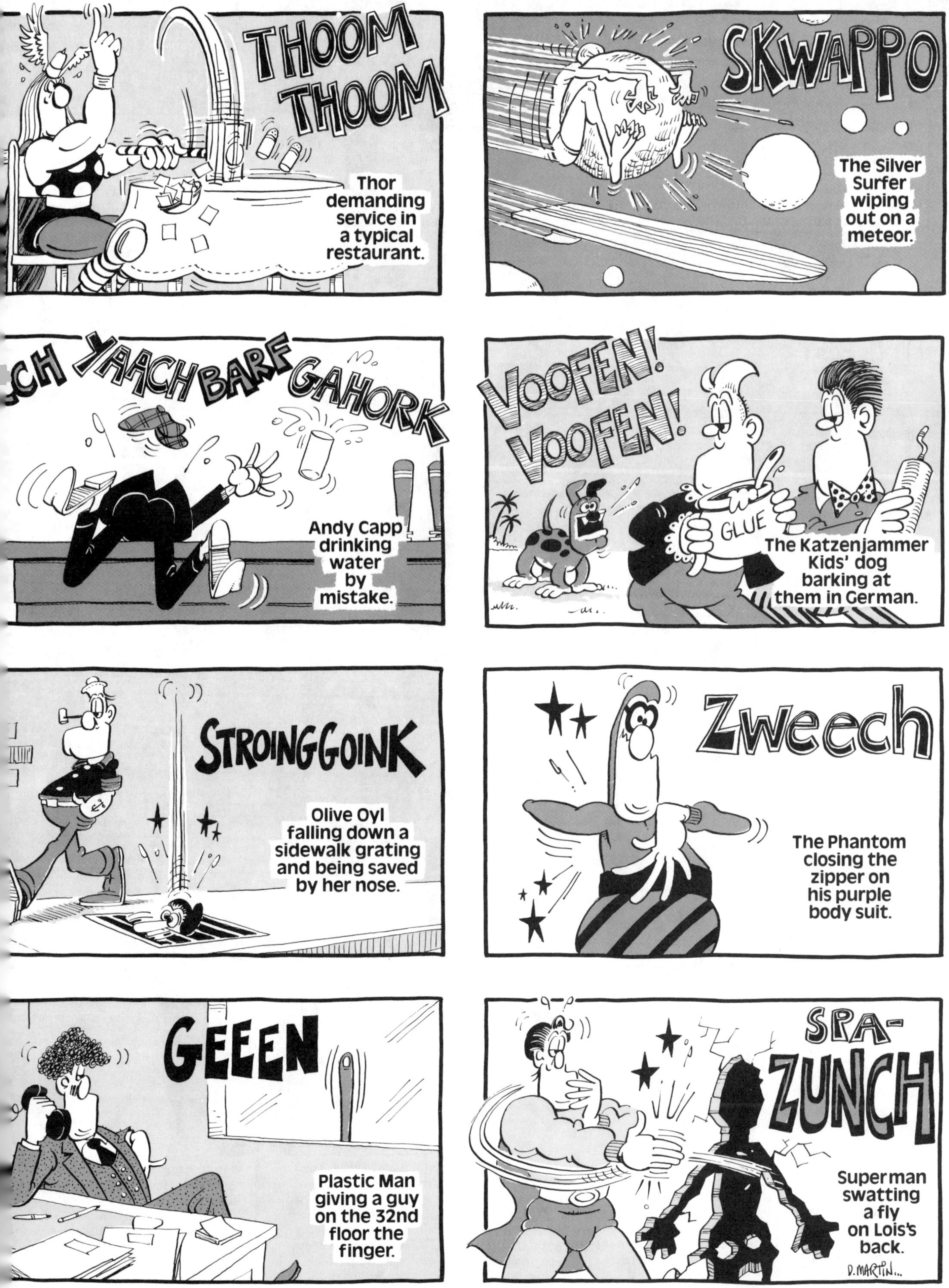
THOOM
THOOM
Thor demanding service in a typical restaurant.
SKWAPPO
The Silver Surfer wiping out on a meteor.
YAACH BARF GAHORK
Andy Capp drinking water by mistake.
VOOFEN!
VOOFEN!
GLUE
The Katzenjammer Kids' dog barking at them in German.
STROINGGOINK
Olive Oyl falling down a sidewalk grating and being saved by her nose.
Zweech
The Phantom closing the zipper on his purple body suit.
GEEEN
Plastic Man giving a guy on the 32nd floor the finger.
SPA-
ZUNCH
Superman swatting a fly on Lois's back.
D. MARTIN...

BRUCE WAYNE'S WORLD DEPT.

1992 is shaping up to be a really miserable year! Our beloved President embarrasses every U.S. citizen by hurling all over the Japanese Prime Minister, Raul Julia is back on Broadwa and Country Music continues to gain in popularity! And if all that weren't bad enough, now

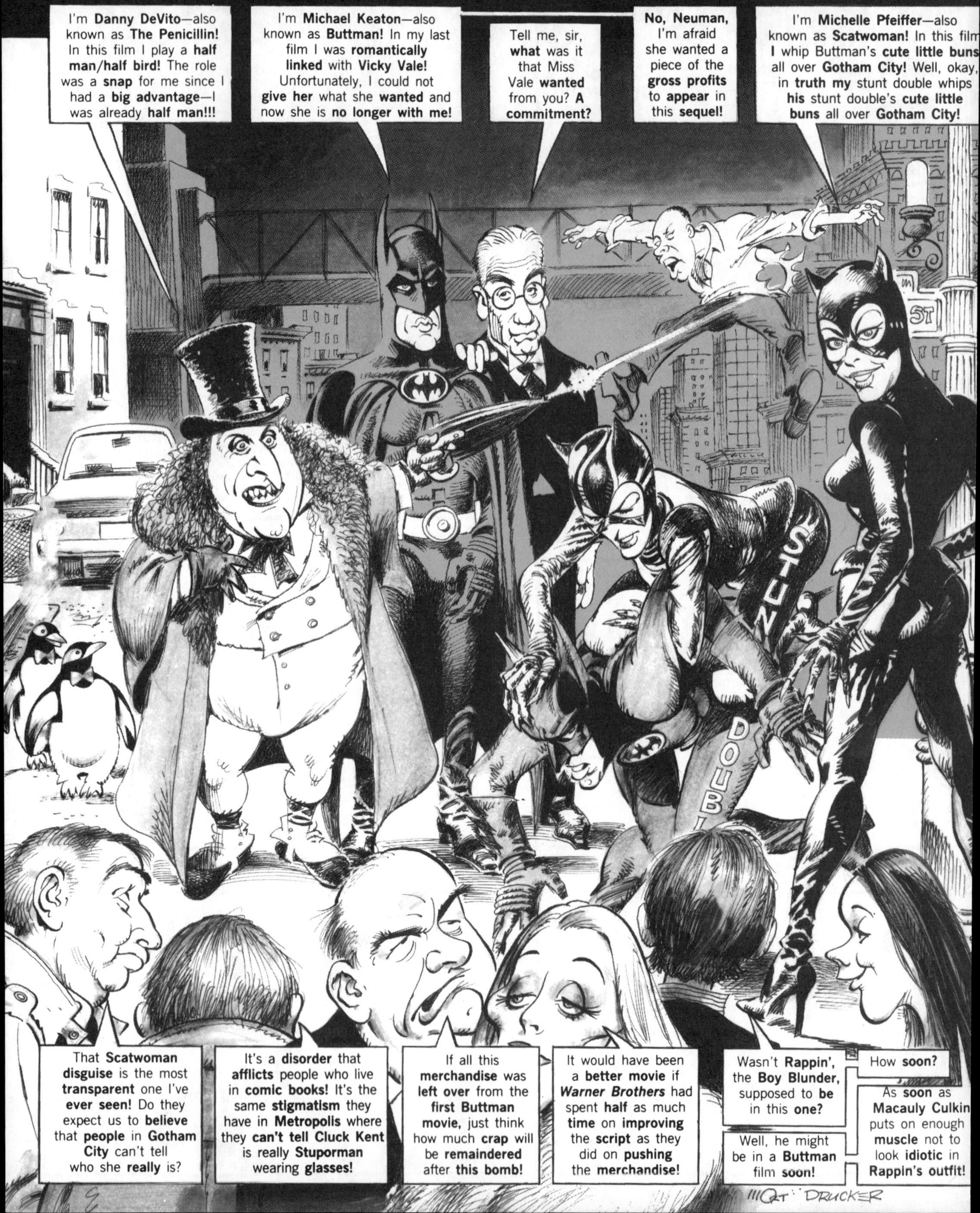

I'm Danny DeVito—also known as The Penicillin! In this film I play a half man/half bird! The role was a snap for me since I had a big advantage—I was already half man!!!
I'm Michael Keaton—also known as Buttman! In my last film I was romantically linked with Vicky Vale! Unfortunately, I could not give her what she wanted and now she is no longer with me!
Tell me, sir, what was it that Miss Vale wanted from you? A commitment?
No, Neuman, I'm afraid she wanted a piece of the gross profits to appear in this sequel!
I'm Michelle Pfeiffer—also known as Scatwoman! In this film I whip Buttman's cute little buns all over Gotham City! Well, okay, in truth my stunt double whips his stunt double's cute little buns all over Gotham City!
That Scatwoman disguise is the most transparent one I've ever seen! Do they expect us to believe that people in Gotham City can't tell who she really is?
It's a disorder that afflicts people who live in comic books! It's the same stigmatism they have in Metropolis where they can't tell Cluck Kent is really Stuporman wearing glasses!
If all this merchandise was left over from the first Buttman movie, just think how much crap will be remaindered after this bomb!
It would have been a better movie if Warner Brothers had spent half as much time on improving the script as they did on pushing the merchandise!
Wasn't Rappin', the Boy Blunder, supposed to be in this one?
Well, he might be in a Buttman film soon!
How soon?
As soon as Macauly Culkin puts on enough muscle not to look idiotic in Rappin's outfit!
STUN
DOUB
MORT DRUCKER

BUTTMAN RETURNS

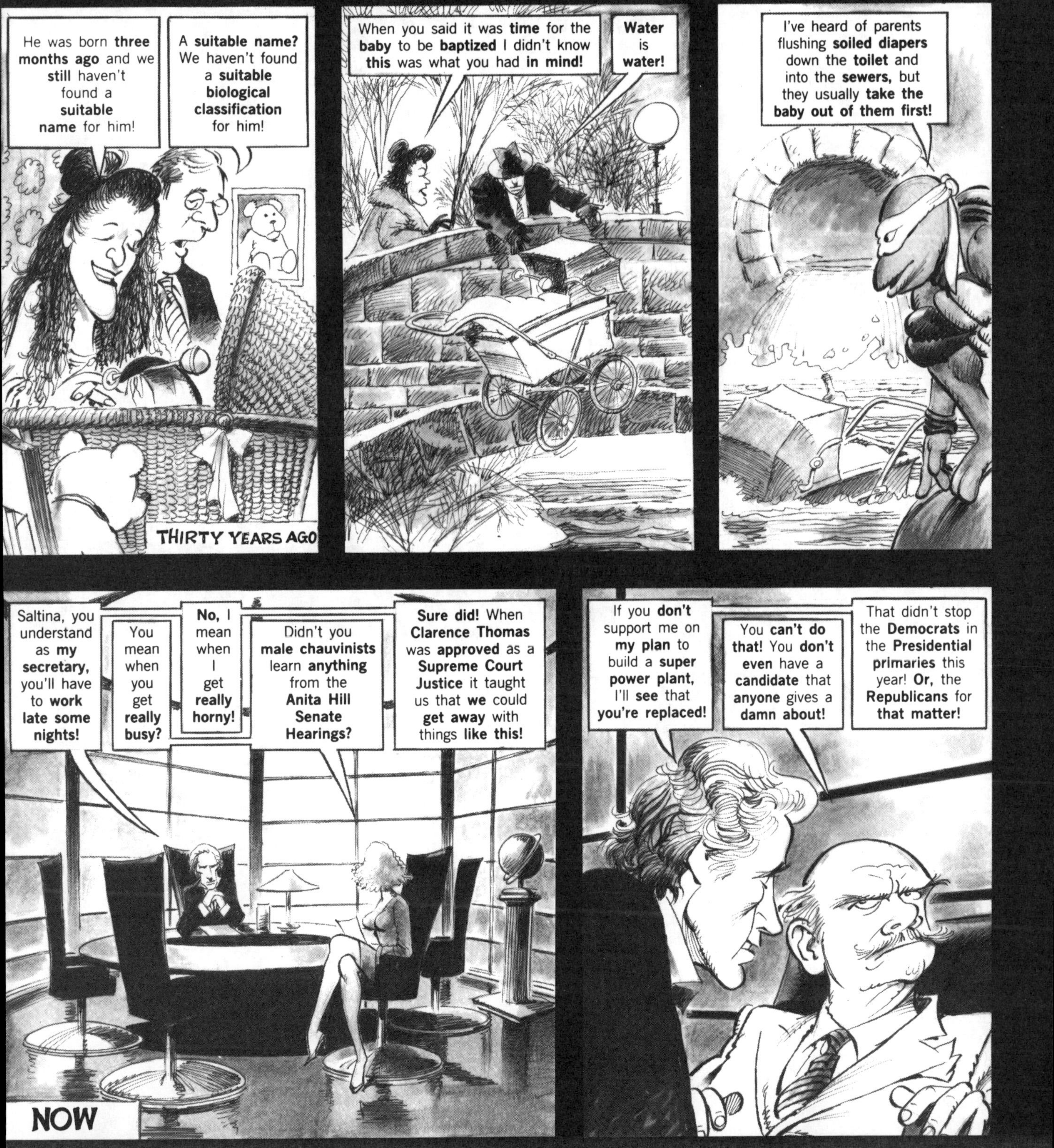
He was born three months ago and we still haven't found a suitable name for him!
A suitable name? We haven't found a suitable biological classification for him!
THIRTY YEARS AGO
When you said it was time for the baby to be baptized I didn't know this was what you had in mind!
Water is water!
I've heard of parents flushing soiled diapers down the toilet and into the sewers, but they usually take the baby out of them first!
NOW
Saltina, you understand as my secretary, you'll have to work late some nights!
You mean when you get really busy?
No, I mean when I get really horny!
Didn't you male chauvinists learn anything from the Anita Hill Senate Hearings?
Sure did! When Clarence Thomas was approved as a Supreme Court Justice it taught us that we could get away with things like this!
If you don't support me on my plan to build a super power plant, I'll see that you're replaced!
You can't do that! You don't even have a candidate that anyone gives a damn about!
That didn't stop the Democrats in the Presidential primaries this year! Or, the Republicans for that matter!

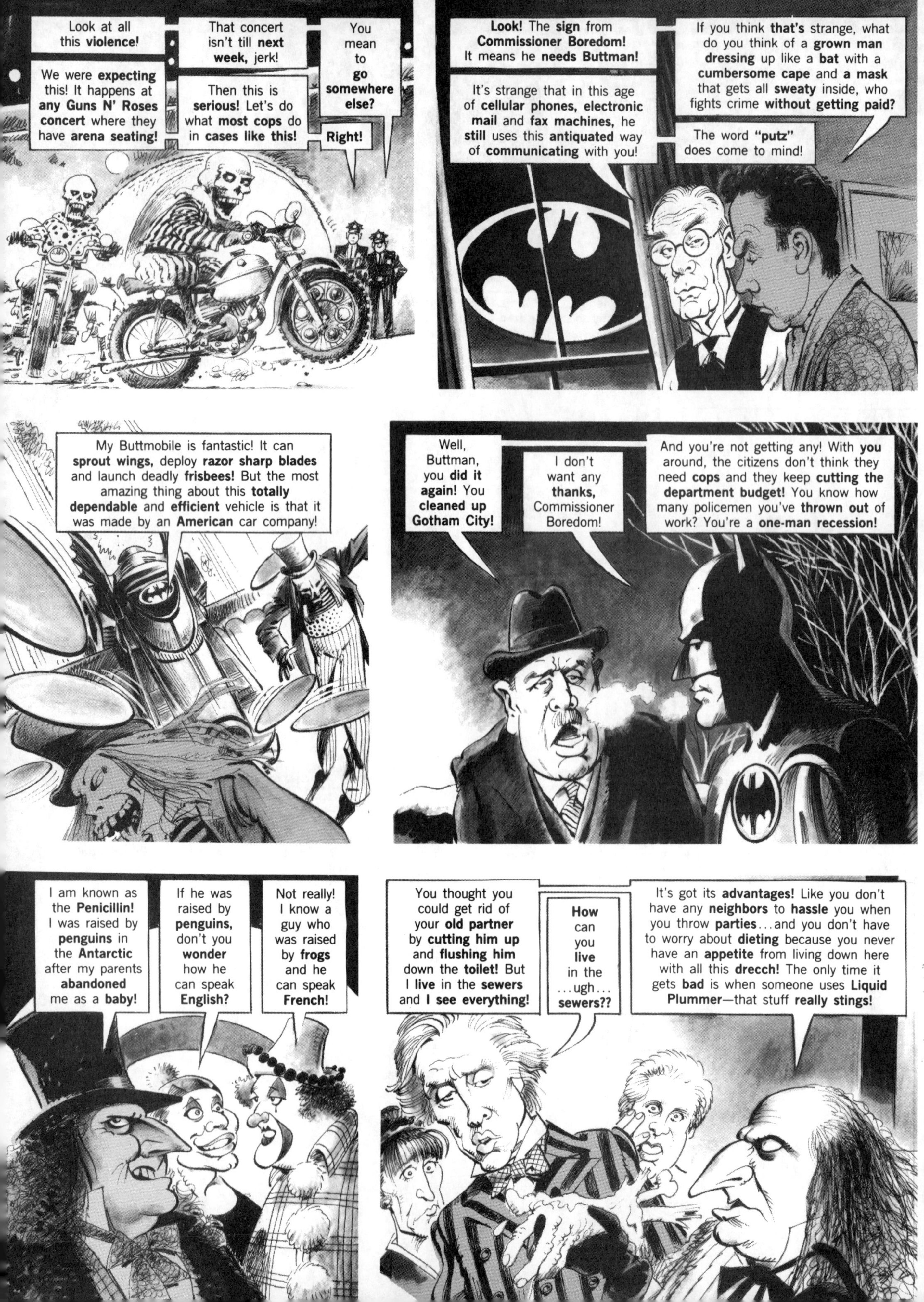
Look at all this violence!
That concert isn't till next week, jerk!
You mean to go somewhere else?
We were expecting this! It happens at any Guns N' Roses concert where they have arena seating!
Then this is serious! Let's do what most cops do in cases like this!
Right!
Look! The sign from Commissioner Boredom! It means he needs Buttman!
It's strange that in this age of cellular phones, electronic mail and fax machines, he still uses this antiquated way of communicating with you!
If you think that's strange, what do you think of a grown man dressing up like a bat with a cumbersome cape and a mask that gets all sweaty inside, who fights crime without getting paid?
The word "putz" does come to mind!
My Buttmobile is fantastic! It can sprout wings, deploy razor sharp blades and launch deadly frisbees! But the most amazing thing about this totally dependable and efficient vehicle is that it was made by an American car company!
Well, Buttman, you did it again! You cleaned up Gotham City!
I don't want any thanks, Commissioner Boredom!
And you're not getting any! With you around, the citizens don't think they need cops and they keep cutting the department budget! You know how many policemen you've thrown out of work? You're a one-man recession!
I am known as the Penicillin! I was raised by penguins in the Antarctic after my parents abandoned me as a baby!
If he was raised by penguins, don't you wonder how he can speak English?
Not really! I know a guy who was raised by frogs and he can speak French!
You thought you could get rid of your old partner by cutting him up and flushing him down the toilet! But I live in the sewers and I see everything!
How can you live in the ...ugh... sewers??
It's got its advantages! Like you don't have any neighbors to hassle you when you throw parties...and you don't have to worry about dieting because you never have an appetite from living down here with all this drecch! The only time it gets bad is when someone uses Liquid Plummer—that stuff really stings!

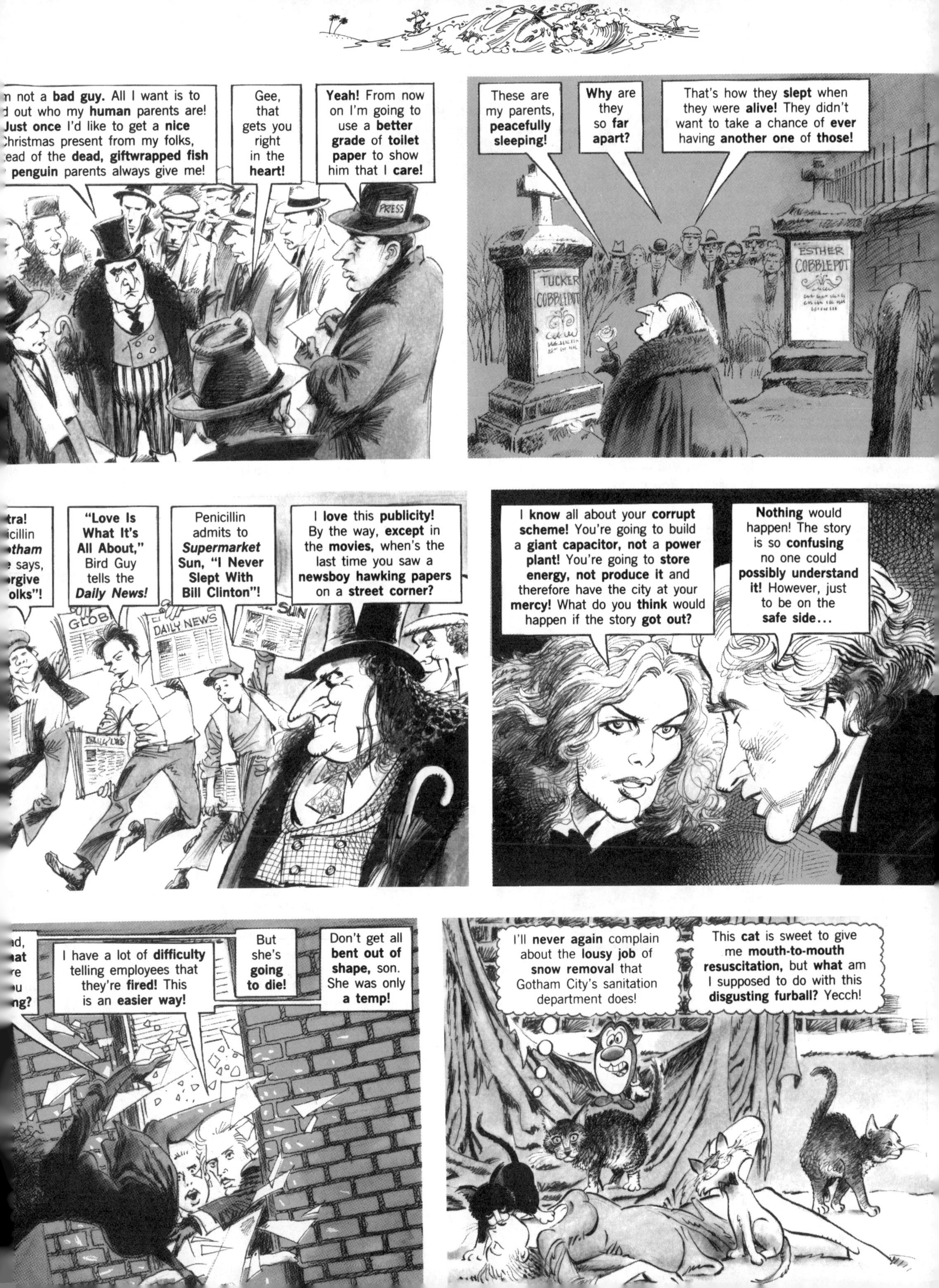
m not a bad guy. All I want is to d out who my human parents are! Just once I'd like to get a nice Christmas present from my folks, ead of the dead, giftwrapped fish penguin parents always give me!
Gee, that gets you right in the heart!
Yeah! From now on I'm going to use a better grade of toilet paper to show him that I care!
PRESS
These are my parents, peacefully sleeping!
Why are they so far apart?
That's how they slept when they were alive! They didn't want to take a chance of ever having another one of those!
TUCKER COBBLEPOT
ESTHER COBBLEPOT
tra! icillin otham e says, orgive olks"!
"Love Is What It's All About," Bird Guy tells the Daily News!
Penicillin admits to Supermarket Sun, "I Never Slept With Bill Clinton"!
I love this publicity! By the way, except in the movies, when's the last time you saw a newsboy hawking papers on a street corner?
GLOB
DAILY NEWS
SUN
I know all about your corrupt scheme! You're going to build a giant capacitor, not a power plant! You're going to store energy, not produce it and therefore have the city at your mercy! What do you think would happen if the story got out?
Nothing would happen! The story is so confusing no one could possibly understand it! However, just to be on the safe side...
ad, hat re u ng?
I have a lot of difficulty telling employees that they're fired! This is an easier way!
But she's going to die!
Don't get all bent out of shape, son. She was only a temp!
I'll never again complain about the lousy job of snow removal that Gotham City's sanitation department does!
This cat is sweet to give me mouth-to-mouth resuscitation, but what am I supposed to do with this disgusting furball? Yecch!

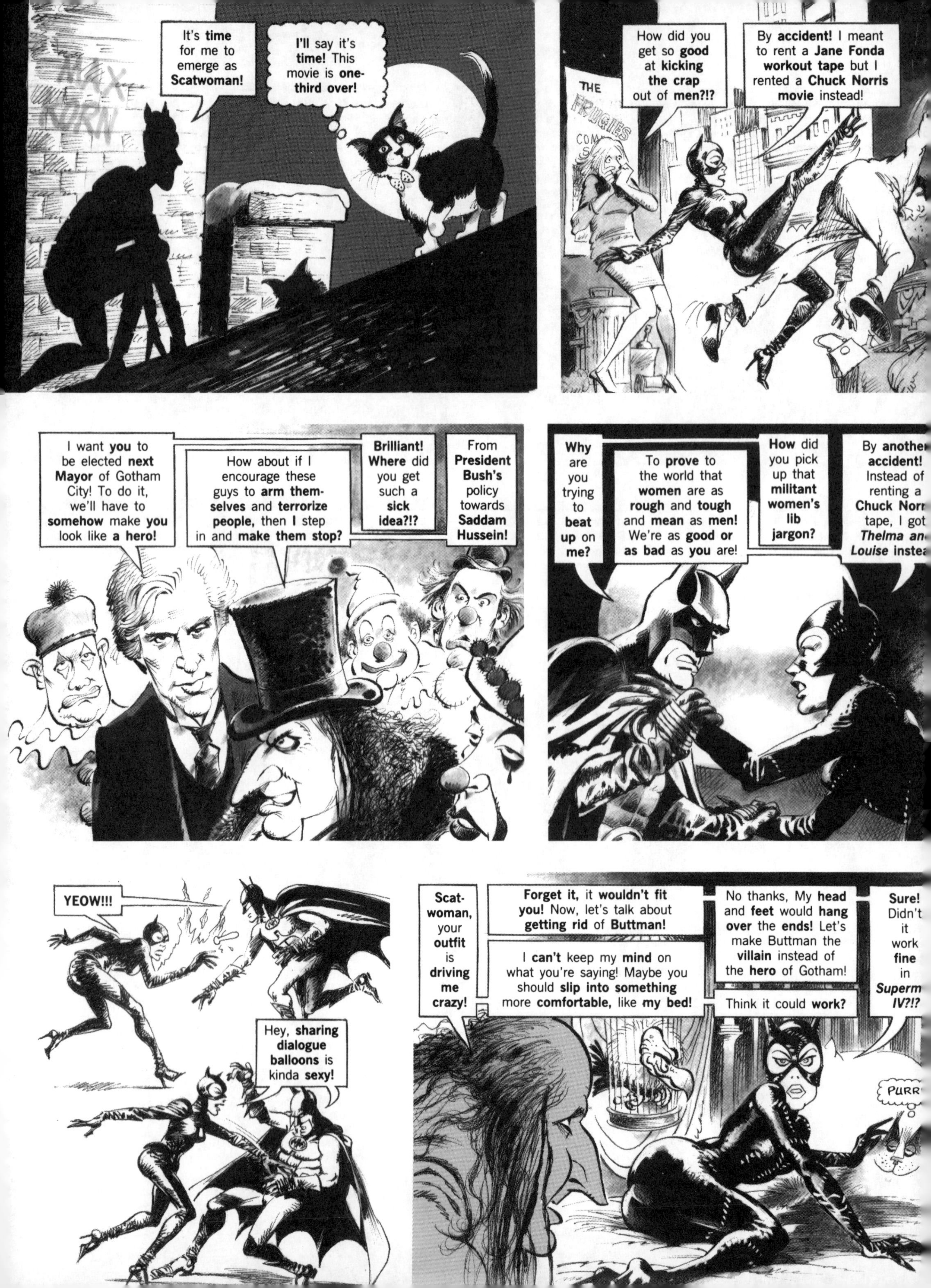
It's time for me to emerge as Scatwoman!
I'll say it's time! This movie is one-third over!
How did you get so good at kicking the crap out of men?!?
By accident! I meant to rent a Jane Fonda workout tape but I rented a Chuck Norris movie instead!
I want you to be elected next Mayor of Gotham City! To do it, we'll have to somehow make you look like a hero!
How about if I encourage these guys to arm themselves and terrorize people, then I step in and make them stop?
Brilliant! Where did you get such a sick idea?!?
From President Bush's policy towards Saddam Hussein!
Why are you trying to beat up on me?
To prove to the world that women are as rough and tough and mean as men! We're as good or as bad as you are!
How did you pick up that militant women's lib jargon?
By anothe accident! Instead of renting a Chuck Norr tape, I got Thelma an Louise instea
YEOW!!!
Hey, sharing dialogue balloons is kinda sexy!
Scat-woman, your outfit is driving me crazy!
Forget it, it wouldn't fit you! Now, let's talk about getting rid of Buttman!
I can't keep my mind on what you're saying! Maybe you should slip into something more comfortable, like my bed!
No thanks, My head and feet would hang over the ends! Let's make Buttman the villain instead of the hero of Gotham!
Think it could work?
Sure! Didn't it work fine in Superm IV?!?
PURR

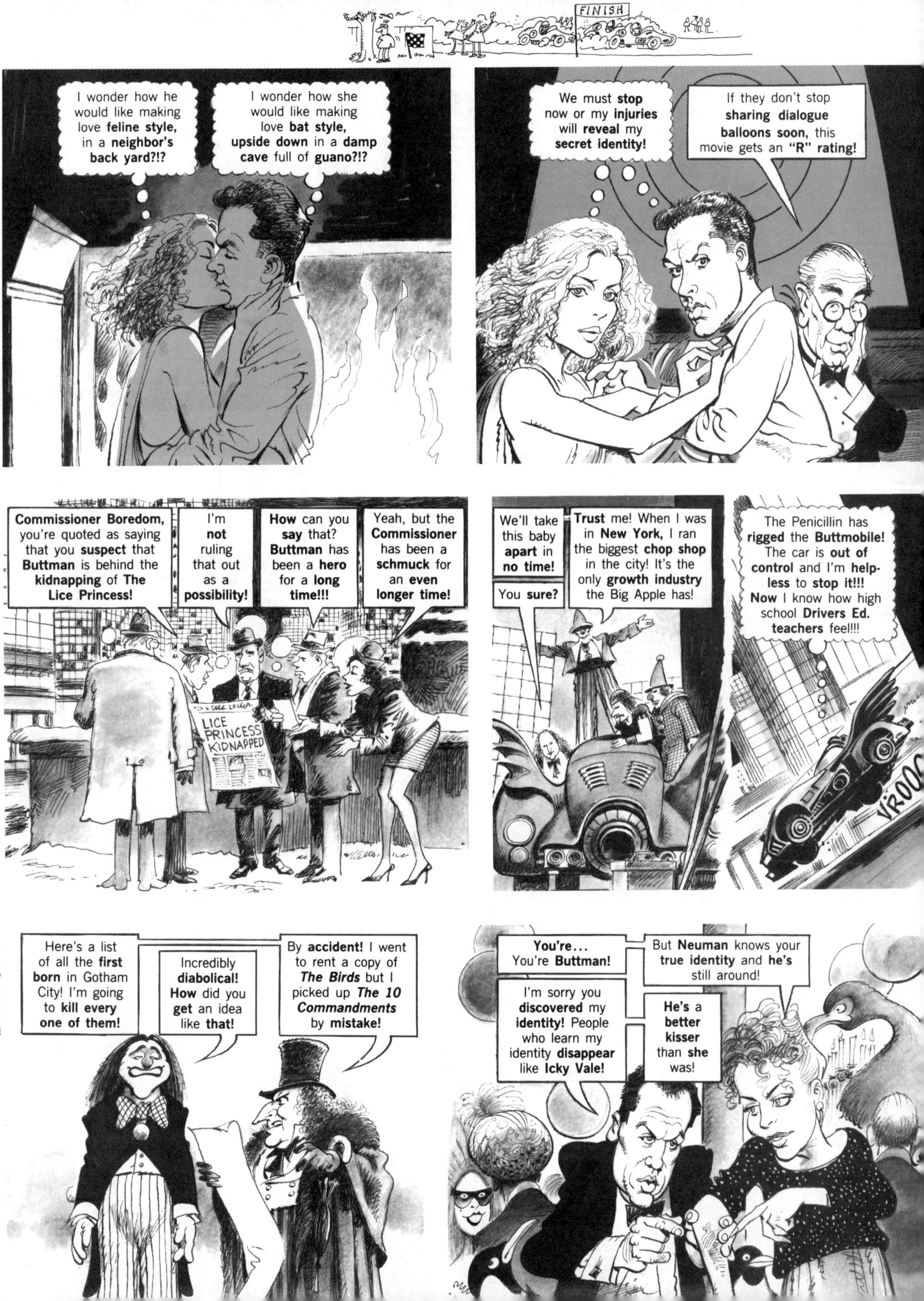
FINISH
I wonder how he would like making love feline style, in a neighbor's back yard?!?
I wonder how she would like making love bat style, upside down in a damp cave full of guano?!?
We must stop now or my injuries will reveal my secret identity!
If they don't stop sharing dialogue balloons soon, this movie gets an "R" rating!
Commissioner Boredom, you're quoted as saying that you suspect that Buttman is behind the kidnapping of The Lice Princess!
I'm not ruling that out as a possibility!
How can you say that? Buttman has been a hero for a long time!!!
Yeah, but the Commissioner has been a schmuck for an even longer time!
LICE PRINCESS KIDNAPPED
We'll take this baby apart in no time!
You sure?
Trust me! When I was in New York, I ran the biggest chop shop in the city! It's the only growth industry the Big Apple has!
The Penicillin has rigged the Buttmobile! The car is out of control and I'm helpless to stop it!!! Now I know how high school Drivers Ed. teachers feel!!!
VROO
Here's a list of all the first born in Gotham City! I'm going to kill every one of them!
Incredibly diabolical! How did you get an idea like that!
By accident! I went to rent a copy of The Birds but I picked up The 10 Commandments by mistake!
You're... You're Buttman!
But Neuman knows your true identity and he's still around!
I'm sorry you discovered my identity! People who learn my identity disappear like Icky Vale!
He's a better kisser than she was!

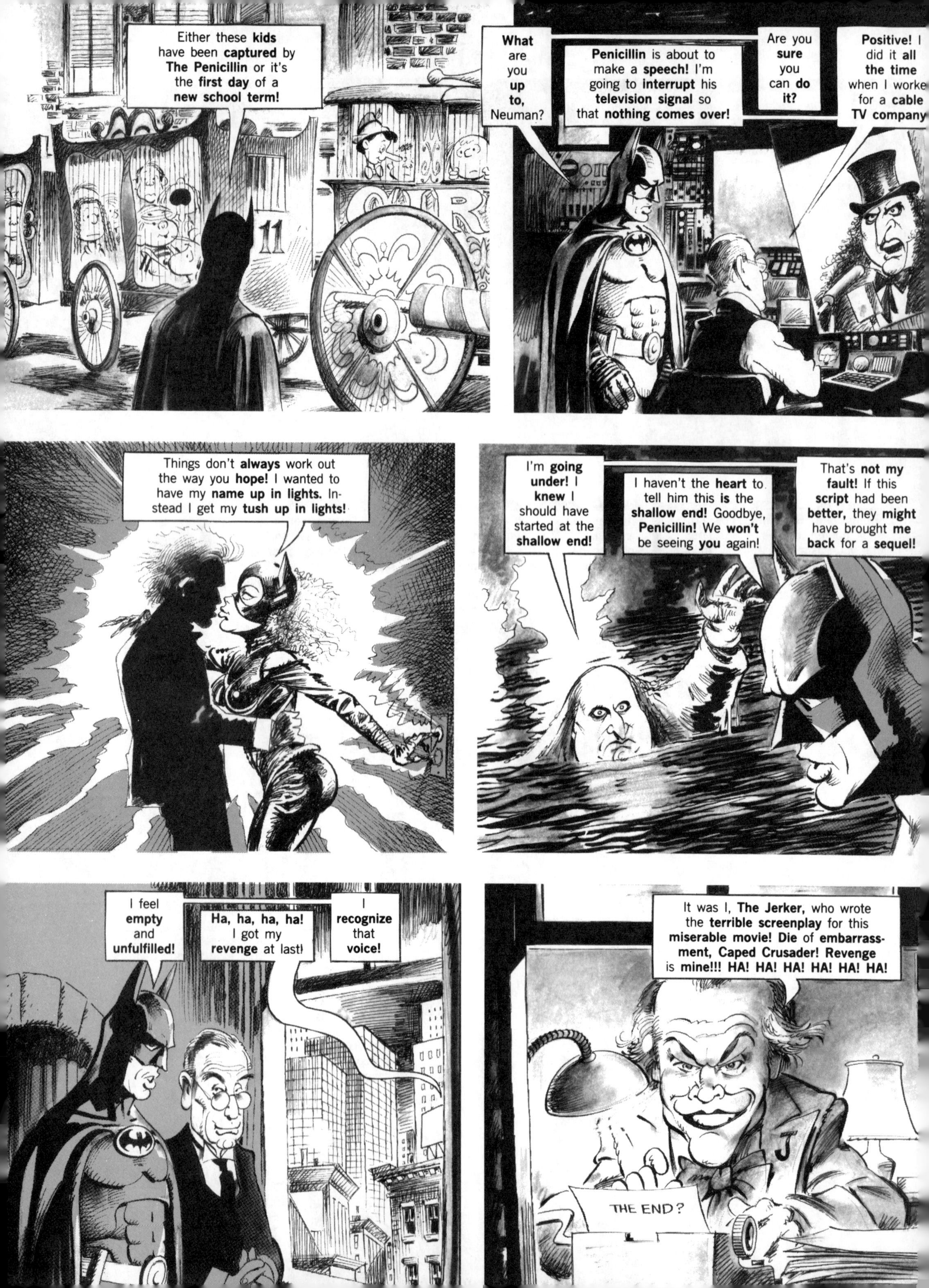
Either these kids have been captured by The Penicillin or it's the first day of a new school term!
What are you up to, Neuman?
Penicillin is about to make a speech! I'm going to interrupt his television signal so that nothing comes over!
Are you sure you can do it?
Positive! I did it all the time when I worke for a cable TV company
Things don't always work out the way you hope! I wanted to have my name up in lights. Instead I get my tush up in lights!
I'm going under! I knew I should have started at the shallow end!
I haven't the heart to tell him this is the shallow end! Goodbye, Penicillin! We won't be seeing you again!
That's not my fault! If this script had been better, they might have brought me back for a sequel!
I feel empty and unfulfilled!
Ha, ha, ha, ha! I got my revenge at last!
I recognize that voice!
It was I, The Jerker, who wrote the terrible screenplay for this miserable movie! Die of embarrassment, Caped Crusader! Revenge is mine!!! HA! HA! HA! HA! HA! HA!
THE END?

RANK ON A ROLL DEPT.

he Caped Crusader is back on the screen, and this time they've signed yet another actor for the title role. He's eorge Clooney, out to scale new heights! How did this come about? Read on as we rhyme you to death with . . .

CLOONEY AS THE BAT

(with apologies – again – to Ernest Lawrence Thayer)

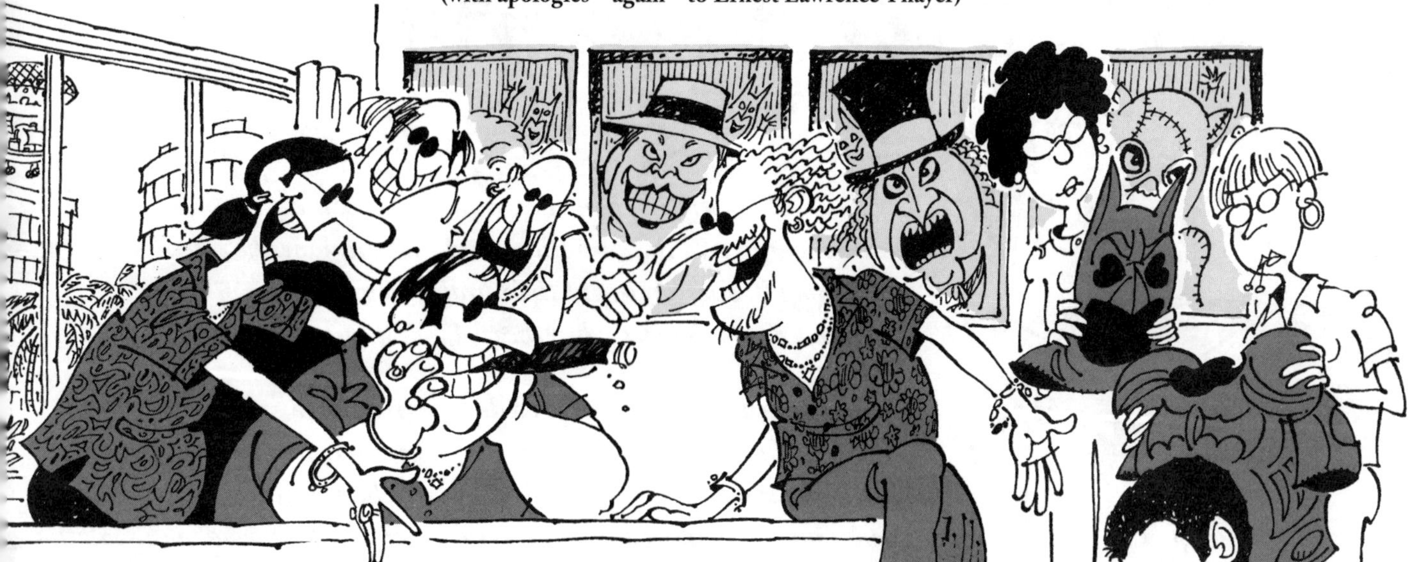

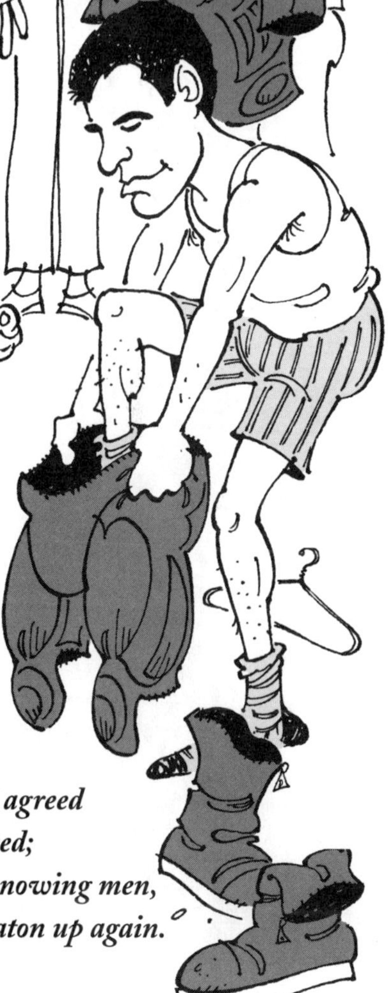

The outlook was depressing on the Warner Brothers lot;
The cost of films was soaring, but the ticket sales were not
And when Who's That Girl *went nowhere and* Young Einstein *had no luck,*
It was clear to all the moguls that their choice of films did suck.

"Let's do Batman," someone murmured – no one knows for sure who said it;
(Although when the flick made millions, each exec would take the credit)
And they shot a mighty epic, betting film fans would go ape
At the sight of Michael Keaton clad in latex and a cape.

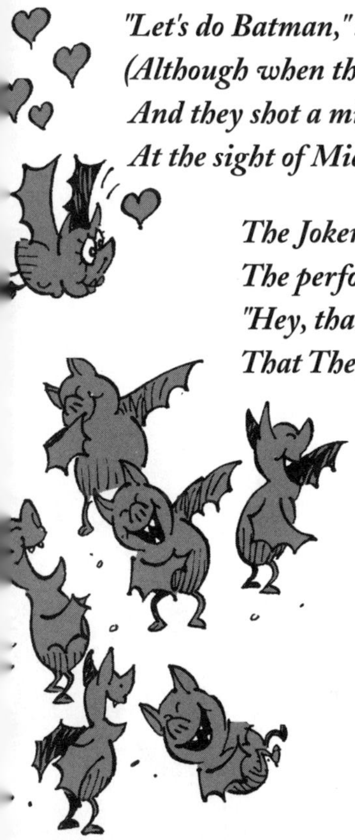

The Joker was the villain and although he wound up beaten,
The performance of Jack Nicholson annihilated Keaton;
"Hey, that's showbiz," said the mogul, for they soon were realizing
That The Joker was the hero when it came to merchandising.

"Strike One!" the critics thundered, and they one and all agreed
That the choice of Michael Keaton was a sorry one indeed;
"How true," concurred the moguls, who were wise and knowing men,
And to show they'd learned their lesson, they signed Keaton up again.

The sequel stumbled forth, a ho-hum epic it was more like;
Twice as drearisome was Keaton – many said he was Al Gore-like.
While The Penguin reeked with evil and Catwoman flashed her whip,
It was clear the Caped Crusader once again had lost his grip.

ARTIST: PAUL COKER WRITER: FRANK JACOBS

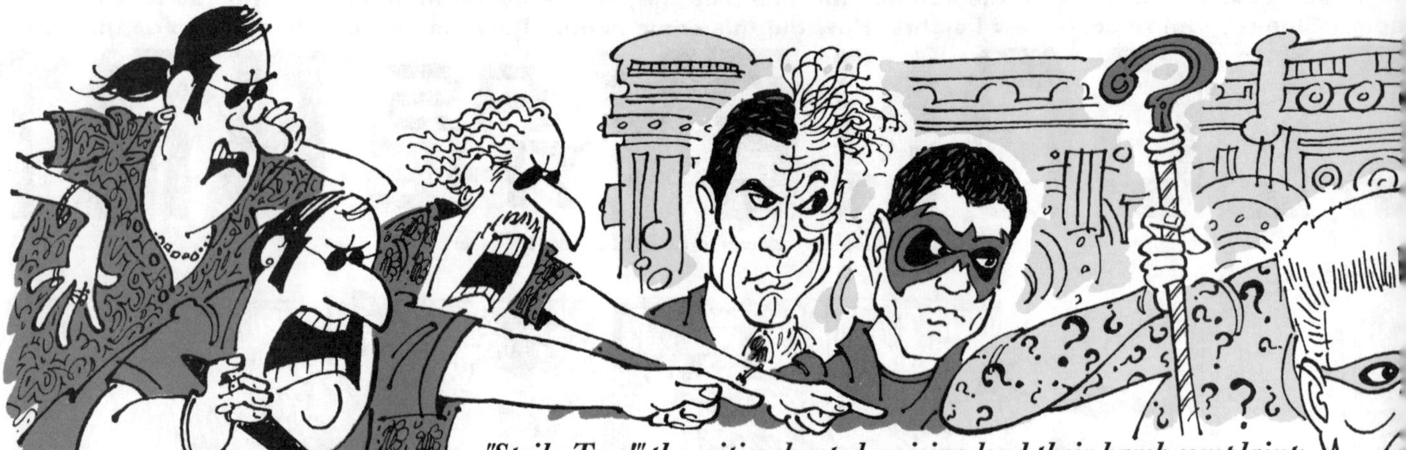

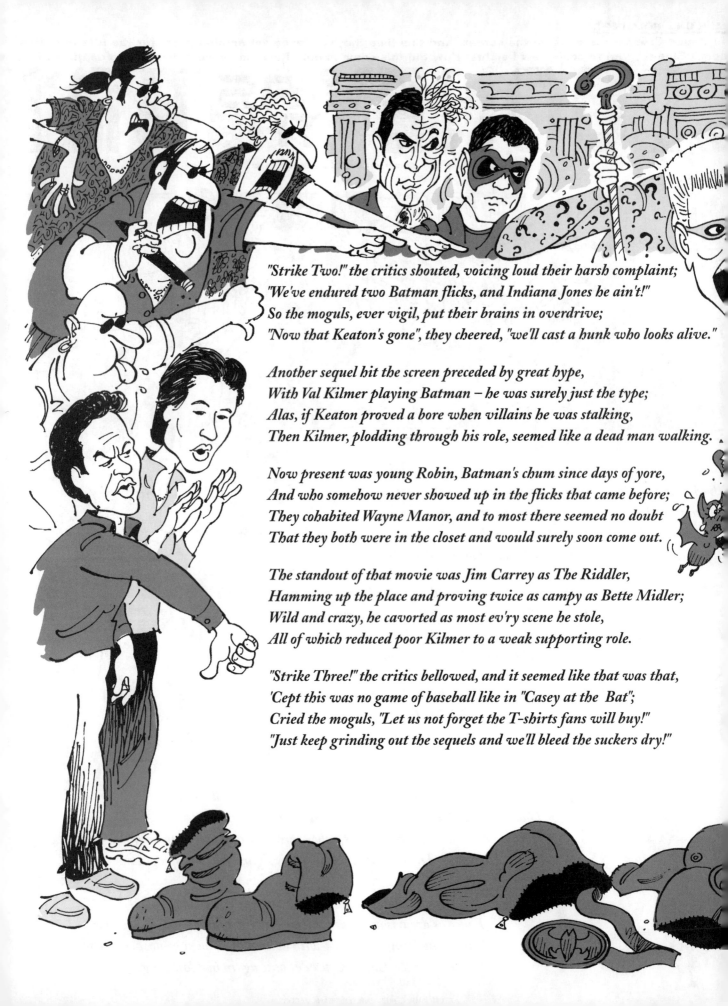

"Strike Two!" the critics shouted, voicing loud their harsh complaint;
"We've endured two Batman flicks, and Indiana Jones he ain't!"
So the moguls, ever vigil, put their brains in overdrive;
"Now that Keaton's gone", they cheered, "we'll cast a hunk who looks alive."

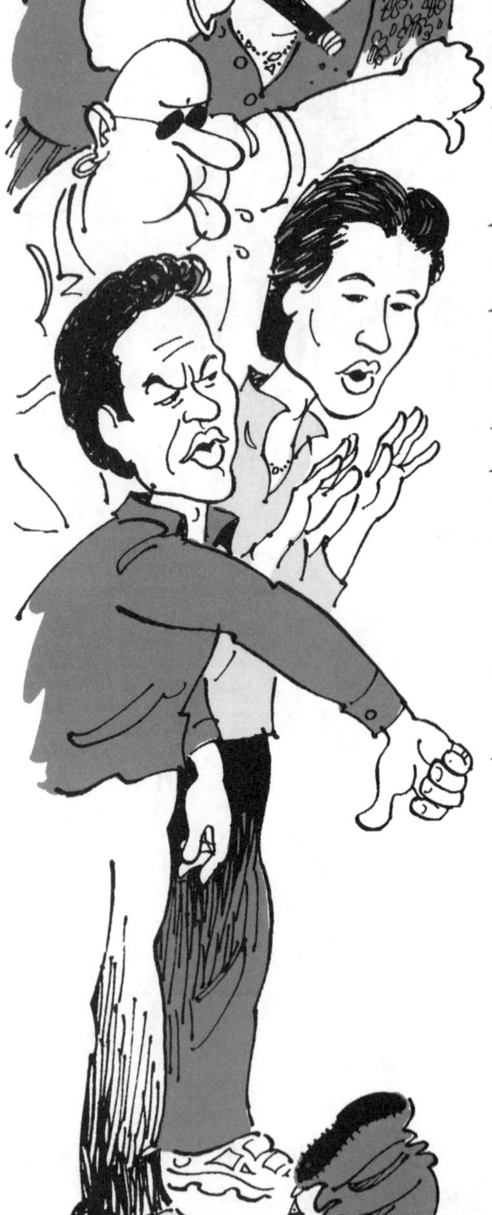

Another sequel hit the screen preceded by great hype,
With Val Kilmer playing Batman – he was surely just the type;
Alas, if Keaton proved a bore when villains he was stalking,
Then Kilmer, plodding through his role, seemed like a dead man walking.

Now present was young Robin, Batman's chum since days of yore,
And who somehow never showed up in the flicks that came before;
They cohabited Wayne Manor, and to most there seemed no doubt
That they both were in the closet and would surely soon come out.

The standout of that movie was Jim Carrey as The Riddler,
Hamming up the place and proving twice as campy as Bette Midler;
Wild and crazy, he cavorted as most ev'ry scene he stole,
All of which reduced poor Kilmer to a weak supporting role.

"Strike Three!" the critics bellowed, and it seemed like that was that,
'Cept this was no game of baseball like in "Casey at the Bat";
Cried the moguls, "Let us not forget the T-shirts fans will buy!"
"Just keep grinding out the sequels and we'll bleed the suckers dry!"

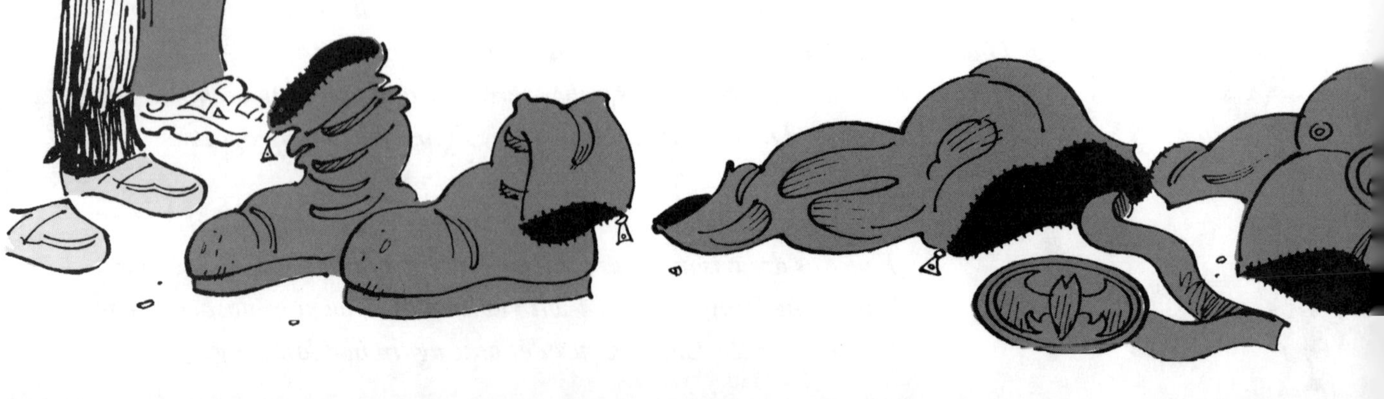

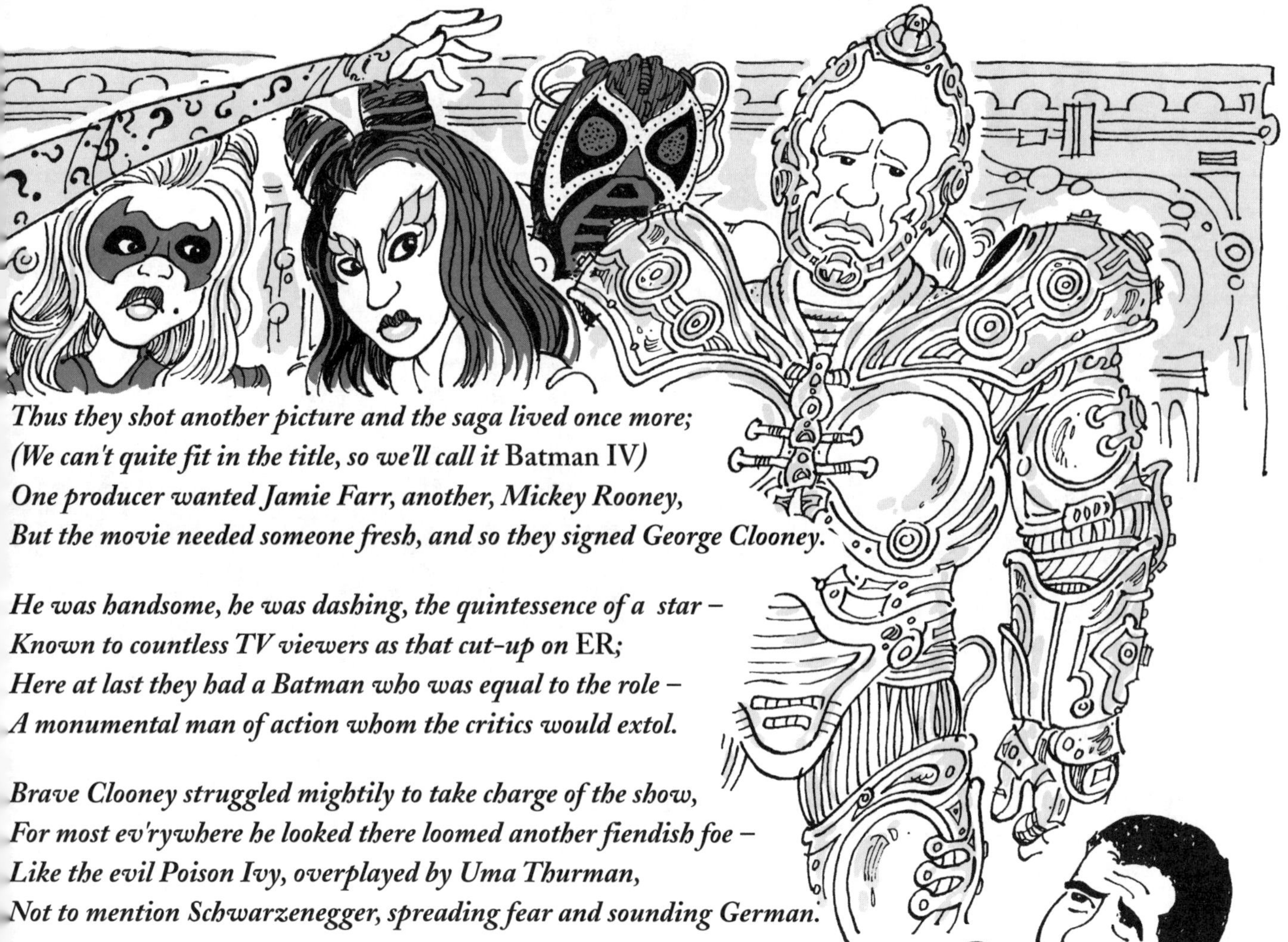

Thus they shot another picture and the saga lived once more;
(We can't quite fit in the title, so we'll call it Batman IV*)*
One producer wanted Jamie Farr, another, Mickey Rooney,
But the movie needed someone fresh, and so they signed George Clooney.

He was handsome, he was dashing, the quintessence of a star –
Known to countless TV viewers as that cut-up on ER;
Here at last they had a Batman who was equal to the role –
A monumental man of action whom the critics would extol.

Brave Clooney struggled mightily to take charge of the show,
For most ev'rywhere he looked there loomed another fiendish foe –
Like the evil Poison Ivy, overplayed by Uma Thurman,
Not to mention Schwarzenegger, spreading fear and sounding German.

"I'm the star!" exulted Clooney, revving up the Batmobile;
"I'll get raves!" he boasted proudly as he crouched behind the wheel;
He would prove he was a hero that the world would not forget;
He'd be praised beyond all measure as the finest Batman yet.

Oh, somewhere there are idols who are worthy of the name,
Winning kudos from the critics, getting showered with acclaim;
And somewhere there are heroes who survive the toughest test,
But there is no joy in filmdom – Clooney struck out like the rest.

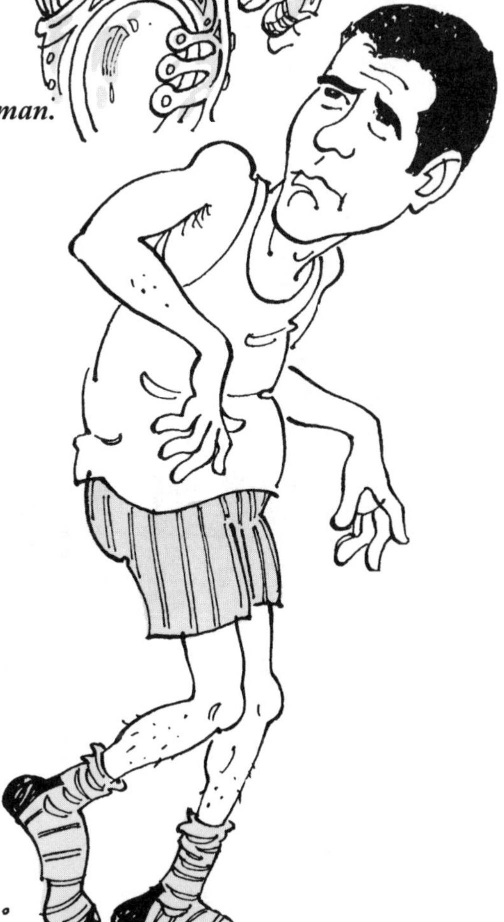

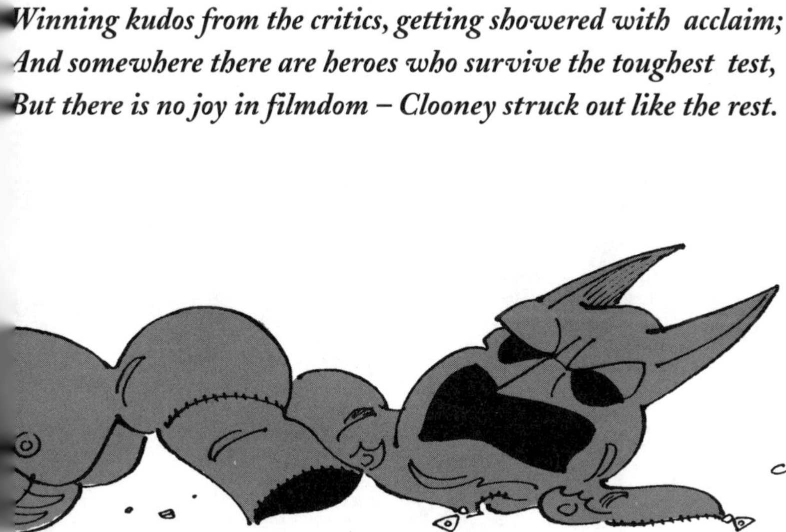

OTHER SUPERHERO DEATHS

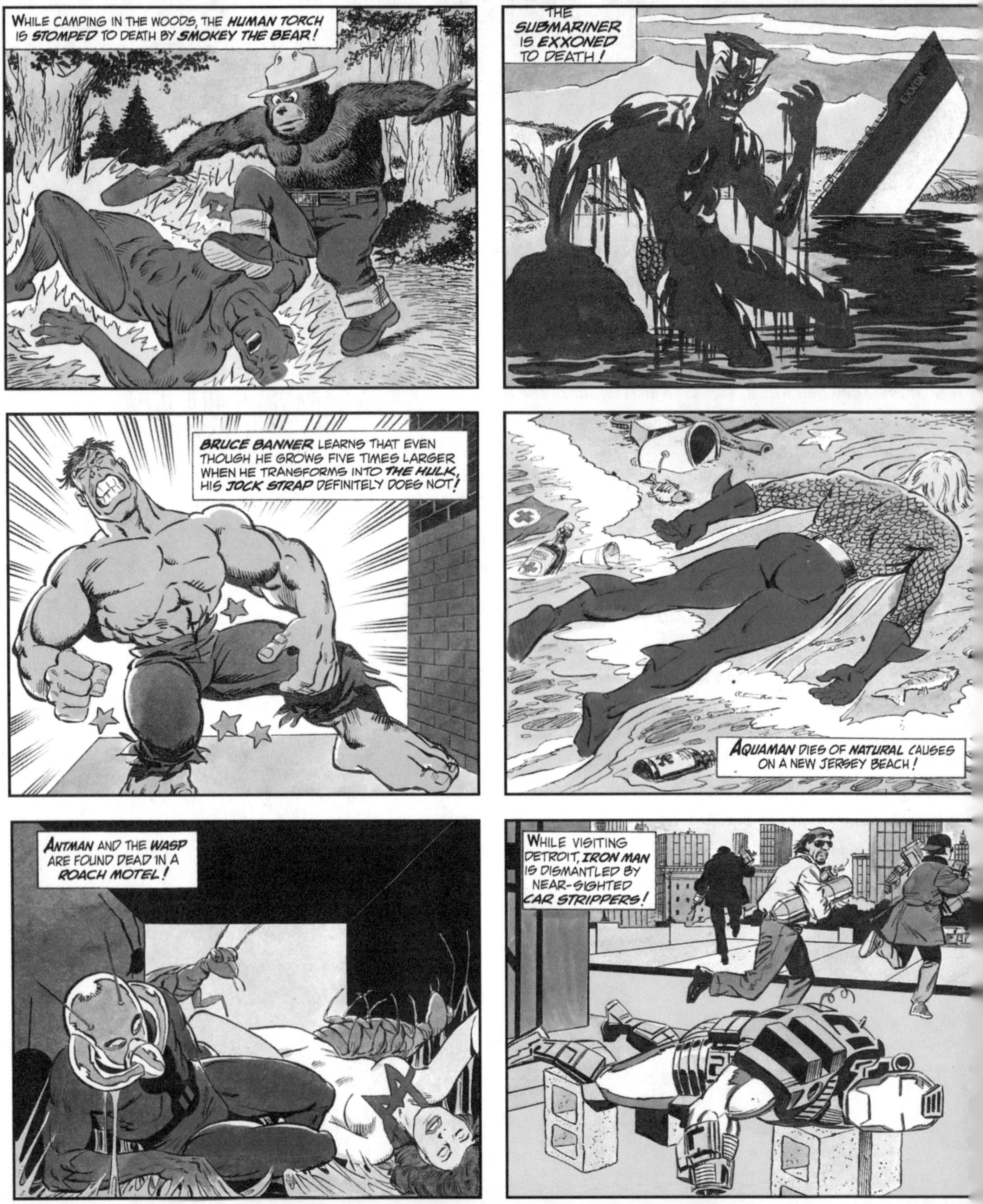
WHILE CAMPING IN THE WOODS, THE HUMAN TORCH IS STOMPED TO DEATH BY SMOKEY THE BEAR!
THE SUBMARINER IS EXXONED TO DEATH!
BRUCE BANNER LEARNS THAT EVEN THOUGH HE GROWS FIVE TIMES LARGER WHEN HE TRANSFORMS INTO THE HULK, HIS JOCK STRAP DEFINITELY DOES NOT!
AQUAMAN DIES OF NATURAL CAUSES ON A NEW JERSEY BEACH!
ANTMAN AND THE WASP ARE FOUND DEAD IN A ROACH MOTEL!
WHILE VISITING DETROIT, IRON MAN IS DISMANTLED BY NEAR-SIGHTED CAR STRIPPERS!

ARTIST: ANGELO TORRES WRITER: BARRY LIEBMANN

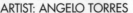

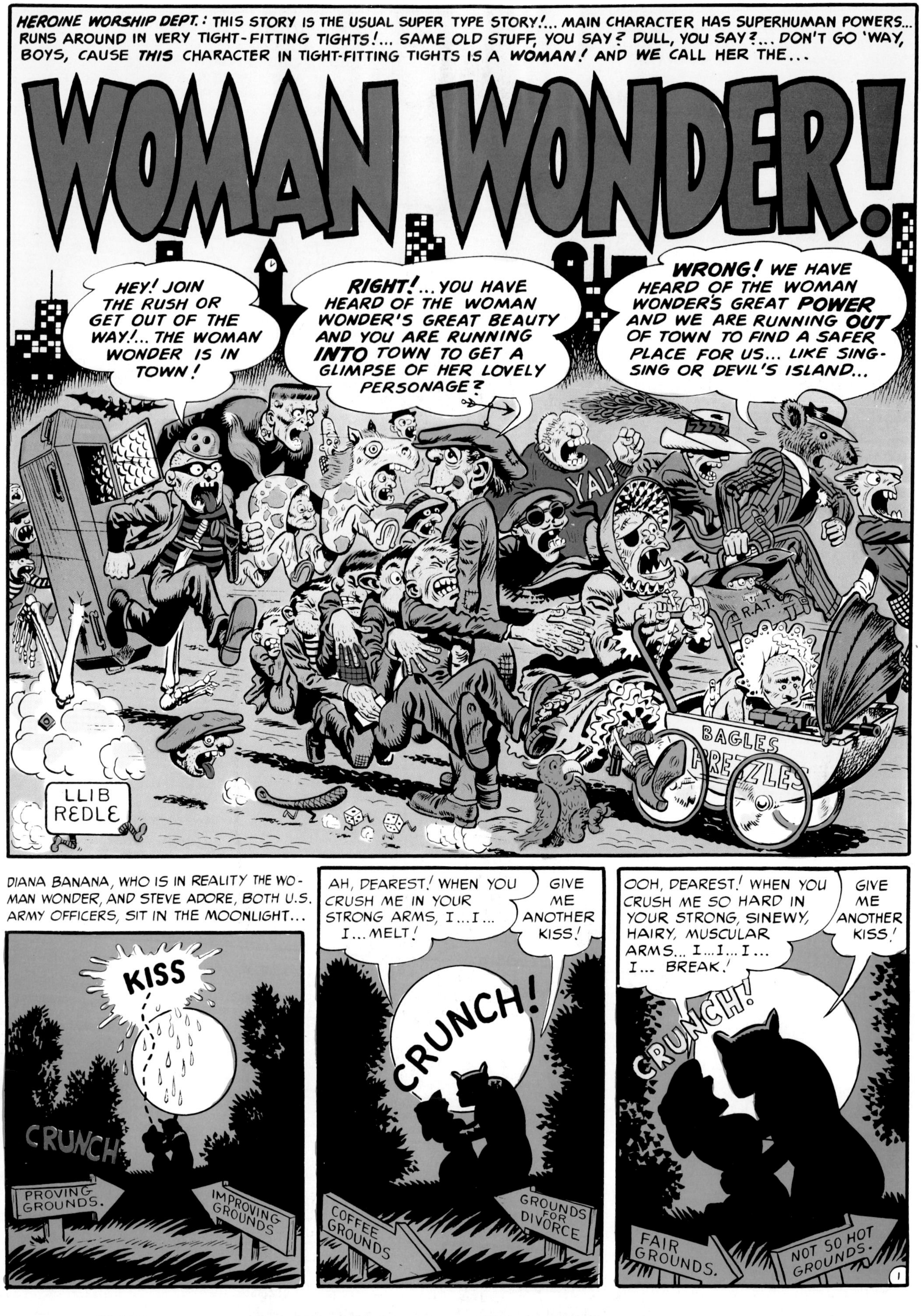
HEROINE WORSHIP DEPT.: THIS STORY IS THE USUAL SUPER TYPE STORY!... MAIN CHARACTER HAS SUPERHUMAN POWERS... RUNS AROUND IN VERY TIGHT-FITTING TIGHTS!... SAME OLD STUFF, YOU SAY? DULL, YOU SAY?... DON'T GO 'WAY, BOYS, CAUSE THIS CHARACTER IN TIGHT-FITTING TIGHTS IS A WOMAN! AND WE CALL HER THE...
WOMAN WONDER!
HEY! JOIN THE RUSH OR GET OUT OF THE WAY!... THE WOMAN WONDER IS IN TOWN!
RIGHT!... YOU HAVE HEARD OF THE WOMAN WONDER'S GREAT BEAUTY AND YOU ARE RUNNING INTO TOWN TO GET A GLIMPSE OF HER LOVELY PERSONAGE?
WRONG! WE HAVE HEARD OF THE WOMAN WONDER'S GREAT POWER AND WE ARE RUNNING OUT OF TOWN TO FIND A SAFER PLACE FOR US... LIKE SING-SING OR DEVIL'S ISLAND...
YALE
R.A.T.
BAGLES
PRETZLES
LLIB REDLE
DIANA BANANA, WHO IS IN REALITY THE WOMAN WONDER, AND STEVE ADORE, BOTH U.S. ARMY OFFICERS, SIT IN THE MOONLIGHT...
KISS
CRUNCH
PROVING GROUNDS.
IMPROVING GROUNDS
AH, DEAREST! WHEN YOU CRUSH ME IN YOUR STRONG ARMS, I...I... I... MELT!
GIVE ME ANOTHER KISS!
CRUNCH!
COFFEE GROUNDS
GROUNDS FOR DIVORCE
OOH, DEAREST! WHEN YOU CRUSH ME SO HARD IN YOUR STRONG, SINEWY, HAIRY, MUSCULAR ARMS... I...I...I... I... BREAK!
GIVE ME ANOTHER KISS!
CRUNCH!
FAIR GROUNDS.
NOT SO HOT GROUNDS.
1

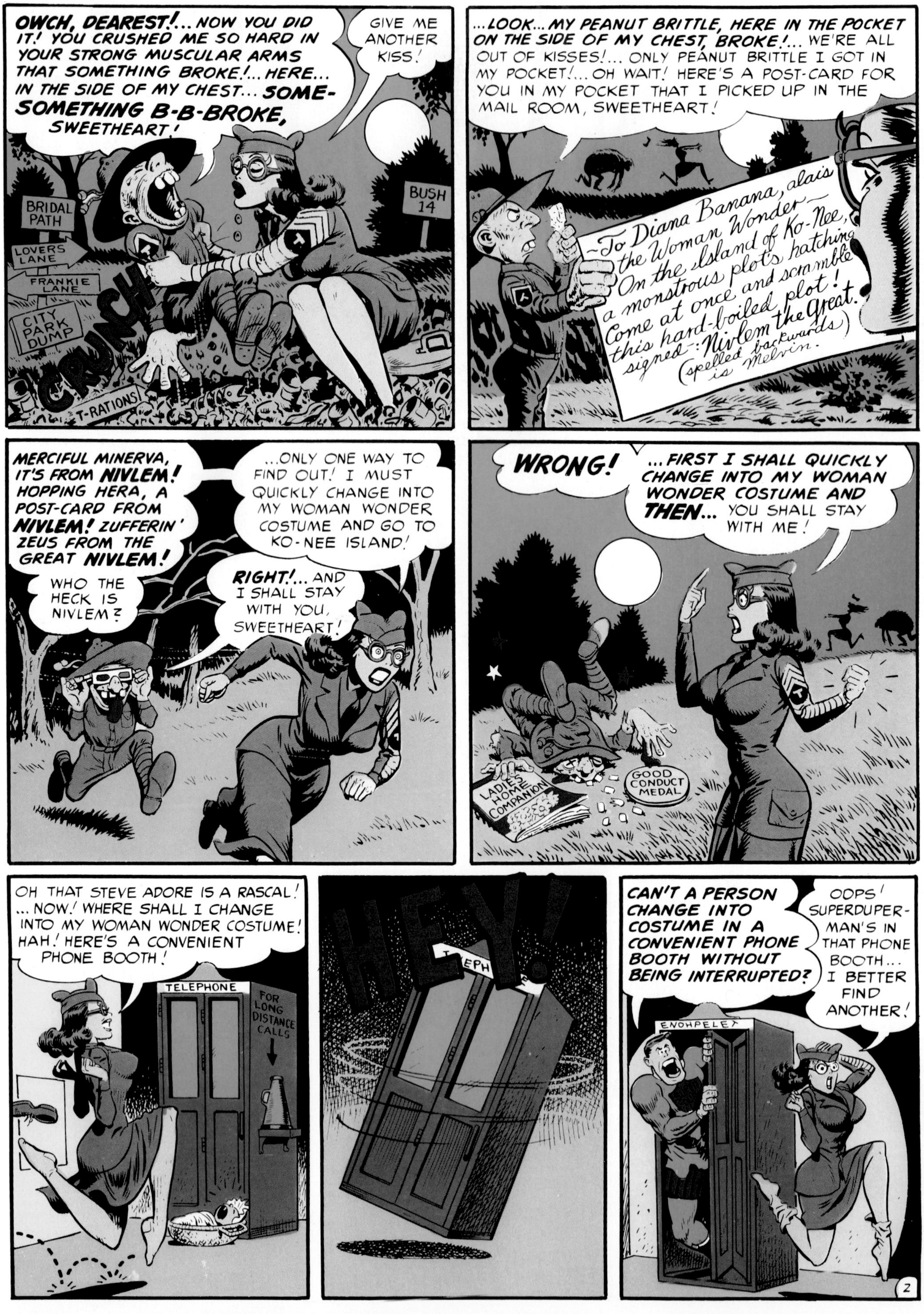
OWCH, DEAREST!... NOW YOU DID IT! YOU CRUSHED ME SO HARD IN YOUR STRONG MUSCULAR ARMS THAT SOMETHING BROKE!... HERE... IN THE SIDE OF MY CHEST... SOME-SOMETHING B-B-BROKE, SWEETHEART!
GIVE ME ANOTHER KISS!
BRIDAL PATH
LOVERS LANE
FRANKIE LANE
CITY PARK DUMP
BUSH 14
CRUNCH
T-RATIONS
...LOOK... MY PEANUT BRITTLE, HERE IN THE POCKET ON THE SIDE OF MY CHEST, BROKE!... WE'RE ALL OUT OF KISSES!... ONLY PEANUT BRITTLE I GOT IN MY POCKET!... OH WAIT! HERE'S A POST-CARD FOR YOU IN MY POCKET THAT I PICKED UP IN THE MAIL ROOM, SWEETHEART!
~To Diana Banana, alais the Woman Wonder~ On the Island of Ko-Nee a monstrous plot's hatching Come at once and scramble this hard-boiled plot! signed~: Nivlem the Great. (spelled backwards is Melvin.)
MERCIFUL MINERVA, IT'S FROM NIVLEM! HOPPING HERA, A POST-CARD FROM NIVLEM! ZUFFERIN' ZEUS FROM THE GREAT NIVLEM!
WHO THE HECK IS NIVLEM?
...ONLY ONE WAY TO FIND OUT! I MUST QUICKLY CHANGE INTO MY WOMAN WONDER COSTUME AND GO TO KO-NEE ISLAND!
RIGHT!... AND I SHALL STAY WITH YOU, SWEETHEART!
WRONG!
...FIRST I SHALL QUICKLY CHANGE INTO MY WOMAN WONDER COSTUME AND THEN... YOU SHALL STAY WITH ME!
LADIES' HOME COMPANION
GOOD CONDUCT MEDAL
OH THAT STEVE ADORE IS A RASCAL! ...NOW! WHERE SHALL I CHANGE INTO MY WOMAN WONDER COSTUME! HAH! HERE'S A CONVENIENT PHONE BOOTH!
TELEPHONE
FOR LONG DISTANCE CALLS
HEY!
CAN'T A PERSON CHANGE INTO COSTUME IN A CONVENIENT PHONE BOOTH WITHOUT BEING INTERRUPTED?
OOPS! SUPERDUPERMAN'S IN THAT PHONE BOOTH... I BETTER FIND ANOTHER!
ENOHPELET
2

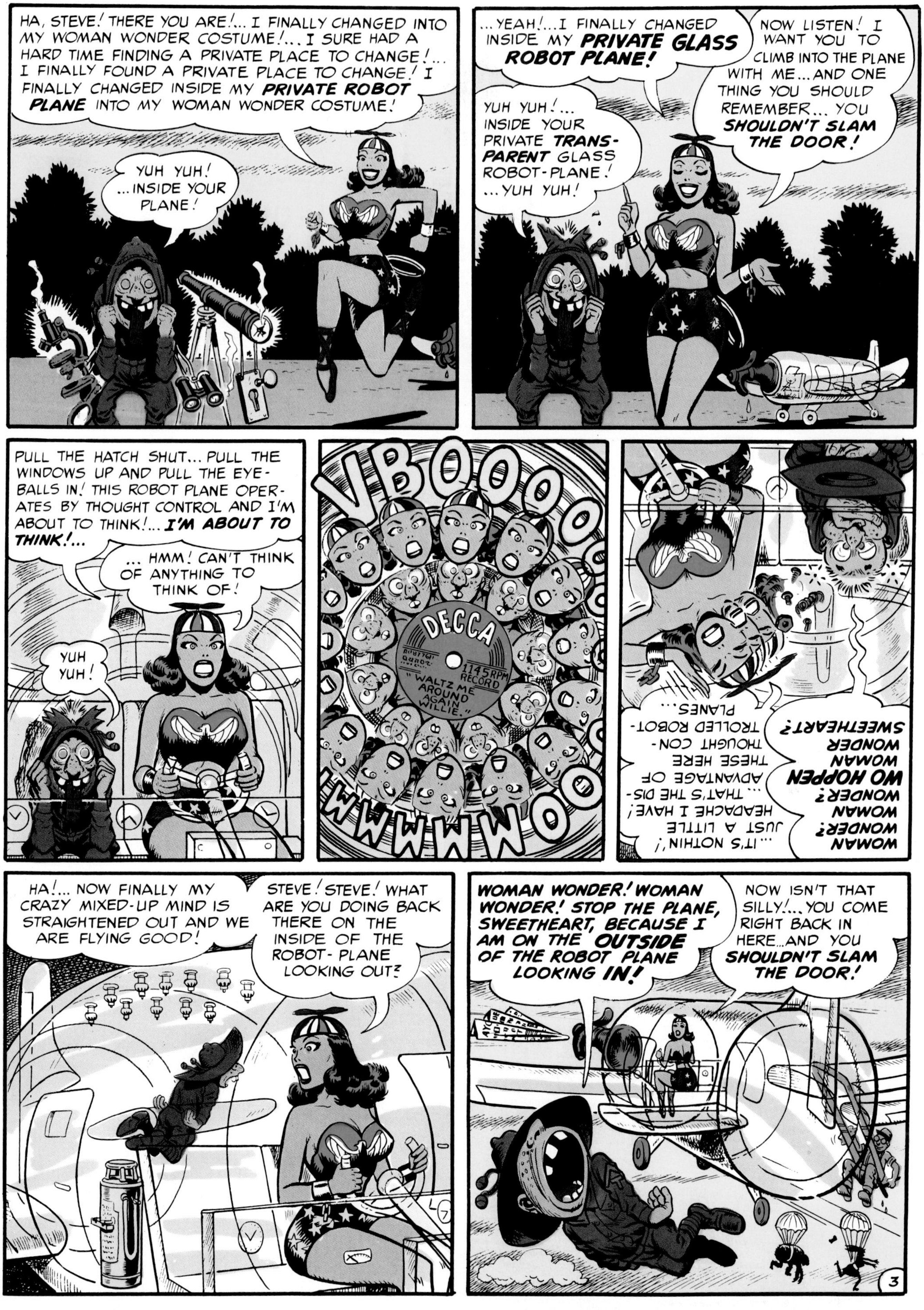

HA, STEVE! THERE YOU ARE!... I FINALLY CHANGED INTO MY WOMAN WONDER COSTUME!... I SURE HAD A HARD TIME FINDING A PRIVATE PLACE TO CHANGE!... I FINALLY FOUND A PRIVATE PLACE TO CHANGE! I FINALLY CHANGED INSIDE MY PRIVATE ROBOT PLANE INTO MY WOMAN WONDER COSTUME!
YUH YUH! ...INSIDE YOUR PLANE!
...YEAH!...I FINALLY CHANGED INSIDE MY PRIVATE GLASS ROBOT PLANE!
YUH YUH!... INSIDE YOUR PRIVATE TRANS-PARENT GLASS ROBOT-PLANE! ...YUH YUH!
NOW LISTEN! I WANT YOU TO CLIMB INTO THE PLANE WITH ME... AND ONE THING YOU SHOULD REMEMBER... YOU SHOULDN'T SLAM THE DOOR!
PULL THE HATCH SHUT... PULL THE WINDOWS UP AND PULL THE EYE-BALLS IN! THIS ROBOT PLANE OPER-ATES BY THOUGHT CONTROL AND I'M ABOUT TO THINK!... I'M ABOUT TO THINK!...
... HMM! CAN'T THINK OF ANYTHING TO THINK OF!
YUH YUH!
VBOOOOOOOOOOOMMMMM!
DECCA
1145 RPM RECORD
"WALTZ ME AROUND AGAIN WILLIE."
WOMAN WONDER? WOMAN WONDER? WO HOPPEN WOMAN WONDER SWEETHEART?
...IT'S NOTHIN'! JUST A LITTLE HEADACHE I HAVE! ...THAT'S THE DIS-ADVANTAGE OF THESE HERE THOUGHT CON-TROLLED ROBOT-PLANES....
HA!... NOW FINALLY MY CRAZY MIXED-UP MIND IS STRAIGHTENED OUT AND WE ARE FLYING GOOD!
STEVE! STEVE! WHAT ARE YOU DOING BACK THERE ON THE INSIDE OF THE ROBOT-PLANE LOOKING OUT?
WOMAN WONDER! WOMAN WONDER! STOP THE PLANE, SWEETHEART, BECAUSE I AM ON THE OUTSIDE OF THE ROBOT PLANE LOOKING IN!
NOW ISN'T THAT SILLY!... YOU COME RIGHT BACK IN HERE...AND YOU SHOULDN'T SLAM THE DOOR!

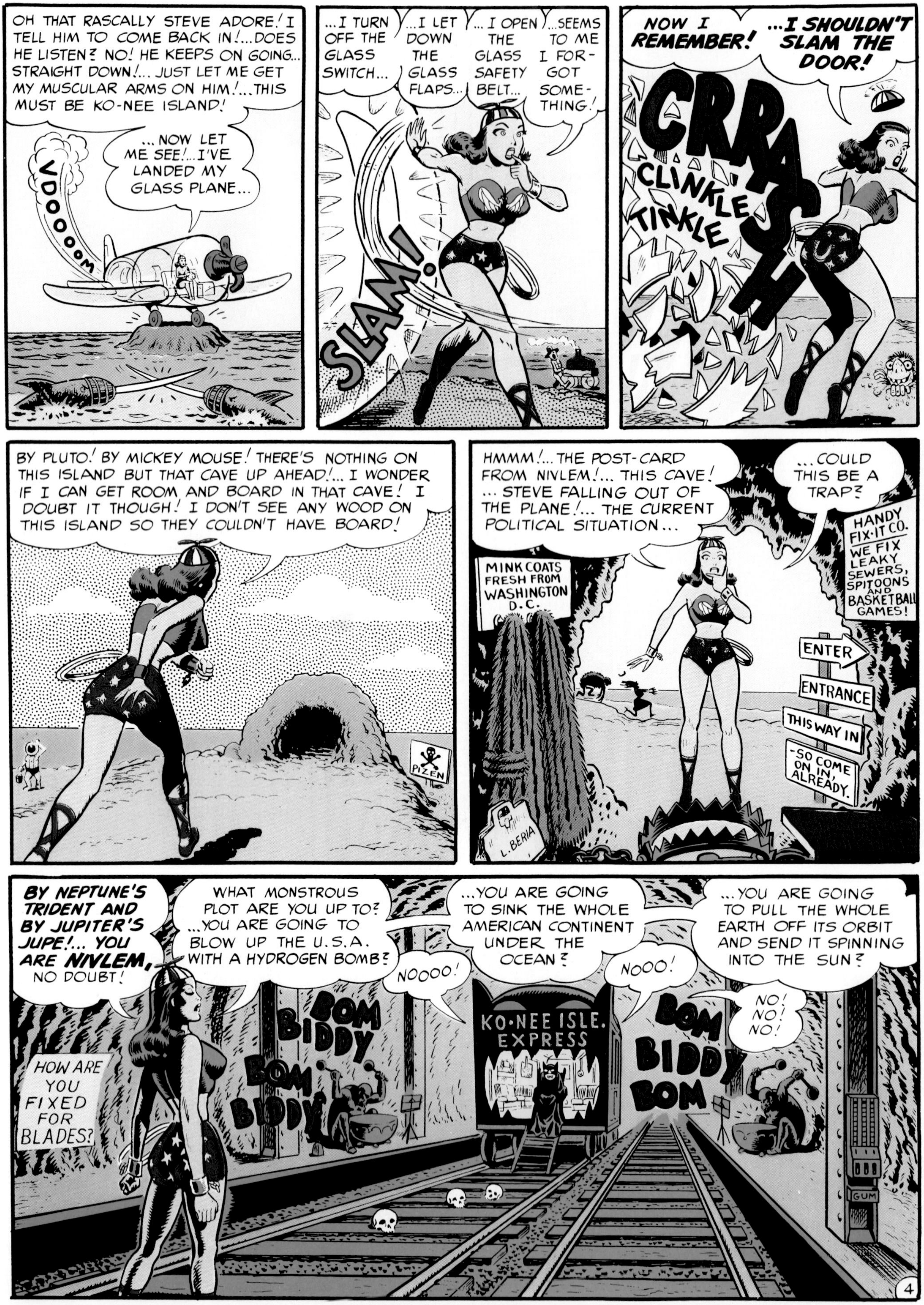
OH THAT RASCALLY STEVE ADORE! I TELL HIM TO COME BACK IN!... DOES HE LISTEN? NO! HE KEEPS ON GOING... STRAIGHT DOWN!... JUST LET ME GET MY MUSCULAR ARMS ON HIM!... THIS MUST BE KO-NEE ISLAND!
... NOW LET ME SEE!... I'VE LANDED MY GLASS PLANE...
VDOOOooom
... I TURN OFF THE GLASS SWITCH...
... I LET DOWN THE GLASS FLAPS...
... I OPEN THE GLASS SAFETY BELT...
... SEEMS TO ME I FOR-GOT SOME-THING!
SLAM!
NOW I REMEMBER!
... I SHOULDN'T SLAM THE DOOR!
CRRASH
CLINKLE
TINKLE
BY PLUTO! BY MICKEY MOUSE! THERE'S NOTHING ON THIS ISLAND BUT THAT CAVE UP AHEAD!... I WONDER IF I CAN GET ROOM AND BOARD IN THAT CAVE! I DOUBT IT THOUGH! I DON'T SEE ANY WOOD ON THIS ISLAND SO THEY COULDN'T HAVE BOARD!
PIZEN
HMMM!... THE POST-CARD FROM NIVLEM!... THIS CAVE! ... STEVE FALLING OUT OF THE PLANE!... THE CURRENT POLITICAL SITUATION...
... COULD THIS BE A TRAP?
MINK COATS FRESH FROM WASHINGTON D.C.
HANDY FIX-IT CO. WE FIX LEAKY SEWERS, SPITOONS AND BASKETBALL GAMES!
ENTER
ENTRANCE
THIS WAY IN
-SO COME ON IN, ALREADY.
L. BERIA
BY NEPTUNE'S TRIDENT AND BY JUPITER'S JUPE!... YOU ARE NIVLEM, NO DOUBT!
WHAT MONSTROUS PLOT ARE YOU UP TO? ... YOU ARE GOING TO BLOW UP THE U.S.A. WITH A HYDROGEN BOMB?
NOOOO!
... YOU ARE GOING TO SINK THE WHOLE AMERICAN CONTINENT UNDER THE OCEAN?
NOOO!
... YOU ARE GOING TO PULL THE WHOLE EARTH OFF ITS ORBIT AND SEND IT SPINNING INTO THE SUN?
NO! NO! NO!
HOW ARE YOU FIXED FOR BLADES?
BOM BIDDY BOM BIDDY
KO·NEE ISLE. EXPRESS
BOM BIDDY BOM
GUM

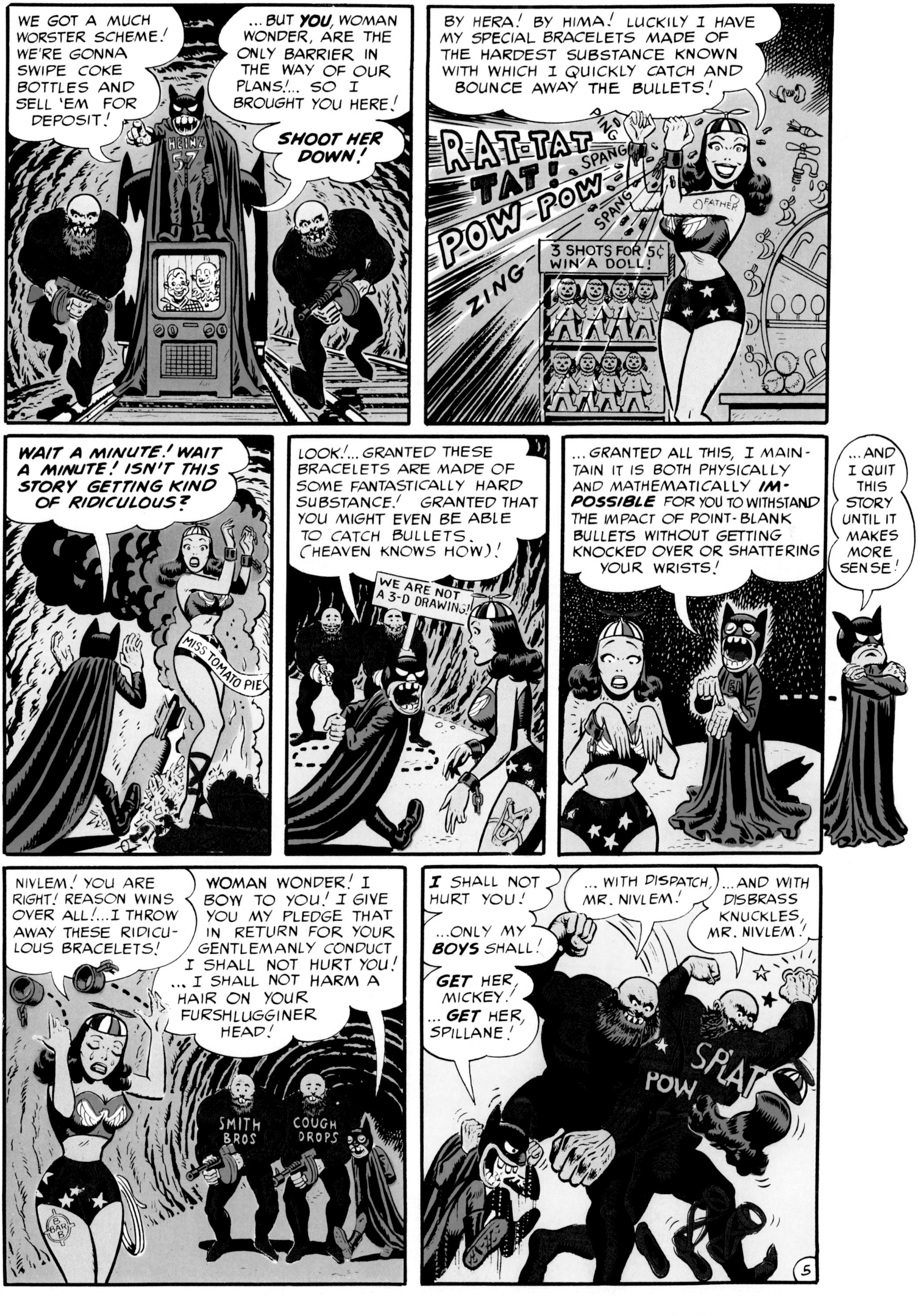
WE GOT A MUCH WORSTER SCHEME! WE'RE GONNA SWIPE COKE BOTTLES AND SELL 'EM FOR DEPOSIT!
...BUT YOU, WOMAN WONDER, ARE THE ONLY BARRIER IN THE WAY OF OUR PLANS!... SO I BROUGHT YOU HERE!
SHOOT HER DOWN!
HEINZ 57
BY HERA! BY HIMA! LUCKILY I HAVE MY SPECIAL BRACELETS MADE OF THE HARDEST SUBSTANCE KNOWN WITH WHICH I QUICKLY CATCH AND BOUNCE AWAY THE BULLETS!
RAT-TAT TAT! POW-POW
PING
SPANG
SPANG
SPANG
ZING
FATHER
3 SHOTS FOR 5¢ WIN A DOLL!
WAIT A MINUTE! WAIT A MINUTE! ISN'T THIS STORY GETTING KIND OF RIDICULOUS?
MISS TOMATO PIE
LOOK!... GRANTED THESE BRACELETS ARE MADE OF SOME FANTASTICALLY HARD SUBSTANCE! GRANTED THAT YOU MIGHT EVEN BE ABLE TO CATCH BULLETS. (HEAVEN KNOWS HOW)!
WE ARE NOT A 3-D DRAWING!
...GRANTED ALL THIS, I MAINTAIN IT IS BOTH PHYSICALLY AND MATHEMATICALLY IMPOSSIBLE FOR YOU TO WITHSTAND THE IMPACT OF POINT-BLANK BULLETS WITHOUT GETTING KNOCKED OVER OR SHATTERING YOUR WRISTS!
...AND I QUIT THIS STORY UNTIL IT MAKES MORE SENSE!
NIVLEM! YOU ARE RIGHT! REASON WINS OVER ALL!...I THROW AWAY THESE RIDICULOUS BRACELETS!
WOMAN WONDER! I BOW TO YOU! I GIVE YOU MY PLEDGE THAT IN RETURN FOR YOUR GENTLEMANLY CONDUCT I SHALL NOT HURT YOU! ... I SHALL NOT HARM A HAIR ON YOUR FURSHLUGGINER HEAD!
SMITH BROS
COUGH DROPS
I SHALL NOT HURT YOU!
...ONLY MY BOYS SHALL!
GET HER, MICKEY! ... GET HER, SPILLANE!
... WITH DISPATCH, MR. NIVLEM!
...AND WITH DISBRASS KNUCKLES, MR. NIVLEM!
POW
SPLAT

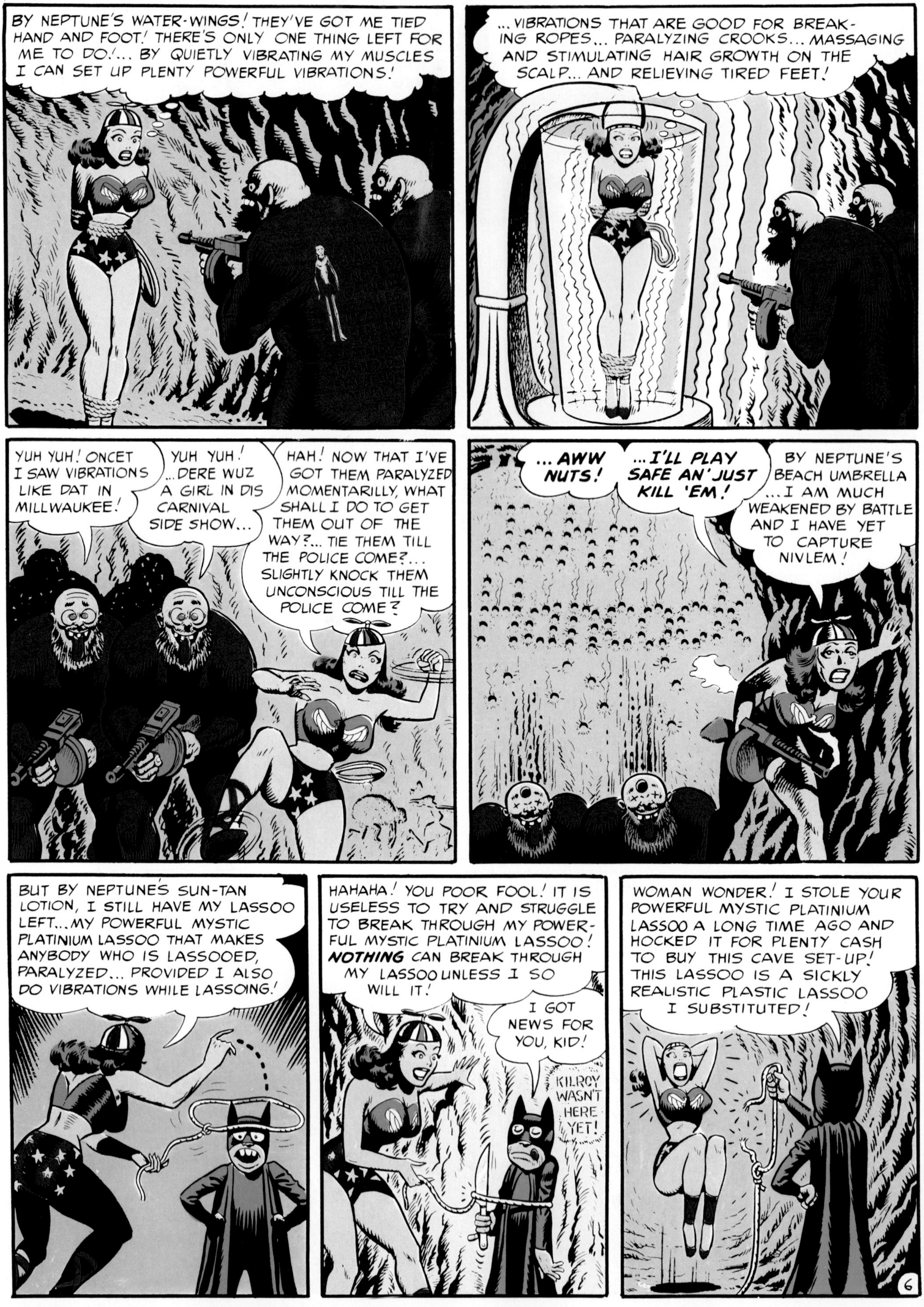

BY NEPTUNE'S WATER-WINGS! THEY'VE GOT ME TIED HAND AND FOOT! THERE'S ONLY ONE THING LEFT FOR ME TO DO!... BY QUIETLY VIBRATING MY MUSCLES I CAN SET UP PLENTY POWERFUL VIBRATIONS!
...VIBRATIONS THAT ARE GOOD FOR BREAKING ROPES... PARALYZING CROOKS... MASSAGING AND STIMULATING HAIR GROWTH ON THE SCALP... AND RELIEVING TIRED FEET!
YUH YUH! ONCET I SAW VIBRATIONS LIKE DAT IN MILLWAUKEE!
YUH YUH! ...DERE WUZ A GIRL IN DIS CARNIVAL SIDE SHOW...
HAH! NOW THAT I'VE GOT THEM PARALYZED MOMENTARILLY, WHAT SHALL I DO TO GET THEM OUT OF THE WAY?... TIE THEM TILL THE POLICE COME?... SLIGHTLY KNOCK THEM UNCONSCIOUS TILL THE POLICE COME?
...AWW NUTS!
...I'LL PLAY SAFE AN' JUST KILL 'EM!
BY NEPTUNE'S BEACH UMBRELLA ...I AM MUCH WEAKENED BY BATTLE AND I HAVE YET TO CAPTURE NIVLEM!
BUT BY NEPTUNE'S SUN-TAN LOTION, I STILL HAVE MY LASSOO LEFT...MY POWERFUL MYSTIC PLATINIUM LASSOO THAT MAKES ANYBODY WHO IS LASSOOED, PARALYZED... PROVIDED I ALSO DO VIBRATIONS WHILE LASSOING!
HAHAHA! YOU POOR FOOL! IT IS USELESS TO TRY AND STRUGGLE TO BREAK THROUGH MY POWERFUL MYSTIC PLATINIUM LASSOO! NOTHING CAN BREAK THROUGH MY LASSOO UNLESS I SO WILL IT!
I GOT NEWS FOR YOU, KID!
KILROY WASN'T HERE YET!
WOMAN WONDER! I STOLE YOUR POWERFUL MYSTIC PLATINIUM LASSOO A LONG TIME AGO AND HOCKED IT FOR PLENTY CASH TO BUY THIS CAVE SET-UP! THIS LASSOO IS A SICKLY REALISTIC PLASTIC LASSOO I SUBSTITUTED!
6

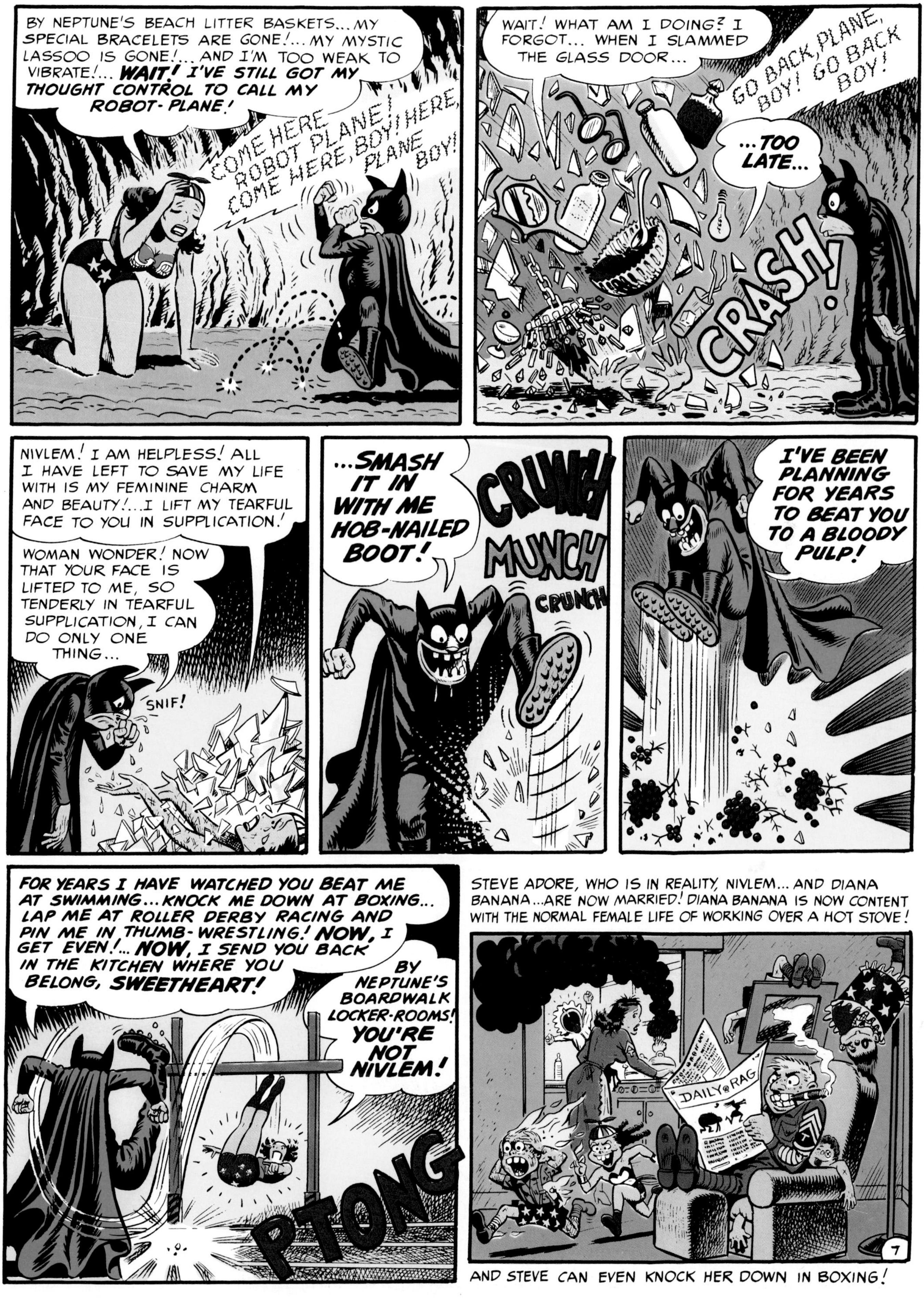
BY NEPTUNE'S BEACH LITTER BASKETS... MY SPECIAL BRACELETS ARE GONE!... MY MYSTIC LASSOO IS GONE!... AND I'M TOO WEAK TO VIBRATE!... WAIT! I'VE STILL GOT MY THOUGHT CONTROL TO CALL MY ROBOT-PLANE!
COME HERE ROBOT PLANE! COME HERE, BOY! HERE, PLANE BOY!
WAIT! WHAT AM I DOING? I FORGOT... WHEN I SLAMMED THE GLASS DOOR...
GO BACK, PLANE, BOY! GO BACK BOY!
...TOO LATE...
CRASH!
NIVLEM! I AM HELPLESS! ALL I HAVE LEFT TO SAVE MY LIFE WITH IS MY FEMININE CHARM AND BEAUTY!... I LIFT MY TEARFUL FACE TO YOU IN SUPPLICATION!
WOMAN WONDER! NOW THAT YOUR FACE IS LIFTED TO ME, SO TENDERLY IN TEARFUL SUPPLICATION, I CAN DO ONLY ONE THING...
SNIF!
...SMASH IT IN WITH ME HOB-NAILED BOOT!
CRUNCH
MUNCH
CRUNCH
I'VE BEEN PLANNING FOR YEARS TO BEAT YOU TO A BLOODY PULP!
FOR YEARS I HAVE WATCHED YOU BEAT ME AT SWIMMING... KNOCK ME DOWN AT BOXING... LAP ME AT ROLLER DERBY RACING AND PIN ME IN THUMB-WRESTLING! NOW, I GET EVEN!... NOW, I SEND YOU BACK IN THE KITCHEN WHERE YOU BELONG, SWEETHEART!
BY NEPTUNE'S BOARDWALK LOCKER-ROOMS! YOU'RE NOT NIVLEM!
PTONG
STEVE ADORE, WHO IS IN REALITY, NIVLEM... AND DIANA BANANA ...ARE NOW MARRIED! DIANA BANANA IS NOW CONTENT WITH THE NORMAL FEMALE LIFE OF WORKING OVER A HOT STOVE!
DAILY RAG
7
AND STEVE CAN EVEN KNOCK HER DOWN IN BOXING!

BATMAN & ROBIN

OUTTAKE #621: THE KISS

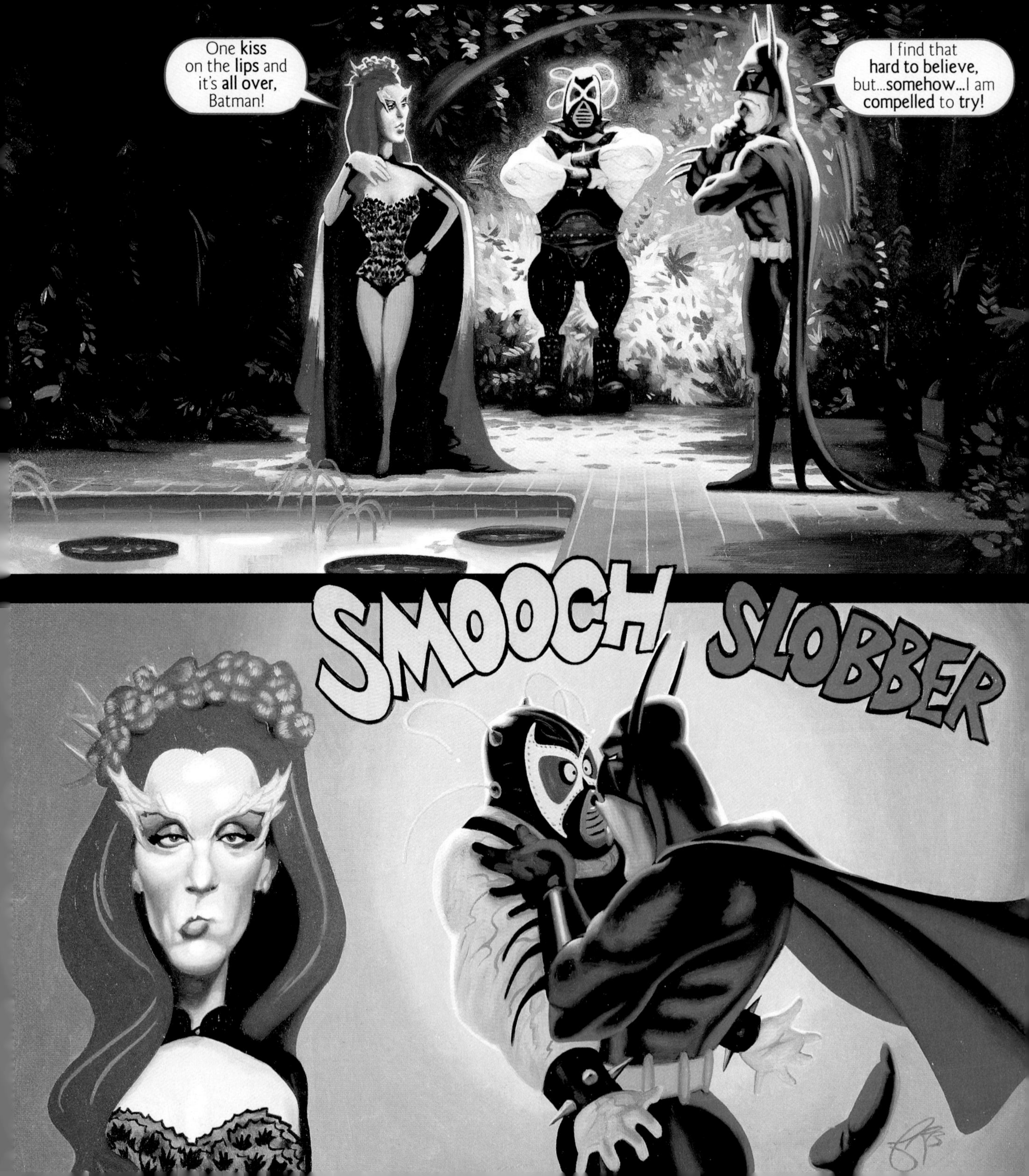
One kiss on the lips and it's all over, Batman!
I find that hard to believe, but...somehow...I am compelled to try!
SMOOCH
SLOBBER

Leonardo! Michelangelo! Donatello! Raphael! Famous painters? Hmm ...yes! But they're also the names of some pizza-chomping reptiles! Well, move over, you shelled schmucks! Here's

MAD'S GALLERY OF LESSER-KNOWN NINJA TURTLES

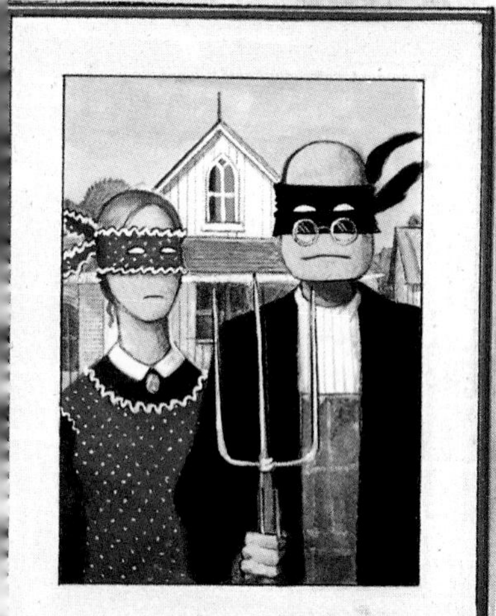
GRANNO & WOODO

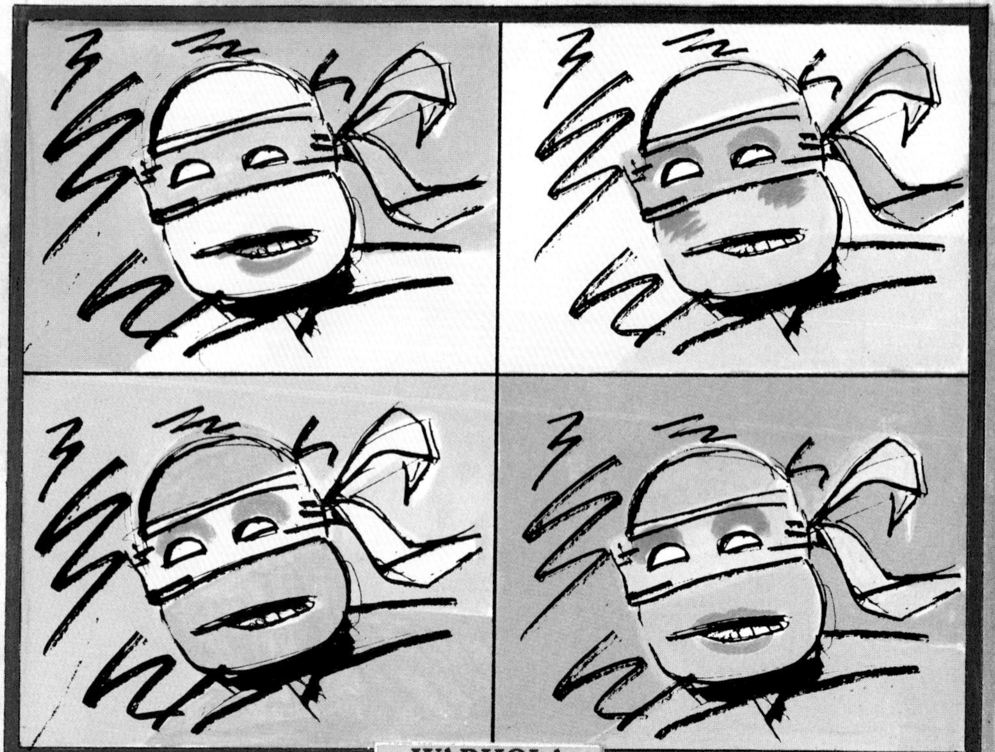
WARHOLA

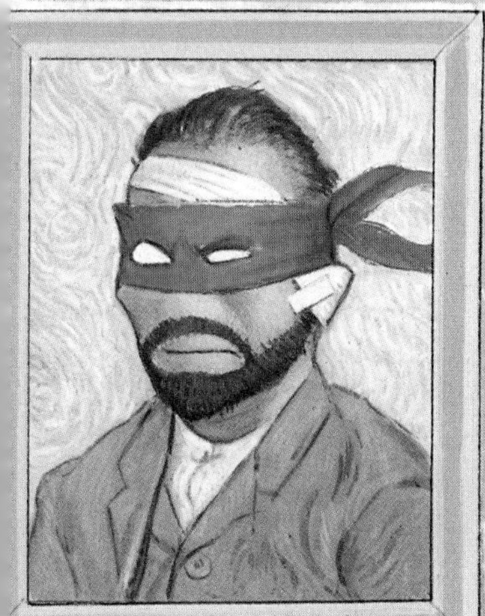
VINCENZO

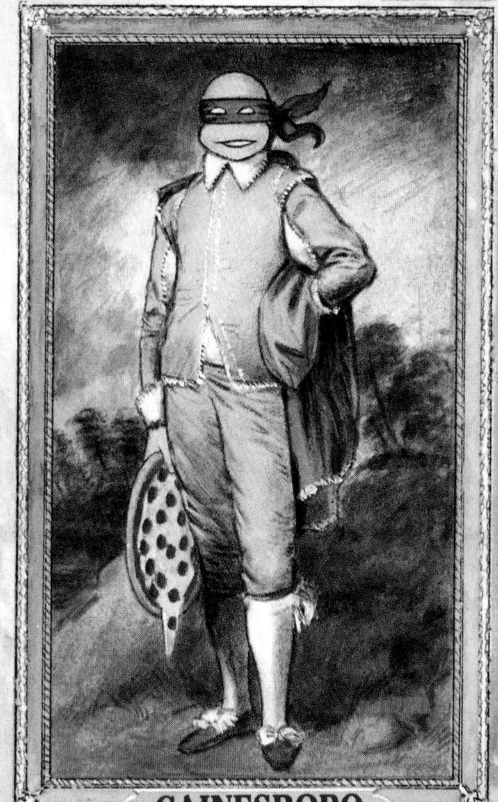
GAINESBORO

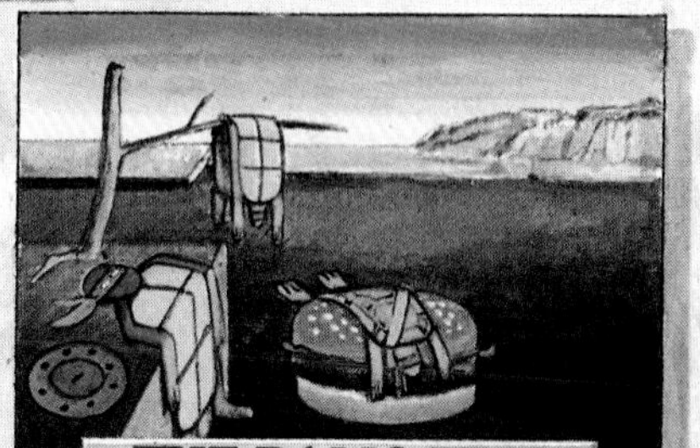
THE DALIO TRIO

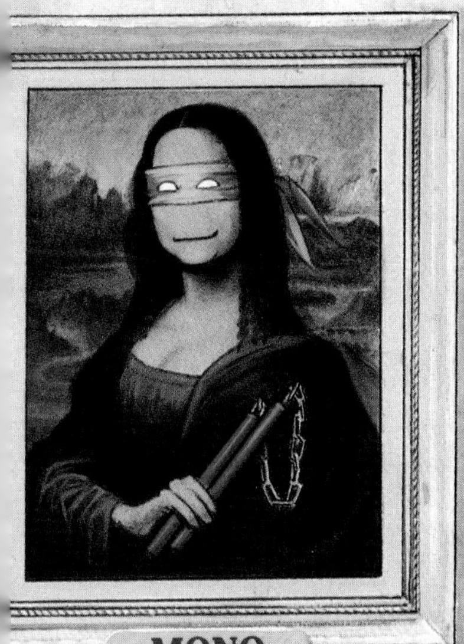
MONO

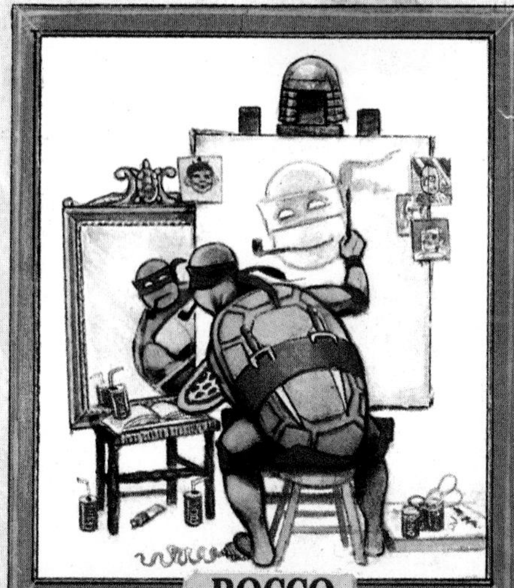
ROCCO

ARTIST: GREG THEAKSTON WRITER: MIKE SNIDER

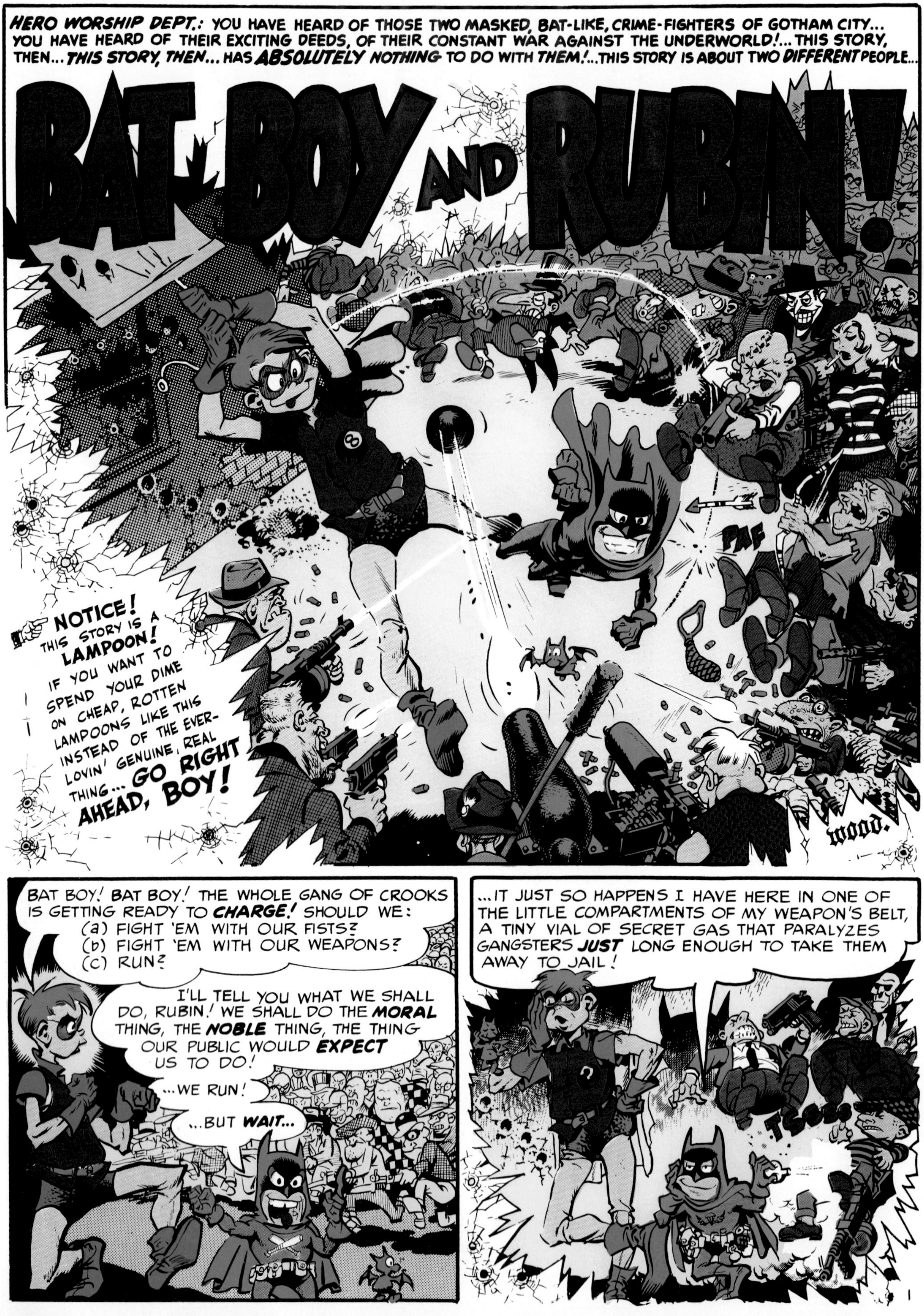
HERO WORSHIP DEPT.: YOU HAVE HEARD OF THOSE TWO MASKED, BAT-LIKE, CRIME-FIGHTERS OF GOTHAM CITY... YOU HAVE HEARD OF THEIR EXCITING DEEDS, OF THEIR CONSTANT WAR AGAINST THE UNDERWORLD!... THIS STORY, THEN... THIS STORY, THEN... HAS ABSOLUTELY NOTHING TO DO WITH THEM!... THIS STORY IS ABOUT TWO DIFFERENT PEOPLE...
BAT BOY AND RUBIN!
PAF
NOTICE! THIS STORY IS A LAMPOON! IF YOU WANT TO SPEND YOUR DIME ON CHEAP, ROTTEN LAMPOONS LIKE THIS INSTEAD OF THE EVER-LOVIN' GENUINE, REAL THING... GO RIGHT AHEAD, BOY!
wood.
BAT BOY! BAT BOY! THE WHOLE GANG OF CROOKS IS GETTING READY TO CHARGE! SHOULD WE: (a) FIGHT 'EM WITH OUR FISTS? (b) FIGHT 'EM WITH OUR WEAPONS? (c) RUN?
I'LL TELL YOU WHAT WE SHALL DO, RUBIN! WE SHALL DO THE MORAL THING, THE NOBLE THING, THE THING OUR PUBLIC WOULD EXPECT US TO DO!
...WE RUN!
...BUT WAIT...
...IT JUST SO HAPPENS I HAVE HERE IN ONE OF THE LITTLE COMPARTMENTS OF MY WEAPON'S BELT, A TINY VIAL OF SECRET GAS THAT PARALYZES GANGSTERS JUST LONG ENOUGH TO TAKE THEM AWAY TO JAIL!

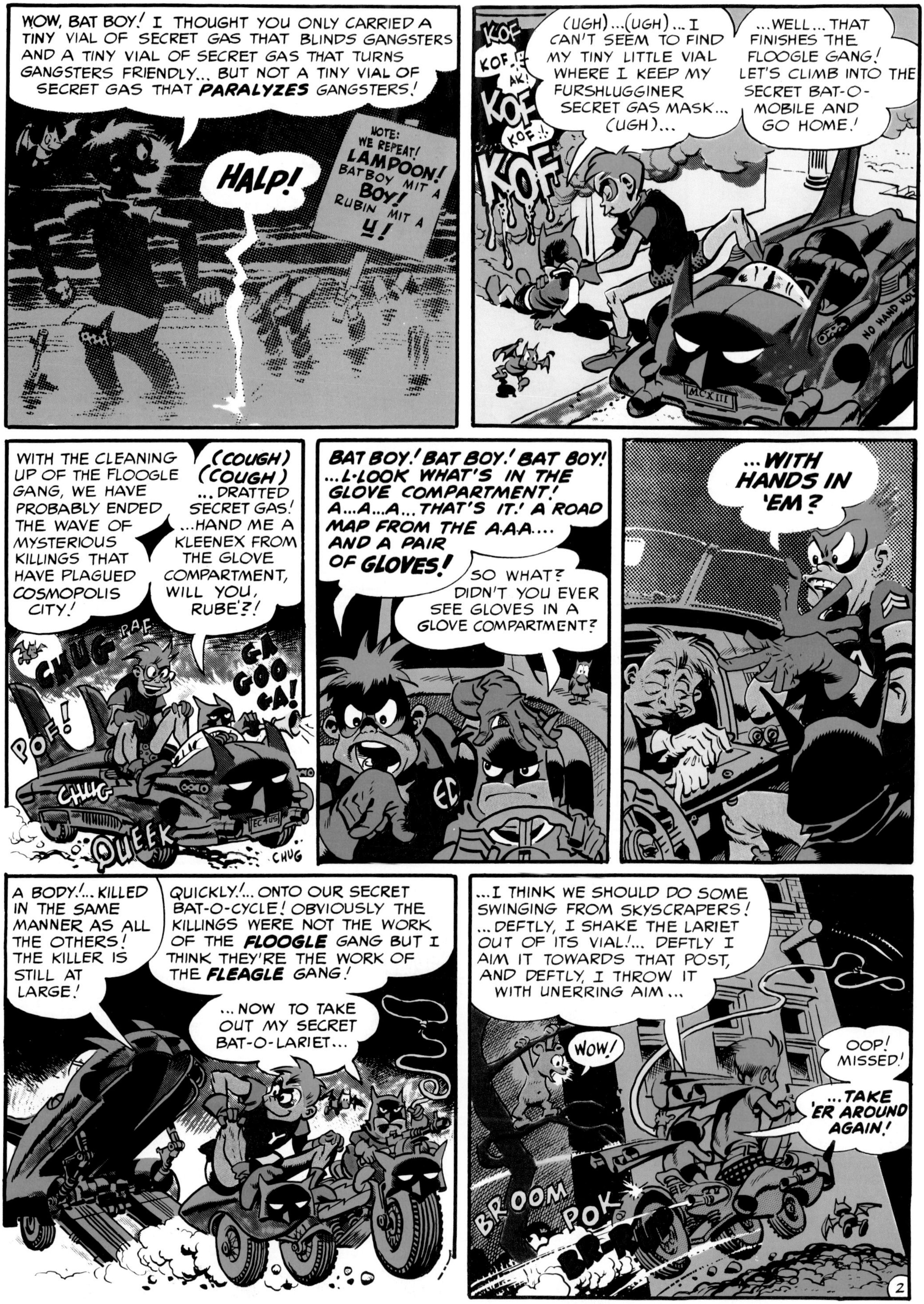
WOW, BAT BOY! I THOUGHT YOU ONLY CARRIED A TINY VIAL OF SECRET GAS THAT BLINDS GANGSTERS AND A TINY VIAL OF SECRET GAS THAT TURNS GANGSTERS FRIENDLY... BUT NOT A TINY VIAL OF SECRET GAS THAT PARALYZES GANGSTERS!
HALP!
NOTE: WE REPEAT! LAMPOON! BATBOY MIT A BOY! RUBIN MIT A U!
KOF KOF! AK! KOF KOF! KOF
(UGH)...(UGH)... I CAN'T SEEM TO FIND MY TINY LITTLE VIAL WHERE I KEEP MY FURSHLUGGINER SECRET GAS MASK... (UGH)...
...WELL... THAT FINISHES THE FLOOGLE GANG! LET'S CLIMB INTO THE SECRET BAT-O-MOBILE AND GO HOME!
NO HAND HOLD
MCXIII
WITH THE CLEANING UP OF THE FLOOGLE GANG, WE HAVE PROBABLY ENDED THE WAVE OF MYSTERIOUS KILLINGS THAT HAVE PLAGUED COSMOPOLIS CITY!
(COUGH) (COUGH) ...DRATTED SECRET GAS! ...HAND ME A KLEENEX FROM THE GLOVE COMPARTMENT, WILL YOU, RUBE?!
CHUG PAF
GA GOO GA!
POF!
CHUG
EC4US
QUEEK
CHUG
BAT BOY! BAT BOY! BAT BOY! ...L-LOOK WHAT'S IN THE GLOVE COMPARTMENT! A...A...A... THAT'S IT! A ROAD MAP FROM THE A.A.A.... AND A PAIR OF GLOVES!
SO WHAT? DIDN'T YOU EVER SEE GLOVES IN A GLOVE COMPARTMENT?
EC
...WITH HANDS IN 'EM?
A BODY!... KILLED IN THE SAME MANNER AS ALL THE OTHERS! THE KILLER IS STILL AT LARGE!
QUICKLY!... ONTO OUR SECRET BAT-O-CYCLE! OBVIOUSLY THE KILLINGS WERE NOT THE WORK OF THE FLOOGLE GANG BUT I THINK THEY'RE THE WORK OF THE FLEAGLE GANG!
...NOW TO TAKE OUT MY SECRET BAT-O-LARIET...
...I THINK WE SHOULD DO SOME SWINGING FROM SKYSCRAPERS! ...DEFTLY, I SHAKE THE LARIET OUT OF ITS VIAL!... DEFTLY I AIM IT TOWARDS THAT POST, AND DEFTLY, I THROW IT WITH UNERRING AIM...
WOW!
OOP! MISSED!
...TAKE 'ER AROUND AGAIN!
BROOM
POK

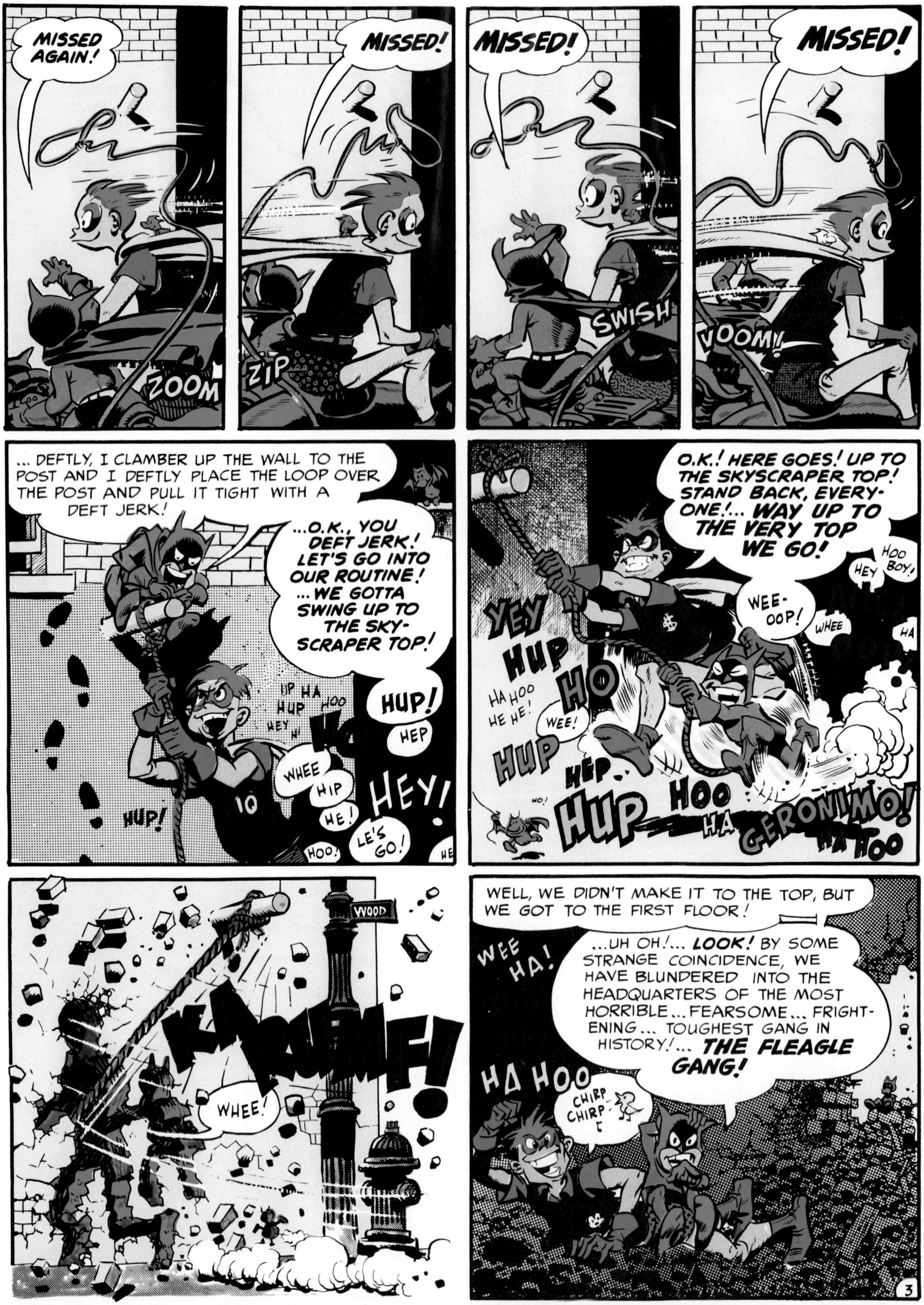
MISSED AGAIN!
ZOOM
MISSED!
ZIP
MISSED!
SWISH
MISSED!
VOOM!
... DEFTLY, I CLAMBER UP THE WALL TO THE POST AND I DEFTLY PLACE THE LOOP OVER THE POST AND PULL IT TIGHT WITH A DEFT JERK!
...O.K., YOU DEFT JERK! LET'S GO INTO OUR ROUTINE! ...WE GOTTA SWING UP TO THE SKY-SCRAPER TOP!
UP HA HUP HOO HEY HI
HUP!
HO
HEP
WHEE
HIP
HE!
HEY!
HUP!
HOO!
LE'S GO!
O.K.! HERE GOES! UP TO THE SKYSCRAPER TOP! STAND BACK, EVERY-ONE!... WAY UP TO THE VERY TOP WE GO!
HOO BOY!
HEY
WEE-OOP!
WHEE
HA
YEY
HUP
HO
HA HOO HE HE!
WEE!
HUP
HEP
NO!
HUP
HOO
HA
GERONIMO!
HA HOO
WOOD
KA-RUMF!
WHEE!
WELL, WE DIDN'T MAKE IT TO THE TOP, BUT WE GOT TO THE FIRST FLOOR!
WEE HA!
...UH OH!... LOOK! BY SOME STRANGE COINCIDENCE, WE HAVE BLUNDERED INTO THE HEADQUARTERS OF THE MOST HORRIBLE... FEARSOME... FRIGHT-ENING... TOUGHEST GANG IN HISTORY!... THE FLEAGLE GANG!
HA HOO
CHIRP CHIRP

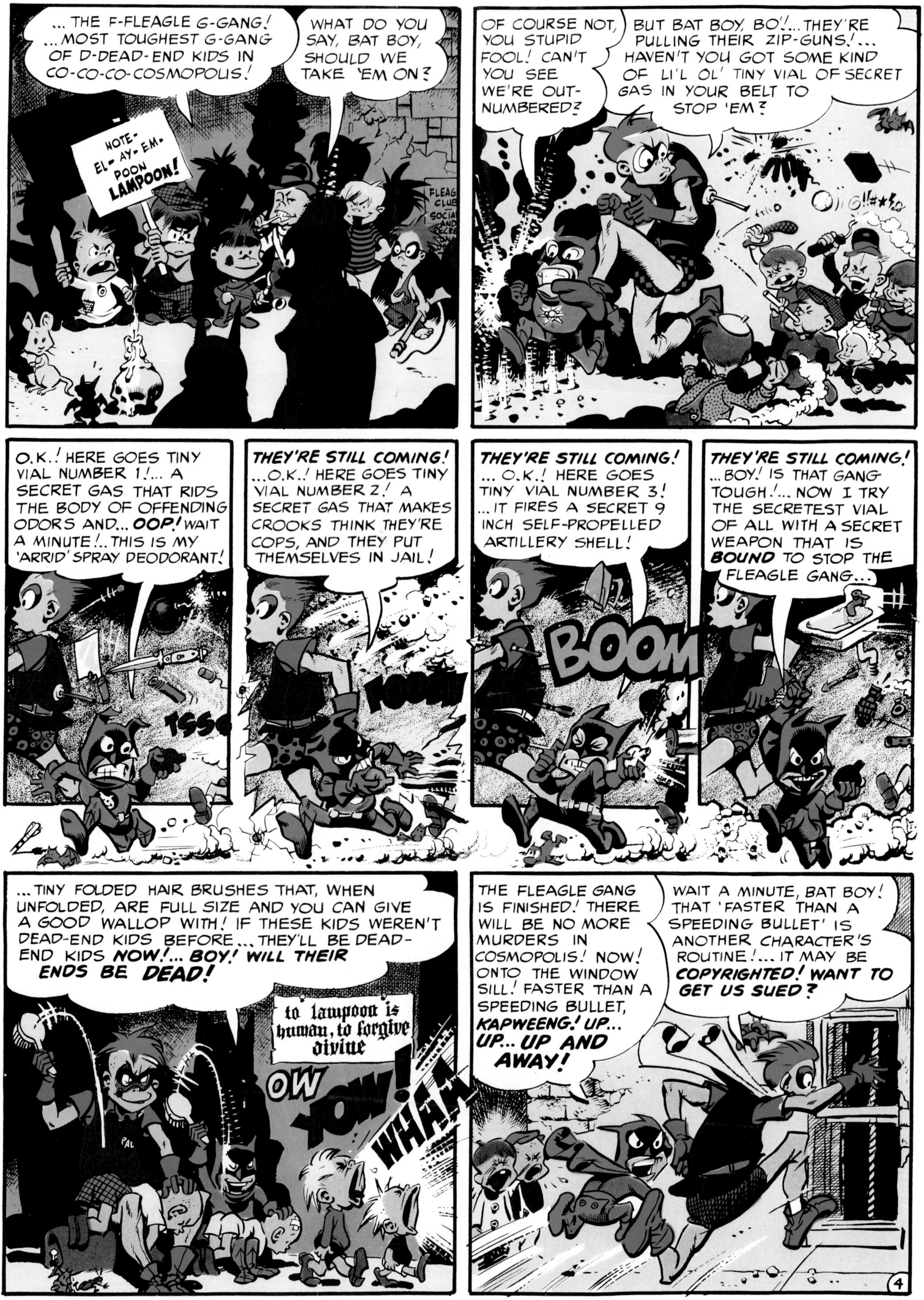

... THE F-FLEAGLE G-GANG! ...MOST TOUGHEST G-GANG OF D-DEAD-END KIDS IN CO-CO-CO-COSMOPOLIS!
WHAT DO YOU SAY, BAT BOY, SHOULD WE TAKE 'EM ON?
HOTE-EL-AY-EM-POON LAMPOON!
OF COURSE NOT, YOU STUPID FOOL! CAN'T YOU SEE WE'RE OUT-NUMBERED?
BUT BAT BOY, BO'! ...THEY'RE PULLING THEIR ZIP-GUNS! ...HAVEN'T YOU GOT SOME KIND OF LI'L OL' TINY VIAL OF SECRET GAS IN YOUR BELT TO STOP 'EM?
O.K.! HERE GOES TINY VIAL NUMBER 1! ... A SECRET GAS THAT RIDS THE BODY OF OFFENDING ODORS AND... OOP! WAIT A MINUTE! ..THIS IS MY 'ARRID' SPRAY DEODORANT!
THEY'RE STILL COMING! ...O.K.! HERE GOES TINY VIAL NUMBER 2! A SECRET GAS THAT MAKES CROOKS THINK THEY'RE COPS, AND THEY PUT THEMSELVES IN JAIL!
THEY'RE STILL COMING! ... O.K.! HERE GOES TINY VIAL NUMBER 3! ...IT FIRES A SECRET 9 INCH SELF-PROPELLED ARTILLERY SHELL!
BOOM
THEY'RE STILL COMING! ...BOY! IS THAT GANG TOUGH! ... NOW I TRY THE SECRETEST VIAL OF ALL WITH A SECRET WEAPON THAT IS BOUND TO STOP THE FLEAGLE GANG...
...TINY FOLDED HAIR BRUSHES THAT, WHEN UNFOLDED, ARE FULL SIZE AND YOU CAN GIVE A GOOD WALLOP WITH! IF THESE KIDS WEREN'T DEAD-END KIDS BEFORE... THEY'LL BE DEAD-END KIDS NOW! ... BOY! WILL THEIR ENDS BE DEAD!
to lampoon is human, to forgive divine
OW
YOW!
THE FLEAGLE GANG IS FINISHED! THERE WILL BE NO MORE MURDERS IN COSMOPOLIS! NOW! ONTO THE WINDOW SILL! FASTER THAN A SPEEDING BULLET, KAPWEENG! UP... UP... UP AND AWAY!
WAIT A MINUTE, BAT BOY! THAT 'FASTER THAN A SPEEDING BULLET' IS ANOTHER CHARACTER'S ROUTINE! ... IT MAY BE COPYRIGHTED! WANT TO GET US SUED?
4

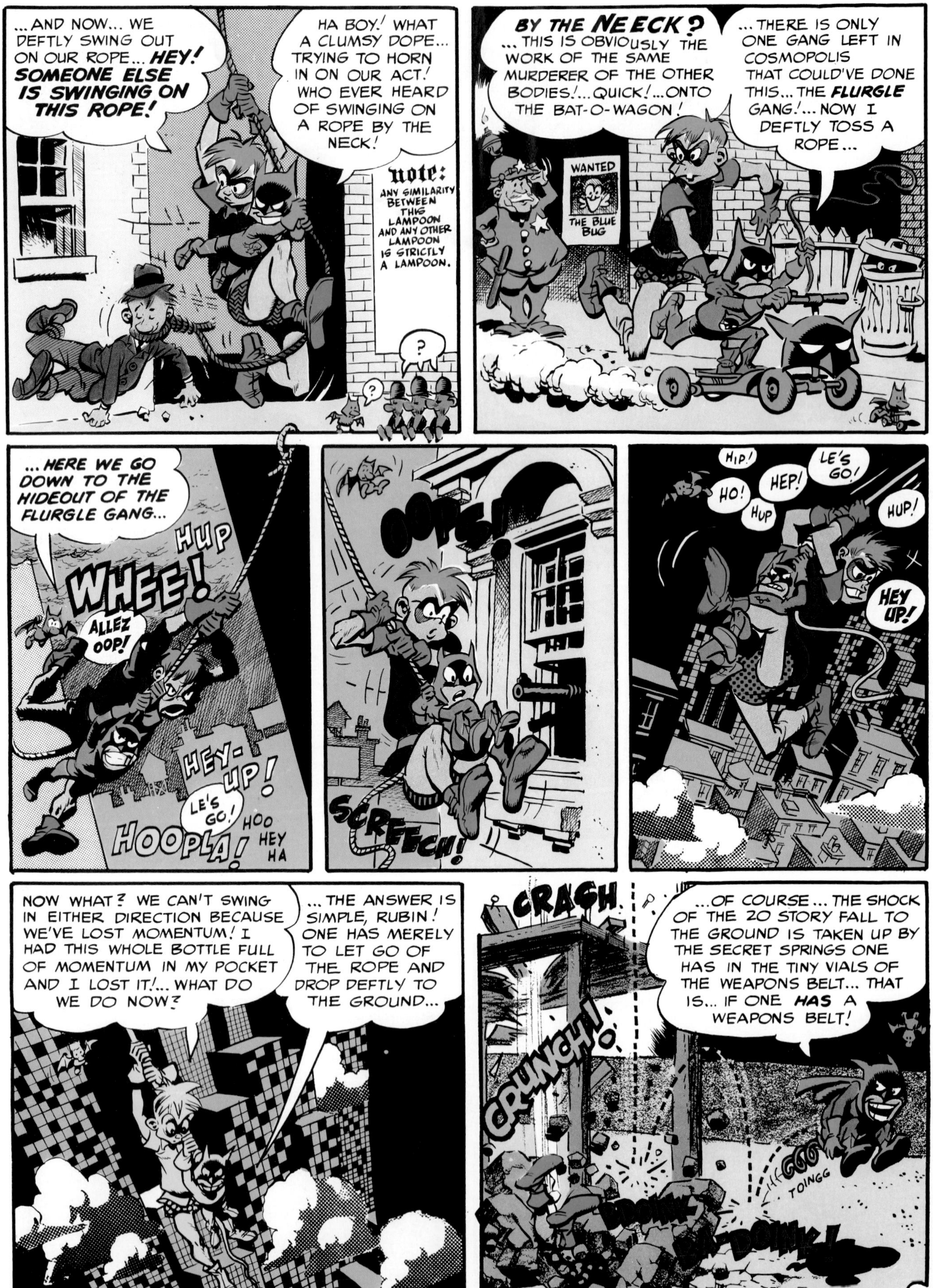
...AND NOW... WE DEFTLY SWING OUT ON OUR ROPE... HEY! SOMEONE ELSE IS SWINGING ON THIS ROPE!
HA BOY! WHAT A CLUMSY DOPE... TRYING TO HORN IN ON OUR ACT! WHO EVER HEARD OF SWINGING ON A ROPE BY THE NECK!
note: ANY SIMILARITY BETWEEN THIS LAMPOON AND ANY OTHER LAMPOON IS STRICTLY A LAMPOON.
?
?
BY THE NEECK? ...THIS IS OBVIOUSLY THE WORK OF THE SAME MURDERER OF THE OTHER BODIES!...QUICK!...ONTO THE BAT-O-WAGON!
WANTED
THE BLUE BUG
...THERE IS ONLY ONE GANG LEFT IN COSMOPOLIS THAT COULD'VE DONE THIS... THE FLURGLE GANG!... NOW I DEFTLY TOSS A ROPE...
...HERE WE GO DOWN TO THE HIDEOUT OF THE FLURGLE GANG...
HUP
WHEE!
ALLEZ OOP!
HEY-UP!
LE'S GO!
HOOPLA!
HOO HEY HA
OOPS!
SCREECH!
HIP!
HO!
HEP!
LE'S GO!
HUP
HUP!
HEY UP!
NOW WHAT? WE CAN'T SWING IN EITHER DIRECTION BECAUSE WE'VE LOST MOMENTUM! I HAD THIS WHOLE BOTTLE FULL OF MOMENTUM IN MY POCKET AND I LOST IT!... WHAT DO WE DO NOW?
...THE ANSWER IS SIMPLE, RUBIN! ONE HAS MERELY TO LET GO OF THE ROPE AND DROP DEFTLY TO THE GROUND...
CRASH
CRUNCH!
...OF COURSE... THE SHOCK OF THE 20 STORY FALL TO THE GROUND IS TAKEN UP BY THE SECRET SPRINGS ONE HAS IN THE TINY VIALS OF THE WEAPONS BELT... THAT IS... IF ONE HAS A WEAPONS BELT!
TOINGG
BA-DOINK!

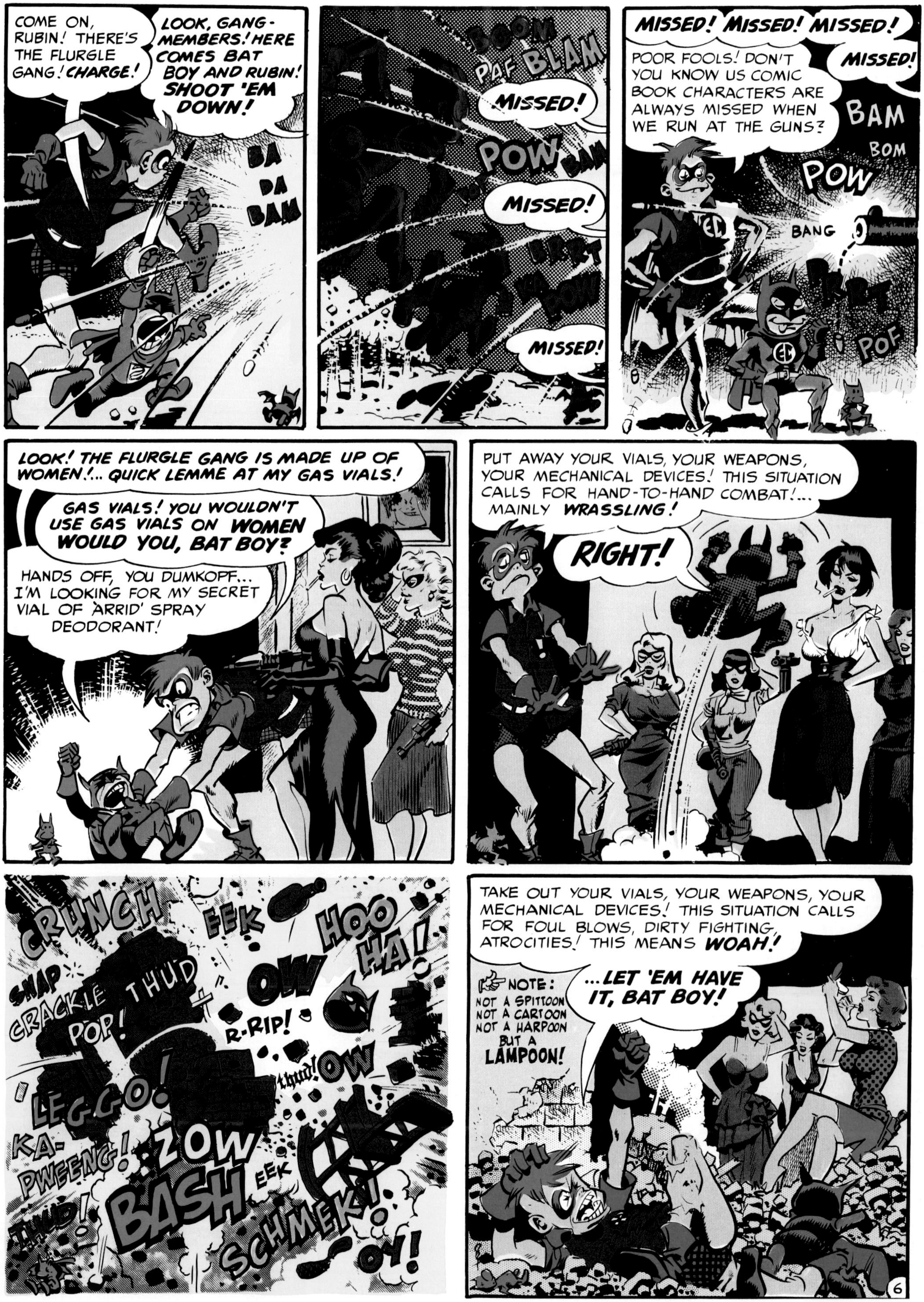

COME ON, RUBIN! THERE'S THE FLURGLE GANG! CHARGE!
LOOK, GANG-MEMBERS! HERE COMES BAT BOY AND RUBIN! SHOOT 'EM DOWN!
BA DA BAM
BOOM
PAF BLAM
MISSED!
POW
MISSED!
MISSED!
MISSED! MISSED! MISSED!
POOR FOOLS! DON'T YOU KNOW US COMIC BOOK CHARACTERS ARE ALWAYS MISSED WHEN WE RUN AT THE GUNS?
MISSED!
BAM
BOM
POW
BANG
POF
LOOK! THE FLURGLE GANG IS MADE UP OF WOMEN!... QUICK LEMME AT MY GAS VIALS!
GAS VIALS! YOU WOULDN'T USE GAS VIALS ON WOMEN WOULD YOU, BAT BOY?
HANDS OFF, YOU DUMKOPF... I'M LOOKING FOR MY SECRET VIAL OF 'ARRID' SPRAY DEODORANT!
PUT AWAY YOUR VIALS, YOUR WEAPONS, YOUR MECHANICAL DEVICES! THIS SITUATION CALLS FOR HAND-TO-HAND COMBAT!... MAINLY WRASSLING!
RIGHT!
CRUNCH
EEK
HOO HA!
SNAP
CRACKLE
POP!
THUD
OW
R-RIP!
thud!
OW
LEGGO!
KA-PWEENG!
ZOW
BASH
EEK
THUD!
SCHMEK!
OY!
TAKE OUT YOUR VIALS, YOUR WEAPONS, YOUR MECHANICAL DEVICES! THIS SITUATION CALLS FOR FOUL BLOWS, DIRTY FIGHTING, ATROCITIES! THIS MEANS WOAH!
...LET 'EM HAVE IT, BAT BOY!
NOTE: NOT A SPITTOON NOT A CARTOON NOT A HARPOON BUT A LAMPOON!

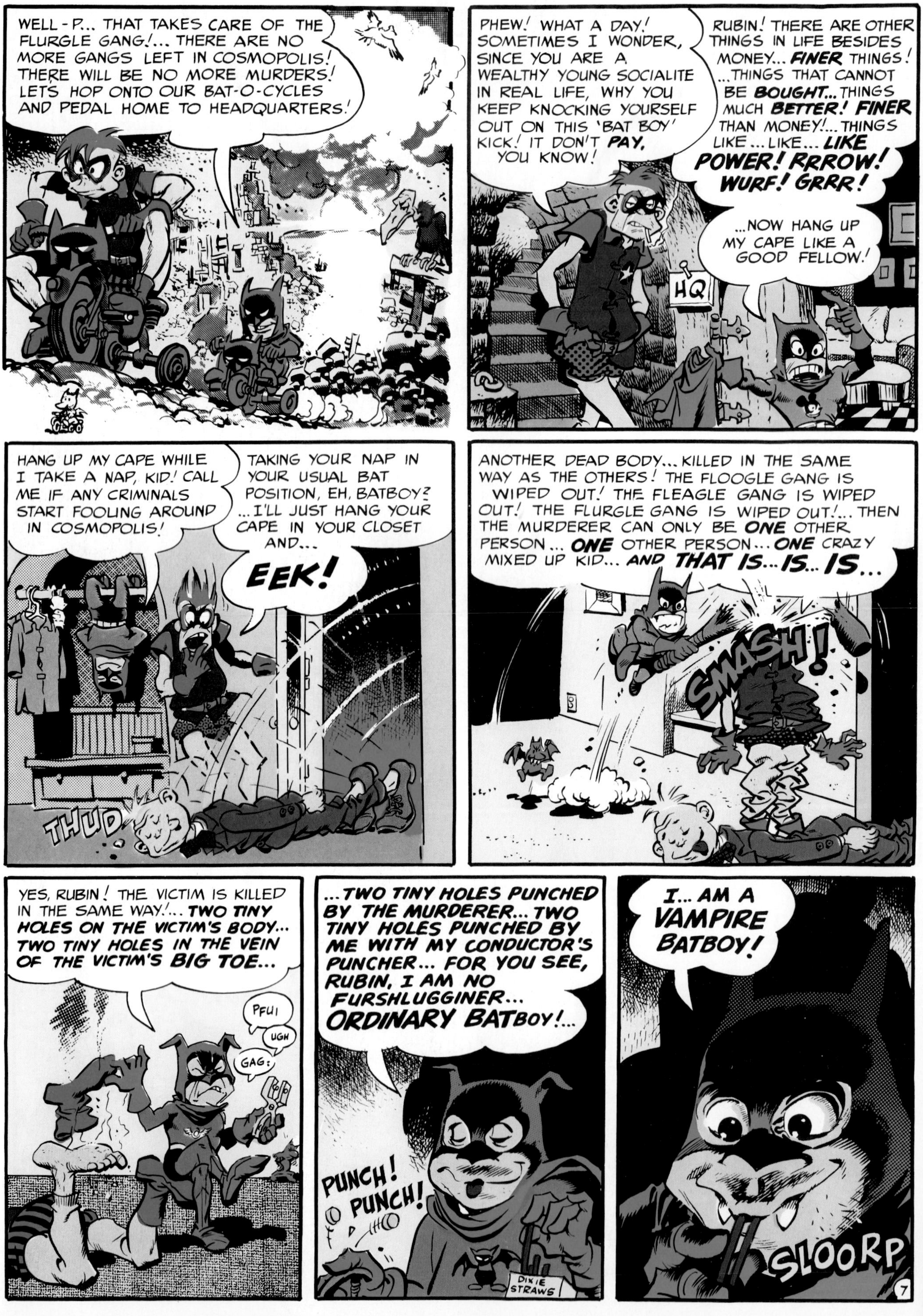
WELL-P... THAT TAKES CARE OF THE FLURGLE GANG!... THERE ARE NO MORE GANGS LEFT IN COSMOPOLIS! THERE WILL BE NO MORE MURDERS! LETS HOP ONTO OUR BAT-O-CYCLES AND PEDAL HOME TO HEADQUARTERS!
PHEW! WHAT A DAY! SOMETIMES I WONDER, SINCE YOU ARE A WEALTHY YOUNG SOCIALITE IN REAL LIFE, WHY YOU KEEP KNOCKING YOURSELF OUT ON THIS 'BAT BOY' KICK! IT DON'T **PAY,** YOU KNOW!
RUBIN! THERE ARE OTHER THINGS IN LIFE BESIDES MONEY... **FINER** THINGS! ...THINGS THAT CANNOT BE **BOUGHT...** THINGS MUCH **BETTER! FINER** THAN MONEY!... THINGS LIKE... LIKE... **LIKE POWER! RRROW! WURF! GRRR!**
...NOW HANG UP MY CAPE LIKE A GOOD FELLOW!
HQ
HANG UP MY CAPE WHILE I TAKE A NAP, KID! CALL ME IF ANY CRIMINALS START FOOLING AROUND IN COSMOPOLIS!
TAKING YOUR NAP IN YOUR USUAL BAT POSITION, EH, BATBOY? ...I'LL JUST HANG YOUR CAPE IN YOUR CLOSET AND...
EEK!
THUD
ANOTHER DEAD BODY... KILLED IN THE SAME WAY AS THE OTHERS! THE FLOOGLE GANG IS WIPED OUT! THE FLEAGLE GANG IS WIPED OUT! THE FLURGLE GANG IS WIPED OUT!... THEN THE MURDERER CAN ONLY BE **ONE** OTHER PERSON... **ONE** OTHER PERSON... **ONE** CRAZY MIXED UP KID... **AND THAT IS... IS... IS...**
SMASH!
YES, RUBIN! THE VICTIM IS KILLED IN THE SAME WAY!... **TWO TINY HOLES ON THE VICTIM'S BODY... TWO TINY HOLES IN THE VEIN OF THE VICTIM'S BIG TOE...**
PFUI
UGH
GAG!
...TWO TINY HOLES PUNCHED BY THE MURDERER... TWO TINY HOLES PUNCHED BY ME WITH MY CONDUCTOR'S PUNCHER... FOR YOU SEE, RUBIN, I AM NO FURSHLUGGINER... ORDINARY BATBOY!...
PUNCH! PUNCH!
DIXIE STRAWS
I... AM A VAMPIRE BATBOY!
SLOORP

ONE RIP-ROARING DAY IN METROPOLIS

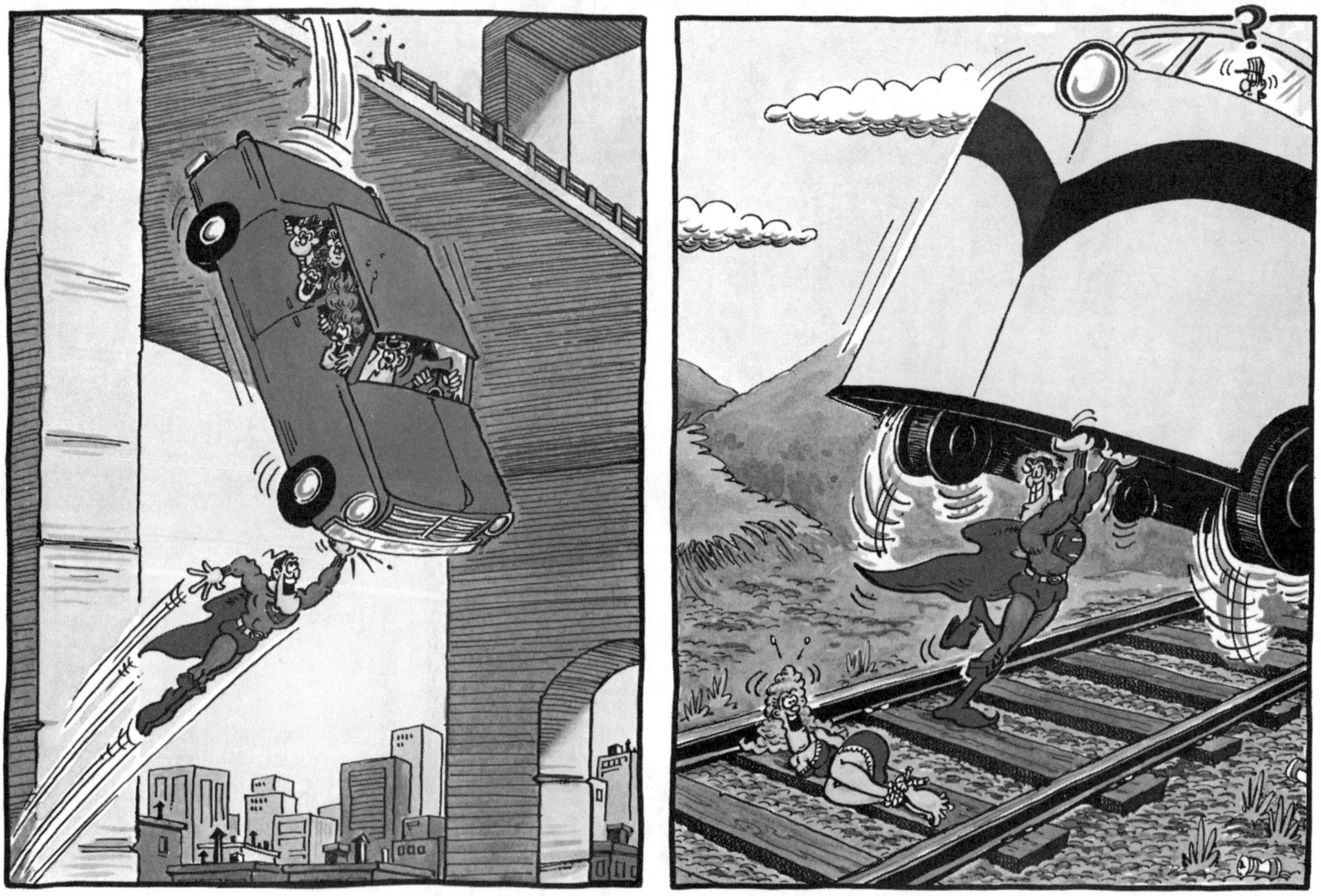

ARTIST: DON MARTIN WRITER: DON EDWING

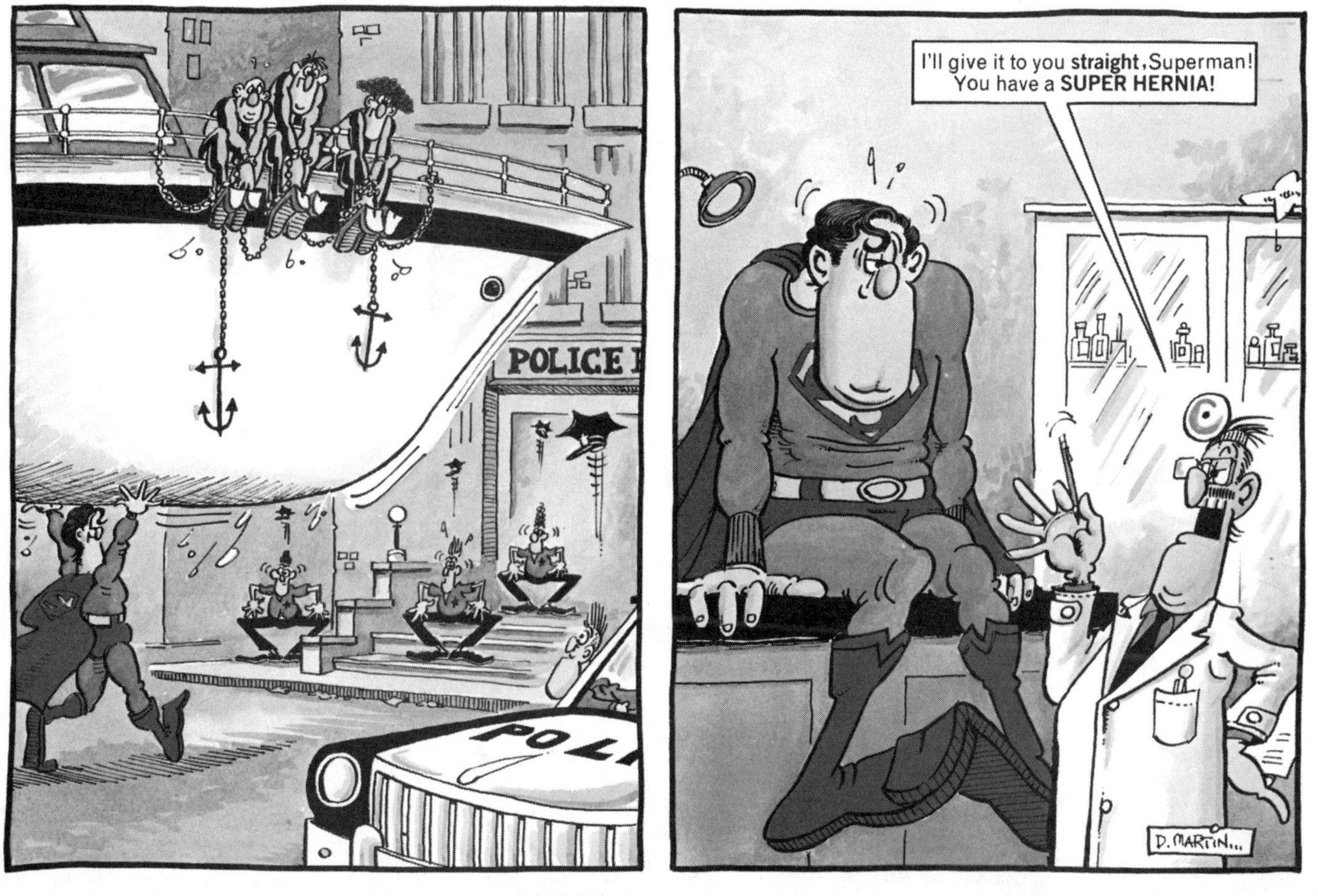
POLICE
I'll give it to you **straight**, Superman! You have a **SUPER HERNIA!**
D. MARTIN...

THE LAST SUPER DEPT.

Did "Superman I" drag a little? A little...?!? And did MAD's satire of that first film drag even more? Are you kidding...?!? And how about "Superman II"? It made you a little bit drow didn't it? And the MAD take-off of that film Close to Dullsville, right? Well, get ready

STUPORM

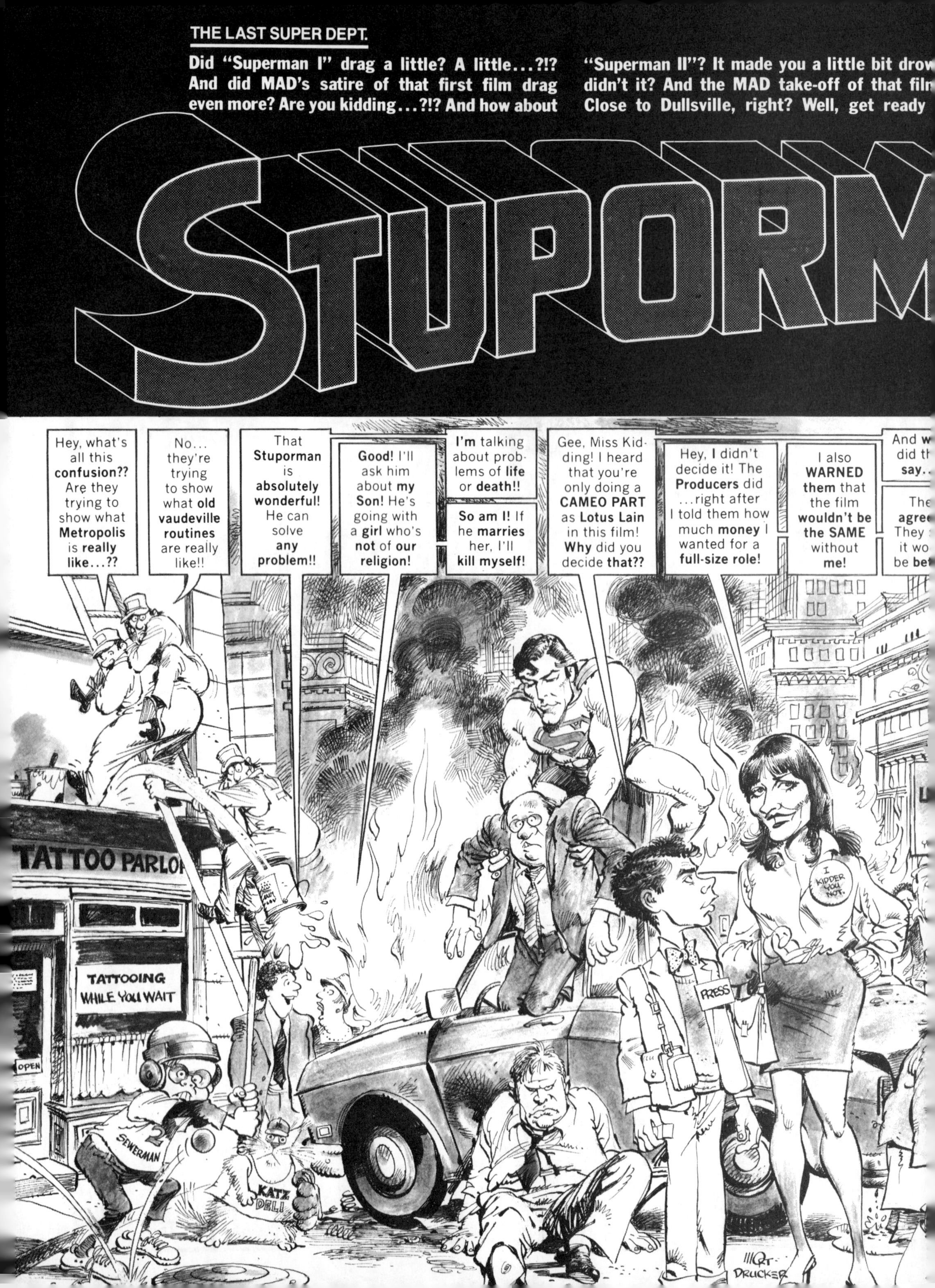

Hey, what's all this **confusion??** Are they trying to show what **Metropolis** is **really like...??**
No... they're trying to show what **old vaudeville routines** are really like!!
That **Stuporman** is **absolutely wonderful!** He can solve **any problem!!**
Good! I'll ask him about **my Son!** He's going with a **girl** who's **not of our religion!**
I'm talking about problems of **life** or **death!!**
So am I! If he **marries** her, I'll **kill myself!**
Gee, Miss Kidding! I heard that you're only doing a **CAMEO PART** as **Lotus Lain** in this film! **Why** did you decide **that??**
Hey, **I** didn't decide it! The **Producers** did ...right after I told them how much **money** I wanted for a **full-size role!**
I also **WARNED them** that the film **wouldn't be the SAME** without **me!**
And w did th say..
The agree They it wo be bet
TATTOO PARLO
TATTOOING WHILE YOU WAIT
OPEN
SEWERMAN
KATZ DELI
PRESS
I KIDDER YOU NOT.
MORT DRUCKER

uperman III"—the ultimate sleeping pill... the following satire of it...which should glehandedly transform the whole shebang into

ANZZZ

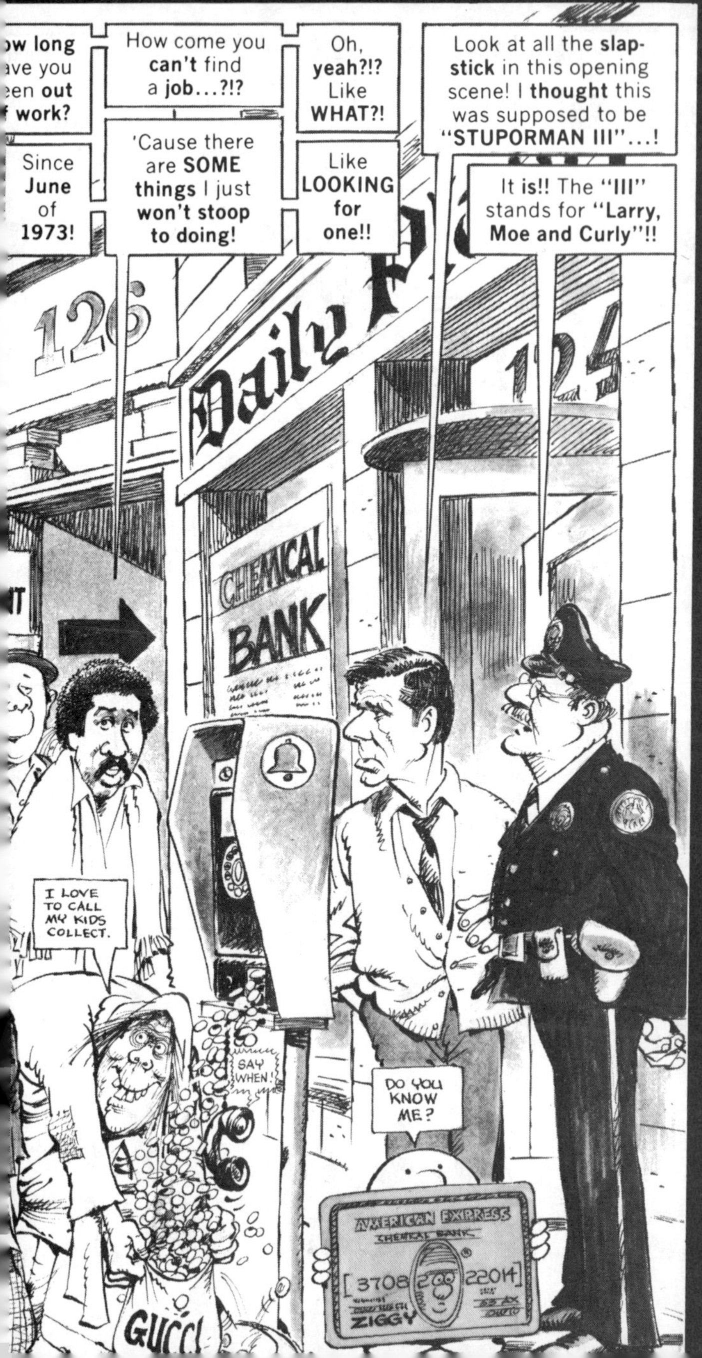

ow long ave you een out f work?
How come you can't find a job...?!?
Oh, yeah?!? Like WHAT?!
Look at all the slapstick in this opening scene! I thought this was supposed to be "STUPORMAN III"...!
Since June of 1973!
'Cause there are SOME things I just won't stoop to doing!
Like LOOKING for one!!
It is!! The "III" stands for "Larry, Moe and Curly"!!
126
Daily
CHEMICAL BANK
I LOVE TO CALL MY KIDS COLLECT.
SAY WHEN!
DO YOU KNOW ME?
AMERICAN EXPRESS
CHEMICAL BANK
3708
2201
ZIGGY
GUCCI

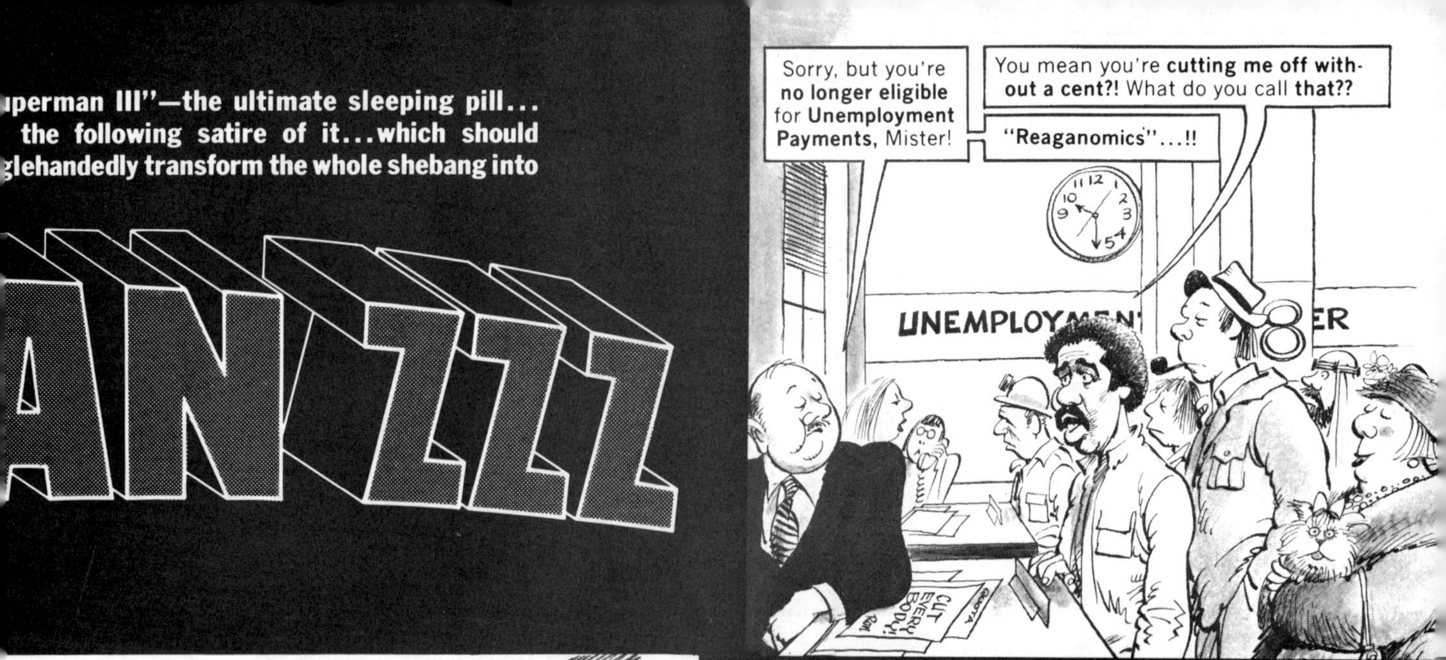

Sorry, but you're no longer eligible for Unemployment Payments, Mister!
You mean you're cutting me off without a cent?! What do you call that??
"Reaganomics"...!!
UNEMPLOYMEN ER
CUT EVERYBODY!

ARTIST: MORT DRUCKER WRITER: STAN HART

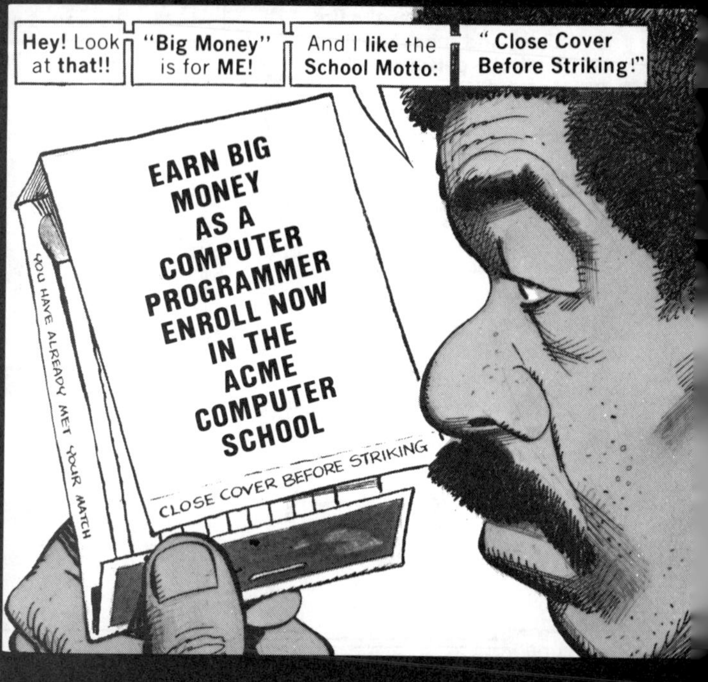

Hey! Look at that!!
"Big Money" is for ME!
And I like the School Motto:
"Close Cover Before Striking!"
EARN BIG MONEY AS A COMPUTER PROGRAMMER ENROLL NOW IN THE ACME COMPUTER SCHOOL
CLOSE COVER BEFORE STRIKING
YOU HAVE ALREADY MET YOUR MATCH

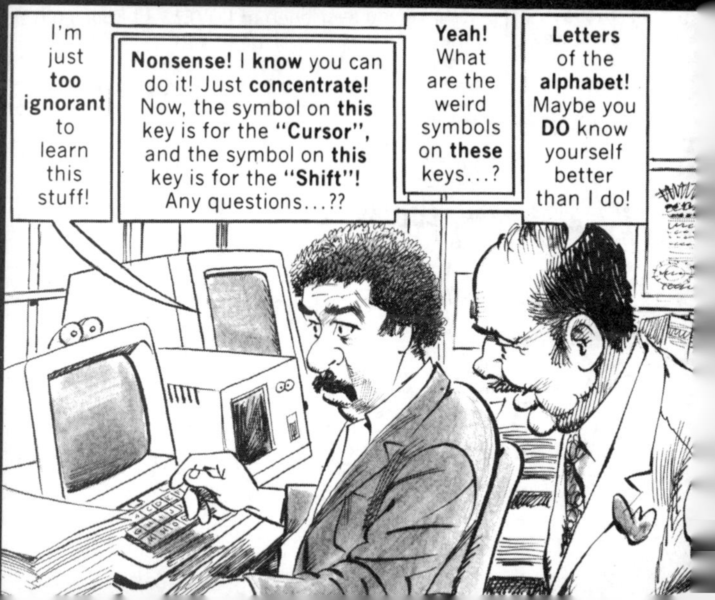

I'm just too ignorant to learn this stuff!
Nonsense! I know you can do it! Just concentrate! Now, the symbol on this key is for the "Cursor", and the symbol on this key is for the "Shift"! Any questions...??
Yeah! What are the weird symbols on these keys...?
Letters of the alphabet! Maybe you DO know yourself better than I do!

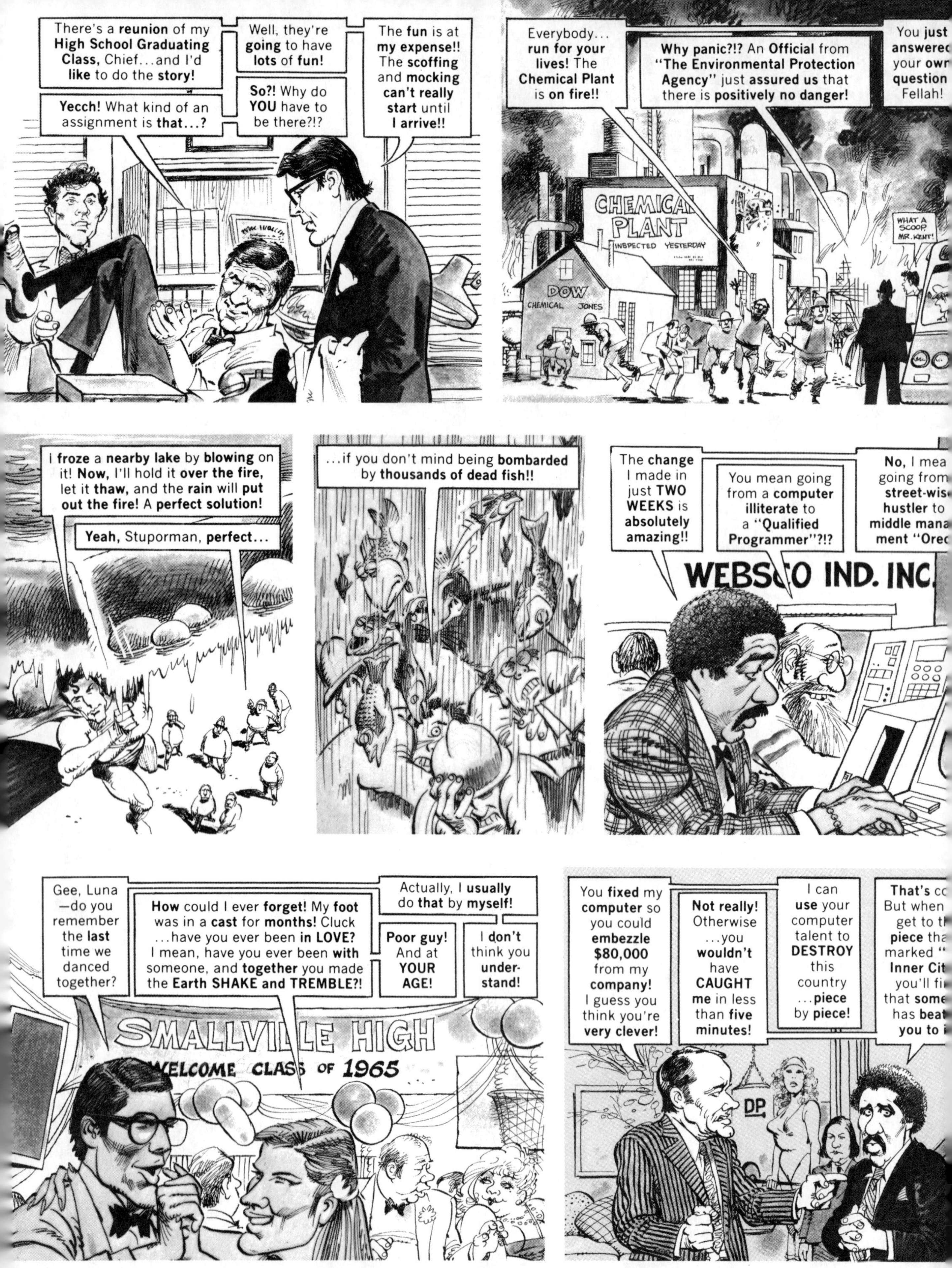

There's a **reunion** of my **High School Graduating Class,** Chief...and I'd **like** to do the **story!**
Yecch! What kind of an assignment is **that...?**
Well, they're **going** to have **lots** of **fun!**
So?! Why do **YOU** have to be there?!?
The **fun** is at **my expense!!** The **scoffing** and **mocking can't really start** until **I arrive!!**
Everybody... **run for your lives!** The **Chemical Plant is on fire!!**
Why panic?!? An **Official** from **"The Environmental Protection Agency"** just **assured us** that there is **positively no danger!**
You **just answered** your **own question** Fellah!
CHEMICAL PLANT
INSPECTED YESTERDAY
DOW CHEMICAL JONES
WHAT A SCOOP, MR. KENT!
I **froze** a **nearby lake** by **blowing** on it! **Now,** I'll hold it **over the fire,** let it **thaw,** and the **rain** will **put out the fire!** A **perfect solution!**
Yeah, Stuporman, **perfect...**
...if you don't mind being **bombarded** by **thousands of dead fish!!**
The **change** I made in just **TWO WEEKS** is **absolutely amazing!!**
You mean going from a **computer illiterate** to a **"Qualified Programmer"?!?**
No, I mea going from **street-wis hustler** to **middle mana** ment **"Orec**
WEBSCO IND. INC.
Gee, Luna—do you remember the **last** time we danced together?
How could I ever **forget!** My **foot** was in a **cast** for **months!** Cluck ...have you ever been **in LOVE?** I mean, have you ever been **with** someone, and **together** you made the **Earth SHAKE and TREMBLE?!**
Actually, I **usually** do **that** by **myself!**
Poor guy! And at **YOUR AGE!**
I **don't** think you **under-stand!**
SMALLVILLE HIGH
WELCOME CLASS OF 1965
You **fixed** my **computer** so you could **embezzle $80,000** from my **company!** I guess you think you're **very clever!**
Not really! Otherwise ...you **wouldn't** have **CAUGHT me** in less than **five minutes!**
I can **use** your computer talent to **DESTROY** this country ...**piece** by **piece!**
That's c But when get to t **piece** tha marked " **Inner Ci** you'll fi that **some** has **beat** you to i
DP

Now, **here's** my **plan!** I want you to **tap** into the **computer** that **controls** the **Weather Satellite** and **re-program** it so that it creates **tornadoes** and **torrential rains** in **Columbia!** That will **ruin** the **coffee crop,** causing a **world-wide shortage!** Meanwhile, **I'll** have **cornered** the **market** in **coffee!**

Ha-ha-ha! Nobody can **stop** my plan!!

That's cause **nobody** can **understand** it!!

I **hate** to ruin his **fun**...so I **won't tell him** that the **Weather Satellite** only **REPORTS** the weather, it **doesn't CONTROL** it!!

Mmm! Now that we're **alone,** Cluck... I wonder if **you're** as excited as **I am!**

Uh—of course, Luna, **Excuse me,** I'll be **right back!!**

Poor darling! Someday, you'll find out that **sex** is even **more fun** when you have it with **another person!**

Gee...**I know** the Government **gives subsidies** to **discourage excessive harvesting,** but who'd think they'd get so **tough** about **enforcing it?!**

The satellite caused a **tornado,** but Stuporman **dispersed** it! Then... after the **torrential rains**...he **dried up** the **entire coffee crop** with his **breath!** What could I **do...?!?**

He's **unbelievable!** We've got to **stop** him! **THINK**...!! What single thing will **finally get rid of Stuporman once** and for **all?!**

If they make "**Stuporman IV**"...**THAT** will do it **for sure!**

You're **right!!** But **KRAPTONITE** will be **faster!**

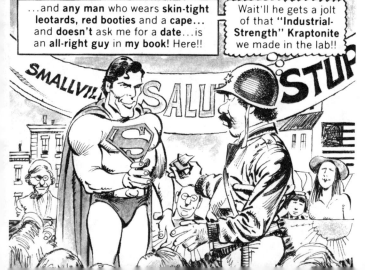

...and **any man** who wears **skin-tight leotards, red booties** and a **cape**... and **doesn't** ask me for a **date**...is an **all-right guy** in **my book!** Here!!

Wait'll he gets a jolt of that "**Industrial-Strength**" Kraptonite we made in the lab!!

I **feel** so **strange!** As if I'd **enjoy** doing **mean, rotten, nasty** things to people! What's to **become** of me?

You could **always** become a **High School Principal!**

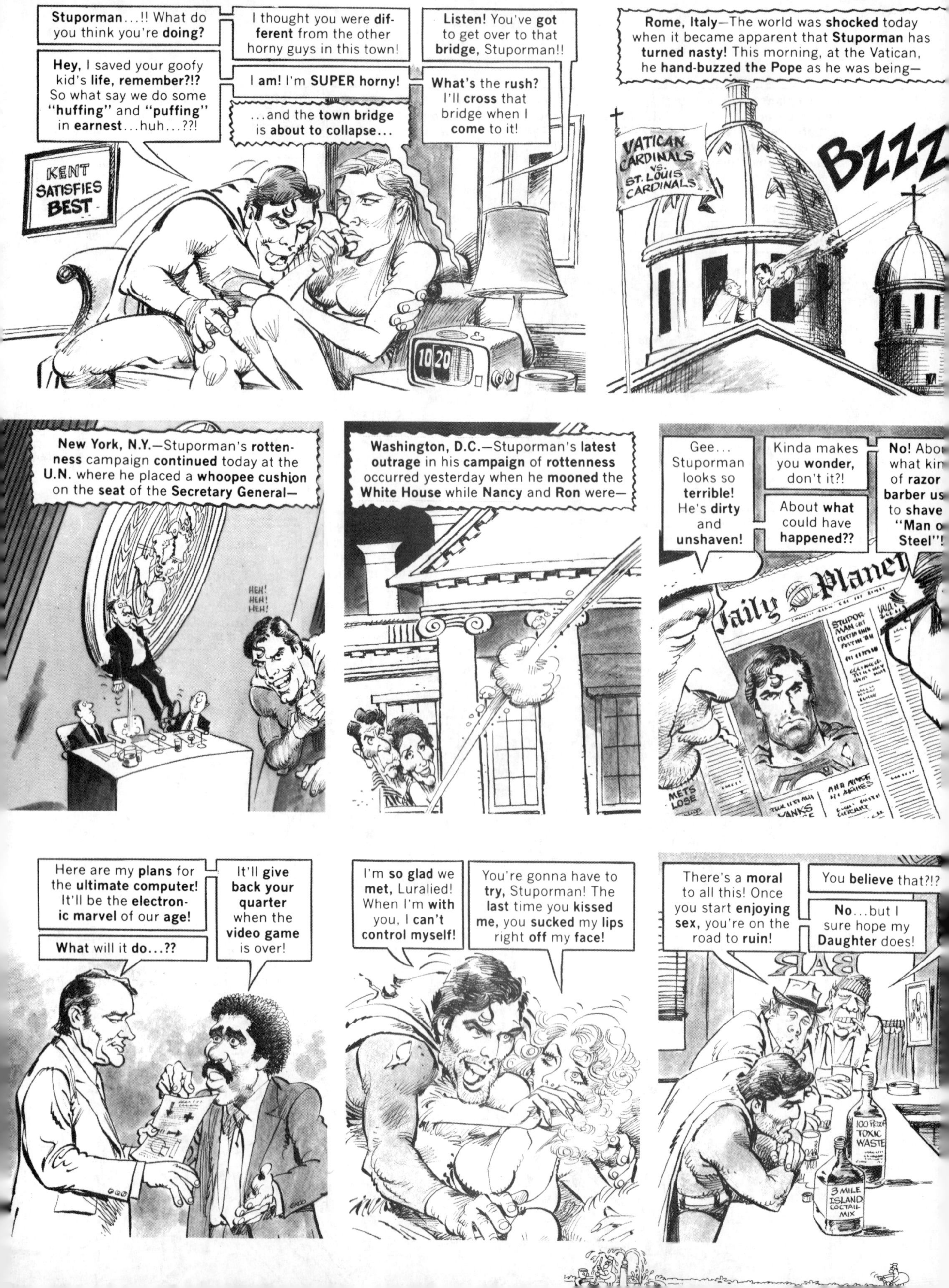
Stuporman...!! What do you think you're doing?
I thought you were different from the other horny guys in this town!
Hey, I saved your goofy kid's life, remember?!? So what say we do some "huffing" and "puffing" in earnest...huh...??!
I am! I'm SUPER horny!
...and the town bridge is about to collapse...
Listen! You've got to get over to that bridge, Stuporman!!
What's the rush? I'll cross that bridge when I come to it!
KENT SATISFIES BEST
10 20
Rome, Italy—The world was shocked today when it became apparent that Stuporman has turned nasty! This morning, at the Vatican, he hand-buzzed the Pope as he was being—
VATICAN CARDINALS VS. ST. LOUIS CARDINALS
BZZZ
New York, N.Y.—Stuporman's rottenness campaign continued today at the U.N. where he placed a whoopee cushion on the seat of the Secretary General—
HEH! HEH! HEH!
Washington, D.C.—Stuporman's latest outrage in his campaign of rottenness occurred yesterday when he mooned the White House while Nancy and Ron were—
Gee... Stuporman looks so terrible! He's dirty and unshaven!
Kinda makes you wonder, don't it?!
About what could have happened??
No! Abou what kin of razor barber us to shave "Man o Steel"!
Daily Planet
STUPORMAN
METS LOSE
Here are my plans for the ultimate computer! It'll be the electronic marvel of our age!
What will it do...??
It'll give back your quarter when the video game is over!
I'm so glad we met, Luralied! When I'm with you, I can't control myself!
You're gonna have to try, Stuporman! The last time you kissed me, you sucked my lips right off my face!
There's a moral to all this! Once you start enjoying sex, you're on the road to ruin!
You believe that?!?
No...but I sure hope my Daughter does!
BAR
100 PROOF TOXIC WASTE
3 MILE ISLAND COCTAIL MIX

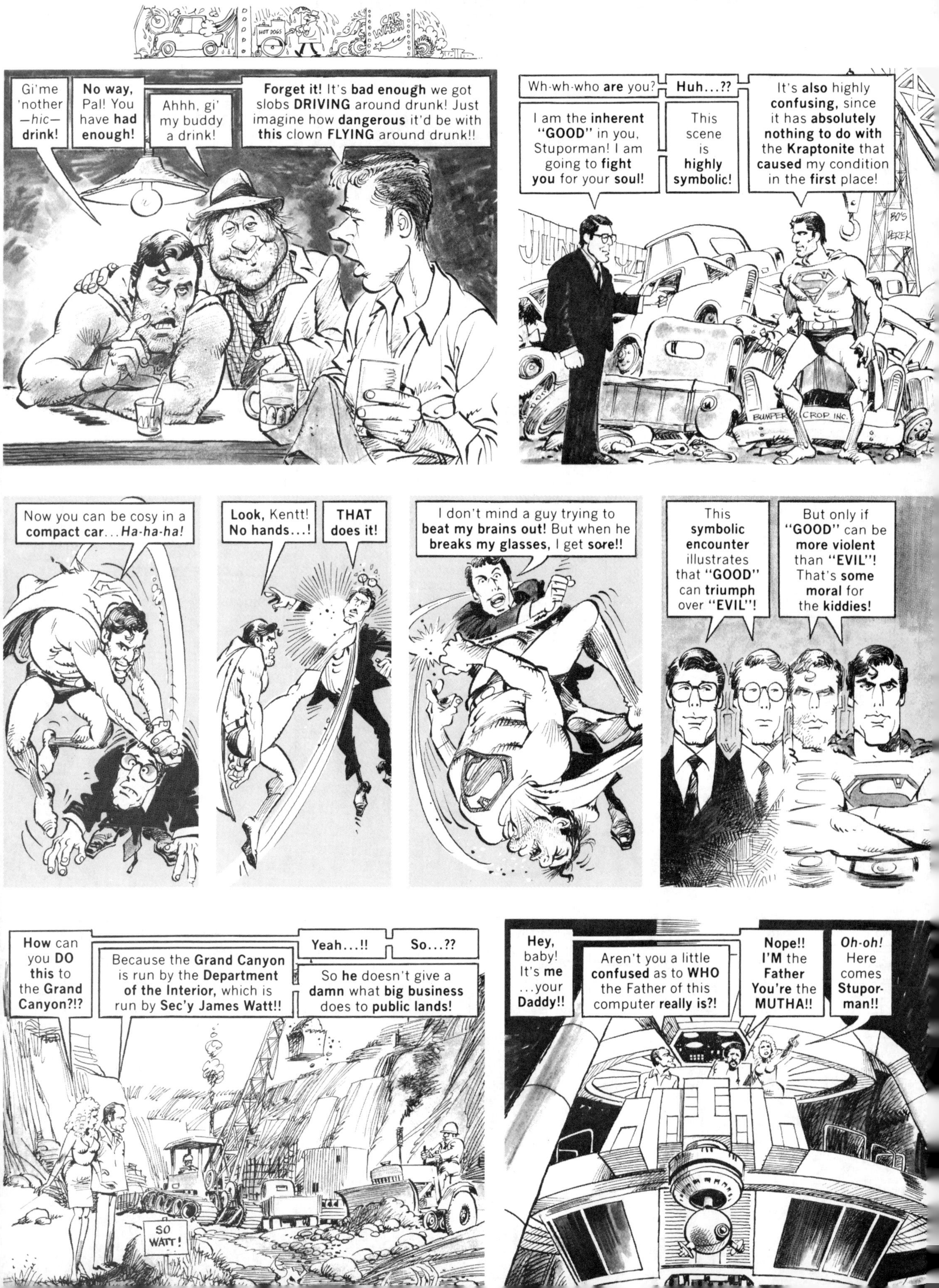
HOT DOGS
CAR WASH
Gi'me 'nother —hic— drink!
No way, Pal! You have had enough!
Ahhh, gi' my buddy a drink!
Forget it! It's bad enough we got slobs DRIVING around drunk! Just imagine how dangerous it'd be with this clown FLYING around drunk!!
Wh-wh-who are you?
I am the inherent "GOOD" in you, Stuporman! I am going to fight you for your soul!
Huh...??
This scene is highly symbolic!
It's also highly confusing, since it has absolutely nothing to do with the Kraptonite that caused my condition in the first place!
BO'S DEREK
BUMPER CROP INC.
Now you can be cosy in a compact car... Ha-ha-ha!
Look, Kentt! No hands...!
THAT does it!
I don't mind a guy trying to beat my brains out! But when he breaks my glasses, I get sore!!
This symbolic encounter illustrates that "GOOD" can triumph over "EVIL"!
But only if "GOOD" can be more violent than "EVIL"! That's some moral for the kiddies!
How can you DO this to the Grand Canyon?!?
Because the Grand Canyon is run by the Department of the Interior, which is run by Sec'y James Watt!!
Yeah...!!
So...??
So he doesn't give a damn what big business does to public lands!
SO WATT!
Hey, baby! It's me ...your Daddy!!
Aren't you a little confused as to WHO the Father of this computer really is?!
Nope!! I'M the Father You're the MUTHA!!
Oh-oh! Here comes Stupor-man!!

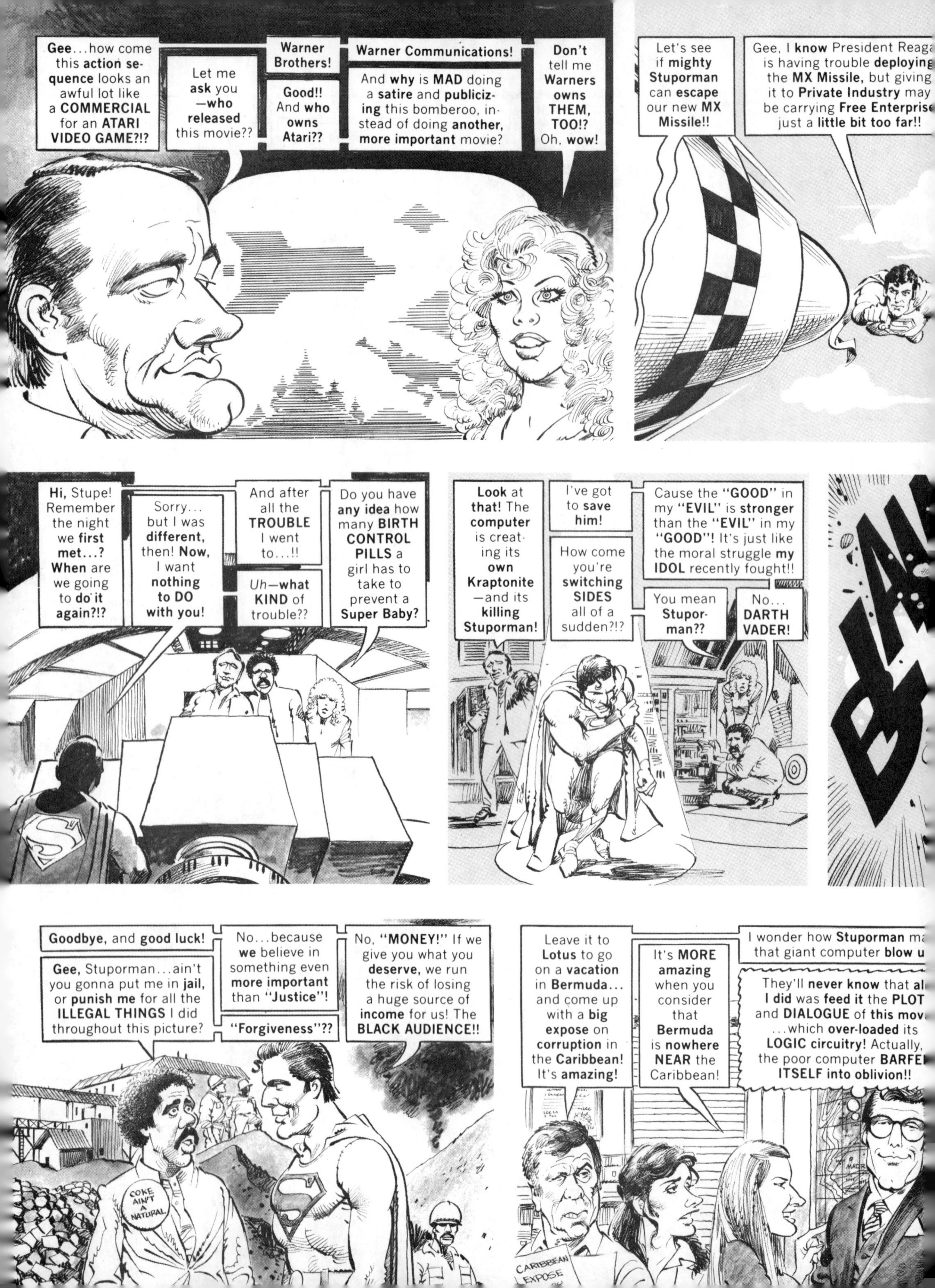

Gee...how come this action sequence looks an awful lot like a COMMERCIAL for an ATARI VIDEO GAME?!?
Let me ask you —who released this movie??
Warner Brothers!
Good!! And who owns Atari??
Warner Communications!
And why is MAD doing a satire and publicizing this bomberoo, instead of doing another, more important movie?
Don't tell me Warners owns THEM, TOO!? Oh, wow!
Let's see if mighty Stuporman can escape our new MX Missile!!
Gee, I know President Reaga is having trouble deploying the MX Missile, but giving it to Private Industry may be carrying Free Enterprise just a little bit too far!!
Hi, Stupe! Remember the night we first met...? When are we going to do it again?!?
Sorry... but I was different, then! Now, I want nothing to DO with you!
And after all the TROUBLE I went to...!!
Uh—what KIND of trouble??
Do you have any idea how many BIRTH CONTROL PILLS a girl has to take to prevent a Super Baby?
Look at that! The computer is creating its own Kraptonite —and its killing Stuporman!
I've got to save him!
How come you're switching SIDES all of a sudden?!?
Cause the "GOOD" in my "EVIL" is stronger than the "EVIL" in my "GOOD"! It's just like the moral struggle my IDOL recently fought!!
You mean Stuporman??
No... DARTH VADER!
Goodbye, and good luck!
Gee, Stuporman...ain't you gonna put me in jail, or punish me for all the ILLEGAL THINGS I did throughout this picture?
No...because we believe in something even more important than "Justice"!
"Forgiveness"??
No, "MONEY!" If we give you what you deserve, we run the risk of losing a huge source of income for us! The BLACK AUDIENCE!!
COKE AIN'T A NATURAL
Leave it to Lotus to go on a vacation in Bermuda... and come up with a big expose on corruption in the Caribbean! It's amazing!
It's MORE amazing when you consider that Bermuda is nowhere NEAR the Caribbean!
I wonder how Stuporman ma that giant computer blow u
They'll never know that al I did was feed it the PLOT and DIALOGUE of this mov ...which over-loaded its LOGIC circuitry! Actually, the poor computer BARFE ITSELF into oblivion!!
CARIBBEAN EXPOSE

COMIC BOOK PREVIEWS

HE greatest comic book hero of all time is Superman. He stood for truth, justice and the American way — emphasis on "truth." But where's the Man of Steel when it comes to the freebie preview newsletters they hand out at the comic book shops? Those things are filled with about as much truth as Clinton's grand jury testimony. Wouldn't it great if just once those weasels at DC and Marvel ve you the *real* low-down on upcoming comic ooks? Well, you have a better chance of see- g Wonder Woman and Batgirl in a top- s romp in the Batcave (hey, now ere's a comic we'd shell out $2.95)! Anyway, since they won't ve you the real low- wn, we will. re's...

IF TRUTH IN ADVERTISING LAWS APPLIED TO COMIC BOOK PREVIEWS

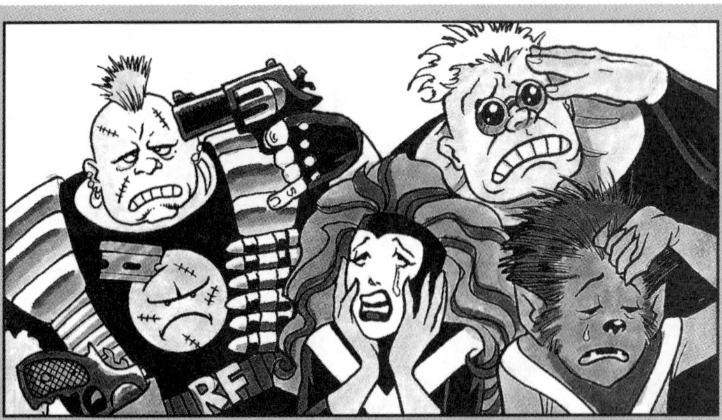

X-FACTOR #98.6

The mutants fight Razorface – a big, tough, ugly-looking, armor-covered villain – for two pages. The rest of the book is padded with scenes of the heroes whining about how society hates them.

On sale Nov.15, we guess.

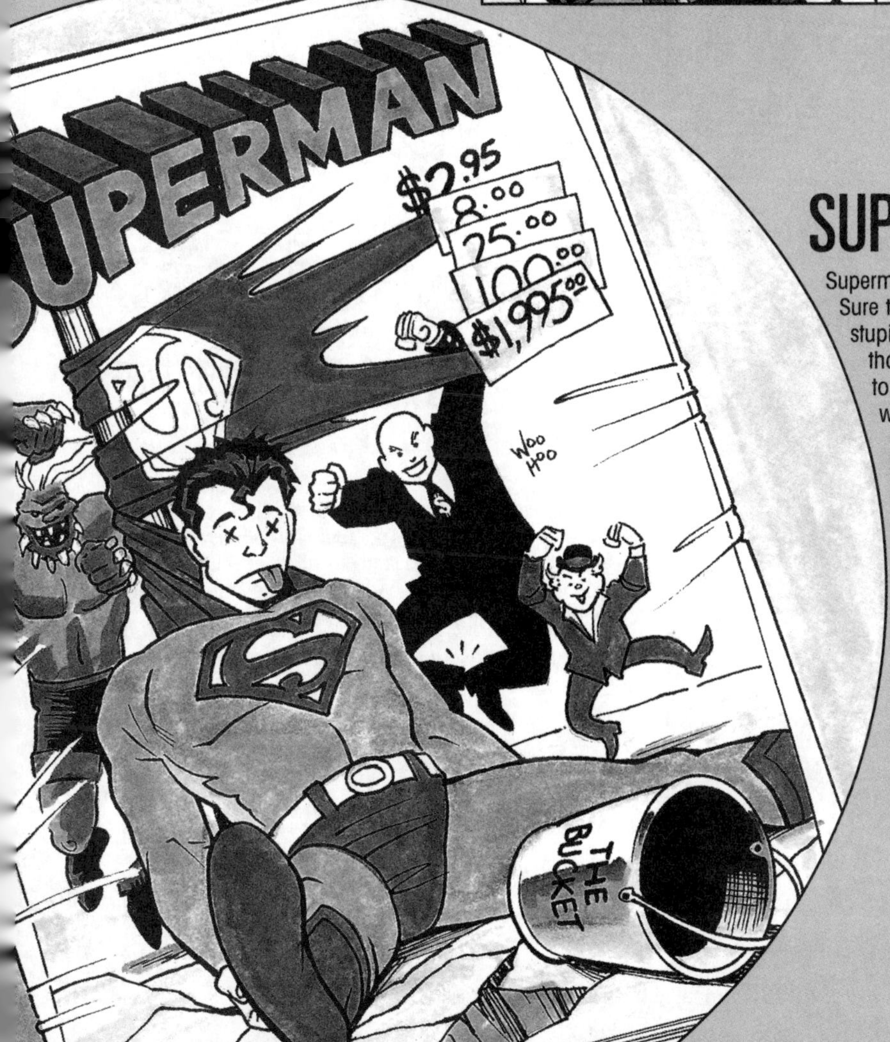
SUPERMAN
$2.95
8.00
25.00
100.00
$1,995.00
WOO HOO
THE BUCKET

SUPERMAN #429

Superman kicks the bucket again. Sure to be a collector's item with stupid fans who actually think that DC Comics is going to kill off a character worth billions of dollars.

On sale Nov. 5...and then off sale the next day so greedy comic shop owners can jack up the price immediately.

ARTIST: AMANDA CONNER WRITER: BARRY LIEBMANN

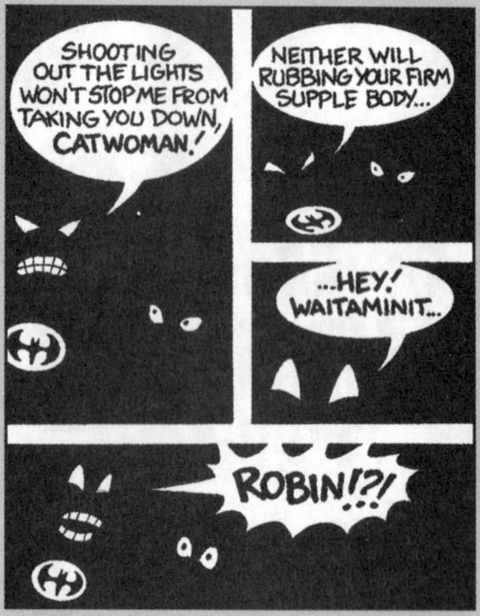
SHOOTING OUT THE LIGHTS WON'T STOP ME FROM TAKING YOU DOWN, CATWOMAN!
NEITHER WILL RUBBING YOUR FIRM SUPPLE BODY...
...HEY! WAITAMINIT...
ROBIN!?!

BATMAN:

TALES OF THE LEGEND OF THE SECRET OF THE BAT – GRAPHIC NOVEL

Pretty much the same "vigilante against the forces of evil" story they do every month, except it's printed on slightly nicer paper, so it's 50 times as expensive. Contains lots of scenes of dark nights and shadows so that readers won't realize the artist can't draw.

On sale Nov. 14, and will remain in the racks forever.

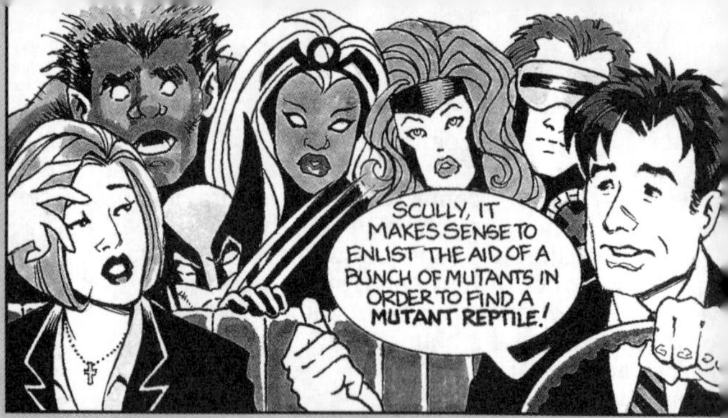
SCULLY, IT MAKES SENSE TO ENLIST THE AID OF A BUNCH OF MUTANTS IN ORDER TO FIND A MUTANT REPTILE!

X-MEN VS. X-FILES

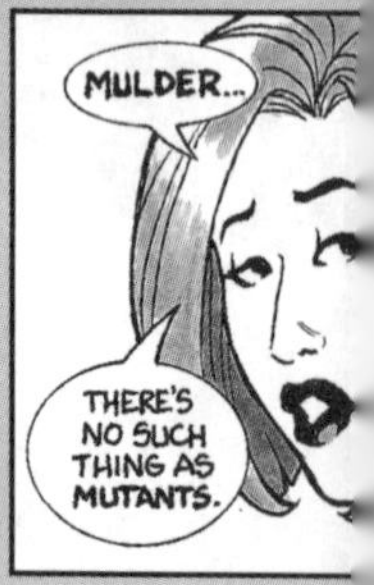
MULDER...
THERE'S NO SUCH THING AS MUTANTS.

In this 97-page crossover, the X-Men meet agents Scully and Mulder while investigating a giant radioactive alligator roaming the sewers of New York. Both teams then fight and argue continuously until the last page, where, with only six panels left to resolve the story, they join forces to kick the main villain's butt easily.

On sale last week. Too bad you missed it.

SUPERMAN #430

Superman is brought back from the dead. Like you didn't see THAT coming.

On sale Dec. 12 between 12:21 and 12:27 p.m. — then it goes directly into the back issue bin.

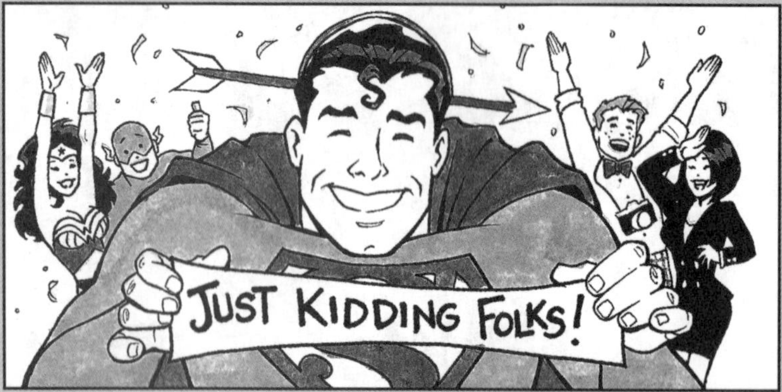
JUST KIDDING FOLKS!

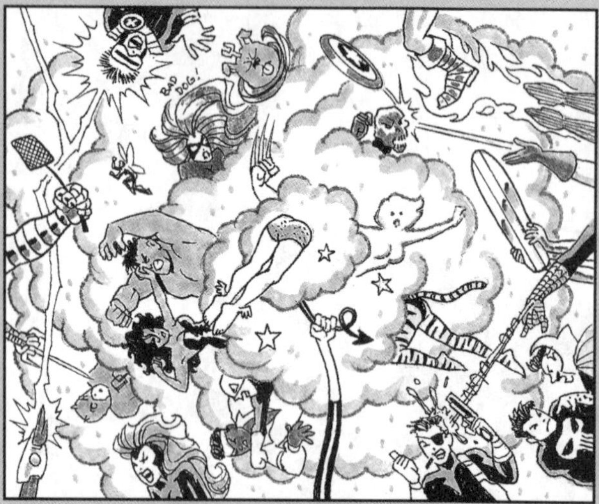
BAD DOG!

EVERY CHARACTER IN THE MARVEL UNIVERSE

FIGHTING ONE ANOTHER

A 926-page special depicting every single character Marvel ever created — no matter how obscure — punching, slapping, kicking and biting one another. The plot is incoherent, the art sucks, and the pages are out of order, but since this volume comes in a vacuum-packed, steel-reinforced, impossible-to-open Mylar bag, who'll ever notice?

On sale just as soon as we figure out what Mylar is.

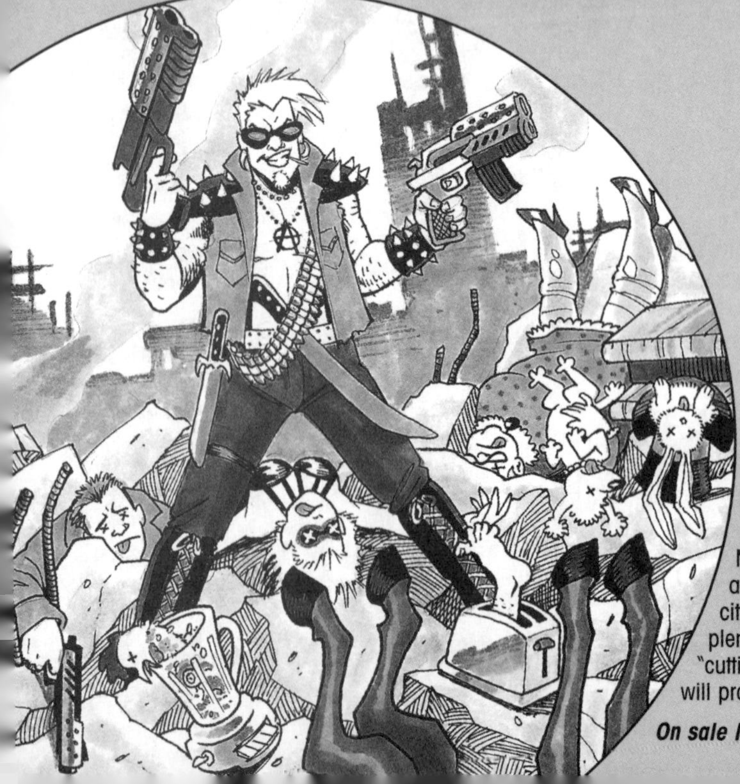

SWITCHBLADE MCGURK

Meet Switchblade McGurk, another punk-looking anti-hero running around a depressing post-apocalyptic city that's ripped off from *Blade Runner*. Crammed with plenty of violence and sleaze that readers will defend as "cutting edge." Number one of a 12-part mini-series that will probably be discontinued by issue #6.

On sale November 32.

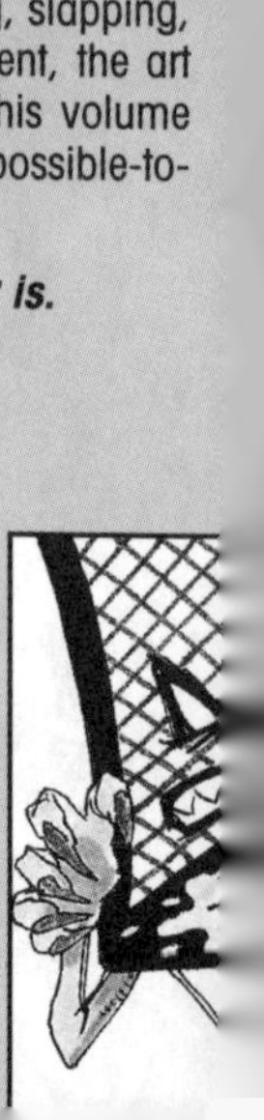

THE HULK VS. ARNOLD SCHWARZENEGGER

A 96-page special in which America's favorite green monster and Hollywood's biggest star kick the living crap out of each other. Though the Hulk can smash mountains with his pinkie, his fight with "Ah-nuld" ends in a tie because otherwise the big, muscle-bound hambone wouldn't allow Marvel to use his image.

On sale whenever Arnold's latest bomb movie is released.

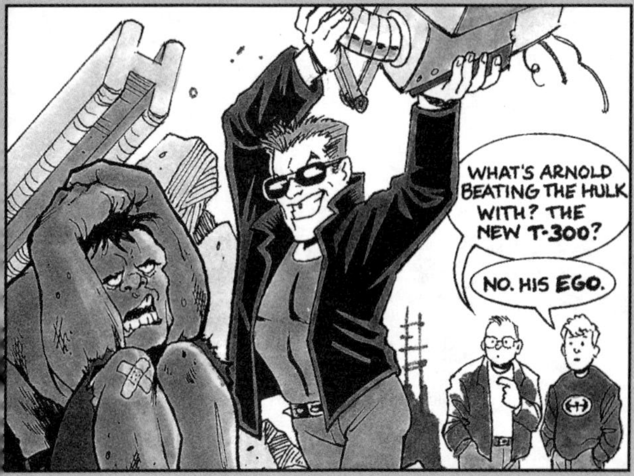
WHAT'S ARNOLD BEATING THE HULK WITH? THE NEW T-300?
NO. HIS EGO.

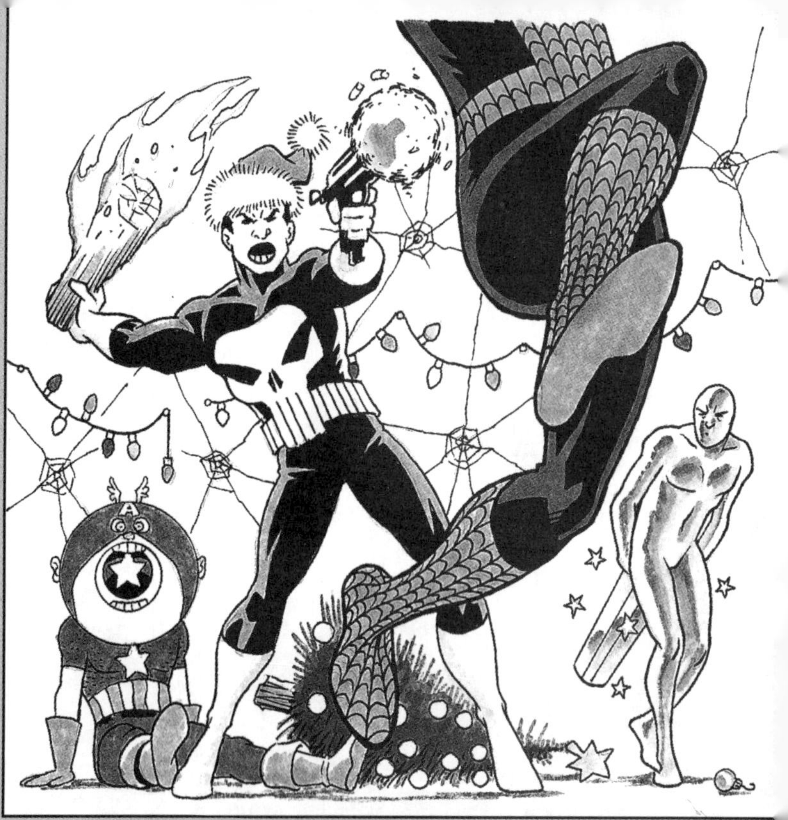

THE PUNISHER CHRISTMAS ANNUAL

After the Punisher is visited by the Ghosts of Christmas Past (Captain America), Christmas Present (Spiderman) and Christmas Future (Silver Surfer), he tries to beat them to death with a Yule log. ***On sale Easter Sunday.***

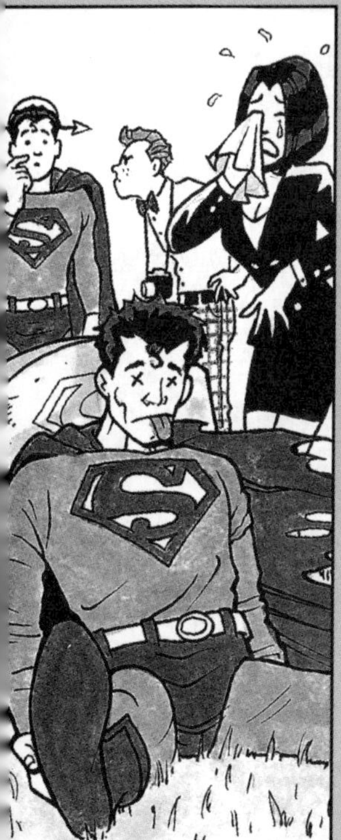

THE NEW ADVENTURES OF SUPERMAN #341

The Superman brought back from the dead in Superman #430 proves to be a clone, so the real Superman is actually still dead.

On sale Dec. 4, March 23 and May 3.

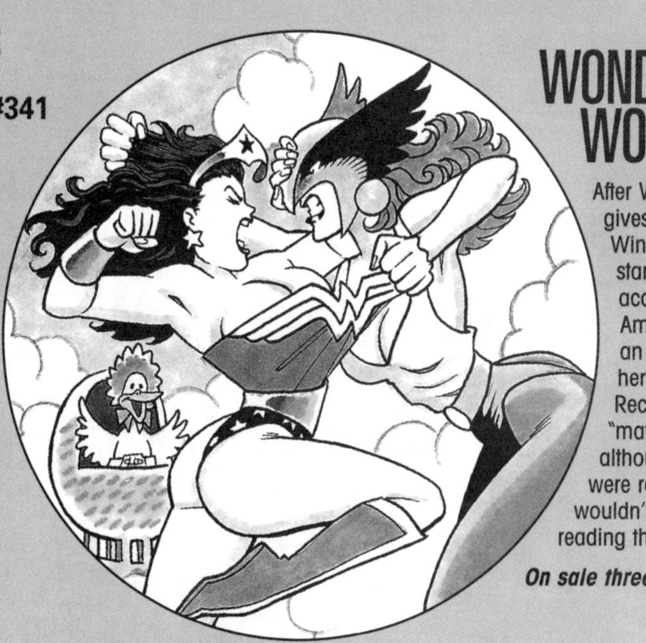

WONDER WOMAN #250

After Wonder woman gives birth to a Winged baby, guest star Hawkwoman accuses the Amazing Amazon of having an affair with her husband. Recommended for "mature readers," although if a reader were really mature, he wouldn't be caught dead reading this trash.

On sale three weeks late.

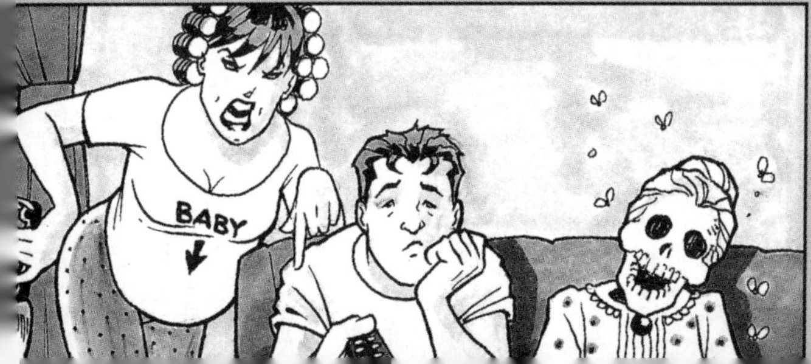
BABY

THE AMAZING SPIDERMAN #1,597,398

Peter Parker frets about Aunt May's health, his finances and his relationship with Mary Jane. After a lot of padding, Spiderman eventually fights a villain known as the Bug Squisher. A so-so issue that will be made to seem special by the fact that it will be released with 46 different covers.

On sale whenever the artist sobers up.

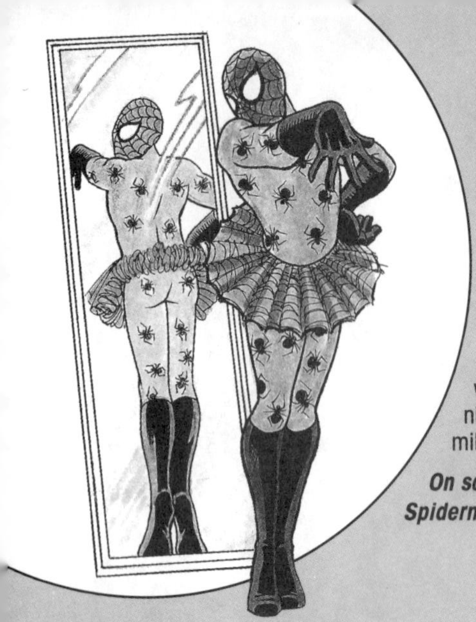

WEB OF SPIDERMAN #93

Spiderman gets a new costume this issue, so the editors decided that since the readers are going to buy it no matter what, they'd just match old Web-Head with some villain who has the same lame-o lightning powers you've seen 320 million times before.

On sale five hours after the last Spiderman book came out.

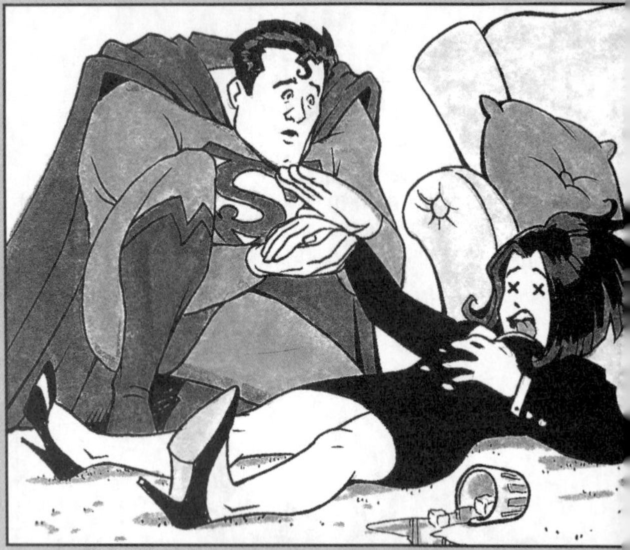

THE OLD ADVENTURES OF SUPERMAN MADE TO LOOK LIKE

NEW ADVENTURES OF SUPERMAN

Superman comes back from the grave. When he shows up outside Lois' window on page two for a romantic rendezvous, she keels over dead from the shock. The rest of the book shows Superman moping inconsolably around the Fortress of Solitude.

On sale five minutes after we print it.

TEENAGE SUSHI HAPPY HAPPY #1

Another Japanese import with artwork that basically looks like a cheap *Johnny Quest* cartoon. The translation is extremely murky (the story might have something to do with a boy who fights a giant squid), but readers won't mind because Japanese anime is hot right now... at least according to the comic shop owners trying to unload the stuff.

On sale as soon as Asian-American anti-defamation groups stop protesting.

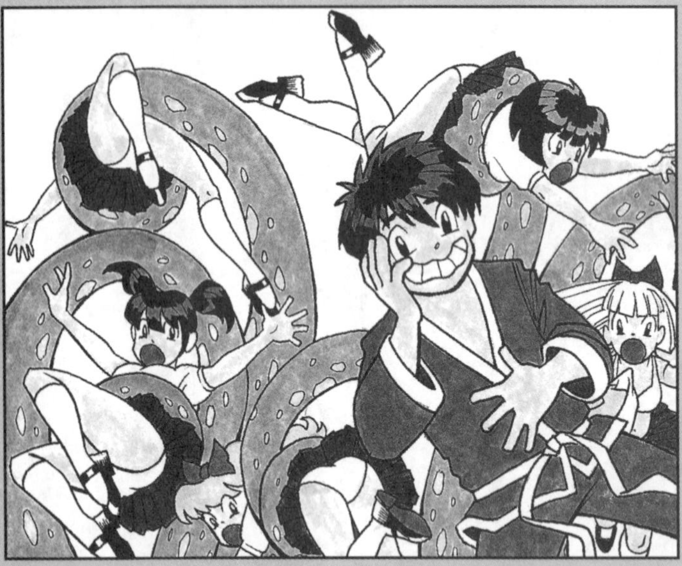

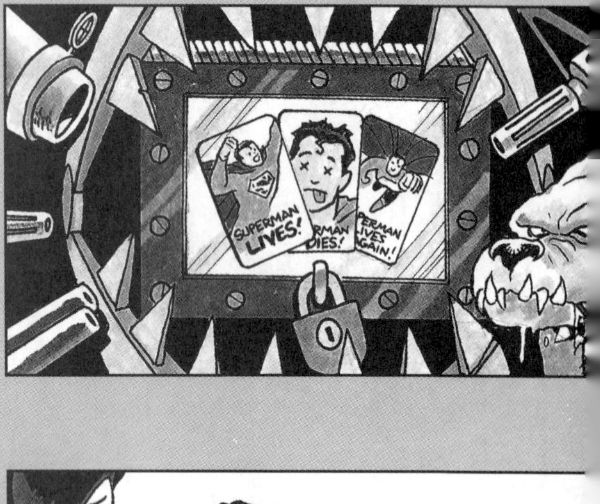
SUPERMAN LIVES!

THE NEWER THAN NEW ADVENTURES OF

SUPERMAN #56

The Man of Steel is still dead, so this issue highlights his funeral. This means lots of splash pages and two-page panels of Superman's friends standing around his grave looking solemn. Lame stuff, but if you don't buy it, you won't own the entire "Superman is Dead" series and lose money on the deal.

On sale whenever we're damn well ready.

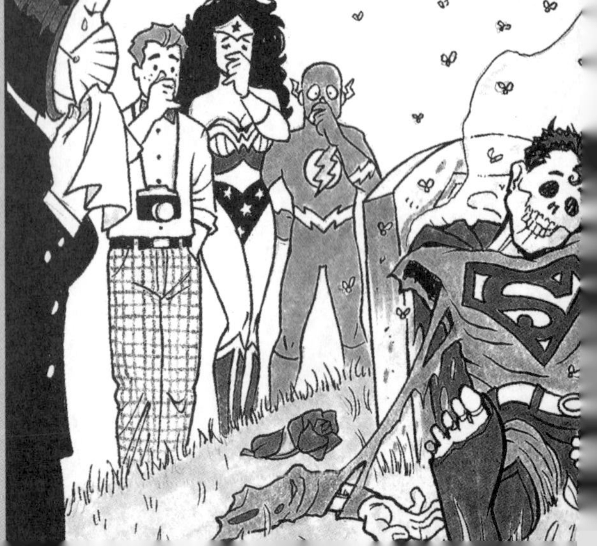

THE "HONEST, SUPERMAN IS STILL DEAD (WE REALLY MEAN IT THIS TIME)" SPECIAL

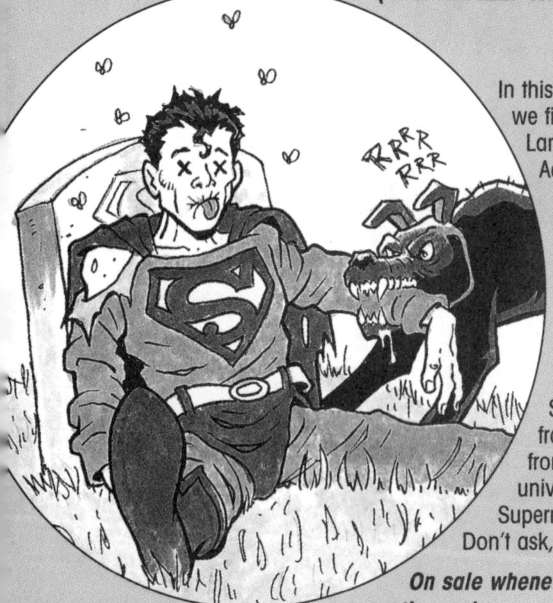
RRRR
RRR

In this 46,798 page special, we find out that the Lois Lane who died in "The Old Adventures of Superman Made to Look Like the New Adventures of Superman #12" was from a parallel universe, which means that the *real* Lois is still alive! Unfortunately, this also means that the Superman who rose from the dead was also from the same parallel universe, so the real Superman is still dead. Don't ask, just buy it!

On sale whenever you cough up the cash.

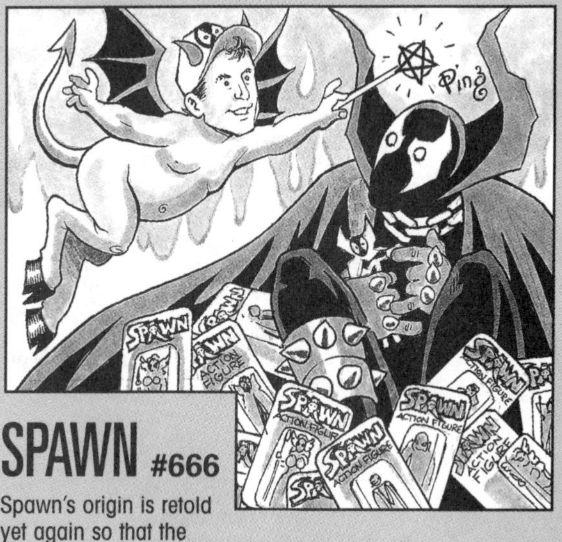
Ping

SPAWN #666

Spawn's origin is retold yet again so that the book's creative team won't have to come up with something fresh. For like the 800th time, we see how Spawn is given his powers from Satan — a fact that should provide inspiration and thrills to psychotic, devil-worshipping creeps everywhere.

On sale the day after Charles Manson's birthday.

C COMICS RADING CARDS

vhat if the market fell out on trading cards
years ago? These babies — lame
nts of old trading cards that used to sell
¢ — are engraved on solid platinum
gold leaf trim. Sure to be thrown out by
parents unless you buy the special bul-
roof, unbreakable, immovable viewing
. Complete set, with case: $300,000

sale when your credit rating arrives.

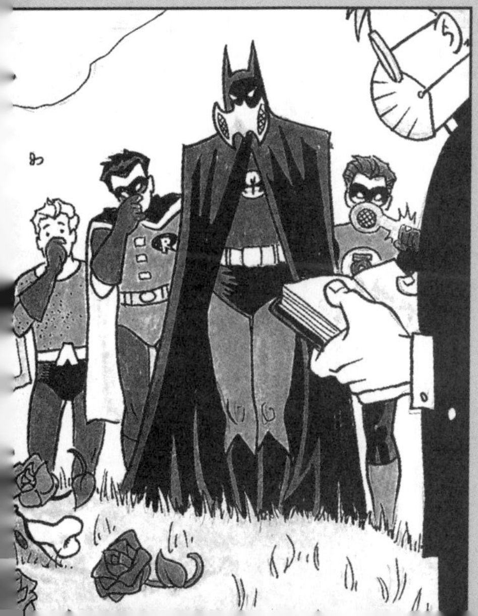

THE JUDGE DREDD/ BATMAN & ROBIN/ STEEL MOVIE SPECIAL

THREE-PACK

Yeah, those films came out years ago, but there's still a ton of these move tie-ins gathering dust in the warehouse, so DC stuffed one of each into a baggie hoping little kids won't know any better.

On sale whenever you're ready, sir!

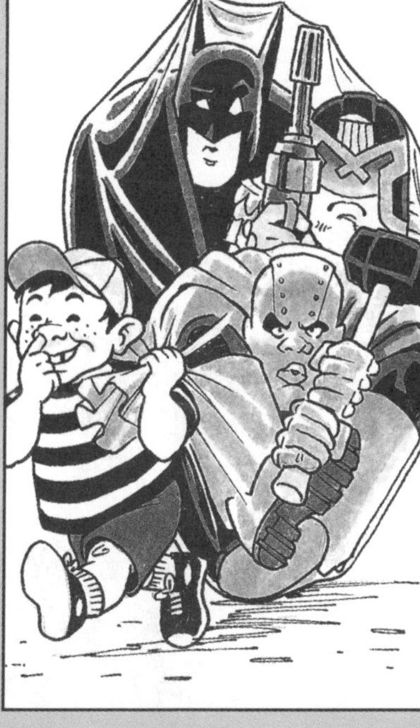

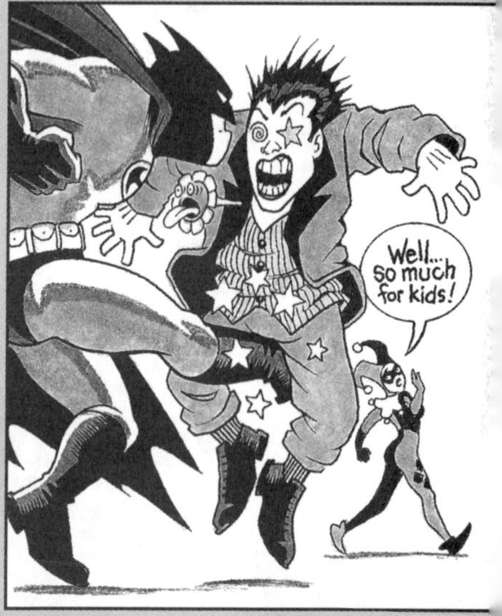
Well... so much for kids!

DETECTIVE COMICS #1

Batman chases the Joker for the umpteenth time and, after twenty tedious pages, finally kicks him in the groin. Though this issue is mediocre at best, you'll want to snap up at least fifty copies. Why? Since DC is arbitrarily starting the numbering system all over again, this issue will be considered #1. Sure to be a collector's item... if all other two million copies mysteriously disappear.

On sale as soon as Batman's creator, Bob Kane, stops spinning in his grave.

GREEN AND BARE IT DEPT.

DON MARTIN LOOKS AT...

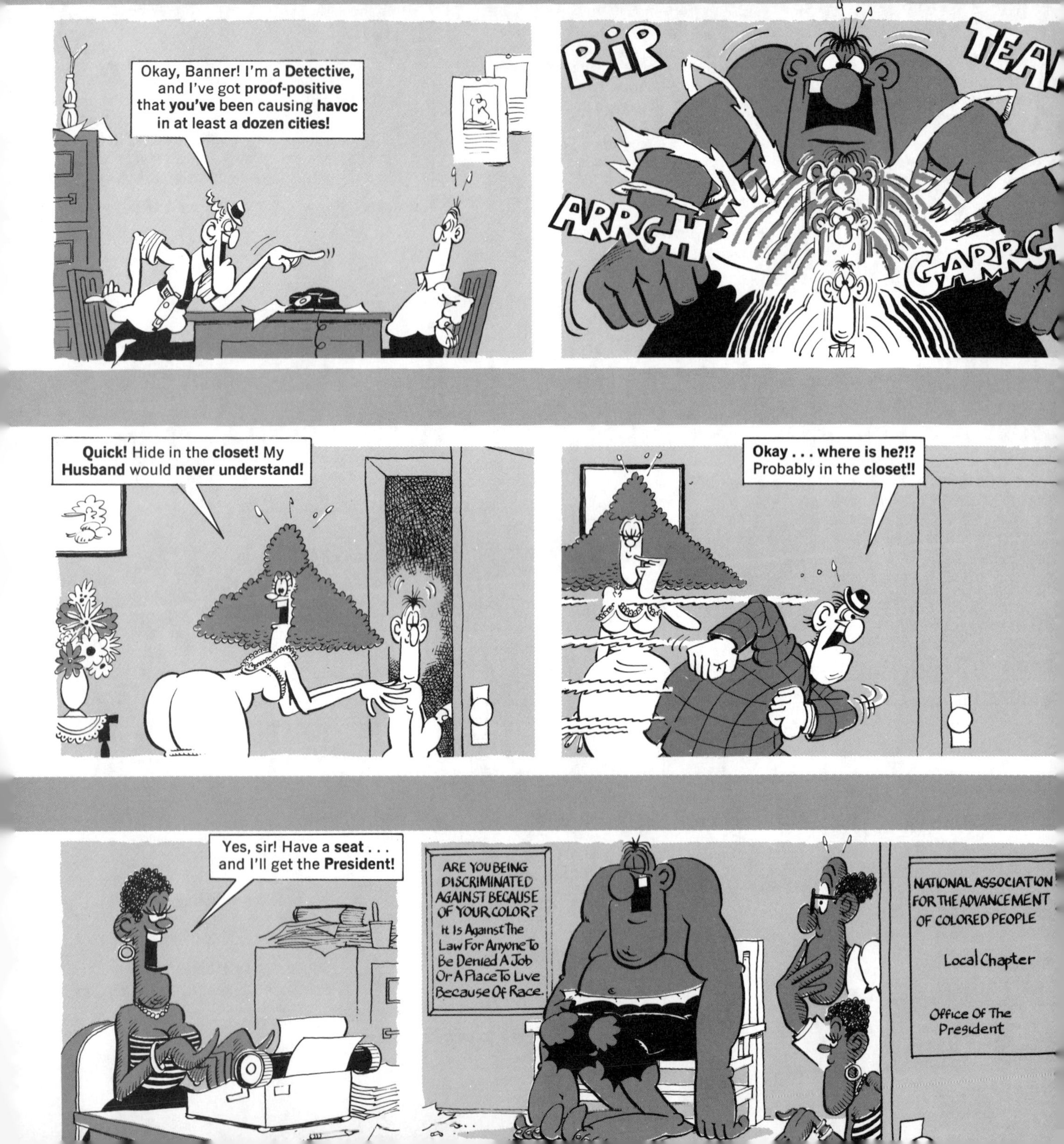

Okay, Banner! I'm a Detective, and I've got proof-positive that you've been causing havoc in at least a dozen cities!
RIP
ARRGH
Quick! Hide in the closet! My Husband would never understand!
Okay . . . where is he?!? Probably in the closet!!
Yes, sir! Have a seat . . . and I'll get the President!
ARE YOU BEING DISCRIMINATED AGAINST BECAUSE OF YOUR COLOR? It Is Against The Law For Anyone To Be Denied A Job Or A Place To Live Because Of Race.
NATIONAL ASSOCIATION FOR THE ADVANCEMENT OF COLORED PEOPLE
Local Chapter
Office Of The President

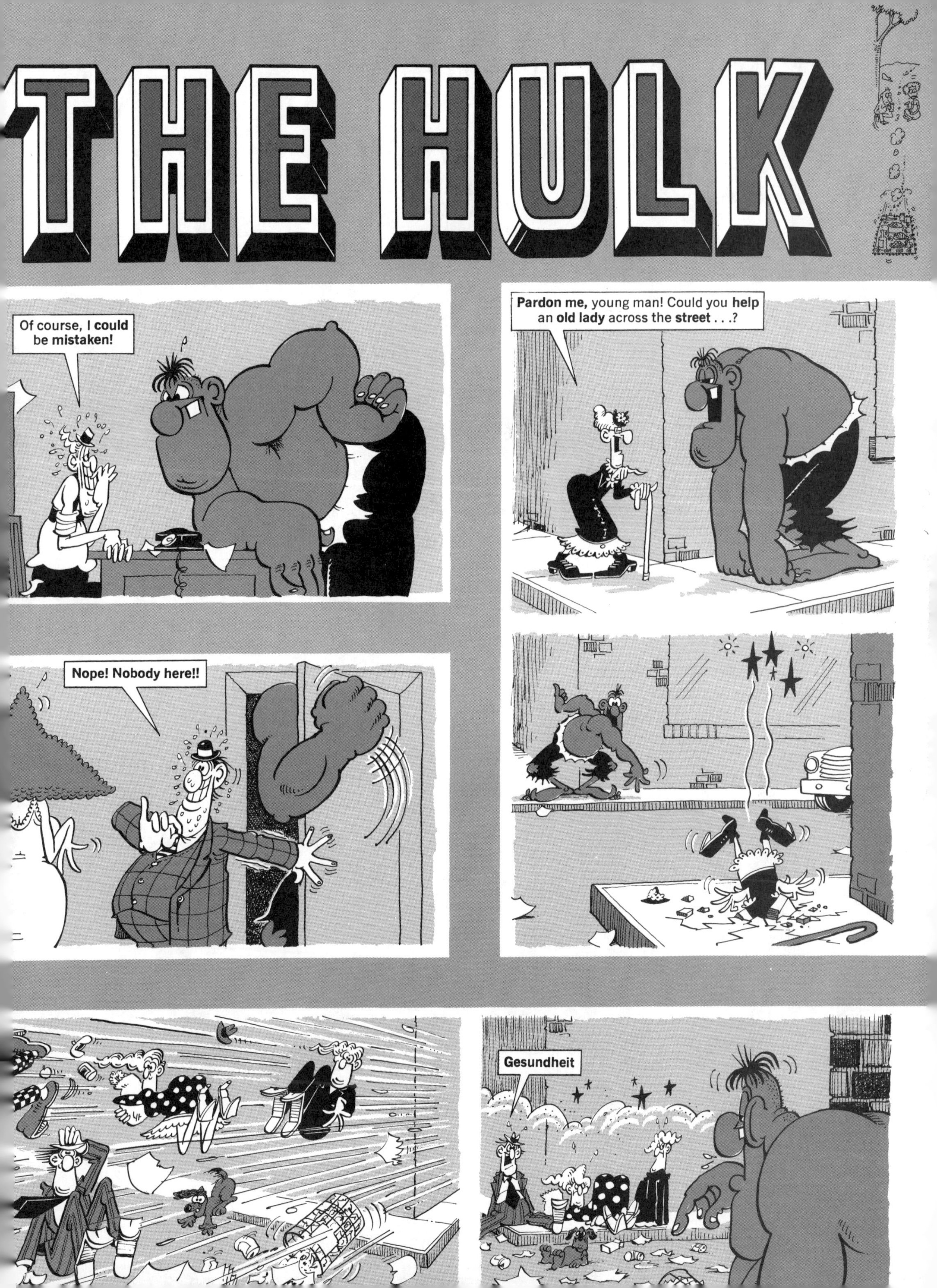
THE HULK
Of course, I could be mistaken!
Pardon me, young man! Could you help an old lady across the street . . .?
Nope! Nobody here!!
Gesundheit

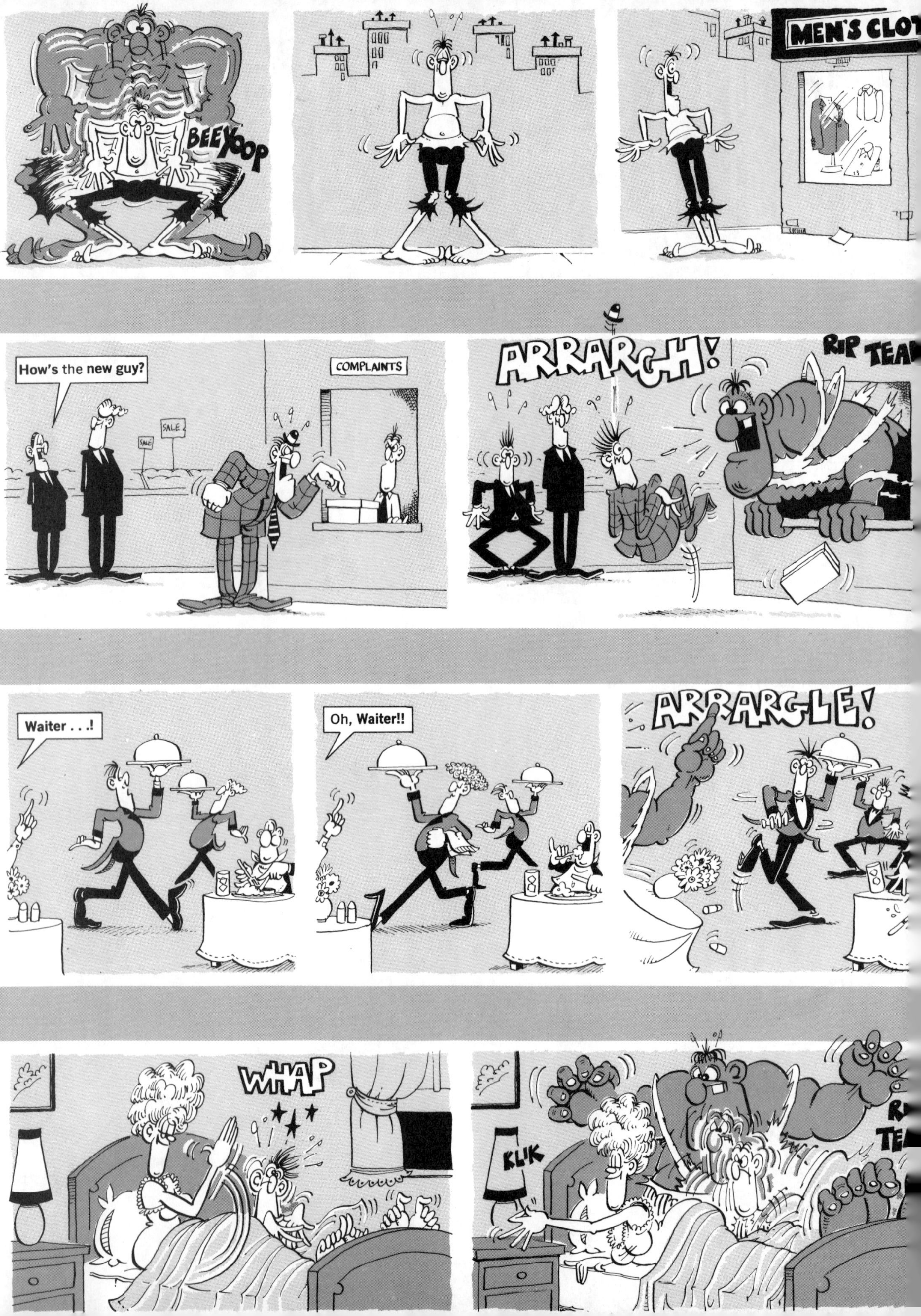
BEEYOOP
MEN'S CLOT
How's the new guy?
SALE
SALE
COMPLAINTS
ARRARGH!
RIP TEA
Waiter . . .!
Oh, Waiter!!
ARRARGLE!
WHAP
KLIK

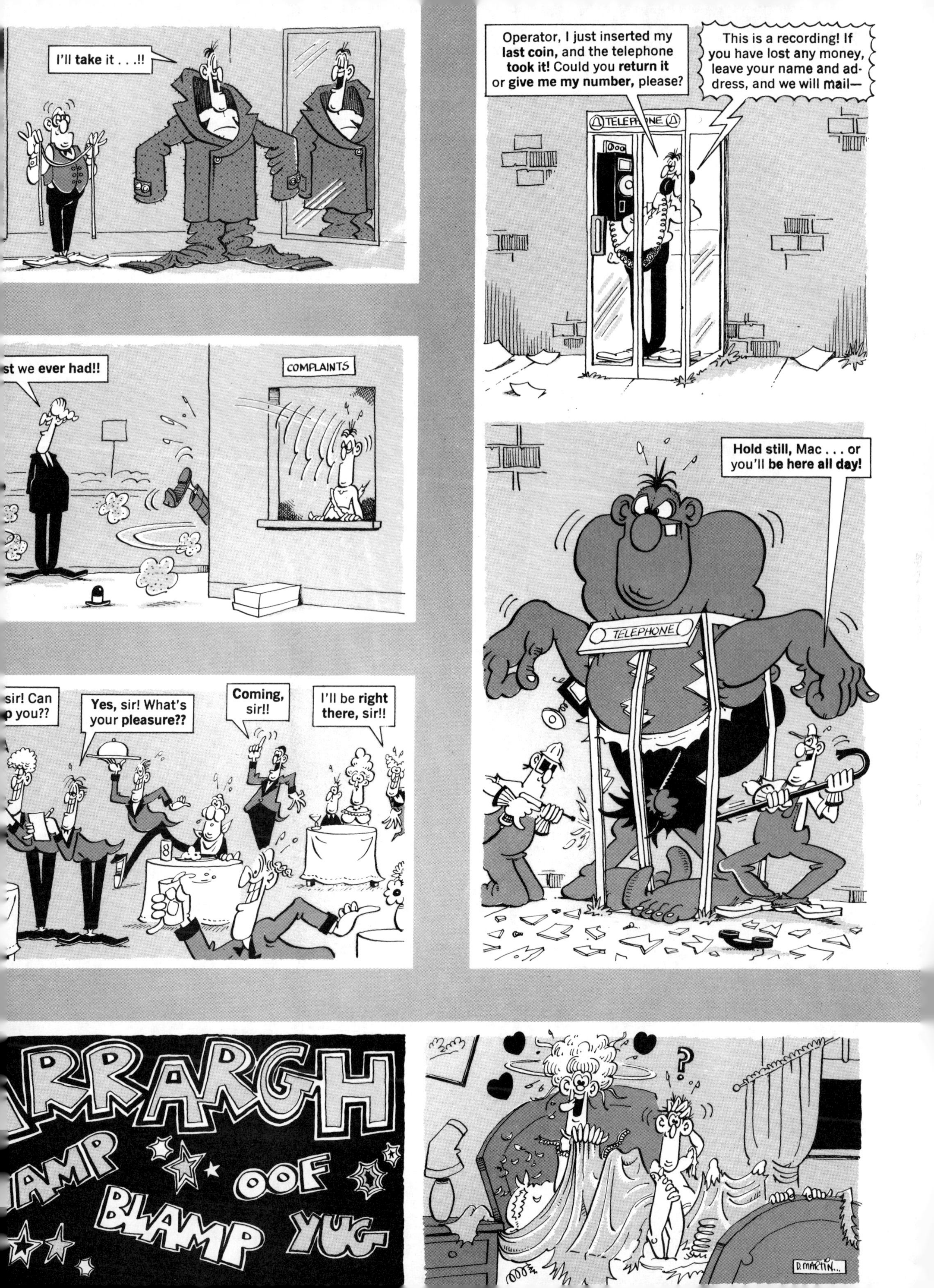

I'll take it . . .!!
st we ever had!!
COMPLAINTS
sir! Can
p you??
Yes, sir! What's your pleasure??
Coming, sir!!
I'll be right there, sir!!
ARRRAGH
AMP
OOF
BLAMP
YUG
Operator, I just inserted my last coin, and the telephone took it! Could you return it or give me my number, please?
This is a recording! If you have lost any money, leave your name and address, and we will mail—
TELEPHONE
Hold still, Mac . . . or you'll be here all day!
TELEPHONE
D. MARTIN..

A sleek new vehicle is roaring out of the Butt-cave this summer! And this time it's featuring dual air bags! Here is our version of...

BUTTMAN

ARTIST: MORT DRUCKER

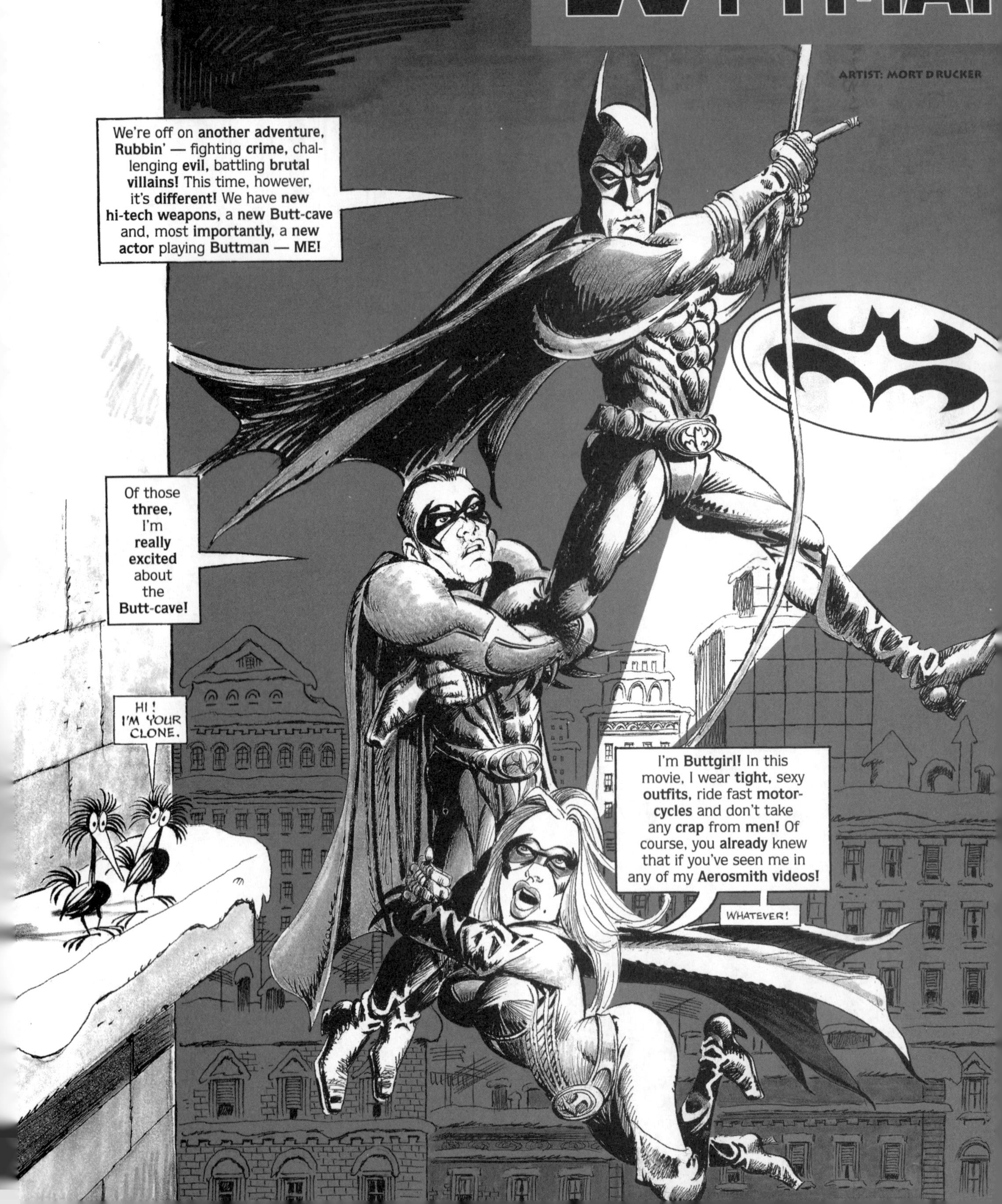
We're off on another adventure, Rubbin' — fighting crime, challenging evil, battling brutal villains! This time, however, it's different! We have new hi-tech weapons, a new Butt-cave and, most importantly, a new actor playing Buttman — ME!
Of those three, I'm really excited about the Butt-cave!
HI! I'M YOUR CLONE.
I'm Buttgirl! In this movie, I wear tight, sexy outfits, ride fast motorcycles and don't take any crap from men! Of course, you already knew that if you've seen me in any of my Aerosmith videos!
WHATEVER!

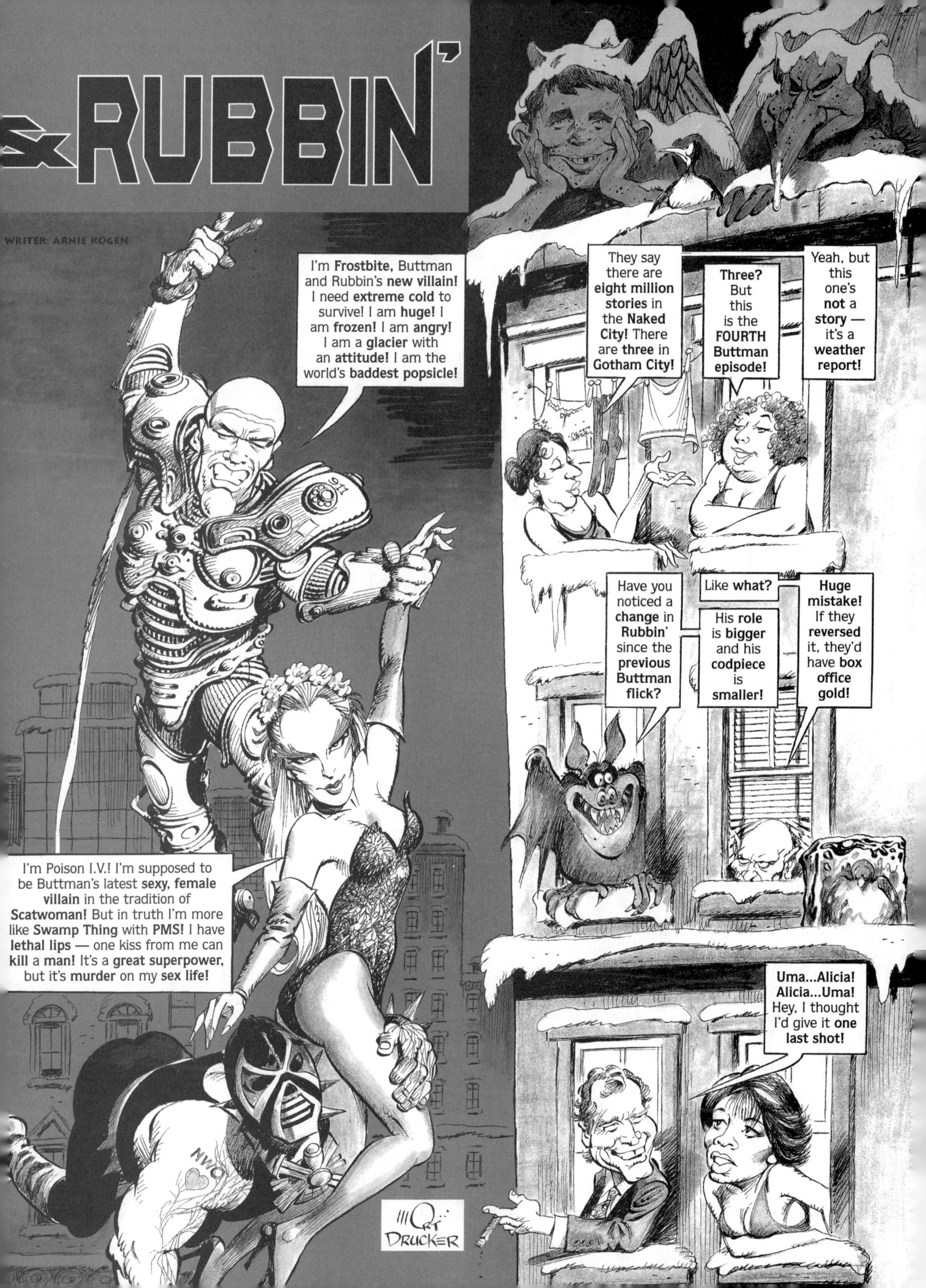
& RUBBIN'
WRITER: ARNIE KOGEN
I'm Frostbite, Buttman and Rubbin's new villain! I need extreme cold to survive! I am huge! I am frozen! I am angry! I am a glacier with an attitude! I am the world's baddest popsicle!
I'm Poison I.V.! I'm supposed to be Buttman's latest sexy, female villain in the tradition of Scatwoman! But in truth I'm more like Swamp Thing with PMS! I have lethal lips — one kiss from me can kill a man! It's a great superpower, but it's murder on my sex life!
They say there are eight million stories in the Naked City! There are three in Gotham City!
Three? But this is the FOURTH Buttman episode!
Yeah, but this one's not a story — it's a weather report!
Have you noticed a change in Rubbin' since the previous Buttman flick?
Like what?
His role is bigger and his codpiece is smaller!
Huge mistake! If they reversed it, they'd have box office gold!
Uma...Alicia! Alicia...Uma! Hey, I thought I'd give it one last shot!
NWO
ART DRUCKER

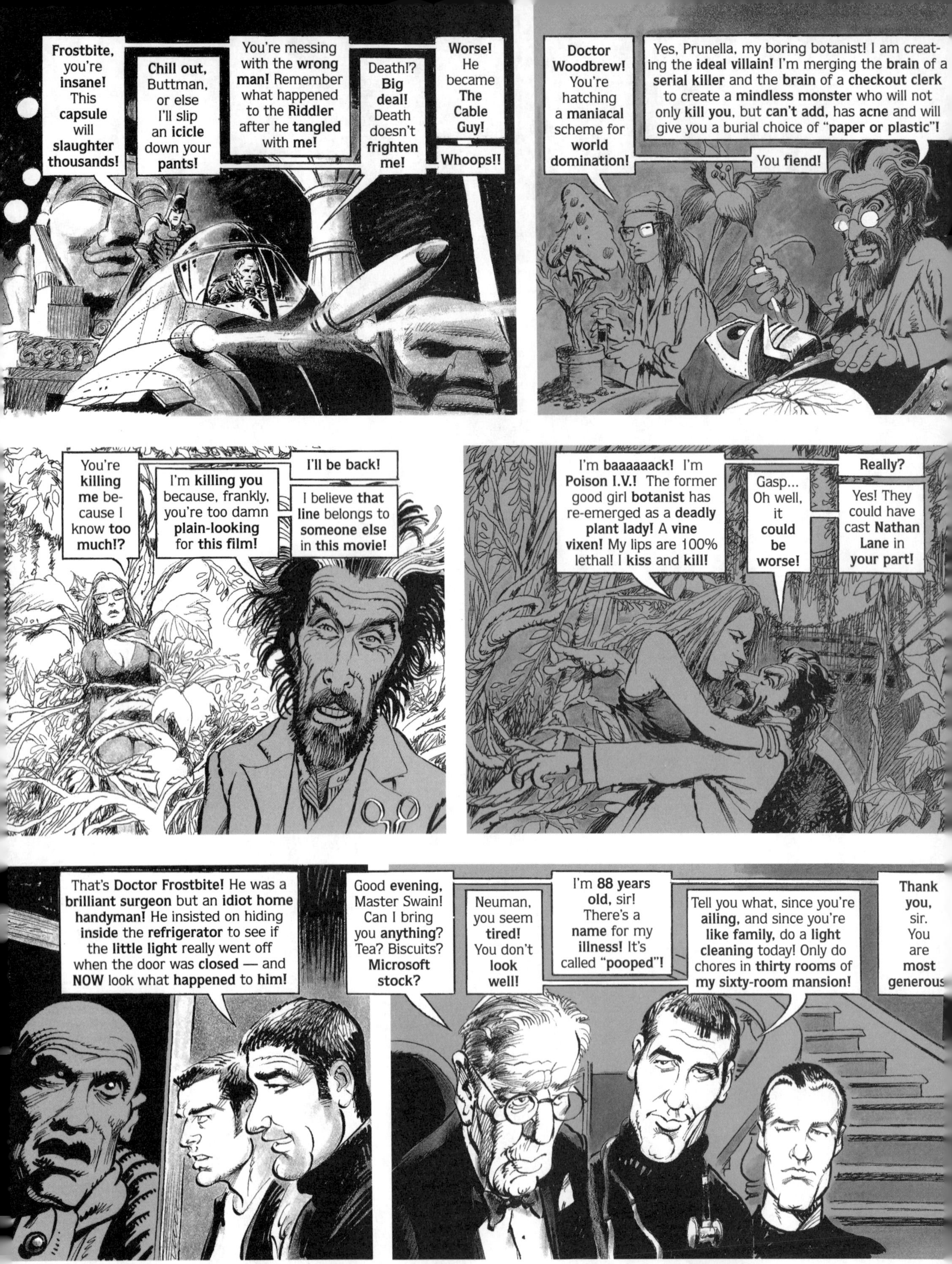
Frostbite, you're insane! This capsule will slaughter thousands!
Chill out, Buttman, or else I'll slip an icicle down your pants!
You're messing with the wrong man! Remember what happened to the Riddler after he tangled with me!
Death!? Big deal! Death doesn't frighten me!
Worse! He became The Cable Guy!
Whoops!!
Doctor Woodbrew! You're hatching a maniacal scheme for world domination!
Yes, Prunella, my boring botanist! I am creating the ideal villain! I'm merging the brain of a serial killer and the brain of a checkout clerk to create a mindless monster who will not only kill you, but can't add, has acne and will give you a burial choice of "paper or plastic"!
You fiend!
You're killing me because I know too much!?
I'm killing you because, frankly, you're too damn plain-looking for this film!
I'll be back!
I believe that line belongs to someone else in this movie!
I'm baaaaaack! I'm Poison I.V.! The former good girl botanist has re-emerged as a deadly plant lady! A vine vixen! My lips are 100% lethal! I kiss and kill!
Gasp... Oh well, it could be worse!
Really?
Yes! They could have cast Nathan Lane in your part!
That's Doctor Frostbite! He was a brilliant surgeon but an idiot home handyman! He insisted on hiding inside the refrigerator to see if the little light really went off when the door was closed — and NOW look what happened to him!
Good evening, Master Swain! Can I bring you anything? Tea? Biscuits? Microsoft stock?
Neuman, you seem tired! You don't look well!
I'm 88 years old, sir! There's a name for my illness! It's called "pooped"!
Tell you what, since you're ailing, and since you're like family, do a light cleaning today! Only do chores in thirty rooms of my sixty-room mansion!
Thank you, sir. You are most generous

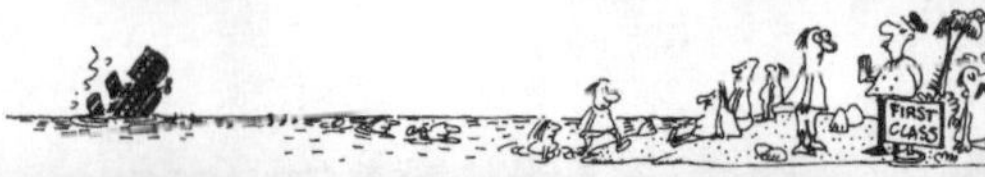

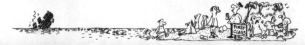

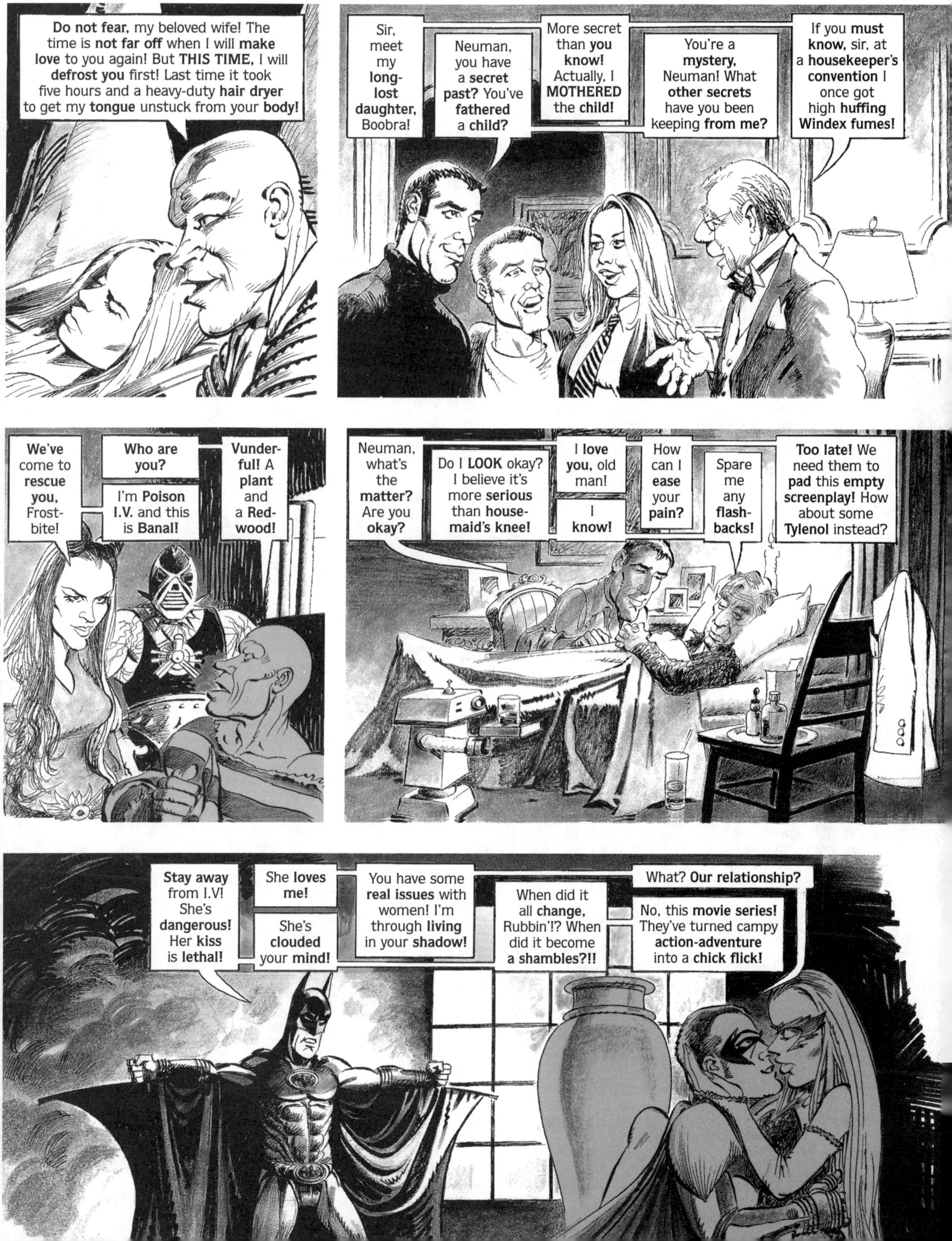

Do not fear, my beloved wife! The time is not far off when I will make love to you again! But THIS TIME, I will defrost you first! Last time it took five hours and a heavy-duty hair dryer to get my tongue unstuck from your body!
Sir, meet my long-lost daughter, Boobra!
Neuman, you have a secret past? You've fathered a child?
More secret than you know! Actually, I MOTHERED the child!
You're a mystery, Neuman! What other secrets have you been keeping from me?
If you must know, sir, at a housekeeper's convention I once got high huffing Windex fumes!
We've come to rescue you, Frost-bite!
Who are you?
I'm Poison I.V. and this is Banal!
Vunder-ful! A plant and a Red-wood!
Neuman, what's the matter? Are you okay?
Do I LOOK okay? I believe it's more serious than house-maid's knee!
I love you, old man!
I know!
How can I ease your pain?
Spare me any flash-backs!
Too late! We need them to pad this empty screenplay! How about some Tylenol instead?
Stay away from I.V! She's dangerous! Her kiss is lethal!
She loves me!
She's clouded your mind!
You have some real issues with women! I'm through living in your shadow!
When did it all change, Rubbin'!? When did it become a shambles?!!
What? Our relationship?
No, this movie series! They've turned campy action-adventure into a chick flick!

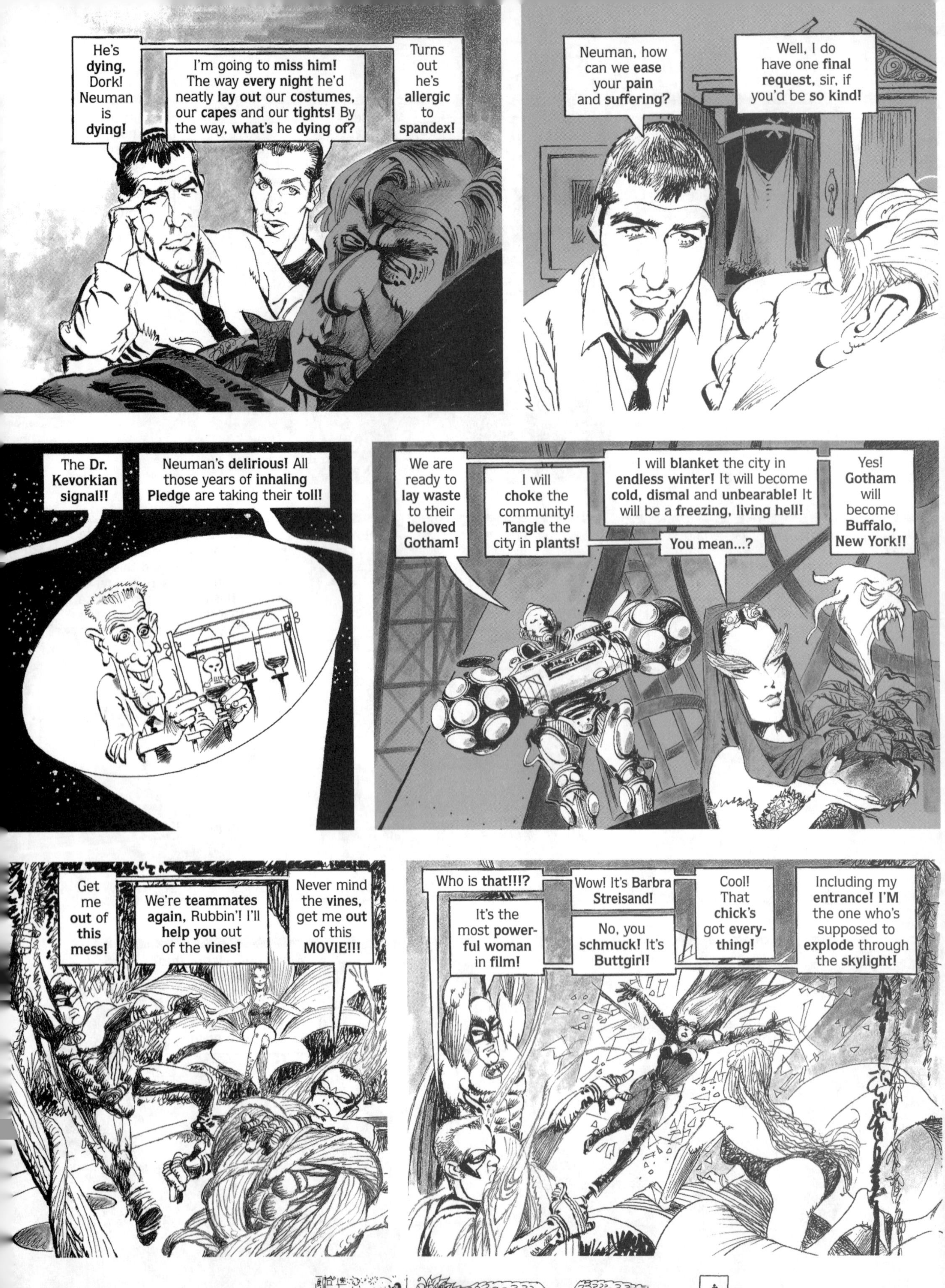
He's dying, Dork! Neuman is dying!
I'm going to miss him! The way every night he'd neatly lay out our costumes, our capes and our tights! By the way, what's he dying of?
Turns out he's allergic to spandex!
Neuman, how can we ease your pain and suffering?
Well, I do have one final request, sir, if you'd be so kind!
The Dr. Kevorkian signal!!
Neuman's delirious! All those years of inhaling Pledge are taking their toll!
We are ready to lay waste to their beloved Gotham!
I will choke the community! Tangle the city in plants!
I will blanket the city in endless winter! It will become cold, dismal and unbearable! It will be a freezing, living hell!
You mean...?
Yes! Gotham will become Buffalo, New York!!
Get me out of this mess!
We're teammates again, Rubbin'! I'll help you out of the vines!
Never mind the vines, get me out of this MOVIE!!!
Who is that!!!?
It's the most power-ful woman in film!
Wow! It's Barbra Streisand!
No, you schmuck! It's Buttgirl!
Cool! That chick's got every-thing!
Including my entrance! I'M the one who's supposed to explode through the skylight!

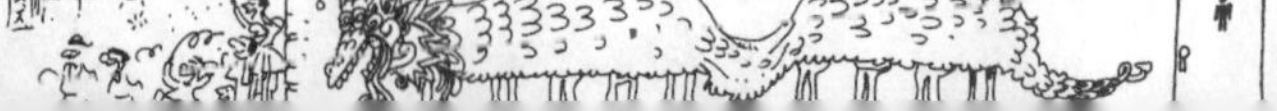

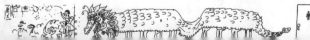

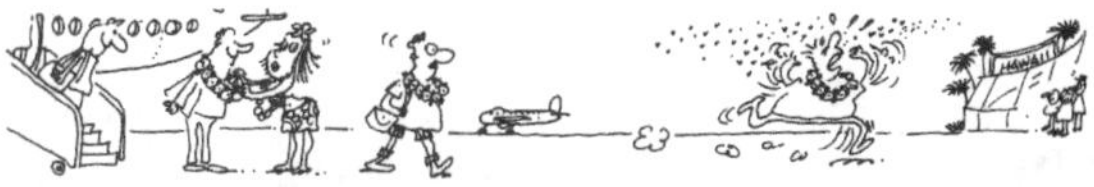

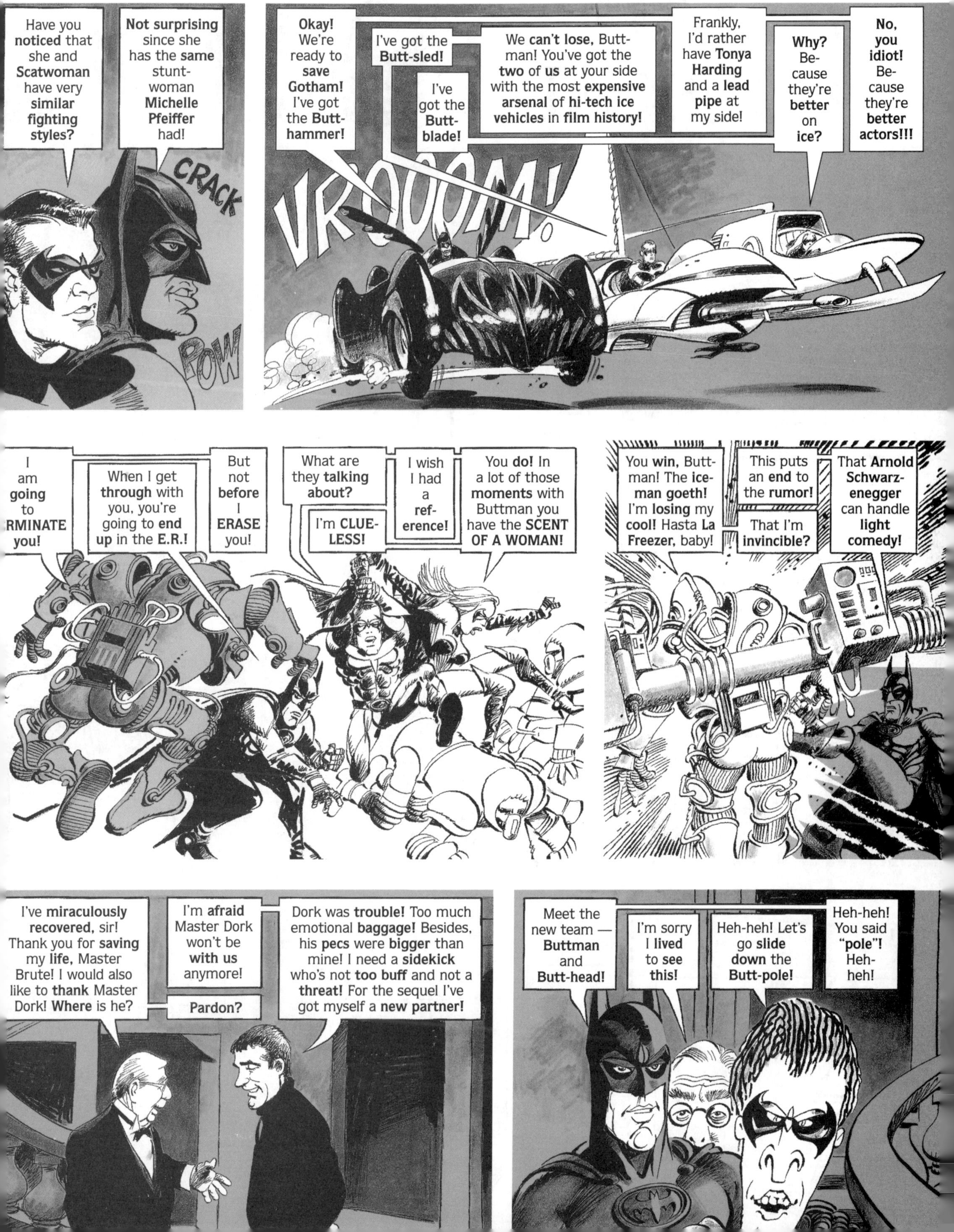

Have you noticed that she and Scatwoman have very similar fighting styles?
Not surprising since she has the same stunt-woman Michelle Pfeiffer had!
CRACK
POW
Okay! We're ready to save Gotham! I've got the Butt-hammer!
I've got the Butt-sled!
I've got the Butt-blade!
We can't lose, Butt-man! You've got the two of us at your side with the most expensive arsenal of hi-tech ice vehicles in film history!
Frankly, I'd rather have Tonya Harding and a lead pipe at my side!
Why? Be-cause they're better on ice?
No, you idiot! Be-cause they're better actors!!!
VROOOM!
I am going to RMINATE you!
When I get through with you, you're going to end up in the E.R.!
But not before I ERASE you!
What are they talking about?
I'm CLUE-LESS!
I wish I had a ref-erence!
You do! In a lot of those moments with Buttman you have the SCENT OF A WOMAN!
You win, Butt-man! The ice-man goeth! I'm losing my cool! Hasta La Freezer, baby!
This puts an end to the rumor!
That I'm invincible?
That Arnold Schwarz-enegger can handle light comedy!
I've miraculously recovered, sir! Thank you for saving my life, Master Brute! I would also like to thank Master Dork! Where is he?
I'm afraid Master Dork won't be with us anymore!
Pardon?
Dork was trouble! Too much emotional baggage! Besides, his pecs were bigger than mine! I need a sidekick who's not too buff and not a threat! For the sequel I've got myself a new partner!
Meet the new team — Buttman and Butt-head!
I'm sorry I lived to see this!
Heh-heh! Let's go slide down the Butt-pole!
Heh-heh! You said "pole"! Heh-heh!

COMIC SHNOOK'S DEPT.

A MAD LOOK AT SUPE

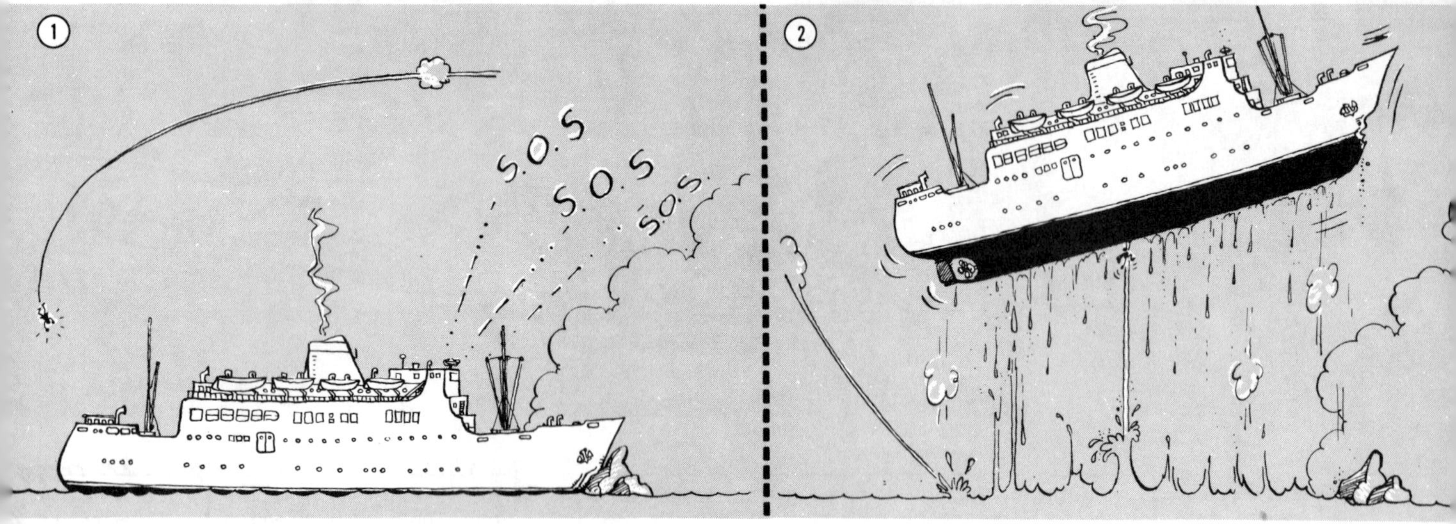
1
2
S.O.S
S.O.S
S.O.S

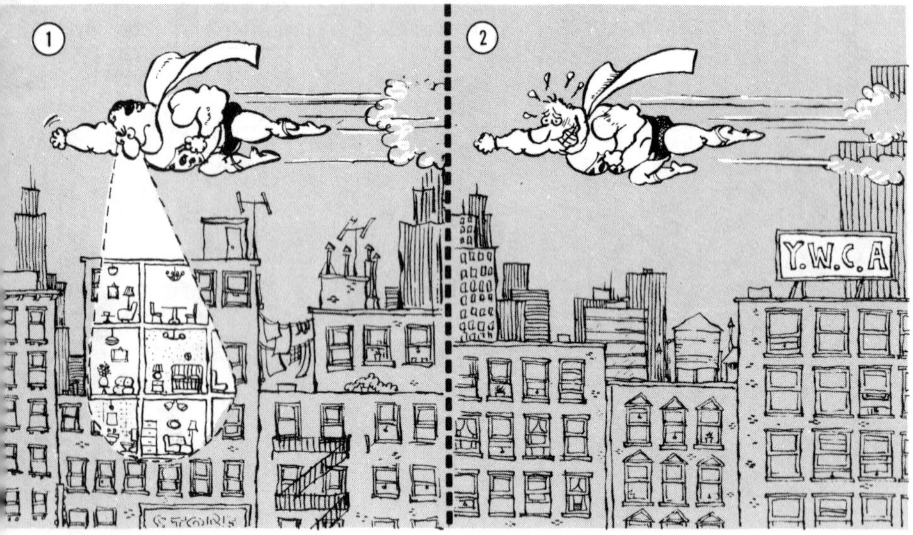
1
2
Y.W.C.A

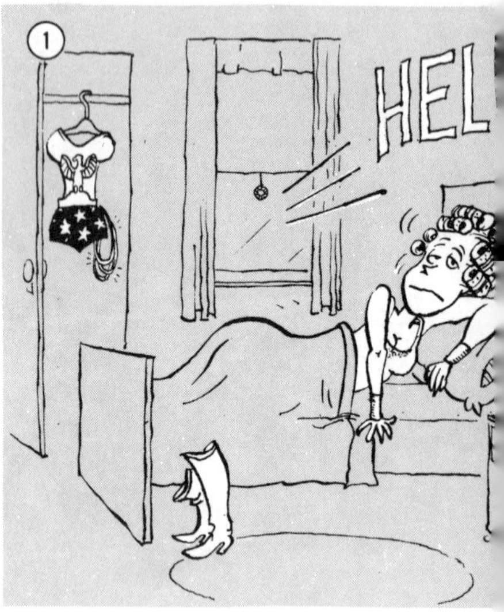
1
HEL

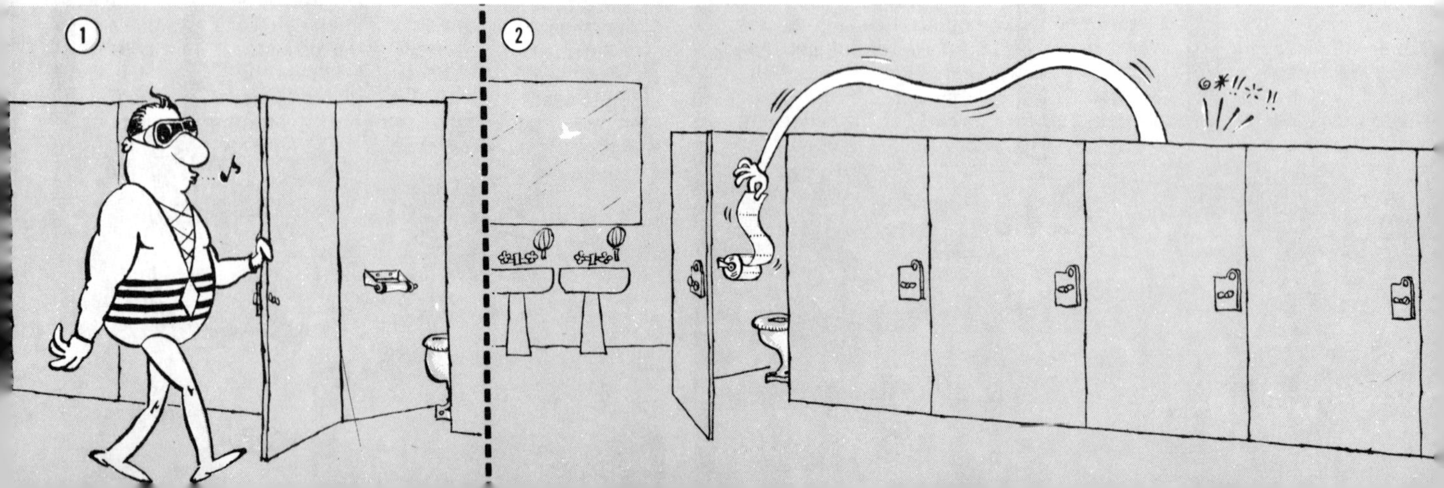
1
2

R HEROES

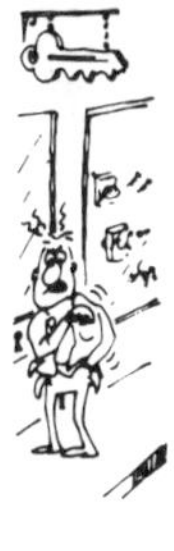

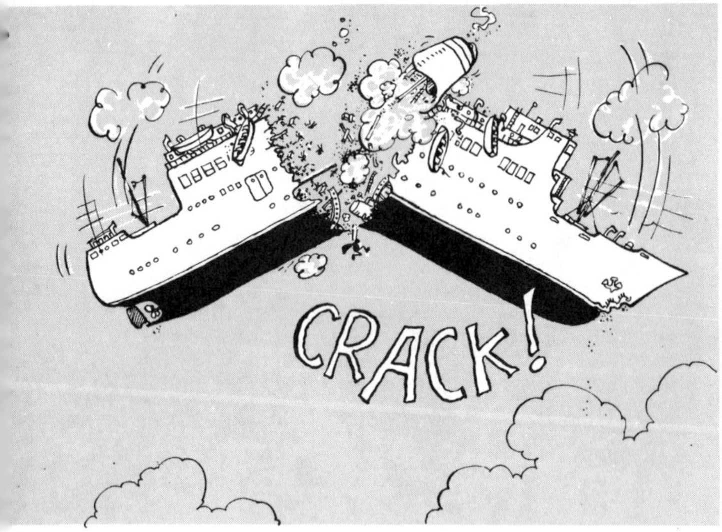
CRACK!

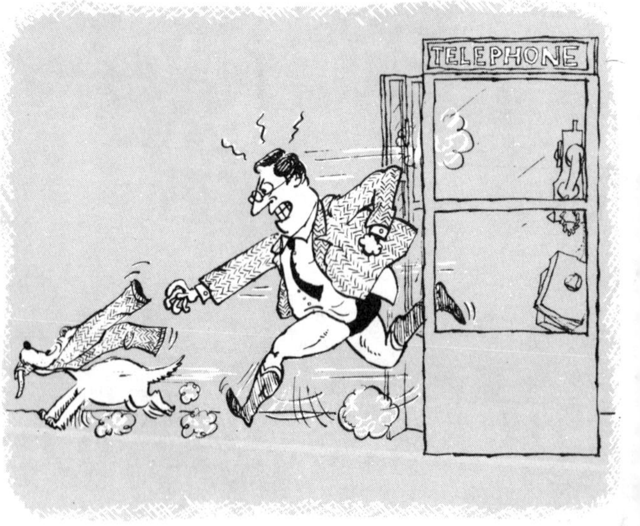
TELEPHONE

ARTIST & WRITER: SERGIO ARAGONES

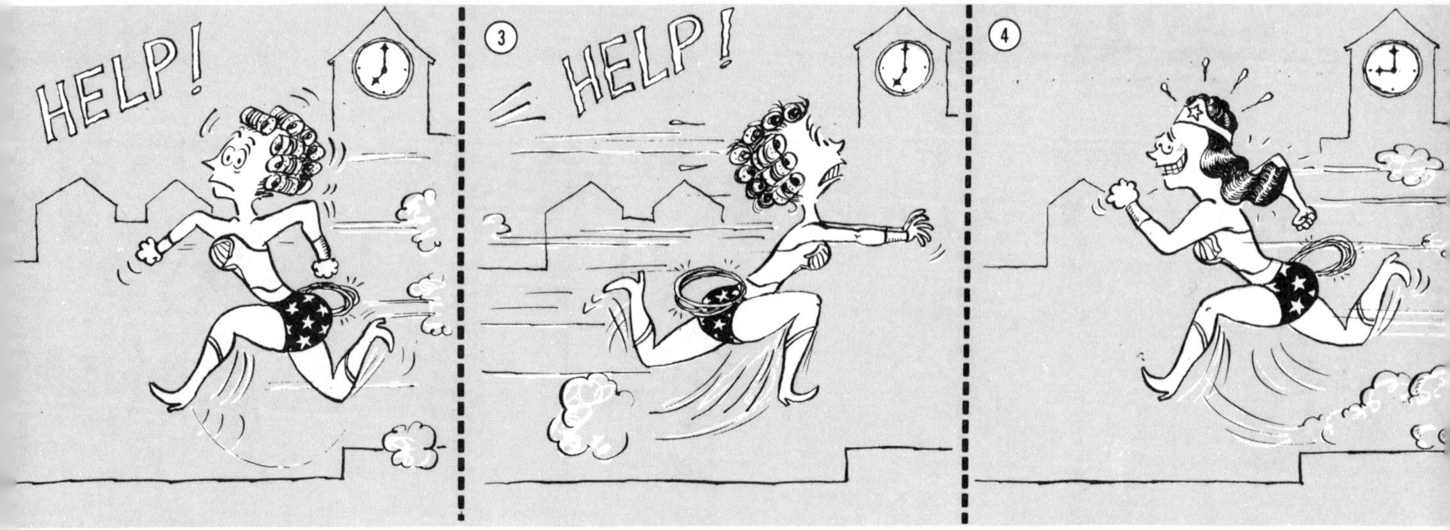
HELP!
3
HELP!
4

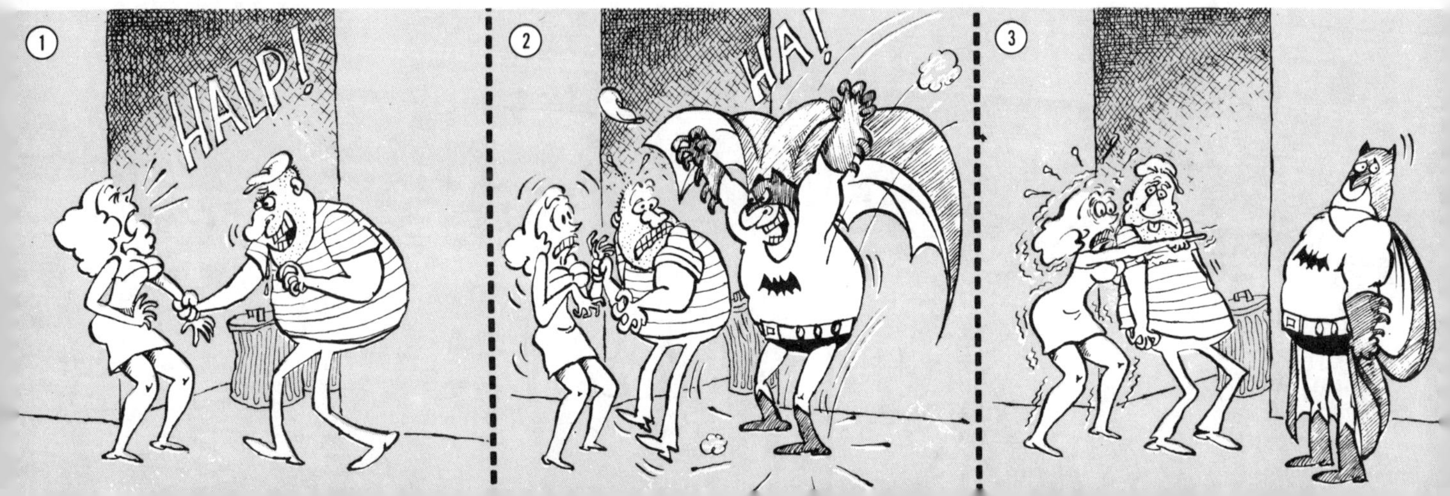
1
HALP!
2
HA!
3

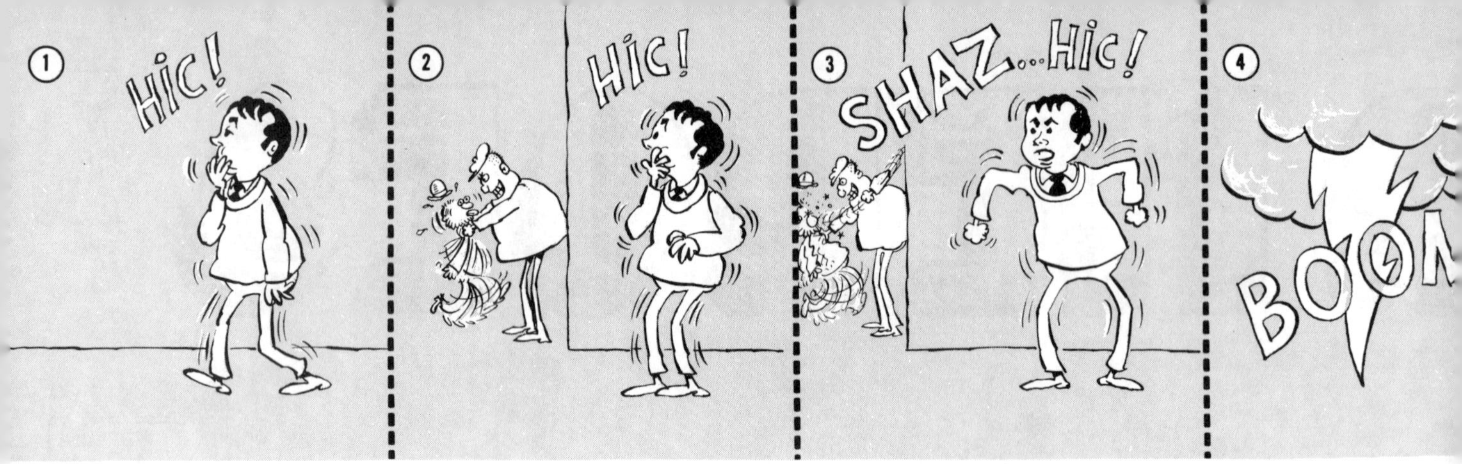
HIC!
HIC!
SHAZ...HIC!
BOO

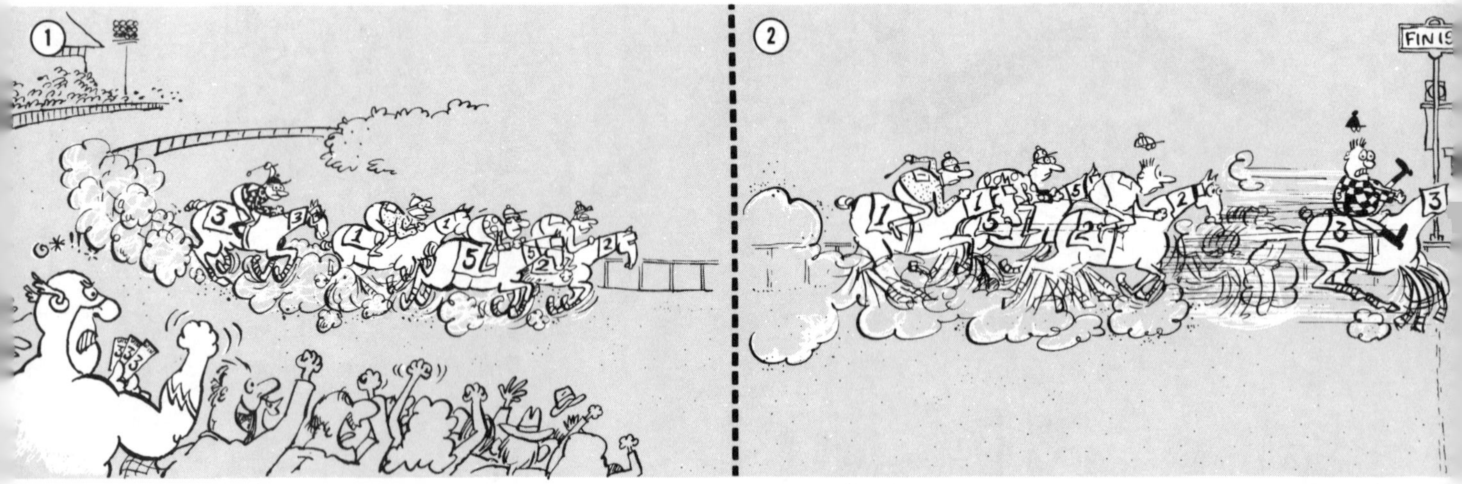
FINIS

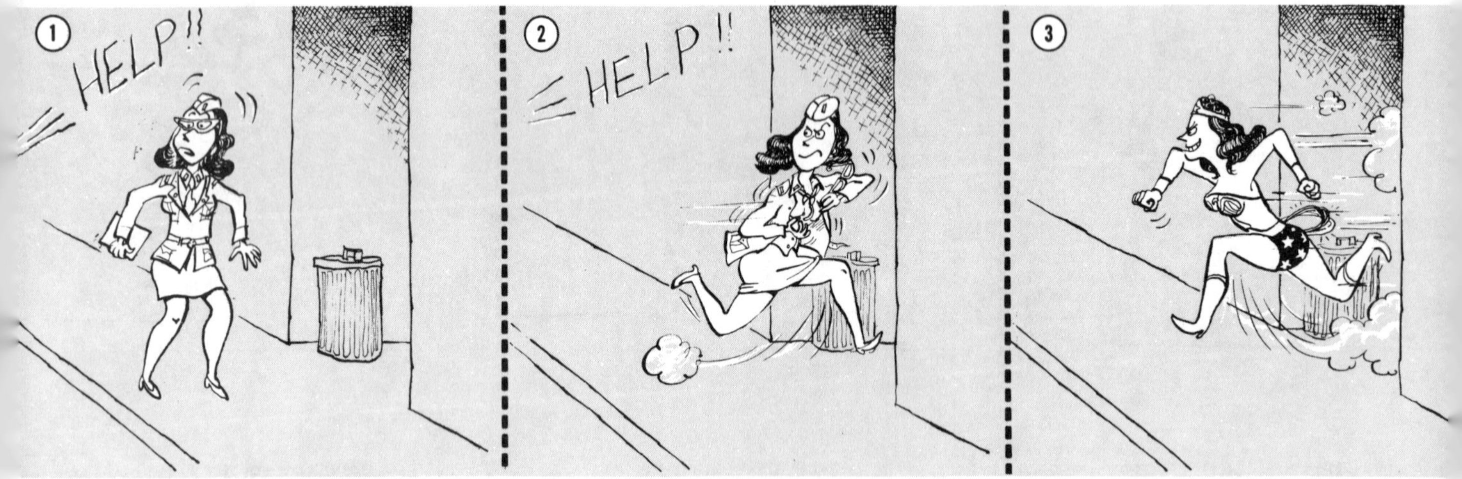
HELP!!
HELP!!

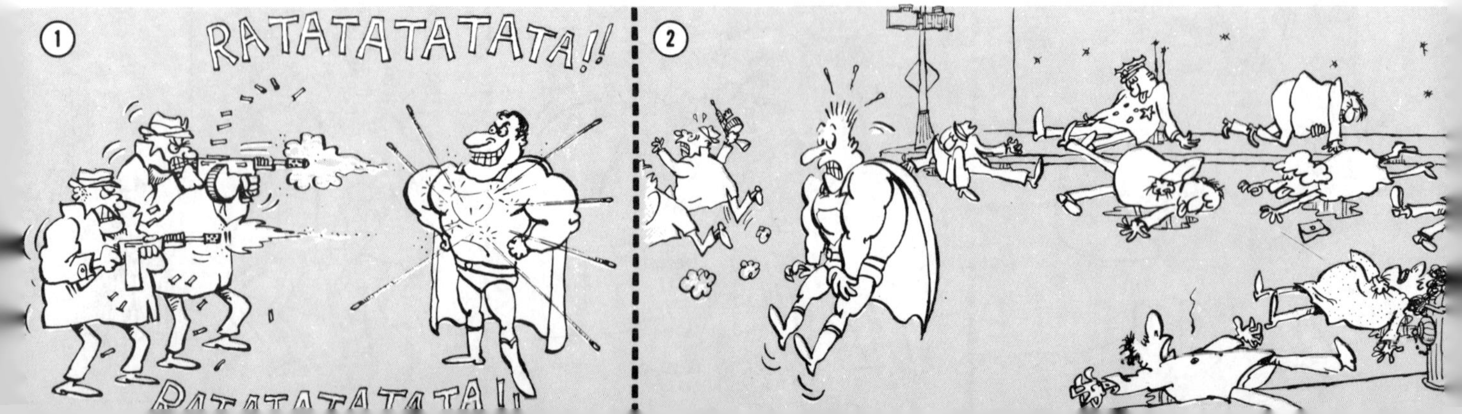
RATATATATATATA!!

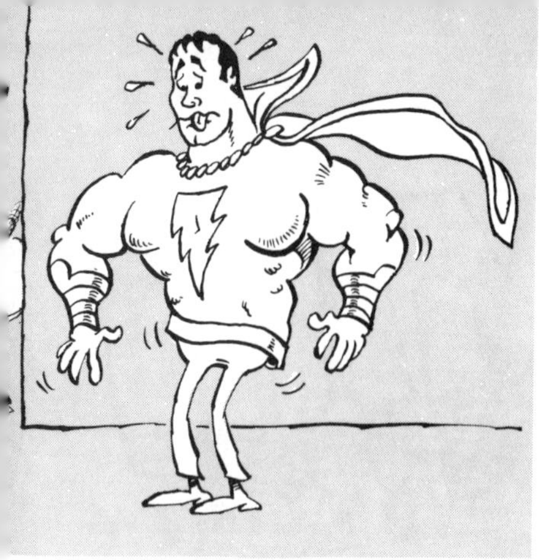

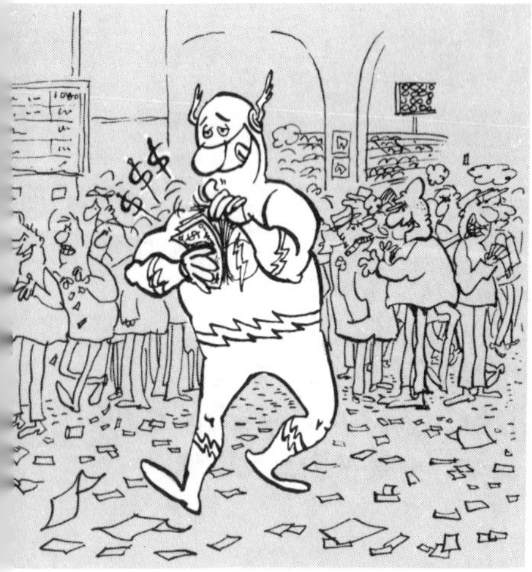

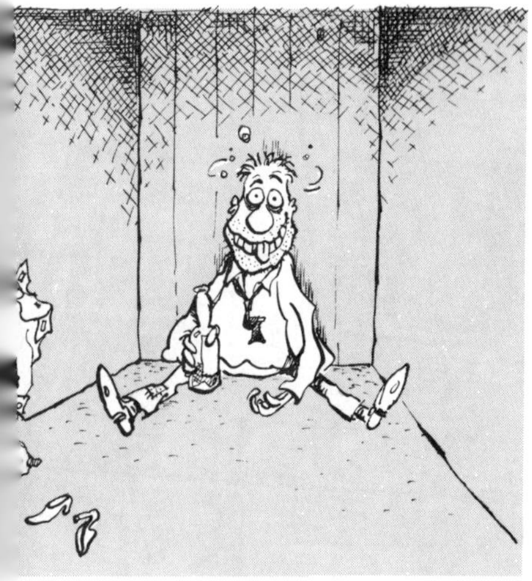

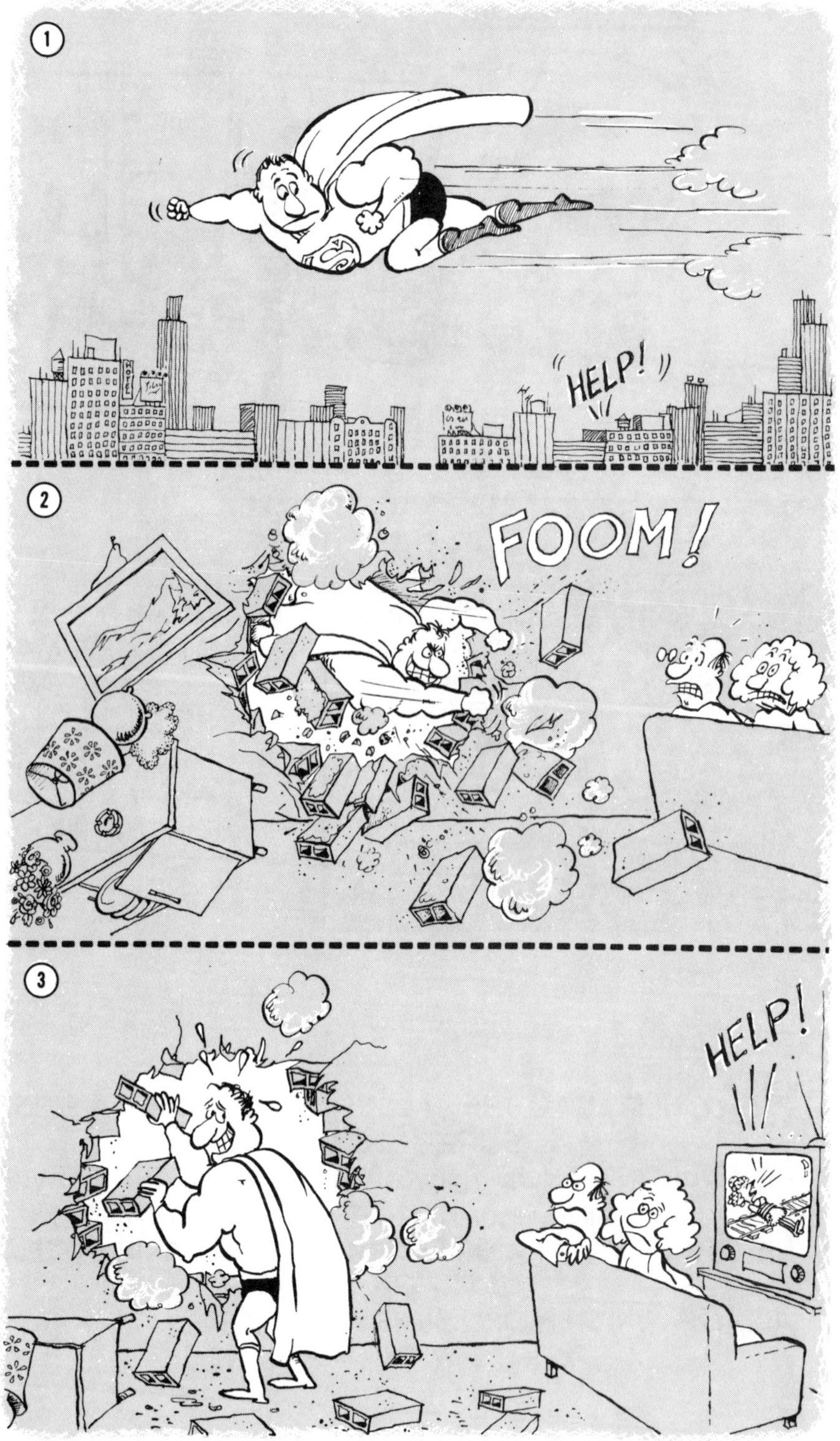
1
HELP!
2
FOOM!
3
HELP!

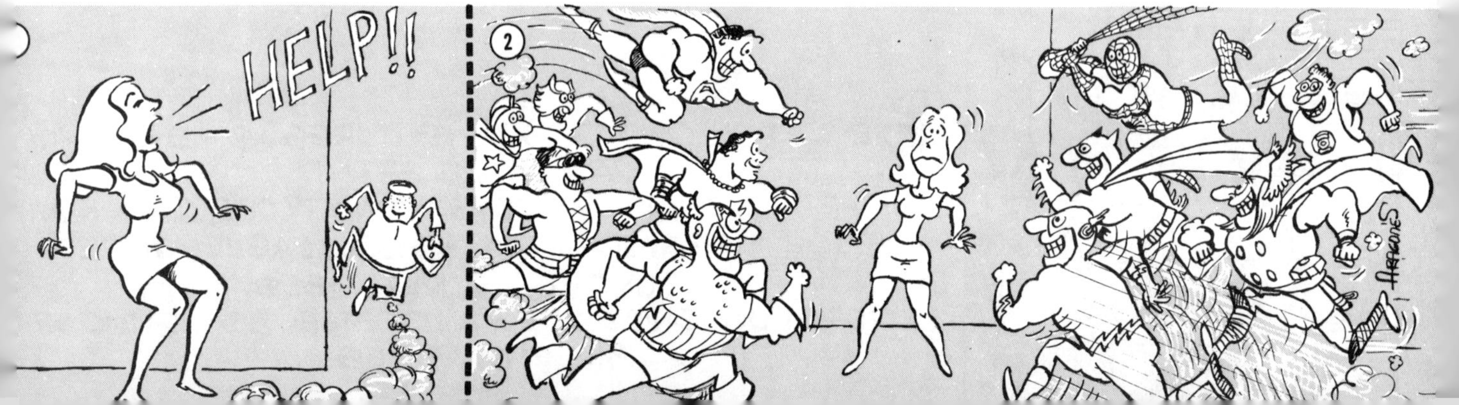
HELP!!
2

FRANK ON A ROLL DEPT.

SUPERMAN R.I.P.

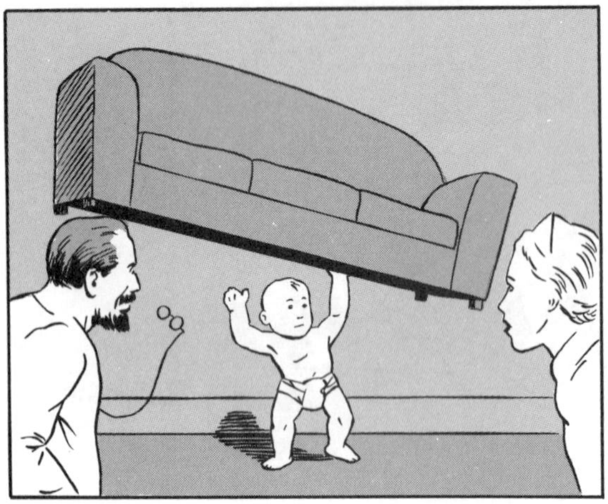

IT WAS BACK IN 1938, FROM KRYPTON OUT IN SPACE,
THAT THE MAN OF STEEL ARRIVED ON EARTH
TO SAVE THE HUMAN RACE;
HE STOOD UP FOR LAW AND ORDER, FILLED
THE FOULEST FIEND WITH FEAR,
AND ALTHOUGH HE LACKED A GREEN CARD,
WE WERE GLAD THAT HE WAS HERE.

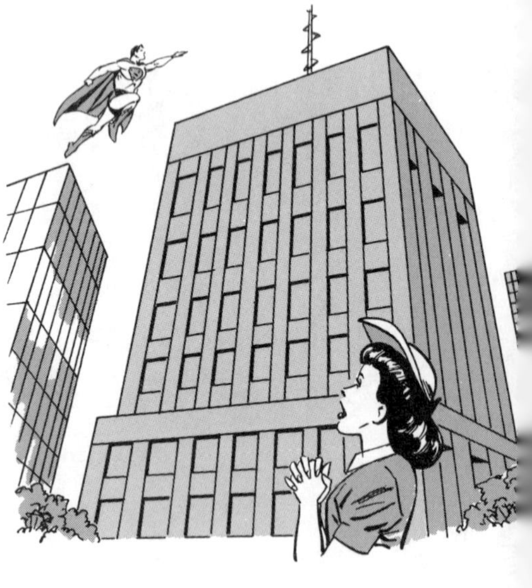

HE COULD LEAP THE TALLEST BUILDING IN A SINGLE
SUPER BOUND;
HE COULD CHANGE THE COURSE OF RIVERS, SWIM
THE DEPTHS AND NOT GET DROWNED;
HE COULD CATCH A SPEEDING BULLET AND OUTFLY
A BIRD OR PLANE.
ALL OF WHICH MOST SURELY HELPED IN MAKING
POINTS WITH LOIS LANE.

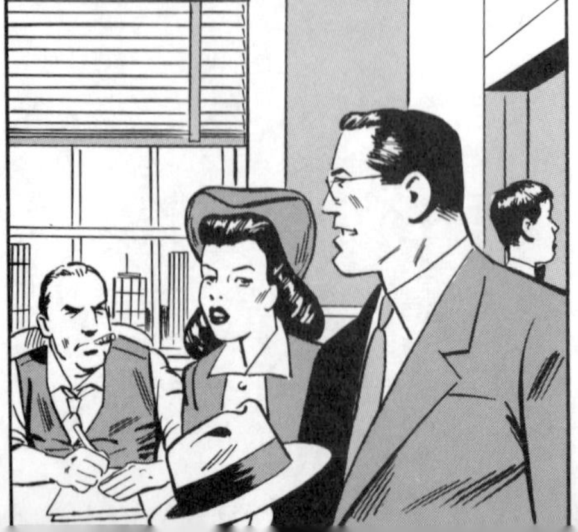

SO WE FOLLOWED HIS ADVENTURES AS HIS EARTHLY
DAYS WERE SPENT
IN THE DAILY PLANET OFFICE AS THE WIMPY ONE, CLARK KENT,
THOUGH IT SEEMED TO US HIS COLLEAGUES WERE A
BUNCH OF STUPID ASSES
NOT TO RECOGNIZE THE MAN OF STEEL BEHIND THOSE
SILLY GLASSES.

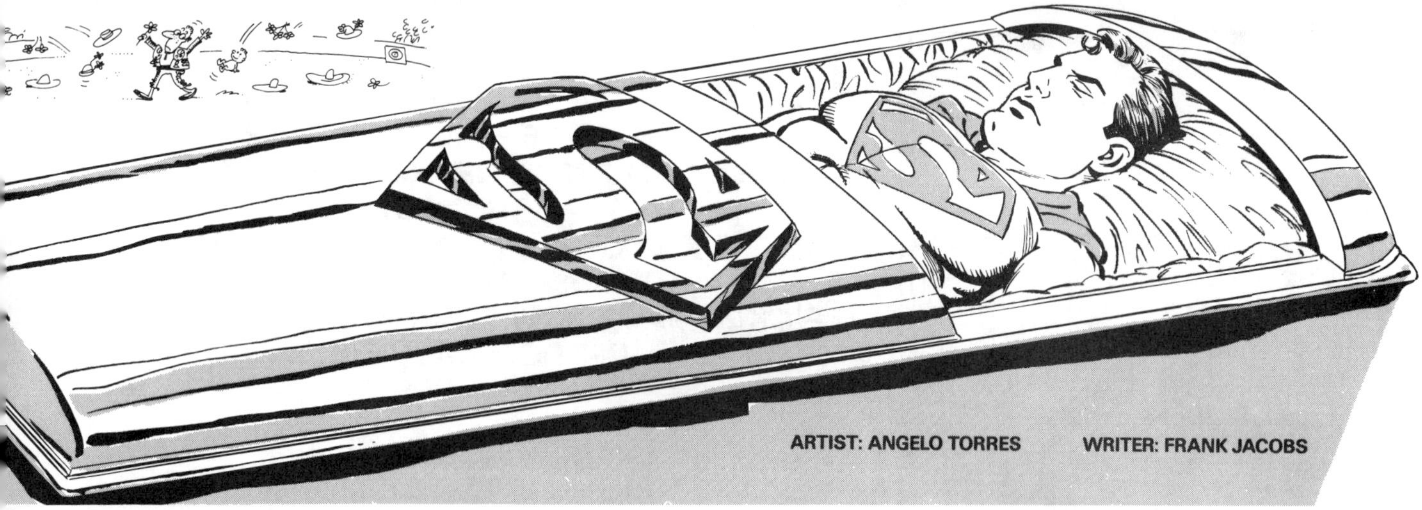
ARTIST: ANGELO TORRES WRITER: FRANK JACOBS

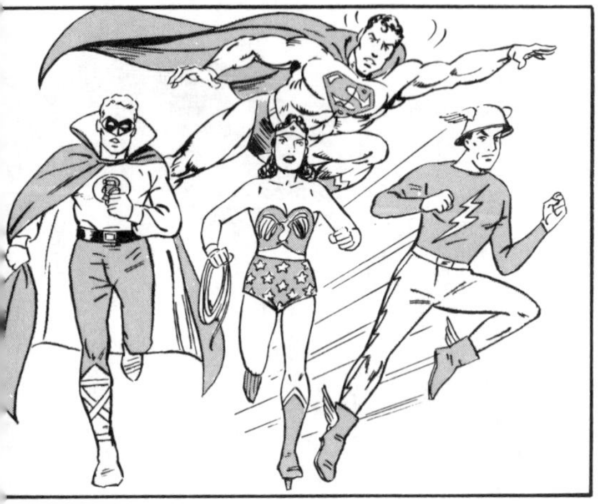

BUT THERE SOON SPRANG UP STRONG RIVALS,
EACH OF WHOM MADE QUITE A SPLASH--
NAMELY BATMAN, WONDER WOMAN, THE GREEN
LANTERN AND THE FLASH;
AND HE WORRIED FOR HIS FUTURE AS THEY
JOINED HIM IN THE CHASE--
WAS HE STILL THE MAN OF STEEL OR JUST
ANOTHER PRETTY FACE?

MORE ANXIETY HE SUFFERED AS HE PAID THE PRICE
OF FAME
TO A BUNCH OF SECOND-RATERS RIPPING OFF
HIS NOBLE NAME:
SUPERGIRL AND SUPER CHICKEN, SUPERMOUSE
AND SUPER TEEN--
EACH ONE CHEAPENING HIS IMAGE, EACH ONE
SCHLOCKING UP THE SCENE.

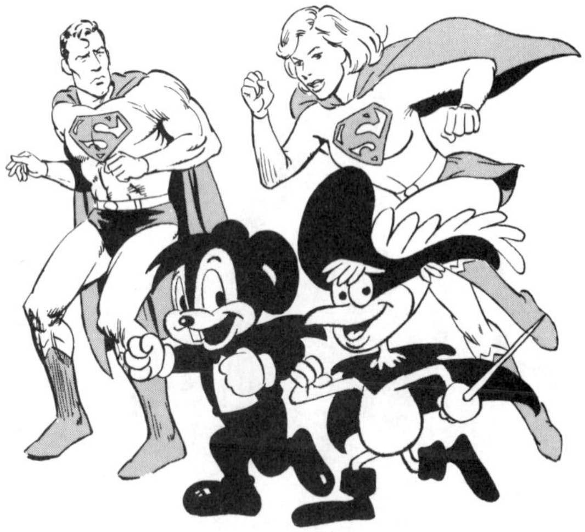

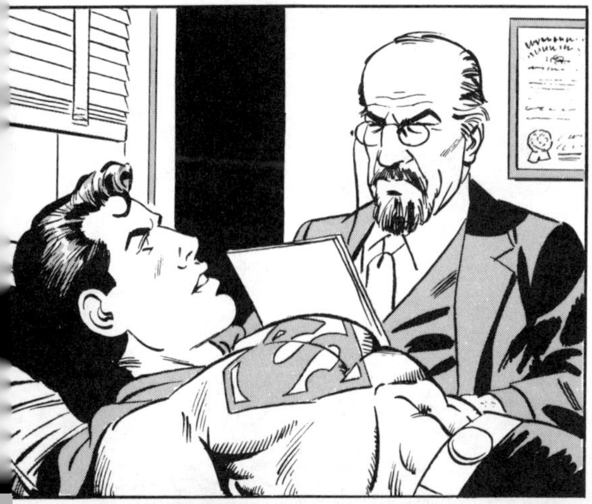

"LIFE'S A BITCH," OUR HERO MUTTERED, IN THE
THROES OF DEEP DEPRESSION
(*which he spilled out to his therapist at
eighty bucks a session*),
BUT THEN HAPPILY HE GOT A BREAK THAT
FILLED HIS HEART WITH CHEER;
IT WAS "*SUPERMAN--THE MOVIE*" AND WOULD
SALVAGE HIS CAREER.

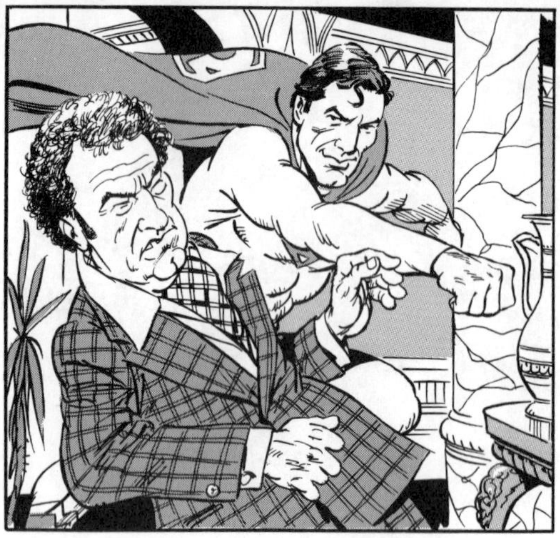

WAS HE BACK IN ALL HIS GLORY? THERE SEEMED
VERY LITTLE DOUBT
AS HE SOCKED IT TO LEX LUTHOR IN A STUNNING
SHOW OF CLOUT,
BUT THE SEQUELS BOMBED SO BADLY THAT A
COMEBACK WAS DENIED HIM;
FICKLE FANS NOW TURNED AGAINST HIM AND THE
CRITICS CRUCIFIED HIM.

HOW IT PAINED HIM SEEING BATMAN TAKE HIS
PLACE AS NUMBER ONE,
MAKING MEGABUCKS FROM MOVIES, SELLING
T-SHIRTS BY THE TON;
HOW HE SUFFERED WHEN THE NINJA CRAZE
ELECTRIFIED THE NATION.
GETTING ACED OUT BY A TURTLE WAS THE
WORST HUMILIATION.

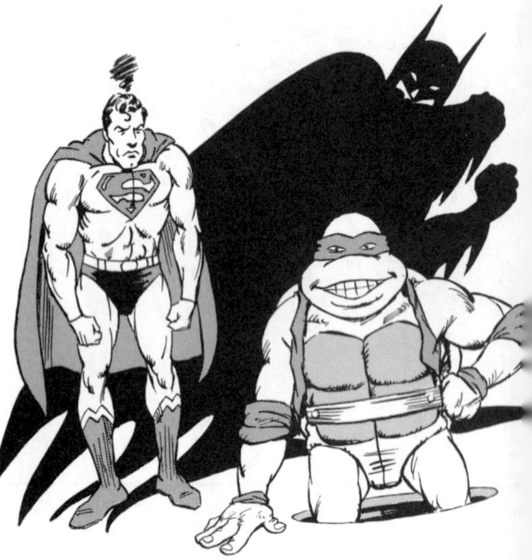

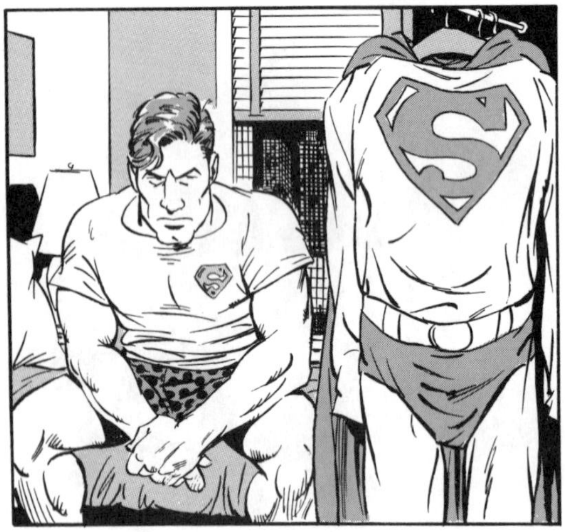

CAST ASIDE, HE HAD TO WONDER IF HIS LIFE HAD
ANY WORTH,
AND HE WISHED HE'D LANDED ANYWHERE BUT
HERE ON PLANET EARTH,
AND HE WALLOWED IN SELF-PITY AS HE CURSED
HIS ROTTEN LUCK--
DID THE "S" HE WORE SO PROUDLY STAND FOR
SUPERMAN OR SCHMUCK?

REST IN PEACE, ONCE MIGHTY SUPERMAN --
FOR YOU THERE'S NO TOMORROW;
YOU WERE SLAIN BY EVIL DOOMSDAY, BUT
OUR HEARTS FEEL LITTLE SORROW;
WHAT A PITY WHEN THE CHIPS WERE DOWN,
YOU CHOSE NOT TO SURVIVE;
SOME MAY SAY YOU DIED COURAGEOUSLY--
WE KNOW YOU TOOK A DIVE.

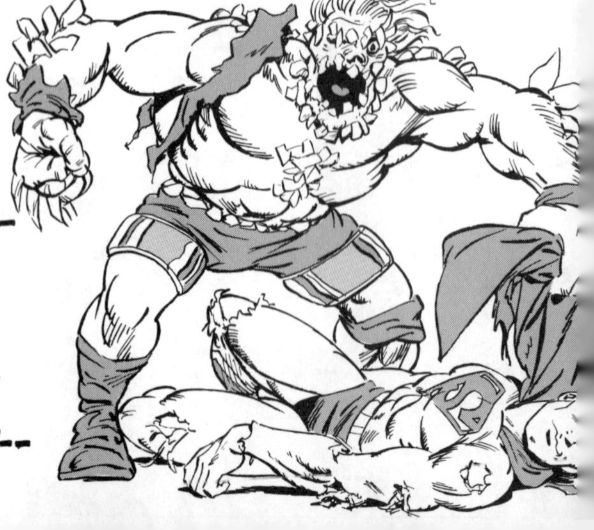

THE MULTIPLEX-MEN DEPT.

ARTIST: AMANDA CONNER
WRITER: DESMOND DEVLIN

Hollywood has a long tradition of spending big bucks on live-action films featuring superheroes! And when you consider turkeys like *Batman and Robin*, *Steel*, *Judge Dredd* and *Spawn*, you kind of wonder why that tradition continues! Simple: The studio heads are nimrods, morons, peabrains and dolts who never learn from their mistakes! Which is why we're sure to see these…

UPCOMING MOVIES BASED ON COMIC BOOKS

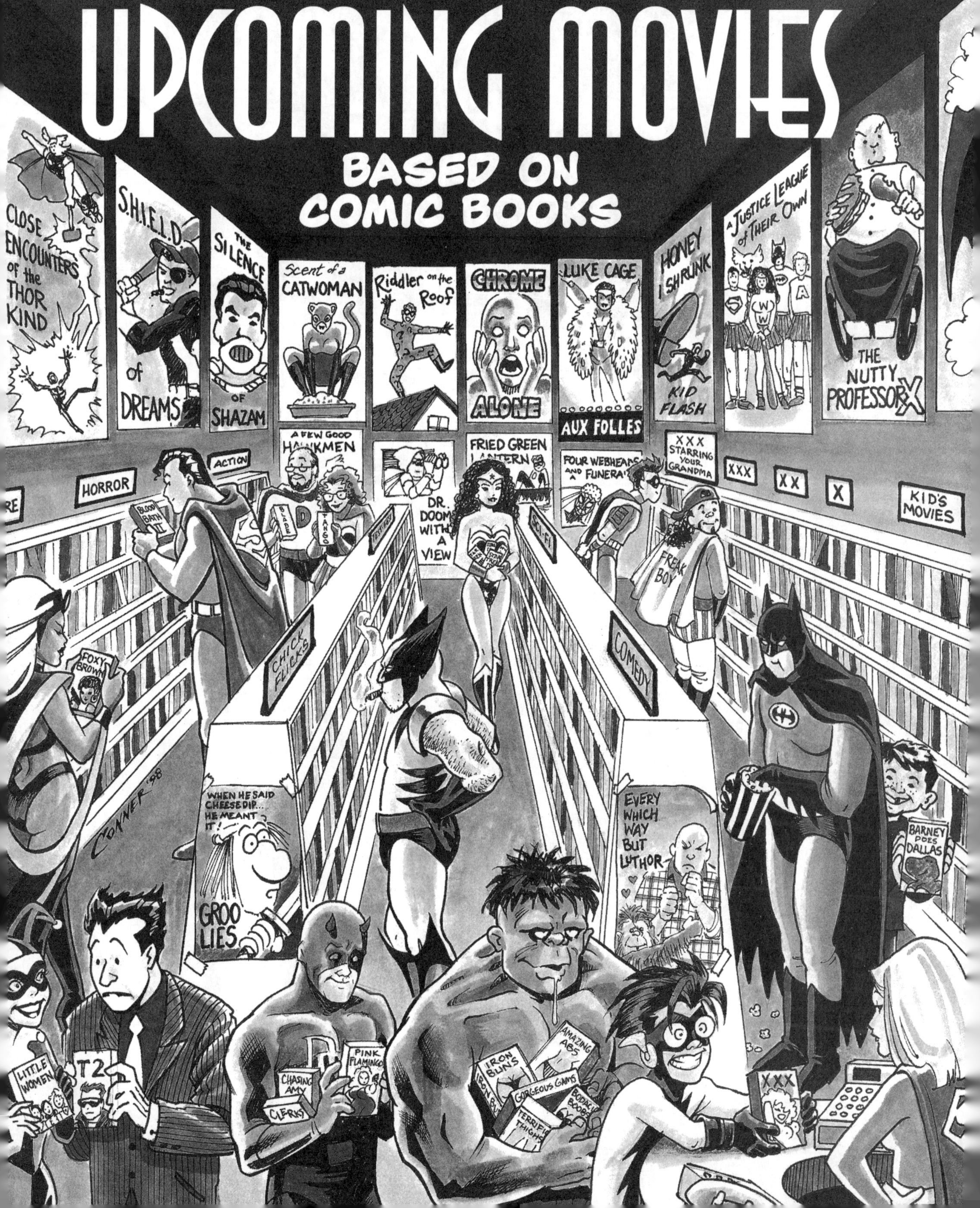
CLOSE ENCOUNTERS of the THOR KIND
S.H.I.E.L.D of DREAMS
THE SILENCE OF SHAZAM
Scent of a CATWOMAN
Riddler on the Roof
CHROME ALONE
LUKE CAGE AUX FOLLES
HONEY I SHRUNK KID FLASH
A JUSTICE LEAGUE of THEIR OWN
THE NUTTY PROFESSOR X
A FEW GOOD HAWKMEN
FRIED GREEN LANTERN
FOUR WEBHEADS AND A
DR. DOOM WITH A VIEW
XXX STARRING YOUR GRANDMA
HORROR
ACTION
XXX
XX
X
KID'S MOVIES
BLOOD BATH II
BLADE
SCI-FI
CHICK FLICKS
COMEDY
FOXY BROWN
FREAK BOY
WHEN HE SAID CHEESE DIP... HE MEANT IT!
GROO LIES
EVERY WHICH WAY BUT LUTHOR
BARNEY DOES DALLAS
LITTLE WOMEN
T2
CHASING AMY
CLERKS
PINK FLAMINGOS
IRON BUNS
AMAZING ABS
GORGEOUS GAMS
TERRIFIC THIGHS
XXX
CONNER '98

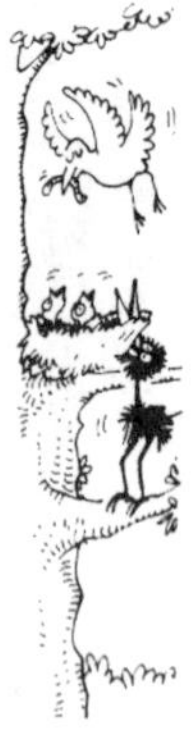

UPCOMING MOVIES

BASED ON COMIC BOOKS

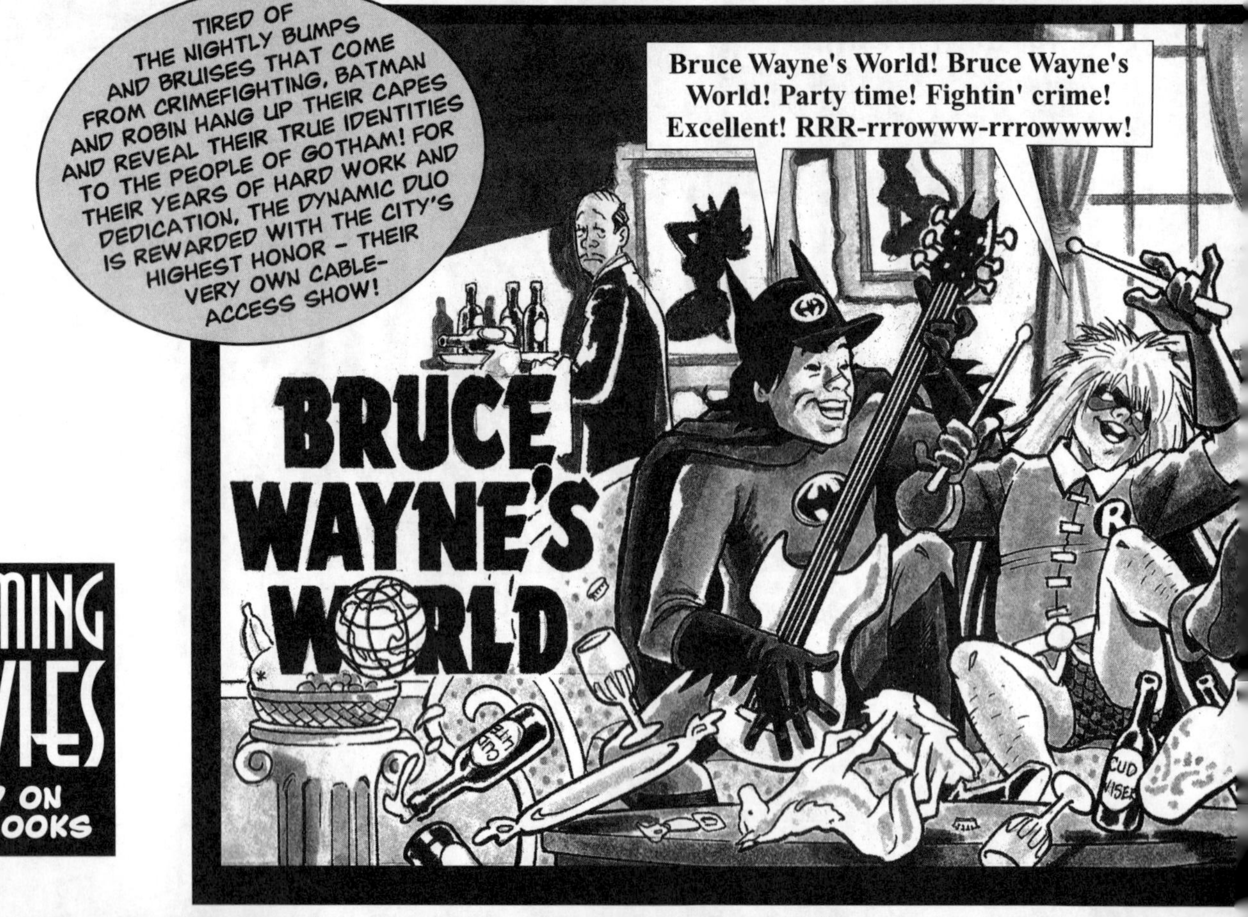
TIRED OF THE NIGHTLY BUMPS AND BRUISES THAT COME FROM CRIMEFIGHTING, BATMAN AND ROBIN HANG UP THEIR CAPES AND REVEAL THEIR TRUE IDENTITIES TO THE PEOPLE OF GOTHAM! FOR THEIR YEARS OF HARD WORK AND DEDICATION, THE DYNAMIC DUO IS REWARDED WITH THE CITY'S HIGHEST HONOR – THEIR VERY OWN CABLE-ACCESS SHOW!
Bruce Wayne's World! Bruce Wayne's World! Party time! Fightin' crime! Excellent! RRR-rrrowww-rrrowwww!
BRUCE WAYNE'S WORLD

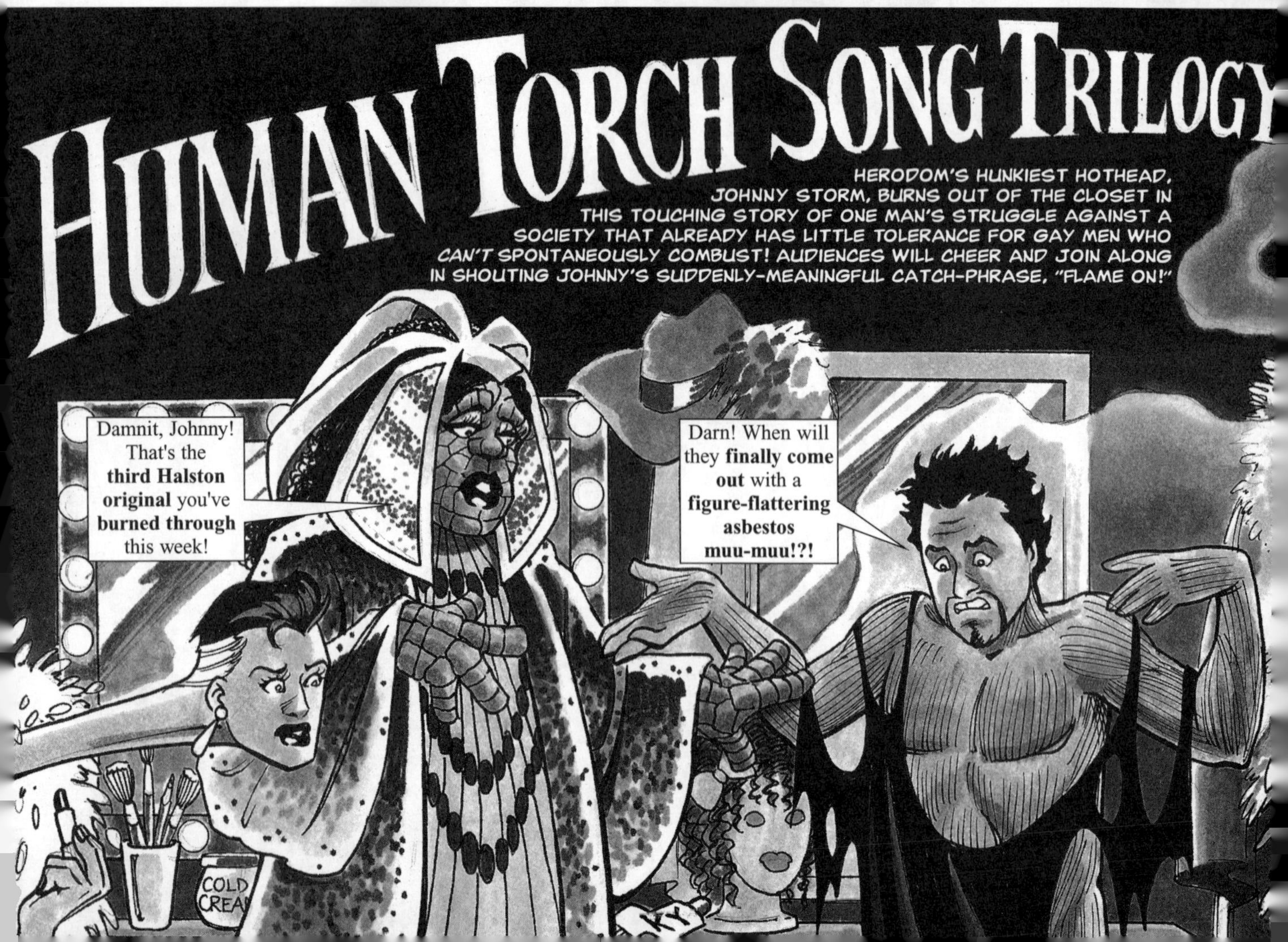
HUMAN TORCH SONG TRILOGY
HERODOM'S HUNKIEST HOTHEAD, JOHNNY STORM, BURNS OUT OF THE CLOSET IN THIS TOUCHING STORY OF ONE MAN'S STRUGGLE AGAINST A SOCIETY THAT ALREADY HAS LITTLE TOLERANCE FOR GAY MEN WHO *CAN'T* SPONTANEOUSLY COMBUST! AUDIENCES WILL CHEER AND JOIN ALONG IN SHOUTING JOHNNY'S SUDDENLY-MEANINGFUL CATCH-PHRASE, "FLAME ON!"
Damnit, Johnny! That's the **third Halston original** you've **burned through** this week!
Darn! When will they **finally come out** with a **figure-flattering asbestos muu-muu!?!**
COLD CREAM

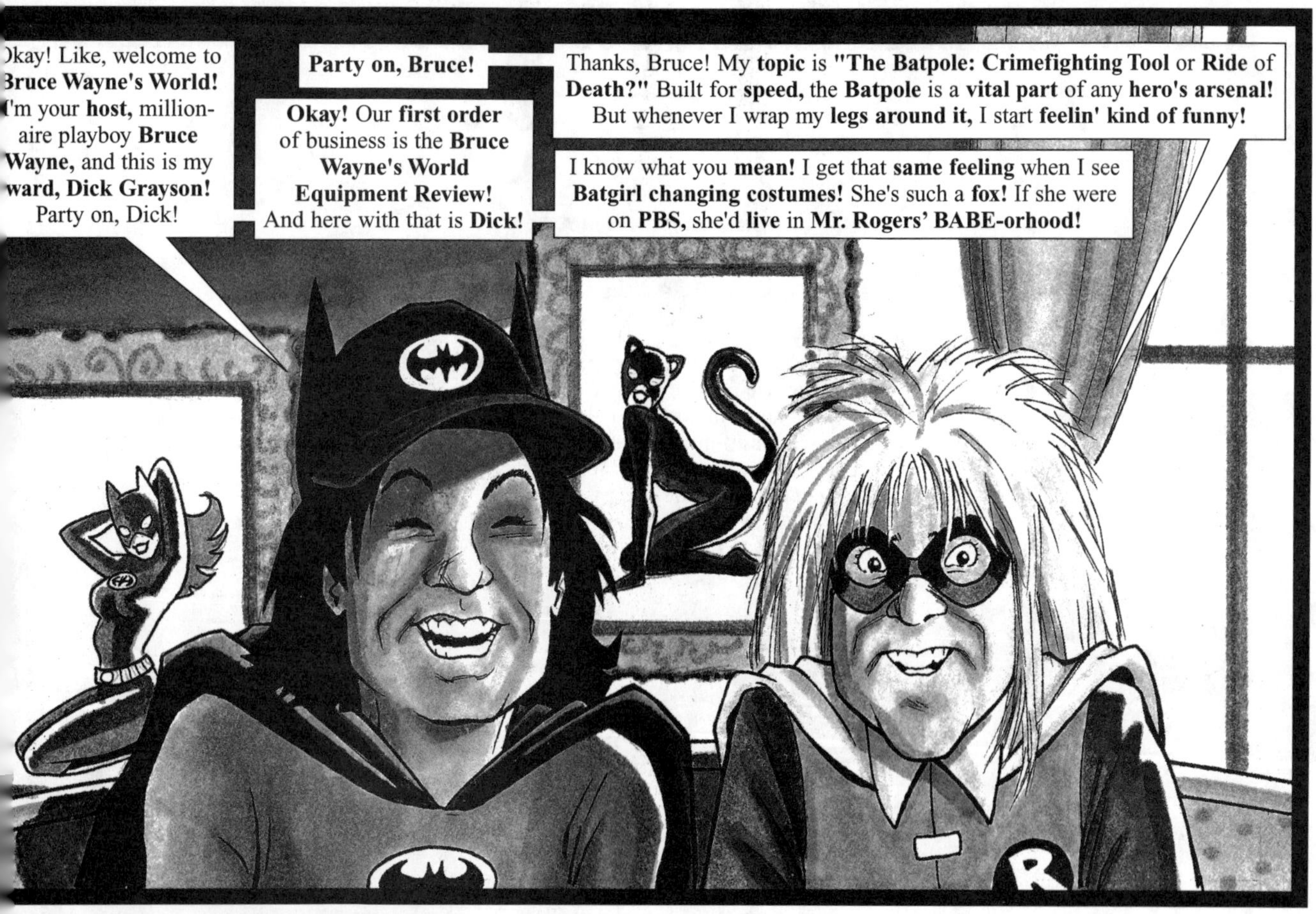
)kay! Like, welcome to Bruce Wayne's World! I'm your host, millionaire playboy Bruce Wayne, and this is my ward, Dick Grayson! Party on, Dick!
Party on, Bruce!
Okay! Our first order of business is the Bruce Wayne's World Equipment Review! And here with that is Dick!
Thanks, Bruce! My topic is "The Batpole: Crimefighting Tool or Ride of Death?" Built for speed, the Batpole is a vital part of any hero's arsenal! But whenever I wrap my legs around it, I start feelin' kind of funny!
I know what you mean! I get that same feeling when I see Batgirl changing costumes! She's such a fox! If she were on PBS, she'd live in Mr. Rogers' BABE-orhood!

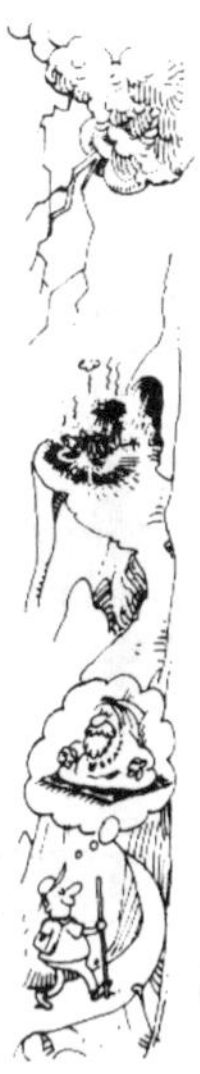

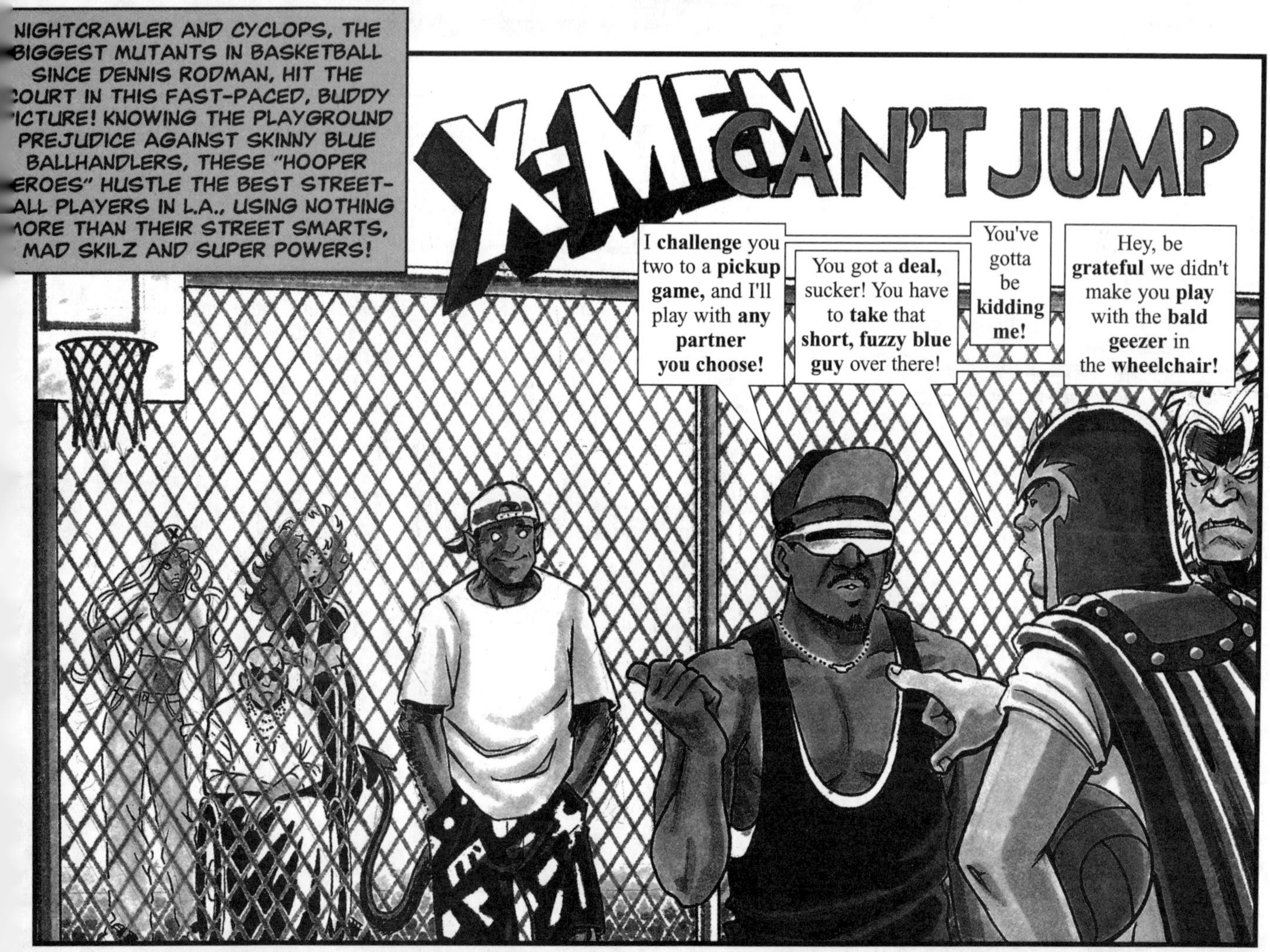
NIGHTCRAWLER AND CYCLOPS, THE BIGGEST MUTANTS IN BASKETBALL SINCE DENNIS RODMAN, HIT THE COURT IN THIS FAST-PACED, BUDDY PICTURE! KNOWING THE PLAYGROUND PREJUDICE AGAINST SKINNY BLUE BALLHANDLERS, THESE "HOOPER HEROES" HUSTLE THE BEST STREET-BALL PLAYERS IN L.A., USING NOTHING MORE THAN THEIR STREET SMARTS, MAD SKILZ AND SUPER POWERS!
X-MEN CAN'T JUMP
I challenge you two to a pickup game, and I'll play with any partner you choose!
You got a deal, sucker! You have to take that short, fuzzy blue guy over there!
You've gotta be kidding me!
Hey, be grateful we didn't make you play with the bald geezer in the wheelchair!

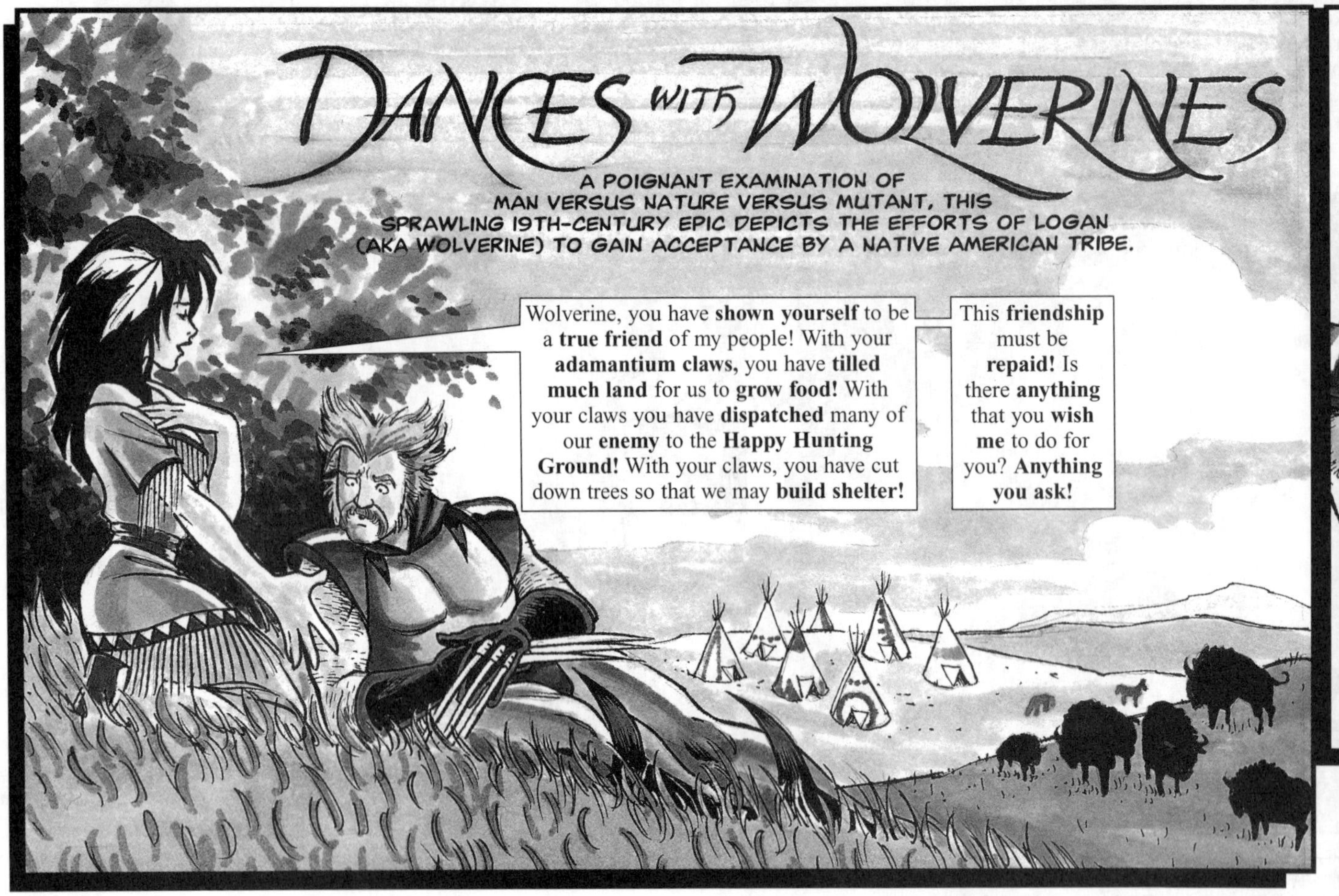
DANCES WITH WOLVERINES
A POIGNANT EXAMINATION OF MAN VERSUS NATURE VERSUS MUTANT, THIS SPRAWLING 19TH-CENTURY EPIC DEPICTS THE EFFORTS OF LOGAN (AKA WOLVERINE) TO GAIN ACCEPTANCE BY A NATIVE AMERICAN TRIBE.
Wolverine, you have **shown yourself** to be a **true friend** of my people! With your **adamantium claws,** you have **tilled much land** for us to **grow food!** With your claws you have **dispatched** many of our **enemy** to the **Happy Hunting Ground!** With your claws, you have cut down trees so that we may **build shelter!**
This **friendship** must be **repaid!** Is there **anything** that you **wish me** to do for you? **Anything you ask!**

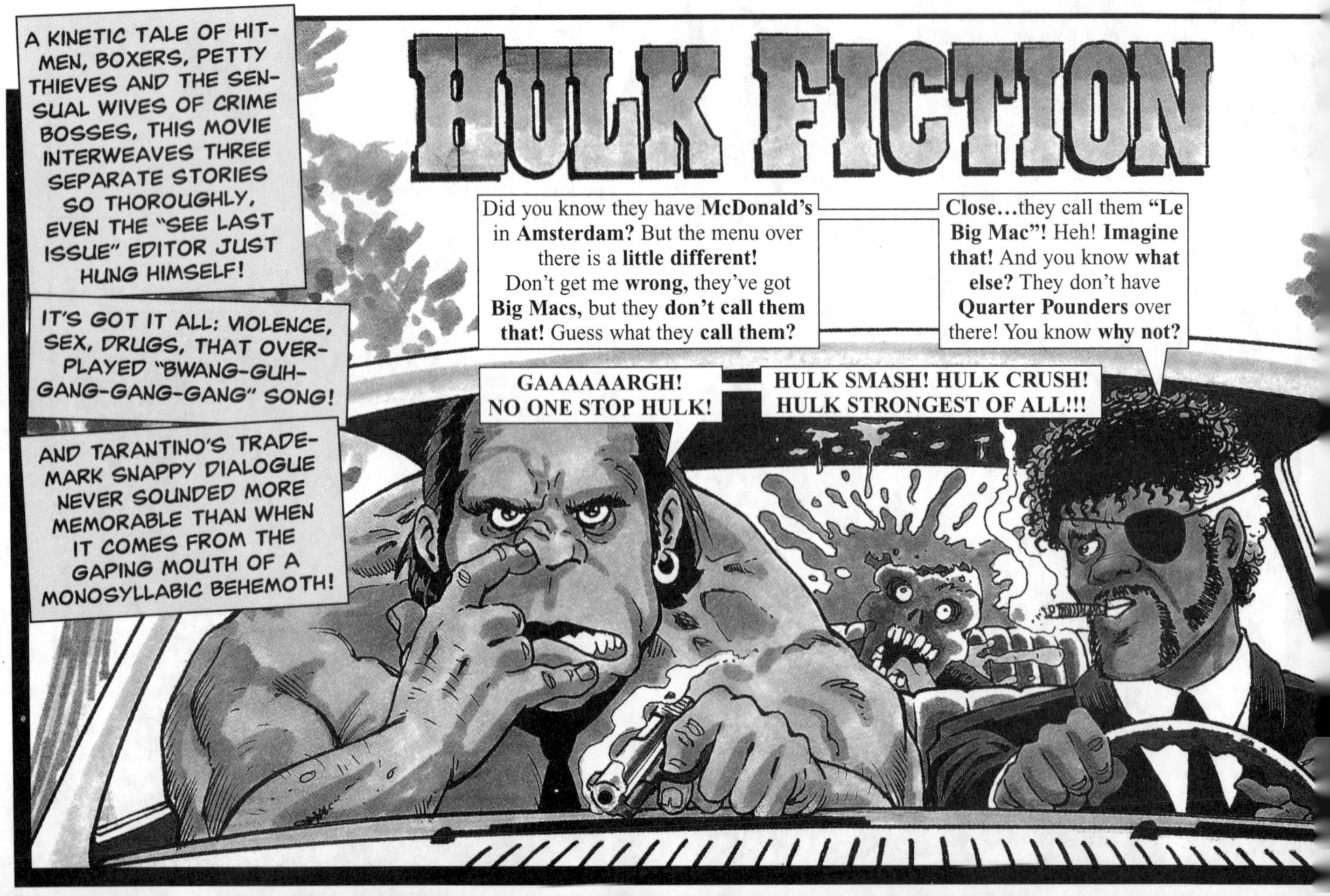
A KINETIC TALE OF HIT-MEN, BOXERS, PETTY THIEVES AND THE SEN-SUAL WIVES OF CRIME BOSSES, THIS MOVIE INTERWEAVES THREE SEPARATE STORIES SO THOROUGHLY, EVEN THE "SEE LAST ISSUE" EDITOR JUST HUNG HIMSELF!
HULK FICTION
IT'S GOT IT ALL: VIOLENCE, SEX, DRUGS, THAT OVER-PLAYED "BWANG-GUH-GANG-GANG-GANG" SONG!
AND TARANTINO'S TRADE-MARK SNAPPY DIALOGUE NEVER SOUNDED MORE MEMORABLE THAN WHEN IT COMES FROM THE GAPING MOUTH OF A MONOSYLLABIC BEHEMOTH!
Did you know they have **McDonald's** in **Amsterdam?** But the menu over there is a **little different!** Don't get me **wrong,** they've got **Big Macs,** but they **don't call them that!** Guess what they **call them?**
GAAAAAARGH! NO ONE STOP HULK!
Close…they call them **"Le Big Mac"!** Heh! **Imagine that!** And you know **what else?** They don't have **Quarter Pounders** over there! You know **why not?**
HULK SMASH! HULK CRUSH! HULK STRONGEST OF ALL!!!

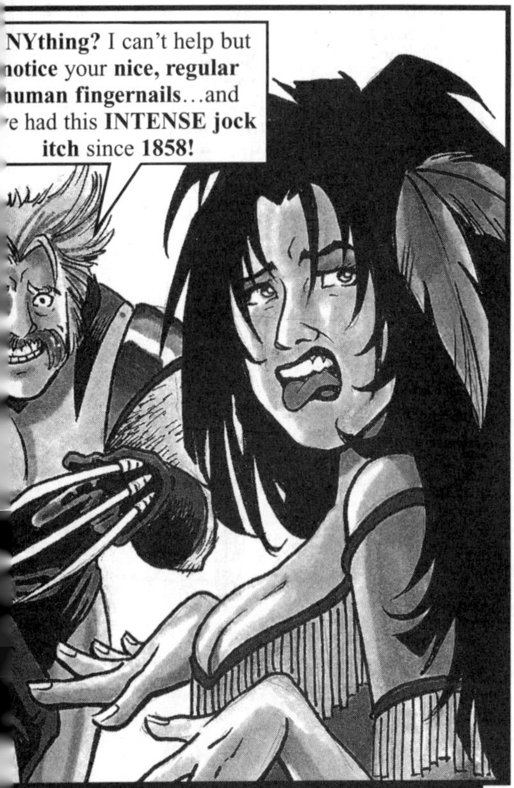
NYthing? I can't help but notice your nice, regular human fingernails…and 'e had this INTENSE jock itch since 1858!

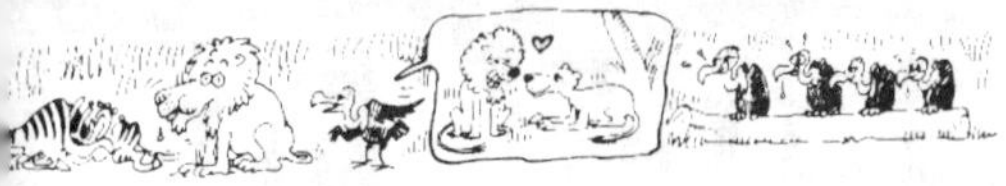

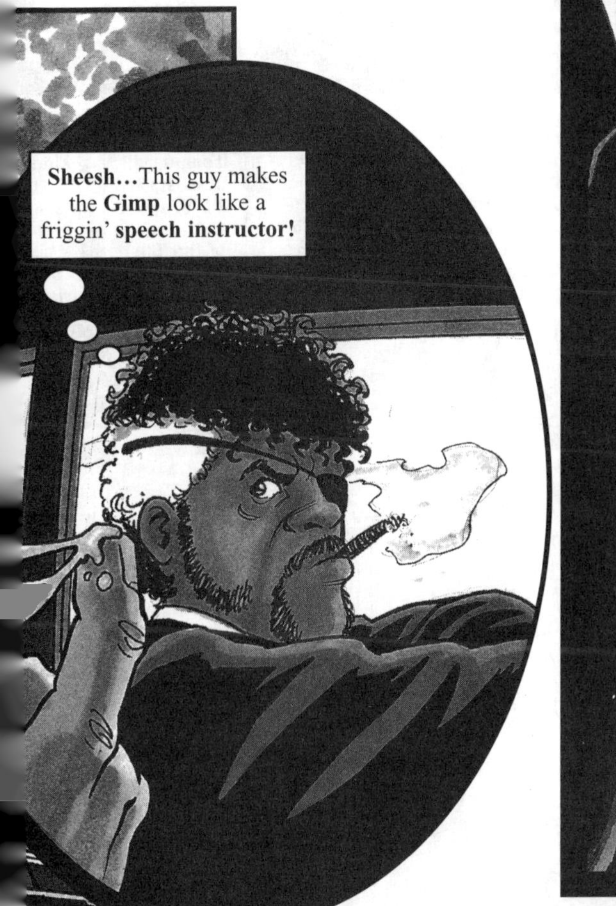
Sheesh…This guy makes the Gimp look like a friggin' speech instructor!

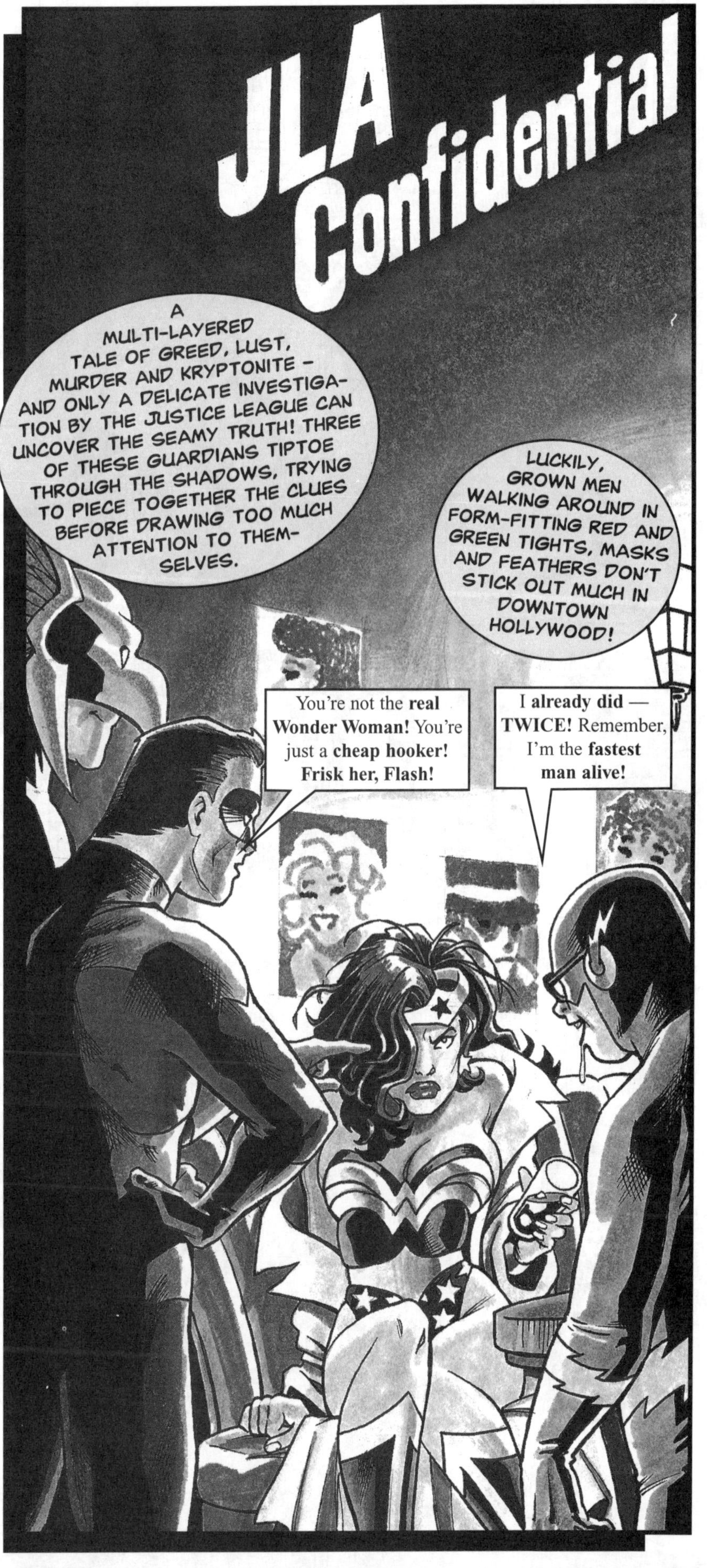
JLA Confidential
A MULTI-LAYERED TALE OF GREED, LUST, MURDER AND KRYPTONITE – AND ONLY A DELICATE INVESTIGATION BY THE JUSTICE LEAGUE CAN UNCOVER THE SEAMY TRUTH! THREE OF THESE GUARDIANS TIPTOE THROUGH THE SHADOWS, TRYING TO PIECE TOGETHER THE CLUES BEFORE DRAWING TOO MUCH ATTENTION TO THEMSELVES.
LUCKILY, GROWN MEN WALKING AROUND IN FORM-FITTING RED AND GREEN TIGHTS, MASKS AND FEATHERS DON'T STICK OUT MUCH IN DOWNTOWN HOLLYWOOD!
You're not the real Wonder Woman! You're just a cheap hooker! Frisk her, Flash!
I already did — TWICE! Remember, I'm the fastest man alive!

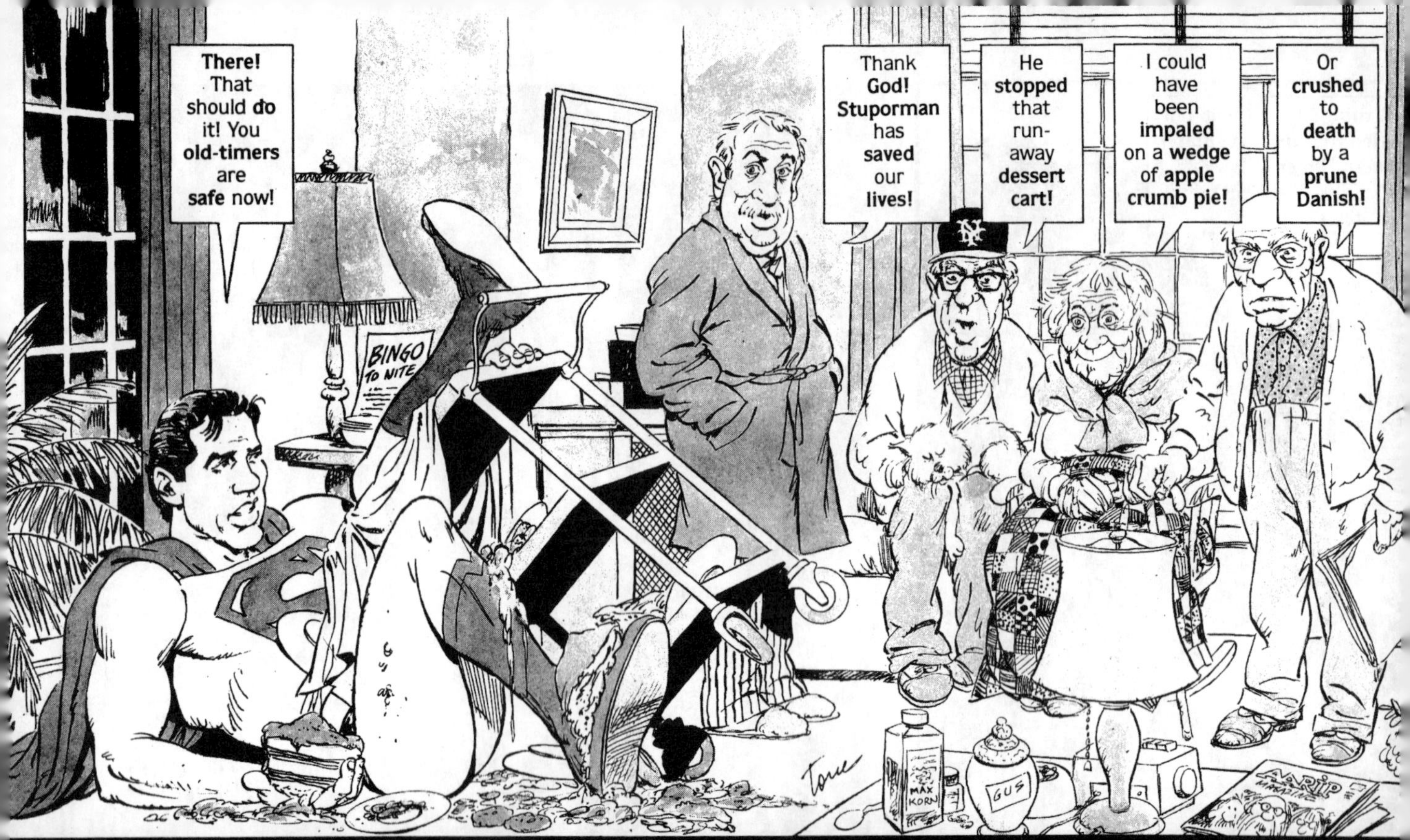
There! That should do it! You old-timers are safe now!
Thank God! Stuporman has saved our lives!
He stopped that run-away dessert cart!
I could have been impaled on a wedge of apple crumb pie!
Or crushed to death by a prune Danish!
BINGO TO NITE
MAX KORN
GUS

TALES FROM THE KRYPTONITE DEPT.

LOTUS & CL

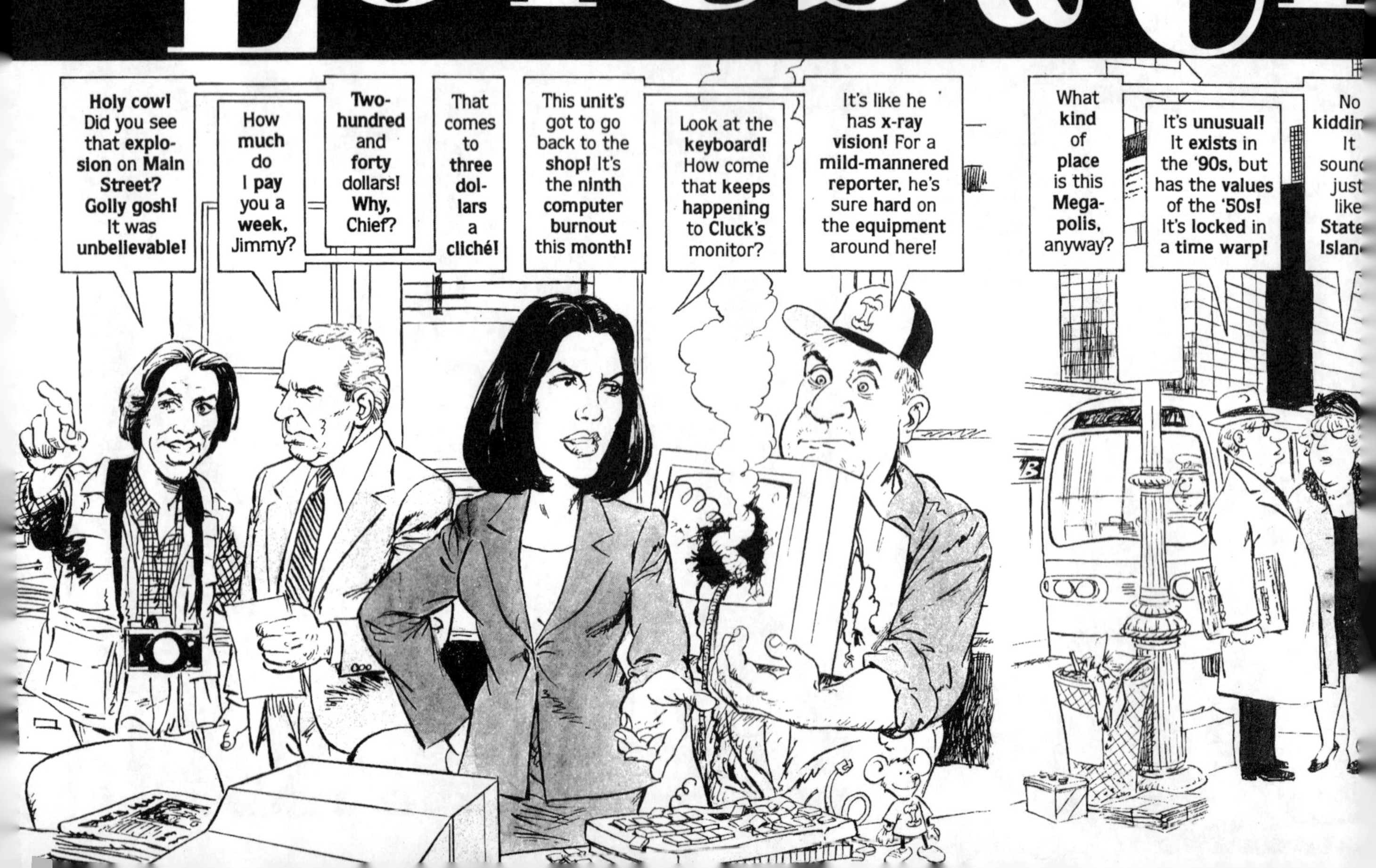
Holy cow! Did you see that explosion on Main Street? Golly gosh! It was unbelievable!
How much do I pay you a week, Jimmy?
Two-hundred and forty dollars! Why, Chief?
That comes to three dollars a cliché!
This unit's got to go back to the shop! It's the ninth computer burnout this month!
Look at the keyboard! How come that keeps happening to Cluck's monitor?
It's like he has x-ray vision! For a mild-mannered reporter, he's sure hard on the equipment around here!
What kind of place is this Megapolis, anyway?
It's unusual! It exists in the '90s, but has the values of the '50s! It's locked in a time warp!
No kiddin It soun just like State Islan

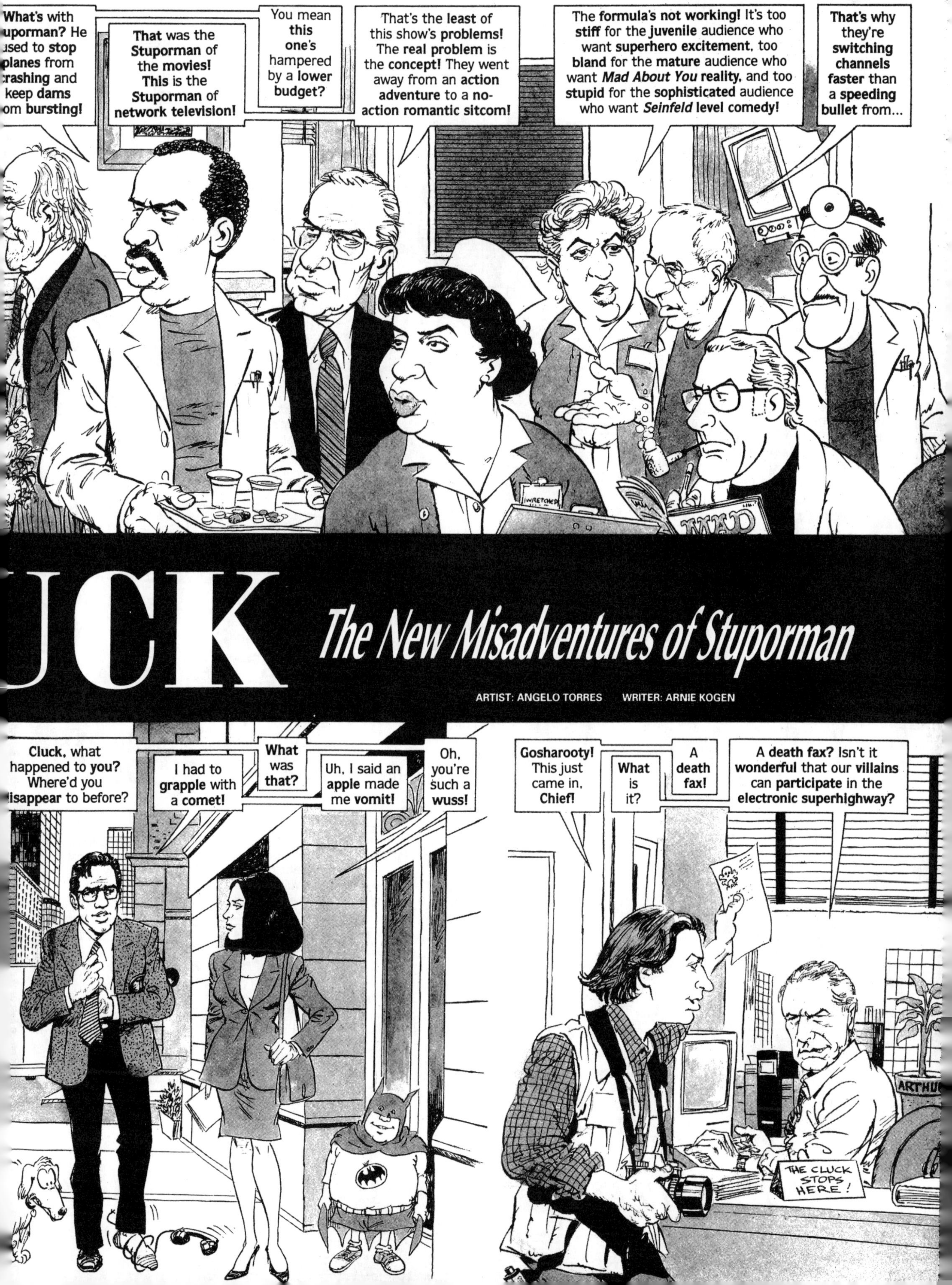
What's with uporman? He used to stop planes from rashing and keep dams om bursting!
That was the Stuporman of the movies! This is the Stuporman of network television!
You mean this one's hampered by a lower budget?
That's the least of this show's problems! The real problem is the concept! They went away from an action adventure to a no-action romantic sitcom!
The formula's not working! It's too stiff for the juvenile audience who want superhero excitement, too bland for the mature audience who want *Mad About You* reality, and too stupid for the sophisticated audience who want *Seinfeld* level comedy!
That's why they're switching channels faster than a speeding bullet from...
WRETCHED
MAD
UCK
The New Misadventures of Stuporman
ARTIST: ANGELO TORRES WRITER: ARNIE KOGEN
Cluck, what happened to you? Where'd you isappear to before?
I had to grapple with a comet!
What was that?
Uh, I said an apple made me vomit!
Oh, you're such a wuss!
Gosharooty! This just came in, Chief!
What is it?
A death fax!
A death fax? Isn't it wonderful that our villains can participate in the electronic superhighway?
ARTHU
THE CLUCK STOPS HERE!

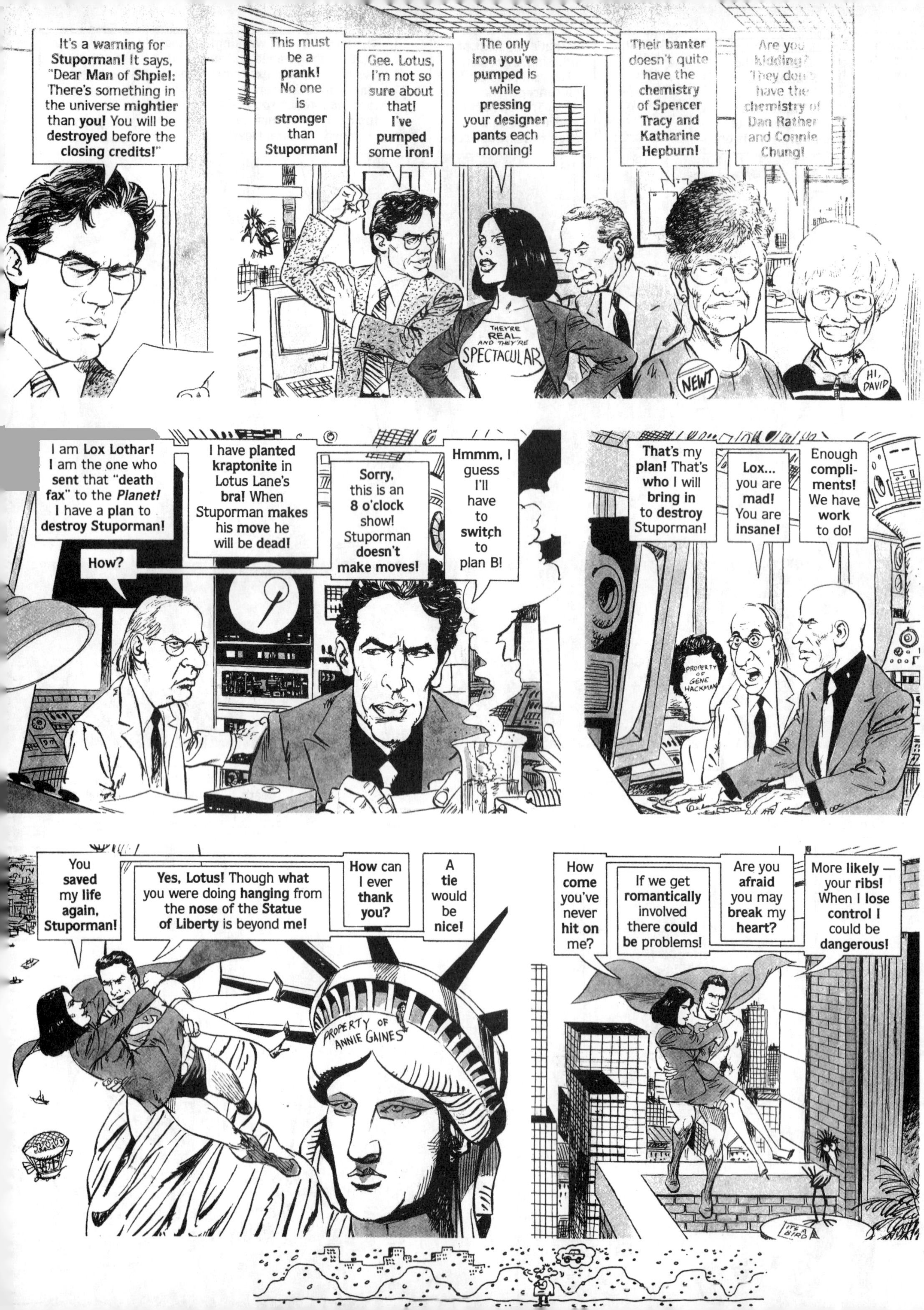
It's a warning for Stuporman! It says, "Dear Man of Shpiel: There's something in the universe mightier than you! You will be destroyed before the closing credits!"
This must be a prank! No one is stronger than Stuporman!
Gee, Lotus, I'm not so sure about that! I've pumped some iron!
The only iron you've pumped is while pressing your designer pants each morning!
Their banter doesn't quite have the chemistry of Spencer Tracy and Katharine Hepburn!
Are you kidding? They don't have the chemistry of Dan Rather and Connie Chung!
THEY'RE REAL AND THEY'RE SPECTACULAR
NEWT
HI, DAVID
I am Lox Lothar! I am the one who sent that "death fax" to the *Planet!* I have a plan to destroy Stuporman!
How?
I have planted kraptonite in Lotus Lane's bra! When Stuporman makes his move he will be dead!
Sorry, this is an 8 o'clock show! Stuporman doesn't make moves!
Hmmm, I guess I'll have to switch to plan B!
That's my plan! That's who I will bring in to destroy Stuporman!
Lox... you are mad! You are insane!
Enough compliments! We have work to do!
PROPERTY OF GENE HACKMAN
You saved my life again, Stuporman!
Yes, Lotus! Though what you were doing hanging from the nose of the Statue of Liberty is beyond me!
How can I ever thank you?
A tie would be nice!
PROPERTY OF ANNIE GAINES
How come you've never hit on me?
If we get romantically involved there could be problems!
Are you afraid you may break my heart?
More likely — your ribs! When I lose control I could be dangerous!
IT'S A BIRD

Box office fiascos like *The Coneheads, Wayne's World 2,* and *It's Pat* have endangered other *Saturday Night Live* movie projects now under consideration...**So What's the Problem?**

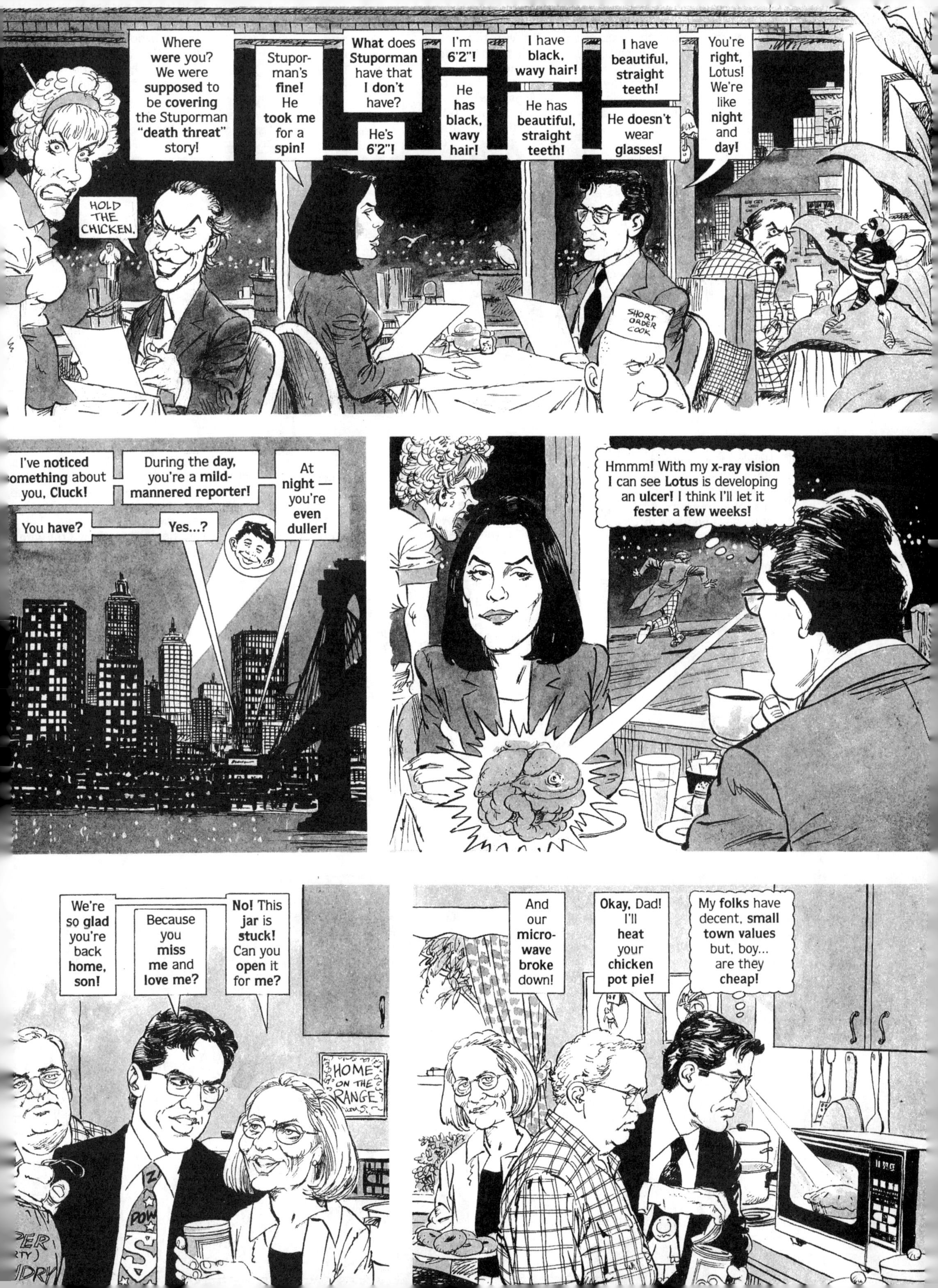
Where were you? We were supposed to be covering the Stuporman "death threat" story!
Stuporman's fine! He took me for a spin!
What does Stuporman have that I don't have?
He's 6'2"!
I'm 6'2"!
He has black, wavy hair!
I have black, wavy hair!
He has beautiful, straight teeth!
I have beautiful, straight teeth!
He doesn't wear glasses!
You're right, Lotus! We're like night and day!
HOLD THE CHICKEN.
SHORT ORDER COOK
I've noticed something about you, Cluck!
You have?
During the day, you're a mild-mannered reporter!
Yes...?
At night — you're even duller!
Hmmm! With my x-ray vision I can see Lotus is developing an ulcer! I think I'll let it fester a few weeks!
We're so glad you're back home, son!
Because you miss me and love me?
No! This jar is stuck! Can you open it for me?
HOME ON THE RANGE
And our micro-wave broke down!
Okay, Dad! I'll heat your chicken pot pie!
My folks have decent, small town values but, boy... are they cheap!

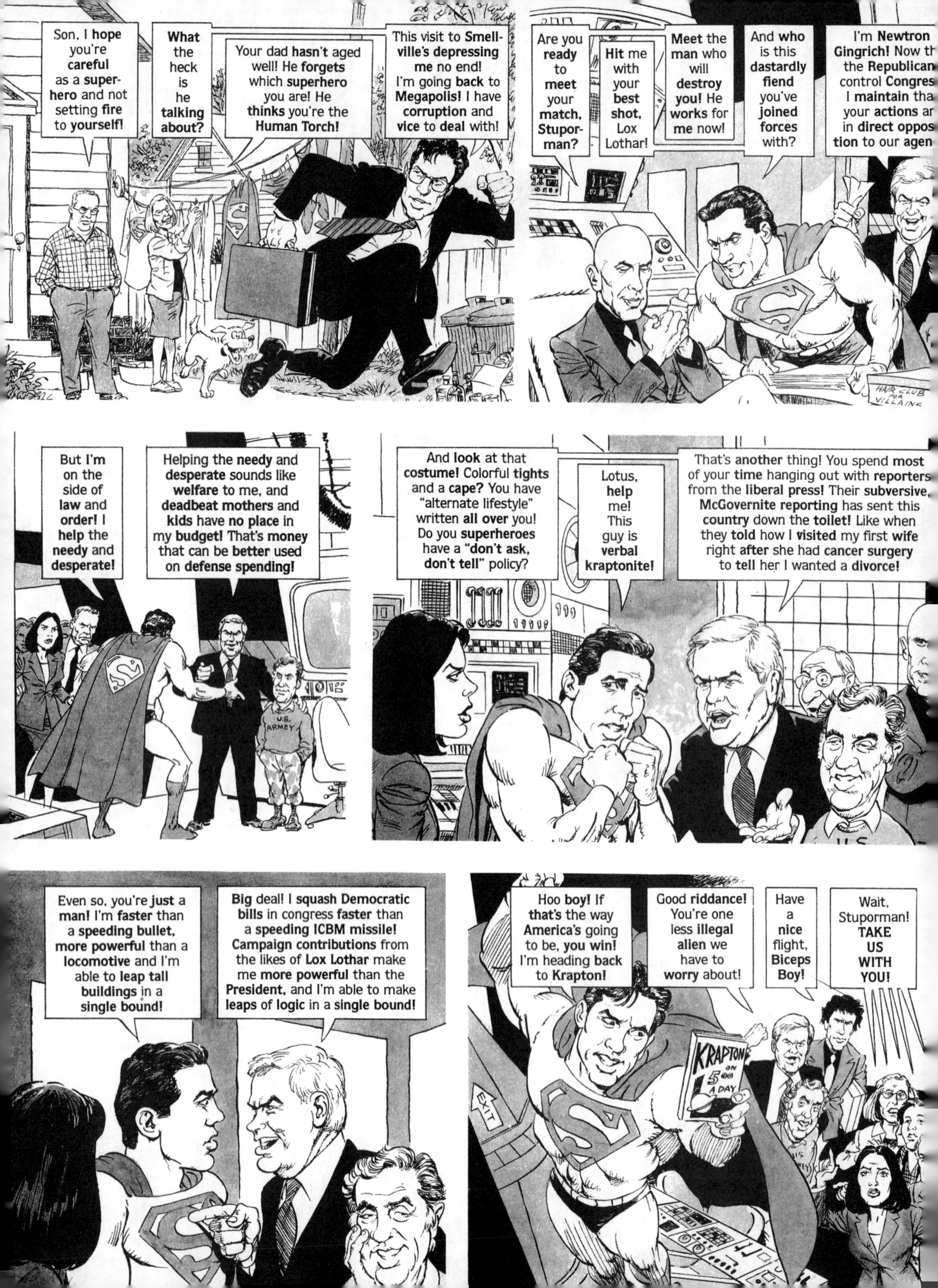
Son, I hope you're careful as a superhero and not setting fire to yourself!
What the heck is he talking about?
Your dad hasn't aged well! He forgets which superhero you are! He thinks you're the Human Torch!
This visit to Smellville's depressing me no end! I'm going back to Megapolis! I have corruption and vice to deal with!
Are you ready to meet your match, Stuporman?
Hit me with your best shot, Lox Lothar!
Meet the man who will destroy you! He works for me now!
And who is this dastardly fiend you've joined forces with?
I'm Newtron Gingrich! Now th the Republican control Congres I maintain tha your actions ar in direct oppos tion to our agen
HAIR CLUB FOR VILLAINS
But I'm on the side of law and order! I help the needy and desperate!
Helping the needy and desperate sounds like welfare to me, and deadbeat mothers and kids have no place in my budget! That's money that can be better used on defense spending!
U.S. ARMEY
And look at that costume! Colorful tights and a cape? You have "alternate lifestyle" written all over you! Do you superheroes have a "don't ask, don't tell" policy?
Lotus, help me! This guy is verbal kraptonite!
That's another thing! You spend most of your time hanging out with reporters from the liberal press! Their subversive, McGovernite reporting has sent this country down the toilet! Like when they told how I visited my first wife right after she had cancer surgery to tell her I wanted a divorce!
Even so, you're just a man! I'm faster than a speeding bullet, more powerful than a locomotive and I'm able to leap tall buildings in a single bound!
Big deal! I squash Democratic bills in congress faster than a speeding ICBM missile! Campaign contributions from the likes of Lox Lothar make me more powerful than the President, and I'm able to make leaps of logic in a single bound!
Hoo boy! If that's the way America's going to be, you win! I'm heading back to Krapton!
Good riddance! You're one less illegal alien we have to worry about!
Have a nice flight, Biceps Boy!
Wait, Stuporman! TAKE US WITH YOU!
KRAPTON ON 5.00 A DAY
EXIT

IF SUPER-HEROES NEEDED EXTRA MONEY

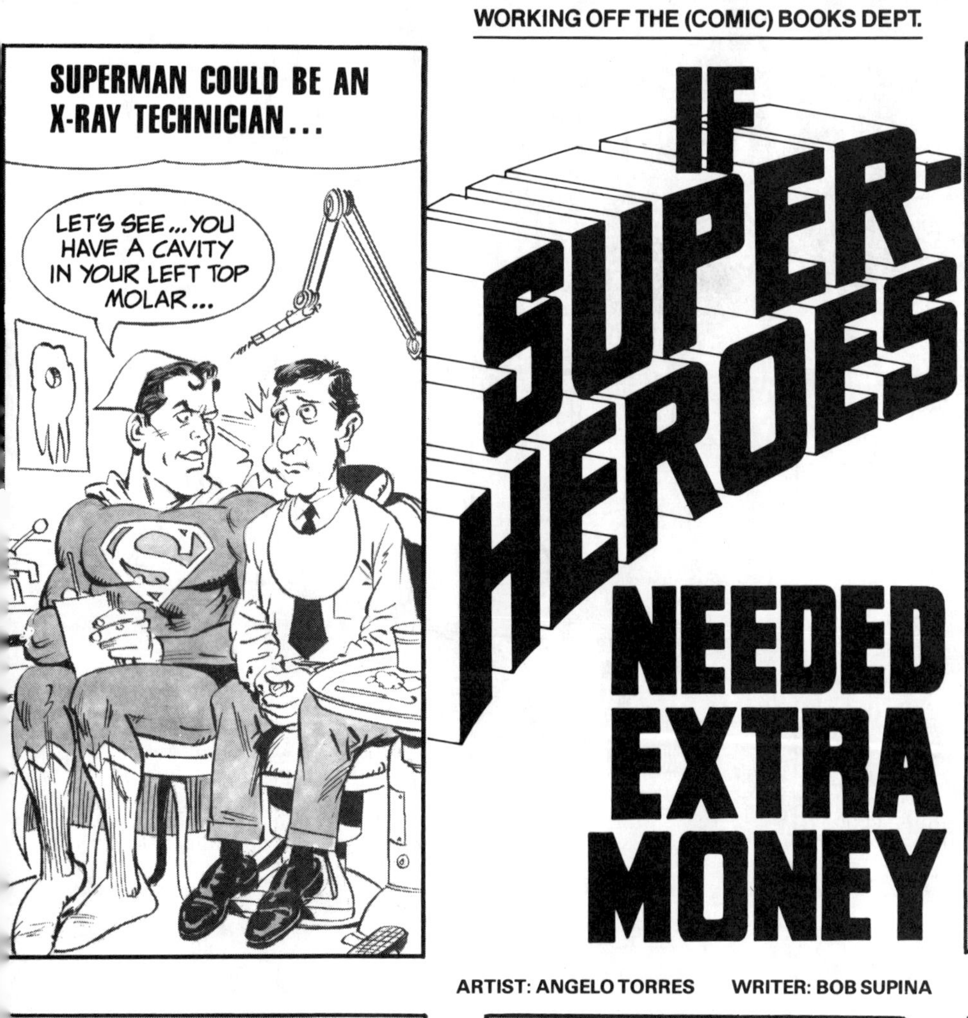
SUPERMAN COULD BE AN X-RAY TECHNICIAN...
LET'S SEE...YOU HAVE A CAVITY IN YOUR LEFT TOP MOLAR...

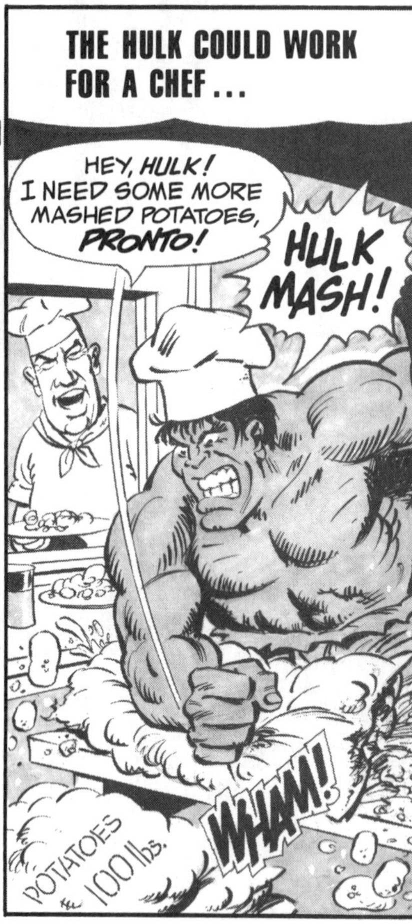
THE HULK COULD WORK FOR A CHEF...
HEY, HULK! I NEED SOME MORE MASHED POTATOES, PRONTO!
HULK MASH!
WHAM!
POTATOES 100 lbs.

ARTIST: ANGELO TORRES   WRITER: BOB SUPINA

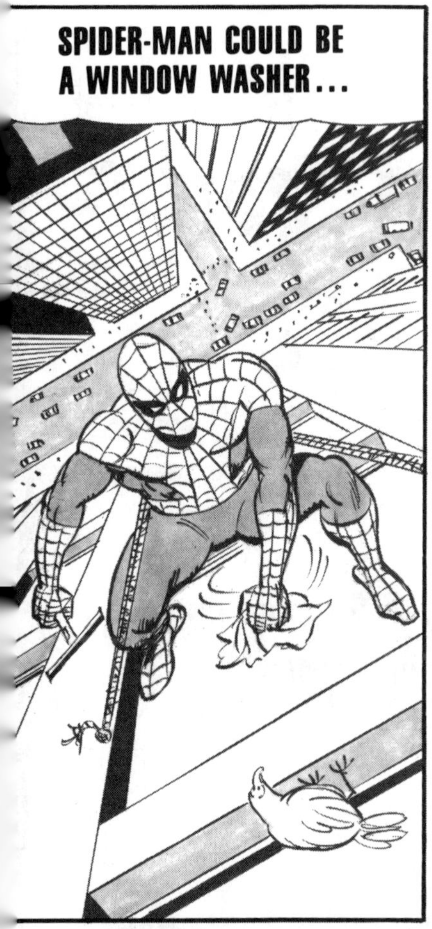
SPIDER-MAN COULD BE A WINDOW WASHER...

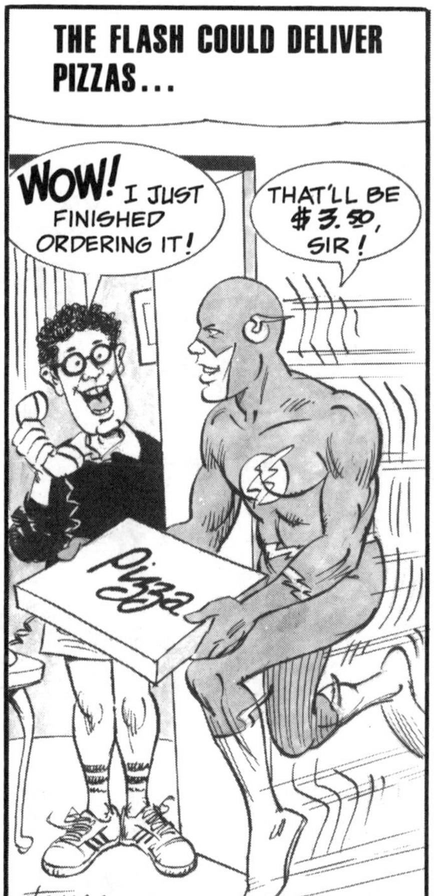
THE FLASH COULD DELIVER PIZZAS...
WOW! I JUST FINISHED ORDERING IT!
THAT'LL BE $3.50, SIR!
Pizza

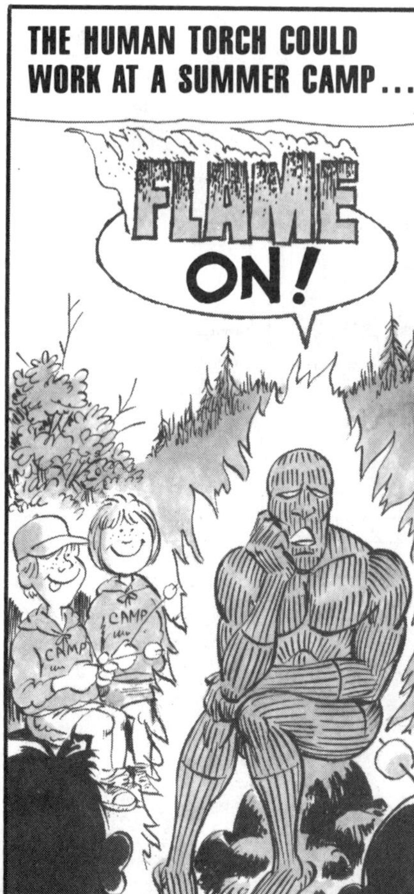
THE HUMAN TORCH COULD WORK AT A SUMMER CAMP...
FLAME ON!
CAMP
CAMP

DON MARTIN LOOKS AT SP

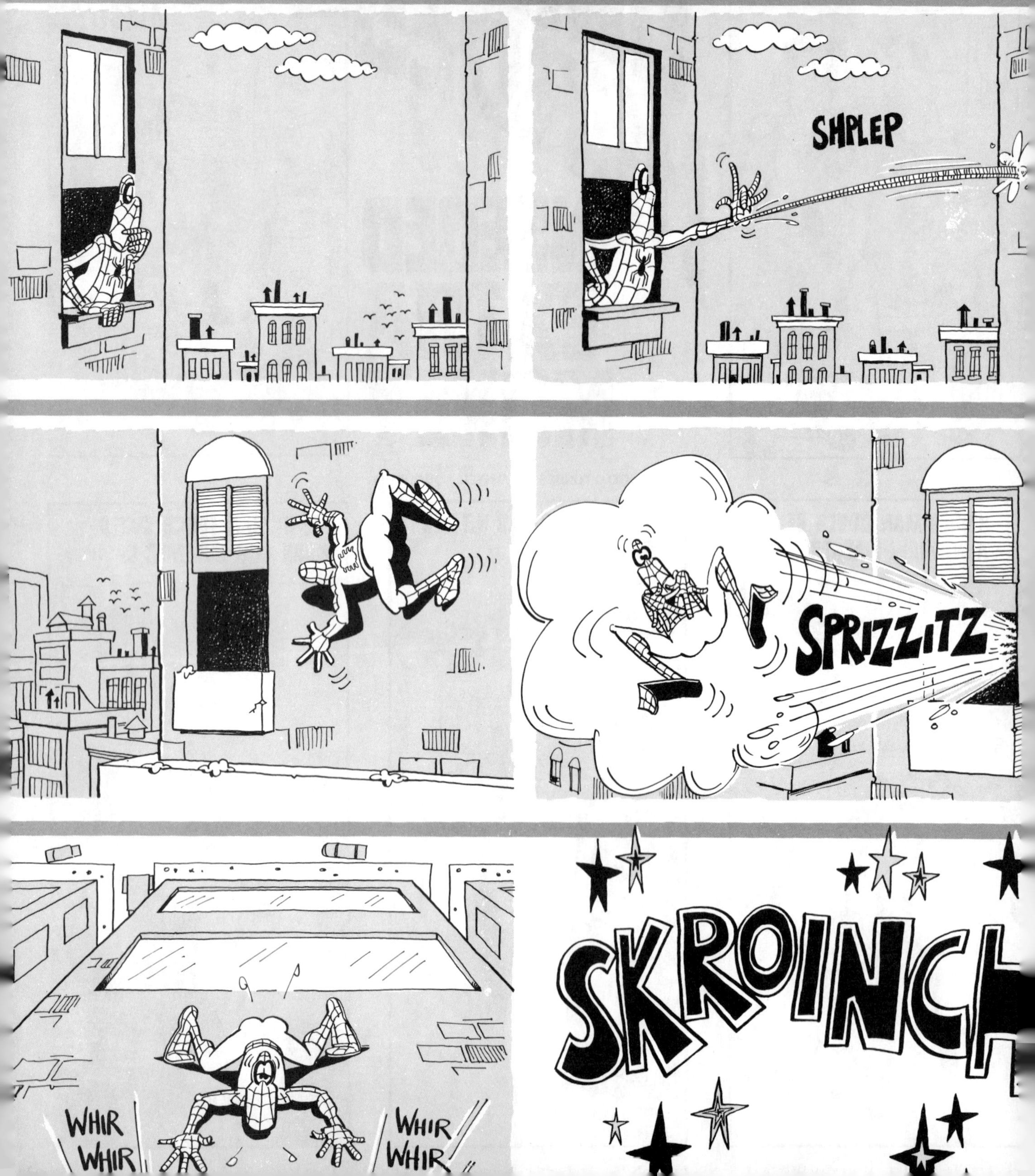
SHPLEP
SPRIZZITZ
WHIR
WHIR
WHIR
WHIR
SKROINCH

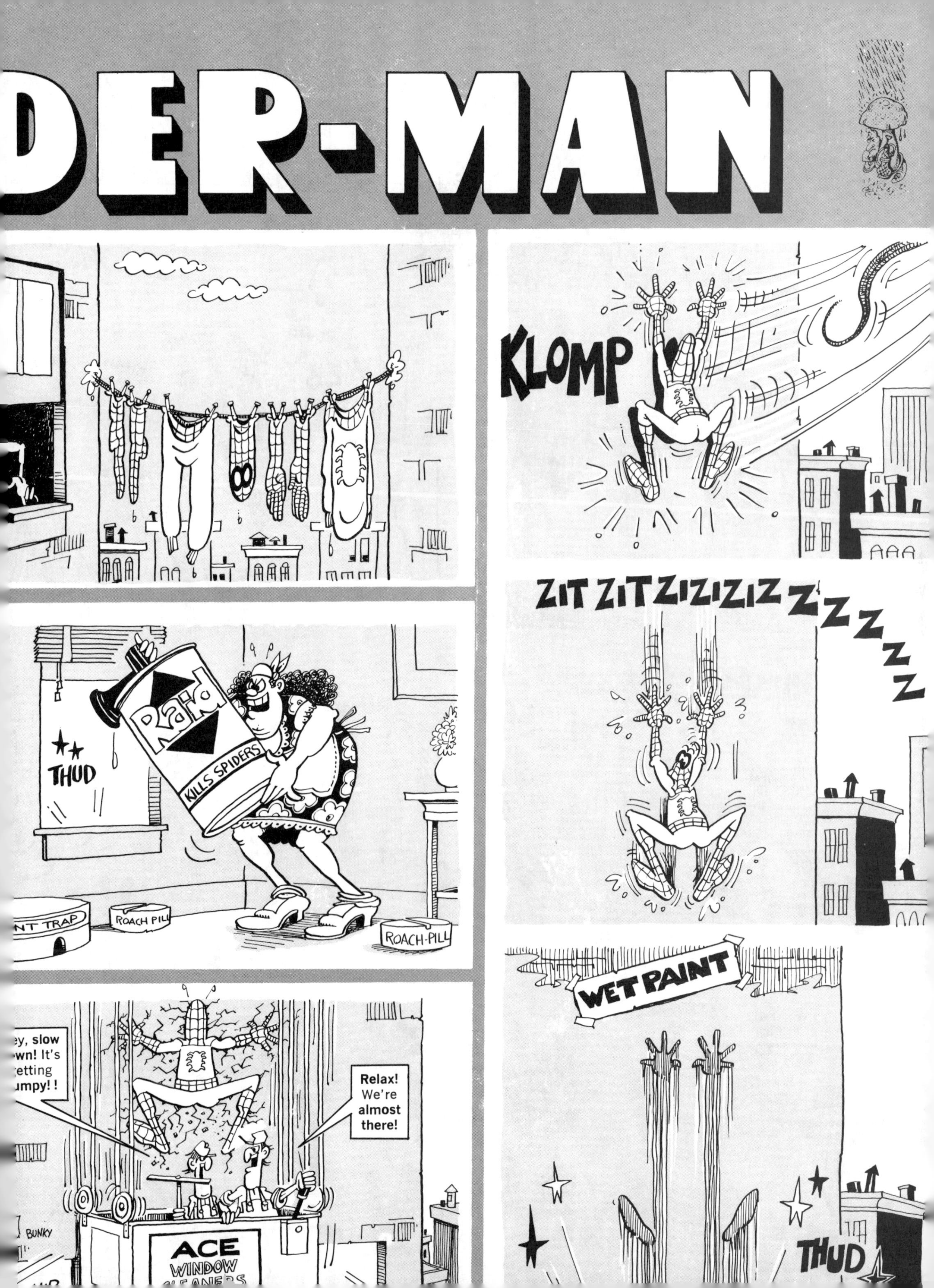
DER-MAN
KLOMP
THUD
Raid
KILLS SPIDERS
NT TRAP
ROACH PILL
ROACH-PILL
ZIT ZIT ZIZIZIZ ZZZZZ
WET PAINT
ey, slow wn! It's etting umpy!!
Relax! We're almost there!
BUNKY
ACE
WINDOW
THUD

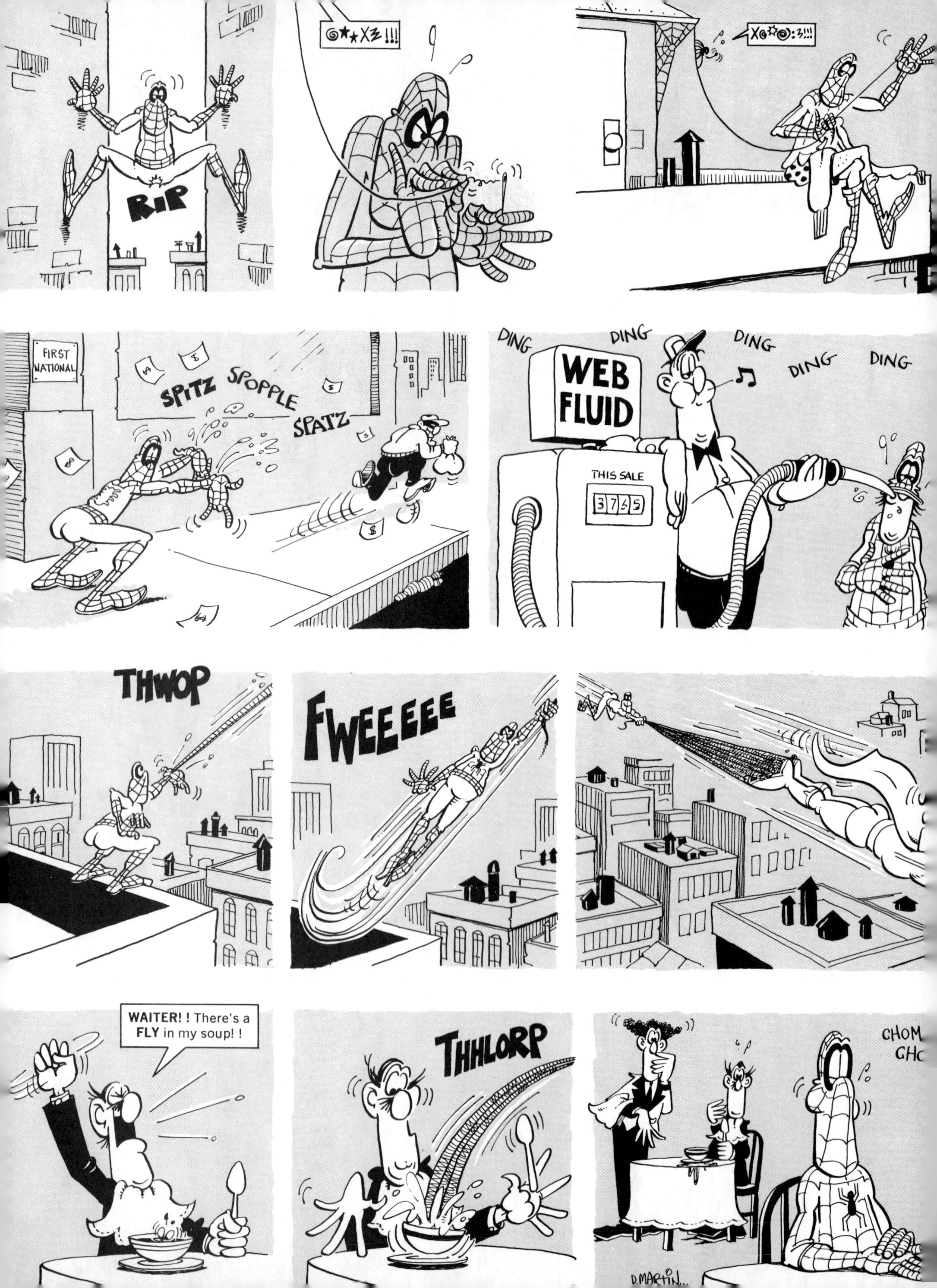
RIP
FIRST NATIONAL
SPITZ
SPOPPLE
SPATZ
DING
DING
DING
DING
DING
WEB FLUID
THIS SALE
3765
THWOP
FWEEEEE
WAITER! ! There's a FLY in my soup! !
THHLORP
CHOM
D.MARTIN...

KENT SATISFIES BEST? DEPT.

A "COMICS" SCENE WE'D LIKE TO SEE

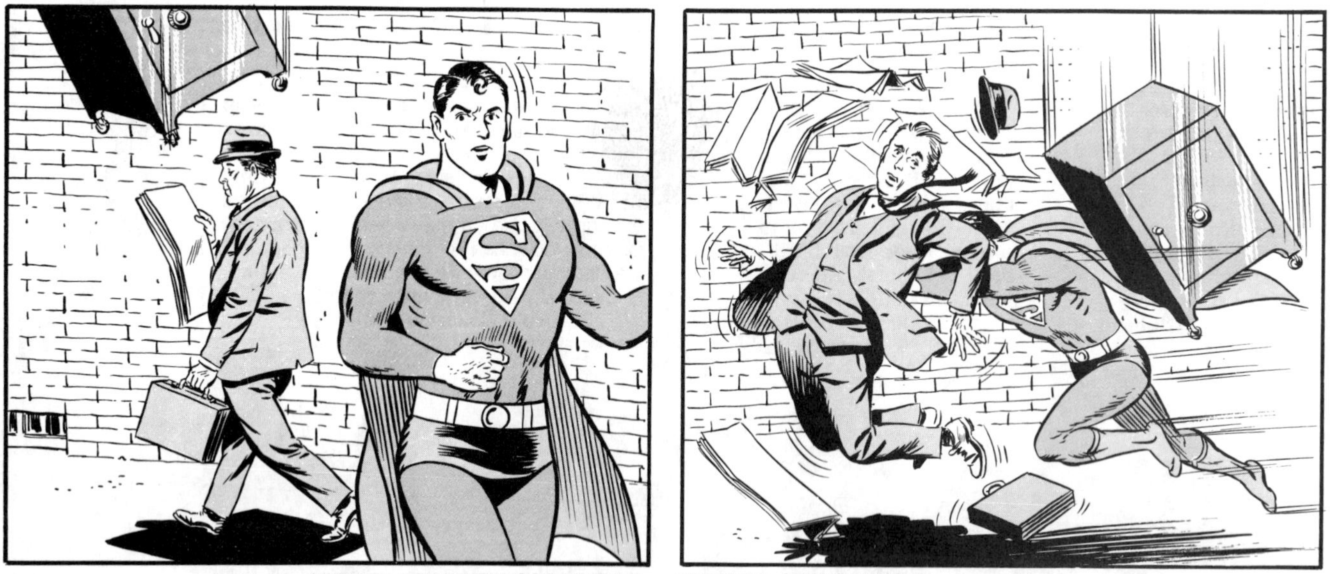

ARTIST: GEORGE WOODBRIDGE WRITER: DON EDWING

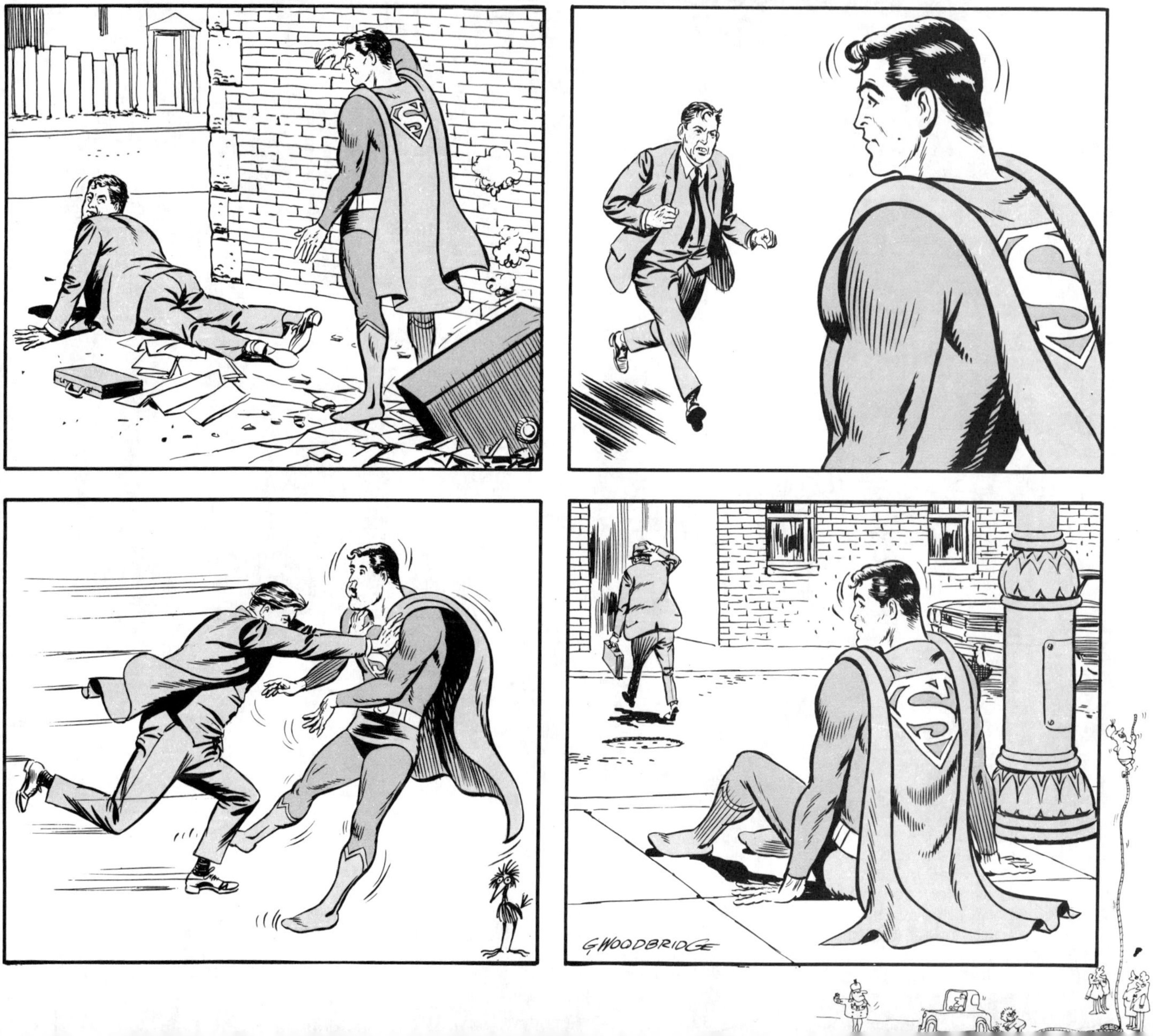
G WOODBRIDGE

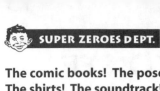

The comic books! The poseable action figures! The trading cards! The graphic novels! The TV special! The shirts! The soundtrack! The videogame! And.... um.... oh yeah, there's a movie somewhere amid all the merchandising! With all those greedy tie-ins, is it any wonder these geeky freaks are called the...

My name is **Professor $,** and I **created** the **$-Men!** I recruited **five bizarre freaks** and **drilled** them like **soldiers** until they could perform **together** as a **single unit!** I **got** the **idea** from the **guy** who started **The Backstreet Boys** and **'N SYNC!**

I'm the **$-Man** called **Cyclod!** I first **knew** I was **different** when I was a **child!** I tried to **read** a **bedtime story,** and I **burned** my **house** down! You might **think** it's **cool** to have **nuclear-powered** eye-balls, but there's a **down-side!** My **weekly Visine** bills are **through the roof!**

They call me **Deform!** I have **supreme power** over the **weather!** I know I'm an **awful actress,** but it could be **worse!** It could have been **Al Roker inside** this **suit!** Although I'll admit that **Willard Scott** has a **much** more **natural** looking **wig** than **mine!** When I **auditioned** for this **role,** I had to **act** like I was **creating** a **killer hurricane! Afterwards,** the **casting director paid** me a **huge** compliment! He said, **"Wow, you really blew!"**

Vasoline's my **monicker, bub!** **Life** is a **highway,** and I've got **road rage!** My **foot,** your **ass...let's do lunch!** As you can see, I have a **crucial** role in **$-Men!** I'm the **only one** who can deliver **dumb catch phrases!**

I'm **Rogaine,** a super-hero with the **ability** to **suck** the **life** out of **anything!** You know, **just like George Clooney** and **Joel Schumacher** did to the *Batman* franchise!

I'm **Jean Greypoupon,** and I'm so **dull** that I don't **even** get to **have** a **super nickname!** I possess the **ability** to **read** other people's **minds!** I can foretell **exactly** what a person **will do next!** That's **not** so **amazing,** though...with the **lousy predictable script** they gave us, **anybody** watching **this** movie can do the **same thing!**

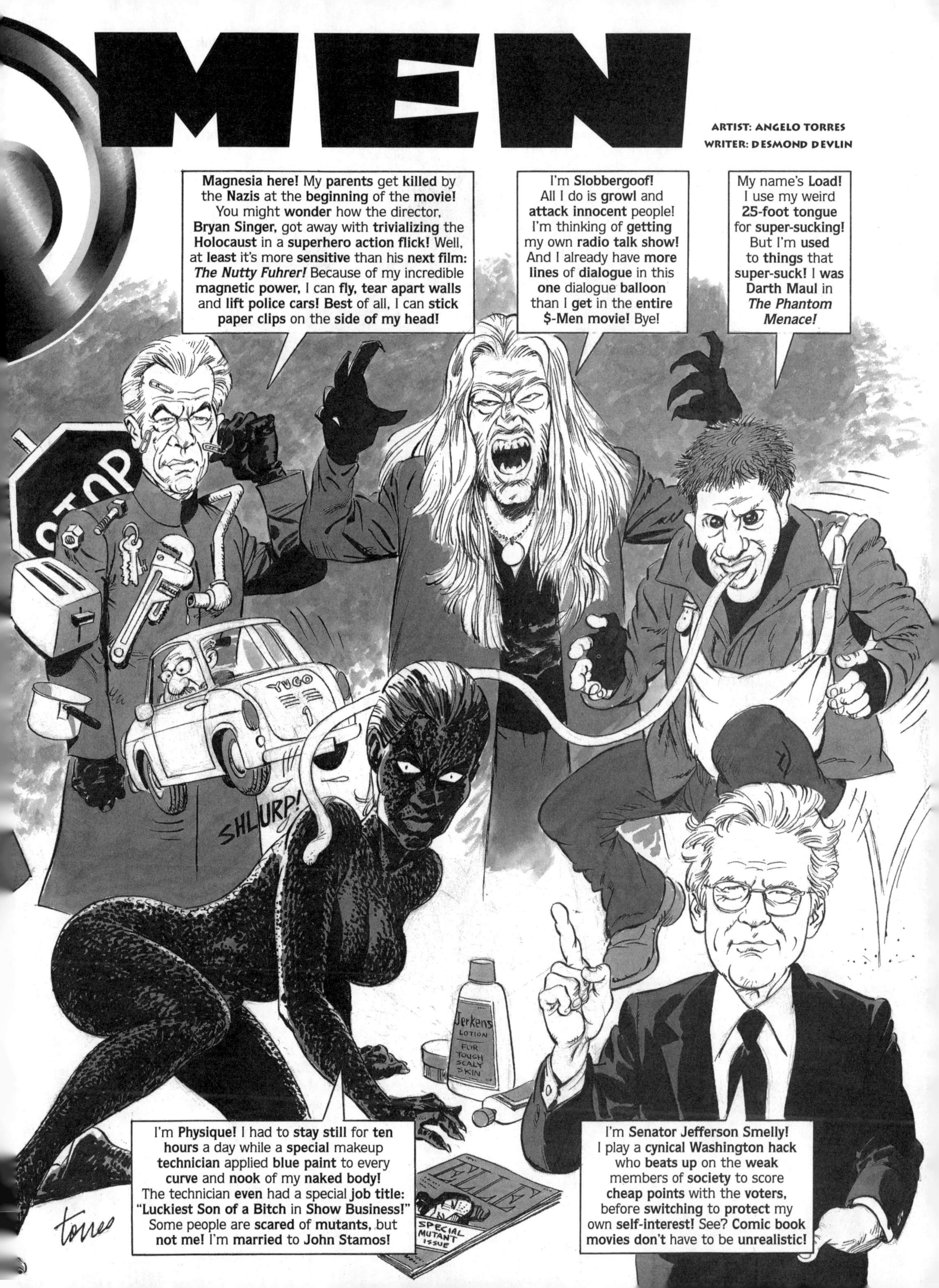
MEN
ARTIST: ANGELO TORRES
WRITER: DESMOND DEVLIN
Magnesia here! My parents get killed by the Nazis at the beginning of the movie! You might wonder how the director, Bryan Singer, got away with trivializing the Holocaust in a superhero action flick! Well, at least it's more sensitive than his next film: The Nutty Fuhrer! Because of my incredible magnetic power, I can fly, tear apart walls and lift police cars! Best of all, I can stick paper clips on the side of my head!
I'm Slobbergoof! All I do is growl and attack innocent people! I'm thinking of getting my own radio talk show! And I already have more lines of dialogue in this one dialogue balloon than I get in the entire $-Men movie! Bye!
My name's Load! I use my weird 25-foot tongue for super-sucking! But I'm used to things that super-suck! I was Darth Maul in The Phantom Menace!
STOP
YUGO
SHLURP!
Jerkens LOTION FOR TOUGH SCALY SKIN
ELLE
SPECIAL MUTANT ISSUE
I'm Physique! I had to stay still for ten hours a day while a special makeup technician applied blue paint to every curve and nook of my naked body! The technician even had a special job title: "Luckiest Son of a Bitch in Show Business!" Some people are scared of mutants, but not me! I'm married to John Stamos!
I'm Senator Jefferson Smelly! I play a cynical Washington hack who beats up on the weak members of society to score cheap points with the voters, before switching to protect my own self-interest! See? Comic book movies don't have to be unrealistic!
torres

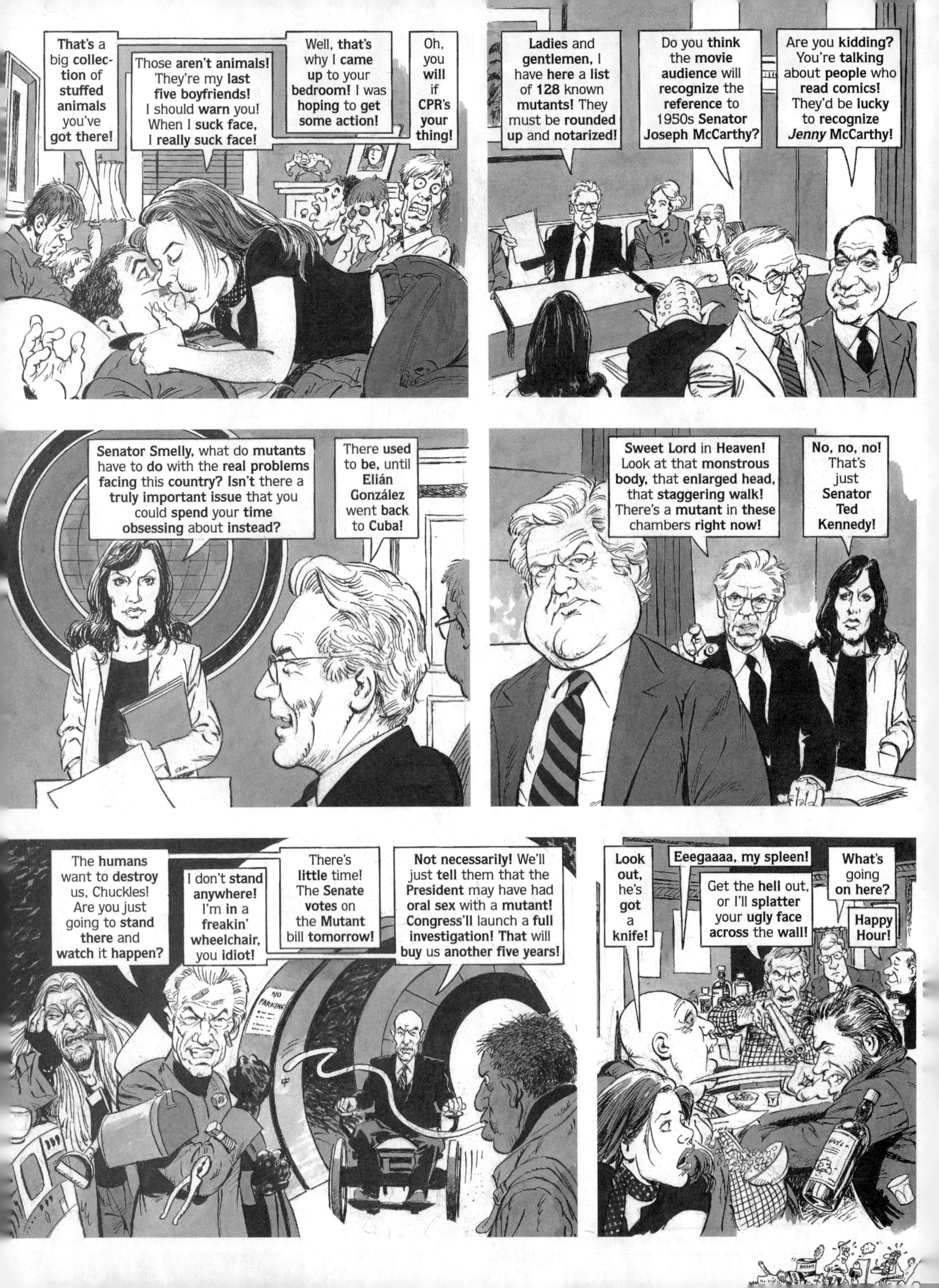
That's a big collection of stuffed animals you've got there!
Those aren't animals! They're my last five boyfriends! I should warn you! When I suck face, I really suck face!
Well, that's why I came up to your bedroom! I was hoping to get some action!
Oh, you will if CPR's your thing!
Ladies and gentlemen, I have here a list of 128 known mutants! They must be rounded up and notarized!
Do you think the movie audience will recognize the reference to 1950s Senator Joseph McCarthy?
Are you kidding? You're talking about people who read comics! They'd be lucky to recognize *Jenny* McCarthy!
Senator Smelly, what do mutants have to do with the real problems facing this country? Isn't there a truly important issue that you could spend your time obsessing about instead?
There used to be, until Elián González went back to Cuba!
Sweet Lord in Heaven! Look at that monstrous body, that enlarged head, that staggering walk! There's a mutant in these chambers right now!
No, no, no! That's just Senator Ted Kennedy!
The humans want to destroy us, Chuckles! Are you just going to stand there and watch it happen?
I don't stand anywhere! I'm in a freakin' wheelchair, you idiot!
There's little time! The Senate votes on the Mutant bill tomorrow!
Not necessarily! We'll just tell them that the President may have had oral sex with a mutant! Congress'll launch a full investigation! That will buy us another five years!
NO PARKING
Look out, he's got a knife!
Eeegaaaa, my spleen!
Get the hell out, or I'll splatter your ugly face across the wall!
What's going on here?
Happy Hour!

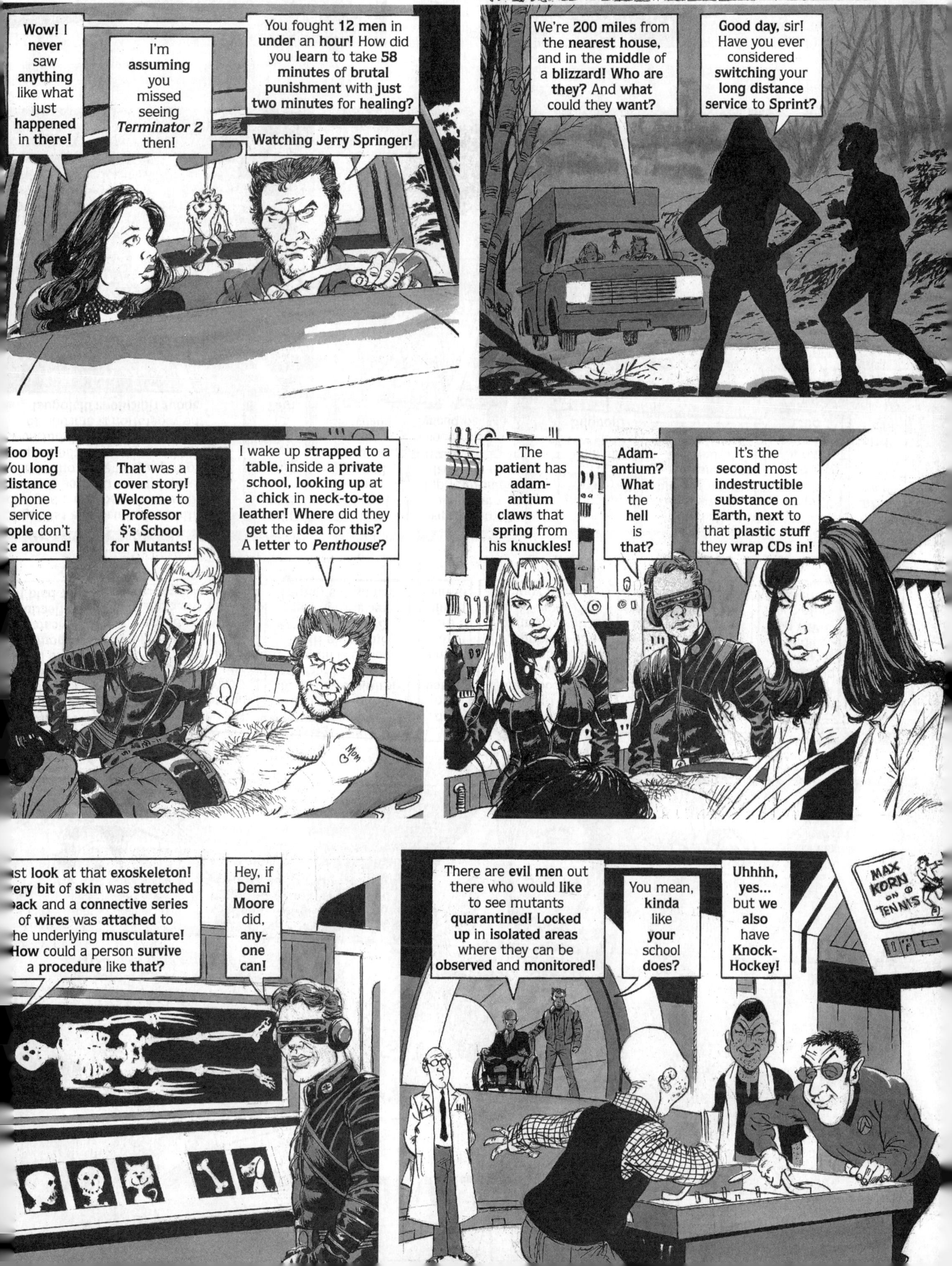
Wow! I never saw anything like what just happened in there!
I'm assuming you missed seeing Terminator 2 then!
You fought 12 men in under an hour! How did you learn to take 58 minutes of brutal punishment with just two minutes for healing?
Watching Jerry Springer!
We're 200 miles from the nearest house, and in the middle of a blizzard! Who are they? And what could they want?
Good day, sir! Have you ever considered switching your long distance service to Sprint?
loo boy! You long distance phone service ople don't e around!
That was a cover story! Welcome to Professor $'s School for Mutants!
I wake up strapped to a table, inside a private school, looking up at a chick in neck-to-toe leather! Where did they get the idea for this? A letter to Penthouse?
Mom
The patient has adamantium claws that spring from his knuckles!
Adamantium? What the hell is that?
It's the second most indestructible substance on Earth, next to that plastic stuff they wrap CDs in!
st look at that exoskeleton! ery bit of skin was stretched ack and a connective series of wires was attached to he underlying musculature! How could a person survive a procedure like that?
Hey, if Demi Moore did, anyone can!
There are evil men out there who would like to see mutants quarantined! Locked up in isolated areas where they can be observed and monitored!
You mean, kinda like your school does?
Uhhhh, yes... but we also have Knock-Hockey!
MAX KORN ON TENNIS

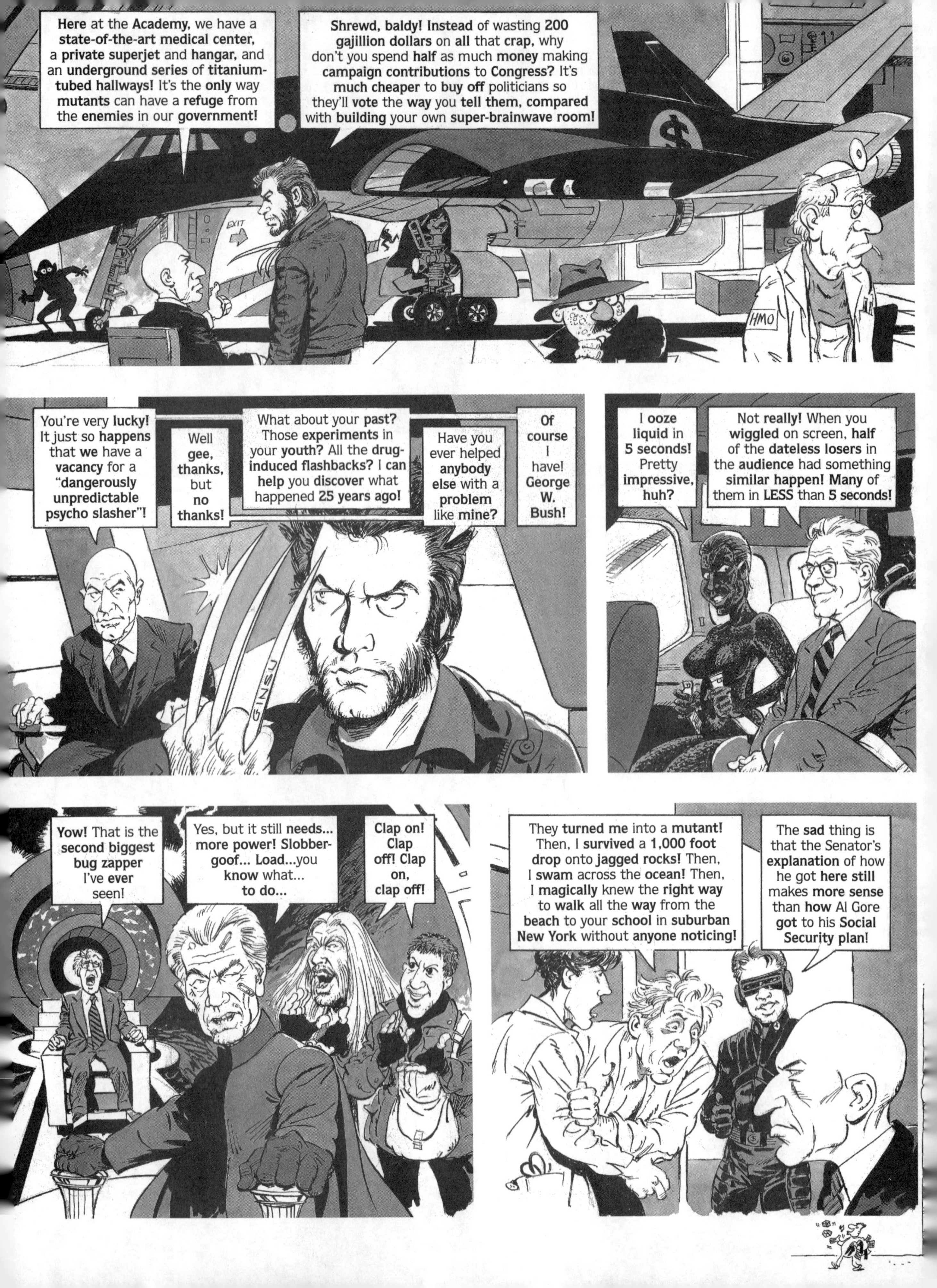
Here at the Academy, we have a state-of-the-art medical center, a private superjet and hangar, and an underground series of titanium-tubed hallways! It's the only way mutants can have a refuge from the enemies in our government!
Shrewd, baldy! Instead of wasting 200 gajillion dollars on all that crap, why don't you spend half as much money making campaign contributions to Congress? It's much cheaper to buy off politicians so they'll vote the way you tell them, compared with building your own super-brainwave room!
EXIT
HMO
You're very lucky! It just so happens that we have a vacancy for a "dangerously unpredictable psycho slasher"!
Well gee, thanks, but no thanks!
What about your past? Those experiments in your youth? All the drug-induced flashbacks? I can help you discover what happened 25 years ago!
Have you ever helped anybody else with a problem like mine?
Of course I have! George W. Bush!
GINSU
I ooze liquid in 5 seconds! Pretty impressive, huh?
Not really! When you wiggled on screen, half of the dateless losers in the audience had something similar happen! Many of them in LESS than 5 seconds!
Yow! That is the second biggest bug zapper I've ever seen!
Yes, but it still needs... more power! Slobber-goof... Load...you know what... to do...
Clap on! Clap off! Clap on, clap off!
They turned me into a mutant! Then, I survived a 1,000 foot drop onto jagged rocks! Then, I swam across the ocean! Then, I magically knew the right way to walk all the way from the beach to your school in suburban New York without anyone noticing!
The sad thing is that the Senator's explanation of how he got here still makes more sense than how Al Gore got to his Social Security plan!

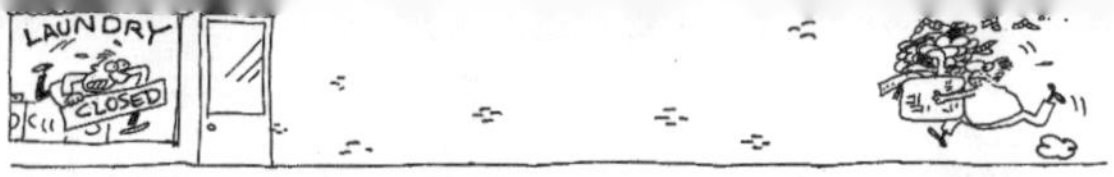
LAUNDRY
CLOSED

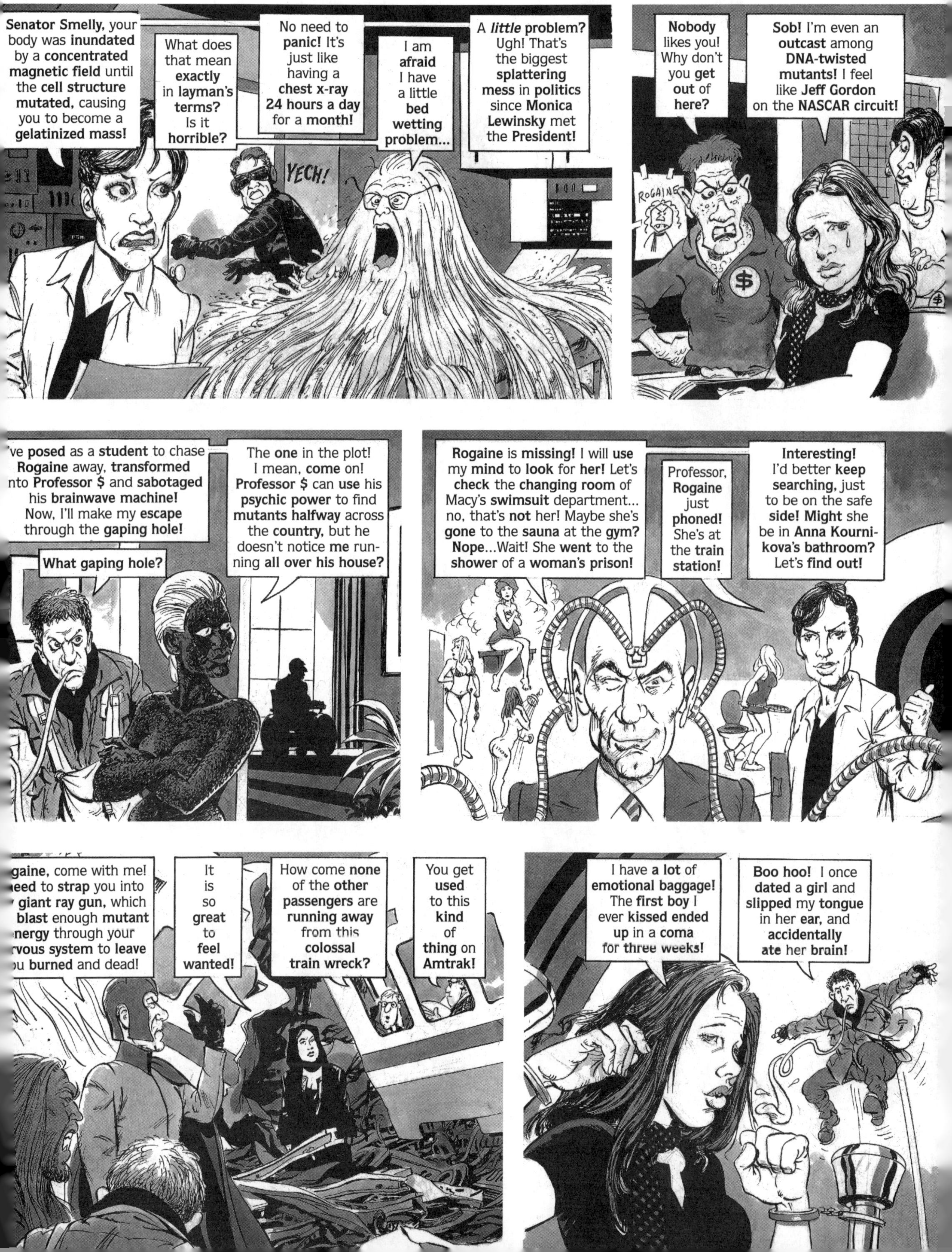
Senator Smelly, your body was inundated by a concentrated magnetic field until the cell structure mutated, causing you to become a gelatinized mass!
What does that mean exactly in layman's terms? Is it horrible?
No need to panic! It's just like having a chest x-ray 24 hours a day for a month!
I am afraid I have a little bed wetting problem...
A little problem? Ugh! That's the biggest splattering mess in politics since Monica Lewinsky met the President!
YECH!
Nobody likes you! Why don't you get out of here?
Sob! I'm even an outcast among DNA-twisted mutants! I feel like Jeff Gordon on the NASCAR circuit!
ROGAINE
$
've posed as a student to chase Rogaine away, transformed nto Professor $ and sabotaged his brainwave machine! Now, I'll make my escape through the gaping hole!
What gaping hole?
The one in the plot! I mean, come on! Professor $ can use his psychic power to find mutants halfway across the country, but he doesn't notice me running all over his house?
Rogaine is missing! I will use my mind to look for her! Let's check the changing room of Macy's swimsuit department... no, that's not her! Maybe she's gone to the sauna at the gym? Nope...Wait! She went to the shower of a woman's prison!
Professor, Rogaine just phoned! She's at the train station!
Interesting! I'd better keep searching, just to be on the safe side! Might she be in Anna Kournikova's bathroom? Let's find out!
gaine, come with me! eed to strap you into giant ray gun, which blast enough mutant nergy through your rvous system to leave u burned and dead!
It is so great to feel wanted!
How come none of the other passengers are running away from this colossal train wreck?
You get used to this kind of thing on Amtrak!
I have a lot of emotional baggage! The first boy I ever kissed ended up in a coma for three weeks!
Boo hoo! I once dated a girl and slipped my tongue in her ear, and accidentally ate her brain!

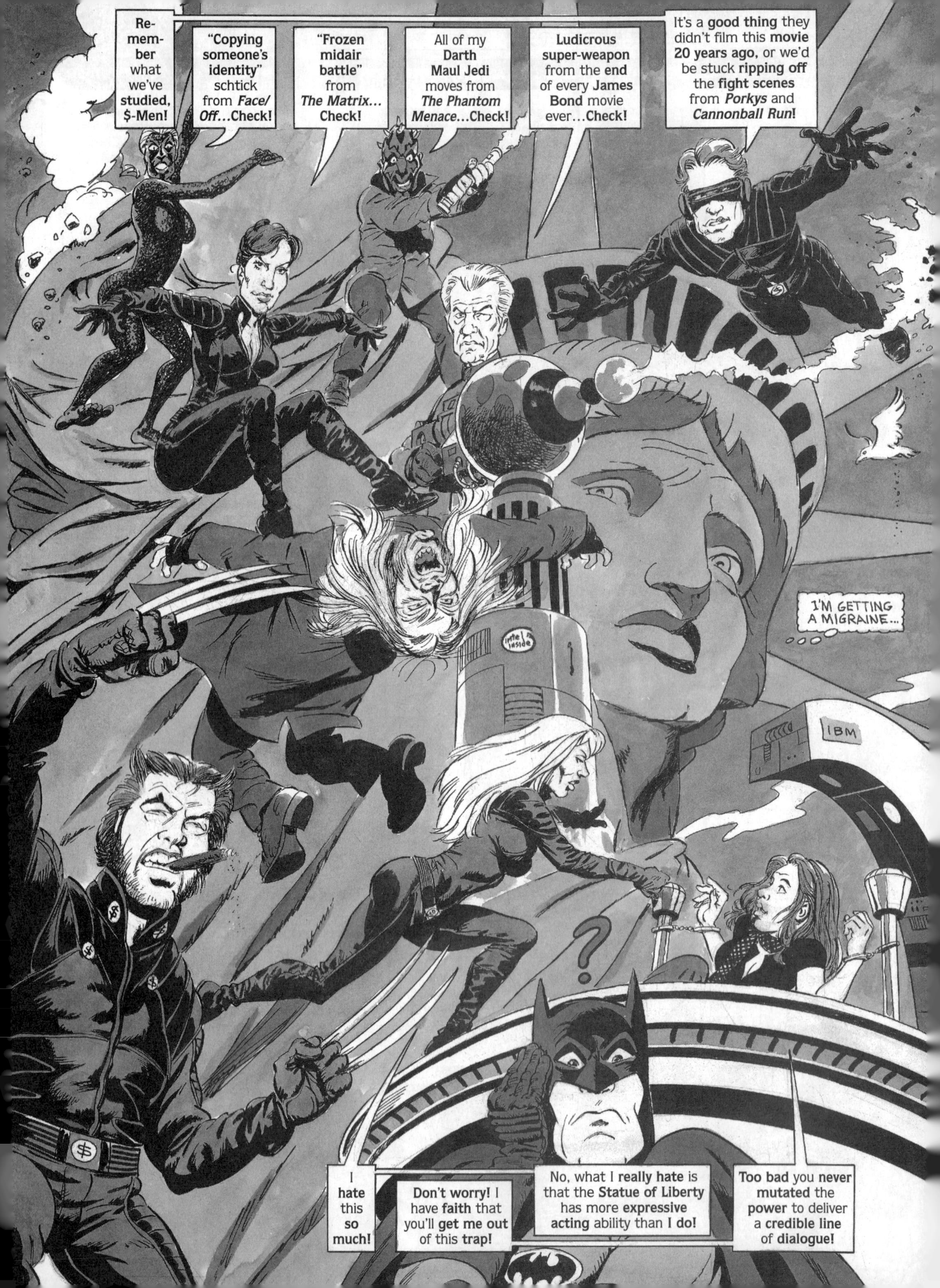

Re-mem-ber what we've studied, $-Men!
"Copying someone's identity" schtick from Face/Off...Check!
"Frozen midair battle" from The Matrix...Check!
All of my Darth Maul Jedi moves from The Phantom Menace...Check!
Ludicrous super-weapon from the end of every James Bond movie ever...Check!
It's a good thing they didn't film this movie 20 years ago, or we'd be stuck ripping off the fight scenes from Porkys and Cannonball Run!
intel inside
I'M GETTING A MIGRAINE...
IBM
?
I hate this so much!
Don't worry! I have faith that you'll get me out of this trap!
No, what I really hate is that the Statue of Liberty has more expressive acting ability than I do!
Too bad you never mutated the power to deliver a credible line of dialogue!

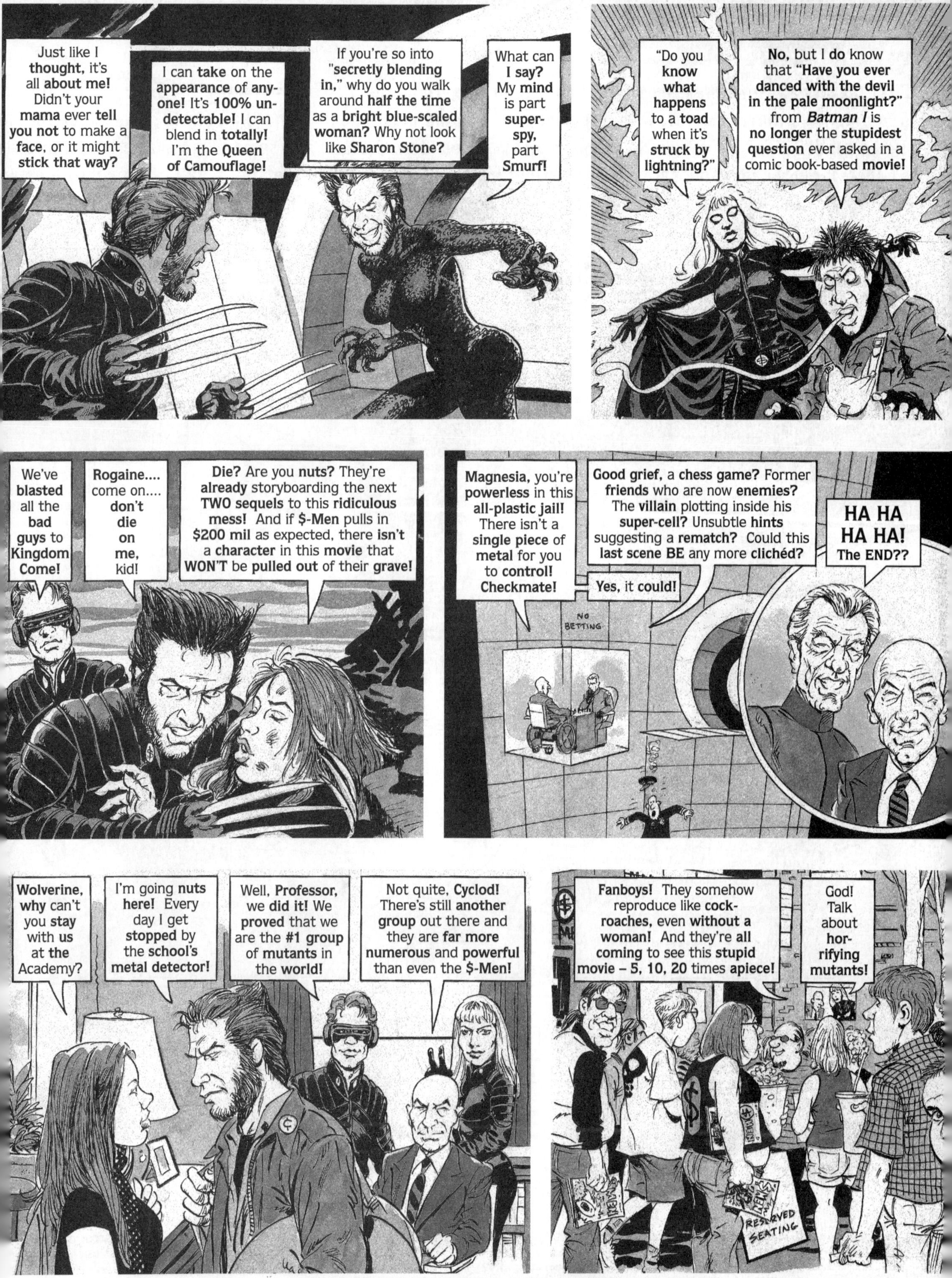

Just like I thought, it's all about me! Didn't your mama ever tell you not to make a face, or it might stick that way?
I can take on the appearance of anyone! It's 100% undetectable! I can blend in totally! I'm the Queen of Camouflage!
If you're so into "secretly blending in," why do you walk around half the time as a bright blue-scaled woman? Why not look like Sharon Stone?
What can I say? My mind is part super-spy, part Smurf!
"Do you know what happens to a toad when it's struck by lightning?"
No, but I do know that "Have you ever danced with the devil in the pale moonlight?" from *Batman I* is no longer the stupidest question ever asked in a comic book-based movie!
We've blasted all the bad guys to Kingdom Come!
Rogaine.... come on.... don't die on me, kid!
Die? Are you nuts? They're already storyboarding the next TWO sequels to this ridiculous mess! And if $-Men pulls in $200 mil as expected, there isn't a character in this movie that WON'T be pulled out of their grave!
Magnesia, you're powerless in this all-plastic jail! There isn't a single piece of metal for you to control! Checkmate!
Good grief, a chess game? Former friends who are now enemies? The villain plotting inside his super-cell? Unsubtle hints suggesting a rematch? Could this last scene BE any more clichéd?
Yes, it could!
HA HA HA HA! The END??
NO BETTING
Wolverine, why can't you stay with us at the Academy?
I'm going nuts here! Every day I get stopped by the school's metal detector!
Well, Professor, we did it! We proved that we are the #1 group of mutants in the world!
Not quite, Cyclod! There's still another group out there and they are far more numerous and powerful than even the $-Men!
Fanboys! They somehow reproduce like cockroaches, even without a woman! And they're all coming to see this stupid movie – 5, 10, 20 times apiece!
God! Talk about horrifying mutants!
RESERVED SEATING

First there was *Superman* the comic book, then *Superman* the TV series, then *Superman* the movie, th *Superman* the movie sequel, then *Superman* the second movie sequel and then (GAK!) *Superman* the thi movie sequel! Then we got another *Superman* TV series (*Lois & Clark*) and somewhere scattered in there we a bunch of poorly animated cartoons (check your local listings)! You'd figure after a half century they'd be do milking this tired, old franchise, but nooooo — now we have to sit through still another *Superman* TV show we call

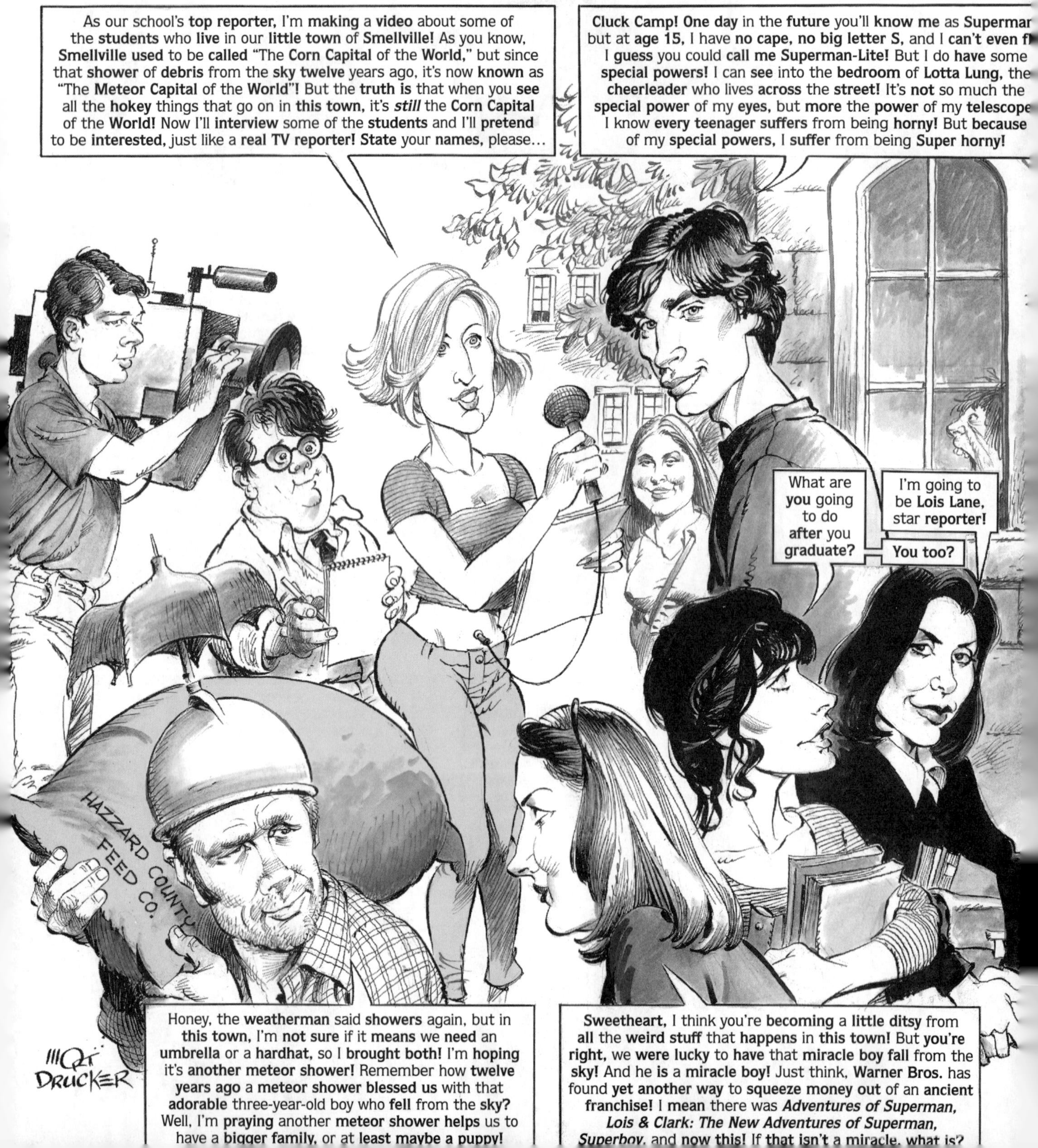
As our school's top reporter, I'm making a video about some of the students who live in our little town of Smellville! As you know, Smellville used to be called "The Corn Capital of the World," but since that shower of debris from the sky twelve years ago, it's now known as "The Meteor Capital of the World"! But the truth is that when you see all the hokey things that go on in this town, it's *still* the Corn Capital of the World! Now I'll interview some of the students and I'll pretend to be interested, just like a real TV reporter! State your names, please...
Cluck Camp! One day in the future you'll know me as Supermar but at age 15, I have no cape, no big letter S, and I can't even fl I guess you could call me Superman-Lite! But I do have some special powers! I can see into the bedroom of Lotta Lung, the cheerleader who lives across the street! It's not so much the special power of my eyes, but more the power of my telescope I know every teenager suffers from being horny! But because of my special powers, I suffer from being Super horny!
What are you going to do after you graduate?
I'm going to be Lois Lane, star reporter!
You too?
HAZZARD COUNTY FEED CO.
Honey, the weatherman said showers again, but in this town, I'm not sure if it means we need an umbrella or a hardhat, so I brought both! I'm hoping it's another meteor shower! Remember how twelve years ago a meteor shower blessed us with that adorable three-year-old boy who fell from the sky? Well, I'm praying another meteor shower helps us to have a bigger family, or at least maybe a puppy!
Sweetheart, I think you're becoming a little ditsy from all the weird stuff that happens in this town! But you're right, we were lucky to have that miracle boy fall from the sky! And he is a miracle boy! Just think, Warner Bros. has found yet another way to squeeze money out of an ancient franchise! I mean there was *Adventures of Superman, Lois & Clark: The New Adventures of Superman, Superboy*, and now this! If that isn't a miracle, what is?
MORT DRUCKER

SMELLVILLE

ARTIST: MORT DRUCKER WRITER: DICK DEBARTOLO

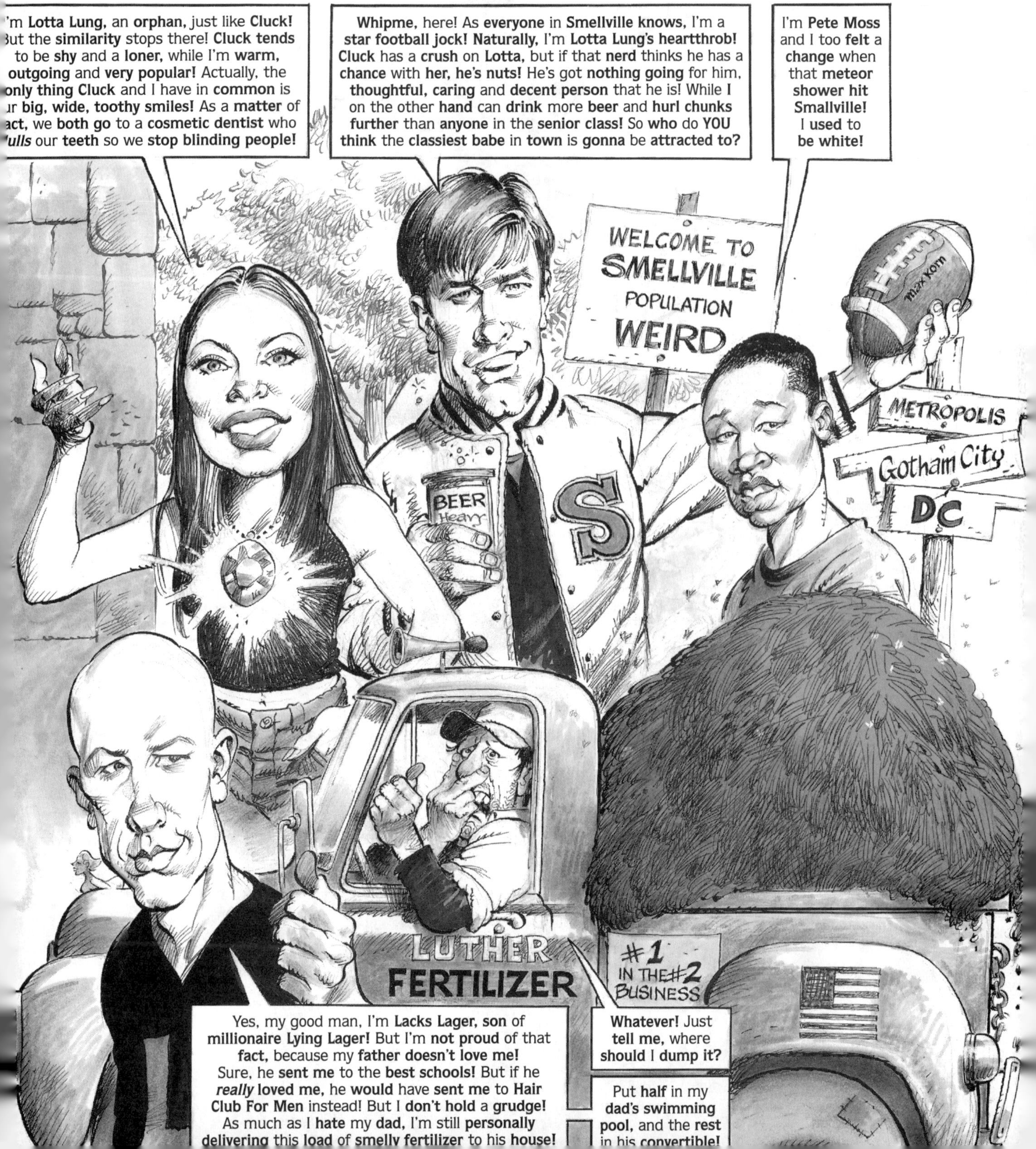
'm Lotta Lung, an orphan, just like Cluck! But the similarity stops there! Cluck tends to be shy and a loner, while I'm warm, outgoing and very popular! Actually, the only thing Cluck and I have in common is ur big, wide, toothy smiles! As a matter of act, we both go to a cosmetic dentist who ulls our teeth so we stop blinding people!
Whipme, here! As everyone in Smellville knows, I'm a star football jock! Naturally, I'm Lotta Lung's heartthrob! Cluck has a crush on Lotta, but if that nerd thinks he has a chance with her, he's nuts! He's got nothing going for him, thoughtful, caring and decent person that he is! While I on the other hand can drink more beer and hurl chunks further than anyone in the senior class! So who do YOU think the classiest babe in town is gonna be attracted to?
I'm Pete Moss and I too felt a change when that meteor shower hit Smallville! I used to be white!
WELCOME TO SMELLVILLE POPULATION WEIRD
METROPOLIS
Gotham City
DC
BEER Heavy
S
LUTHER FERTILIZER
#1 IN THE #2 BUSINESS
Yes, my good man, I'm Lacks Lager, son of millionaire Lying Lager! But I'm not proud of that fact, because my father doesn't love me! Sure, he sent me to the best schools! But if he really loved me, he would have sent me to Hair Club For Men instead! But I don't hold a grudge! As much as I hate my dad, I'm still personally delivering this load of smelly fertilizer to his house!
Whatever! Just tell me, where should I dump it?
Put half in my dad's swimming pool, and the rest in his convertible!

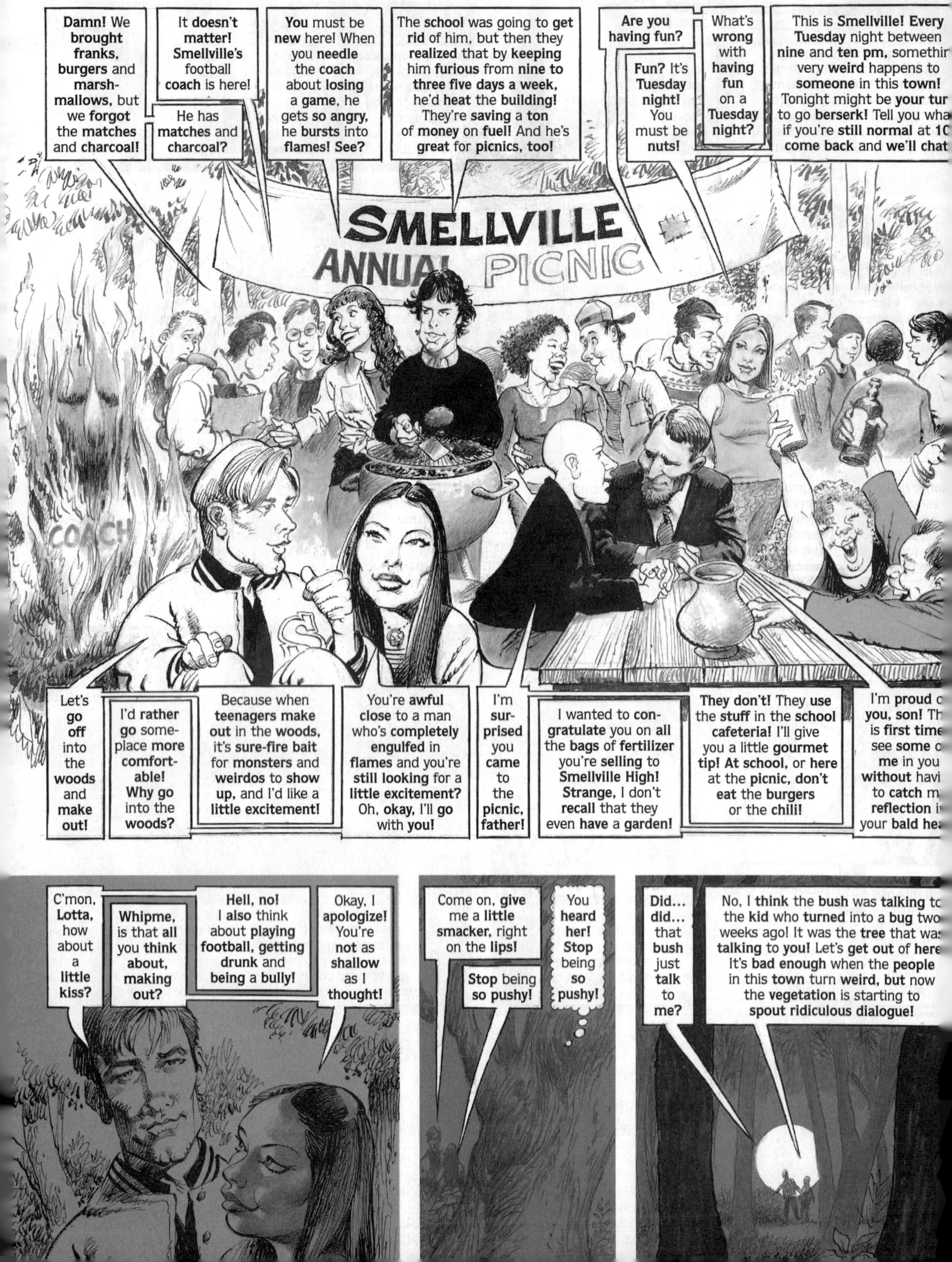

Damn! We brought franks, burgers and marshmallows, but we forgot the matches and charcoal!
It doesn't matter! Smellville's football coach is here!
He has matches and charcoal?
You must be new here! When you needle the coach about losing a game, he gets so angry, he bursts into flames! See?
The school was going to get rid of him, but then they realized that by keeping him furious from nine to three five days a week, he'd heat the building! They're saving a ton of money on fuel! And he's great for picnics, too!
Are you having fun?
Fun? It's Tuesday night! You must be nuts!
What's wrong with having fun on a Tuesday night?
This is Smellville! Every Tuesday night between nine and ten pm, somethi very weird happens to someone in this town! Tonight might be your tu to go berserk! Tell you wha if you're still normal at 1 come back and we'll chat
SMELLVILLE
ANNUAL PICNIC
COACH
Let's go off into the woods and make out!
I'd rather go someplace more comfortable! Why go into the woods?
Because when teenagers make out in the woods, it's sure-fire bait for monsters and weirdos to show up, and I'd like a little excitement!
You're awful close to a man who's completely engulfed in flames and you're still looking for a little excitement? Oh, okay, I'll go with you!
I'm surprised you came to the picnic, father!
I wanted to congratulate you on all the bags of fertilizer you're selling to Smellville High! Strange, I don't recall that they even have a garden!
They don't! They use the stuff in the school cafeteria! I'll give you a little gourmet tip! At school, or here at the picnic, don't eat the burgers or the chili!
I'm proud o you, son! Th is first time see some o me in you without havi to catch m reflection i your bald he
C'mon, Lotta, how about a little kiss?
Whipme, is that all you think about, making out?
Hell, no! I also think about playing football, getting drunk and being a bully!
Okay, I apologize! You're not as shallow as I thought!
Come on, give me a little smacker, right on the lips!
Stop being so pushy!
You heard her! Stop being so pushy!
Did... did... that bush just talk to me?
No, I think the bush was talking to the kid who turned into a bug two weeks ago! It was the tree that was talking to you! Let's get out of here! It's bad enough when the people in this town turn weird, but now the vegetation is starting to spout ridiculous dialogue!

First I have to **fight off** Whipme, and **now** a tree! I've **got** to **stop flashing** my **sexy smile every** ten seconds! It's **getting** me in **too much trouble!** No matter where I go, **someone** or **something** is wrapping their **limbs** around me!

Come on, don't **fight** me! My **bark** is **worse** than my **bite!**

Whipme, please **do something** to **help** me **here!**

I **will!** I'm **gonna** go **home**, get a **saw** and **cut** you **free!** My **cordless saw!** But the **battery** needs a **complete charge**, so I'll be **back** in **24 hours! Good luck!**

If you're **looking** for **Lotta**, she **went off** into the **woods** with **Whipme!**

The woods! Some creepy, crawling, unspeakable things hang out there!

Don't worry, she's with **Whipme!**

HE'S the creepy, crawly, unspeakable thing I'm **talking** about!

Help, help! Someone please help me!

No one else **seems** to **hear** anything, but I **swear** that's **Lotta** calling for help! My **super duper** hearing is getting **better** daily!

Next stop on this **train**, Grand Central Station!

My **super duper** hearing is **definitely** getting **better!** We're **more** than **2,000** miles from Grand Central Station, and I can **hear** that conductor **perfectly** too!

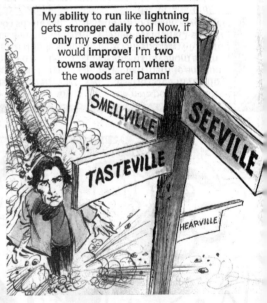

My **ability** to **run** like **lightning** gets **stronger** daily too! Now, if only my **sense of direction** would **improve!** I'm **two towns** away from **where** the woods are! **Damn!**

SMELLVILLE

SEEVILLE

TASTEVILLE

HEARVILLE

Go back to the **second light**, **make** a **right**, and when you **see** the **piece** of land with **nothing** but trees, that's the **woods!**

BEER

BAIT

GAS

FREE TUMS

WITH EVERY FILL UP

Cluck, you've **come** to **help** me! Thank goodness!

Oh, **my knees**, I'm **weak**, I... I can't **stand**... I'm **shaking**... I'm **collapsing!**

It must be this **necklace** with the **Kraptonite!**

No, it's that tight **sweater!** Man, **what** a **rack!** I get **weak** when I get **close** to **them!**

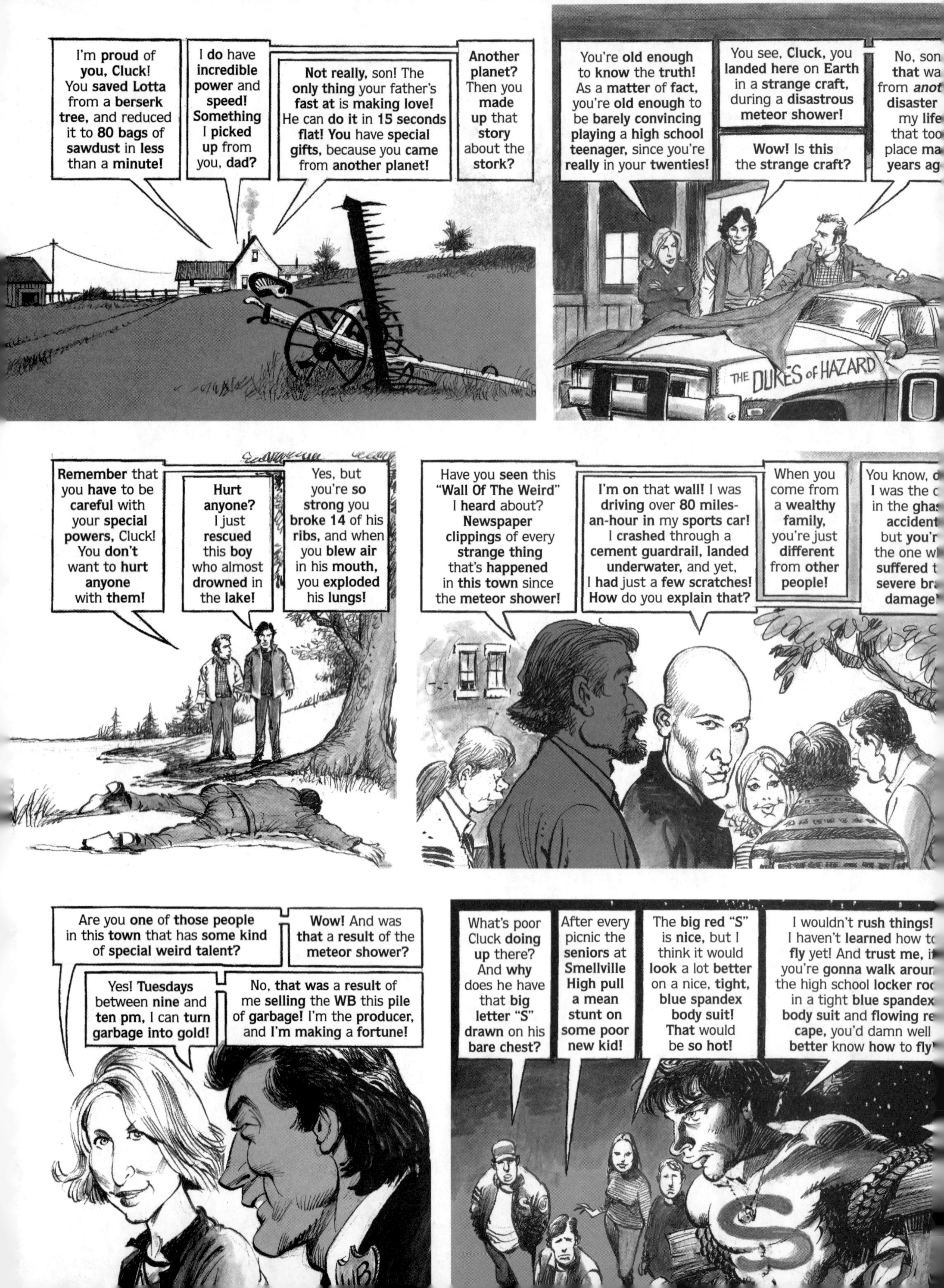

I'm proud of you, Cluck! You saved Lotta from a berserk tree, and reduced it to 80 bags of sawdust in less than a minute!
I do have incredible power and speed! Something I picked up from you, dad?
Not really, son! The only thing your father's fast at is making love! He can do it in 15 seconds flat! You have special gifts, because you came from another planet!
Another planet? Then you made up that story about the stork?
You're old enough to know the truth! As a matter of fact, you're old enough to be barely convincing playing a high school teenager, since you're really in your twenties!
You see, Cluck, you landed here on Earth in a strange craft, during a disastrous meteor shower!
Wow! Is this the strange craft?
No, son that wa from anot disaster my life that too place ma years ag
THE DUKES of HAZARD
Remember that you have to be careful with your special powers, Cluck! You don't want to hurt anyone with them!
Hurt anyone? I just rescued this boy who almost drowned in the lake!
Yes, but you're so strong you broke 14 of his ribs, and when you blew air in his mouth, you exploded his lungs!
Have you seen this "Wall Of The Weird" I heard about? Newspaper clippings of every strange thing that's happened in this town since the meteor shower!
I'm on that wall! I was driving over 80 miles-an-hour in my sports car! I crashed through a cement guardrail, landed underwater, and yet, I had just a few scratches! How do you explain that?
When you come from a wealthy family, you're just different from other people!
You know, d I was the c in the ghas accident but you'r the one w suffered t severe bra damage
Are you one of those people in this town that has some kind of special weird talent?
Yes! Tuesdays between nine and ten pm, I can turn garbage into gold!
Wow! And was that a result of the meteor shower?
No, that was a result of me selling the WB this pile of garbage! I'm the producer, and I'm making a fortune!
What's poor Cluck doing up there? And why does he have that big letter "S" drawn on his bare chest?
After every picnic the seniors at Smellville High pull a mean stunt on some poor new kid!
The big red "S" is nice, but I think it would look a lot better on a nice, tight, blue spandex body suit! That would be so hot!
I wouldn't rush things! I haven't learned how t fly yet! And trust me, i you're gonna walk aroun the high school locker roo in a tight blue spandex body suit and flowing re cape, you'd damn well better know how to fly

TURTLE WHACKS DEPT.

A MODERN DAY FAIRY TALE

The Turtle and the Hare

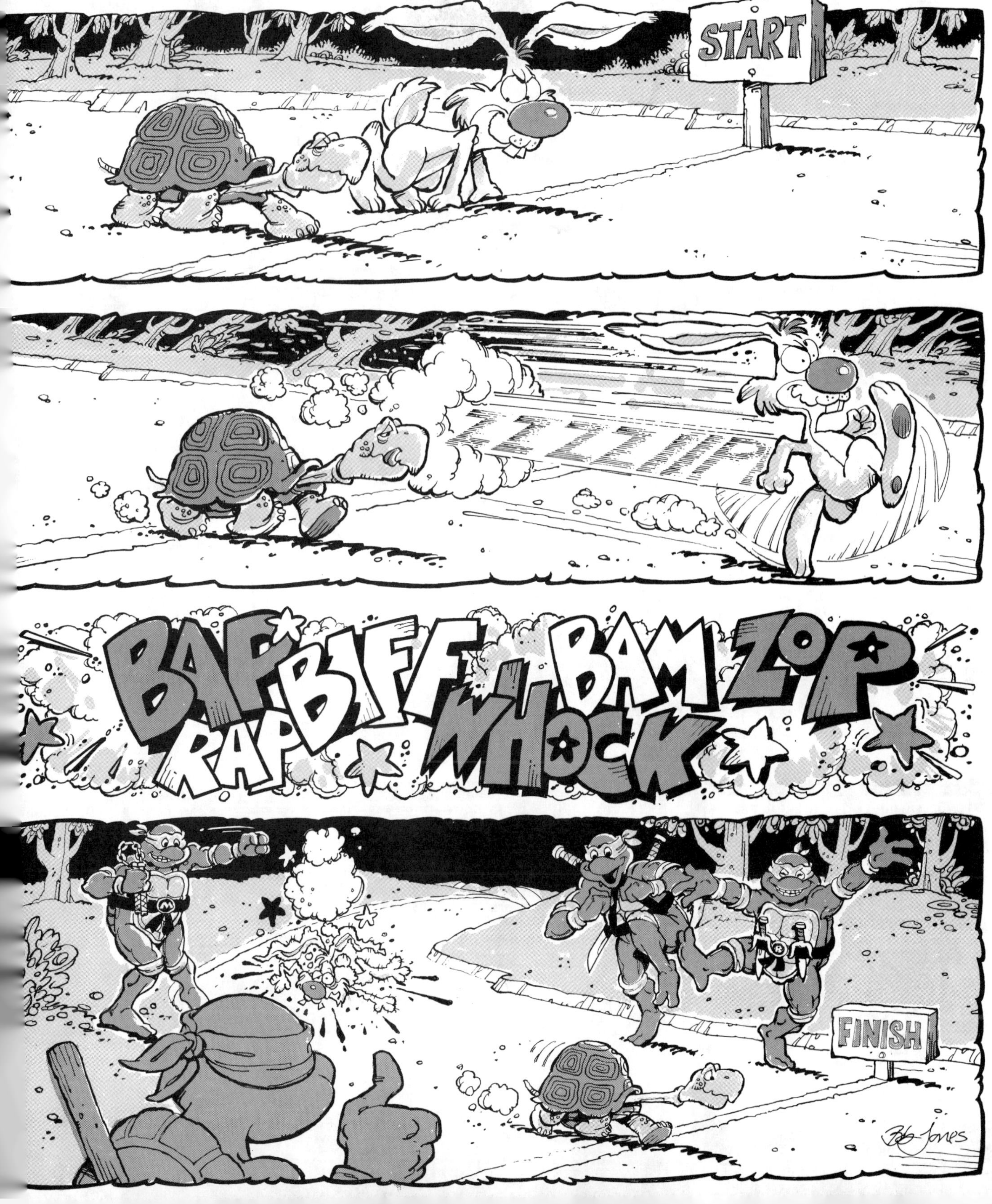
START
ZZZZIP
BAP
BIFF
BAM
ZOP
RAP
WHOCK
FINISH
Bob Jones

THE DORK KNIGHT DEPT.

The new Batsman cartoon series on TV is said to be bas on the dark, moody Batsman movies. (Personally, think it's based on DC Comics' insatiable desi to milk even more money from the Dynamic Duo!) B since we desire to fill five pages regardless of t worthiness of the subject, here's our version of

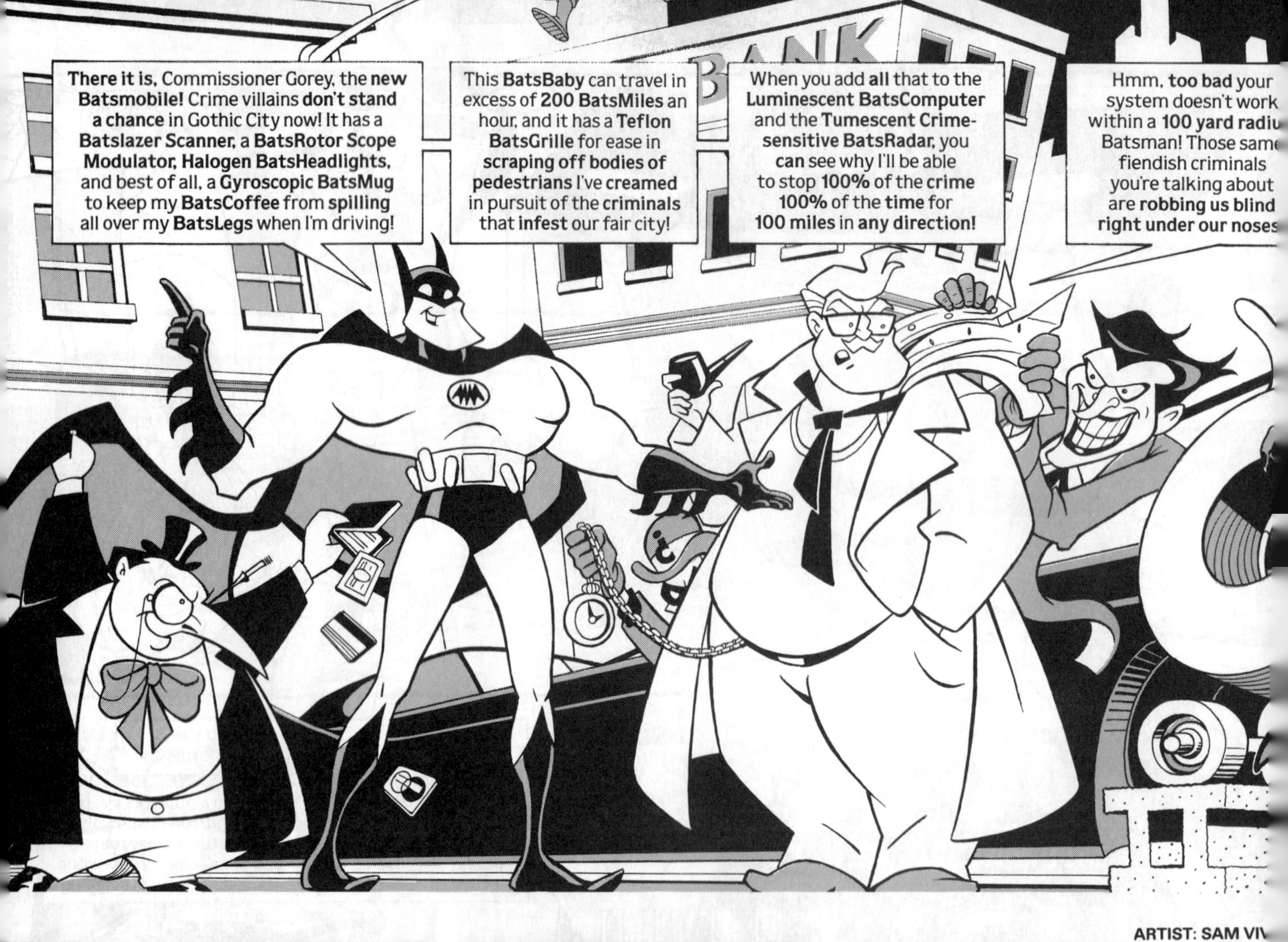

BANK
There it is, Commissioner Gorey, the new Batsmobile! Crime villains don't stand a chance in Gothic City now! It has a Batslazer Scanner, a BatsRotor Scope Modulator, Halogen BatsHeadlights, and best of all, a Gyroscopic BatsMug to keep my BatsCoffee from spilling all over my BatsLegs when I'm driving!
This BatsBaby can travel in excess of 200 BatsMiles an hour, and it has a Teflon BatsGrille for ease in scraping off bodies of pedestrians I've creamed in pursuit of the criminals that infest our fair city!
When you add all that to the Luminescent BatsComputer and the Tumescent Crime-sensitive BatsRadar, you can see why I'll be able to stop 100% of the crime 100% of the time for 100 miles in any direction!
Hmm, too bad your system doesn't work within a 100 yard radiu Batsman! Those same fiendish criminals you're talking about are robbing us blind right under our noses

ARTIST: SAM VIV

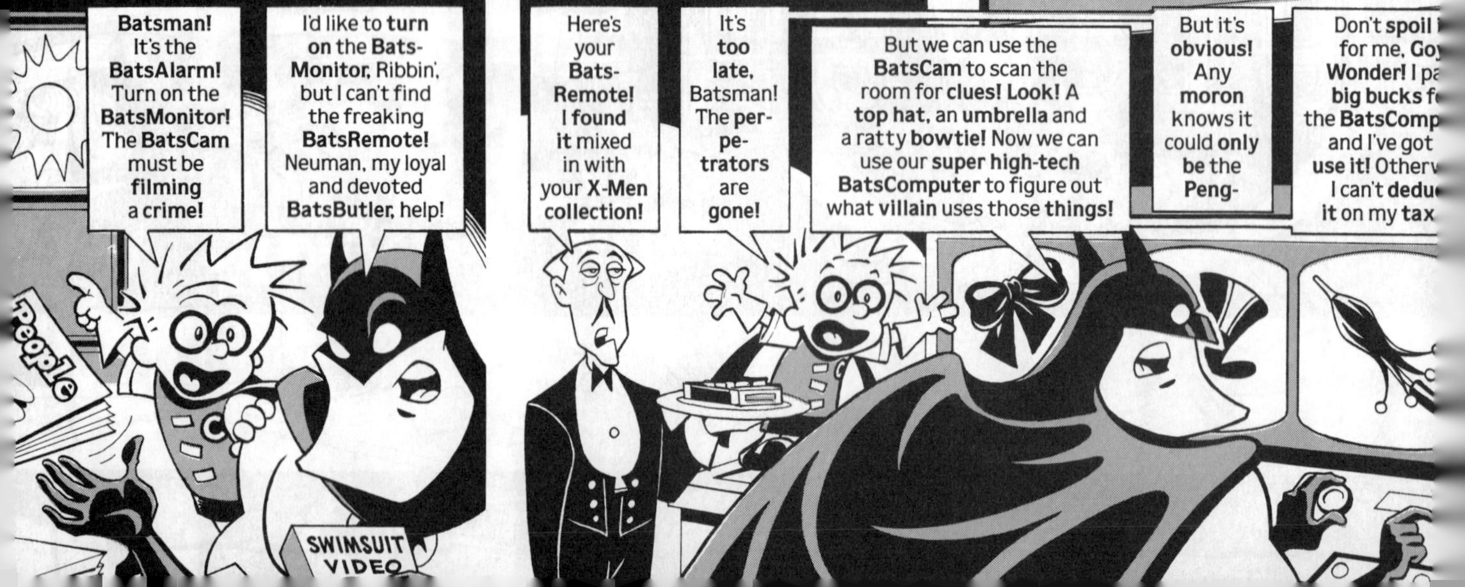

Batsman! It's the BatsAlarm! Turn on the BatsMonitor! The BatsCam must be filming a crime!
I'd like to turn on the Bats-Monitor, Ribbin', but I can't find the freaking BatsRemote! Neuman, my loyal and devoted BatsButler, help!
Here's your Bats-Remote! I found it mixed in with your X-Men collection!
It's too late, Batsman! The per-pe-trators are gone!
But we can use the BatsCam to scan the room for clues! Look! A top hat, an umbrella and a ratty bowtie! Now we can use our super high-tech BatsComputer to figure out what villain uses those things!
But it's obvious! Any moron knows it could only be the Peng-
Don't spoil for me, Goy Wonder! I pa big bucks f the BatsComp and I've got use it! Otherv I can't dedu it on my tax
People
SWIMSUIT VIDEO

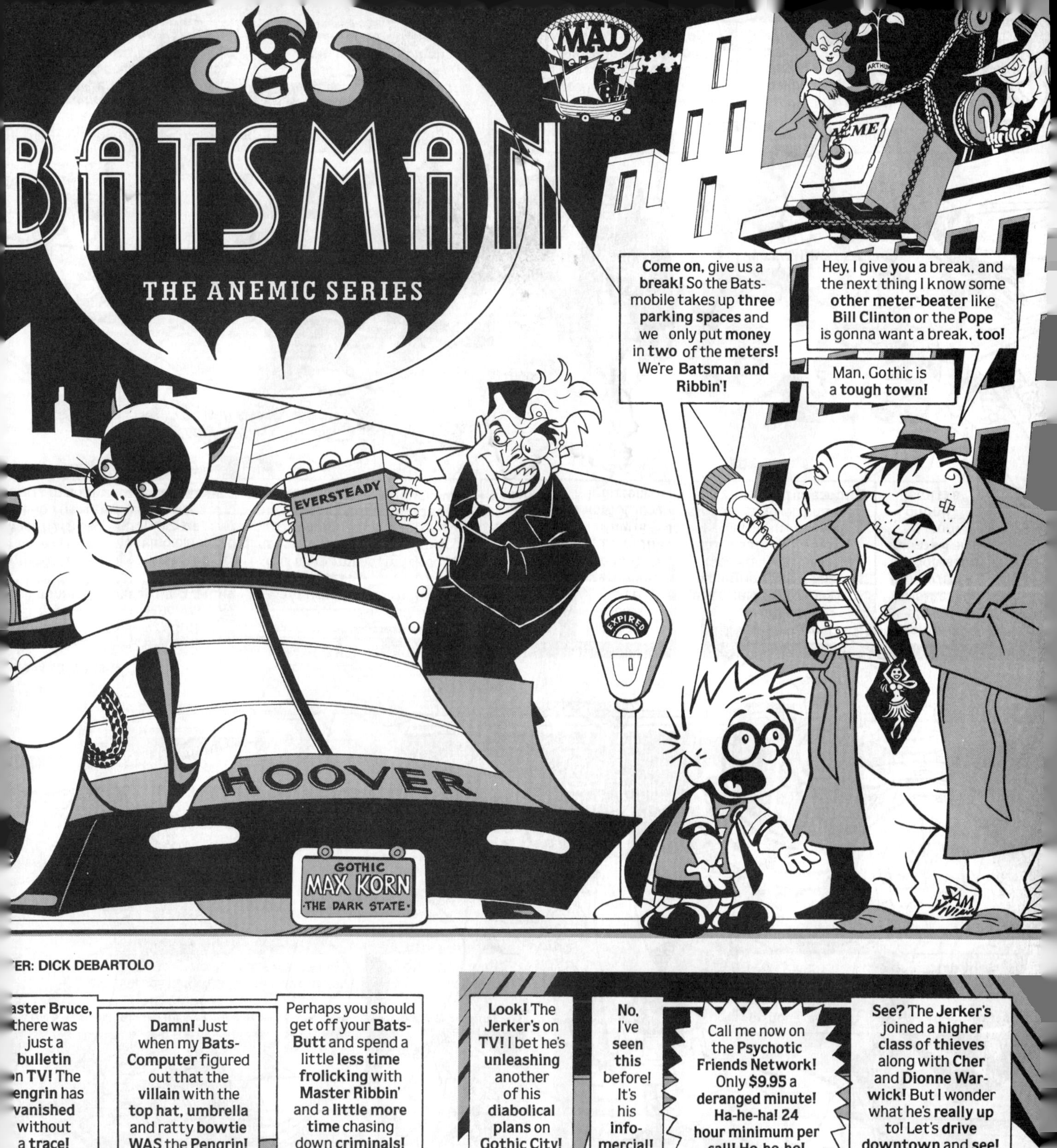
MAD
BATSMAN
THE ANEMIC SERIES
ACME
EVERSTEADY
Come on, give us a break! So the Batsmobile takes up three parking spaces and we only put money in two of the meters! We're Batsman and Ribbin'!
Hey, I give you a break, and the next thing I know some other meter-beater like Bill Clinton or the Pope is gonna want a break, too!
Man, Gothic is a tough town!
EXPIRED
HOOVER
GOTHIC
MAX KORN
THE DARK STATE

TER: DICK DEBARTOLO

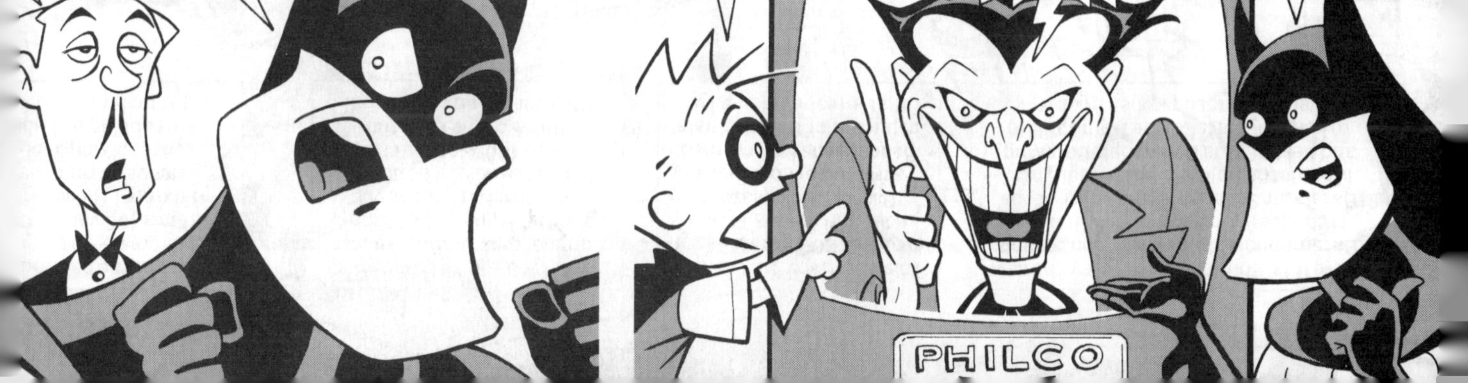
aster Bruce, there was just a bulletin n TV! The engrin has vanished without a trace!
Damn! Just when my Bats-Computer figured out that the villain with the top hat, umbrella and ratty bowtie WAS the Pengrin!
Perhaps you should get off your Bats-Butt and spend a little less time frolicking with Master Ribbin' and a little more time chasing down criminals!
Look! The Jerker's on TV! I bet he's unleashing another of his diabolical plans on Gothic City!
No, I've seen this before! It's his info-mercial!
Call me now on the Psychotic Friends Network! Only $9.95 a deranged minute! Ha-he-ha! 24 hour minimum per call! Ho-ho-ho!
See? The Jerker's joined a higher class of thieves along with Cher and Dionne Warwick! But I wonder what he's really up to! Let's drive downtown and see!
PHILCO

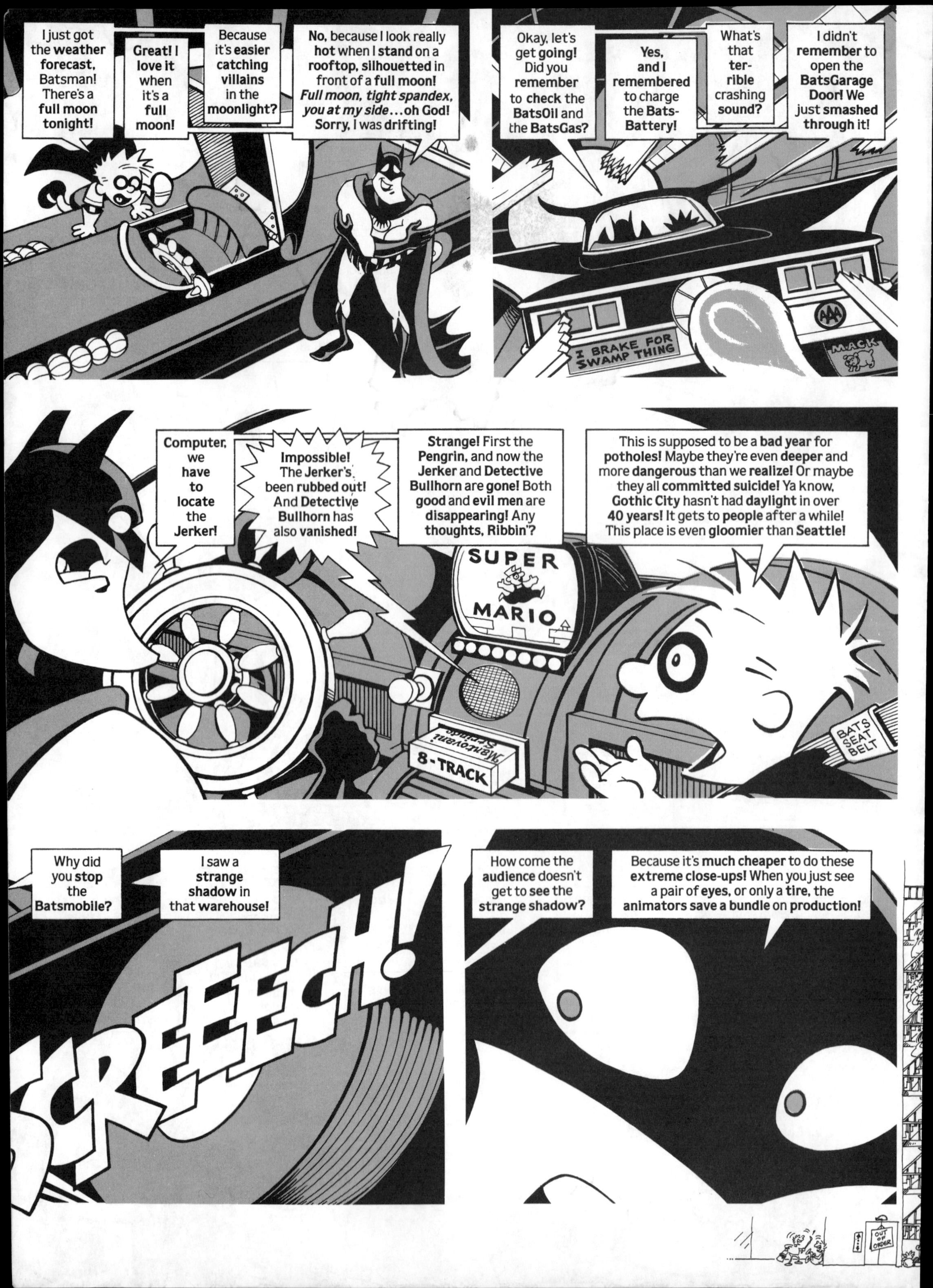

I just got the weather forecast, Batsman! There's a full moon tonight!
Great! I love it when it's a full moon!
Because it's easier catching villains in the moonlight?
No, because I look really hot when I stand on a rooftop, silhouetted in front of a full moon! Full moon, tight spandex, you at my side...oh God! Sorry, I was drifting!
Okay, let's get going! Did you remember to check the BatsOil and the BatsGas?
Yes, and I remembered to charge the Bats-Battery!
What's that ter-rible crashing sound?
I didn't remember to open the BatsGarage Door! We just smashed through it!
I BRAKE FOR SWAMP THING
AAA
MACK
Computer, we have to locate the Jerker!
Impossible! The Jerker's been rubbed out! And Detective Bullhorn has also vanished!
Strange! First the Pengrin, and now the Jerker and Detective Bullhorn are gone! Both good and evil men are disappearing! Any thoughts, Ribbin'?
This is supposed to be a bad year for potholes! Maybe they're even deeper and more dangerous than we realize! Or maybe they all committed suicide! Ya know, Gothic City hasn't had daylight in over 40 years! It gets to people after a while! This place is even gloomier than Seattle!
SUPER MARIO
8-TRACK
BATS SEAT BELT
Why did you stop the Batsmobile?
I saw a strange shadow in that warehouse!
SCREEECH!
How come the audience doesn't get to see the strange shadow?
Because it's much cheaper to do these extreme close-ups! When you just see a pair of eyes, or only a tire, the animators save a bundle on production!
OUT OF ORDER

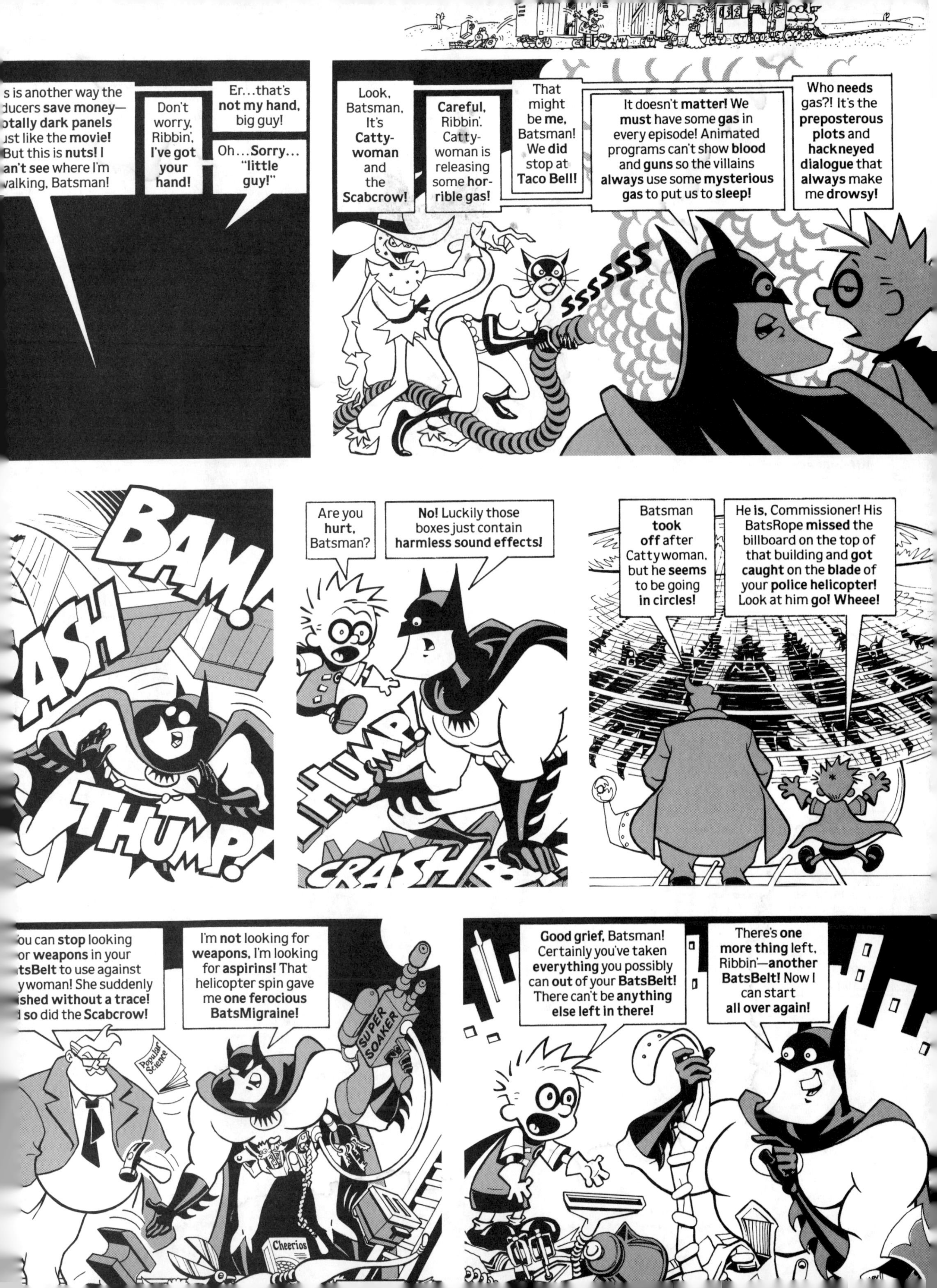

s is another way the ducers **save money**—otally dark panels ust like the **movie!** But this is **nuts!** I an't see where I'm valking, Batsman!
Don't worry, Ribbin', **I've got your hand!**
Er...that's **not my hand,** big guy!
Oh...**Sorry...** **"little guy!"**
Look, Batsman, It's **Catty-woman** and the **Scabcrow!**
Careful, Ribbin'. Catty-woman is releasing some **hor-rible gas!**
That might be **me,** Batsman! We **did** stop at **Taco Bell!**
It doesn't **matter!** We **must** have some **gas** in every episode! Animated programs can't show **blood** and **guns** so the villains **always** use some **mysterious gas** to put us to **sleep!**
Who **needs** gas?! It's the **preposterous plots** and **hackneyed dialogue** that **always** make me **drowsy!**
SSSSSS
BAM!
ASH
THUMP!
Are you **hurt,** Batsman?
No! Luckily those boxes just contain **harmless sound effects!**
THUMP!
CRASH!
Batsman **took off** after Cattywoman, but he **seems** to be going **in circles!**
He **is,** Commissioner! His BatsRope **missed** the billboard on the top of that building and **got caught** on the **blade** of your **police helicopter!** Look at him **go! Wheee!**
ou can **stop** looking or **weapons** in your tsBelt to use against ywoman! She suddenly ished **without a trace!** d **so** did the **Scabcrow!**
I'm **not** looking for **weapons,** I'm looking for **aspirins!** That helicopter spin gave me **one ferocious BatsMigraine!**
Popular Science
SUPER SOAKER
Cheerios
Good grief, Batsman! Certainly you've taken **everything** you possibly can **out** of your **BatsBelt!** There can't be **anything else left in there!**
There's **one more thing** left, Ribbin'—**another BatsBelt!** Now I can start **all over again!**

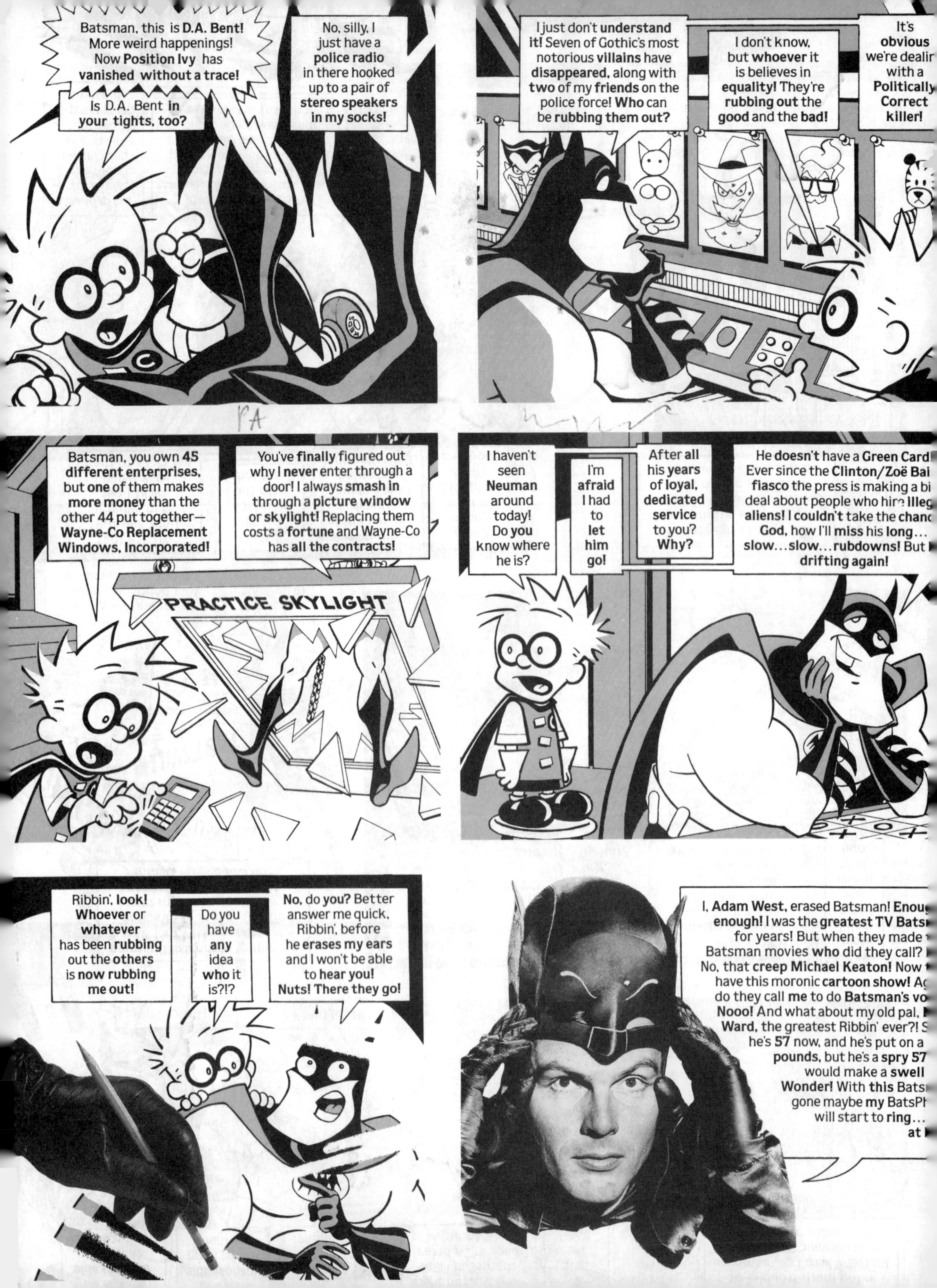

Batsman, this is D.A. Bent! More weird happenings! Now Position Ivy has vanished without a trace!
Is D.A. Bent in your tights, too?
No, silly, I just have a police radio in there hooked up to a pair of stereo speakers in my socks!
I just don't understand it! Seven of Gothic's most notorious villains have disappeared, along with two of my friends on the police force! Who can be rubbing them out?
I don't know, but whoever it is believes in equality! They're rubbing out the good and the bad!
It's obvious we're dealin with a Politically Correct killer!
PA
Batsman, you own 45 different enterprises, but one of them makes more money than the other 44 put together—Wayne-Co Replacement Windows, Incorporated!
You've finally figured out why I never enter through a door! I always smash in through a picture window or skylight! Replacing them costs a fortune and Wayne-Co has all the contracts!
PRACTICE SKYLIGHT
I haven't seen Neuman around today! Do you know where he is?
I'm afraid I had to let him go!
After all his years of loyal, dedicated service to you? Why?
He doesn't have a Green Card Ever since the Clinton/Zoë Bai fiasco the press is making a bi deal about people who hire illeg aliens! I couldn't take the chanc God, how I'll miss his long… slow…slow…rubdowns! But drifting again!
Ribbin', look! Whoever or whatever has been rubbing out the others is now rubbing me out!
Do you have any idea who it is?!?
No, do you? Better answer me quick, Ribbin', before he erases my ears and I won't be able to hear you! Nuts! There they go!
I, Adam West, erased Batsman! Enou enough! I was the greatest TV Bats for years! But when they made Batsman movies who did they call? No, that creep Michael Keaton! Now have this moronic cartoon show! A do they call me to do Batsman's vo Nooo! And what about my old pal, Ward, the greatest Ribbin' ever?! he's 57 now, and he's put on a pounds, but he's a spry 57 would make a swell Wonder! With this Bats gone maybe my BatsP will start to ring… at